OTHER TITLES IN THE RESEARCH METHODS IN LINGUISTICS SERIES

Research Methods in Applied Linguistics

A Practical Resource

EDITED BY BRIAN PALTRIDGE AND AEK PHAKITI

Bloomsbury Academic
An imprint of Bloomsbury Publishing Plc

BLOOMSBURY

LONDON · NEW DELHI · NEW YORK · SYDNEY

Bloomsbury Academic

An imprint of Bloomsbury Publishing Plc

50 Bedford Square	1385 Broadway
London	New York
WC1B 3DP	NY 10018
UK	USA

www.bloomsbury.com

BLOOMSBURY and the Diana logo are trademarks of Bloomsbury Publishing Plc

First published 2015

British Library Cataloguing-in-Publication Data

A catalogue record for this book is available from the British Library.

ISBN: PB: 978-1-4725-2501-7
HB: 978-1-4725-2456-0
ePDF: 978-1-4725-3424-8
ePub: 978-1-4725-2481-2

Library of Congress Cataloging-in-Publication Data

Research Methods in Applied Linguistics : A Practical Resource /
edited by Brian Paltridge and Aek Phakiti.
pages cm
Includes bibliographical references and index.
ISBN 978-1-4725-2501-7 (pb) – ISBN 978-1-4725-2456-0 (hb) –
ISBN 978-1-4725-2481-2 (epub) – ISBN 978-1-4725-3424-8 (epdf)
1. Applied linguistics–Research. 2. Applied linguistics–Methodology.
I. Paltridge, Brian, editor. II. Phakiti, Aek, editor.
P129.R475 2015
418.0072–dc23
2014046974

Series: Research Methods in Linguistics

Typeset by Integra Software Services Pvt. Ltd.
Printed and bound in India

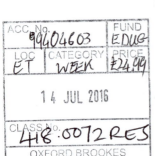

CONTENTS

NOTES ON CONTRIBUTORS

Gary Barkhuizen is Head of the School of Cultures, Languages and Linguistics at the University of Auckland, New Zealand. His research and teaching interests are in the areas of language teacher education, learner language, sociolinguistics and narrative inquiry, and he has published widely on these topics in a range of international journals. He is co-author of *Analysing Learner Language* (Oxford University Press, 2005), *Narrative Inquiry in Language Teaching and Learning Research* (Routledge, 2014) and editor of *Narrative Research in Applied Linguistics* (Cambridge University Press, 2013).

David Block is ICREA (*Institució Catalana de Recerca i Estudis Avançats*) Research Professor in Sociolinguistics at the University of Lleida (Spain). He is interested in the impact of political economic and social phenomena on multimodal identity-making practices of all kinds (including social movements, multiculturalism, bi/multilingualism and the acquisition and use of languages) and, in recent years, he has focused specifically on neoliberalism as the dominant ideology in contemporary societies and social class as a key dimension of identity. His books include *The Social Turn in Second Language Acquisition* (2003), *Second Language Identities* (2007) and *Social Class in Applied Linguistics* (2014). He is editor of the Routledge book series *Language, Society and Political Economy*.

Simon Borg has been involved in English Language Teaching (ELT) for over twenty-five years, working as a teacher, teacher educator, lecturer, examiner, researcher and consultant in a range of international contexts. After fifteen years at the University of Leeds, where he was a professor of TESOL, Simon now works full time as an ELT consultant. He specializes in the design, delivery, evaluation and study of teacher education and development programs, teacher research initiatives and research methods training. He is recognized as a leading scholar in the study of language teachers and teacher education and maintains a strong academic profile through research, publications and speaking at international conferences. He is also an editorial board member for leading language education journals.

Anne Burns is Professor of TESOL at the University of New South Wales, Sydney and an Honorary Professor at the University of Sydney. She has been a visiting professor in New Zealand, Sweden and Hong Kong. She has published extensively on action research, teacher education and the teaching of speaking from discourse perspectives. She is co-editor (with Jack Richards) of *The Cambridge Guide to Pedagogy and Practice in Second Language Teaching* (Cambridge University Press, 2012) and (with Roger Barnard) of *Researching Language Teacher Cognition and Practice: International Case Studies* (Multilingual Matters, 2012) and the co-author (with Christine Goh) of *Teaching Speaking: A Holistic Approach* (Cambridge University Press, 2012). She is also academic advisor to the Applied Linguistics Series published by Oxford University Press.

Christine Pearson Casanave taught at a Japanese university from 1990 to 2003 after receiving her PhD at Stanford University. Since 2004, she has been affiliated with Temple University in Japan, mainly advising doctoral students on their qualitative dissertation projects. Her primary interests and publications concern advanced academic literacy practices, such as graduate level writing and writing for publication. Since 2012, she has been visiting scholar at her M.A. alma mater, the Monterey Institute of International Studies, where she helped design the MATESOL program in the early 1980s. She does most of her academic reading while walking.

Peter De Costa is Assistant Professor in the Department of Linguistics, Germanic, Slavic, Asian and African Languages at Michigan State University. He is part of the core faculty within the Second Language Studies PhD Program and the Master of Arts in TESOL Program. His primary area of research is the role of identity and ideology in second language acquisition (SLA). Much of his current work focuses on conducting ethical applied linguistic research and sociolinguistic scales.

Susan Gass is University Distinguished Professor at Michigan State University where she serves as Chair of the Department of Linguistics and Germanic, Slavic, Asian and African Languages, Director of the English Language Center, Director of the Second Language Studies Program and Co-Director of the Center for Language Education and Research and of the Center for Language Teaching Advancement. She has published widely in the field of second language acquisition, including the recent book with Jennifer Behney and Luke Plonsky: *Second Language Acquisition: An Introductory Course* (Routledge, 2013). She has served as president of the American Association for Applied Linguistics and the International Association of Applied Linguistics.

Jennifer L. Greer is Lead Instructor, Academic Writing, in the Professional Development Program, The Graduate School, at the University of Alabama at Birmingham (UAB). A former journalist and Peace Corps Volunteer (Costa Rica) in Adult Education, Jennifer is bilingual in English and Spanish. She taught English as a Second Language in K-12 prior to joining UAB. She currently designs and teaches ethics, writing and presenting curricula for graduate students, research staff and post-doctoral fellows.

Lesley Harbon is Professor and Head of the School of International Studies at The University of Technology, Sydney, Australia. She has taught in languages education units of study and supervised research higher degree projects at both Masters and Doctoral levels. Her research interests include linguistic landscape research, language teacher professional development, intercultural language education and bilingual/CLIL language education. With Robyn Moloney, she edited *Language Teachers' Narratives of Practice* (Cambridge Scholars Publishing, 2013).

David Hirsh is Associate Professor in TESOL and Associate Dean (postgraduate programs) in the Faculty of Education and Social Work at the University of Sydney. His research focuses on vocabulary development, international education and indigenous language revitalization. His work has appeared in the journals *Reading in a Foreign Language* and the *Journal of Research in International Education*, and in the texts *Teaching Academic Writing: An Introduction for Teachers of Second Language Writers* (University of Michigan Press, 2009) and *Current Perspectives in Second Language Vocabulary Research* (Peter Lang, 2012).

Adrian Holliday is Professor of Applied Linguistics at Canterbury Christ Church University, where he supervises doctoral research in the critical sociology of English language education and intercultural communication. His book, *The Struggle to Teach English as an International Language* (Oxford University Press, 2005), deals with the cultural chauvinism hidden beneath English language teaching professionalism and 'native speaker' politics. He wrote *Doing and Writing Qualitative Research* (2nd edn, Sage, 2007) to take ownership of a postmodern methodology for understanding hidden cultural realities. *Intercultural Communication* (2nd edn, Routledge, 2010, with Hyde and Kullman) begins an exploration of cultural difference when the established essentialist paradigm is put aside. *Intercultural Communication & Ideology* (Sage, 2011) employs a critical cosmopolitan approach to understand the Western ideologies which inhibit our understanding of the crucial, modern contribution of non-Western cultural realities. His recent book, *Understanding Intercultural Communication* (Routledge, 2013), provides a detailed exploration of his new 'grammar of culture'.

Ken Hyland is Chair Professor of Applied Linguistics and Director of the Centre for Applied English Studies at the University of Hong Kong. He is best known for his research into second language writing and academic discourse, having published over 180 articles and twenty books on these topics. His most recent books include *Academic Publishing* (Oxford University Press, 2015), *Disciplinary Identity* (Cambridge University Press, 2012) and *Innovation and Change in English Language Education* (edited with Lillian Wong, Routledge, 2013). He is a foundation fellow of the Hong Kong Academy of the Humanities, was founding co-editor of the *Journal of English for Academic Purposes* (Elsevier) and was co-editor of *Applied Linguistics*.

Rebecca Hughes is Global Head of Education at the British Council and holds an Honorary Professorship of Applied Linguistics at the University of Nottingham, Malaysia Campus. Prior to this Rebecca was Director of the Centre for English Language Education at the University of Nottingham from 2000 to 2010 gaining a personal Chair in 2007. She was subsequently the first Pro-Vice Chancellor (International) at The University of Sheffield during which time she also led the Worldwide Universities Network Global Challenge on the Globalisation of Higher Education and Research. Rebecca has published widely in her personal research interest of spoken language and also contributed to on-going debates about the role of language policy in International Higher Education.

Nataliya V. Ivankova is Associate Professor in the Department of Health Services Administration (School of Health Professions) and the Department of Acute, Chronic and Continuing Care (School of Nursing) at the University of Alabama at Birmingham. She teaches graduate-level research methods courses including research design, survey, qualitative and mixed methods research. Her primary research focus is on the applications of mixed methods research in social and behavioural sciences including community-based participatory action research and implementation science. Professionally, she serves as a member of several editorial boards, including the *Journal of Mixed Methods Research* and is a founding co-editor of a book series, *Mixed Methods Research Series*, with Sage Publications. During the first twenty years of her professional career, she taught ESL and contrastive linguistics at the Izmail State Pedagogical Institute in Ukraine.

Lourdes Ortega is Professor in the Department of Linguistics at Georgetown University. Her main area of research is in second language acquisition, particularly bilingual, usage-based and educational dimensions of adult language learning in classroom settings. Her 2000 meta-analysis (co-authored with John M. Norris) won the Pimsleur and the TESOL Research Awards. Her most recent book is *Understanding Second Language Acquisition* (revised version to be published by Routledge).

Brian Paltridge is Professor of TESOL at the University of Sydney. With Sue Starfield he is co-author of *Thesis and Dissertation Writing in a Second Language* (Routledge, 2007) and with his TESOL colleagues at the

University of Sydney *Teaching Academic Writing* (University of Michigan Press, 2009). With Ken Hyland, he edited the *Companion to Discourse Analysis* (Continuum, 2011); and with Diane Belcher and Ann Johns, *New Directions in English for Specific Purposes Research* (University of Michigan Press, 2011). His most recent publications are the second edition of his book *Discourse Analysis* (Bloomsbury, 2012), the *Handbook of English for Specific Purposes*, edited with Sue Starfield (Wiley-Blackwell, 2013) and *Ethnographic Perspectives on Academic Writing*, with Sue Starfield and Christine Tardy (Oxford University Press, 2016).

Aek Phakiti is Senior Lecturer in TESOL at The University of Sydney. His research focuses on language testing and assessment, second language acquisition and research methods in language learning. He is an author of *Strategic Competence and EFL Reading Test Performance* (Peter Lang, 2007), *Experimental Research Methods in Language Learning* (Bloomsbury, 2014) and with Carsten Roever, *Quantitative Methods for Second Language Research: A Problem-Solving Approach* (Routledge, in press, 2016). He was a recipient of the TOEFL Outstanding Young Scholar and a Faculty of Education and Social Work Teaching Excellence Award in 2010.

Annamaria Pinter is Associate Professor at the Centre for Applied Linguistics, University of Warwick, United Kingdom. She has published widely in the area of teaching English to young learners. She is the author of *Teaching Young Language Learners Oxford Handbooks for Language Teachers* (Oxford University Press, 2006) and *Children Learning Second Languages* (Palgrave Macmillan, 2011). She is also an editor of an e-book series entitled *Teaching English to Young Learners* (http://www.candlinandmynard.com/series.html). She has published extensively in ELT/Applied Linguistics journals and has given numerous plenary talks worldwide.

John Read is Associate Professor in Applied Language Studies at the University of Auckland, New Zealand. He has taught postgraduate courses in applied linguistics in tertiary institutions in New Zealand, Singapore and the United States. His primary research interests are in second language vocabulary assessment and the testing of English for academic and professional purposes. He is the author of *Assessing Vocabulary* (Cambridge University Press, 2000). He was co-editor of *Language Testing* from 2002 to 2006 and served as President of the International Language Testing Association in 2011–2012.

Carsten Roever is Associate Professor in Applied Linguistics in the School of Languages and Linguistics at the University of Melbourne. His research interests include interlanguage pragmatics, Conversation Analysis, second language testing and testing of second language pragmatics. His recent publications have focused on testing of sociopragmatic knowledge, pragmatics of less commonly taught languages and learners' developing ability to engage in extended discourse. His work has appeared in journals such as *Applied Linguistics, Language Testing, ELT Journal* and *Intercultural Pragmatics*. He is co-editor of the *Australian Review of Applied Linguistics*.

Heath Rose is Associate Professor of Applied Linguistics in the Department of Education at Oxford University. His research interests include language learner strategies, second language education, Japanese as a foreign language and the pedagogical implications of the spread of English as a global language. He has published in *Applied Linguistics, Modern Language Journal, Foreign Language Annals* and *ELT Journal*. With Nicola Galloway, he is co-author of *Introducing Global Englishes* (Routledge, 2015).

Huizhong Shen is Associate Professor in TESOL/Languages at the Faculty of Education and Social Work, the University of Sydney. He has served the role of Associate Dean, International, Director of China Education Centre and Founding Director of Confucius Institute at the University of Sydney. He has undertaken research, teaching and PhD supervision in TESOL and foreign language education, teacher education, cross-cultural pedagogies, language and identities and ICT-based language instruction. His publications include books, monographs, articles and curriculum materials. His recent publications are *Teaching Academic Writing* (with colleagues from the University of Sydney, University of Michigan Press, 2008), *Developments and Prospects of English Teaching in China* (edited volume, Fudan University Press, 2009) and *Postmodernism and Process Pedagogy* (Fudan University Press, 2008).

Sue Starfield is Associate Professor in the School of Education and Director of The Learning Centre at the University of New South Wales. With Brian Paltridge, she is co-author of *Thesis and Dissertation Writing in a Second Language: A Handbook for Supervisors* (Routledge, 2007) and co-editor of the *Handbook of English for Specific Purposes* (Wiley-Blackwell, 2013). She is co-editor of the journal *English for Specific Purposes*. She is co-editor with Brian Paltridge of two new book series: *Routledge Introductions to English for Specific Purposes* and *Routledge Research in English for Specific Purposes* and is currently co-authoring a book with Brian Paltridge and Christine Tardy titled *Ethnographic Perspectives on Academic Writing* to be published by Oxford University Press. Her research and publications cover tertiary academic literacies, advanced academic writing, postgraduate pedagogy, ethnographic methodologies, identity in academic writing and access and equity in higher education.

Marie Stevenson is Lecturer in TESOL at the University of Sydney. She lectures in the areas of literacy, grammar, discourse and teaching methodology. Her main areas of research are second language reading and writing, and she has extensive experience in various facets of these, particularly in the measurement of second language reading and writing processes. She participated in Project NELSON, a large-scale project conducted at the University of Amsterdam that investigated the transfer of reading and writing skills and processes from L1 (Dutch) to L2 (English). She has published in journals such as *Language Learning*, *Journal of Educational Psychology* and *International Journal of Bilingualism*.

Neomy Storch is Senior Lecturer in ESL and Applied Linguistics in the School of Languages and Linguistics, the University of Melbourne. Her research focuses on issues related to second language (L2) pedagogy, including collaborative writing, feedback, writing development and the nature of peer interaction. She has published widely on these issues and presented her findings at national and international conferences and invited plenaries. She has published a book on *Collaborative Writing in L2 Classrooms* (Multilingual Matters, 2013) and co-author of a book with John Bitchener entitled *Written Corrective Feedback for SLA: Theoretical Perspectives and Empirical Research* (Multilingual Matters, 2014). She is the co-editor of the *Australian Review of Applied Linguistics*.

Jane Sunderland is Reader in Gender and Discourse (Honorary) at Lancaster University, United Kingdom. She is interested in a range of issues surrounding gender, language and discourse including classroom talk; gender representation in language textbooks and in young children's fiction; multimodality; gendered discourses; literacies and the Harry Potter series; and gender and language in African contexts. Her most recent research monographs are *Language, Gender and Children's Fiction* (Continuum, 2011) and *Gendered Discourses* (Palgrave Macmillan, 2004). She is currently co-authoring a book on Harry Potter and children's reading (Routledge).

Steven Talmy is Associate Professor in the Department of Language and Literacy Education at the University of British Columbia, where he is involved in both graduate education and K-12 teacher certification. His research has focused on so-called generation 1.5 English language learners in K-12 public school settings, integrating close analyses of classroom talk and critical ethnography to examine classroom resistance, linguicism, language ideologies about ESL and the stigma of ESL as a social identity category.

Larry Vandergrift is Professor Emeritus at the Official Languages and Bilingualism Institute of the University of Ottawa. He has published widely on the theory and pedagogy of L2 listening comprehension and continues to be actively engaged in research and professional writing. He has been a co-editor of the *Canadian Modern Language Review*. In 2009, the Canadian Association of Second Language Teachers honoured him with the

Robert Roy Award for his teaching, research, writing and dedication to the improvement of L2 teaching and learning in Canada.

Elvis Wagner is Associate Professor of TESOL in the Teaching and Learning Department at Temple University in Philadelphia, United States. His research interests include the teaching and testing of L2 oral proficiency, focusing on how the non-verbal components of spoken language affect L2 listeners' comprehension of spoken texts as well as the use of unscripted spoken texts for teaching and testing L2 listening. He has published in *Language Testing, Language Assessment Quarterly, Applied Linguistics, System, Language Learning and Technology* and *TESOL Journal.*

Wei Wang is Senior Lecturer in Chinese Studies at the University of Sydney. Being educated in China, Singapore and Australia, he has undertaken research and publications in modern Chinese and English discourse studies, applied linguistics and translation studies. He is the author of *Genre across Languages and Cultures: Newspaper Commentaries in China and Australia* (VDM, 2007). His publications appear in *Discourse Studies,* the *Australian Review of Applied Linguistics, Translation and Interpreting Review* and other academic journals. He also published book chapters with Continuum, Benjamins, the University of Michigan Press and Wiley-Blackwell.

Lindy Woodrow is Senior Lecturer (Honorary) in TESOL at the University of Sydney, Australia. Her research focus is second language motivation particularly of Confucian Heritage Culture learners. She has published motivation research in *The Modern Language Journal, Language Learning, System* and *Foreign Language Annals.* She has also published in the area of academic writing and has a book *Writing about Quantitative Research in Applied Linguistics* (Palgrave Macmillan, 2014).

PREFACE

This volume aims to serve as a comprehensive resource that covers both research methodological and content overviews of selected topics in applied linguistics research, particularly those relevant to language learning and teaching. It aims to provide accessible, manageable and practical guidance for people new to research as well as for those who wish to expand their knowledge of other research methodologies.

The book is divided into two parts: (1) approaches and methods and (2) research areas. We have done this so that readers can see specific examples of research methods as they have been applied in the field of applied linguistics. It was not, unfortunately, possible for us to include everything about applied linguistics research in the one volume. We have therefore selected research approaches and methods that have been frequently adopted in recent years. We have also chosen topics in applied linguistics that have been frequently researched. Much of what we cover in this volume, then, is more or less relevant to applications to language teaching and learning, although other areas are touched on as well.

The intended audience for the book is third-year (or above) undergraduate and postgraduate students (e.g. masters and doctoral students) in Applied Linguistics, TESOL and Second Language Studies. The book is also suitable for experienced researchers wishing to expand their knowledge in research areas they are less familiar with. It is also intended as a resource for research supervisors and educators to recommend to their students for information and advice on possible research designs and possible research topics.

Despite our best attempts, some errors may appear in this book. An up-to-date list of corrections will be kept for future editions of the book. The editors would be grateful if you could send your comments or suggestions to them so that they can improve the book in future editions. You can contact Brian Paltridge at brian.paltridge@sydney.edu.au or Aek Phakiti at aek.phakiti@sydney.edu.au.

Brian Paltridge
Aek Phakiti

ACKNOWLEDGEMENTS

We would like to thank the many people who have helped us with this project. Key among these are Gurdeep Mattu and Andrew Wardell at Bloomsbury and Rajakumari Ganessin at Integra who supported us throughout this project. We are also indebted to the students who have taken part in our research methods courses at the University of Sydney. Their questioning of what we have taught them has helped us refine our thinking in the area as well as improve our actual research practices. There are many other people we also wish to thank who have contributed to this book. These include each of the authors of the chapters in the volume. We thank them all for agreeing so readily to write for the book, and for so patiently and promptly responding to our requests for clarification on their chapters. We note though with sadness the passing of Richard Baldauff, who was to write a chapter for the book. He is greatly missed, in our book, as he is missed everywhere else.

We also wish to thank Fran Waugh, the Acting Dean of the Faculty of Education and Social Work and Sue Goodwin, the Associate Dean for Research in our faculty, for their support for TESOL activities and for creating the environment which enables us to do the kind of work that we do. And we thank our families and life partners for their support, without which, none of what we do would be possible.

PART ONE

Research Approaches and Methods

Overview

There are fifteen chapters in this section of the book. In each chapter, authors have included a sample study which illustrates the points they are making. Topics that the authors have addressed include assumptions which underlie the particular method or approach, issues of validity or trustworthiness and research techniques and instruments appropriate to the goal and method of research. The authors have also identified resources for further reading on the particular method or issue under discussion.

- In *Chapter One* (Approaches and Methods in Applied Linguistics), Aek Phakiti and Brian Paltridge present issues and interests in applied linguistics studies. They discuss the nature of academic research, including various dimensions of research.

- In *Chapter Two* (Quantitative Research and Analysis), Aek Phakiti introduces quantitative research methods in language learning and use and presents steps involved in quantitative data analysis. Two types of statistical analyses (descriptive and inferential statistics) are presented.

- In *Chapter Three* (Qualitative Research and Analysis), Adrian Holliday describes the basic premises of qualitative research as a mainstream research approach in applied linguists studies, particularly in the area of language education. His chapter also presents key techniques and instruments of analysis.

- In *Chapter Four* (Mixed Methods Research and Analysis), Nataliya Ivankova and Jennifer Greer explain the nature of mixed methods research (MMR) and the philosophical assumptions and methodological characteristics underlying this research approach. They also present three major MMR designs and their graphic representations, followed by how to implement these designs in research studies.

- In *Chapter Five* (Survey Research), Elvis Wagner discusses the methodology and underlying assumptions of survey research in applied linguistics. Key stages for doing survey research (e.g. planning the project, designing the survey) are outlined.

- In *Chapter Six* (Experimental Research), Susan Gass introduces underlying assumptions of experimental research and important considerations in working with this approach such as the importance of clarifying research questions and research hypotheses and the issue of random assignment.

- In *Chapter Seven* (Case Studies), Christine Casanave presents characteristics and assumptions of case studies, followed by several types of case studies. Procedures for conducting a case study are outlined.

- In *Chapter Eight* (Ethnographic Research), Sue Starfield discusses how ethnography as a qualitative methodology allows researchers to examine issues in everyday contexts, using multiple sources such as observation and participation by the researcher. She also introduces critical ethnography which examines the impacts of inequality in social and educational settings with a view to promoting social change.

- In *Chapter Nine* (Critical Research in Applied Linguistics), Steven Talmy provides a methodological overview of critical applied linguistics research which explores the role of language in producing, sustaining, challenging and transforming power asymmetries, discrimination, inequality, social injustice and hegemony.

- In *Chapter Ten* (Narrative Inquiry), Gary Barkhuizen discusses underlying assumptions associated with narrative inquiry which aims to make sense of the meaning people make of their life experience. He describes a range of techniques for collecting and analysing narrative data.

- In *Chapter Eleven* (Action Research), Anne Burns discusses the philosophical and paradigmatic orientations and methods of action research. She elaborates on issues of reliability and validity in action research which are, still often, contested.

- In *Chapter Twelve* (Discourse Analysis), Brian Paltridge and Wei Wang outline major approaches to the analysis of spoken and written texts such as speech act theory, cross-cultural pragmatics, conversation analysis, genre analysis, critical discourse analysis, corpus approaches to discourse analysis, classroom discourse analysis and multimodal discourse analysis.

- In *Chapter Thirteen* (Research Synthesis), Lourdes Ortega presents the principles and methodology of research synthesis which takes an empirical approach to conducting secondary reviews of the research literature. She highlights the importance of validity and trustworthiness in research syntheses (e.g. sampling relevance, publication bias and primary research quality).

- In *Chapter Fourteen* (Ethics and Applied Linguistics Research), Peter De Costa focuses on ethical considerations in applied linguistics research. He examines the distinction between *macroethics* (i.e. the protocols and principles articulated in professional codes of conduct) and *microethics* (i.e. everyday dilemmas that arise in specific research contexts) which need to be considered in all research designs.

- Finally, in *Chapter Fifteen* (Developing a Research Project), Brian Paltridge and Aek Phakiti discuss research processes and provide guidelines for how a research proposal might be developed and evaluated.

CHAPTER ONE

Approaches and Methods in Applied Linguistics Research

Aek Phakiti and Brian Paltridge

This chapter introduces approaches and methods in applied linguistics research. First, it discusses how applied linguistics has been defined and presents key research areas in the field. Next, it discusses dimensions such as primary versus secondary, cross-sectional versus longitudinal, and quantitative versus qualitative research. It then outlines the notion of research paradigms which underlie choices in research approaches and methods. The concepts of validity, trustworthiness, reliability and research ethics are also introduced.

Defining applied linguistics

Applied linguistics (AL) is an interdisciplinary field of study that aims to understand the multifaceted roles and nature of language use and/or language problems in social contexts (see e.g. Berns & Matsuda 2006; Cook 2003; Davies & Elder 2004; Hall, Smith & Wicaksono 2011; McCarthy 2001; Pawlak & Aronin 2014; Pennycook 2001; Schmitt 2002 for detailed discussions). AL researchers are interested, for example, in understanding how language is used or learnt as well as what problems or difficulties people face when using language to communicate in a variety of situations and contexts. To achieve this, applied linguistics researchers draw on a range of theories and research methodologies not only from linguistics, but also from other disciplines such as education, psychology and sociology.

AL researchers would agree that it is not straightforward to precisely define applied linguistics. This is because language, human characteristics (e.g. behaviours, thoughts, beliefs) and social contexts (e.g. cultures, religions) are highly complex. Cambridge English Language Teaching (ELT) (n.d) has asked leading scholars in the fields of applied linguistics to define applied linguistics. Here are excerpts from what some of these scholars have written that reflect the diversity of opinion regarding how applied linguistics is conceived:

> For me, applied linguistics means taking language and language theories as the basis from which to elucidate how communication is actually carried out in real life, to identify problematic or challenging issues involving language in many different contexts, and to analyse them in order to draw out practical insights and implications that are useful for the people in those contexts. (Anne Burns, p. 1)
>
> Applied linguistics (AL) is one of several academic disciplines focusing on how language is acquired and used in the modern world. It is a somewhat eclectic field that accommodates diverse theoretical approaches, and its interdisciplinary scope includes linguistic, psychological and educational topics. Although the field's original focus was the study of foreign/second languages, this has been extended to cover first language issues, and nowadays many scholars would consider sociolinguistics and pragmatics to be part of the AL rubric. (Zoltán Dörnyei, p. 3)
>
> Applied linguistics (AL) provides the theoretical and descriptive foundations for the investigation and solution of language-related problems, especially those of language education (first-language, second-language and foreign language teaching and learning), but also problems of translation and interpretation, lexicography, forensic linguistics and (perhaps) clinical linguistics. The main distinguishing characteristic of AL is its concern with professional activities whose aim is to solve 'real-world' language-based problems, which means that research touches on a particularly wide range of issues – psychological, pedagogical, social, political and economic as well as linguistic. As a consequence, AL research tends to be interdisciplinary. (Richard Hudson, p. 4)

Under the applied linguistics umbrella, there are many sub-fields, including first and second language acquisition (FLA/SLA), language teaching, language testing and assessment, world Englishes and critical applied linguistics, to name a few (see Davies & Elder 2004 for a wide range of topics that are discussed under the general heading of applied linguistics). Each of these sub-fields asks a variety of research questions and utilizes particular research methodologies to answer these questions.

Topics in applied linguistics

Given the nature of applied linguistics research and the wide range of contexts in which it is carried out, the range of topics examined by applied linguists is vast. Below, ordered alphabetically, is a list of academic journals that have the term *applied linguistics* in their title and which illustrate the diversity of topics that are examined in the area of applied linguistics.

Annual Review of Applied Linguistics (http://journals.cambridge.org/action/display Journal?jid=APL)

This journal provides reviews of research in key areas of applied linguistics. Most articles are state-of-the-art reviews and allow readers to understand current issues and research approaches that have used to examine them. In every fourth or fifth issue, this journal publishes a survey of research in a specific area. Previous issues have focused on topics such as language learning and pedagogy, discourse analysis, teaching innovations, SLA, computer-assisted instruction, language use in professional contexts, sociolinguistics, language policy and language assessment.

Applied Linguistics (http://applij.oxfordjournals.org/)

This journal publishes research into language that is associated with real-world problems. It views applied linguistics not only as the link between theory and practice, but also as the study of language and language-related problems in situations in which people use and learn languages. Areas of research published in this journal include bilingualism and multilingualism, computer-mediated communication, conversation analysis, corpus linguistics, critical discourse analysis, deaf linguistics, discourse analysis and pragmatics, first and additional language learning, teaching and use, forensic linguistics, language assessment, language planning and policies, language for special purposes, lexicography, literacies, multimodal communication, rhetoric and stylistics and translation.

Australian Review of Applied Linguistics (http://www.alaa.org.au/page/aral_journal.html)

This is the journal of the Applied Linguistics Association of Australia. It aims to promote the development of links between language-related research and its application in education, professional and other language-related settings. Articles published in this journal include articles on first and second language teaching and learning, bilingualism and bilingual education, discourse analysis, translation and interpreting, language testing and language planning and policy.

European Journal of Applied Linguistics (http://www.degruyter.com/view/j/eujal)

This journal focuses on problems that are relevant to the language situation in Europe. The topics of interest for this journal include language testing for citizenship, language choice in European Union (EU) institutions, the age factor, consequences of the supremacy of EU legislation for legal terminology in the languages of member states, language contact in Europe, language policies at the national and EU levels, the linguistic needs of migrants and minorities, multilingualism in the workplace, multilingual families and bilingual first language acquisition in Europe and European approaches to foreign language teaching.

International Journal of Applied Linguistics (http://onlinelibrary.wiley.com/journal/10.1111/ (ISSN)1473-4192)

This journal publishes research addressing the links between expertise in language and the experience of people using language. Thus, research areas may include the way language works, how it affects peoples' lives and what interventions are desirable and feasible in differing domains of language use and learning. This journal focuses on areas most closely related to language use and learning in society such as language policy, language in the professions, language in public discourse, and media and translating between languages and registers.

ITL International Journal of Applied Linguistics (http://poj.peeters-leuven.be/content.php?journal _code=ITL&url=journal)

This journal publishes research in the broad area of applied linguistics, with a strong preference for contributions relating to language acquisition such as SLA, foreign/second language teaching and educational linguistics.

Modern Journal of Applied Linguistics (http://www.mjal.org/)

This journal publishes work in all areas of language and linguistics studies including language teaching, language testing, English for specific purposes, pragmatics, computer-assisted language learning, sociolinguistics, language learning problems, discourse analysis, curriculum development, classroom research and language policy.

Aims of applied linguistics research

AL aims to gain an understanding of language learning, the use of and problems associated with language in particular social contexts. There are various aims to applied linguistics research. For example:

- To gain basic knowledge or theory about language learning or use (e.g. first, second, third, bilingualism, multilingualism) generally or in a specific context or for a specific purpose.

- To confirm existing knowledge, theories or ideas about language learning, use or problems through the gathering of empirical evidence.

- To understand the roles of individuals and real-world contexts affecting the nature of language learning or use generally or in a particular context.

- To address problems in language learning, use or communication worldwide (e.g. in particular sociopolitical contexts, or in relation to educational policies and practices).

- To assess or evaluate a situation involving language learning or use such as language teaching, language testing and assessment, language program evaluation, translation, discourse and conversation analysis.

- To reduce or minimize issues concerning unfairness or inequality among people due to language and language-related issues and barriers.

Defining research in applied linguistics

Having introduced some of the aims of applied linguistics research, we now turn to how research is defined in the area of applied linguistics. We start with definitions of *research* provided by a number of applied linguists:

- Research is a systematic process of inquiry consisting of three elements or components: (1) a question, problem or hypothesis; (2) data; and (3) analysis; and interpretation of data (Nunan 1992, p. 3).

- Research is the organized, systematic search for answers to the questions we ask (Hatch & Lazaraton 1991, p. 1).

- 'Research' simply means trying to find answers to questions, an activity every one of us does all the time to learn more about the world around us (Dörnyei 2007, p. 15).

The above definitions are useful to help conceptualize what is involved in research. For the purpose of this chapter, research in applied linguistics can be defined as *an investigation, examination or inquiry that requires planning, organizing and ethical considerations as well as systematic and careful analysis of data, sound interpretations and conclusions on the basis of evidence and inferences being made.* To unpack this definition:

- *Investigation* means paying vigilant, methodical attention to every step in the research process, from the beginning to the end. Care is essential since it helps researchers avoid mistakes or errors in collecting and analysing data, for example.

- *Planning* and *organizing* include identifying what questions are worth asking, how they have been researched to date and why and how they need to be further researched.

- *Systematic* and *careful investigation* include the need to understand what research methods are appropriate and feasible, what approaches to data analysis have been taken by other methodologists or researchers in analysing similar kinds of data and what is acceptable or not in the analysis of the data.

- *Putting forward sound interpretations and conclusions* means not making a claim beyond the available evidence. It is thus essential to consider any limitations in the research that may influence the findings, inferences and conclusions that have been made.

Dimensions of research

Research can be classified into various dimensions. This section of the chapter examines the distinction between *primary* and *secondary* research, *basic* and *applied* research, *cross-sectional* and *longitudinal* research and *quantitative* and *qualitative* research. *Mixed methods* research is also discussed.

Primary versus secondary research

The distinction between *primary* and *secondary* research is determined by whether a new set of data is needed (primary research) or not (secondary research) to answer a research question. *Primary research* requires that empirical data be collected to answer the research question(s). For example, if the aim is to understand people's attitudes or beliefs about something, their motivation to learn a particular language or the typical processes or procedures they use to do something, primary data needs to be collected to provide insights into these questions. The research, thus, might employ particular instruments (e.g. questionnaires) or techniques (e.g. interviews) to collect data which is then analysed in order to answer the research question.

If, however, the aim is to find out what other scholars have done on a particular topic, academic books and journals might be examined in order to do this. This form of inquiry is sometimes termed *secondary research* as it relies on other research and sources to answer the research question(s). Students are likely to begin with secondary research before they move on to conducting primary research. Secondary research can also be described as *library study* or a *review of the literature* on a particular topic. This form of research can be about existing theories or the status of current knowledge on a particular issue that can then be used to form the basis of a primary research project. In recent years, a new form of secondary research has become known as *research synthesis*, which includes a *meta-analysis* (see Ortega this volume) that aims to gain information about the current status of knowledge through a systematic analysis of empirical findings in a particular research area. This form of systematic review is useful as it is able to inform researchers as to what still needs to be done in future research.

Basic versus applied research

Most applied linguistics research can be placed on a basic-applied research continuum. The key distinction between *basic* and *applied* research lies in what researchers aim to achieve in their research. *Basic research* aims to produce fundamental knowledge about something that we currently lack, to refine or to fine-tune current knowledge, so that explanations of a phenomenon are meaningful, sufficient or robust. For example, in SLA research, researchers aim to understand the basic processes involved in language learning (e.g. morpheme acquisition, the roles of long-term and working memories, cross-linguistic influences, and individual and social differences affecting language learning and use; see e.g. Lightbown & Spada 2013; Ortega 2009). Research in these areas has the primary intent of gaining knowledge of or developing theories regarding what underlies individuals' processes or behaviours.

Applied research is related to situations in which researchers or practitioners aim to make use of or apply knowledge or theories from basic research to address a problem by systematically applying them through activities with a group of individuals and observing how they work to, for example, enhance learning or improve a process. In applied research, therefore, researchers aim to seek solutions to a problem.

Action research (see Burns this volume) is an example of applied research. Experimental research can be either basic or applied research depending on the research topics, aims and designs (see Gass this volume). It is important to note, however, that most studies in applied linguistics contain elements of both basic and applied research. It is often difficult to say that an applied linguistics study is basic or applied research due to the nature of the study design employed, which can have both basic and applied purposes.

Cross-sectional versus longitudinal research

The distinction between cross-sectional and longitudinal research relates to the *time* at which the data is collected and the *length* of time taken for the data collection. *Cross-sectional research* refers to research in which researchers collect data from one or more cohorts (a person, group of people) at a single point in time or within a short period of time (e.g. using questionnaires, one-off interviews). Cross-sectional research is often described as a *snapshot of data collection*. Survey research (see Wagner this volume) often adopts a cross-sectional data collection design.

Longitudinal research refers to research in which researchers gather the same aspects of information from the same participant(s) over a period of time. This allows researchers to observe changes or stability in behaviours, learning, abilities and/or other cognitive/social development. Longitudinal research can help researchers establish sequences of events or changes (see Dörnyei 2007 who discusses cross-sectional and longitudinal research distinctions in applied linguistics research; also Flick 2014 who addresses cross-sectional and longitudinal research with a qualitative orientation).

Quantitative versus qualitative research

The key distinction between *quantitative* and *qualitative* research lies in the types of data collected by the researchers. Quantitative data are *numerical data* that researchers obtain to answer research questions, such as test scores, Likert-scale questionnaire responses and academic grades (see Phakiti this volume), whereas qualitative data are data that can be described or conceptualized in words and these include data collected through interviews, observations, texts or pictures, rather than in numbers (see Holliday this volume). It is not, however, sufficient to classify research as just quantitative or qualitative due to the diversity of underlying philosophies and perspectives about what constitutes reality or knowledge that underlie various (so-called) research paradigms (see Research Paradigms below).

Quantitative research generally seeks to *explore* or *determine the relationship* between variables. Such relationships can be linear (two variables can increase or decrease in value in tandem) and causal (one variable can change the characteristics of another variable). Quantitative researchers use *variables* to represent what they are investigating (e.g. language proficiency, anxiety) and objective measures or tests to elicit variables as sources of research data. The researchers attempt to control the object of their investigation by, for example, manipulating or varying conditions of learning and standardizing research instruments and data-collection procedures. Quantitative researchers stress the importance of *objectivity* throughout their research processes (e.g. by avoiding personal opinions, values or judgments). Quantitative researchers often aim to have a *large sample size*, so that they can make better inferences about the variables under investigation and generalize their findings in light of an associated theory or to other populations or settings. Quantitative researchers analyse their data by means of numerical or *statistical* analysis. A statistical analysis can be descriptive (e.g. average scores, frequency counts or percentages) or inferential (e.g. it may employ a *probability* test to investigate the likelihood of a theoretical relationship). There are different quantitative research designs in applied linguistics including experimental research (see Gass this volume) and survey research (see Wagner this volume). Phakiti (this volume) provides an overview of quantitative research and data analysis.

Qualitative research in applied linguistics typically seeks to make sense of language, language learning or use in context, or a social phenomenon as it occurs in *natural settings* such as social and classroom settings. Unlike quantitative researchers, qualitative researchers do not aim to control the research setting. Qualitative researchers take the position that human behaviours such as language learning and use or actions are bound to the context in which they occur. Consequently, social reality within cultures, institutions and values cannot be interpreted in the same manner as physical reality. Qualitative researchers stress the importance of *meaning* and *holistic concerns* rather than discrete variables, statistics and standardization. Qualitative researchers allow themselves to be involved in formulating meanings and interpretations of what they have observed. In some situations, findings are viewed in light of insights from study participants as in ethnographic research (see Starfield this volume). Qualitative researchers employ techniques such as individual or group interviews, naturalistic observations and a range of qualitative data (see Holliday this volume) to help them develop an understanding of the research issue. They may also use research tools such as notes and audio or video recordings in their data collection. Case studies (Casanave this volume), ethnographic research (Starfield this volume) and narrative inquiry (Barkhuizen this volume) are typical examples of qualitative research designs.

Mixed methods research

In recent years, applied linguistics research has begun to combine quantitative and qualitative research methodologies in a single study. This is described as *mixed methods research* (MMR). Creswell and Plano Clark (2011), Ivankova and Greer (this volume) and Riazi and Candlin (2014) provide comprehensive discussions of mixed methods research design. This approach argues that employing both quantitative and qualitative methodologies can strengthen the quality of a study because one can support, complement or expand the other. A mixed methods design is, however, not simply a matter of quantitative data plus qualitative data (see Dörnyei 2007). The rationale and decisions for combining two distinct methodologies are needed for a mixed methods study to be appropriate. Riazi and Candlin (2014) point out that issues involved in MMR designs are highly complex as, for example, they need to be dealt with at the level of research paradigms (e.g. postpositivism and constructivism; further discussed below), purposes of mixed methods research (e.g. triangulation, complementarity, development) and parallelism or sequences of quantitative or qualitative phases. It should also be noted that while *survey research* (Wagner this volume) has a tradition of being quantitative research and *action research* (Burns this volume) has a tradition of being qualitative research, in recent years, both have the potential to be seen as MMR designs since researchers can collect both quantitative and qualitative data while still working with the same approach.

There are three common mixed methods designs in applied linguistics research.

- Researchers can use one research method to complement another; that is, a one-after-the-other design (Flick 2014). The study, thus, may commence with a research question that can be answered through quantitative analysis. On the basis of the findings of the quantitative component of the study, qualitative data may be collected through, for example, individual and group interviews or observations. The researchers then analyse the qualitative data to add to or counterbalance the quantitative findings.

- Researchers use one research approach as a starting point for another; that is, a dominance design (Flick 2014). In this design, the emphasis is more often on the latter method of the two. For example, researchers may interview a group of learners and, on the basis of qualitative analysis of the data, develop a Likert-scale questionnaire that is used with a much larger group of learners to examine the question from a quantitative perspective.

- Researchers ask a set of research questions and use one method to answer each question separately and independently, that is, a side-by-side design (Flick 2014). For example, the question 'what is the relationship between intrinsic motivation and self-efficacy?' could be answered via the use of correlational analysis of questionnaire data. The question 'what are the key factors influencing their relationship?' could then be answered via qualitative analysis of individual interviews with high-, medium- and low-ability students who were part of the questionnaire phase of the study.

People new to research methods can find it difficult to understand the difference between *data triangulation* and *mixed methods research*. Although a mixed methods design may allow researchers to triangulate research results, data triangulation refers only to the strategy of collecting information from different or multiple sources to help gain a deeper understanding of a particular matter. For example, ethnographic researchers who use a combination of interviews, observations and document analysis to answer their research questions are not necessarily employing a mixed methods design since they analyse the data qualitatively, not mixing quantitative and qualitative methods. Similarly, experimental researchers who collect data from language tests, academic grades, self-assessment and various kinds of questionnaire are not necessarily using a mixed methods design since they may choose to analyse all the data statistically. In both examples, data triangulation is not the same as mixed methods research.

Research paradigms

This section of the chapter expands the discussion of research to the level of (so-called) *research paradigms*. Understanding and making sense of research paradigms can be one of the most challenging tasks for new researchers. Indeed, it may take a whole book to address a single research paradigm. Nevertheless, students and other people new to research need to be aware of the research paradigm that underlies the approach(es) to uncovering knowledge that is being used in the research. There is, of course, no good or bad research paradigm, since research is judged on the basis of the topic it investigates, its aims and the methodology being used. Researchers using different paradigms have the same basic mission: to improve knowledge on a particular topic.

A research paradigm is the underlying philosophical view of what constitutes knowledge or reality as the researcher seeks to gain an understanding of a particular topic. The paradigm directs researchers to collect data and/or evidence that can be viewed as valid, legitimate or trustworthy. Predominant research paradigms include positivism, postpositivism, constructivism and critical-realism (see Guba & Lincoln 2005 for a comprehensive review of research paradigms across academic disciplines). A researcher's adopted paradigm is not something that is always boldly stated or labelled by the researcher. Researchers hardly ever say 'I am a postpositivist' or 'This research takes a constructivist perspective' in their published research. However, we can speculate and infer a researcher's paradigm by observing the principles they follow and how they go about their pursuit of knowledge.

So far, this chapter has discussed various approaches to and methods employed in applied linguistics research, including a discussion of both quantitative and qualitative methods. This leads to the question of *why* researchers collect data in a particular way. For example, why do experimental researchers attempt to control or manipulate the research setting? Why do ethnographic researchers not attempt to control or manipulate the research setting, but take it as it is? According to Guba and Lincoln (2005), the question of *why* leads us to the twin concepts of *paradigm* and *strategy*. A research paradigm is a set of beliefs or a philosophical view that underlies the approach to research, whereas a research strategy is the way in which researchers go about trying to understand what they aim to investigate.

There are three key concepts that help us understand the different dimensions of a research paradigm: *ontology* (i.e. our views on the nature of reality), *epistemology* (i.e. our views on the nature of knowledge and how it can be acquired) and *methodology* (i.e. the research approach we use to investigate reality) (Guba & Lincoln 2005). At an ontological level, we ask: what do we think we can know? What is reality? At an epistemological level, we ask: what is our relationship to the thing we are trying to know? Do we need to be *objective* or *subjective* in order to better know it? At a methodological level, we ask: how do we go about our pursuit of knowledge? Is a case study appropriate, for example?

It is important to note that when research authors mention 'quantitative and qualitative research paradigms', what they are actually referring to only distinguishes research at the methodological level, and not at the overarching research paradigm level. We now provide brief definitions of key research paradigms (positivism, postpositivism, constructivism) and pragmatism:

- *Positivism* is a research philosophy that believes that reality can be understood objectively. There is a set of immutable laws or theories that govern reality. Reality is seen as quantifiable and measurable.

- *Postpositivism* is a modified version of positivism that believes reality can only be approximated and cannot be perceived with total accuracy. Objectivity is viewed as an ideology to guide researchers.

- *Constructivism* is a research philosophy that views social realities (e.g. cultures, cultural objects, institutions, values) as multiple and dependent on who is involved, what is being studied and the context in which a study takes place. Reality is typically seen as being socially co-constructed.

- *Pragmatism* is a pluralistic approach to research that stresses the importance of *problem solving* over the adoption of a particular approach to research methods. Pragmatism is not a paradigm in the traditional sense. This research approach adopts methods (quantitative and/or qualitative) that work best to address a particular research problem, rather than committing to a particular research philosophy which may have a specific view of what constitutes reality. Pragmatism seeks an application of multiple methods, types of data and data analyses that can fully provide answers to research questions or problems. This paradigm can be said to underpin mixed methods research.

Ontology

In a *positivist paradigm*, evidence takes on a *realist* perspective. Positivists believe that the object of their inquiry exists objectively. Positivism assumes that physical or social reality is governed by immutable laws that are essentially independent of by whom, when and how it is examined (Guba & Lincoln 2005). This paradigm is the basis of several types of quantitative research, including experimental research and survey research.

A modified positivist or what is now known as a *postpositivist paradigm* would maintain that, although the object of inquiry exists independently of the human mind, researchers cannot observe and perceive it with total accuracy. This view can be regarded as a *critical realist ontology*. Positivists and postpositivists, for example, strive for testable and confirmable theories that explain phenomena by showing how they are derived from theoretical assumptions. They, for example, posit that there is a cause–effect relationship between two variables and seek scientific explanations and laws governing human behaviours, thoughts and behaviours.

Unlike positivism and postpositivism, *constructivism* does not share the realist or critical realist perspective. That is, it takes the *relativist* stance that realities are multiple and exist in people's minds. Although there is no one way to describe constructivism due to varying perspectives of what constitute the truth and diverse starting points of research inquiry (Flick 2014; LeCompte & Schensul 2010), constructivists would agree in their assertion that the subject matter of social sciences differs fundamentally from the subject matter of physical or natural sciences and, therefore, requires a different goal for inquiry and a different set of methods for investigation. They further argue that social reality (e.g. cultures, cultural objects, institutions, values) cannot be reduced in the same manner as physical reality. Hence, perceived reality can be multiple depending on who is involved and the context in which the study takes place. It is the task of the researcher to understand and portray social settings or events as they are, rather than trying to manipulate them.

Pragmatism does not necessarily view truth or reality as something independent of human minds or something socially co-constructed. Pragmatists do not have to commit to a traditional system of reality arguments. Rather, they focus on the need to use a variety of methods from various research paradigms to advance their knowledge about the research problem under investigation.

Epistemology

In relation to its ontology, *positivism* assumes an *objectivist* stance towards research inquiry. That is, positivists must remove their influence from the research setting and distance themselves from their object of inquiry, so that they can determine an accurate correspondence between their observations and this reality. Unlike positivists, *postpositivists* argue that complete objectivity is nearly impossible to achieve. They do, nonetheless, retain the notion of objectivity as an idea to regulate their research. That is, they can never absolutely know the truth, but they can approximate it, and can get closer to it with better theories, and through their experiences of conducting research.

Unlike positivism and postpositivism, the *constructivist paradigm* takes the *subjectivist* position that attempts to know things are inherently and unavoidably subjective. Reality, as they perceive it, is dependent upon, rather than independent of, their inquiry. They argue that facts cannot be established as aspects of knowledge independent of a researcher's values and background. Taking the epistemological aspect into consideration when examining research in applied linguistics, significant differences can be seen in the way in which researchers collect data. In a language classroom, for example, an observer may choose to sit at the back of the classroom and observe quietly what is going on using a structured observation scheme. He or she would try to be as objective as possible and be aware of the need to avoid any personal bias during the observation. Another observer may choose to be actively involved in the classroom activities and attempt to establish *trust* with the participants. This method of being involved, he/she argues, allows him/her to gain deeper insights into the participants' minds and perspectives.

Proponents of pragmatism are aware of the issues related to objectivity and subjectivity in research. They acknowledge that research takes place in a social setting and to be objective or subjective depends on what is socially accepted. For example, when the setting involves testing and assessment, which may have high-stakes implications on individuals and/or society, objectivity is needed. However, when the object of inquiry is related to individuals' feelings or attitudes towards some sociocultural activities, subjectivity will be critical to facilitate insight into participants' minds.

Pragmatically speaking, objectivity and subjectivity need to be considered in relation to real-world research topics and traditional views of methods associated with such topics.

Methodology

Positivists conduct their research by defining and controlling variables and manipulating the research setting. In experimental research, researchers vary the independent variable (the variable believed to influence other variables) under various conditions to test its effect. Participants are randomly assigned to different conditions to avoid subjective selection by the researchers and to minimize the impact of other independent variables that might coexist during the experimental study (e.g. the different ages and levels of language proficiency of participants). In survey and correlational research, research instruments (e.g. questionnaires and tests) and data-collection procedures should be validated (trialled and analysed) before actually being used in the main study. These are examples of control and manipulation.

Postpositivists take a similar stance to the positivists. However, they modify the positivists' position by promoting the use of multiple strategies for gathering and analysing data (including qualitative data such as interviews and observations). It should be noted that within postpositivism, data collection and analysis must still be carried out within the critical realist ontology (to maintain as much objectivity as possible). For example, qualitative data such as interview data must be coded by two or more trained coders, and intra- and inter-coder reliability estimates must be calculated and reported.

The constructivist paradigm, in contrast, adopts a non-experimental, non-manipulative set of research procedures including the range of techniques associated with participant observation and in-depth interviews. The term *hermeneutics* is used to describe a research process in which the researcher forms interpretations or constructions, from a close understanding of the data (e.g. observation notes, interview recordings). This initiates a cycle (potentially never-ending the hermeneutic circle) of interpreting these constructions and then refining and forming new constructions.

Finally, pragmatists look for various approaches and methods to address a real-world research problem. They attempt to use the best of both quantitative and qualitative research methods to maximize their understanding. Pragmatists might combine a traditional survey research method using a large sample size, followed by a case study utilizing individual interviews (with students, teachers and administrators) and classroom observations using both structural observation schemes and qualitative observations.

Owing to the complexity of paradigm dimensions and research specificities, there are other research paradigms that we have not included here (e.g. the ecological paradigm, the critical paradigm, the social network paradigm, the feminism and the participatory paradigm; see e.g. Flick 2014; Guba & Lincoln 2005). Some authors in this volume do however touch on some of these research paradigms in their chapters.

Table 1.1 summarizes the differences between key research paradigms at the ontological, epistemological and methodological levels (e.g. Creswell 2014; Flick 2004, 2014; Guba & Lincoln 2005; LeCompte & Schensul 2010).

Validity, reliability and ethics

The adopted research paradigm plays a significant role in defining what is considered to be valid research. In this volume, various authors describe what they see as valid or trustworthy within a particular research design. Here, we introduce the concept of validity/trustworthiness, reliability and ethics.

The term *validity* is largely associated with traditional quantitative research. However, some qualitative researchers do use the term 'validity' to describe the legitimacy of their research. An alternative term adopted in qualitative research, however, is *trustworthiness*. Regardless of a preference for one term or the other, validity and trustworthiness are related to the extent to which we can trust the research findings; that is, what the researchers claim as knowledge and understanding of a research problem. See Gass (this volume) and Wagner (this volume) for further types of validity of quantitative research; see Casanave (this volume) and Burns (this volume) for discussions of trustworthiness in qualitative research.

Reliability is driven by quantitative research and is about *consistency* in measuring something of interest. Often, reliability is associated with research instruments. In quantitative research, research validity cannot be attained when the research instruments used are unreliable. However, reliable instruments may not be valid. For example, an English grammar test may be reliable because students will get similar scores if they take the test on multiple occasions. However, if the scores from the grammar test are used to make claims about how well students can write in English, an invalid claim is being made because writing ability involves more than just grammatical knowledge. In qualitative research, researchers use the concept of *dependability*, which allows readers to understand any shifting conditions that are associated with the participants and the setting being researched

Table 1.1 Differences between four research paradigms (e.g. Creswell 2014; Flick 2014; Guba & Lincoln 2005; LeCompte & Schensul 2010)

Level	Positivism	Postpositivism	Constructivism	Pragmatism
Ontology	Realism: Reality is 'out there' and can be known; hypothetical linear or cause–effect relationships	Critical realism: Reality is out there but probable facts; no absolute truth about relationships	Relativism: Multiple realities as constructed by the local and specific; co-construction of knowledge or understanding of relationships	Not committed to one system of reality
Epistemology	Objective; context- and value-free; to prove or test theory; generalize findings; to establish universal theory	Objective; context-bound; to prove, test and/or falsify theory	Subjective; value-bound; to portray people, social settings or events	Objectivity and subjectivity depends on the real-world problem being focused.
Methodology	Control and manipulation of variables, testing and measurement of variables, quantitative research methods such as experimental, survey, statistical research; quantitative instrument (e.g. tests, questionnaires); stress reliability and validity of measurement and analysis	Similar to positivism, but modified quantitative research designs; multiple strategies (including qualitative techniques, but must be objective)	Hermeneutical; dialectical; qualitative research methods (e.g. case studies, ethnographies, narrative inquiry); qualitative techniques (e.g. interviews, observation, documents); employ trustworthiness criteria	Flexible to adopt a variety of methods and techniques across other research paradigms. It takes a problem-centred approach.

and any research modifications researchers make as they progress through their study. Such explicit and honest accounts of research methods can help both researchers and their readers understand the research findings. Dependability, thus, in qualitative research is analogous to *reliability* in quantitative research.

Ethical considerations are critical to all research. If knowledge is gained through research processes that might harm human beings (physically or psychologically), intentionally or unintentionally, then the price of this knowledge may be considered too high. With regard to research participants, some points researchers should consider include whether *informed consent should be sought* (i.e. should all research participants be informed of the potential risks and benefits of the research before giving their consent, and is this consent required?), should *anonymity* be maintained (i.e. should the identities of research participants remain undisclosed, potentially even to the researcher?) and should *confidentiality* be respected? (e.g. in the case in which the researcher is aware of the identities of research participants, should these identities be revealed or not in the reporting of the data). Ethics approval needs to be obtained from the institution where the study is being carried out prior to the data collection. In most academic institutions, there is a research ethics committee that considers research projects and makes sure that a high ethical standard in the research has been met (see De Costa this volume for a discussion of this).

Peer-reviewed journals in applied linguistics

The following refereed journals publish on a variety of research topics in applied linguistics:

Applied Linguistics; Bilingualism: Language and Cognition; English for Specific Purposes; English Language Teaching Journal; International Review of Applied Linguistics; Journal of Bilingualism; Language Learning; Language Teaching; Language Teaching Research; Second Language Research; Studies in Second Language Acquisition; System; TESOL Quarterly; The Modern Language Journal; World Englishes.

A further useful resource for locating applied linguistics journals is the document published each year by the International TESOL Association titled *How to Get Published in TESOL and Applied Linguistics Serials* which is available at:

http://www.tesol.org/docs/default-source/books/how-to-get-published-in-applied-linguistics-serials.pdf?sfvrsn=4

Resources for further reading

Each of the chapters of this book recommends further reading on the particular approaches, methods or topics being discussed. Here, we list a number of books on research methods that readers will find useful.

Allison, D 2002, *Approaching English Language Research*, Singapore University Press, Singapore.

Allison presents the process of carrying out research. This book discusses practical problems in undertaking research, reading and reporting on research, data analysis and the interpretation of findings. There is a chapter on writing a research proposal as well as a section on problems that students often meet in carrying out research.

Brown, JD & Rodgers, TS 2002, *Doing Second Language Research*, Oxford University Press, Oxford.

This book discusses both qualitative and quantitative research. Specific topics include case study research, introspective methods, classroom-based research, the use of statistics and language program evaluation. There are many self-study exercises in the book.

Dörnyei, Z 2007, *Research Methods in Applied Linguistics*, Oxford University Press, Oxford.

This book provides an extensive discussion of quantitative, qualitative and mixed method research. There are also chapters on data analysis and reporting on research.

Flick, U 2014, *An Introduction to Qualitative Research*, 5th edn, Sage, London.

Now in its fifth edition, this book comprehensively presents approaches to qualitative research and methodologies involved in conducting qualitative research. Although this book is not written specifically for applied linguistics research, it is accessible and extremely useful for researchers who are new to qualitative research.

Gass, S & Mackey, A 2007, *Data Elicitation for Second and Foreign Language research*, Lawrence Erlbaum, Mahwah.

This book presents a detailed discussion of data elicitation techniques for second and foreign language research. This includes a discussion of psycholinguistics-based research, research which examines cognitive processes, survey research, pragmatics-based research and classroom-based research.

McKay, SL 2006, *Researching Second Language Classrooms*, Lawrence Erlbaum, Mahwah.

This book provides a very good overview of methods for researching second language classrooms. It contains chapters on different types of research, ways of researching classroom discourse, and provides guidance for writing research reports. Particular attention is given to action research, survey research, introspective research, case studies and ethnographic studies.

Mackey, A & Gass, S 2005, *Second Language Research: Methodology and Design*. Lawrence Erlbaum, Mahwah.

This book discusses issues in data gathering, common data-collection techniques and the coding of data. It also discusses qualitative and quantitative research, classroom-based research and issues in the reporting of research.

Mackey, A & Gass, SM (eds) 2012, *Research Methods in Second Language Acquisition: A Practical Guide*, Wiley-Blackwell, Malden.

This edited book provides a comprehensive, step-by-step guide to various research designs in second language research. There are two parts to this book: data types (e.g. areas of research including learner corpora, instructed SLA, second language writing and reading), and data coding, analysis and replication (e.g. how to code qualitative data and run statistical analysis, how to do a meta-analysis and replication study).

Richards, K, Ross, S & Seedhouse, P 2012, *Research Methods for Applied Language Studies: An Advanced Research Book for Students*, Routledge, London.

This book presents quantitative, qualitative and mixed methods research designs in applied language studies, particularly in the areas of foreign language learning, teaching and assessment. In each chapter, the authors provide a range of tasks and discussion points to help readers understand some specific research concepts and topics.

Walliman, N 2011, *Research Methods: The Basics*, Routledge, London.

This book introduces various aspects of research principles, theories and methodologies. Topics include types of data, data-collection procedures, data analysis and research writing.

References

Berns, M & Matsuda, PK 2006, 'Applied linguistics: Overview and history', in K Brown (ed.), *The Encyclopedia of Language and Linguistics*, 2nd edn, Elsevier, Oxford, pp. 394–405.

Cambridge English Language Teaching (ELT) n.d, 'What is applied linguistics?', viewed 30 July 2014 http://www.cambridge.org.br/for-teachers/applied -linguistics?uk_url=/servlet/file/store7/item5633198/version1/Article_What%20 is%20applied%20linguistics.pdf.

Cook, G 2003, *Applied Linguistics*, Oxford University Press, Oxford.

Creswell, JW 2014, *Research Design: Qualitative, Quantitative, and Mixed Methods Approaches*, 4th edn, Sage, Thousand Oaks, CA.

Creswell, JW & Plano Clark, VL 2011, *Designing and Conducting Mixed Methods Research*, 2nd edn, Sage, Thousand Oaks, CA.

Davies, A & Elder, C (eds), 2004, *Handbook of Applied Linguistics*, Blackwell, London.

Dörnyei, Z 2007, *Research Methods in Applied Linguistics: Quantitative, Qualitative, and Mixed Methodologies*, Oxford University Press, Oxford.

Flick, U 2004, 'Constructivism', in U Flick, Ev Kardorff & I Steinke (eds), *A Companion to Qualitative Research*, Sage, London, pp. 88–94.

———— 2014, *An Introduction to Qualitative Research*, 5th edn, Sage, London.

Guba, EG & Lincoln, YS 2005, 'Paradigmatic controversies, contradictions, and emerging confluences', in NK Denzin & YS Lincoln (eds), *The Sage Handbook of Qualitative Research*, 3rd edn, Sage, Thousand Oaks, CA, pp. 191–215.

Hall, CJ, Smith, PH & Wicaksono, R 2011, *Mapping Applied Linguistics: A Guide for Students and Practitioners*, Routledge, London.

Hatch, E & Lazaraton, A 1991, *The Research Manual: Design and Statistics for Applied Linguistics*, Newbury House, Rowley, MA.

LeCompte, MD & Schensul, J 2010, *Designing and Conducting Ethnographic Research: An Introduction*, AltaMira Press, Plymouth.

Lightbown, PM & Spada, N 2013, *How Languages are Learned*, 4th edn, Oxford University Press, Oxford.

McCarthy, M 2001, *Issues in Applied Linguistics*, Cambridge University Press, Cambridge.

Nunan, D 1992, *Research Methods in Language Learning*, Cambridge University Press, Cambridge.

Ortega, L 2009, *Understanding Second Language Acquisition*, Hodder, London.

Pawlak, M & Aronin, L 2014, *Essential Topics in Applied linguistics and Multilingualism: Studies in Honor of David Singleton*, Springer, New York, NY.

Pennycook, A 2001, *Critical Applied Linguistics: A Critical Introduction*, Lawrence Erlbaum Associates, London.

Riazi, M & Candlin, CN 2014, 'Mixed-methods research in language teaching and learning: Opportunities, issues and challenges', *Language Teaching*, vol. 47, no. 2, pp. 135–173.

Schmitt, N 2002, *An Introduction to Applied Linguistics*, Arnold, London.

CHAPTER TWO

Quantitative Research and Analysis

Aek Phakiti

A good deal of research in applied linguistics and language acquisition research involves quantifying aspects of language learning and use and factors that are part of or influence language learning and/or use (e.g. knowledge about language, first language, motivation, self-regulation and anxiety (see Lightbown & Spada 2013; Macaro 2010; Ortega 2009 for topics of language learning research). Lazaraton (2005), Loewen and Gass 2009, Plonsky and Gass (2011) and Plonsky (2013, 2014) present and discuss issues and applications of quantitative methods and designs in applied linguistics and language learning research. This chapter introduces quantitative research methods in language learning and use and discusses issues involved in quantitative data analysis. It also presents two types of statistical analyses (descriptive and inferential statistics) that are used in quantitative research. The chapter concludes with the presentation of a sample study, paying particular attention to quantitative data analysis.

Underlying assumptions and methodology

Quantitative research usually involves numbers, quantification and statistics to address a research problem or objective, and it typically requires a large sample size. There are two kinds of statistics which determine the nature of quantitative research: descriptive statistics and inferential statistics (discussed below). Quantitative research that aims to investigate the characteristics of a population (e.g. Census survey, a national literacy test) or opinions, perceptions and attitudes of learners (e.g. perceived effectiveness of a language program, learning anxiety and language needs) may simply aim to report an *average score*, a *percentage* or a *rank* of something for all participants. This kind of quantitative research uses *descriptive statistics*.

Another type of quantitative research aims to do more than just reporting an average score, ranked score or a percentage. For example, researchers may aim to examine a causal-like or linear relationship between two or more variables, such as aspects of language learning (e.g. the age, gender, language proficiency and/or aptitude of students and the teaching methods employed to teach them). This kind of quantitative research uses *inferential statistics*.

The origin of quantitative research was *positivism* – a philosophical perspective that strives to understand universal principles or rules that govern human behaviours. A positivist takes a *realist stance* and believes that reality is essentially independent of who is examining it and when and how it is being examined. Today's quantitative researchers generally take a *postpositivistic* position, which is a modified version of positivism. It distinguishes ideology from reality. According to proponents of this position, an object of inquiry cannot be understood with complete accuracy. Instead, they believe that objectivity is a *regulative* principle which reminds researchers to be aware of potential influences of their personal bias or values as well as those of others involved in a research setting on research outcomes. See Guba and Lincoln (2005) and Phakiti and Paltridge (this volume) for a discussion of research paradigms.

Types of quantitative research

Examples of research where a quantitative approach is usually taken are experiments, surveys, correlational studies, individual differences research and language testing research. It should be noted that although today's research may be qualitative or quantitative or mixed, in this chapter each of these designs is discussed in the situation in which researchers employ a quantitative method.

Experimental research

Experimental researchers consider two types of variables (i.e. aspects or characteristics of something that can take different values or scores): independent and dependent variables. An *independent variable* is a variable that exists freely and is hypothesized to have an effect on other variables that are described as *dependent variables*. For example, if an instruction is an independent variable, students' learning performance in the classroom may be considered a dependent variable. Experimental research typically examines causal-like relationships between independent variables and dependent variables of interest. Instructed second language acquisition research can test a theory using an experimental research design, which should be considered and planned in its entirety prior to its implementation. Researchers strictly control the conditions under which an independent variable of interest (e.g. types of feedback or instructions) is to be tested for its effects on language learning behaviours or outcomes (e.g. better writing performance and increased positive attitude towards learning). *Random assignment* is used to allocate participants into experimental and control groups. Random assignment is a technique in which researchers assign participants into two or more groups using a by-chance technique (e.g. a coin-toss or randomized computer program). Through this technique, each participant will have an equal chance of being placed in any one group (see Gass this volume). Inferential statistics, such as *t*-tests and analysis of variance (ANOVA), are used to answer research questions (see e.g. Gass this volume; Phakiti 2014; Read this volume; Vandergrift this volume). In recent years, experimental research has begun to utilize a mixed methods approach.

Survey research

Survey research often focuses on a snapshot of a particular topic of interest (i.e. it is cross-sectional) with a large sample size. It can be longitudinal when researchers aim to collect the same data from the same participants at different points of time. Researchers typically adopt *Likert-scale questionnaires* which ask respondents to choose a scale ranging, for example, from 1 to 5, or *structured interviews* which allow all respondents to answer the same questions. It is important to note that survey research is not always purely quantitative, because researchers can gather qualitative data (e.g. through open-ended questions or survey interviews) and analyse them qualitatively. Survey research can, therefore, be quantitative, qualitative or mixed, depending on a researcher (see Wagner this volume). When survey researchers analyse quantitative questionnaire data, they typically use statistics to examine the reliability of the questionnaire, correlations between pairs of variables of interest and to make comparisons among different groups of participants.

Correlational research

Correlational research aims to explore whether a relationship between two variables exists, and if so, to what extent they are related. It is conducted without manipulating the research setting. Survey research can adopt correlational analysis, but correlational research is broader than survey research in that the data are not always gathered from survey instruments. Data may be from an existing database (e.g. students' grades, test scores and hours of study) or participants may be asked to complete test tasks so that their test performance data can be used for correlational analysis. Research that focuses on a particular language skill (e.g. reading, listening, speaking and writing) also uses correlational analysis (see several chapters in Part 2 of this volume).

Individual differences research

Individual differences research (also known as *ex post facto* research) examines whether a variable (e.g. motivation, aptitude, anxiety, language learning strategies, reading ability and attitude towards something) differs among different groups of learners (e.g. defined by gender, age, years of language exposure, language background and native versus non-native speakers). Data may be collected using similar methods to those used in correlational analysis or using survey research instruments. As in experimental research, groups of learners are treated as independent variables for the purpose of statistical comparison. However, unlike in experimental research, researchers do not manipulate, modify or control the research setting. They explore differences among learners as they exist, as in survey and correlational research.

Language testing and assessment research

Language testing is a key area of research in applied linguistics. It aims to measure language learners' proficiency or language skills. The number of language testing studies is quantitative because it examines test reliability, scoring methods and test validity (see below). Test validation research that aims to verify and improve the quality of test questions or tasks before its actual use in testing language learners is predominant in this type of quantitative research. Several specific statistical procedures, such as Item Response Theory, Generalizability Theory and Differential Item Functioning analysis are used (see Purpura 2011; Read this volume for further discussion of this).

Validity and reliability

There are two interconnected levels of validity in quantitative research: the validity of a research instrument and the validity of a research result. The *validity of a research instrument* (e.g. a test, a questionnaire and an observation scheme) is related to how accurately the instrument yields information about the aspect under investigation. An evaluation of the validity of a research instrument includes, for example, considering the theory underlying the behaviours to be measured, the characteristics of the instruments (e.g. types and number of questions or items), the manner in which it is used to collect the data and its reliability (i.e. consistency of the scoring, rating or reporting).

Reliability is related to the concept of *consistency*. To understand the concept of reliability, let us take a clock as an example. A clock with a good battery is likely to be consistent, thereby reliable. Suppose one clock is five minutes faster and the other is ten minutes slower than the actual time. Both clocks are consistent in their timing. In this example, the clocks are reliable, but they do not tell us the correct (let us say 'valid') time. The concept of reliability is closely related to validity in the sense that a quantitative study cannot be valid if it uses unreliable data to analyse and answer its research questions. It is important to note that something that is valid in one context may not be valid in another. Take a watch as another example. Three students have just arrived in Sydney (Australia) from Shanghai (China), Barcelona (Spain) and Tokyo (Japan). They have not adjusted their watches yet. Their watches' times are not valid to show Sydney's time but are valid in their home countries.

In quantitative research, the reliability of the data is often determined by reliability coefficients or measures of internal consistency. In language test data, researchers usually report KR-20 (Kuder–Richardson 20) as a reliability estimate of objective tests (Brown 1996). In rating-scale and Likert-scale questionnaires, researchers report a correlation coefficient or Cronbach Alpha coefficient (Dörnyei 2007). Generally speaking, a reliability estimate ranges from 0 (0 per cent reliable) to 1 (100 per cent reliable). A reliability coefficient of 0.90 upwards is desirable, although a coefficient of 1 is rare. In general, a reliability coefficient of 0.70 for a questionnaire is taken to be acceptable (Dörnyei 2007).

The *validity of a research finding* is concerned with the *accuracy* of the finding. This validity depends on how valid and reliable research instruments in a particular study are as well as on the statistical validity of the data analysis. *Statistical validity* is related to the *probability value* that researchers set to reject a *null hypothesis* (a null hypothesis states that no relationship or difference among groups exists). Statistical validity also depends on whether researchers use an appropriate statistical test to investigate a research question and whether the statistical assumptions of a particular statistical test are met or not. The considerations of both the validity of the research instruments being used and the research outcomes reflect the extent to which a quantitative study is *sound* and is likely to yield useful information or knowledge (see Gass this volume, which presents specific aspects of quantitative validity including construct, content and face validity).

Techniques and instruments

There is a wide range of quantitative data types in applied linguistics research. Quantitative data can derive from measurement instruments that quantify variables and factors, such as the results of language tests or responses on Likert-scale questionnaires. They can also derive from qualitative data collection techniques such as think-aloud protocols, retrospective interviews, diaries and written, visual, audio or spoken texts (see Gass & Mackey 2007; Mackey & Gass 2005). Several chapters in this volume present and discuss quantitative research instruments and techniques in detail (e.g. Hyland, Stevenson, Vandergrift, Wagner).

Key stages in quantitative data analysis

There are a number of stages researchers typically move through in the preparation of quantitative data for analysis.

Checking and organizing data

In the checking and organizing data stage, the data need to be checked to see whether each study participant has fully completed all sections or items in the data collection procedure. Interview data, for example, need to be transcribed and organized prior to quantification processes (such as tally and frequency counts). Once all data (quantitative or qualitative) have been double-checked, participant identification (ID) codes need to be assigned, so that the data can be easily referred to when checking the accuracy of the data entry.

Coding data

The aim of data coding is to classify or group the data, thereby making it easier to analyse. Coding allows the researcher to quantify and represent the area under investigation using numbers. To achieve validity in the data coding, the data needs to be coded in a systematic and principled way.

How quantitative data is coded depends on the nature of the scales used to measure the variables. There are three basic types of quantitative data, *nominal data*, *ordinal data* and *interval data* (Dörnyei 2007). The distinctions among these are important when selecting appropriate statistical techniques to use to analyse the data. *Nominal data* (also referred to as categorical data) are used for classification and group comparison purposes.

We may, for example, ask participants to report whether they are native or non-native speakers of English. For statistical analysis, we can code this data by assigning 1 to native speakers of English and 2 to non-native speakers of English. Nominal data do not have mathematical properties. For example, we cannot say that people assigned 2 have higher scores than people assigned 1.

Ordinal data (meaning 'ordering' the data) are known as *rank-ordered* data. Examples of this include academic grades, Likert-scale data, rank of class achievement and ranking on the basis of personality or psychological traits. For example, academic grades can be coded as follows: A (coded 5), B (coded 4), C (coded 3), D (coded 2) and F (coded 1). Although ordering data in this way allows us to express differences in individuals' characteristics, it does not allow us to express the degree of these differences. For example, in an agreement scale ranging from 1 (strongly disagree) to 5 (strongly agree), we can see that one is greater or lesser than another in terms of level of agreement, but we cannot say that the distance between the scores of 4 (agree) and 5 (strongly agree) is the same as the distance between the scores of 1 (strongly disagree) and 2 (disagree), for example. Whether ordinal data can be seen as interval data (discussed next) has been an ongoing debate among statisticians and quantitative researchers.

Interval data are data measured on an interval scale, which is a scale of measurement in which the distance between any two adjacent units of measurement is the same. Examples of interval data include language test scores, the number of years of study and age. Interval data are suitable for inferential statistics (discussed below) because they have continuous values.

Coding qualitative data, such as think-aloud, written, oral or interview data for quantitative data analysis involves the development of coding systems to quantify the variables of interest. Much of the coding of qualitative data is subjective in the sense that each coder or rater may interpret the meaning of the qualitative data differently. Hence, we need to be mindful of the consistency of coding for each individual coder or rater (intra-coder or -rater reliability) and between two or more coders or raters (inter-coder or -rater reliability; see Mackey & Gass 2005). Data coding training and moderation of coding need to be implemented to achieve consistency. There are some inter-coder reliability estimates that can be used, including: (1) percentage agreement (the ratio of the number of items coded the same to the total number of items coded) and (2) *Cohen's kappa* (a statistic indicating the average rate of agreement for an entire set of data, taking into account both agreement and disagreement between coders). Cohen's kappa is preferred over percentage agreement as it takes into consideration the random chance of coding agreement and the quantity of data coded. A Cohen's kappa coefficient ranges between 0 and 1. A Cohen's kappa of 0.75 or above indicates a good to very good level of the agreement between two coders (see Altman 1991; Cohen 1960; Fleiss 1981).

Entering data into a computer program

Once the data have been coded and numerical values have been assigned, the data can be keyed into a statistical software program such as IBM SPSS (Statistical Package for Social Sciences), which allows us to handle quantitative data from a large sample. Issues relevant to data entry include naming data files, defining variables for data recording and entering data into a designated file. The data entry process needs to be managed to reduce the chance of errors (see Dörnyei 2007). During data entry, the issues of missing data and potential outliers (i.e. extreme cases which can distort statistical results) will need to be dealt with.

Screening and cleaning data

The screening and cleaning stage concerns the accuracy of data entry and involves the use of a decision-making process for dealing with missing data and incorrect data entry. For example, SPSS can be used to compute a minimum and maximum value for each variable. If, for example, the maximum value of an item is 5 but SPSS reports it as 55 instead, it means that there is a data entry error for this item. We then need to check where the mistake occurred in the data file and correct it.

Data screening can also be performed through the use of diagrams, such as histograms or charts that can be produced by SPSS. Through a visual inspection of these diagrams, impossible values in the data set can be detected. Data screening allows us to identify and correct data entry problems and remove outliers.

Analysing the reliability of data

Quantitative researchers need to make sure that their data are derived from reliable instruments or measures. Reliability is a necessary yet insufficient condition for validity because a study cannot be valid if its instruments are not reliable. As discussed above, the reliability of an instrument is related to its *consistency* in capturing the target construct of the investigation across points in time and its ability to discriminate among participants who possess different levels of the construct of interest of the research (e.g. writing ability, motivation levels). SPSS can analyse research instrument reliability.

Reducing data

It is often the case that there are numerous variables in the same data file for analysis (e.g. test score variables, strategy use items and motivation items). In this case, we will experience difficulty in managing and analysing the data, so we should seek to reduce the number of variables to a reasonable level. If we do a correlational analysis (discussed in the sample study), there can be hundreds of correlation coefficients to interpret, report and discuss. Hence, we need some theoretical rationale to help us reduce the number of variables for quantitative data analysis to answer our research questions. Many psychological and cognitive constructs, such as language proficiency, metacognition, motivation and anxiety, can be inferred through observation of various behaviours or thoughts. Therefore, we can use multiple items to assess one construct. For example, we may be able to understand metacognitive strategy use by devising questionnaire items measuring planning, monitoring and evaluating strategy use. Within each of these subscales, there are a number of items which can be combined to form a single score (or a *composite*). This is done to ensure that the construct of interest is not under-represented by our measurements. By aggregating items, we gain richer information about the construct under examination.

There are different statistical techniques that can minimize the chance of aggregating irrelevant or problematic items with reliable ones. First, *correlation coefficients* (discussed below) can inform us as to whether the items measure the same construct. Here, we should expect a strong correlation among them. Second, reliability analysis in SPSS can help us decide whether items are suitable for inclusion. In *Cronbach alpha analysis*, SPSS allows us to check whether the reliability of each subscale will increase or decrease if we exclude a particular item in the subscale. This information can help us decide whether we should include a particular item to form a composite. Third, we can employ *exploratory factor analysis* (EFA) to help us reduce the number of items for further inferential statistics.

Performing inferential statistics

Quantitative researchers choose appropriate statistical tests (e.g. parametric or non-parametric, discussed below) to answer the research question. Researchers need to know which statistical test can yield the answer to a particular research question. For example, if they aim to address a linear relationship, a Pearson correlation may be suitable, if the statistical assumptions are met. If they aim to examine group differences, an independent-samples *t*-test, an ANOVA or a multivariate analysis of variance (MANOVA) may be employed. Some of these statistical tests will be introduced below.

Basic statistical concepts

Much of what we do in quantitative data analysis involves *statistics* because we do not always have the information we need from the entire population of interest. If the data are from all members of the population, we deal with *parameters*. However, in most circumstances, such as in a classroom context, we only have access to a sample of the target population. In order to estimate the parameters of the population from the sample, we use inferential statistics. Sometimes in our research, we need only basic statistics such as frequency counts, percentages or means (average scores) to answer our research questions. Here we use *descriptive statistics* (i.e. statistics for describing, summarizing and explaining the distribution of a data set). At other times, we need to go through detailed statistical procedures to answer our research questions because of the complex nature of the issue we are researching and the nature of the research. Here, we work with inferential statistics (i.e. statistics for making inferences about population parameters). We now explore the differences between descriptive and inferential statistics and how they are related in quantitative research.

Descriptive statistics

Descriptive statistics are used to describe individual variables. A mean score is an example of a descriptive statistic. Instead of using raw test data to show how students performed in an exit test, we can calculate the mean score which shows how well the students did in the test as a group. Descriptive statistics can be divided into measures of frequency, central tendency and dispersion.

Measures of frequency are mostly used with nominal data. Frequencies can be represented using a histogram, a sector graph or a bar chart. Frequencies can also be represented in a table with percentages calculated cumulatively. *Measures of central tendency* provide an overall picture of the data. The three common measures of central tendency are the mean, the median and the mode. The *mean* is the most common indicator of central tendency. It can be calculated by summing all the scores of a variable in the data set and dividing the result by the number of scores. For example, the mean of the data set 1, 2, 3, 4, 5 is 3 (i.e. 15 ÷ 5). The *median* is the value that divides the data set exactly into two parts of equal size, the data being arranged in ascending order. In the data set described above, the median is also 3. The median can be more appropriate as a descriptor if the mean is distorted by an outlier. For the data set 6, 7, 8, 9, 11, 76, the mean is 19.5 while the median is 8.5. 76 is an example of an outlier. The *mode* is the value that occurs most frequently in the data set. In the data set 12, 13, 14, 14, 14, 16, 18, the mode is 14.

Measures of dispersion describe the *variability* of the data away from the measure of central tendency. However, measures of central tendency do not necessarily tell the entire story of the data. For example, a mean of 24.66 could be achieved in a *homogenous* data set, such as 24, 24, 24, 25, 25, 26, or by a *heterogeneous* data set, such as 2, 7, 15, 28, 46, 50. The mean also depends on the sample size and hence we cannot always compare the means of two different learner groups if the sample sizes differ greatly. Hence, we may need other measures of dispersion. The *standard deviation* is a statistic that describes the variability of the data. The standard deviation indicates by how much the data varies from the mean. A low standard deviation implies the data points may be clustered around the mean, while a high one shows the data points are more spread out away from the mean.

Inferential statistics

Inferential statistics are used when we try to connect individual variables in terms of their relationships. Inferential statistics help us make inferences about population parameters. To perform inferential statistics, however, there are some other statistical concepts we need to understand, including the normal distribution, probability and parametric and non-parametric tests (see Brown 1991, 1992 for an accessible discussion of these terms).

Normal distribution

Whether a data set has a normal distribution or not is related to the spread of the data points around the mean. A normal distribution has a bell-shaped figure. In a perfect normal distribution, the mean, median and mode have equal values. Variables that determine whether a data set has a normal distribution include sample size and the range of scores. Hatch and Lazaraton (1991) suggest a minimum of 30 participants for quantitative data analysis. However, in general, the more data points used, the greater the stability of the data distribution. It is also important that the data set exhibits a range of scores. This is perhaps why interval data are desirable for statistical analysis. A dichotomous variable that takes on values such as yes (coded 1) or no answer (coded 2) cannot lead to a normal distribution regardless of sample size. However, some sets of ordinal scores which appear continuous due to their large sample sizes may have a normal distribution.

SPSS can produce a histogram that may indicate the presence of a normal distribution. Perfect distribution is scarce in applied linguistics data, so we need some criteria to help us determine if the distribution is considered acceptably normally distributed. There are two statistical measures which SPSS can produce to help us decide this. The first is the *skewness statistic*, which tells us the extent to which a score distribution deviates from perfect symmetry (i.e. mode = median = mean). A negative skewed value suggests that the distribution is skewed towards the right (i.e. mode > median > mean), while a positive value suggests that the distribution is skewed towards the left (i.e. mode < median < mean). The *kurtosis statistic* is related to the peakedness of a distribution (i.e. whether it is flat or sharp). A kurtosis value of 0 suggests that the data set is normally distributed. A negative kurtosis statistic suggests that the distribution tends to be flat, whereas a positive kurtosis statistic suggests that the distribution is peaked. Conservatively, values of skewness and kurtosis statistics within *plus and minus 1* suggest that the data set is acceptably normally distributed (see Carr 2008 for an accessible discussion of this through the use of Microsoft Excel).

Probability and significance values

Probability is related to the degree to which the statistical finding occurs by chance (i.e. due to random variation). This is related to *statistical validity*, which asks whether or not the statistical finding is true or incidental (i.e. found by chance). The *p*-value (*p* = probability) is the likelihood that we will be wrong in the statistical inferences that we make from the data (i.e. when we reject the null hypothesis). $p < 0.05$ (i.e. there are 5 in 100 chances of being wrong) or $p < 0.01$ (i.e. there are 1 in 100 chances of being wrong) are commonly used or found in applied linguistics research.

To clarify the difference between a probability value and a significance value, we need to remember that the significance value will be *fixed* (e.g. the researcher specifies that it must be less than or equal to 0.05 or 0.01). The *probability value*, on the other hand, is *data-driven* and produced by the test statistics. For example, when we set a *p*-value to be less than 0.01 and when a *p*-value of 0.04 is obtained from the data, this data-driven *p*-value is *not statistically significant* at 0.01 because 0.04 is larger than 0.01. However, if we set a probability value at 0.05, the obtained *p*-value is statistically significant at 0.05 because 0.04 is smaller than 0.05. It is important to note that the word *significant(ce)* is not the same as the word *important(ce)* that we normally use. The word *significant(ce)* in quantitative research is associated to hypothesis testing.

Effect sizes

The statement in the Publication Manual of the American Psychological Association (APA 2010) points out that statistical significance *p-values* are not acceptable indices of effect. In several situations, researchers may find a statistical significance, but the finding yields little meaning, leading to *no theoretical or pedagogical practicality*, thereby not always worthy in a practical sense. An effect size is a *magnitude-of-effect estimate* that is independent of sample size (see Ortega this volume). A magnitude-of-effect estimate highlights the distinction between *statistical* and *practical significance* (see the Sample Study). Larson-Hall (2010, pp. 118–119) provides a table of effect sizes, their formulas and interpretations).

Parametric or non-parametric tests

There are two types of inferential statistics. These are *parametric* and *non-parametric statistics*. The distinction between the two lies in the different sets of statistical assumptions (i.e. preconditions essential for accurate applications of a statistical test) that must be met before the statistical analysis can be undertaken. These assumptions are *not optional,* and if they are not met, there is a heightened risk of making a false inference/claim (e.g. in rejecting the null hypothesis). The main assumptions for parametric tests are (1) the data is normally distributed, (2) the data is interval or continuous and (3) data scores are independent across measures.

A non-parametric test (i.e. a distribution-free test) is suitable for the analysis of frequency data or data that does not meet the normal distribution assumption. A non-parametric test can analyse discrete variables or ranked-order data. Although parametric tests are preferable in quantitative research, non-parametric tests are important for applied linguistics research because some data are not interval or continuous. Furthermore, in some cases in which the data is categorical or dichotomous (e.g. pass or fail scores), we cannot employ parametric tests because the normal distribution assumption. For example, we may want to see if gender, with male learners (coded 1) and female learners (coded 0), is relevant to passing (coded 1) or failing (coded 0) an English test. With this kind of data, there can be a connection between two different dichotomous variables, and a non-parametric test will be required to detect it.

Statistical tests

Although there are various reliable statistical programs available for use in applied linguistics (e.g. Microsoft Excel, IBM SPSS and Statistical Analysis System (SAS)), it is important to note that researchers need to know and understand the logic behind statistical analysis and the standards for a particular statistical test. There is a wide range of statistical tests that are used in applied linguistics research. Some common statistical tests are introduced here.

Correlations

Correlational analysis is used to examine systematic relationships between two variables. The nature of the data (e.g. continuous or categorical data) determines the kind of correlational analysis that can be used. Examples of correlational tests include Pearson Product Moment correlations, Spearman Rho correlation, Phi correlations and Point–Biserial correlations (see Phakiti 2014). A correlation test is expressed on a scale from 0 to 1. If two variables are strongly correlated, this means that an increase or decrease in one variable will be accompanied by an increase or decrease in the other variable. If two variables are uncorrelated (i.e. 0), there is no systematic relationship between them. A positive (+) correlation suggests a positive association between two variables (i.e. the two variables are associated and move in the same direction in a systematic way). A negative (–) correlation suggests a negative relationship (i.e. the two variables are associated and move systematically in opposite directions).

Factor analysis

Factor analysis is related to the correlational approach because it is used to determine how the observed variables from questionnaires or tests (responses to items) are linked to a common factor which underlies observed behaviours. In quantitative research, an underlying factor of language learner behaviours (e.g. motivation, strategy use and anxiety) is hypothetically assumed to influence how individuals answer questionnaire items. This hypothetical assumption can be tested empirically through the use of factor analysis. There are two types of factor analysis. The first is known as EFA, which is used to explore the clustering of questionnaire items (i.e. to explore whether the items are relatively homogeneous or highly correlated). EFA is useful when researchers are not certain about a particular construct, especially in a new research area. EFA can help researchers reduce the data and can be used during a pilot study, so that researchers can develop a more rigorous research instrument.

The second type of factor analysis is *confirmatory factor analysis* (CFA). CFA is used when researchers are confident that a particular construct underlies a set of questionnaire or test items. CFA is closely connected to quantitative research that employs a structural equation modelling (SEM) approach, which allows researchers to confirm a theory or hypothesis empirically (see Phakiti 2007; Ockey 2014; Woodrow this volume).

Regression analysis

Regression analysis is also an extension of the correlational analytical method. It is used to examine the prediction of one dependent, continuous-scale variable (e.g. reading comprehension scores) based on values of another one or more independent variables (either categorical or continuous in nature; e.g. genders, age groups, motivation). *Simple regression* uses only one independent variable, whereas *multiple regression* uses two or more independent variables that are correlated with each other, to predict a dependent variable. In a multiple regression, researchers can identify the independent variable that is the best prediction of a dependent variable. A regression coefficient, which ranges from 0 to 1, tells us the extent to which a dependent variable can be predicted, given a one unit change in an independent variable.

Chi-square test

A *chi-square test* is a non-parametric test that indicates whether a relationship between two categorical variables exists statistically. For example, male and female language learners may differ in their preferred choice of English language learning activity (e.g. reading versus speaking). In a contingency table (often referred to as a *cross-tabulation*), a row represents categories of the gender variable and a column represents categories of the subject variable. This table can be constructed by using frequency counts. A chi-square test can inform researchers whether male students are more likely than their female counterparts to choose a particular English language learning activity.

T-tests

There are two types of *t-test* that are used in applied linguistics: a repeated-measures *t*-test and an independent-samples *t*-test. A *paired-samples t-test* examines whether *two* mean scores from the same group of participants differ significantly. For example, we may want to see whether learners' attitudes to writing feedback have changed after a two-month period. We will have pre- and post-instruction questionnaires investigating their attitudes. An *independent-samples t-test* is used to determine whether the mean scores between two groups of students are significantly different.

Analysis of variance

Analysis of variance (ANOVA) has a similar logic to the *t*-tests mentioned above. A *within-group ANOVA* is similar to a paired-samples *t*-test and a *between-groups ANOVA* is similar to an *independent-samples t-test*. The key difference is that ANOVAs can compare more than two group mean scores or levels of an independent variable. A within-group ANOVA can compare the mean scores among pre-, post- and delay-post tests. A between-groups ANOVA can compare three or more groups of participants (e.g. high-ability, intermediate-ability and low-ability) in terms of their self-regulation. When more than two means are compared in ANOVAs, a *post-hoc* test will be used to identify exactly which groups significantly differ from each other. That is, the ANOVA can flag a statistical significance, but it does not indicate where the mean difference lies.

Ethical considerations

Different types of quantitative research have different ethical considerations due to their differing research aims and designs. For example, experimental researchers need to carefully consider the potential negative impact of their treatments on participants (see e.g. Gass this volume; De Costa this volume). Generally speaking, quantitative researchers (as with all researchers) need to follow ethical protocols to safeguard their research participants in terms of *confidentiality* and their *right to privacy*. Participants have the right to know what is involved in the research and what they will be doing in the study. They need to voluntarily agree to take part. In survey research, *anonymity* is important because it encourages participants to be truthful in expressing their thoughts and attitudes. Researchers can protect their participants' identities through the use of *pseudonyms* (made-up names) to refer to them and the research site (e.g. school, college, university or company) in the study. Researchers should submit their research ethics application forms to the relevant research ethics review committees in their institution, and it should be approved prior to the data collection.

A sample study

Phakiti (2003) illustrates quantitative data analysis. This study investigated the nature of cognitive and metacognitive strategy use and its relationship to English as a foreign language (EFL) reading test performance. Three hundred and eighty-four Thai university students participated in the study. The study employed an 85-item, multiple-choice reading test to assess the students' English reading achievement on a course in which they were enrolled and a 35-item, 5-point Likert-scale strategy use questionnaire to measure their cognitive and metacognitive strategy use (e.g. 0 = never to 5 = always). The participants first took a 3-hour reading test, which was followed by the completion of the questionnaire. For the purpose of data matching, the questionnaire was put together with the test answer sheet. In the first part of the questionnaire, participants were asked to provide demographic information, including their gender, age and the number of years they had been learning English. In the second part, they were asked to report on the extent of their strategy use during the test completion.

Data preparation

In order to key the test score data and strategy use data into SPSS, each participant was assigned an ID code, so that the data could be checked at a later stage. With regard to the questionnaire data, these were coded according to different types of data as discussed above. For example, for the data relating to gender, males were coded as 1 and females as 2. All this data were then keyed into SPSS. Two people took turns in entering the data to reduce the chance of an error being made. On average, it took about two and a half minutes to enter one set of questionnaire responses into SPSS. The researcher double-checked for accuracy in the data entry at the end by scanning the data file as well as by randomly checking the data against the actual questionnaires.

After the completion of the data entry, descriptive statistics were calculated, including the mean, median, mode, maximum, minimum and skewness and kurtosis statistics of the reading test and questionnaire data. This process allowed the researcher to check whether there were missing data or outliers in the data and to determine whether the data exhibited a normal distribution. Because it was important to see if the data in the reading test and questionnaire were reliable, a reliability analysis was performed. The reliability estimate of the overall test (like KR-20) was 0.88. The Cronbach alpha coefficients (as discussed earlier) for the cognitive strategy and metacognitive strategy variables were 0.75 and 0.85, respectively.

Data analysis and results

In Phakiti's study, three research questions were asked. However, for the purpose of this chapter, only research question 2 will be discussed. This research question was: what is the relationship of cognitive and metacognitive strategies to EFL reading comprehension test performance? In this chapter, the relationship between cognitive strategy use and reading comprehension performance will be discussed. There were two key inferential steps in the correlational analysis that was conducted. The first was to find out whether there was a relationship between cognitive strategy use and reading test performance. To carry out this step, the p-value was set to be 0.05 (i.e. 5 per cent was attributed to the limit of the probability of erroneously rejecting the null hypothesis that stated there was no relationship). If the p-value from the data was found to be less than 0.05 (e.g. 0.02), the null hypothesis could be rejected, thereby accepting that a relationship between the two variables existed. The rejection of the null hypothesis is known as *statistical significance*. In Phakiti's study, the p-value was found to be less than 0.05. It would be premature to conclude at this stage that a significant correlation has been found. This is because correlations depend on sample sizes and the number of behavioural observations that constitute the numerical data to be used. The second step in the analysis is an evaluation stage in which the researcher asks whether the detected correlation coefficient is *useful* (e.g. Can it inform teaching practice? Can it confirm a theory?).

The second key step concerns the *practical significance of the study*. Researchers typically examine the effect size of a correlation coefficient. In a Pearson correctional analysis (Cohen 1988), Pearson *r* values of 0.10 (small), 0.30 (medium) and 0.50 (large) indicate the extent to which a detected effect size is practical (i.e. the larger the value, the higher the practical significance of the study). It is important not to confuse statistical significance with practical significance. Sometimes it is useful to know that there is no statistical significance since it can confirm a theory that states that two variables are not related. That is, when researchers cannot reject the null hypothesis (i.e. when $p > 0.05$), it does not always mean that the finding is unuseful. A non-statistical finding may confirm a theory. For example, if there is no statistical significance between a learning style and success in language learning, it may be useful to confirm a theory of learning that claims that while learning styles vary from individual to individual, they are not a major contributor to learning success.

Prior to the first key step, Phakiti examined the distribution of the data (by examining descriptive statistics and graphical displays to investigate whether there were two modes in the data distribution, which could affect the *r* coefficient). A *scatterplot* was used which matched the score of one variable with the score of the other variable for all participants, to check whether the two variables (i.e. cognitive strategy use and test performance) were related. Based on the examination of the scatterplot, it was observed that the relationship was linear and positive. After these steps had been carried out, the Pearson correlation was calculated ($p < 0.05$) and it was found that this indicated a positive relationship between cognitive strategy use and test performance. The correlation coefficient between cognitive strategy use and test performance was found to be 0.39. Researchers also examine the value of r^2 (i.e. r × r) to interpret the strength of the relationship between two variables. r^2 is known as *shared variance* and indicates the degree of overlap between the sets of observations (i.e. the strength of the relationship). A shared variance can also be treated as an *effect size* of a correlation.

In this study, the shared variance (r^2) between cognitive strategy use and reading comprehension performance was 0.15 (0.39 × 0.39); that is, there was 15 per cent shared variance. In this study, it was argued that this degree was reasonable because there were other factors influencing language test performance, including communicative language ability, test-taker characteristics, test-method facets and random error as outlined by Bachman and Palmer (1996). It was also argued that although this correlation coefficient appeared to be weak, it was an important one because if cognitive use could contribute to 15 per cent of the language test performance, we knew that learners who successfully used this strategy would be at an advantage. In summary, Pearson's correlation allowed Phakiti to evaluate to what extent the two variables were related and whether the detected relationship was meaningful and interpretable.

Resources for further reading

Bachman, L 2004, *Statistical Analyses for Language Assessment*, Cambridge University Press, Cambridge.

This book presents both conceptual and statistical procedures useful for general applied linguistics research. It discusses the basics of quantitative data analysis and statistical tests.

Dörnyei, Z 2007, *Research Methods in Applied Linguistics: Quantitative, Qualitative, and Mixed Methodologies*, Oxford University Press, Oxford.

This book treats quantitative research comprehensively from the design stage through to the analysis and reporting stages.

Larson-Hall, J 2010, *A Guide to Doing Statistics in Second Language Research using SPSS*, Routledge, New York, NY.

This book is comprehensive in the treatment of statistics in second language research. It also provides procedures of how to perform statistical analyses in SPSS.

Lowie, W & Seton, B 2013, *Essential Statistics for Applied Linguistics*, Palgrave Macmillan, Hampshire.

This book explains both descriptive and inferential statistics in applied linguistics. It presents how to use SPSS for common statistical tests with examples of how a particular analysis can be done.

Mackey, A & Gass, S 2005, *Second Language Research*. Lawrence Erlbaum Associates, Mahwah, NJ.

This book provides an accessible account of the procedures of quantitative data analysis. Chapter 9 provides a discussion of issues involved in quantitative data analysis and procedures for carrying out statistical analysis.

Roever, C & Phakiti, A in press, 2016, *Quantitative Methods for Second Language Research: A Problem-solving Approach*, Routledge, London.

This book introduces quantitative approaches to data analysis in applied linguistics with particular emphasis on second language learning and assessment research.

Woodrow, L 2014, *Writing about Quantitative Research in Applied Linguistics*, Palgrave Macmillan, London.

This book is an accessible reference text which aims to help people write about quantitative research in applied linguistics. It explains different types of statistical analyses with annotated examples drawn from published and unpublished sources.

References

Altman, DG 1991, *Practical Statistics for Medical Research*, Chapman and Hall, London.

American Psychological Association (APA) 2010, *Publication Manual of the American Psychological Association*, 6th edn, American Psychological Association, Washington, DC.

Bachman, LF & Palmer, AS 1996, *Language Testing in Practice*, Oxford University Press, Oxford.

Brown, JD 1991, 'Statistics as a foreign language – Part1: What to look for in reading statistical language studies', *TESOL Quarterly*, vol. 25, no. 4, pp. 569–586.

———— 1992, 'Statistics as a foreign language – Part2: More things to consider in reading statistical language studies', *TESOL Quarterly*, vol. 26, no. 4, pp. 629–664.

———— 1996, *Testing in Language Programs*, Prentice Hall, Upper Saddle River, NJ.

Carr, N 2008, 'Using Microsoft Excel to calculate descriptive statistics and create graphs', *Language Assessment Quarterly*, vol. 5, no. 1, pp. 43–62.

Cohen J 1960, 'A coefficient of agreement for nominal scales', *Educational and Psychological Measurement*, vol. 20, no. 1, pp. 37–46.

Cohen, J 1988, *Statistical Power Analysis for the Behavioral Sciences*, Sage, Newbury Park, CA.

Dörnyei, Z 2007, *Research Methods in Applied Linguistics: Quantitative, Qualitative, and Mixed Methodologies*. Oxford University Press, Oxford.

Fleiss, JL 1981, *Statistical Methods for Rates and Proportions*, 2nd edn, John Wiley, New York, NY.

Gass, SM & Mackey, A 2007, *Data Elicitation for Second and Foreign Language Research*. Lawrence Erlbaum Associates, Mahwah, NJ.

Guba, EG & Lincoln, YS 2005, 'Paradigmatic controversies, contradictions, and emerging confluences', in NK Denzin & YS Lincoln (eds), *The Sage Handbook of Qualitative Research*, 3rd edn, Sage, Thousand Oaks, CA, pp. 191–215.

Hatch, E & Lazaraton, A 1991, *The Research Manual: Design and Statistics for Applied Linguistics*, Heinle and Heinle, Boston, MA.

Larson-Hall, J 2010, *A Guide to Doing Statistics in Second Language Research using SPSS*, Routledge, New York, NY.

Lazaraton, A 2005, 'Quantitative research methods', in E. Hinkel (ed.), *Handbook of Research in Second Language Teaching and Learning*, Lawrence Erlbaum Associates, Mahwah, NJ, pp. 209–224.

Lightbown, PM & Spada, N 2013, *How Languages are Learned*, 4th edn, Oxford University Press, Oxford.

Loewen, S & Gass, S 2009, 'The use of statistics in L2 acquisition research', *Language Teaching*, vol. 42, no. 2, pp. 181–196.

Macaro, E 2010, *Continuum Companion to Second Language Acquisition*, Continuum, London.

Mackey, A & Gass, S 2005, *Second Language Research*. Lawrence Erlbaum Associates, Mahwah, NJ.

Ockey, GJ 2014, 'Exploratory factor analysis and structural equation modeling', in AJ Kunnan (ed.), *The Companion to Language Assessment*, John Wiley & Sons, London, pp. 1–21.

Ortega, L 2009, *Understanding Second Language Acquisition*, Hodder, London.

Phakiti, A 2003, 'A closer look at the relationship of cognitive and metacognitive strategy use to EFL reading achievement test performance', *Language Testing*, vol. 20, no. 1, pp. 26–56.

—— 2007, *Strategic Competence and EFL Reading Test Performance*, Peter Lang, Frankfurt am Main.

—— 2014, *Experimental Research Methods in Language Learning*, Bloomsbury, London.

Plonsky, L 2013, 'Study quality in SLA: An assessment of designs, analyses, and reporting practices in quantitative L2 research', *Studies in Second Language Acquisition*, vol. 35, no. 4, pp. 655–687.

—— 2014, 'Study quality in quantitative L2 research (1990–2010): A methodological synthesis and call for reform', *The Modern Language Journal*, vol. 98, no. 1, pp. 450–470.

Plonsky, L & Gass, S 2011, 'Quantitative research methods, study quality, and outcomes: The case of interaction research', *Language Learning*, vol. 61, no. 2, pp. 325–366.

Purpura, P 2011, 'Quantitative research methods in assessment and teaching', in E Hinkel (ed.), *Handbook of Research in Second Language Teaching and Learning*, vol 2. Routledge, New York, NY, pp. 731–751.

CHAPTER THREE

Qualitative Research and Analysis

Adrian Holliday

In this chapter, I will first set out some of the basic premises of qualitative research as a mainstream research approach which is used by applied linguists as they develop their interests in wider social and political issues connected with language and language education. It is important to begin in this way because analysing qualitative data is very much integrated with other stages of the research approach. The central section on techniques and instruments of analysis will demonstrate this, and the extended example in the final section will show how the basic issues connected with the approach come back again and again during analysis.

Underlying assumptions and methodology

There are a wide range of approaches to qualitative data analysis. The field is however moving increasingly towards a postmodern acknowledgement of the inevitability of qualitative research being subjective (Walford 1991, p. 1). While in quantitative research the emphasis is on controlling variables to the extent that the influence of the researcher is minimized, the aim of qualitative research is to search for the richest possible data. It is recognized that the ideas and presence of the researcher will be influential in what the data looks like and the way in which it is interpreted. Postmodernism acknowledges that 'truth' is mediated by ideology. Therefore, the outcomes of the research will always be influenced by the researcher's beliefs. There are also strong indications that quantitative research is itself increasingly recognizing these influences and becoming less naïve in its attitudes towards data.

The basic aim of qualitative research is to get to the bottom of what is going on in all aspects of social behaviour. It tends to do this within specific social settings such as schools, factories, hospital wards and so on, which are treated as cultures of activity, and pose basic ethnographic questions to do with power structures, tacit behavioural rules and modes of organization. Its roots are therefore closely associated with social and cultural anthropology and with the sister discipline of ethnography (see Starfield this volume), which is more precisely concerned with describing human communities, but from which it borrows much of its method. Within applied linguistics, qualitative research has been more traditionally applied to the linguistic aspects of communication and as such has been quite limited; but it is now being applied to a wide range of scenarios from the politics of language teaching to the non-linguistic environment of language behaviour (e.g. Holliday 2005, 2006).

The types of data that can be collected are very varied, and it could be said that the data comprises whatever can be seen or heard which helps the researcher to get to the bottom of the issues implicit in the research questions. Such types of data are listed in Table 3.1. It needs to be noted here that interviews, observations, diaries and so on, as listed in the third column, are not really types of data, but means of collecting it.

Table 3.1 Types of data

Type	Characteristics	How collected
Description of behaviour	What people are seen or heard doing or saying	Observation notes, research diary etc.
Description of event	Piece of behaviour, defined either by the people in the setting (e.g. wedding, meeting) or by the researcher (e.g. bus journey, argument)	Observation notes, research diary etc.
Description of institution	The way the setting operates in terms of regulations, tacit rules, rituals	Observation notes, research diary etc.
Description of appearance	What the setting or people in it look like (e.g. space, buildings, clothing, arrangement of people or objects, artefacts)	Observation notes, research diary, drawings, diagrams

(*continued*)

Type	Characteristics	How collected
Description of research event	What people say or do in interview, focus group etc.	Observation notes, research diary etc.
Personal narrative	Reconstruction of experience that aids understanding	Narrative, research diary etc.
Account	What people say or write to the researcher – actual words	Interview, audio recording, questionnaire, participant's diary, transcription, verbatim notes
Talk	What people are heard saying – actual words	Audio recording, transcription, verbatim notes
Visual record	What is actually seen	Film, video recording
Document	Piece of writing belonging or pertaining to the setting	Photocopy, scan

As the data is collected, it begins to indicate a picture of what is going on. Each piece of data, in itself a single instance of behaviour, contributes to this emerging picture. The outcome needs to be a *thick description*, which is a narrative of what has been found that shows the full complexity and depth of what is going on. For example, a thick description of the roles and aspirations of a school head teacher was created by juxtaposing a description of her dealing with a pupil, a description of what happens when she enters a class, a description of her role in the school, a description of her office and its artefacts, her own account of her mission in the school, a pupil's account of her effect on timekeeping and a clause on the role of headmistresses in a ministry document (Holliday 2007, p. 74, citing Herrera).

Central to the process of data collection and analysis is gradual focusing. Ideally, decisions about what sort of data should be collected will not be made until the researcher has entered the field, the place where the research will be carried out. An initial broad observation of what is going on will enable the researcher to establish what sorts of data will be relevant. More focused data collection then begins, but there should still be room for further refinement of focus and data collection choices.

Validity and trustworthiness

Because of the inevitability of subjectivity, the validity and trustworthiness of the research will depend on how this subjectivity is managed. Good research therefore depends on three principles. The first principle is *transparency* of method, which requires a description of how the research was carried out, from decisions regarding data collection and analysis to how the beliefs and influence of the researcher were excavated and addressed.

The second principle is *submission*, which requires that while being aware that she or he is the designer of the process, the researcher must submit to the data in such a way that the unexpected is allowed to emerge and perhaps change the direction of the research. A good piece of research will have built into the research design something which will enable the research to take on a life of its own. There is therefore an inherent weakness in qualitative research which tries to imitate quantitative research by starting with research questions, asking these questions in interviews and then reporting the answers. In such a design, the researcher will only be able to get answers to questions she has thought of, and which have led the interviewees' responses. An important discipline is for the researcher to put aside professional preoccupations. For example, while carrying out classroom research, the researcher must try as hard as possible to stop thinking like a teacher or a teacher trainer and try and see the classroom from a stranger's point of view. Another connected discipline is that of *making the familiar strange* in which the researcher tries as hard as possible to take on the role of a stranger in order to experience what it is like to approach a situation for the first time and to be acutely aware of how it operates as a culture.

Two ways of allowing the research to take on a life of its own are through a holistic thematic analysis (see below) and attending to detail. This can best be illustrated in descriptive data. The following description of classroom behaviour, while clearly being subjective in what the researcher has chosen to describe, contains detail which travels beyond his initial questions and leads him to look further:

> The teacher walks around at the back monitoring while the students work. Those writing seek comment from their peers.... A student near the camera leans back to speak to friend. One girl student is arranging her hair. Several students talk to peers while the teacher explains. This does not seem to be a problem. The student who has been 'talking' is also clearly getting on with her work (Holliday 2005, p. 90).

The research question which drove this description was 'what are the students' role and behaviour in the classroom?' By noticing certain types of informal behaviour and being prepared to think laterally about it, the researcher was driven to consider that communicative activity took place outside and sometimes in conflict with the teacher's plan. I shall return to the issue of detail in methods of analysis below.

The third principle is that of *making appropriate claims*. Qualitative research looks at instances of behaviour rather than broad tendencies in that it cannot prove, for example, that certain percentages of people believe certain things. An appropriate claim would therefore be that in a particular location at a particular time, certain things *seem* to be the case. This shows that the purpose of qualitative research is not to prove anything, but to generate ideas which are sufficient to make us think again about what is going on in the world. It is not therefore possible to use qualitative studies to prove or disprove other studies by means of replication. Three different researchers looking at the same set of qualitative data may easily arrive at three very different interpretations, and it may well be the case that the data can only be made sense of by a researcher who has taken part in the total experience of collecting it.

Techniques and instruments

The process of analysing qualitative data is not always separate from collecting data. Indeed, an ongoing dialogue between collecting data, writing and analysis should be encouraged. A research diary should be kept throughout the whole process, in which comments made at the time of data collection are kept. An example of these is in the right hand column of Table 3.2. Even though it must be acknowledged that the data is already itself a product of the researcher's interpretation, it is important that the researcher should learn to separate this from what can be said about it.

Table 3.2 Data and comment

Data: what can be seen or heard	Comment: what this seems to mean at the time of data collection
The women tended to sit down the right of the room while the men tended to sit down the left of the room. Down the centre of the room there were many instances where the division was not precise, as men and women sit shoulder to shoulder and talk to each other.	This might connect with gender segregation seen in other parts of the society – e.g. on buses. But, the men and women sitting together in the centre seem comfortable. Other factors might therefore easily override the segregation principle. This connects with observation of men and women working together in small groups.

The classic method for analysing qualitative data is to begin by taking the following steps:

1   Coding: convert the comments on each piece of data to key words or phrases – for example, 'informal behaviour', 'gender division' and 'teacher control'. There may be more than one such code for each

piece of data, but basically this is a method for seeing how each code is distributed throughout the data.

2   Determining themes: The codes which occur with significant frequency are then grouped within themes.

3   Constructing an argument: The themes are then used as the headings and subheadings for constructing an argument about what can be learnt from the data. Under each thematic heading, extracts from the data which exemplify the theme are collected and used as evidence for the points made in the argument.

4   Going back to the data: Collecting extracts to support the argument will involve going back to the data, reassessing the codes and refining or possibly changing the themes. The process of drafting and redrafting the argument will also add to this process of refinement.

There is a parallel here with writing a literature review, where the literature as a whole is like the data, and where extracts from the data are used in the same way as quotations from the literature, to provide evidence for what is being said about it. Note that I refer to data throughout as an uncountable noun – 'data is' rather than 'data are' – because in qualitative research, it is not a sequence of items, but collectively a single body of experience. For this reason, for the purpose of analysis, it is better not to divide the data into parts (e.g. according to stages or types), but to deal with it holistically.

There is a range of computer software for analysing qualitative data. This can be very helpful in and collating codes and determining themes. However, I would not personally recommend using software as it cannot replace the intuition of the researcher who was there when the data was collected. The entire meaning may not be confined to the data, as the research diary is also an important source of interpretation. Also some data is so complex that it defies coding, and the narrative needs to be written in a more creative manner directly from the data and the research diary.

The following extract from a dissertation (Duan 2007, pp. 156–157) shows the resulting interaction between (a) extracts of data (double indented), (b) comment made specifically about the extract (indented) and (c) the broader argument about what the data means (italicized). *Teachers* is the thematic heading for this part of the analysis. The three dots indicate that material is missing.

Teachers

...The reasons for Teacher Liang passing the letter to us were, I thought, to teach us something from the letter, to offer us encouragement, and hard-working spirit. I felt that Teacher Liang was a good teacher. The reasons for her to hit us or scold us were to nurture and educate us – to enable us to become useful, successful people. She did everything for our own good! (Diary, Wang Yang, 7 March 2002)

This Teacher Liang is the same one that scolded Wang Yang in the first extract. It seemed that he had already changed his view regarding this teacher. In the incident above, Wang Yang seemed to dislike the teacher. But in this extract, it seems that he tries to find some justification for his teacher's ill treatment of him, even defending his teacher for what she had done to him, showing his understanding for her scolding him. This does not necessarily mean that he has changed his view. It may indicate consistently ambivalent feelings towards her. On the one hand, he hated his teacher for scolding him in public. On the other hand, he showed consent in witnessing his teacher's recital of the discourse. *This may suggest that there is evidence of the dominant discourse within the students' discourse.* The following extract shows just such a feeling:

I know that Teacher Liang is a good teacher, that she always wants the best for us and that she has been doing all these things for our own good. But I could still not forget that she had scolded me in front of the other students, that she scolded me for 'grinning cheekily', saying that I did not study hard. Thinking of these events, I felt heavy and painful. It was difficult for me to forget these things. When she did these things, I really hated her because I thought she should not have scolded me in public, she could do it privately in her office instead of in public. That really hurt my self-esteem. It made me lose face.

It also seemed that teachers have contradictory feelings towards students. As Teacher Xiao comments:

Student life is really hard. They have too much homework to do every day. All their subject teachers compete with each other regarding the amount of the homework they assign to the students. They want the students to spend most of their time after school on the subject *they* teach. As a result, the students have to suffer from over-assigned homework. Take my daughter, for instance. She is only in Year One in N1MS. But she has to work until the middle of each night to try to finish her homework, sometimes even until 1.00 o'clock in the following morning. I feel sorry for them, these poor students. (Individual Interview, Teacher Xiao, 1 August 2004)

Teacher Xiao seems here to show her empathy for the students in their suffering. This may be because she has an interested daughter. But it seemed that she even complained on the students' behalf about this homework issue. *And this may suggest that there is indeed a student's discourse within the teachers' dominant discourse.*

It is important to note how the data extracts are carefully referenced, so that they can be traced back to the larger corpus of data. Also, the extracts are cross-referred to other extracts to show how meaning is built through their interconnection within the thick description, and the researcher goes into considerable detail in explaining what each extract means, while showing due caution through the use of phrases like 'not necessarily' and 'seem'. It may well be the case that there are other interpretations. In this discussion, Duan first of all exercises restraint from jumping too quickly into an interpretation. He sets the extract from the diary against another 'incident above' and uses this juxtaposition to move gradually from one possible interpretation to another.

Qualitative researchers need to be excellent writers. It may be the case that small extracts of data are not sufficiently effective in expressing the richness and complexity of what the researcher experienced. Researchers may decide to present longer extracts of data, or reconstructions, or even fictionalized representations. There is no restriction on what can be done as long as it is explained and justified in the text, and as long as it is made clear in what way faithfulness to the data is maintained, and what sense is being made of the data. Many novice qualitative researchers make the mistake of thinking that presenting raw data will speak for itself. What is important to understand is that because the reader was not there, the data left alone will never be sufficient to communicate what was going on.

Ethical considerations

There are clearly considerable ethical issues in qualitative research. At the most basic level, the integrity and privacy of the people taking part in the research must be preserved at all costs. It is not however always a matter of getting permission. The following points need to be considered: (a) People will very likely have far more important things to do and think about than taking part in your research project. Involving them in extended procedures for getting permission, collaborating or checking interpretations may in itself be an unfair imposition. (b) It may be unfair to expect that the people in the research setting should understand or be interested in the research project. (c) Different cultural settings will require different forms of consent, with different degrees of formality, informality and understanding. (d) What people are prepared to say, or how they are prepared to appear in front of a researcher may have as much to do with their perceptions of the researcher as with the questions the researcher is asking. They may be researching you as much as you are researching them – if they care to take the time. Researchers are usually far more unusual than the people they are researching. (e) It may be unfair to develop relationships within a research setting which cannot be sustained in their own terms. (f) Whatever claims you may have to being an insider, these will always be contaminated by the fact that you are a researcher.

A sample study

The study I have chosen for this section is reported in Holliday (2010, 2011) and involved my investigation into the politics of established descriptions of national cultures.

My driving suspicion was that these descriptions are not as neutral as they purport to be, and I was led into this by previous work on the way dominant English teaching methodology employs negative stereotypes of 'other cultures'. The purpose of the research was thus to question an established belief. My data comprised (a) email interviews with thirty informants from a range of countries, (b) reconstructions of intercultural events from a range of ethnographic sources and (c) research and training literature on intercultural communication as examples of academic or professional ideology. Here, I will focus on my initial analysis of the interview data, while being aware that eventually it was looked at holistically along with the rest of the data. I am happy with email as a means for interviewing because it allows my informants the space to take their time, solves the issue of distance, has the (so far unused) potential for group discussion and produces written responses which do not need to be transcribed. It also means that the social setting does not have to be a physical one but could be a community of people. I am open about the fact that my informants are friends, colleagues and students who are hand-picked for having encountered cultural difference, and I kept this in mind when I began to make claims at the end of my research.

I asked each person the same three questions: (1) 'What are the major features of your cultural identity?' (2) 'What role does nation play in this?' (3) 'Are you comfortable with how others define your cultural identity?' These are purposefully very broad to allow maximum richness, and I invited each person to use them simply as starting points, with the possibility that I would get back to them later with further questions which may grow out of their responses. My aim as a qualitative researcher is not to attempt to control variability, but to invite complexity.

The data I received, about 22,000 words, defied classic thematic analysis. I began by following the procedure described above, by first marking the interview text directly with a number of codes, as exemplified in Table 3.3.

Table 3.3 Example of coding

Sample of data from question 1	Codes
First of all, what is my cultural identity? … I suppose it is defined according to a set of identifiable features that I share with others who belong to the world I most frequently inhabit. These features can only be described in terms that I am familiar with and that I consider important because of where I come from culturally. This sounds a rather circular approach: I define my cultural identity according to factors which are recognized as important for the group I see myself as part of.	Relative to group
Defining factors seem to be language, education, ancestry, religion and profession (I left language till last, but it seems to have emerged as number one, and although there is more to be said about everything else, I will leave it for now!)	Small culture Religion Ancestry
Most people can claim a first language, and it helps us to establish ourselves within a particular discourse community, but I am not sure how to explain the role of an English native speaker as part of my cultural identity. If I think about cultural identity as a set of features I share with others, language is too broad, or maybe it is that English is too widely spoken to indicate a particular culture.	Language

It needs to be noted here that this was not a linguistic analysis of the interview responses, but an analysis of opinion. The total list of twenty-five codes which emerged from this initial exercise were as follows, some of which I have glossed in brackets: (1) Ancestry, (2) Gender/sexuality, (3) Geography (other than nation), (4) Language, (5) Layered (different realities at the same time), (6) Moral (judgements about the world), (7) Multicultured, (8) Multi-loyal (to more than one 'culture'), (9) Nation first (the most important category), (10) Nation complex (too complex to be an easy category), (11) Nation insufficient (too simple to be an easy category), (12) Nation limiting (too stereotypical to be realistic), (13) National imagery, (14) Nation repressive (repressive ideologies), (15) Nation critical (critical of what it means), (16) Non-exclusive (others can join and can join others), (17) Othered (negatively stereotyped), (18) Reflexive (defined in response to others), (19) Relative to audience, (20) Religion, (21) Politics, (22) Small cultures (family, work, class, group, etc.), (23) Shifting, (24) History (personal) and (25) Uncertain. The large number concerning nation (9–15) resulted from their being a specific question about it – for the reason that I was concerned with how far national culture is problematic.

I, then, began to rationalize these codes into a smaller and more manageable group of subthemes, each of which could be grouped under a smaller number of themes, as shown in Table 3.4. At this point, it became very clear that this approach to coding and deriving themes was *very unsatisfactory*. The problem was that: (a) every time I looked back at the data, I found something different, *because* what people were saying was so complex; (b) this totally invalidated my attempt, in the final column of Table 3.4, to try and validate themes on the basis of the percentage of times they were indicated; (c) and as a result, trying to be too systematic in the analysis was actually taking me progressively further away from what the informants were actually saying, which in itself was far from clear.

Table 3.4 Deriving themes

Themes	Subthemes	Codes subsumed	Percentage of informants mentioned
The significance and ambivalence of nation	Nation as the most important category	(9)	50
	Nation as complex, insufficient and only a part of one's identity	(10–11)	50
	Nation as limiting, confining, repressive or morally distasteful	(12–15)	50
Other locational categories	Language as a means of distinguishing group boundaries	(4)	50
	Ancestry and personal and family history	(1, 24)	30
	Small or large entities other than nation	(3, 22)	25
	Religion	(20)	25
Complexity	The shifting and multiple nature of cultural identity and its ability to be different things at the same time	(5, 8, 23, 25)	75
	Reflexivity and relativity to changing circumstances and other groups	(18, 19)	50
	Loyalties and memberships transcending group boundaries	(7, 8)	25
Struggling with otherness	Being reduced by majority and inaccurate imaginations of who one really is	(17)	50

There was something else, which initially seemed problematic but then took me in a direction I had not expected – which was the truly validating element of the research, as I have referred to above. I had chosen informants partly because of their range of nationalities, which was in turn led by my interest in the way in which the West negatively stereotypes the rest of the world. However, ethically, I could not declare their nationality unless they gave me permission. I, therefore, had to ask them in my next question –

> To help me to preserve privacy, would you like to be referred to either as yourself or with a pseudonym? Can you then provide a phrase about who you are – something like 'Adrian – a British academic living in Britain'.

This prompt was purposefully tentative because I was aware of my agenda and of the dangers of pushing it. The responses I got back gave names or pseudonyms, followed by phrases, several of which avoided clear reference nationality:

> '... a young academic from Oaxaca, Mexico' '... an English teacher living in France'
> '... an Iranian-Australian Academic'
> '... who currently lives and teaches in the UAE'
> '... an ESL academic working in Saudi Arabia'

There was also one response which explicitly raised the question of how far it was important to refer to 'profession, nationality, residence, etc'.

Other questions which arose as a result of this initial analysis were to do with the type of informants who had been approached. Were they too special *because* of being at 'cultural interfaces', of having travelled, of being good at expressing their complex ideas in writing, of being middle class, academics or students – or were they just particular examples of what many of us, everywhere, are like? This in turn led to thoughts about whether or not to interview other types of people. I also decided to leave behind the coding approach to analysis and derive themes directly from reading the interview text. However, the most significant outcome was a stronger appreciation of the moral imperative embedded in how we should deal with data – taking disciplined care to refrain from imposing meaning, not only on data, but also on the people who it represents.

The purpose of this example has been to illustrate that qualitative data analysis is far from a straightforward process. Rather than bringing the research to neat closure, it can raise as many questions as it seeks to answer and is always unfinished. On the one hand, there is comfort in its extreme open-endedness, and other the other hand, immense caution has to be applied.

Resources for further reading

All the texts listed below deal with mainstream qualitative research methodology and provide a holistic picture within which data analysis is part. None of them are specific to applied linguistics because I feel the mainstream is where the best roots for the research approach can be obtained.

Denzin, NK & Lincoln, YS (eds), 2005, *Handbook of Qualitative Research*, 3rd edn, Sage, Thousand Oaks, CA.

Though expensive, this is an essential body of work for any serious qualitative researcher. Fairly short chapters between them cover the whole range of qualitative research activity, from an overview of approaches through such methods as action research, grounded theory, narrative inquiry and so on.

Geertz, C 1993, *The Interpretation of Cultures: Selected Essays*, Fontana, London.

This is a classic text for those who wish to get into the intricacies of thick description.

Hammersley, M & Atkinson, P 1995, *Ethnography: Principles in Practice*, Routledge, London.

This is an excellent description of the scope and use of qualitative research methodology. While the title refers to ethnography, this is treated liberally, and it becomes clear that ethnography, grounded theory, phenomenology and so on are different sides of a common approach.

Holliday, AR 2007, *Doing and Writing Qualitative Research*, 2nd edn, Sage, London.

This is the text from which most of this chapter is taken. It is a practical introduction while also dealing with theoretical issues, and based on an analysis, with interviews and examples of how a number of researchers, from undergraduate to doctoral students, have carried out their studies. Though these studies are taken from a range of disciplines, a significant number are within applied linguistics.

Spradley, JP 1980, *Participant Observation*, Holt, Rinehart and Winston, New York, NY.

Though now old, this is an excellent manual for classic qualitative research methodology. It works gradually through the basic steps from broad to gradual narrowing of focus.

References

Duan, YP 2007, 'The influence of the Chinese university entrance exam (English)', PhD thesis, Department of Language Studies, Canterbury Christ Church University, Kent, United Kingdom.

Holliday, AR 2005, *The Struggle to Teach English as an International Language*, Oxford University Press, Oxford.

—————— 2006, 'The value of reconstruction in revealing hidden or counter cultures', *Journal of Applied Linguistics*, vol. 1, no. 3, pp. 275–294.

—————— 2007, *Doing and Writing Qualitative Research*, 2nd edn, Sage, London.

—————— 2010, 'Complexity in cultural identity', *Language & Intercultural Communication*, vol. 10, no. 2, pp. 165–177.

—————— 2011, *Intercultural Communication & Ideology*, Sage, London.

Walford, G 1991, 'Reflexive accounts of doing educational research', in G Walford, (ed.), *Doing Educational Research*, Routledge, London, pp. 1–17.

CHAPTER FOUR

Mixed Methods Research and Analysis

Nataliya V. Ivankova and Jennifer L. Greer

In support of evidence-based teaching, educators around the world are increasingly turning to mixed methods research (MMR) to seek answers to complex research questions. Indeed, one could argue that MMR has become a research approach of choice in the field of applied linguistics (Ivankova & Creswell 2009; Riazi & Candlin 2014), given the many factors – linguistic, social, cultural and political – involved in global language learning. In the United Kingdom, for example, MMR was used to explore the challenges of teaching English globally to learn how to best prepare primary school teachers worldwide for the local classroom setting (Copland, Garton & Burns 2013). In Belgium, researchers employed MMR to understand if corrective feedback via a 3-D avatar-based game would help improve language learning in students from middle school to college (Cornellie, Clarebout & Desmet 2012). In Taiwan, an investigator conducted an MMR study about the impact of new English exit testing requirements on the pedagogy of instructors in technical schools with teacher certification programs (Pan 2011). In the United States, MMR helped address the issue of Latino parental involvement in the learning of dual-language children in Head Start programs by providing insight into cultural, social and language questions as well as effective family engagement strategies (McWayne et al. 2013).

When conceptualizing those research studies educators and researchers all wondered: *What is the best approach to studying these multi-layered problems so that we understand what is really occurring in the language and learning setting? What methods should we use that will allow us to simultaneously explore the breadth and the depth of these issues and will give us the most comprehensive answers?* Instead of conducting separate studies to examine trends and relationships using quantitative methods, or to explore individuals' experiences and perceptions about the problem using qualitative methods, researchers can combine or mix different methods within one study using an MMR approach (Creswell & Plano Clark 2011; Teddlie & Tashakkori 2009). Such mixing of methods within MMR creates a more complete picture of a problem in practice (Greene 2007; Johnson & Onwuegbuzie 2004; Tashakkori & Creswell 2007). In the field of applied linguistics, the application of MMR potentially provides a more multidimensional and accurate view of the processes of learning a language as well as social, cultural and political factors that influence the development of communicative competence as individuals cross boundaries, real and virtual.

In this chapter, you will learn what MMR is, what its primary philosophical assumptions and methodological characteristics are and why it is used in applied linguistics. We will introduce you to three basic MMR designs and their graphic representations. We will also discuss how to implement basic designs effectively and ethically. Finally, we will discuss a sample study in one of the most common MMR designs used in the field of applied linguistics and provide some points to remember when conducting MMR.

What is mixed methods research?

In the late 1970s and the 1980s, social science researchers began to study larger, multi-faceted questions by moving beyond a single-strategy approach – either quantitative or qualitative methods – and integrating the two methods within one study. Interestingly, scholars had been experimenting with combining quantitative and qualitative methods for a long time, with Aristotle, perhaps, being the first 'proto-mixed methodologist' (Teddlie & Tashakkori 2009, p. 47). Nevertheless, MMR was only recognized as a legitimate research approach around the end of the twentieth century (Creswell 2014; Ivankova & Kawamura 2010; Tashakkori & Teddlie 2003). At the same time, because MMR has united researchers from different social and behavioural disciplines, many definitions of MMR exist based on the different criteria researchers use to explain the nature of this approach (Johnson, Onwuegbuzie & Turner 2007). These criteria also include the situations when researchers mix different types of data or analytical strategies within the same approach, for example, surveys and numerical measures in quantitative research, and in-depth interviews and analysis of documents and artefacts in qualitative research. In 2007 Tashakkori and Creswell (2007), the founding editors of the *Journal of Mixed Methods Research*, advanced a broad definition of MMR that emphasizes the use of both quantitative and qualitative data and a meaningful integration of quantitative and qualitative methods within a study to generate more credible and persuasive conclusions about the research issue:

> As an effort to be as inclusive as possible, we have broadly defined mixed methods here as research in which the investigator collects and analyzes data, integrates the findings, and draws inferences using both qualitative and quantitative approaches or methods in a single study or a program of inquiry (p. 4).

Why do we use mixed methods research?

In their seminal paper on mixed methods evaluation designs, Greene, Caracelli and Graham (1989) identified five broad reasons for using MMR: (1) triangulation – to seek corroboration of results from different methods, (2) complementarity – to seek clarification of the results from one method with the results from the other method, (3) development – to use the results from one method to help develop or inform the other method, (4) initiation – to seek the discovery of new perspectives from one method with questions or results from the other method and (5) expansion – to extend the breadth and range of inquiry by using different methods for different inquiry components. Other mixed methods researchers (Creswell & Plano Clark 2011; Morse & Niehaus 2009; Teddlie & Tashakkori 2009) have further elaborated the rationales for applying MMR. For applied linguistics, MMR offers clear benefits in the following ways:

- Employing qualitative methods to determine the meaning and understanding of constructs and quantitative methods assessing the magnitude and frequency of constructs, as exemplified in the MMR study on family engagement among Latino Head Start parents by McWayne et al. (2013).

- Combining multiple methods compatible with the discipline (e.g. pre-post test, survey, questionnaire, case study, learning log, writing sample, focus group, in-depth interview, translation and observation) to gain comprehensive answers to research questions, as illustrated by Danzak's (2011) MMR study that used multiple methods to study the impact of adolescent English language learners' language and literacy experiences on their identities as bilingual writers.

- Combining quantitative and qualitative methods to draw on the strengths of each, as reflected in the MMR study by Cornillie, Clarebout and Desmet (2012) of corrective feedback in a digital game for the purposes of English language learning.

- Framing the investigation within synergistic philosophical and theoretical positions, such as Wesely (2010) did in her MMR study of motivation as a psycho-social learning construct in early adolescents who left language immersion programs in public schools.

- Offering ways to work more inclusively to study phenomena across disciplines and cultures, as did Copland, Garton and Burns (2013) in their MMR study of the challenges faced when teaching English by teachers in five different primary schools in five countries.

The utility and strength of MMR are emphasized by its recognition as the third research paradigm (Johnson & Onwuegbuzie 2004), the third methodological movement (Teddlie & Tashakkori 2003), the third research community (Teddlie & Tashakkori 2009) and the third research approach (Creswell 2014). As a result, signs of growth abound with MMR textbooks and reference books, published studies, methodological articles, reviews and special peer-reviewed journal issues devoted to this research approach. This media includes the *Journal of Mixed Methods Research*, the *International Journal of Multiple Research Approaches*, the *Sage Handbook of Mixed Methods in Social & Behavioral Research* (Tashakkori & Teddlie 2003, 2010) and Sage's Mixed Methods Research Series. Additionally, professional conferences offer mixed methods researchers a chance to exchange ideas in forums such as the American Educational Research Association Special Interest Group 'Mixed Methods Research', the American Evaluation Association Topical Interest Group 'Mixed Methods Evaluation' and the annual international MMR conference since 2006. The new Mixed Methods International Research Association (MMIRA) (http://mmira .wildapricot.org/, viewed 28 January 2015) has formed to unite mixed methods researchers around the world. Finally, US and internationally based funding agencies have begun to promote an MMR approach in their grant award guidelines.

What are philosophical assumptions and issues associated with MMR?

Implicit in the definition of MMR are certain philosophical assumptions that have preoccupied scholars for centuries as they debated how to best generate and assess new knowledge (Teddlie & Tashakkori 2009). For example, is knowledge constructed from many sources in a holistic fashion (a constructivist paradigm advocated by qualitative researchers), or is it a single, concrete truth based on a proven hypothesis or cause and effect (a positivist paradigm advocated by quantitative researchers)? These are important paradigm distinctions to consider when qualitative and quantitative methods are integrated or mixed (Maxcy 2003). In particular, two paradigms – transformative and pragmatic – underlie MMR (Mertens et al. 2010; Teddlie & Tashakkori 2009). The transformative paradigm is guided by the principles of social justice, whereas pragmatism argues that what has practical and functional value is ultimately important and valid. Both philosophical paradigms justify the integration of epistemological practices associated with quantitative and qualitative research approaches when conducting MMR in applied linguistics.

Implementing MMR is not void of challenges. In recent years, leading MMR scholars (Creswell & Plano Clark 2011; Greene 2007; Tashakkori & Teddlie 2010) have identified a series of issues related to MMR, including differences in researchers' epistemological practices related to quantitative and qualitative research paradigms; the nature of true MMR research questions; unique aspects of MMR design and analysis; assessing quality of MMR studies; and collaborating on MMR projects with researchers from other disciplines, paradigms and cultures. More recently, Riazi and Candlin (2014) raised similar issues in their review of forty published MMR papers in language teaching and learning. They cited a general lack of exposure to or understanding of basic MMR concepts and principles and noted a tendency for the use of methodological procedures that do not always draw on the best of the MMR process. Riazi and Candlin also noted an absence of clear MMR purpose statements, although they identified triangulation, or cross-validation of findings, as the primary methodological aim in the papers studied, followed by complementarity. The authors cautioned that 'theorizing and conceptualizing a problem as an integrated but multi-layered whole … is not an easy task, and is likely to present challenges for researchers' (p. 154).

What are the methodological characteristics of mixed methods research?

The key to successfully implementing MMR is understanding that it has distinct methodological characteristics that make it different from other research approaches. These characteristics or methodological dimensions refer to the number of quantitative and qualitative study strands and the timing, weighting and mixing of quantitative and qualitative methods, which vary strategically based on specific MMR designs (Creswell & Plano Clark 2011; Teddlie & Tashakkori 2009). Figure 4.1 summarizes and explains these methodological characteristics. The sum of these decisions – about study strands, timing, weighting and mixing – further defines the type of an MMR study and explains the variety of available MMR designs that can be employed in the field of applied linguistics.

- *Strand* – component of an MMR study that encompasses the basic process of conducting quantitative or qualitative research: posing a question, collecting and analysing data and interpreting results:

  - An MMR study includes at least one quantitative and one qualitative strand, and may consist of two or more varied strands.

- *Timing* – temporal relationship between the quantitative and qualitative strands within an MMR study:

  - *Concurrent:* collecting and analysing both quantitative and qualitative data at the same point in time or independently.

  - *Sequential:* collecting and analysing quantitative data first, followed by qualitative data or collecting and analysing qualitative data first, followed by quantitative data.

- *Weighting* – relative importance of quantitative and qualitative methods for answering the study's research questions:

  - *Equal* weighting - equal emphasis is placed on quantitative and qualitative methods.

  - *Quantitative* weighting – greater emphasis is placed on quantitative methods; qualitative methods perform a secondary role.

  - *Qualitative* weighting – greater emphasis is placed on qualitative methods; quantitative methods perform a secondary role.

- *Mixing* – explicit interrelating of the quantitative and qualitative methods in an MMR study:

  - *Combining:* mixing quantitative and qualitative methods during the interpretation of both quantitative and qualitative results.

  - *Connecting:* mixing quantitative and qualitative methods during data collection, that is, quantitative or qualitative data is collected based on the results of data analysis in the previous qualitative or quantitative strand.

  - *Merging:* mixing quantitative and qualitative methods during data analysis, that is, quantitative and qualitative data from different study strands are analysed together.

FIGURE 4.1 *Key methodological characteristics of MMR (adapted from Ivankova 2015)*

How do we design and conduct a mixed methods research study?

Ivankova and Creswell (2009) outlined a set of logical steps for researchers in applied linguistics to follow when designing and conducting an MMR study:

1 Determine if mixed methods research is the best approach to address the research problem that you want to study and identify the rationale for using MMR.

2 Select a specific mixed methods design to best address this problem.

3 Write a detailed mixed methods purpose statement that reflects the intent of the study and guides the selection of the methods.

4 Write specific research questions to address the quantitative and qualitative components of your study.

5 Choose the quantitative and qualitative data to collect. Draw a visual diagram of the methodological procedures to be employed in your study.

6 Collect and analyse the quantitative and qualitative data for your study.

7 Write the final report reflecting the mixed methods design you used in the study.

As in any research approach, the study design is guided by the study purpose and the research questions, whereas the selected MMR design informs the selection of the study participants, types of data to be collected and means of their analysis. Based on the variation of the methodological characteristics discussed above, three basic types of MMR designs can be used to address the purposes and needs of researchers in applied linguistics:

- Concurrent Quan + Qual MMR design

- Sequential Quan → Qual MMR design

- Sequential Qual → Quan MMR design

In the following sections, we discuss the methodological characteristics of these MMR designs, provide their conceptual diagrams, illustrate their use in applied linguistics and explain some advantages and limitations that novice mixed methods researchers should consider when selecting these designs. To better understand the design conceptual diagrams, we included a notation system for visual presentation of MMR study procedures (Creswell & Plano Clark 2011; Morse 1991) in Figure 4.2.

- QUAN, QUAL: uppercase letters indicate increased weight for either quantitative and qualitative method.

- quan, qual: lowercase letters indicate decreased weight for either quantitative and qualitative method.

- Plus sign: + indicates that quantitative and qualitative data are collected and analysed concurrently.

- Arrow: → indicates that quantitative and qualitative data are collected and analysed in a sequence.

- Rectangle: ☐ indicates a stage in quantitative and qualitative data collection and analysis.

- Oval: ◯ indicates a stage in quantitative and qualitative methods integration and results interpretation.

- Hexagon: ⬡ indicates a stage where researchers create integrated conclusions from the quantitative and qualitative strands.

FIGURE 4.2 *A notation system for visual presentation of MMR study procedures (adapted from Ivankova 2015)*

Concurrent Quan + Qual MMR design

A concurrent Quan + Qual MMR design is used when it is necessary to compare or merge quantitative and qualitative results to produce well-validated conclusions. It typically includes two strands, during which quantitative and qualitative data are collected and analysed separately or independently of each other. Figure 4.3 presents a conceptual diagram of this design. The weight is typically given to both study strands, because each strand addresses related aspects of the same research question in a complementary way. The mixing of the quantitative and qualitative methods occurs when quantitative and qualitative results are compared or synthesized to find corroborating evidence and to produce a more complete understanding of the research problem (Creswell & Plano Clark 2011).

For example, Miyazoe and Anderson (2010) used a concurrent Quan + Qual design to examine the effectiveness of three different online writing activities – forums, blogs and wikis – in an English as foreign language (EFL) blended learning course in a university in Japan. They concurrently surveyed sixty-one second-year students from three course

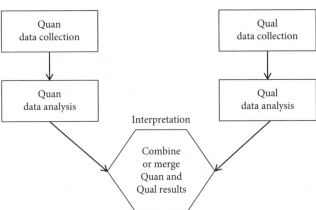

FIGURE 4.3 *Conceptual diagram of concurrent Quan + Qual MMR design (reprinted from Ivankova (2015), with permission of SAGE Publications, Inc.)*

sections and interviewed eighteen volunteer students. They also analysed writing assignments from all students. The researchers equally emphasized quantitative (survey) and qualitative (interview and written text) data because both data sets were used to explain different aspects of EFL learning. The results from quantitative and qualitative analysis were combined 'to provide a triangulated interpretation' (p. 190) of learning outcomes and students' perceptions of learning EFL online.

An advantage of this concurrent design is that both quantitative and qualitative data can be collected and analysed within a short period of time. Thus, it helps save time and the associated cost for conducting the study (Creswell & Plano Clark 2011; Morse & Niehaus 2009). It can also result in well-validated and substantiated findings, because concurrent strand implementation allows for obtaining 'different but complementary data on the same topic' (Morse 1991, p. 122). However, this design may be challenging for a sole researcher because of the need to concurrently implement quantitative and qualitative study strands that often require different sets of research skills (Creswell & Plano Clark 2011; Teddlie & Tashakkori 2009).

Sequential Quan ⟶ Qual MMR design

A sequential Quan → Qual design is used when there is a need for follow-up qualitative data to elaborate, explain, or confirm initial quantitative results. It consists of two chronological strands with a quantitative strand occurring first in sequence. Figure 4.4 presents a conceptual diagram of this design. The weight is typically given to the first, quantitative, study strand because this design is mostly used when the research problem and related purpose require examination by quantitative methods (Creswell & Plano Clark 2011). The mixing of the quantitative and qualitative methods typically occurs chronologically at the completion of the first, quantitative, strand and beginning of the second, qualitative, strand. For example, the results from quantitative survey in the first study strand can help identify the individuals to follow-up with qualitative interviews as well as inform the content of these interview questions. Additionally, the results from both study strands are interpreted together so that the qualitative findings can provide better understanding of the initial quantitative results.

For example, Kissau (2012) used a sequential Quan → Qual design to examine the relationship between online second language (L2) methodology instruction and the sense of teaching efficacy of teacher-candidates in a licensure program in a US university. In the first study strand, quantitative, the researcher surveyed 62 L2 teacher-candidates twice – before the start of the course and upon its completion. In the second study strand, qualitative, at the end of the course, the researcher conducted follow-up individual interviews with eight teacher-candidates who completed the survey about their experiences in the course. The purpose was 'to elaborate upon the survey data and to better understand the quantitative results' (p. 302). The weight was given to initial quantitative survey data because they revealed teacher-candidates' attitudes about the effectiveness of L2 methodology instruction. The two study strands were connected when the results of the survey data were used to inform the selection of the teacher-candidates for follow-up interviews and to inform the interview questions. The two sets of results were also mixed during the discussion of the overall integrated study conclusions.

An advantage of this sequential design is that the chronological nature of the quantitative and qualitative data collection and analysis makes it more straightforward and easy to implement by one researcher (Creswell & Plano Clark 2011; Ivankova, Creswell & Stick 2006; Morse & Niehaus 2009). This design also provides an opportunity for the exploration of the initial quantitative results in more detail, especially when unexpected results arise

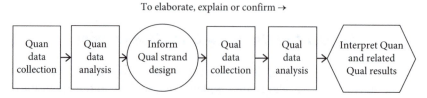

FIGURE 4.4 *Conceptual diagram of sequential Quan → Qual MMR design (reprinted from Ivankova (2015), with permission of SAGE Publications, Inc.)*

from a quantitative strand (Morse 1991). The limitations of this design are related to the length of time and feasibility of resources to collect and analyse both sets of data. Additionally, because many of the research aspects of the second qualitative strand are yet unknown at the study design stage, another approval for continuation of the study is required from the institution's ethical review board once the first quantitative strand is completed. This, ultimately, may extend the overall time of the study.

Sequential Qual → Quan MMR design

A sequential Qual → Quan design is used when it is necessary to use initial qualitative data to develop new measures and identify unknown variables and relationships. It consists of two chronological strands with a qualitative strand occurring first in sequence. Figure 4.5 presents a conceptual diagram of this design. The weight is typically given to the first, qualitative, study strand, because in this design 'the researcher starts by qualitatively exploring a topic before building to a second, quantitative phase' (Creswell & Plano Clark 2011, p. 86). The mixing of the qualitative and quantitative methods typically occurs chronologically at the completion of the first, qualitative, strand and the beginning of the second, quantitative, strand. For example, the results from the qualitative individual or focus group interviews can inform the development of a new survey instrument that will be further administered to a large group of people (Morse & Niehaus 2009). Additionally, the results from both study strands are interpreted together so that the quantitative results can verify, confirm or generalize the initial exploratory qualitative findings.

For example, Ghorbani and Alavi (2014) used a sequential Qual → Quan design to explore the possibilities of implementing English as the medium of instruction (EMI) at Iranian universities. In the first study strand, qualitative, the researchers conducted email interviews with six undergraduate students and six lecturers at the University of Bojnord to explore their perceptions of adopting EMI and to inform the development of a quantitative survey to explore these perceptions

To identify, measure or test →

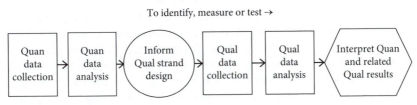

FIGURE 4.5 *Conceptual diagram of sequential Qual → Quan MMR design (reprinted from Ivankova (2015), with permission of SAGE Publications, Inc.)*

with more students and faculty. In the second study strand, quantitative, the researcher administered the new survey to 344 undergraduate and graduate students and thirty-six lecturers. The weight was given to initial qualitative interview data because their analysis 'leads to detailed generalizable results through the second quantitative phase' (Creswell 2005, as cited in Ghorbani & Alavi 2014, p. 4). The two study strands were connected when the themes from qualitative interviews were used to inform the development of the survey items and scales. The two sets of results were also mixed during the discussion of the overall integrated study conclusions.

The sequential nature of the qualitative and quantitative data collection and analysis in this design makes it more straightforward and easy to implement by one researcher. This design is specifically advantageous for situations when a researcher wants to explore the phenomenon in depth with a few individuals and wants to expand these findings to a larger population. The sequential nature of this design also may require lengthy time and more resources to collect and analyse both sets of data. Additionally, developing a measurement instrument is a complex process that requires adherence to special psychometric procedures. The sequential nature of this design also necessitates the need to submit an amendment to the existing research protocol, seeking another approval from the institution's ethical review board, once the first qualitative strand is completed to test the new instrument.

What research issues should we consider when implementing an MMR study?

As with any research study, researchers conducting MMR in applied linguistics should ensure that their studies produce accurate or valid conclusions and meet accepted ethical standards for research. Assessing quality of an MMR study can be especially challenging because of the intended mixing of the results from quantitative and qualitative study strands (Teddlie & Tashakkori 2009). It is also important to consider MMR design characteristics, such as concurrent and sequential timing of quantitative and qualitative data collection and analysis, the order of quantitative and qualitative study strands in sequential designs (quantitative or qualitative first) and the type of mixing procedures (Creswell & Plano Clark 2011; Ivankova 2014). These design-related decisions may either compromise or increase the overall validity of an MMR study. Therefore, it is recommended that MMR researchers first evaluate the methodological rigour of each quantitative and qualitative study strand using the procedures adopted in each research approach; after that, they should assess the quality of the integrated study conclusions using approaches described in MMR literature (Creswell & Plano Clark 2011; O'Cathain 2010; Onwuegbuzie

& Johnson 2006; Teddlie & Tashakkori 2009). Assessing the quality of an MMR study should be included in the study design plan and should be an ongoing process.

Likewise, consideration of ethical issues should be a critical component of the whole research process from the study design to reporting of results. Researchers conducting MMR studies in applied linguistics should observe general ethical principles for research, such as obtaining an approval for the research protocol from the institution's ethical review board, securing informed consent from study participants, ensuring their voluntary participation and preserving their anonymity and confidentiality. There are also several ethical considerations that relate to the process of conducting MMR. Because collecting quantitative and qualitative data entails different levels of data sensitivity, an institution's ethical review board may require explanations of different details related to these processes. Additionally, as discussed earlier, in sequential designs that build one study strand on another, it is necessary to file an amendment to the initial research protocol to seek further institutional approval for the study.

A sample study

In this section, we will look closely at an MMR study conducted by Yu, Sun and Chang (2010) in Taiwan. The study employed the most commonly used MMR design in applied linguistics – concurrent Quan + Qual design – and illustrates many of the characteristics essential to a good model MMR study. In this study, the researchers addressed the timely topic of how online course management systems (CMSs), once assumed to be content-neutral, might influence learning outcomes in unexpected ways in the language classroom.

Yu and colleagues structured their study report in a traditional manner, including a thorough introduction to the benefits and possible downsides of modern CMSs, a study purpose statement, research questions, description of the study methods, results merged with discussion of findings and a conclusion with implications. Of note is the researchers acknowledged use of MMR in the paper's abstract, a move that is highly useful to readers and considered a best practice if the study is true to its design. Further, they justified the use of MMR, citing MMR literature in support of their methodological choice when they discussed the study methodology: 'With a mixed method approach – "a natural complement to traditional qualitative and quantitative research" (Johnson & Onwuegbuzie 2004, p. 14) – the study utilizes a collection of data from both questionnaires and face-to-face interviews with CMS users (teachers and students)' (p. 335). In creating a rationale for the use of MMR, Yu and colleagues identified gaps in the research with most CMS studies being strictly quantitative and too little CMS research in the language learning classroom to indicate how instructors and students perceive value in online systems. Noting that the study of human perception is deepened and made more comprehensive by qualitative research, the authors set the stage for their study purpose and research questions, which are both framed in an MMR context. In particular, the study purpose statement is clear and direct: 'to address the gaps and enrich our understanding of college teachers' and students' use of CMSs for the purpose of language teaching and learning' (p. 335). The research questions included:

1   How are CMs and other computer programs adopted in language courses?
2   What motivates the use of CMSs in language courses?
3   What are the perceived limitations of and desired technical and professional support for using CMs in language courses? (p. 335)

The target population was native Mandarin speakers from a variety of disciplines at two Taiwanese universities. In keeping with MMR philosophy, Yu and colleagues included multiple perspectives by studying both teachers and students. The study consisted of two concurrent strands and quantitative and qualitative methods received equal weighting. The researchers did not include a visual representation of their MMR design, so we developed a visual diagram of the study procedures based on their report (see Figure 4.6).

The quantitative strand included the administration of a questionnaire (through email and in person) to university English teachers (n = 53) and university students (n = 241) who had already been using their existing CMSs (Blackboard, Moodle and a local Taiwanese system, E-Campus 3) for several months. The questionnaire covered questions about (a) demographics, (b) usage experience with CMSs and computer assisted language learning and teaching and (c) perceptions of CMSs in language learning and teaching with items structured around five variables: self-efficacy, enjoyment, usefulness, intention and quality. These data were analysed using descriptive statistics, including means, percentages, frequencies and rankings.

For the qualitative strand, the researchers conducted 45 minute face-to-face, post-hoc interviews with seven teachers and seven students. They also used text data from the open-ended questions in the questionnaire. The interview questions addressed four main topics: definitions of and attitudes about CMSs; learning/teaching approaches and beliefs; strengths and limitations of CMSs in English language courses; and new ideas and suggestions for using CMSs. Both the responses to open-ended questions and interview transcripts were coded and analysed around the three research questions to produce categories and themes.

The results from both quantitative and qualitative strands were then combined and discussed in an integrated fashion around the posted research questions. In particular, the researchers integrated presentation of

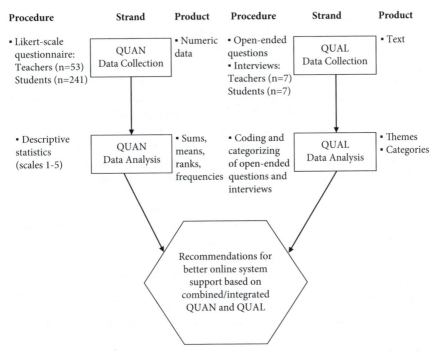

FIGURE 4.6 *Visual diagram of concurrent Quan + Qual MMR design (original diagram by Ivankova and Greer, based on a study by Yu, Sun & Chang 2010)*

quantitative results in numeric data tables with the description of major qualitative themes. For example, a numeric table on commonly used functions is followed by a paragraph of text that includes a quote to show why teachers only use those features that support the language learning objectives and do not feel compelled to be high-end users of all CMS tools. Such consistent merging of the findings from both quantitative and qualitative strands allows the readers to appreciate the synthesis of research evidence in this report. Based on the integrated study conclusions, Yu and colleagues provided recommendations for better online system support for CMS users in language learning.

What should we remember when conducting MMR?

Researchers conducting MMR in the field of applied linguistics should remember that a true MMR study requires mixing of quantitative and qualitative methods at different stages in the study process (Teddlie & Tashakkori 2009). Given this need for seamless integration, researchers should systematically apply the steps necessary for designing and conducting an MMR study. They should also learn how to assess MMR study quality and any ethical issues that may be new to them.

Additionally, considering the relatively recent interest in MMR from the field of applied linguistics, researchers need to educate their audiences about MMR when preparing such studies for publication. In structuring reports, they could follow O'Cathain, Murphy and Nicholl's (2008) guidelines for Good Reporting of a Mixed Methods Study, known as GRAMMS, and clearly articulate an MMR approach, explain a rationale for it and provide a purpose statement and research questions that reflect the MMR orientation of the study. They could also visualize the study design and procedures in a diagram; explain how they attend to critical issues of timing, weighting and mixing; and describe any insights gained from mixing methods.

Finally, researchers could consider networking with other MMR researchers in their field at conferences, through publications, in online forums and via other professional outlets that emphasize development of MMR research. Although times of innovation and shifting paradigms can be difficult and challenging, they also offer opportunities for making what Kuhn (1962, p. 84) called 'a decisive difference' in finding new solutions to problems in a field. With the current dynamism in the field of applied linguistics, no time is more apt than now for decisive differences in research solutions.

Resources for further reading

Books

Creswell, JW & Plano Clark, VL 2011, *Designing and Conducting Mixed Methods Research*, 2nd edn, Sage, Thousand Oaks, CA.

This text provides a practical, step-by-step guidance in designing and implementing an MMR study, covering different topics from the nature of mixed methods; the type of research problems that fit this new approach; the advantages and challenges of using MMR; the foundations of MMR (historical, philosophical and theoretical); specific details and examples of different designs; and guidelines for a proposal, dissertation and journal article.

Greene, JC 2007, *Mixed Methods in Social Inquiry*, Jossey-Bass, San Francisco, CA.

This text examines multiple ways of looking at MMR and provides a clear and coherent perspective to guide new researchers as well as inform experienced scholars. The text includes numerous examples that facilitate understanding of some of the more difficult aspects of MMR.

Morse, JM & Niehaus, L 2009, *Mixed Method Design: Principles and Procedures*, Left Coast Press, Walnut Creek, CA.

This text provides a discussion about what constitutes a true MMR design and offers step-by-step instructions for conducting MMR. Easy to use, this text introduces and discusses key concepts that new scholars will need to implement in a study and write up their findings, drawing on the authors' bank of published studies.

Tashakkori, A & Teddlie, C (eds), 2010, *Sage Handbook of Mixed Methods in Social & Behavioral Research*, Sage, Thousand Oaks, CA.

This handbook addresses all MMR topics, such as use of integrated design, monitoring and evaluation, methods teaching and pedagogy, intervention studies, grant proposals and publishing and draws on an international team of scholars to offer diverse perspectives on this dynamic field.

Teddlie, C & Tashakkori, A 2009, Foundations of *Mixed Methods Research: Integrating Quantitative and Qualitative Approaches in the Social and Behavioral Sciences*, Sage, Thousand Oaks, CA.

This book provides a discussion of the evolution of MMR, setting it in the context of both historical and contemporary methodological thought. Well-sourced and filled with numerous interdisciplinary examples, visuals and charts, this text offers a comprehensive approach to executing an MMR study, from strategy and research design to implementation techniques and reporting.

Journal

Journal of Mixed Methods Research (JMMR).

This is a peer-reviewed flagship journal in the field with an interdisciplinary and an international scope. It publishes both empirical MMR research and methodological and review articles within the social, behavioural, health and human sciences. (http://mmr.sagepub.com/, viewed 28 January 2015)

Association

Mixed Methods International Research Association (MMIRA).

This is a global professional community for promoting methodological quality and innovation. Members receive an online subscription to the Journal of Mixed Methods Research, networking and training opportunities and access to scholarly MMR resources. (http://mmira.wildapricot.org/, viewed 22 March 2015)

References

Copland, F, Garton, S & Burns, A 2013, 'Challenges in teaching English to young learners: Global perspectives and local realities', *TESOL Quarterly*, article first published online: 27 December 2013. DOI: 10.1002/tesq.148.

Cornillie, F, Clarebout, G & Desmet, P 2012, 'Between learning and playing? Exploring learners' perceptions of corrective feedback in an immersive game for English pragmatics', *ReCALL*, vol. 24, no. 3, pp. 257–278.

Creswell, JW 2014, *Research Design: Qualitative, Quantitative, and Mixed Methods Approaches*, 4th edn, Sage, Thousand Oaks, CA.

Creswell, JW & Plano Clark, VL 2011, *Designing and Conducting Mixed Methods Research*, 2nd edn, Sage, Thousand Oaks, CA.

Danzak, RL 2011, 'The interface of language proficiency and identity: A profile analysis of bilingual adolescents and their writing', *Language, Speech, and Hearing Services in Schools*, vol. 42, no. 4, pp. 506–519.

Ghorbani, MR & Alavi, SZ 2014, 'Feasibility of adopting English-medium instruction in Iranian universities', *Current Issues in Education*, vol. 17, no. 1, pp. 1–17.

Greene, JC 2007, *Mixed Methods in Social Inquiry*, Jossey-Bass, San Francisco, CA.

Greene, JC, Caracelli, VJ & Graham, WF 1989, 'Toward a conceptual framework for mixed-method evaluation designs', *Educational Evaluation and Policy Analysis*, vol. 11, no. 3, pp. 255–274.

Ivankova, NV 2014, 'Implementing quality criteria in designing and conducting a sequential QUAN→QUAL mixed methods study of student engagement with learning applied research methods online', *Journal of Mixed Methods Research*, vol. 8, no.1, pp. 25–51.

―――― 2015b, *Mixed Methods Applications in Action Research: From Methods to Community Action*, Sage, Thousand Oaks, CA.

Ivankova, NV & Creswell, JW 2009, 'Mixed methods', in J Heigham & RA Croker (eds), *Qualitative Research in Applied Linguistics: A Practical Introduction*, Palgrave Macmillan, New York, NY.

Ivankova, NV, Creswell, JW & Stick, SL 2006, 'Using mixed methods sequential explanatory design: From theory to practice', *Field Methods*, vol. 18, no. 1, pp. 3–20.

Ivankova, NV & Kawamura, Y 2010, 'Emerging trends in the utilization of integrated designs in the social, behavioral, and health sciences', in A Tashakkori & C Teddlie (eds), *Sage Handbook of Mixed Methods in Social & Behavioral Research*, 2nd edn, Sage, Thousand Oaks, CA.

Johnson, RB & Onwuegbuzie, AJ 2004, 'Mixed methods research: A research paradigm whose time has come', *Educational Researcher*, vol. 33, no.7, pp. 14–26.

Johnson, RB, Onwuegbuzie, AJ & Turner, LA 2007, 'Toward a definition of mixed methods research', *Journal of Mixed Methods Research*, vol. 1, no. 2, pp. 112–133.

Kissau, S 2012, 'Perceptions of self-efficacy for two types of second language methods instruction', *Computer Assisted Language Learning*, vol. 25, no. 4, pp. 295–317.

Kuhn, TS 1962, *The Structure of Scientific Revolutions*, 3rd edn, The University of Chicago Press, Chicago, IL.

Maxcy, SJ 2003, 'Pragmatic threads in mixed methods research in the social sciences: The search for multiple modes of inquiry and the end of the philosophy of formalism', in A Tashakkori & C Teddlie (eds), *Handbook on Mixed Methods in the Behavioral and Social Sciences*, Sage, Thousand Oaks, CA.

McWayne, CM, Melzi, G, Schick, AR & Kennedy, JL 2013, 'Defining family engagement among Latino Head Start parents: A mixed methods measurement development study', *Early Childhood Research Quarterly*, vol. 28, no. 3, pp. 593–607.

Mertens, DM, Bledsoe, KL, Sullivan, M & Watson, A 2010, 'Utilization of mixed methods for transformative purposes', in A Tashakkori & C Teddlie (eds), *Sage Handbook of Mixed Methods in Social & Behavioral Research*, 2nd edn, Sage, Thousand Oaks, CA.

Miyazoe, T & Anderson, T 2010, 'Learning outcomes and students' perceptions of online writing: Simultaneous implementation of a forum, blog, and wiki in an EFL blended learning setting', *System*, vol. 38, pp. 185–199.

Morse, JM 1991, 'Approaches to qualitative-quantitative methodological triangulation', *Nursing Research*, vol. 40, no. 1, pp. 120–123.

Morse, JM & Niehaus, L 2009, *Mixed Method Design: Principles and Procedures*, Left Coast Press, Walnut Creek, CA.

O'Cathain, A 2010, 'Assessing the quality of mixed methods research: Toward a comprehensive framework', in A Tashakkori & C Teddlie (eds), *Sage Handbook of Mixed Methods in Social & Behavioral Research*, 2nd edn, Sage, Thousand Oaks, CA.

O'Cathain, A, Murphy, E & Nicholl, J 2008, 'The quality of mixed methods studies in health services research', *Journal of Health Services Research Policy*, vol. 13, no. 2, pp. 92–98.

Onwuegbuzie, AJ & Johnson, RB 2006, 'The validity issue in mixed research', *Research in the Schools*, vol. 13, no. 1, pp. 48–63.

Pan, Y 2011 'Teacher washback from English certification exit requirements in Taiwan', *Asian Journal of English Language Teaching*, vol. 21, pp. 23–42.

Riazi, AM & Candlin CN 2014, 'Mixed methods research in language teaching and learning: Opportunities, issues, and challenges', *Language Teaching*, vol. 47, no. 2, pp. 135–173.

Tashakkori, A & Creswell, J 2007, 'The new era of mixed methods', *Journal of Mixed Methods Research*, vol. 1, no. 1, pp. 3–8.

Tashakkori, A & Teddlie, C (eds), 2003, *Handbook of Mixed Methods in Social & Behavioral Research*, Sage, Thousand Oaks, CA.

—— (eds), 2010, *Sage Handbook of Mixed Methods in Social & Behavioral Research*, Sage, Thousand Oaks, CA.

Teddlie, C & Tashakkori, A 2009, *Foundations of Mixed Methods Research: Integrating Quantitative and Qualitative Approaches in the Social and Behavioral Sciences*, Sage, Thousand Oaks, CA.

Wesely, PM 2010, 'Language learning motivation in early adolescents: Using mixed methods research to explore contradiction', *Journal of Mixed Methods Research*, vol. 4, no. 4, pp. 295–312.

Yu, W, Sun, Y & Chang, Y 2010, 'When technology speaks language: An evaluation of course management systems used in a language learning context', *ReCALL*, vol. 22, no. 3, pp. 332–355.

CHAPTER FIVE

Survey Research

Elvis Wagner

Virtually everyone is familiar with survey research. People are constantly surveyed about their buying habits, political views, personal beliefs and just about everything else, and the results of this type of research are published and consumed constantly in newspapers, magazines, on television and on the internet. Survey research is a very powerful tool that is used extensively by governments, businesses, educational institutions and by individual researchers, and it has long had an important role in the field of applied linguistics. Researchers have used survey research to investigate the characteristics, attitudes and opinions of language learners. Perhaps most prominently, applied linguistics survey research has provided valuable insights in the areas of learner beliefs (e.g. Kormos et al. 2011), learning strategies (e.g. Chamot & Küpper 1989; Purpura 1999), learner motivation (e.g. Dörnyei 2001; Gardner 1985) and language learning anxiety (Horwitz 2010), among others. As Brown (2001) describes, these notions (i.e. beliefs, strategies, motivation, anxiety) are psychological constructs, abstract notions that are assumed to exist, although they cannot be observed directly. Therefore, survey research instruments allow researchers to operationalize (and consequently, measure) these constructs.

Underlying assumptions and methodology

Survey research differs from experimental research in that the researcher does not manipulate the setting or environment in order to investigate how this affects particular variables or the relationship between variables (see Gass this volume; Nunan 1992). Instead, the goal of survey research is to get information about learners' characteristics, beliefs or attitudes; information that is usually not available from production data, such as performance or observational data (Mackey & Gass 2005). Brown (2001) describes survey research as primary research distinct from both qualitative and statistical research, although survey research will often have both qualitative and quantitative components.

Steps in doing survey research

Because survey research is so prevalent in the social sciences, virtually everyone is familiar with the methodology. In many ways, this presents advantages to the beginning applied linguistics researcher who wants to conduct survey research. The methodology is familiar, and the experience of taking surveys can be useful in creating survey instruments. However, this familiarity can also present unique challenges. Because people are familiar with the methodology, they sometimes gloss over or skip entirely some of the important steps in planning and creating viable research projects. Therefore, a framework for the steps a researcher should follow might be useful. In reality, these steps are not very different from research projects utilizing other methodologies:

- Planning the project
- Designing the survey
- Administering the survey
- Analysing the data

It is very important to note, however, that while these are useful steps to follow when conducting survey research, it is vital that the researcher consider all of these steps during the 'planning the project' phase. That is, unless the researcher has considered how she will administer the survey and analyse the data *before* designing the survey, the research project is almost certainly destined for failure.

Planning the project

When doing the initial planning of the project, the researcher must consider *what* she wants to investigate (reviewing the literature and formulating the research questions), *why* she wants to investigate this topic (identifying the gap in the literature) and *who* she wants to investigate (the population and the sampling techniques that will be used). Based on this planning and research, the researcher then must decide *how* she is going to investigate this topic (the methodology that will be used; the instruments that will be used for the data collection; whether the data will be qualitative, quantitative or both; and how the data will be analysed).

One of the fundamental underlying assumptions to consider when planning survey research is the issue of sampling. Survey research involves trying to find out information about a particular population (e.g. all ESL learners in Great Britain; all university EFL (English as foreign language) learners in Malaysia; all of the EFL learners in a particular language program in Korea). Rarely is an entire population surveyed (an obvious exception is a national census, where a government seeks to obtain information from every member of the population). Because of the huge amount of resources needed to actually complete a census, most research utilizes surveys, in which information is obtained from a sample of the population. While it might be possible for a government to attempt to survey all L2 language users in a country, it is much more feasible (and often useful) to sample from this population. The notion of sampling is a very important consideration in survey research, because the quality and representativeness of the sampling determines the extent of the generalizability of the results of the research of the sample to the larger population (Vogt 2007). Unfortunately, sampling is a consideration that is often overlooked or neglected by educational researchers (including applied linguistics researchers). Because of its importance in a sound research design, a quick overview of the two basic sampling procedures, probability and nonprobability sampling, is provided here.

Types of sampling

Probability sampling techniques (i.e. random, stratified random, systematic and cluster) are used to select a small group (the sample) from a larger group (the population), in order to create samples that are representative of the population. These techniques can be utilized according to the needs, resources, size of the population and quest for generalizability of the individual research projects. *Random sampling* is a variety of sampling in which the researcher seeks to include a truly representative sample of the population in the study. The goal is to assure that every member of the population has an equal chance of being included in the sample. Unfortunately, it is actually very difficult to obtain a truly random sample, and the representativeness of the sample will always be affected by sampling error. A *stratified random sample* is a version of random sampling in which subgroups are selected from within a particular population, and samples are then generated for each of these subgroups. *Systematic sampling*, a more widely used technique, is a sampling technique in which every *nth* person is selected. Finally, *cluster sampling* is a technique in which natural subgroups (clusters) within a population can be identified, and then random samples are generated for each of the clusters.

An example might serve to make the notion of sampling clearer. Say that a researcher is hoping to explore why students at a particular university are studying English as a foreign language. If a list of all the EFL students existed, the researcher could survey each of these learners (in essence, conduct a census) about their motivation for learning English. However, this list might include 1,000 learners, and surveying 1,000 participants would require huge amounts of resources, so the researcher instead chooses to survey a random sampling of these learners. She could have a computer randomly choose 100 participants from the list. If the researcher were interested in comparing particular groups within this population of EFL learners (e.g. to compare the motivation of English majors with non-English majors), she might choose instead to perform stratified random sampling by having a computer randomly choose fifty English majors and fifty non-English majors). She could also perform systematic sampling by generating a list of the 1,000 EFL learners in alphabetical order, randomly choosing one of the first ten names on the list and then selecting every tenth learner to survey.

Random sampling, stratified random sampling and systematic sampling all assume that a 'list' of all the learners in the population exists (in this example, all of the EFL students in this particular university). In reality, however, for many researchers, no such list of all the individuals in a chosen population exists or else the researcher does not have access to this list. If this is the case, then cluster sampling is an option. Again, using the example of our university EFL students, it is possible or even probable that a list of all the current EFL students does not exist (or is out of date or the researcher does not have access to the list). But the researcher does know that there are eight different levels of EFL classes offered at the university. The researcher might then choose to sample eight different classes of students, randomly choosing one class from each of the eight different levels. She could also randomly choose twelve students within each class to survey.

Using appropriate probability sampling helps support the generalizability of the results of survey research. Nevertheless, much of the survey research conducted in applied linguistics utilizes nonprobability sampling – convenience samples. As its name implies, *convenience sampling* involves surveying individuals who are readily available and who the researcher has access to. The use of convenience samples can be informative and can yield interesting and useful results. However, the drawback is that it is not possible to generalize the results to a larger population. Returning to our EFL university student example, if a researcher surveyed the students in her own two classes (a convenience sample) about their motivation for learning English, she might find useful information about the students in these classes, but she could not generalize her results to the rest of the population (all of the university EFL students).

The survey researcher must also be concerned with other sampling issues, including *nonresponse bias*, *sampling error*, *self-selection* and *sampling with replacement* (see Fink 1995; Fowler 1993; Perry 2011; Vogt 2007).

Designing the survey

After the initial planning stage, the researcher needs to design the survey instruments that will be used in the data collection. The design process includes selecting the instruments to be used (see the section below for the different types of survey instruments), creating the instruments (or adapting instruments used by other researchers), piloting the instruments and revising the instruments based on the piloting process.

Questionnaires and interviews

There are two different types of survey data collection instruments: questionnaires and interviews. Questionnaires and interviews are differentiated by the mode in which they are administered and the type of information that each are designed to elicit. Typically, questionnaires are given in written form and are used in order to get information from or about a large number of individuals, while interviews are administered orally and are used to get more in-depth information from a smaller sample of individuals. A questionnaire is a written instrument in which respondents read questions or statements and respond to these questions by selecting a choice offered or writing their own response. Interviews are conducted orally by a researcher in order to elicit oral responses from a participant. An interview schedule refers to the list of questions that the interviewer will ask the participant and serves to ensure that all participants will be asked all of the same questions, in the same order.

In many ways, questionnaires and interviews reflect the larger quantitative versus qualitative data analysis continuum. Questionnaires are designed for efficiency; they can be administered to a large number of participants easily, they can be objectively scored, and the data can be analysed quantitatively. The shortcomings of questionnaires, however, are also readily apparent. The data derived from questionnaires often provide only a superficial assessment of sometimes very complex constructs. Conversely, the data derived from interviews can be quite rich and in-depth. However, this richness comes at a cost of efficiency, in that the researcher (usually) has to meet individually with the participant to administer the interview. The data elicited must then be transcribed and then analysed qualitatively. Questionnaires and interviews are not mutually exclusive – many survey research projects will employ both instrument types in order to get richer interview data that complement the broader questionnaire data. The purpose of the study and the research questions investigated will dictate the type of data collection instruments used. Because of space constraints, the focus here will be on the design of questionnaires.

Questionnaires can be either closed or open-ended. Closed-ended questionnaires have a stimulus (these can be questions or statements, although I will refer to these from this point on as questions) that the participants read and then choose the most appropriate response from a list of possible responses. These possible responses can be in a variety of formats. They can be dichotomous choices (e.g. *yes/no, true/false, agree/disagree*); they can be in multiple-choice format where all of the possible answers are listed; or they can be Likert scale items, in which the respondents have a number of possible responses to choose from. Open-ended questionnaires require the participant to write an answer in response to the stimulus question. The responses elicited with open-ended questionnaires can vary from one word (in response to 'What is your native language?') to extensive written texts (e.g. in response to 'What is your motivation for learning English?').

Questionnaires (closed and open-ended) can be designed to elicit objective data – information about the characteristics of the participants such as age, length of residence in an English speaking country, years of English study, etc., and they can elicit subjective data – information about the beliefs, attitudes and values of the participants. Often, a particular survey will elicit both types of information, such as the background characteristics of the participants as well as their attitudes about learning English.

One of the most commonly used items in survey research is the Likert scale item. This type of item usually includes a statement and then generally has four or five response options, typically including *strongly agree, agree, don't know* (or *no opinion* or *neutral*), *disagree* and *strongly disagree* or some variation of these. These response options are then assigned a number by the researcher (typically 5 for *strongly agree* and 1 for *strongly disagree*), which can be used for quantitative analysis. Some researchers prefer to use more than five categories, with response options such as *somewhat* agree, *slightly* agree, *somewhat* disagree, etc. Including a larger range of response options can serve to improve the psychometric properties of the questionnaire but can also serve to make it more difficult for participants to respond in that they might have difficulty differentiating between the different degrees of agreement or disagreement. There is no consensus among researchers about the use of the *no opinion* or *don't know* response. Some researchers suggest not giving the survey takers this option, because participants who do not have strong feelings about the material in the survey tend to select this category, and if many of the participants choose this category, the results of the overall survey often will not reach statistical significance. Thus, not giving the participants this option can lead to more interpretable results. However, Vogt (2007) argues that respondents choose this neutral response because it most accurately describes their response to the statement and that it is inappropriate to not offer this response simply because it is inconvenient for the researcher.

One of the reasons that these Likert scale items are particularly useful is that a number of items can be used to try and assess the same construct. So, to return to our motivation example, the researcher might want to investigate a particular population's motivation for learning English. Based on her personal experience and the review of the literature conducted in planning the project, she might want to investigate a number of possible external motivators (e.g. *needed for a good job, desire to communicate with English speakers, desire to live or travel in an English speaking country*). The researcher can then create a number of Likert scale items to assess the participants' attitudes for each of these different components of the motivation construct. Then, the items measuring a particular component can be summed or averaged to form a composite scale, although the idea of Likert scale items being treated as composite variables is not universally accepted by statisticians. Likert scales are not really interval scales in that the intervals between the different responses are probably not equal intervals, and thus they are more accurately seen as ordinal data. Nevertheless, many, if not most, applied linguists do treat Likert scale items as interval data.

Generally speaking, the more items that are used to measure a particular concept, the more reliable and accurate is the overall scale. Often, items that are measuring the same construct will include *reverse-coded* items. So, for example, one item in the 'job' motivation scale might state: 'Speaking English is necessary for my job', while the reverse coded item would be something like, 'Learning English is not important for my occupation.'

After the individual items have been created, the questionnaire is then compiled and formatted. The importance of the formatting cannot be underestimated. Brown (2001) and Dörnyei (2010) stress the importance of creating a questionnaire that looks professional, with no typographical errors or formatting inconsistencies. The respondents will automatically make a number of assumptions about a questionnaire based on its appearance. If the questionnaire looks professional, participants are more likely to respond to it seriously. For more information on formatting issues, the reader is urged to consult Brown (2001), Dörnyei (2010), Gillham (2007) and Phakiti (2014).

For reliability purposes, the goal for the researcher is to standardize the questionnaire so that every one of the respondents gets the exact same items, in the same order. Brown (2001) suggests that questions should be ordered from shortest and easiest to answer to longest and most difficult to answer. He also suggests keeping together all questions of a single type, of a single function, of a single response format and question form and all questions on a given topic.

After the initial questionnaire has been created, it is important to pilot the questionnaire to see how it performs. Ideally, the questionnaire can be piloted on participants that are members of the target population and then analysed statistically (see the 'analysis' section below). Based on this analysis of which items seem to be working well and which items are problematic, the developer can revise or delete certain items and add different items if necessary. Then the researcher can do another pilot administration of the questionnaire, analyse the results and revise as needed.

Unfortunately, this extensive piloting and revision process is not always feasible. Nevertheless, it is imperative that some sort of piloting is performed. Resources spent piloting the instrument at this phase of the project are generally resources well spent. It is vital that someone other than the questionnaire developer actually take the questionnaire. At the very least, the researcher can trial the questionnaire on friends or colleagues and get their feedback about the questionnaire. Even if these respondents are not part of the population for which the questionnaire is intended, they can give the researcher valuable information that will assist in the revision process. Often the developer is too close to the questionnaire – he or she cannot see the problems or issues that might be obvious to someone who has not spent many hours researching and developing this survey instrument.

Administering the survey

Only after the instrument has been piloted and revised should it be administered to actual participants. With interviews, the researcher should make sure to schedule enough time to complete the interview. The piloting process should help make clear how much time is needed, but in my experience interviews often take longer than anticipated, and the data from a rushed interview is suspect. The researcher should always strive to be professional, and the interview space should be clean, quiet and unobtrusive. Part of being professional is to be familiar with the interview schedule and rehearsing the questions to be asked. For reliability purposes, it is important that the interviewer follow the interview question wording exactly (Brown 2001). The interviewer should strive to make the interviewee comfortable, welcoming the interviewee at the beginning of the session, thoroughly explaining the research purposes and interview procedure and answering any questions the participant may have. If audio- or video-recording equipment is used to record the interview, it should be as unobtrusive as possible and tested beforehand to make sure it is recording properly.

For questionnaire administration, which often includes larger groups of participants, if at all possible, the researcher should attend the administration in person. While it might be possible for a classroom teacher to administer the questionnaires to his or her class of students, the classroom teacher will invariably not be as invested in the research as the primary researcher nor will he or she be as knowledgeable about the research or able to answer all the questions participants might have. Administering the questionnaire in person, in a polite and professional manner, generally leads to a higher response rate and better results.

It is very important that the researcher anticipate issues that might arise during the administration. Again, the process of piloting the questionnaire should help the researcher anticipate possible problems. A useful suggestion is, as much as possible, to prepare the participants for the questionnaire *before* they appear for the large-scale administration. This can be accomplished by providing participants in advance with information about the study and its purpose (email is often useful for this) and about the questionnaire procedure itself. The researcher should check out the space where the administration will occur, making sure that there is adequate and comfortable space for the respondents. While it may seem obvious to mention that the researcher should double-check that she has enough copies of the questionnaire, and that these copies are collated and in the appropriate order, numerous questionnaire administrations have been scuttled by photocopying problems. As with interviews, when the participants arrive for the administration, the researcher should welcome them, make them feel as comfortable as possible and explain the purpose of the research, the instructions for responding to the questionnaire and answer any questions respondents might have. Again, this might seem obvious, but large-scale administrations can be quite stressful, and if not adequately prepared, the researcher can forget to make the respondents as comfortable as possible. The goal, of course, is to make participants want to respond to the interview or questionnaire as fully and truthfully as possible. Respondents who feel unwanted or unwelcome are much less likely to devote their time and attention to the survey, and the results will be of dubious value. After the administration is completed, the researcher should thank the respondents for their participation.

Sampling issues were described in the 'Planning the Project' section, but sampling is also an administration issue. Appropriate sampling procedures necessitate that the researcher try to get everyone that was targeted in the sampling procedure to actually perform the interview or complete the questionnaire. Even the most conscientious sampler can end up with an unrepresentative sample if not everyone in the targeted sample completes the survey. This is called *nonresponse bias*. For example, if a researcher is exploring students' motivation for learning English and uses a sampling procedure that randomly chooses four classes in a language program to be surveyed, it is important that every student in those four classes be surveyed. If the researcher administers the questionnaire in the four classes in which seventy-five of the eighty students are present, it is very important that the researcher follow up and try to get the remaining five students who were not present in their classes that day to complete the questionnaire. This might sound trivial, but these missing five students could represent serious nonresponse bias. Perhaps these five students often skip class because they are not motivated to learn English. By not getting these students' input, the results of the study are of questionable value.

Questionnaires do not have to be administered in person, of course. Often, questionnaires are sent through the mail to possible respondents, so that the respondent can complete the questionnaire and return it to the researcher. This presents special problems related to response rate and is beyond the purview of this chapter (see Vogt 2007 for further information about postal surveys and questionnaires).

Surveys and questionnaires can also be conducted on the internet or via email. This type of survey research has a number of advantages, the most obvious being the lower costs involved. Rather than having to create and administer physical questionnaires (either in person or via postal mail), the questionnaires can be presented on a website or emailed to potential participants, allowing the participants to respond to the questionnaires when it is convenient for them. The other major advantage is that much of the data entry can be done automatically. When using a web-based survey service, the participants usually complete the questionnaires online, the data is entered automatically, and the results are immediately available for the researcher. Web-based surveys do pose special research problems that have to be addressed, however. Like all other surveys, it is important that adequate sampling procedures be followed, and the researcher must endeavour to follow up with potential participants who did not respond to the initial solicitation. Web-based surveys might be especially prone to bias issues like self-selection bias. Another issue is the need to make online surveys password protected. When participants are solicited for participation in the survey, they should be given a special password that is only able to be used once or else participants might skew the results of the survey by responding multiple times. Web-based surveys also present security issues, and special care should be taken to ensure that secure connections be used so that anonymity can be ensured, especially if the survey is of a sensitive nature.

Analysing the data

After the interviews or questionnaires have been administered, it is necessary to analyse the data. For interviews, the data needs to be transcribed and then coded and analysed qualitatively (see Holliday this volume for more information about analysing qualitative data). Questionnaire data, however, usually entails larger sample sizes and generally necessitate inputting the data into a spreadsheet such as Excel or a statistical program such as SPSS, so that the data can be analysed statistically. One of the most important things to consider is the issue of *reverse-coded items*. Although it might seem obvious, it is imperative that the researcher remember to reverse-code these items when inputting the data. That is, if a Likert scale was used with 5 for *strongly agree* and 1 for *strongly disagree*, when inputting the values for the reverse-coded items, it is necessary to input 1 for *strongly agree*, 2 for *agree*, etc.

After the data are inputted, descriptive statistics (mean, standard deviations, skewness and kurtosis) can be computed. If statistical procedures that require a normal distribution are going to be used in the analysis, these descriptive statistics can be consulted to check that the assumptions regarding normality are met (see Phakiti this volume).

It is also important to examine (and report) the reliability of the questionnaire. Usually, the internal consistency reliability will be estimated using Cronbach's alpha. Internal consistency reliability is used to estimate the extent to which scores on the different items correlate with each other, and Cronbach's alpha is a coefficient (ranging from 0 to 1) that indicates the extent to which the items are measuring a single (unidimensional) construct. The closer this coefficient is to 1, the more consistently the items are measuring the same thing. Depending on what the questionnaire is intended to assess, the reliability can be estimated for the overall questionnaire, for each subsection of the questionnaire or for the individual scales. If the questionnaire is narrow in scope, composed of ten items that are all intended to assess the unidimensional construct 'Learners' motivation in their English classroom', for example, then the reliability should be assessed for the overall questionnaire. If the questionnaire is broader in scope, with three subsections, all designed to measure different components of motivation for learning English (e.g. 'English in the classroom', 'English on the job' and 'English for tourism'), then it would be appropriate to estimate reliability for each of the distinct subsections. If the questionnaire is very broad in scope, with numerous scales all designed to measure different components of motivation, then it would be most appropriate to estimate reliability for each scale. Internal consistency reliability is an estimate of the degree to which the different items are consistently measuring a single construct (see Phakiti 2003). If the questionnaire is designed to measure different things (multiple constructs), then one would expect that the individual items indeed are not measuring consistently.

One of the difficulties with estimating internal consistency reliability for a composite scale (that might be measured by only three or four items) is that often the reliability estimate will be quite low, because Cronbach's alpha is affected by the number of items in the scale. While it is impossible to give a pre-determined cut-off on how high the alpha should be for a questionnaire, Dörnyei (2010) suggests that even short scales composed of only three or four items should have a reliability coefficient alpha of at least 0.70 (i.e. 70 per cent of the items are reliable in terms of measuring the construct), and he suggests that an alpha that is less than 0.60 is problematic. Similarly, Perry (2011) advises that while questionnaires tend to have lower reliability coefficients than test instruments, a reliability coefficient below 0.60 is considered low. Vogt (2007) is even more stringent, stating that an alpha of 0.70 is the minimum acceptable. A reliability coefficient much below 0.70 indicates that the items are not consistently measuring the same unidimensional construct but may in fact be measuring a number of different things.

If the questionnaire has a large number of items and a large number of scales, and if the questionnaire has been given to a large group of respondents, it is more appropriate to use factor analysis in addition to internal consistency reliability to investigate the extent to which the different items designed to measure a specific component of the construct are indeed measuring the same thing. Factor analysis is a more sophisticated statistical technique than reliability analyses and can give the researcher more information about what the different items in the questionnaire are actually measuring (see Vogt 2007 for more information about factor analysis).

Factors affecting the validity of survey research

There are a number of issues that the survey researcher must be aware of and address in order to make the results of survey research as trustworthy and valid as possible. Perhaps the most important consideration involves the issue of sampling. This has been addressed above, but it is worth stressing the notion that unless adequate sampling procedures have been instituted, the research is of little use outside the immediate context of the research and generalizing to a larger population is inappropriate.

Research construct

Another difficulty inherent in much survey research is related to the nature of what is being investigated. As noted, much survey research in applied linguistics is aimed at exploring abstract constructs like motivation, strategy use, attitudes and the anxiety of language learners. Dörnyei, perhaps the pre-eminent researcher of L2 motivation and who uses questionnaires extensively in his research, describes how motivation is an abstract term for a construct that is unobservable, multidimensional and inconstant (Dörnyei 2001). Needless to say, it is no easy task to measure an unobservable, multidimensional and inconstant construct using only a number of statements or questions that a participant has to respond to. To complicate matters even further, many of the constructs being investigated in survey research include behaviours that are unconscious – automatized behaviours that the language learner may do without even being consciously aware of doing so. There is disagreement about whether unconscious behaviours can actually be accessed by conscious recollection, thus calling into doubt the validity of the results of this type of survey research. In addition, questionnaires using Likert scale items to measure these abstract constructs compound the difficulty in that they require respondents to note the strength of choice (e.g. the extent that they *strongly agree* versus just *agree* with the statement). As argued by Vogt (2007), one participant's conception of *agree* might be very different from another participant's conception of *agree*. Even *yes* or *no* answers are problematic in that for many statements, they provide a false dichotomy. For example, a participant asked to respond *Yes* or *No* to a statement 'I listen to the radio to learn English' might become frustrated if she used to listen to the radio in English, but does not anymore, or if she has listened only once or twice. What is the correct answer? While the researcher needs to try and anticipate these types of issues, often they will only become apparent in the trialling and piloting phase.

Again, investigating these abstract constructs is difficult under the best of conditions, but the applied linguistics survey researcher also has to address language and literacy issues. By definition, language learners have an imperfect control of language. If the interviews or questionnaires are presented to the participants in the target language, it is imperative that the language used in eliciting the data be at a level comprehensible to the respondents. This is, of course, much easier said than done. One way around this issue is to elicit the data in the native language of the participants, but this is not always feasible and also introduces translation issues. Dörnyei (2010) describes the two main challenges in translating questionnaires as the need to create a very close translation so that the versions are equivalent; and to produce a text that sounds natural in the target language. Dörnyei (2010, p. 51) provides two possibilities for doing this. The first includes the use of a team of external reviewers who review the two versions of the questionnaire and assess the equivalence of the two versions and the naturalness of the language. The second possibility involves back-translation, in which the questionnaire is translated from the original language to the target language, and then a different person (or persons) translates the target language version of the questionnaire back into the original version. These two original language versions are then compared to ensure the accuracy of the translation.

Fatigue

Another issue that can affect the validity and trustworthiness of survey research is the issue of fatigue. As a general rule of thumb, the more items on a data collection instrument (e.g. a test, questionnaire or interview), the more reliable that instrument will be. That is, the Cronbach's alpha for a questionnaire that has twenty items will tend to be higher than for a questionnaire that has ten items. There is a point, however, where additional items will lead to diminishing returns. Anyone who has ever completed a questionnaire that was too long can attest to this phenomenon. Respondents can read and answer the questionnaire items for only so long before they become fatigued and lose concentration. At this point, the responses provided by the participant become suspect, the reliability of the responses suffers and the validity of the research is questionable. With respondents who are reading and responding in a second language, it is likely that fatigue will set in even sooner. Obviously, the point at which fatigue sets in will vary by the individual respondent, but Dörnyei (2010) suggests that no survey or questionnaire require more than 30 minutes to complete.

Bias

Yet another issue that the applied linguistics survey researcher has to acknowledge and try to address is the issue of respondents who are unmotivated or unreliable. Often, a survey researcher will contact a teacher or a language program administrator and get permission to administer her survey or questionnaire to a classroom of students. These students are a captive audience for the researcher, and while they might complete the questionnaire as instructed, if they are unmotivated to concentrate on the questionnaire and answer truthfully, the reliability and validity of the results are questionable. At the same time, survey research is prone to many different forms of bias. That is, the respondents will often respond (consciously or unconsciously) to the survey prompts by giving answers that will enhance their own standing (*prestige bias*) or their responses will reflect how they would like to think of themselves as acting rather than how they really act (*self-deception bias*). Some respondents are also prone to responding to the interview or questionnaire according to how they think the researcher wants them to respond (*acquiescence bias*).

The point here is thus twofold. It is vital that the researcher pilot and validate the instruments used in survey research (see Brown 2001 for further information about validating survey instruments). In addition, while survey research can be quite informative, the inherent limitations in this type of research must always be remembered and acknowledged by the researcher.

A sample study

Purpura (1999) employed questionnaires to investigate low-ability and high-ability learners' cognitive and metacognitive strategy use and how strategy use affected second language test performance. Drawing on a review of the literature of previous strategy use studies, Purpura created cognitive strategy and metacognitive strategy use questionnaires based on a model of human information processing. The cognitive strategy use questionnaire contained forty questionnaire items designed to measure twelve different cognitive strategy types (e.g. *analysing contrastively, linking with prior knowledge, practising naturalistically*). Each cognitive strategy type was measured by at least two different questionnaire items, although some strategy types were measured by up to five items. The items that were measuring the same cognitive strategy type were averaged to create a composite scale of that variable. Similarly, the metacognitive strategy use questionnaire contained forty questionnaire items designed to measure five different metacognitive strategy types (e.g. *setting goals, assessing the situation, formulating a plan*). Each metacognitive strategy type was measured by at least three items, and one metacognitive strategy type was measured by ten questionnaire items. Again, the items that were measuring the same metacognitive strategy type were averaged to create a composite scale of that variable.

These strategy questionnaires were then administered to 1,382 English language learners. The participants also took the First Certificate of English Anchor Test, so that the strategy use of the learners could be investigated in conjunction with second language test performance. Purpura used a number of statistical procedures to analyse the questionnaire data. He first calculated descriptive statistics (including the means, standard deviations, skewness and kurtosis). Calculating these statistics allowed him to check that the assumptions regarding normality for each variable were met and that statistical procedures requiring a normal distribution would be appropriate for these data. He then performed a series of reliability analyses using Cronbach's alpha for the strategy use questionnaires, estimating the reliability coefficient for both the cognitive questionnaire (alpha = 0.84) and metacognitive questionnaires (alpha = 0.89) as well as the reliability coefficient for each of the scale variables (the twelve different cognitive strategy types and the five different metacognitive strategy types). These reliability analyses allowed Purpura to investigate the extent to which the different items within each scale were actually measuring the same underlying trait, in the hopes of validating the questionnaire. In other words, if three items were designed to measure the strategy *analysing contrastively*, then it would be expected that these three items would have a very high internal consistency. And indeed, a number of the scale reliability coefficients were relatively high (above 0.70), suggesting that the items in these scales were measuring the same construct. However, a number of the composite scale variables were much lower, suggesting that while the items measuring these strategies were designed to measure the same trait, they might in fact have been measuring different traits.

Purpura then used exploratory factor analysis to examine the underlying factorial structure of the two questionnaires. These factor analyses suggested that the cognitive strategy questionnaire was measuring eleven different factors, rather than the twelve different factors (hypothesized cognitive strategies) that Purpura had expected and that the metacognitive strategy questionnaire appeared to be measuring four different factors, rather than the five different factors (hypothesized metacognitive strategies) that he had originally expected.

Based on the results of these exploratory factor analyses, substantive rationale and a rethinking of the original theoretical models, Purpura then used confirmatory factor analysis to test a number of competing models of cognitive strategy use and metacognitive strategy use. In other words, he used these reliability and factor analyses in order to 'generate empirically-based, composite variables, which could then be used to posit a model of strategy use' (Purpura 1999, p. 67), which could be related to a model of second language test performance.

Resources for further reading

Brown, JD 2001, *Using Surveys in Language Programs*, Cambridge University Press, Cambridge.

This book, by a leading authority on statistics and research in applied linguistics, is aimed at teachers and researchers in language programs that are interested in conducting survey research. It provides in-depth coverage of issues related to survey research. The book is organized according to the steps involved in conducting survey research (*planning, designing the instrument, gathering data, analysing data statistically, analysing data qualitatively* and *reporting*). The chapter devoted to statistical analysis is especially thorough and useful for researchers interested in using survey methodology.

Dörnyei, Z with Taguchi, T 2010, *Questionnaires in Second Language Research: Construction, Administration, and Processing*, 2nd edn, Routledge, New York, NY.

This book is a very practical guide to the construction and administration of questionnaires in L2 research from a researcher who has used questionnaires extensively in his research, especially pertaining to the cognitive components of language learning. Perhaps the book's greatest strength is its practical nature – the author gives specific instructions and suggestions for creating reliable, valid and useful questionnaires.

Some useful websites for hosting online surveys
    www.surveymonkey.com, viewed 6 May 2014
    www.questionpro.com, viewed 6 May 2014
    www.KeySurvey.com, viewed 6 May 2014
    www.polldaddy.com, viewed 6 May 2014
    http://freeonlinesurveys.com, viewed 6 May 2014

There are numerous websites and software packages devoted to the creation and administration of surveys and questionnaires. Most of these websites allow users to try out the service for free.

http://nces.ed.gov/statprog/2002/stdtoc.asp, viewed 6 May 2014

Part of the United States Department of Education, The National Center for Educational Statistics administers this website that provides and sets standards for survey data sampling and collection. The Center provides these standards in order to ensure the quality of statistical surveys and their analyses.

References

Brown, JD 2001, *Using Surveys in Language Programs*, Cambridge University Press, Cambridge.

Chamot, A & Küpper, L 1989, 'Learning strategies in foreign language instruction', *Foreign Language Annals*, vol. 22, no. 1, pp. 13–24.

Dörnyei, Z 2001, *Teaching and Researching Motivation*, Longman, Harlow.

Dörnyei, Z withTaguchi, T 2010, *Questionnaires in Second Language Research: Construction, Administration, and Processing*, 2nd edn, Routledge, New York, NY.

Fink, A 1995, *How to Sample in Surveys*, Sage, Thousand Oaks, CA.

Fowler, F, Jr. 1993, *Survey Research Methods*, 2nd edn, Sage, Newbury Park, CA.

Gardner, R 1985, *Social Psychology and Second Language Learning: The Role of Attitudes and Motivation*, Edward Arnold, London.

Gillham, B 2007, *Developing a Questionnaire*, 2nd edn, Continuum, London.

Horwitz, E 2010, 'Foreign and second language anxiety', *Language Teaching*, vol. 43, no. 2, pp. 154–167.

Kormos, J, Kiddle, T & Csizér, K 2011, 'Systems of goals, attitudes, and self-related beliefs in second-language-learning motivation', *Applied Linguistics*, vol. 32, no. 5, pp. 495–516.

Mackey, A & Gass, S 2005, *Second Language Research: Methodology and Design*, Lawrence Erlbaum, Mahwah, NJ.

Nunan, D 1992, *Research Methods in Language Learning*, Cambridge University Press, Cambridge.

Perry, F 2011, *Researching Applied Linguistics: Becoming a Discerning Consumer*, 2nd edn, Lawrence Erlbaum, Mahwah, NJ.

Phakiti, A 2003, 'A closer look at the relationship of cognitive and metacognitive strategy use to EFL reading comprehension test performance', *Language Testing*, vol. 20, no. 1, pp. 26–56.

—— 2014, 'Questionnaire development and analysis', in A Kunnan (ed.), *Companion to Language Assessment*, Wiley-Blackwell, Oxford.

Purpura, J 1999, *Learner Strategy Use and Performance on Language Tests: A Structural Equation Modeling Approach*, Cambridge University Press, Cambridge.

Vogt, W 2007, *Quantitative Research Methods for Professionals*, Pearson, Boston, MA.

CHAPTER SIX

Experimental Research

Susan Gass

Experimental research is a way of determining the effect of something on something else. In other words, a researcher begins with an idea of why something happens and manipulates at least one variable, controls others, to determine the effect on some other variable. To take a simple example from everyday life, let's suppose that an individual has developed a rash, but the source of the rash is not known. There are a number of possibilities: (1) something eaten, (2) a medication taken, (3) touching an object that causes an allergic reaction. We might eliminate one factor at a time, let's say, a particular medication taken to see if the rash disappears. If it does not, then one eliminates a medication taken as the source of the problem. This continues until the culprit is discovered. There is, of course, a fallacy in this reasoning because the rash could disappear on its own, given the many unknown workings of the human body. Nonetheless, experimental research, in this case, is a way of determining, to the extent possible, what the source of the rash is.

We turn to an example from language. Let's assume that we want to know whether focusing a learner's attention on some aspect of language increases that individual's learning of that aspect of language. One way to do this is to find two groups of learners which are matched on their pre-experiment knowledge of this aspect of language. There is then a treatment session in which the experimental group receives focused attention on the particular part of language under investigation, while the control group receives exposure to the same part of language, but their attention is not intentionally directed. A post-test measures improvement from the pre-test. In sum, experimental research involves the manipulation of at least one variable, known as an independent variable, while keeping other relevant variables constant, and observing the effect of the manipulation on some other variable (known as a dependent variable), for example, a test score.

Underlying assumptions of the methodology

Even though a discussion of the philosophy of science is beyond the scope of this chapter, it is important to at least acknowledge some of the philosophical underpinnings when considering what experimental research is and why some individuals are 'married' to this approach and others do not see its value. In the history of second language acquisition (SLA) research, there are those who tend to be what might be called rationalists in their approach to research and others who are considered relativists in their approach (see Jordan 2005 for a disentanglement of these and other related terms). In the former approach, one finds a strong role for experimental quantitative research. The latter group sees the value of multiple realities and more frequently uses qualitative data; in other words, there is no objective reality – only our perceptions of reality.[1] These divisions in recent years are becoming blurred with many studies using both quantitative and qualitative data. These are known as mixed methods studies (see Hashemi & Babahii 2013 for a review; see also the *Journal of Mixed Methods Research*).

Larsen-Freeman and Long (1991) discuss two approaches to research that are differentiated by whether they might be considered inductive or deductive. Conducting research and then coming up with a theory (research-then-theory) is inductive, whereas a theory-then-research approach is deductive. Experimental research with its rationalist underpinnings falls into this latter category.

Specifics of experimental research

With experimental research, there are a number of components that researchers include. First, there is a specific and precise research question. This research question follows from some theoretical vantage point and is generally based on something that remains unanswered from previous research. Second is a set of explicitly stated variables, that is, what is being varied and what is being measured. These must reflect the construct under investigation. Third is a randomly selected group of participants who are randomly assigned to various treatment conditions and/or control groups. Additionally, in reporting research results, the treatment must be described explicitly and must relate in a direct way to the research question. Interpretation of the results, that is, of the effects of the treatment is generally done through statistical means. Finally, to ensure that the interpretation of the treatment effects is accurate, there must be controls and there must be appropriate counterbalancing. In the following section, we elaborate on each of these parts.

Research questions

Research questions must be stated explicitly and must have some basis in previous literature. For example, consider the following two examples:

1 Does focused attention on noun–adjective agreement in Italian promote learning to a greater extent than focused attention on *wh*-movement in Italian for beginning learners of Italian?

Prior research (Gass, Svetics & Lemelin 2003) argued that focused attention promoted learning in some parts of the grammar and not in others and differentially affected learners at different proficiency levels.

2 Should language classes be introduced early in a school's curriculum?

The first question is explicitly stated, although as we will see below, there are variables that are in need of further elaboration and greater explicitness. The second question, while interesting and one which school districts are constantly debating, is not researchable given the vagueness as well as the word *should* which implies some sort of right or wrong and which, as a result, cannot be empirically evaluated.

In sum, in experimental research, there need to be answerable questions. There are a number of characteristics that one can think of when determining whether a question is answerable or researchable. Given the limited resources (time and money) of most researchers, questions must be feasible in relation to the time and budget of the problem. This often entails scaling back on the level of complexity of the research question. As is implied from the discussion above, the question needs to be significant in relation to current research in the field of inquiry. And, of course, ethics must play a role in the questions that are asked. This topic is dealt with in greater detail below. Question 2 above fails in that it would probably not be feasible given the never-ending number of variables involved, even though it is significant in that it is an important question for all school districts.

Research hypothesis

In experimental research, there are not only research questions, but also hypotheses. Hypotheses are predictions based on the research question. For example, in research question 1 above, the following hypothesis might obtain.

1   Focused attention on noun–adjective agreement in Italian will promote learning to a greater extent than focused attention on *wh*-movement in Italian for beginning learners of Italian.

Alternatively, if there is no reason to expect anything other than a difference, the hypothesis might be phrased as follows:

2   Focused attention on noun–adjective agreement in Italian will promote learning to a different degree than focused attention on *wh*-questions in Italian for beginning learners of Italian.

Often, these are expressed as *null* hypotheses which state that there are no differences between/among groups. The research goal is to reject the null hypothesis.

Variables

Variables are characteristics of a class of objects that vary, as in the variable of eye colour or height or weight for humans. In experimental research, variables need to be made explicit. This is actually one of the most difficult parts of a research project. To take research question 1 above, there are a few variables about which decisions need to be made to render those variables sufficiently explicit, so that a researcher can conduct his/her research. For example, how will focused attention be operationalized (by colouring instances of noun–adjective agreement in a written text? By providing an explicit grammatical description? By frequency – that is by introducing numerous instances of noun–adjective agreement in a passage)? When conducting and reporting experimental research, researchers must be clear on how they are defining their terms.

A second variable in the research question under consideration is the notion of learning. In the history of SLA, different definitions have been used and here too numerous decisions have to be made. Is learning measured by a paper/pencil (or computer) test or by spontaneous use? If by a paper/pencil or computer test, what kind of test? If the latter, how does one elicit spontaneous use? And, what does it mean if a form is not used? Does it mean that the learner does not know it or does it mean that the learner does not think she or he needs to use it? If the latter, then learning may have taken place as a result of the treatment, but there may be extraneous reasons for it not being used. Further, if spontaneous use is the criterion for learning, how many instances of the structure/sound/lexical item need to occur? Mackey (1999), for example, required 'the presence of at least two examples of structures in *two* different posttests' (p. 567). Is learning being operationalized only through a test given immediately following the treatment, or will the test be given one week later, or a month later? Other variables relate specifically to the question being considered. For example, investigating noun–adjective agreement in Italian requires further decisions. Are only feminine nouns to be included, only masculine nouns or both? Because nouns that end in -*a* or in -*o* almost invariably indicate what the gender of the noun is, will nouns that do not obviously indicate gender (e.g. *ponte*, m. bridge) be included? Similarly, for questions (*wh*-movement), one will have to determine which questions to include; does one include questions that include prepositions (e.g. *for whom, with what*)?

In sum, variables are characteristics that vary. In experimental research, there are essentially two primary variables of concern: independent variables and dependent variables. Independent variables are the object of investigation. They are those variables that the researcher is investigating in order to determine their effect on something else. In the above example, focused attention on the two grammatical structures is the independent variable. Dependent variables are those variables that the independent variable is having an effect on. Thus, learning is the dependent variable in the above example. In addition to these variables are extraneous variables; these variables are independent variables that the researcher has not controlled for. In essence, they can seriously interfere with the results of a study. In the above example of focused attention, let's assume that a researcher has operationalized focused attention by colouring red all instances of noun–adjective agreement in a reading passage. Let's also assume that the researcher did not test for possible colour-blindness of the participants. Then, colour-blindness is an uncontrolled variable that could have interfered with the interpretation of the results.

Random assignment

A third hallmark of experimental research is the random assignment of participants to one group or another. Random assignment of individuals means that each individual has an equal chance of being assigned to any of the conditions of the study (experimental or control). That is, the process of assignment is random. Randomization is intended to eliminate the possibility that extraneous variables will creep into the research design. To take the above example, had there been randomization, there would have been an equal chance of having colour-blind individuals in both the adjective–noun group and the *wh*-question group.

In general, in educational settings, we cannot always have random assignment of individuals and we are more often dependent on the contexts that already exist (e.g. intact classes) for our research. This is known as quasi-experimental research (as opposed to true experimental research) because not all variables can be completely controlled; in particular, we are dependent on assignment of participants based on class placement rather than on random assignment. But, in such instances, there should be random assignment of the group/class to one condition or another.

Statistical analysis

Interpretation of results is done as a first step through statistical analyses. A discussion of different kinds of statistics and designs is beyond the scope of this chapter, but there are numerous books that deal with these topics (see Dörnyei 2007; Mackey & Gass 2005, 2012, 2015). In general, for most research in the field of SLA or applied linguistics more generally, the significance level (α level) is generally set at 0.05. This means that when we look at statistical results, there is a 95 per cent chance that our results are due to the experimental treatment and only 5 per cent chance that the results are due to chance alone. In many studies, researchers will talk about the results *approaching significance* when the statistical analysis is slightly about 0.05 (e.g. 0.06 – 0.09). In disciplines where the consequences of a chance finding are greater (e.g. life-altering medical treatment), different α levels are required. In other words, the α level is a generally accepted guide that is used by researchers in a discipline. When we are accepting or rejecting hypotheses, we want to avoid any errors in interpretation. There are two noteworthy error types, known as Type I (also known as an α error) and Type II (also known as a β error). The former refers to the rejection of a (null) hypothesis when it should not be rejected, and the latter refers to the acceptance of a (null) hypothesis when it should be rejected. Both of these errors are minimized through rigorous and appropriate use of statistics.

Statistical significance gives us a 'yes/no' indication of the significance of one's results. In most cases, a dichotomous decision is insufficient; one wants to know instead how strong findings are. Effect sizes, because they are not dependent on sample size, are frequently used (many journals require an effect size as part of reporting). Probability levels are highly dependent on sample size, whereas effect sizes are not. Plonsky and Oswald (2014) provide a full discussion of effect sizes and their interpretation.

As part of the interpretation process, one has to be able to eliminate with a reasonable degree of confidence that other factors did not enter into the picture. There are ways to minimize this possibility. One, we have already discussed and that is randomization. Another was hinted at with the colour-blindness example and that is by testing for that variable and eliminating those participants who have that characteristic. One could also include that variable into the design by including it as a variable and then testing for its influence. And, a variation of the latter is to match participants, so that one has a particular characteristic and another does not. This latter is perhaps better understood if one took the variable of gender. Let's assume that in the focused-attention experiment we have reason to believe that males might behave differently than females, we then would want to balance males and females in all groups.

Validity and reliability

With all research, we need to be able to be confident in our results; our results need to be trustworthy and valid. Validity encompasses many of the concepts already discussed in this chapter. In the following section, we refer to a concept that is often discussed together with validity and that is reliability. *Validity* refers to the correctness and appropriateness of the interpretations that a researcher makes of his/her study. Reliability refers to score consistency across administrations of one's instrument. For both concepts, accurate and appropriate instruments are at the core. Thus, if our hypothesis involves learning, we need to have an accurate and appropriate instrument to measure learning. For example, if we are looking at knowledge representation, we need to have a measure that appropriately reflects that and not something that just measures an ability to use the language. In many instances (see discussions in Gass & Mackey 2007; Gass with Behney & Plonsky 2013), part of the theoretical discussions in the literature involve how best to represent particular constructs.

Often variables cannot be measured directly. In these instances, we come up with a working definition that allows us to identify the variable in question with something that is understandable and measurable. This is known as an operationalization. Thus, in our example presented earlier of focused attention, we cannot directly measure this construct, but we can come up with a reasonable surrogate (e.g. colouring or highlighting in some way). Once we have operationalized a variable, we can more easily work with it.

The last thing that a researcher wants is to spend time, effort and money on a project and then realize that the study itself did not reflect what we had thought it would and might apply only to the population of the study and not to the broader community at large. Validity comes in many different colours; in this section, we discuss the most common types of validity: content, face, construct, criterion-related and predictive validity. Following that brief introduction, we turn to a discussion of internal and external validity.

Content validity

Content validity refers to the representativeness of our measurement regarding the phenomena that we want information about. If, for example, we want information about noun–adjective agreement in Italian, we cannot generalize these findings to say that we have fully investigated all types of agreement (article–noun, singular–plural, regular–irregular, nouns that end in –*a-o* and those that are not morphologically marked as masculine/ feminine). In other words, if we want to claim that we have investigated agreement, we need to ensure that our instruments include a representative range of what constitutes agreement.

Face validity

Face validity is closely related to the notion of content validity and takes us into the realm of the consumers of research. Is our instrument readily recognizable as measuring what we claim it measures? For example, the construct of intelligence can be measured in various ways, but there are certain instruments that are well-accepted as measuring this construct, even if it is a somewhat elusive construct. Thus, face validity refers to the familiarity of our instrument, and how easy it is to convince others that there is content validity to it. If a school district wants to measure intelligence with a newly developed instrument, there may be a perception by the community (e.g. parents) that this instrument is not valid (unless of course their child receives a high score!). If the participants do not perceive a connection between the research activities and other educational or second language activities, they may be less likely to take the experiment seriously.

Construct validity

Construct validity refers to the extent to which the research adequately captures the concept in question. In second language and applied linguistic research, construct validity is of great concern because a great deal of what we investigate is not easily quantifiable and not directly measurable. Some variables, such as height, weight and shoe size, are easily measureable and there is little controversy over what they reflect. Thus, a weight of fifty-two kilos is clear to everyone who uses this scale, but in second language research, we are dealing with such constructs as proficiency. What precisely does this mean? How can we measure it, so that we can compare individuals on a common scale? Because these constructs are not directly measurable, their validity can be called into question. One way to enhance construct validity is to have multiple measures. Thus, if we were to measure proficiency, we might have measures that reflect oral use, written use, extent of vocabulary knowledge and so forth. If we were to use these measures as an aggregate, we could have greater confidence in our ability to differentiate individuals along a scale of proficiency.

Criterion-related validity

Criterion-related validity refers to the relationship that a given measure has with some other well-established measure. For example, if a researcher develops an overall measure of language proficiency, it will have criterion-related validity if it measures language students in much the same way as another well-established test. To be more specific, if we are doing a study using first-, second- and third-year English learners of Spanish and develop a test that measures oral proficiency, criterion-related validity would be increased if we could show that on our test, third-year students did better than second-year students who did better than first-year students. Our test, then, would correspond to some other reasonably accepted measure, that of class placement.

Predictive validity deals with how well the measure we are using predicts performance on some other measure. In other words, if we have a test that measures working memory capacity, it has predictive validity if it predicts performance in class performance in a language class.

Internal and external validity

In addition to these five types of validity, there are two other types of validity that are noteworthy: internal validity and external validity. Each of these is important when conducting experimental research.

To what extent are the results of a study truly reflective of what we believe they reflect? This is known as *internal validity*. In other words, are our dependent and independent variables related in the way we think they are? A researcher must control for (i.e. rule out) all other possible factors that could potentially account for the results. This was discussed in the example above in relation to colour-blindness. In that study, had we not controlled for colour-blindness, we would have been left with the unfortunate conclusion that the study had little internal validity. Before conducting any research study, we need to think carefully through the design to ensure that we eliminate or minimize threats to internal validity (see Mackey & Gass 2005, 2015 for a more thorough treatment of this topic and for ways to minimize threats to internal validity).

External validity refers to the potential generalizability[2] of a study. We can make conclusions about the behaviour of the participants in a study, but this is not particularly interesting unless the results have broader implications and are relevant to a wider range of language learners and language learning contexts. Thus, if we conduct a study with English-speaking learners of Italian studying at University ABC, we are interested not just in those specific learners, but also the extent to which the results are applicable to learners of other languages possibly in different contexts. This is the case because we are interested in general principles of learning and not just a particular group of learners.

External validity can be increased with appropriate sampling procedures, as mentioned above. In particular, it is important that our sample be selected randomly, which, in essence, means that each member of the population to be studied has an equal and independent chance of being selected. This is the ideal situation, but one which, in reality, is not always practical. Rather, in second language research, nonrandom sampling is frequently used. Researchers often seek volunteers to participate in a study, as is required by most university ethics review boards. Even when intact classes are used, students can opt out of participation according to university ethical requirements. Sufficiently large sample sizes are always a goal as a way to increase the likelihood of true differences between groups (e.g. experimental and control). Small sample sizes leave the researcher with the uncertainty of interpreting the results. Are the differences between groups true or just coincidental? Many statistical tests help researchers avoid drawing unwarranted conclusions.

Because true random sampling is not always likely in second language research, it is important for researchers to fully and accurately describe the population studied as well as provide details about the materials, methods and procedures. In this way, a particular study can be replicated by others which, in a way, broadens the population base of the original study (see Polio & Gass 1997; Porte 2012 for a fuller description and discussion of replication and reporting). Mackey and Gass (2005, 2015) provide additional discussion on issues of external validity and outline ways of minimizing threats to external validity.

Reliability

Reliability refers to consistency and is a way of ensuring that our constructs are being measured appropriately. In applied linguistics research, it is frequently used when raters are making judgements about data. This is referred to as interrater reliability (when more than one rater is involved) and intrarater reliability (when only one researcher's evaluations are used). In the former instance (e.g. judging oral speech samples on a scale of 1–10), consistency across raters indicates that raters are measuring the same construct in the same way. In the latter case, one might rate the same speech sample at two different points in time to ensure consistency.

Both validity and reliability are ways of ensuring quality in research. As noted, experimental research is a way of finding answers to questions in a disciplined way. These results may have far-reaching impact (including decisions relating to educational practices), and it is incumbent on the research community to ensure that research (experimental and other) is carried out in as careful a way as possible, ensuring quality at each step of the way.

Techniques and instruments

There are as many techniques and instruments as there are research projects. A description of even a few would go beyond the scope and appropriate length of this chapter. Two recent books (Ellis & Barkhuizen 2005; Gass & Mackey 2007) deal with data elicitation methods and methods of analysis respectively and can serve as useful sources of information.

Ethical considerations

As with all research, ethical considerations abound. The most obvious concerns the protection of human subjects and will not be dealt with here (see Mackey & Gass 2005, 2015, Chapter 2; see also De Costa, in press, this volume) as they are elaborated on by each institution's ethical review board. In brief, in most educational settings, one must obtain permission from a human research committee before conducting any research or before recruiting volunteers for a research project (see https://www.citiprogram.org/citidocuments/forms/Responsible%20 Conduct%20of%20Research%20(RCR)%20Catalog.pdf for information on responsible conduct of research, viewed 26 January 2015). The overriding concern is that no harm comes to participants with the ideal being that there be benefits.

As researchers design studies, there is often a control group against which to measure the effects of a particular treatment. But, here too, there is an ethical question. If we have reason to believe that our treatment is beneficial, then we have recruited volunteers who will not receive the treatment. One possibility is to provide the treatment to the control group after all data have been collected. Polio and Gass (2007) designed a study in just this way, although even in this study, there were limitations to equal treatment. The main research question was: Can a brief intervention study in which pre-service teachers are instructed on how to interact with learners promote learning in a subsequent interaction? The design involved an experimental and a control group. The experimental group received a 15–20 minute session with a researcher who went over ways to increase student output (e.g. asking open-ended questions rather than yes/no questions). This was followed by an interactive session with an ESL learner in which they were asked to put into practice what they had learned. So as not to disadvantage the control group and maintain the integrity of the study, the training session with the control group was conducted following the interactive session. Thus, all pre-service teachers had the benefit of a training session which had been hypothesized to be beneficial in the promotion of learning. Yet, the control group's training was conducted after the experiment so as not to influence the research results. This, of course, does not take into account the benefits that the ESL students in the experimental group had over those in the control group. Unfortunately, the complete balancing of benefits would have required the control group of ESL students to return for a second round, and this was not logistically possible. In general, it is important to strictly follow the guidelines established by one's institution regarding all aspects of a study, including modes of recruiting, actual treatment and assessment details and the reporting of information in such a way as to respect privacy and anonymity issues. In addition to local review boards, the American Psychological Association (2010) has important guidelines for many aspects of the research process.

A final point to be made which has ethical ramifications has to do with honesty in reporting, and in particular with the elimination of participants. When elimination takes place, it has to be done judiciously and with justification. For example, in studies which measure reaction time, it may be the case that a participant is not focused on the task. This may be determined by inordinately fast reaction times which make it clear that she or he is just pushing a response button without processing the required material. Often, in such studies, a cut-off point will be determined, such as two standard deviations[3] above or below the mean, with individuals falling on the outside limits of this cut-off point being eliminated from analysis. Whatever criteria are used, it is important that a detailed and principled justification be provided to avoid any question of impropriety.

A sample study

The study that I have chosen to highlight is a study by Alison Mackey, Susan Gass and Kim McDonough, 'How do learners perceive interactional feedback' published in 2000 in *Studies in Second Language Acquisition*. This study was selected because it is an empirical quantitative study, bolstered with qualitative data. The study illustrates the problem of a possible uncontrolled variable cropping up in the study which in this case led to a further study. Thus, it illustrates the cycle of conducting a study, analysing the results (including a post-hoc analysis – an analysis that did not result from the research questions that guided the study) and postulating an uncontrolled variable that led to a further quantitative study (Gass & Lewis 2007).

Description and research questions

As stated in Mackey et al. (2000, p. 477)

> The focus of the current study is an exploration of the claim that, through negotiated interaction, learners' attention may be directed toward particular aspects of language. In order to explore whether interactional feedback and the allocation of focal attention to feedback play a role in the development of L2 knowledge, it is important to first investigate the extent to which that feedback is in fact perceived as such by learners and whether their perceptions about the target of the feedback are correct.

The specific research question was: how do learners perceive the feedback they receive in the course of interaction?

Participants

There were seventeen ESL learners and eleven Italian as a foreign language (IFL) learners in this study.

Task

Each learner carried out an interactive task with a speaker of the language they were learning (English or Italian). When there were errors, the researcher provided corrective feedback to the learner. Following the interaction (which had been videotaped), the video was replayed to the learner who, using a Stimulated Recall procedure (see Gass & Mackey 2000), was asked to comment on what they were thinking during the moments of feedback. These tapes were coded by two raters with the rating being based on the feedback given and the perception of that feedback. Interrater reliability was calculated and reported. There were four (excluding those that were unclassifiable or had no classifiable content) categories of feedback: (1) phonological, (2) morphosyntactic, (3) lexical and (4) semantic. The responses were then paired according to whether the intent of the feedback corresponded with the perception of the feedback. In other words, was phonological feedback perceived as phonological feedback?

The study did not have a control group–experimental group design; rather, it dealt with static perception, that is, perception of an event. Results were presented in terms of percentages (no statistics in the main study) of feedback of phonology, of morphosyntax and of lexis (semantics had too few responses to comment on).

There are times when the data from a study reveal possibilities of interpretation that had not been planned for from the outset. In this study, there were two post-hoc analyses that were conducted as well as a suggestion that led to a further study.

The post-hoc analyses first analysed the type of feedback (recast, negotiation or a combination) in relation to the error type. This analysis was necessary (but not planned) because the interactions had not been scripted and the feedback was naturally occurring. The second post-hoc analysis related learners' perceptions about feedback and their immediate uptake.

Results

The results of this study showed that learners perceive different error types differentially, that there was a different distribution of feedback type depending on error type and that uptake was different depending on error type. Interestingly, there were differences between the ESL group and the IFL group. It was speculated that the difference might relate to the heritage population[4] that had been included in the IFL group.

Further research

Much research leaves as much unanswered as answered. This research was no exception and, in fact, spawned a different study (Gass & Lewis 2007) which dealt with the variable that 'snuck' into the study (also known as an intervening variable), and which may have influenced the results, that of heritage versus non-heritage learners.

Notes

1   Other terms that are used are constructvist/interpretivists who primarily use qualitative research methods and positivists or empiricists who rely primarily on quantitative methods. In reality, research today crosses both camps and it is not uncommon – yours truly included – to find researchers using both quantitative (experimental) and qualitative methods in their quest to answer research questions.

2   There are instances where generalizability may not be a goal of a study. This might be the case within a particular instructional context in which curricular changes are being debated. In such instances, there is a need to determine the extent to which a proposed curricular change (e.g. inserting a technological component into the curriculum) results in increased learning, although in the case of a technological component, the goal might be 'no decrease in learning' because the purpose behind a technological component in a curriculum might be financial.

3   A standard deviation is a measure of dispersion. It is a numerical value that indicates how the scores in a sample are spread out in relation to the mean and therefore indicates the homogeneity or lack thereof of a sample.
4   Heritage learners are those who come to the learning situation with some degree of exposure to the language being learned through their family background. There is a wide range of learner profiles within this category, ranging from the target language being spoken exclusively as a home language to only infrequent use of that language, as for example, visiting relatives abroad during summer visits.

Resources for further reading

Brown, JD & Rodgers, T 2002, *Doing Second Language Research*, Oxford University Press, Oxford.

This book covers a range of research topics including qualitative (case studies, introspective data, classroom data) and quantitative research. In the latter category, there is a discussion of descriptive statistics, correlational research and quasi-experimental research. Within these categories is information about compiling and analysing data as well as guidelines for designing and interpreting data.

Dörnyei, Z 2007, *Research Methods in Applied Linguistics*, Oxford University Press, Oxford.

This text covers a range of research types (quantitative, qualitative, longitudinal). Included are discussions of theoretical and philosophical underpinnings of research types. Basic issues such as data collection and analysis are discussed, as are guidelines for reporting research.

Gass, S & Mackey, A 2007, *Data Elicitation for Second and Foreign Language Research*, Lawrence Erlbaum, Mahwah, NJ.

This book is an extension of Mackey and Gass' (2005) book on research methods (see below). The book focuses extensively on ways of collecting second language data. Chapters, organized around research approaches (e.g. psycholinguistics, formal approaches, interaction), include a discussion of research questions and historical underpinnings of some of the techniques. Each research approach is exemplified with data elicitation techniques including naturalistic language, prompted linguistic production and non-linguistic experimental responses.

Mackey, A & Gass, S 2015, *Second Language Research: Methodology and Design*, 2nd edn, Routledge, New York, NY.

This book, targeted towards students of SLA, addresses basic issues related to research design, providing step-by-step instructions for how to carry out studies. Topics include identifying research problems and questions; selecting elicitation measures; dealing with ethical issues related to data gathering; validity and reliability in research; research in classroom contexts; qualitative research, mixed methods research, data description and coding; and data analysis. Also included is a chapter on writing research reports with suggestions about preparing research results for publication.

Mackey, A & Gass, S (eds), 2012, *Research Methods in Second Language Acquisition: A Practical Guide*, Wiley-Blackwell, Malden, MA.

This edited collection consists of fifteen chapters (including an introductory chapter by the editors), each of which deals with the *how* of *a* particular area of second language research (e.g. reading, writing) or of particular types of data (e.g. corpus, classroom, survey, case study, qualitative, psycholinguistic, formal theory-based). In addition, the second part of the book provides practical information about how to code quantitative and qualitative data, how to conduct appropriate statistical analyses and how to conduct meta-analyses. Finally, there is a paper that focuses on the *why, when* and *how of replication studies*.

Porte, G 2002, *Appraising Research in Second Language Learning: A Practical Approach to Critical Analysis of Quantitative Research*, John Benjamins, Amsterdam.

Porte's book focuses on understanding and interpreting research reports. The goal of the book is to produce critical readers of research. The book is organized around research reports, namely, the abstract, introduction, review of literature, participants, materials, procedures, results, discussion and conclusion. Questions are peppered throughout each of the sections leading the reader to a critical understanding of appropriate content for a sound research article.

Porte, G (ed.), 2012, *Replication Research in Applied Linguistics*, Cambridge University Press, Cambridge.

Porte's edited volume deals specifically with replication research. It consists of nine chapters written by scholars in the field and introductory and concluding chapters by Porte. The book focuses on definitions of replication, arguments for the importance of replication, practical considerations when conducting replication studies as part of graduate programs and in practice. Porte's forward-looking final chapter focuses on the numerous challenges involved in conducting and publishing replication studies, not the least of which is the role of journals and other publication venues in the process.

References

American Psychological Association 2010, *Publication Manual of the American Psychological Association*, 6th edn, American Psychological Association, Washington, D.C.

De Costa, P (ed.), in press, *Ethics in Applied Linguistics Research: Language Researcher Narratives*, Routledge, New York, NY.

Dörnyei, Z 2007, *Research Methods in Applied Linguistics*, Oxford University Press, Oxford.

Ellis, R & Barkhuizen, G 2005, *Analyzing Learner Language*, Oxford University Press, Oxford.

Gass, S with Behney, J & Plonsky, L 2013, *Second Language Acquisition: An Introductory Course*, 4th edn, Routledge, New York, NY.

Gass, S & Lewis, K 2007, 'Perceptions of interactional feedback: Differences between heritage language learners and non-heritage language learners', in A Mackey (ed.), *Conversational Interaction in Second Language Acquisition: A Series of Empirical Studies*, Oxford University Press, Oxford, pp. 173–196.

Gass, S & Mackey, A 2000, *Stimulated Recall Methodology in Second Language Research*, Lawrence Erlbaum Associates, Mahwah, NJ.

—— 2007, *Data Elicitation for Second and Foreign Language Research*, Lawrence Erlbaum, Mahwah, NJ.

Gass, S, Svetics, I & Lemelin, S 2003, 'Differential effects of attention', *Language Learning*, vol. 53, no. 3, pp. 497–545.

Hashemi, M & Babaii, E (eds), 2013, 'Mixed methods research: Toward new research designs in applied linguistics', *The Modern Language Journal*, vol. 97, no. 4, pp. 828–852.

Jordan, G 2005, *Theory Construction in Second Language Acquisition*, John Benjamins, Amsterdam.

Larsen-Freeman, D & Long, M 1991, *An Introduction to Second Language Acquisition Research*, Longman, London.

Mackey, A 1999, 'Input, interaction and second language development', *Studies in Second Language Acquisition*, vol. 21, no. 4, pp. 557–587.

Mackey, A & Gass, S 2005, *Second Language Research: Methodology and Design*, Lawrence Erlbaum, Mahwah, NJ.

—— 2012, *Research Methods in Second Language Acquisition: A Practical Guide*, Wiley-Blackwell, Malden, MA.

—— 2015, *Second Language Research: Methodology and Design*, 2nd edn, Routledge, New York, NY.

Mackey, A, Gass, S & McDonough, K 2000, 'How do learners perceive interactional feedback?', *Studies in Second Language Acquisition*, vol. 22, no. 4, pp. 471–497.

Plonsky, L & Oswald, F 2014, 'How big is "big"? Interpreting effect sizes in L2 research', *Language Learning*, vol. 64, no. 4, pp. 878–912.

Polio, C & Gass, S 1997, 'Replication and reporting', *Studies in Second Language Acquisition*, vol. 19, no. 4, pp. 499–508.

—— 2007, 'Getting students to talk: preservice teacher intervention and learner output', Paper presented at the Fifth International Conference on Language Teacher Education, University of Minnesota.

Porte, G (ed.), 2012, *Replication Research in Applied Linguistics*, Cambridge University Press, Cambridge.

CHAPTER SEVEN

Case Studies

Christine Pearson Casanave

In this chapter, I describe some characteristics of case studies, discuss some methods that are commonly used in case study research, point out some issues in ethics, validity and generalizability and give an example of case study work in the applied linguistics field.

Characteristics and assumptions of case study research

In spite of the fact that case studies are often referred to as a method (e.g. Yin 2009), 'case study' is better thought of as an approach, a strategy or a multidisciplinary research tradition (Creswell 2013; Hesse-Biber & Leavy 2011; Simons 2009; Van Wynsberge & Khan 2007), with a long history across many disciplines. Case studies are also often characterized as part of a qualitative research tradition; however, many methods and techniques can be used in conducting a case study, both quantitative and qualitative (Swanborn 2010; Yin 2009). Case study has been described as 'transparadigmatic', capable of being conducted within postpositivistic, critical theory and interpretivist paradigms (Van Wynsberge & Khan 2007, p. 8). Although differences abound on the precise definition of case study, a generally accepted aspect is that it is an approach in which the object of inquiry is set in a natural context, is unique (in the sense of singular) and bounded. It is also an approach in which the researcher's interest is in an in-depth investigation of the particular rather than the general. By 'bounded' we mean that the phenomenon we are investigating is delimited – we are pretty sure we know what is and is not the case (Stake 2005), and the context in which the case is situated is also particular and delineated. Without attention to context, we do not have a case (Yin 2009). So, the research approach and the written report that results can be called a case study if it investigates one person, one group, one institution or one community in depth (Merriam 1998; Simons 2009; Stake 1995, 2005), with a goal of understanding a phenomenon or a process as exemplified by the person(s) or institution (Swanborn 2010). A multiple case study investigates several particular groups, institutions or individuals (Stake 2006).

The purpose of most case studies is to enhance our understanding of a phenomenon, process, person or group, not to experiment and generalize to other populations in the tradition of larger-scale survey research. Nevertheless, misunderstandings about case study still exist, causing some people to dismiss it as overly subjective, ungeneralizable, too practical and not sufficiently theoretical, with a bias towards verification, and in general unscientific. These myths about case study have been persuasively countered and 'corrected' (Flyvbjerg 2006, 2011). Simons (2009, pp. 164–167), among others, discusses the strengths of a case study's subjectivity, numerous kinds of generalization that are possible from case study research (cross-case, naturalistic, concept, process and situated generalization, as well as in-depth particularization that contributes to 'universal understanding') and the usefulness of case studies in generating theory and evaluating policies.

Perhaps the primary feature of case studies that distinguishes them from other types of research is that they use multiple data sources (interviews, documents, observations) to explore (describe, analyse) particular bounded phenomena. We assume that there is something unique about the case we choose to investigate and are interested in the particulars of what makes the case special, not necessarily what makes it representative of larger processes or groups of people (Simons 2009; Stake 2005). When we speak of generalization, it is to theoretical propositions (Yin 2009) or concepts (Simons 2009), to the kind of vicarious experience in readers that Stake (2005) calls naturalistic generalization or to the situation being studied (situated generalization; Simons 2009). However, by choosing to investigate a case, we presume to be able to identify what makes the case particular and bounded, and therefore what is not a case. But, identifying boundaries may not always be straightforward (Creswell 2013). Researchers often fudge here and there and draw some artificial lines around a case. This is a normal part of case study research.

Second, by choosing a case study tradition, we demonstrate an interest in in-depth portrayals of phenomena associated with particular people or sites, rather than in a broader, more superficial sampling of the phenomena we are investigating (see some examples in Yin 2012). This choice usually requires a commitment of time and a mix of data types. For instance, in applied linguistics, people who are interested in the L2 language acquisition of just one person can conduct a longitudinal study of the language learner (see a discussion of some of these studies in Duff 2008; Van Lier 2005), and people who are interested in L2 writers (for example) can follow one or more individual writers over time as they learn how to write in particular settings for particular purposes (e.g. Berkenkotter et al. 1988; Blakeslee 1997; Casanave 1998, 2010; Leki 2007; Li 2005, 2007, 2013; Prior 1998). In education, researchers who wish to evaluate particular programs or institutions can learn from documents, observations and multiple interviews over time (Simons 2009). The point is that depth and detail over time, of the kind not available from survey research, are essential in a good case study.

A third characteristic of case studies, whatever methods are employed, is that the case study's small n – a person, program, institution – is clearly situated or embedded in a particular context (which may be physical, historical, temporal) (Van Wynsberge & Khan 2007). Without a thorough understanding of context, we will not be able to interpret what the particulars of the case mean.

Types of case studies

Many types of case studies can be imagined, such as descriptive case studies, explanatory case studies, cross-case syntheses and case study evaluations (Yin 2012), but I find Stake's (1995, 2005) discussion especially useful. He distinguishes between intrinsic and instrumental case studies. Intrinsic case studies hold our interest because the case itself is interesting. It can be difficult to convince dissertation committees and journal reviewers that we are doing a study solely because the case fascinates us and because we want to gain deep understanding of it for its own sake. We typically need to produce a rationale that argues why a study will benefit others or contribute to larger bodies of research. But, Stake (2005, p. 445) tells us that an intrinsic case study

> is not undertaken primarily because the case represents other cases or because it illustrates a particular trait or problem, but instead because, in all its particularity *and* ordinariness, this case itself is of interest.

He insists that intrinsic case studies contribute to knowledge even if they do not follow typical 'rules' of scientific research.

With an instrumental case study, on the other hand, something external to the case itself holds our interest, and the case study is conducted in order to further our understanding of the external interest. The case itself may or may not be typical but is chosen 'to advance understanding of that other interest' (Stake 2005, p. 445).

Procedures in case study research

Because there is so much variability in how case study research can be conducted, I can give only the briefest of overview of procedures here. I urge readers who are attracted to the qualitative case study tradition to read more widely and to distinguish between approaches that are more traditionally scientific and *positivistic* (Yin's work; Miles & Huberman 1994; Swanborn 2010), those that are *realist* without being positivistic (Maxwell 2012) and those that lean more towards the interpretive camp (Lincoln & Guba 1985; Simons 2009). Useful examples for second language acquisition (SLA) research are described in Duff (2008), although her descriptions focus more on the outcomes of her and others' research than on the discourse-analytic procedures she used. For examples of case studies in education and educational evaluation, see Merriam (1998) and Simons (2009). Many other examples from applied linguistics and second language education exist as published articles rather than books. In this section, I consider how L2 researchers might choose a case, collect and analyse data and write up a case study report. The section concludes with some comments on researcher roles and responsibilities.

Choosing a case

As is advised for all research, case study research begins with questions and curiosities that the applied linguistics scholar has, rather than with the tradition or method. Perhaps the most pervasive mistake of novice researchers is to start with pronouncements such as: 'I plan to do a mixed-method study', or 'I will do a case study'. As attractive as one approach or the other may look, this is putting the cart before the horse.

So, start with questions, puzzles and curiosities. These will lead to an appropriate choice of approach and method, and if case study is called for, to choosing a case or cases.

For instance, when I was looking for a dissertation topic in graduate school, I was attracted to issues in academic literacy (both first and second language) but was not sure why. With some reading and thinking, mainly about myself and my struggles to read and write in graduate school, I realized that I was not interested in ESL writing as much as I was in the role that writing was playing in disciplinary socialization. I was struck that when people entered graduate school, they often did not have clear identities as particular kinds of scholars who fit within disciplinary communities or communities of practice. Then, some years into their programs, they had taken on previously unfamiliar ways of thinking, using language, writing and researching. The one activity that they seemed to be doing all the time was reading and writing. Moreover, we were all evaluated in graduate school on our writing rather than on tests. Writing and interacting with written texts must hold the key to this miraculous transformation of identity in graduate school.

My curiosity was about the individual's experience of the role of writing in this transformation, not in general processes of the acquisition of academic literacy or in text analysis of academic writing. I wanted to know what specific people were experiencing. In those days, we did not talk about studying ourselves (doing autoethnographies, for example), so I had to find some people to follow around for a while, at least a year – long enough to begin to see some transformations. A case study approach was thus well-suited to my curiosities. I requested permission in writing from the head of the sociology department nearby and from some of his students and ended up studying a first-year doctoral cohort (cf. Prior 1998, for a comparable study of disciplinary socialization). I observed their core classes for several terms, collected samples of their writing, looked at what they were reading and conducted many interviews over time to get a sense of how individual students were changing (Casanave 1990).

But, of course, this is not the only way to choose a case, nor are individual people the only examples of what a good case might be. A researcher might have a strong instrumental purpose for doing research and want to select case study participants and sites or programs much more systematically and purposefully. An applied linguistics researcher, for example, may wish to learn how a beginning L2 learner, or an especially successful learner, strategizes learning over time. It should be noted that in case study research, comparisons are not needed; we could focus on a successful or unsuccessful learner only. Another researcher may be interested in how a particular language program functions. The researcher also needs to make decisions about a case based on many practical factors: How much time will participants have to spend with you without their feeling pressed or resentful? Where are participants and programs located – close to or far from home? Will you and the participants share a language or will one of you be using an L2? Is the particular program you are curious about one that you are affiliated with or are you an outsider? Will administrators or teachers whom you wish to learn from consider you a spy or an ally? These are just a few of the practical questions to consider in choosing a case.

The main point is to start with strong curiosities about some phenomenon associated with particular people, processes and programs, beginning with yourself.

Collecting and analysing data

Unlike some other research approaches, almost any data can be used in case study research. However, particularly in qualitative inquiry, case study data are typically collected over time, in some depth, and from a limited number of people and settings. If the study is of one or more individuals, then interview data, recorded and transcribed (and possibly translated), will be central, as will be other sources of information from the participants (email, journals, casual conversation, documents). See Yi (2007) for a nice description of multiple data sources that she used in her study of a Korean high-school student's out-of-class composing. Interviews with key people who interact with the participant(s) may also play a part. Depending on the topic, data may also include multiple observations of classroom learning or teaching or other group settings (e.g. meetings) in which the participant is involved. Depending on circumstances, these observations may or may not be videotaped. The researcher's own reflections, in the form of research memos and write-ups of early responses to participants and their experiences, also become data (see Maxwell 2013 on research memos). In a case study, the researcher can be seen as one of the participants.

If the case study is of a program or a school rather than of one individual, the researcher needs to gain access to key people in the organization (this can be tricky). Data may consist of interviews or even a survey of people in the organization, documents of many types and a great deal of observation recorded as fieldnotes and research memos. The researcher may also collect visual data in the form of photographs or videos. The point in a case study is to come to know the case well, thoroughly and from different perspectives. Any data that contribute to this effort are included.

Analyses of many types can be used in case study research. Quantitative analyses can be done of surveys, content analyses of documents and linguistic and content analyses of interview transcripts, classroom transcripts and writing samples. Observations, interviews and documents can also be analysed by means of prose descriptions of themes and narrative analyses of stories in which themes, impressions or narrative structures of a story become the main focus.

Finally, a good analysis proceeds to and from concepts at a higher level of abstraction – a conceptual framework – that helps readers see the connections between the individual study of one person or place and others that may be similar or different. The analysis may also be used to help build or modify theoretical concepts. It is in these senses that case study findings can be generalized or at least transferred to other contexts and made use of by others (Simons 2009, p. 164).

Writing a case study report

A case study needs to be written in a detailed and accessible way, so that readers can be in some sense transported into the world(s) of the case. As I mentioned earlier, Stake (1995) calls this kind of connection with readers 'naturalistic generalization', in the absence of the type of generalization we find in statistical studies:

> Naturalistic generalizations are conclusions arrived at through personal engagement in life's affairs or by vicarious experience so well constructed that the person feels as if it happened to themselves. (Stake 1995, p. 85)

As Stake (p. 85) says, even if we cannot generalize to a larger population, 'people can learn much that is general from single cases'.

Therefore, the standard technical report style is usually not appropriate for a case study report because it will lack the kinds of details needed, even though comparable sections are usually present in a case study (e.g. an introduction, description of context and methods, examples and interpretations of data, and discussion, regardless of what headings the writer uses). The case study report includes the writer's reasons for doing the study, and his or her roles in the interaction with the participants, class or program are made clear. Descriptions abound and may include visuals – readers need to vicariously see and experience contexts, people and events. Case studies may include quite a bit of narrative – what happened in the research process and what happened in the participants' lives or in the group, program or organization being studied. There may also be photographs or drawings in the report, or in a website established by the researcher. The website can also include full transcripts and sound recordings, assuming that participants have given permission for their data to be used in this way and that their confidentiality is protected. In the report, alternative interpretations may be offered, and conclusions about a person or program tend to be tentative. In all write-ups, the case report needs to be presented with enough convincing detail, so that readers can judge for themselves whether the insights and observations of this particular object of investigation pertain to their own situations.

Some people believe that a good case report, in the naturalistic or qualitative tradition, requires better writing skills than does a technical report. Lincoln and Guba (1985) mention this, and certainly their criteria for evaluating a case study report (see below) focus primarily on qualities of writing. After all, a case report must persuade readers of its credibility. Persuasiveness will happen not only as a result of the quality of the research, but also through the writing (Ely et al. 1997). As Simons (2009, p. 153) pointed out, 'To have the impact on our readers we desire, vignettes, cameos and narratives need to be well written.' But novice scholars or L2 speakers should not despair: Most of us are not inherently good writers. We learn to write better as we practice; we get feedback from others; and if our research questions lead us to a naturalistic case study project, we will be required to write. See Chapter 9 in Simons (2009), which is devoted to techniques designed to help students with reporting and writing. See also Belcher and

Hirvela (2005), who found that some of the L2 doctoral students they worked with were obligated by their research interests to write qualitative dissertations. They succeeded admirably.

Researcher roles and responsibilities

In conducting all research, researchers need to be alert to how their investigation might possibly harm participants. Qualitative inquiry in particular often depends on close contact with and descriptions of particular people and places and thus needs to pay attention to qualities of 'honesty, justice, and respect for persons' (Soltis 1991, p. 247) and to the fundamental principle of 'doing no harm' (Simons 2009, p. 96). Case-study research that adopts qualitative methods places the researcher in an especially sensitive position: The case study is by definition an in-depth study of a particular person, group or program. As the study becomes more and more particularized, it becomes difficult to protect participants' identities and to separate private issues from those that can be written about without risk. A written agreement with case study participants (*informed consent*) that alerts them to possible risks, that assures them of anonymity, that informs them that all data are confidential and that gives them the right to withdraw from the study at any time should be made early in the research process. It is also a good idea, whenever possible, to share transcripts, descriptions and drafts with participants and to check with them regularly about whether they want any material excluded in the interest of *privacy* and *confidentiality*. It should be noted that interpretations, as opposed to descriptions and transcripts, usually remain the prerogative of the researcher, even when they are negotiated with participants.

It behooves researchers as well to consider not only the risks to their participants, but the possible benefits. Researchers who only take, and do not give something back, are deservedly looked at sceptically by those they research. For example, L2 students in a case study project might benefit by receiving special long-term attention from researchers, and if the study is done even partially in the L2, they will benefit from extra language practice. In one of my case study projects, I requested quite a bit of interview time from one of my Japanese participants, a busy professor (Casanave 1998). She benefited by being able to use me to check the English in some of her professional papers.

Researchers themselves develop complex and sometimes personal relationships with case study participants and sites and thus need to reflect constantly (e.g. in research memos) on the roles they are playing in their own study. For example, to what extent are researchers viewed as insiders or outsiders to the community they are involved in (Richards 2003)? To what extent does a close or intimate friendship influence a researcher's choices and interpretations (Taylor 2011)? Power, gender and status differences need to be attended carefully. L2 students, young or old, may feel especially vulnerable to the requests by and interactions with an interviewer, even if the interactions take place in the students' L1. Students may not be able to express their discomfort or resistance. An open discussion of the investigators' roles and relationships in the project will wisely take place with participants and become part of the case study report as well.

Issues of validation

A standard question about the need for validation in all research asks what Maxwell (2013) has asked: How might you be wrong? Why should we believe what you have said about your case? Responses to these questions have been debated for decades, and range from traditional criteria adapted from the sciences to radical rejection in certain kinds of qualitative inquiry of any criteria that look too *realist* or too scientific. Whether qualitative researchers believe that we should retain (Maxwell 2013; Morse et al. 2002) or reject (Wolcott 1990) notions of validity as a fundamental evaluative criterion, most are committed to a criterion of rigour (however defined) that is applied during the process of research, not just to evaluate the results.

For both quantitatively and qualitatively based case studies, one way that researchers can address issues of validity is from a modernist or realist position. This traditional position claims there is a real world out there, that our job is to represent it as accurately and objectively as we can, knowing that there is no pure Truth to be known or found, and yet that there are ways to check on the accuracy of our interpretations and representations. In his discussion of threats to validity (bias and reactivity), Maxwell (2012, 2013) acknowledges that he is a realist, not a postmodernist, and as such, he uses a very common-sense definition of validity, which, as realists, we could adopt for a case study:

> [...] I use validity in a fairly straightforward, commonsense way to refer to the correctness or credibility of a description, conclusion, explanation, interpretation, or other sort of account. (Maxwell 2013, p. 122)

He then points out that we do not need to believe in *objective truth* to hold this common-sense view, and that most researchers are not seeking such truth. Rather, most of them want 'some grounds for distinguishing accounts that are credible from those that are not' (p. 122; see also Creswell 2013; Phillips & Burbules 2000). This view recognizes that we cannot eliminate researcher bias or the influence of researchers on participants and settings, but that we can openly acknowledge that bias in our interpretations and writing. Some or all of the items in Maxwell's validity checklist can be applied to case study research if we see ourselves as realists-modernists. The checklist includes long-term involvement in the field, detailed and varied data, participants' feedback on our interview transcripts and interpretations (*member checking*), informal intervention by the researcher (and recognizing that our presence is always an intervention), searching actively for discrepant cases, triangulating (primarily by collecting data from multiple sources), using numbers (tables, etc.) where appropriate (*quasi-statistics* – a term coined by Howard Becker many years ago to refer to 'the use of simple numerical results that can be readily derived from the data' Maxwell 2013, p. 128) and comparing one case with others (Maxwell 2013, Chapter 6). This perspective on validity in qualitative case study projects will not usually raise eyebrows with dissertation committee members or with journal editors. It is quite widely accepted.

However, Denzin's (1997) take on the validation issue may raise both eyebrows and hackles. Given that some of the changes and flux that are being experienced in qualitative inquiry are influencing research in applied linguistics and second language education, I believe that we need to listen to arguments for viewing evaluation criteria in new ways. Denzin uses the term 'legitimation' rather than validity. From his critical post-structural perspective, he sees the 'crisis of legitimation' in qualitative inquiry (with ethnography as his example) as one in which we can no longer rely on traditional scientific claims of authority and empirical credibility in the texts we write from our research. Rather, post-structural legitimation must be seen as subjective, emotional, moral and political performances (including drama and poetry) of words and texts that draw audiences in and move them in some way (emotionally, to take action). The text or performance will be endlessly contested. The researcher's goal, in other words, is to present multiple versions of 'reality' and to deal openly with contested views.

I conclude this section by presenting the ideas of Lincoln and Guba (1985, 2002; also covered by Simons 2009), on judging the processes and products of qualitative inquiry, and case studies in particular. In their 1985 book, Lincoln and Guba recommended multiple criteria concerning trustworthiness to evaluate the research *process* for all naturalistic inquiry. These criteria concern the ways data are collected and treated. They offer the criteria of credibility, transferability, dependability and confirmability as replacement criteria for the traditional criteria for evaluating scientific and technical projects (e.g. reliability, validity, generalizability). Like Maxwell, they assert that to know a particular case well, researchers need to spend a great deal of time getting to know the case, observing contexts and events and triangulating data by looking at the case from multiple perspectives (diverse data, methods and investigators). They also suggest that we share ideas in interim reports with peers and with participants themselves and create some kind of archive (tapes, videos, documents) against which we can check findings. Their point is that, even though we can never prove anything, we need to find ways to help make case study findings believable, applicable to readers and dependable and confirmable to the extent possible by our system of record keeping. Because case study research, focusing as it does on a particular and bounded case such as an individual or a program, is even more susceptible to criticism by traditional researchers than other naturalistic inquiry, these techniques for legitimating the research process take on special importance.

In a later publication, Lincoln and Guba (2002) ask how to judge the *products* of naturalistic inquiry, case reports in particular, at a time when innovations and alternatives in approaches to research are proliferating. They comment on four qualities of the product (the case report itself) that can be used to evaluate it (see my comments above on the importance of writing).

First, they state that resonance criteria should be used to assess the fit between the written report and the belief system or philosophical assumptions that underlie the report. A naturalistic case study would reflect multiple realities, for instance, including reflection by the researcher on his or her role, whereas a more traditional study would seek more unified and distanced explanations and representations. Second, rhetorical criteria would be applied to the report that reflects qualities of good writing: unity, organization, simplicity and clarity, craftsmanship (elegance and creativity of the writing, involvement of the writer). Third, empowerment criteria are used to judge whether the report moves readers to undertake some action, even if it is just consciousness-raising. Finally, applicability criteria ask whether the case study can be applied to readers' own contexts. This is a way that case study research can be *generalized*.

In all three of these views of evaluation criteria, researchers no longer presume that interview transcripts or observation fieldnotes represent uncontested or unmitigated facts, truth or unbiased perspectives of participants and observation sites. All case studies result in texts, not accurate representations of reality, and all are constructed by researchers in the act of doing research and writing and must be judged in this light. As texts, they can always be contested and reinterpreted. The good news here is that we exist in an era of methodological, representational and evaluative diversity. All approaches require rigorous attention to both research procedures and to writing. The researcher's task is therefore one of knowing what is out there, making reasoned choices and explaining those choices clearly.

A sample study

In this section, I summarize one case study to exemplify some of the characteristics of a case study of one individual. The study concerns a Korean 'study abroad' (*jogi yuhak*) adolescent, 'Hoon', who was struggling with identity and academic writing in a Midwestern U.S. high school (Yi 2013). It comes from a larger study of the bilingual literacy practices of Korean teenagers in a Midwestern city. This approach to case study, selecting a focal individual from a larger project, is quite common, particularly when the researcher has conducted a major project as part of a doctoral dissertation. The study focuses on interactions between identities and literacy practices and is framed in part with perspectives from New Literacy Studies (Gee 1992; Street 1995) and academic literacies (Lea & Street 1998; Lillis & Scott 2007, all cited in Yi 2013, p. 211).

In this spin-off case study, Yi wished to understand the interactions between Hoon's identities and his inability to write successfully in his advanced ESL class, which he was forced to repeat three times, in spite of doing well in other high school (classes that required little writing). Following good case study procedures, Yi used numerous data sources within a bounded context to document Hoon's experiences and attitudes over time (approximately two years). Yi's data included:

> observations, interviews, transcripts, field notes, Hoon's literacy activity checklists, and artifacts, such as his literacy autobiography, e-mails, online chatting with me, reading materials, writing samples, quizzes, and the work he produced for such courses as Advanced ESL, math, biology, and Japanese. (p. 213)

These multiple data sources provided Yi with invaluable insights unavailable in a shorter or more superficial study. She analysed her data by inductively immersing herself in the various sources multiple times and identifying patterns and themes. She also documented her own biases and interpretations to check how those might have influenced her findings. Finally, she reviewed her findings periodically with Hoon ('member checks'), including staying in touch with him after he returned to Korea.

Yi found that Hoon felt trapped in his ESL classes, believing that his identity was stigmatized by the ESL label. Yi also discovered that his literacy skills were poor in both Korean and English, and that he resisted devoting effort to improving. Not a success story, this study revealed Hoon's resistance and resentment at his ESL status, and thus his many missed opportunities to develop academic literacy skills even in Korean.

In long-term, in-depth case studies like this one, the researcher is always faced with more data than can possibly be used even in a dissertation, let alone in a short journal article. Yi devoted quite a bit of space to her review of literature, her framework and her discussion, so readers might be frustrated not to see more actual data excerpts, but this is a choice that all authors of journal articles must make. Nonetheless, we trust her findings for a number of reasons: how long she worked with Hoon, the varied data sources, a suitable framework from which to interpret her findings, the possibility of connecting core issues to readers and to her framework and attention to the quality of her writing.

Strengths and limitations of case study research

If researchers want to understand deeply a particular person or a site (a class, a program), with the primary goal of understanding and interpreting rather than of experimenting, hypothesis testing or generalizing to other populations, then a case study, particularly in the qualitative tradition, is an appropriate choice of approach. Moreover, the case study approach benefits by being able to accommodate many different methods, mainly qualitative but also quantitative, including detailed linguistic analyses of L2 development (Duff 2008). In applied linguistics, a case study is able to look closely at contexts, people and change over time (Van Lier 2005, p. 195). For researchers who enjoy uncovering the particulars of a person or phenomenon and spending time doing so, case studies will suit them.

On the other hand, case studies often involve more time than some researchers have and require social skills that they may not be comfortable with. Moreover, if researchers really want to say something about a population of people, rather than about an individual, then a case study may not be the best choice. The case study report itself requires good writing skills in order that rich and varied details can be presented in a convincing way. Readers need such details to be able to apply the case study findings to their own lives and settings. We can all polish our writing skills, however, so this should not deter us as researchers unless we truly hate to write. Additionally, qualitative case studies are still finding their way into the applied linguistics repertoire of valued research approaches in dissertations, journals and books. Therefore, researchers who feel they need to please gatekeepers should assess the political scene before committing to a qualitative case study project.

Speaking for myself, I find nothing quite so engaging as a case study when I am curious about an aspect of another person's life. Moreover, we look closely at ourselves in this kind of research and can include personal reflections as part of the case study report. Both self and others become characters in the stories we tell.

Resources for further reading

Duff, PA 2008, *Case Study Research in Applied Linguistics*, Routledge, New York, NY.

This readable book provides an introduction to case study research in applied linguistics. It includes many examples from well-known case studies from the 1970s and 1980s as well as more recent examples, focusing more on findings than on methods. It also features how-to chapters on doing and writing up case study research. Most of the discussion presumes that researchers will be investigating language acquisition, but Duff also refers to research on topics such as identity and socialization.

Flyvbjerg, B 2011, 'Case study', in NK Denzin & YS Lincoln (eds), *The Sage Handbook of Qualitative Research*, 4th edn,Sage, Thousand Oaks, pp. 301–316.

This chapter is adapted from Flyvbjerg's previous publications (e.g. Flyvbjerg 2006), all of which are important for their systematic dispelling of myths about qualitative case study research. One of his points is that context-dependent research is the only kind of research that we have in the social sciences.

Leki, I 2007, *Undergraduates in a Second Language: Challenges and Complexities of Academic Literacy Development*, Lawrence Erlbaum, New York, NY.

Leki's case studies look at how individual L2 undergraduates in a US university find their way into the literacy practices of their subject matter areas. Even for those not interested in L2 literacy, the case studies provide models of how to conduct and write up one kind of case study research.

Prior, PA 1998, *Writing/Disciplinarity: A Sociohistoric Account of Literate Activity in the Academy*, Lawrence Erlbaum, Mahwah, NJ.

Although Prior's book can be quite densely theoretical in places, his case studies of second language writers provide good models for one kind of case study research that includes analysis of L2 writers' texts and the many social and personal factors that help shape those texts. See also Casanave's (2002) collection of case studies.

Simons, H 2009, *Case Study Research in Practice*, Sage, Thousand Oaks, CA.

In addition to introducing the basics of case study approaches, this very readable book from the field of education and educational evaluation benefits from focused attention to ethics, writing and to dispelling myths about case study research. It is less 'positivist' in orientation than Yin (2009).

Stake, RE 1995, *The Art of Case Study*, Sage, Thousand Oaks, CA.

Stake's work on case study is perhaps the most frequently cited in the education, sociology and applied linguistics literature. It is rather prescriptive, but those who are new to case study research will appreciate its guidelines. See also his later publication, Stake 2006, on multiple case study analysis.

Van Wynsberghe, R & Khan, S 2007, 'Redefining case study', *International Journal of Qualitative Methods*, vol. 16, no. 2, pp. 80–94.

In this important article, the authors review the main issues in and critiques of case study research. They then offer a 'transparadigmatic and transdisciplinary' prototype view of case study that includes seven features: a small n, contextual detail, natural settings, boundedness, working hypotheses and lessons learned, multiple data sources and extendability of readers' understanding (p. 4).

Yin, R K 2009, *Case Study Research: Design and Methods*, 4th edn, Sage, Thousand Oaks, CA.

This often cited book gives readers in a variety of disciplines a systematic introduction, with examples, to designs and methods that can be used in case studies, particularly of organizations. Notable is Yin's more traditionally scientific perspective, and his point that case studies do not inherently call for qualitative methods but can utilize many quantitative and computer-associated methods. Exercises are included at the end of each chapter.

References

Belcher, D & Hirvela, A 2005, 'Writing the qualitative dissertation: What motivates and sustains commitment to a fuzzy genre?', *Journal of English for Academic Purposes*, vol. 4, no. 3, pp. 187–205.

Berkenkotter, C, Huckin, TN & Ackerman, J 1988, 'Conventions, conversations, and the writer: case study of a student in a rhetoric PhD program', *Research in the Teaching of English*, vol. 22, no. 1, pp. 9–45.

Blakeslee, AM 1997, 'Activity, context, interaction, and authority: learning to write scientific papers in situ', *Journal of Business and Technical Communication*, vol. 11, no. 2, pp. 125–169.

Casanave, CP 1990, 'The role of writing in socializing graduate students into an academic discipline in the social sciences', Doctoral dissertation, Stanford University, California.

———— 1998, 'Transitions: the balancing act of bilingual academics', *Journal of Second Language Writing*, vol. 7, no. 2, pp. 175–203.

———— 2002, *Writing Games: Multicultural Case Studies of Academic Literacy Practices in Higher Education*, Lawrence Erlbaum, Mahwah, NJ.

———— 2010, 'Taking risks?: A case study of three doctoral students writing qualitative dissertations at an American university in Japan', *Journal of Second Language Writing*, vol. 9, no. 1, pp. 1–16.

Creswell, JW 2013, *Qualitative Inquiry and Research Design: Choosing among Five Approaches*, 3rd edn, Sage, Los Angeles, CA.

Denzin, NK 1997, *Interpretive Ethnography: Ethnographic Practices for the 21st Century*, Sage, Thousand Oaks, CA.

Duff, PA 2008, *Case Study Research in Applied Linguistics*, Routledge, New York.

Ely, M, Vinz, R, Downing, M & Anzul, M 1997, *On Writing Qualitative Research: Living by Words*, Routledge, New York, NY.

Flyvbjerg, B 2006, 'Five misunderstandings about case-study research', *Qualitative Inquiry*, vol. 12, no. 2, pp. 219–245.

———— 2011, 'Case study', in NK Denzin & YS Lincoln (eds), *The Sage Handbook of Qualitative Research*, 4th edn, Sage, Thousand Oaks, CA, pp. 301–316.

Hesse-Biber, SN & Leavy, P 2011, *The Practice of Qualitative Research*, 2nd edn, Sage, Thousand Oaks, CA.

Leki, I 2007, *Undergraduates in a Second Language: Challenges and Complexities of Academic Literacy Development*, Lawrence Erlbaum, New York, NY.

Li, Y 2005, 'Multidimensional enculturation: The case study of an EFL Chinese doctoral student', *Journal of Asian Pacific Communication*, vol. 15, no. 1, pp. 153–170.

———— 2007, 'Apprentice scholarly writing in a community of practice: An intraview of an NNES graduate student writing a research article', *TESOL Quarterly*, vol. 41, no. 1, pp. 55–79.

———— 2013, 'Seeking entry to the North American market: Chinese management academics publishing internationally', *Journal of English for Academic Purposes*, vol. 13, no. 1, pp. 41–52.

Lincoln, YS & Guba, EG 1985, *Naturalistic Inquiry*, Sage, Beverly Hills, CA.

———— 2002, 'Judging the quality of case study reports', in AM Huberman & MB Miles (eds), *The Qualitative Researcher's Companion*, Sage, Thousand Oaks, CA, pp. 205–215.

Maxwell, JA 2012, *A Realist Approach for Qualitative Research*, Sage, Thousand Oaks, CA.

———— 2013, *Qualitative Research Design: an Interactive Approach*, 3rd edn, Sage, Thousand Oaks, CA.

Merriam, SB 1998, *Qualitative Research and Case Study Applications in Education*, Jossey-Bass, San Francisco, CA.

Miles, MB & Huberman, AM 1994, *Qualitative Data Analysis: An Expanded Sourcebook*, 2nd edn, Sage, Thousand Oaks, CA.

Morse, JM, Barrett, M, Mayan, M, Olson, K & Spiers, J 2002, 'Verification strategies for establishing reliability and validity in qualitative research', *International Journal of Qualitative Methods*, vol. 1, no. 2, pp. 13–22.

Phillips, DC & Burbules, NC 2000, *Postpositivism and Educational Research*, Rowman & Littlefield, Lanham, MD.

Prior, PA 1998, *Writing/disciplinarity: A Sociohistoric Account of Literate Activity in the Academy*, Lawrence Erlbaum, Mahwah, NJ.

Richards, K 2003, *Qualitative Inquiry in TESOL*, Palgrave MacMillan, New York, NY.

Simons, H 2009, *Case Study Research in Practice*, Sage, Thousand Oaks, CA.

Soltis, JF 1991, 'The ethics of qualitative research', in EW Eisner & A Peshkin (eds), *Qualitative Inquiry in Education: The Continuing Debate*, Teachers College Press, New York, NY, pp. 247–257.

Stake, RE 1995, *The Art of Case Study*, Sage, Thousand Oaks, CA.

———— 2005, 'Qualitative case studies', in NK Denzin & YS Lincoln (eds), *The Sage Handbook of Qualitative Research*, 3rd edn, Sage, Thousand Oaks, CA, pp. 443–446.

———— 2006, *Multiple Case Study Analysis*, The Guilford Press, New York, NY.

Swanborn, P 2010, *Case Study Research: What, Why and How?*, Sage, Los Angeles, CA.

Taylor, J 2011, 'The intimate insider: Negotiating the ethics of friendship when doing insider research', *Qualitative Research*, vol. 11, no. 3, pp. 3–22.

Van Lier, L 2005, 'Case study', in E Hinkel (ed.), *Handbook of Research in Second Language Teaching and Learning*, Lawrence Erlbaum, Mahwah, NJ, pp. 195–208.

Van Wynsberghe, R & Khan, S 2007, 'Redefining case study', *International Journal of Qualitative Methods*, vol. 16, no. 2, pp. 80–94.

Wolcott, HF 1990, 'On seeking–and rejecting–validity in qualitative research', in EW Eisner & A Peshkin (eds), *Qualitative Inquiry in Education: The Continuing Debate*, Teachers College Press, New York, NY, pp. 121–152.

Yi, Y 2007, 'Engaging literacy: A biliterate student's composing practices beyond school', *Journal of Second Language Writing*, vol. 16, no. 1, pp. 23–39.

———— 2013, 'Adolescent multilingual writer's negotiation of multiple identities and access to academic writing: A case study of a *jogi yuhak* student in a US high school', *The Canadian Modern Language Review*, vol. 69, no. 2, pp. 207–231.

Yin, RK 2009, *Case Study Research: Design and Methods*, 4th edn, Sage, Thousand Oaks, CA.

———— 2012, *Applications of Case Study Research*, 3rd edn, Sage, Thousand Oaks, CA.

CHAPTER EIGHT

Ethnographic Research

Sue Starfield

Why adopt an ethnographic approach to research in applied linguistics? The broad research questions you have in mind as well as your understanding of language, learning and communication shape your choice of methodology. If you see writing, reading, speaking and listening and language learning as primarily shaped by the social contexts in which they occur and you are interested in uncovering the meanings that participants in these processes bring to the communicative events in which they engage, then ethnography may be an appropriate methodology for your research project. As ethnography privileges the direct observation of human behaviour within particular 'cultures' and settings and seeks to understand a social reality from the perspectives of those involved in the observed interactions, it also has implications for the role of the researcher which will be discussed further below. If, moreover, you see your role as researcher as encouraging social change in the community within which you are carrying out your research, you may be more interested in what is known as *critical* ethnography (Talmy 2013).

Ethnographic work, as Hesse-Biber and Leavy (2006) point out, is labour-intensive and requires time, energy and resources. However, the rewards of prolonged engagement within a specific community and the richness of data generated via 'fieldwork' make it a methodology worthy of serious consideration by those seeking to engage in qualitative research. According to Harklau (2005) and Davis (2013), ethnography is currently one of the major approaches to research on second language learning and teaching. Moreover, ethnography is seen as distinct from other qualitative approaches; for example, one of the leading journals in the field, *TESOL Quarterly*, provides separate sets of substantial guidelines to authors on conversation analysis, case studies and (critical) – their parentheses – ethnography (see Resources for Further Reading).

In this chapter, I consider the different strands or traditions and methodological assumptions that inform contemporary ethnographic approaches to applied linguistics research, including critical ethnography, and discuss various methods that are typically used. This leads to a discussion of ethical issues, particularly pertinent to ethnographic research. As the writing of ethnographic texts and the key role of the researcher have been topics of much discussion over the last two decades, I also provide explicit consideration of these two areas. The chapter concludes with an account of an ethnographic study of academic writing that I carried out at a South African university.

Underlying assumptions and methodology

Ethnography's home is within qualitative research as 'qualitative researchers study things in their natural settings, attempting to make sense of, or interpret, phenomena in terms of the meanings people bring to them' (Denzin & Lincoln 2005, p. 3). However, as Watson-Gegeo (1988) pointed out, ethnography is not synonymous with qualitative research. Impressionistic accounts, fixed category observations, brief engagement or a study based on a few in-depth, semi-structured interviews should neither be considered ethnography nor ethnographic[1] (Lazaraton 2003).

According to Hammersley (1990, pp. 2–3), the key features of a broadly defined ethnographic method include studying people's behaviour in everyday rather than experimental contexts, gathering data from a range of sources chiefly by 'observation and/or relatively informal conversation' and collecting data that are not based on pre-set categories or explicit hypotheses but that arise out of a general interest in an issue or problem. Ethnographic research is typically small in scale and focused on a single setting or group. Prolonged engagement by the researcher in the research setting is also a defining feature of ethnography.

Whereas positivist researchers who use questionnaires and surveys assume that they already know what is important, participant observation, in contrast, makes no such assumptions. Researchers are encouraged to immerse themselves in the everyday activities of the group of people whose meaning-making (also known as 'emic' or insider perspectives) practices they are attempting to understand. Rather than testing preformed ideas or theories (as in deductive research), ideas are developed inductively from the observations. This is not to suggest that ethnography is atheoretical; rather, it is seen as hypothesis generating, with theory being *emergent*,[2] leading to the development of theorization and possible generalization (also called 'etic' or outsider perspectives) as the research progresses. Participant observation therefore allows for the possibility of 'surprise' – that is the emergence of knowledge that is not predetermined by the original research position or paradigm (Willis 1980). For example, through Grimshaw's (2007) extended observation of Chinese students in a Chinese university setting, he was able to develop a set of arguments that draw on postcolonial theory to challenge commonly held views in much Western literature of 'the Chinese learner' as passive, uncritical and lacking in autonomy.

While these methods can be identified as 'core' characteristics of ethnographic approaches, the meanings attached to the status of the data collected vary according to different epistemologies and theoretical frameworks adopted by the researchers. It is therefore important that those embarking on ethnographic research have an understanding of the differing histories of ethnography that inform current approaches. In the section that follows, I provide an outline of this history and its implications as I understand them.

The origins of ethnography

Ethnography as a research methodology has its roots in the cultural and linguistic anthropology of the early twentieth century and certain branches of sociology and has, more recently, been adopted by educational researchers concerned about school failure of certain groups (Harklau 2005; Lazaraton 2003). While Western anthropology's object of study was distant, 'foreign' cultures, the sociologists, who practised ethnography in the West from the early twentieth century on, adapted anthropology's approach to understanding culture 'from the inside' to intensive observations of everyday urban environments, often studying 'subcultures' in economically and socially disadvantaged communities. From the 1960s, under the influence of Hymes's call for an ethnography of communication (Hymes 1972; Saville-Troike 1982) and the development of the broad field of sociolinguistics, ethnographic approaches have been embraced by some in the newer field of applied linguistics. Work that draws on the ethnography of communication has looked at teacher–learner classroom interactions and differences between home and school literacies (e.g. Cazden et al. 1972; Heath 1983) and, more recently, Duff (2002).

The use of ethnographic approaches has been encouraged by what has been called the 'social turn' in language study which has led to the desire to develop in-depth understandings of language learning and teaching events in the specific (and frequently unequal) social contexts within which they are taking place. The combination of long-term observation and the collection of diverse forms of data provide understandings of participants' perspectives and meaning-making practices within the complex sociocultural worlds they inhabit that more traditional methodologies may not have succeeded in capturing.

Applied linguists typically use ethnographic approaches to study language practices within communities and institutions that are familiar to the researcher rather than exotic and strange as in traditional ethnography. Applied linguistics is almost by definition interdisciplinary, and a number of applied linguists are now working collaboratively with colleagues in fields such as health, the workplace, organizations of various types, the justice system and education broadly defined, carrying out ethnographic work on the communication practices at these sites (see e.g. Sarangi & Roberts 1999). While acknowledging the diversity of perspectives and traditions that inform ethnography as well as the variety of sites that applied linguists may be asked to investigate, Rampton (2007) and colleagues (see Maybin & Trusting 2011) in the United Kingdom have developed what they call 'Linguistic Ethnography' – an interdisciplinary approach influenced by *inter alia* critical discourse analysis: the new literacy studies and interactional sociolinguistics (see *Linguistic Ethnography Forum* in Resources for further reading below).

While some stress the need for those embarking on ethnographic research to locate themselves within a 'tradition' (Harklau 2005; *TESOL Quarterly Guidelines* in Further Reading and Resources Below), others argue that the 'traditions' or 'perspectives' have always been characterized by their 'own cultural diversity' (Atkinson et al. 2001, p. 3) and encourage researchers to be aware of and open to this richness. Whatever alignments and identifications are ultimately chosen, Ramanathan and Atkinson's (1999, p. 48) claim in their study of ethnographic approaches and methods in L2 writing research that few ethnographically oriented L2 writing studies 'make their theoretical bases explicit' should be at the forefront of the researcher's thinking and writing (see also Lillis 2008, Peirce 1995, Starfield 2011).[3]

The impact of postmodernism – the researcher's role and authority

Postmodernism and post-structuralism (see Clifford & Marcus 1986; Harklau 2005), sometimes called the 'linguistic' or 'textual' turn in ethnography, have had a profound effect on the production of ethnographic texts, particularly with regard to undermining 'realist' accounts and focusing on the subjectivity of the ethnographer as the writer/producer of an ethnographic text (see van Maanen 1988). By realist accounts, I am referring to the belief that ethnography can provide 'holistic, richly detailed descriptions' (Watson-Gegeo 1988, p. 588) that 'present' an observed 'reality' or 'culture'. Watson-Gegeo's very useful account of ethnography in ESL does not problematize the role of the researcher in the construction of the ethnographic account – a central preoccupation of post-structural approaches in which issues of identity, subjectivity and the production of multivoiced accounts come to the fore.

The original meaning of the term 'ethnography' is 'writing culture', highlighting the significance of both the textual nature of the ethnographic account and its construction by a researcher who is also a writer. The applied linguistics researcher who adopts an ethnographic approach needs to be aware that an extensive literature has discussed both representation and authority in ethnographic writing (see Van Maanen 1988). As Clifford (1986, p. 23) argued in his introduction to *Writing Cultures*: 'the grounds from which persons and groups securely represent each other' have been dislodged. This has led to what has been called the 'reflexive turn' in ethnographic writing. Reflexivity refers to the researcher/writer's ability to reflect on their own positioning and subjectivity in the research and provide an explicit, situated account of their own role in the project and its influences over the findings. Reflexivity is a counter to the positivist construct of the dispassionate, objective researcher who is absent from the account produced (see Foley 2002; Starfield 2013). Cameron et al. (1992) stress that textual representation is power as the writer/researcher is a member of a powerful social group who selects and mediates the talk and identities of the research participants in the act of writing.

The *TESOL Quarterly Qualitative Research: (Critical) Ethnography Guidelines* encourage writers of ethnographic studies to 'develop a mode of textual representation that suits your research experience, objectives, beliefs about the nature of ethnographic knowledge, and preferences' (see Resources for Further Reading). I would urge readers who have a desire to explore alternative forms of representation to examine recent issues of *TESOL Quarterly* and other relevant journals to assess for themselves the extent to which practice is following espoused theory in this instance. This said, Richardson's (2000) criteria for evaluating ethnographic research (see Resources for Further Reading) clearly indicate that it is not a case of 'anything goes'.

Critical ethnography

When Tara Goldstein (1997) sought to understand the meanings that particular language practices had for immigrant workers in a Canadian factory and how these related to their experiences of living in an ethnically stratified society, she chose a research approach that was not only ethnographic in the traditional sense of carrying out observation and describing the meanings language usage had for the workers but that would also take into account the influence of class, gender and power relations in a post-industrial capitalist society, both at work and outside the workplace. Her critical ethnography helps us understand why it is that many immigrant workers in Canada do not take up the English language courses on offer.

Critical ethnographic researchers therefore consider the social location of the group they are studying through 'examining their access to economic, political and cultural resources' (Carspecken 1996, p. 204) and consciously employ macro-perspectives such as sociological theory to examine 'micro' ethnographic data gathered by the researcher. In turn, the macro-theories may be challenged, refined and altered. For example, the detailed microethnographic analyses of classroom discourse carried out by Bloome et al. (2005) locate classroom language and literacy events within broader social and historical contexts. As in Goldstein's study, critical ethnographic research accounts acknowledge the complex relationships between social structures and human agency (Anderson 1989). For Brodkey (1987, p. 67), 'the goal of critical ethnography is always the same: to help create the possibility of transforming such institutions as schools.'

Motha's (2006) year-long critical feminist ethnography embodies these meanings of the term 'critical' in 'critical ethnography' and is located within a post-structural theoretical framework that draws on critiques of multiculturalism, whiteness studies, identity theory and the intersection of native speaker status, race and colonialism. She studied the racial meanings that student and teacher identities and language acquire in a North American school context. Race, whiteness and the status of native speaker teachers of English in linguistically and racially diverse classrooms are sensitive and complex issues that have been underexplored in applied linguistics. Her data were collected in a range of contexts and included classroom observation, interviews and regular 'afternoon teas' with the four novice teachers who participated in her research. She provided the teachers with drafts of all her writing, discussed her interpretations and representations of events with them and has also co-presented at conferences with them. Her work moves through the description of classroom interactions to interpretation and analysis to suggest implications both for pedagogies that seek to confront racism in the ESOL classroom and for the TESOL profession more broadly.

Validity and trustworthiness

In *Critical Ethnography in Educational Research*, Carspecken (1996, pp. 87–89) lists six techniques to support validity claims if qualitative researchers are to produce reports in which the findings can be considered sufficiently trustworthy for colleagues to rely on them in their own research. These are: using multiple recordings devices and multiple observers, using a flexible observations schedule, practising prolonged engagement, using a vocabulary in the fieldnotes that is not overly coloured by the writer's interpretations, using peer-debriefing and using member checking. Most of these techniques are self-explanatory I believe and should be part of the methods of those engaging in ethnographic research, however critical.

Member checking refers to sharing your fieldnotes and interpretations with the people one is studying. In what they called 'collaborative ethnography', Barton and Hamilton (1998) shared their interview transcripts and thematic analyses of participants' literacy practices with them, partly to check the validity of their own analyses. To the extent, however, that participants' involvement in the research process altered their self-understandings and empowered them to explore new literacy practices, the study can be seen to have achieved 'catalytic validity' (Lather 1991): a type of validity that many critical researchers would argue is an important outcome of the research process.

It could however be argued (and other chapters in this volume do so) that validity is a concern inasmuch as researchers still seek to justify their work in relation to the positivist paradigm. Rather than use the term 'validity', ethnographic research as with much qualitative research prefers to talk of 'trustworthiness'. Multiple methods of data collection are seen to contribute to the trustworthiness of the research (Maykut & Morehouse 1994). Triangulation or the collation of data from a range of sources and/or gathered through a range of research methods such as participant observation, informal and formal interviewing and document collection strengthens the validity (or credibility) of the analyses and interpretations (see Watson-Gegeo 1988). Triangulation is further used to ascertain participant's perspectives on their own meaning-making practices. These emic perspectives also contribute to the trustworthiness of the findings.

Clifford Geertz (1975) saw ethnography as being 'thick description': description that goes beyond simple description to include interpretation. Thick description can also be seen as providing greater trustworthiness and may also allow for 'transferability' of findings to different contexts. At the same time, generalizability as conceived of in quantitative research is not necessarily the aim of ethnographic research but rather to 'understand deeply, through a thorough, systematic, iterative analysis' (Duff 2007, p. 983).

Techniques and instruments

Ethnographic research methods of data collection include the techniques of observation through fieldwork, with participant observation (observation that entails interaction with those being studied) being commonly used, the keeping of fieldnotes, formal and informal interviewing of informants/participants, typically using either audio- or videotaping and the collection of relevant documents available at the site or archivally. These multiple methods help the researcher provide the thick description considered essential for ethnographic research and enable triangulation. As indicated earlier, one of the distinguishing features of ethnographic research is that the researcher is the primary instrument of data collection. The awareness that the researcher gains through 'being present' in the setting brings a great richness of understanding. Goldstein (1997) writes that her role as an English teacher in the factory enhanced her access to the Production Departments as many of the workers were her students. This view would obviously run counter to views of the researcher as detached and objective. In the following section, I discuss participant observation and ethnographic interviewing in more detail as they can be seen to form the cornerstone of the ethnographic approach.

Participant observation and fieldwork

Participant observation is carried out through prolonged engagement by the researcher in a setting or field, hence the use of the term 'fieldwork'. Fieldwork aims to provide a description and interpretive explanatory account of what people do in a particular setting and what meaning their interactions have for them. Goldstein (1997) for example observed bilingual workers' interactions on the production line, at the t-shirt printing machines, in the warehouse, in the offices, in language classes, at breaks and at lunch over a two-year period. Her observation included details of the language choices made by the workers in these different contexts. She would stand next to the production line and note down the communication patterns in use, building up an extensive set of fieldnotes in the different settings. Her fieldnotes were both audio-recorded and handwritten, particularly on the noisy production lines. They also included sketches of where participants were standing at the time and a description of the activity being done.

These rich observational data in combination with data from thirty-nine audio-recorded ethnographic interviews enabled her to generate broad hypotheses about language choices on the shop floor which she was able to check with workers and employers. Goldstein's critical framework and commitment to transformation enabled her to understand why it was that many factory workers were resistant to English language classes when it would have seemed obvious that learning English would improve their life chances.

Ethnographic interviews

While numerous approaches to research utilize interviewing, ethnographic interviews can be distinguished by their duration, frequency of contact and, with the influence of post-structuralism and feminism, an awareness that the interview is itself a site of meaning construction and that the interview 'produces' a text for interpretation (Heyl 2001). According to Heyl (2001, p. 370), the core components of ethnographic interviews are listening well and with respect; developing an ethical engagement with the participants at all stages; acquiring self-awareness of one's role in the co-construction of meaning; being aware of ways the ongoing relationship and broader social context affect participants, processes and outcomes; and acknowledging that 'dialogue is discovery' and that only partial knowledge is possible. More critical approaches recognize that many interview situations involve unequal power relations and are sites of identity negotiation. In multilingual contexts, a decision may need to be made as to whether to use an interpreter. In applied linguistics research, language is not only the medium of communication but frequently the topic of study as well, requiring perhaps an even greater level of reflexivity on the part of the researcher.

Ethical considerations

As Murphy and Dingwall (2001) point out, ethnographic researchers share the same minimal responsibility to protect participants from harm that all research with human participants requires with particular regard to anonymity, identification and informed consent that emergent research design may complexify. For example, it may not be possible to specify in advance who will be interviewed or what sorts of information or documentation will be sought as issues that emerge in the course of the research mean that fully informed consent was not possible at the outset (Fox et al. 2006).

While it should be evident that ethnographic research requires approval from a University ethics committee and that permission to conduct observation and interviews, particularly in classrooms, must be sought, Duff (2007, p. 977) points out that gaining permission may be difficult to obtain because of the 'perceived invasiveness' of such practices. Ironically, perhaps, newer technologies such as video recording may increase the perception of invasiveness in groups that may feel vulnerable. Furthermore, it is considered by many ethics committees that seeking informed consent from one's current students in order to carry out classroom-based inquiry is coercive (Duff 2007) as they are in what is termed a 'dependent' relationship with the researcher.

At all times, informed consent must be sought and most universities provide guidelines in this regard. Those new to the field should study the comprehensive and clear *TESOL Quarterly* Informed Consent Policy Statement and Release http://www.tesol.org/read-and-publish/journals/tesol-quarterly/tesol-quarterly-research-guidelines/informed-consent-policy-statement-and-release, viewed 4 December 2013. Have you, for example, considered whether the participants in your study speak English well enough to understand the informed consent form? Would you consider making the form available in the participants' first language or perhaps using an interpreter? If the participants are not literate in any language, could you obtain oral consent?

A sample study

In this section, I discuss a year-long ethnographic study of students' writing development within a disciplinary context that I carried out at a South African university in the final years of official apartheid. My attempts to better understand why it was that black students who spoke English as an additional language and who were learning to write in a course called Sociology One were much less successful than their white peers led me to adopt a critical ethnographic perspective. As the research evolved, I became more aware of how broader socio-economic and political inequalities shaped the possibilities available to students to negotiate successful identities for themselves.

In my professional academic life, I was working in the field of student academic support and was concerned that generic academic writing skills were not helping the students sufficiently. I wanted to find out more about the lived experience of students learning to write within a specific discipline and knew that the Department of Sociology was concerned about the inequitable pass rates of black and white students.

As is common in ethnographic research, my initial question was broadly based. Drawing on Saville-Troike (1982, p. 2), it asked: 'What does a writer need to know to communicate appropriately within a particular discourse community and how does he or she learn?' As the research progressed, several more focused questions emerged, again fairly typical of ethnographic research:

- What is the nature of the written genres which students in Sociology One are expected to produce?

- How do students from apartheid schools learn and teachers teach these genres?

- What are the processes whereby students are initiated into the new discourse community?

- What are considered to be successful texts and what are the processes whereby students do or do not 'succeed'?

Eleven students participated in my year-long study. Nine of the students were African, three were women and two were white, one male and one female. They were all new to Sociology One. All of the African students were from socio-economically disadvantaged apartheid schooling backgrounds.

To ensure trustworthiness, I used a combination of observation – along the full continuum from non-participant to participant – within as many teaching and learning contexts as possible, in-depth semi-structured interviews and document collection, including copies of students' written texts. I triangulated by checking my evolving understandings of their reality with the different participants as I built my thick description of the students' experiences of learning to write in Sociology One.

I collected data from multiple sites that included lecture halls, tutorials of different kinds, markers' meetings, weekly tutor briefings, one of the tutor's offices and corridor conversations. I took extensive fieldnotes.

In some respects, I was like a student. I attended all four weekly lectures in a hall with several hundred students, and one weekly tutorial of about thirty students. I read the materials included in the *Course Reader* which enabled me to trace different student interpretations (or misinterpretations) of the readings and develop the concept of what I called (after Bourdieu) 'textual capital' (see Starfield 2002).

Each student took part in a semi-structured interview of about one-and-a-half hours which included discussion of their essays and tests. Eight of the students took part in a second interview and some were interviewed a year later. In addition, I had numerous less formal conversations with the students in the course of the year. I collected copies of all eleven students' essays, tests and exams.

I conducted an in-depth semi-structured interview with all academic staff who taught on the first-year course of at least one hour. Some were later approached to review students' essays and exams that they had marked and to discuss criteria employed and feedback as part of the process of triangulation (Starfield 2002, 2004). I audio-taped and transcribed all interviews including the two markers' meetings that I observed.

I also collected relevant documents such as the student newspaper and political pamphlets distributed by the various student organizations on campus. I use some of this data in support of my analysis of the ways in which a student whom I called Ben negotiates his textual identity in his successful essay (Starfield 2004). I draw on arguments in favour of the anonymous marking of student essays to reduce perceived bias in the assessment of black students that appeared in the student newspaper.

I used critical discourse analysis (Fairclough 1992) combined with systemic functional linguistics (Halliday 1994) as my main analytic tool for textual analysis. I examined the linguistic and discursive resources students drew on as they wrote their assignments in order to create identities in written texts that were more or less successful. A critical discourse analysis of the *Student Handbook* enabled me to see how the department positioned and constructed students from disadvantaged backgrounds vis-à-vis students from 'mainstream' backgrounds. Thematic analysis of interview data provided insights into student perceptions of their experiences of success and failure which complemented the textual data. I was able to argue that successful texts were the outcome of complex identity negotiations (see Ivanič 1998) and that key academic genres were not 'fixed' or easily identifiable.

Data collected at one of the markers' meeting and analysed using the work of Bourdieu (1982) helped me develop a critique of the concept of discourse community as used in English for Academic Purposes – challenging my initial conceptualizations. I came to view academic discourse communities as being themselves sites of power and contestation: a view not reflected in much of the literature on the teaching of writing (Starfield 2001). While I had titled my project 'Making and sharing meaning', by the end of my year in Sociology One, I was to conclude that the effects of apartheid were such that meaning could not be shared equally by all.

Future developments in ethnographic research

The attention currently being paid to multimodal literacies and the ever-increasing impact of technology in schools, workplaces and other sites of communication is beginning to give rise to applied linguistics ethnographic studies of the multimodal communicative practices of their inhabitants (see e.g. Davies 2006; Scollon et al. 1999). Relatedly, the development of virtual communities facilitated by technology and the impact of globalization have the potential to produce ethnographic studies that call into question the notion of community as based in a single setting (see Slembrouck 2005).

Autoethnography – a blend of autobiography and ethnography – has become a popular approach in a number of fields including education (see Foley 2002). Will such studies begin to emerge in applied linguistics or will they struggle to be published? We may begin to see more attempts at different reporting formats (see Lee & Simon-Maeda 2006). Goldstein's (2003) ethnographic playwriting is a rare example of such an attempt. *Hong Kong, Canada*, a play that is included in an appendix to her book-length critical ethnography of a multilingual Toronto high school, invites readers to perform/read the play which creatively raises many of the issues examined in the research itself.

Of course, challenging the dominant genres in any academic field is potentially risky, but I would encourage readers of this chapter contemplating ethnographic work to read widely and consider how best to represent their work and the voices of those who participate.

Notes

1   The term 'ethnography' is contested. Educational researchers have been urged by many to not use the term unless studying a culture 'holistically', and critical researchers have problematized the notion of culture, cultural description and the impossibility of 'holistic' accounts. 'Ethnographic' is often a preferred alternative.

2 The theoretical perspectives derived from this data are sometimes known as grounded theory.

3 The sustained engagement in a 'field' that ethnographic work requires makes it a suit able methodology for a doctoral study. Journal articles that describe ethnographic work (often the outcome of such a study) are however typically constrained by length requirements to limit details of the methodological framework and methods adopted. It is therefore worth reading the dissertation in its entirety to obtain an understanding of the researcher's engagement in the field.

Resources for further reading

Ethnography and Education is an international, peer-reviewed journal. More information can be found at http://www.tandfonline.com/toc/reae20/current# .Up_vWL_q4cs, viewed 7 May 2014.

The Centre for Urban Ethnography, Graduate School of Education, University of Pennsylvania, convenes the Ethnography in Education Research Forum, an annual meeting of qualitative researchers in education. See http://www.gse.upenn.edu/cue/, viewed 7 May 2014.

The Ethnograph is a software package that allows you to store, code, search data, write and store analytic memos. More information is available at http://www .qualisresearch.com/, viewed 7 May 2014.

The *Ethnography and Education* website: www.ethnographyandeducation.org, viewed 7 May 2014, is run by the group that started the journal and who host an annual *Oxford Ethnography and Education Conference*.

The Linguistic Ethnography Forum: www.lingethnog.org, viewed 7 May 2014. This website hosts the *UK Linguistic Ethnography Forum*, a Special Interest Group of the British Association for Applied Linguistics (BAAL). There is information about participants; past and planned events and discussion papers they have produced.

Richardson, L 2000, 'Evaluating ethnography', *Qualitative Inquiry*, vol. 6, no. 2, pp. 253–255.

Richardson, who describes herself as a 'poststructural ethnographer', shares five of the criteria she uses when reviewing papers or monographs. These are: substantive merit, aesthetic merit, reflexivity, impact and expressing a reality. The criteria are described in more detail in the article.

Scott Jones, J & Watt, S (eds), 2010 *Ethnography in Social Science Practice*, Routledge, London.

This is a very helpful introductory text for students interested in understanding ethnography as a research methodology within a broader social sciences perspective.

TESOL Quarterly Qualitative Research: (Critical) Ethnography Guidelines http://
www.tesol.org/read-and-publish/journals/tesol-quarterly/tesol-quarterly-research
-guidelines/qualitative-research-%28critical%29-ethnography-guidelines, viewed 7
May 2014.

These extensive guidelines are essential reading for anyone beginning ethnographic
research within the broad fields of language and education. They also offer an
open-minded perspective on what they call the 'critical ethnography report',
suggesting that the traditional Introduction-Method-Results-Discussion format
of the research article embodies a positivist attitude to research that may not be
appropriate for ethnographic writing when the researcher was not a detached
'objective' observer but an active participant.

References

Anderson, GL 1989, 'Critical ethnography in education: Origins, current status and
    new directions', *Review of Educational Research*, vol. 59, no. 3, pp. 249–270.
Atkinson, P, Coffey, A, Delamont, S, Lofland, J & Lofland, L 2001, 'Editorial
    introduction', in P Atkinson, A Coffey, S Delamont, J Lofland & L Lofland
    (eds), *Handbook of Ethnography*, Sage, London, pp. 1–7.
Barton, D & Hamilton, M 1998, *Local Literacies*, Routledge, London.
Bloome, D, Carter, SP, Christian, BM, Otto, S & Shuart-Faris, N 2005, *Discourse
    Analysis and the Study of Classroom Language and Literacy Events:
    A Microethnographic Perspective*, Lawrence Erlbaum, Mahwah, NJ.
Bourdieu, P 1982, *Ce que parler veut dire*, Fayard, Paris.
Brodkey, L 1987, 'Writing critical ethnographic narratives', *Anthropology and
    Education Quarterly*, vol. 18, no. 2, pp. 67–76.
Cameron, D, Frazer, E, Harvey, P, Rampton, MBH & Richardson, K 1992,
    Researching Language: Issues of Power and Method, Routledge, London.
Carspecken, PF 1996, *Critical Ethnography in Educational Research*, Routledge,
    New York, NY.
Cazden, C, John, V & Hymes, D 1972, *Functions of Language in the Classroom*,
    Waveland Press, Prospect Hills, IL.
Clifford, J 1986, 'Introduction: partial truths', in J Clifford & G Marcus (eds),
    Writing Culture, University of California Press, Berkeley, pp. 1–26.
Clifford, J & Marcus, G (eds), 1986, *Writing Culture*, University of California
    Press, Berkeley, CA.
Davies, J 2006, 'Affinities and beyond! Developing ways of seeing in online spaces',
    E-learning, vol. 3, no. 2, pp. 217–234.
Davis, KA 2013, 'Ethnographic approaches to second language acquisition
    research', in CA Chappelle (ed.), *Encyclopedia of Applied Linguistics*, Wiley-
    Blackwell, Oxford, pp. 1–8.
Denzin N & Lincoln, Y 2005, 'Introduction: the discipline and practice of
    qualitative research', in N Denzin & Y Lincoln (eds), *The Sage Handbook of
    Qualitative Research*, 3rd edn, Sage, Thousand Oaks, CA, pp. 1–32.
Duff, PA 2002, 'The discursive co-construction of knowledge, identity, and
    difference: An ethnography of communication in the high school mainstream',
    Applied Linguistics, vol. 23, no. 3, pp. 289–322.

———— 2007, 'Qualitative approaches to classroom research with English language learners', in J Cummins & C Davison (eds), *International Handbook of English Language Teaching*, Springer, New York, NY, pp. 973–986.

Fairclough, N 1992, *Discourse and Social Change*, Polity Press, Cambridge.

Foley, D 2002, 'Critical ethnography: The reflexive turn', *Qualitative Studies in Education*, vol.15, no. 5, pp. 469–490.

Fox, J, Artemeva, N, Darville, R & Woods, D 2006, 'Juggling through hoops: Implementing ethics policies in applied linguistic studies', *Journal of Applied Ethics*, vol. 4, no. 1–4, pp. 77–79.

Geertz, C 1975, *The Interpretation of Cultures*, Hutchinson, London.

Goldstein, T 1997, *Two Languages at Work: Bilingual Life on the Production Floor*, Mouton de Gruyter, Berlin.

———— 2003, *Teaching and Learning in a Multilingual School: Choices, Risks and Dilemmas*. Lawrence Erlbaum, Mahwah, NJ.

Grimshaw, T 2007, 'Problematizing the construct of "the Chinese learner": Insights from ethnographic research', *Educational Studies*, vol. 33, no. 3, pp. 299–311.

Halliday, MAK 1994, *An Introduction to Functional Grammar*, 2nd edn, Edward Arnold, London.

Hammersley, M 1990, *Reading Ethnographic Research: A Critical Guide*, Longman, London.

Harklau, L 2005, 'Ethnography and ethnographic research on second language teaching and learning', in E Hinkel (ed.), *Handbook of Research in Second Language Teaching and Learning*, Lawrence Erlbaum, Mahwah, NJ, pp. 179–194.

Heath, SB 1983, *Ways with Words*, Cambridge University Press, New York, NY.

Hesse-Biber, SN & Leavy, P (2006), *The Practice of Qualitative Research*, Sage, Thousand Oaks, CA.

Heyl, BS 2001, 'Ethnographic interviewing' in P Atkinson, A Coffey, S Delamount, J Lofland & L Lofland (eds), *Handbook of Ethnography*, Sage, London, pp. 368–383.

Hymes, D 1972. 'Toward ethnographies of communication', in PP Giglioli (ed.), *Language and Social Context*, Penguin, Harmondsworth, pp. 21–44.

Ivanič, R 1998, *Writing and Identity: The Discoursal Construction of Identity in Academic Writing*, John Benjamins, Amsterdam.

Lather, P 1991, *Getting Smart: Feminist Research and Pedagogy with/in the Postmodern*, Routledge, New York, NY.

Lazaraton, A 2003, 'Evaluative criteria for qualitative research in applied linguistics: Whose criteria and whose research?', *The Modern Language Journal*, vol. 87, no. 1, pp. 1–12.

Lee, E & Simon Maeda, A 2006, 'Racialized research identities in ESL/EFL research', *TESOL Quarterly*, vol. 40, no. 3, pp. 573–594.

Lillis, T 2008, 'Ethnography as method, methodology and "deep theorising": Closing the gap between text and context in academic writing research', *Written Communication*, vol. 25, no. 3, pp. 353–388.

Maybin, J & Trusting, K 2011, 'Linguistic ethnography', in J Simpson (ed.), *Routledge Handbook of Applied Linguistics*, Routledge, Abingdon, pp. 515–528.

Maykut, P & Morehouse, R 1994, *Beginning Qualitative Research: A Philosophical and Practical Guide*, Falmer Press, London.

Motha, S (2006), 'Racializing ESOL teacher identities in U.S. K-12 public schools', *TESOL Quarterly*, vol. 40, no. 3, pp. 495–517.

Murphy, E & Dingwall, R 2001, 'The ethics of ethnography' in P Atkinson, A Coffey, S Delamount, J Lofland & L Lofland (eds), *Handbook of Ethnography*, Sage, London, pp. 339–351.

Peirce, BN 1995, 'The theory of methodology in qualitative research', *TESOL Quarterly*, vol. 29, no. 3, pp. 569–576.

Ramanathan, V & Atkinson, D 1999, 'Ethnographic approaches and methods in L2 writing research: A critical guide and review', *Applied Linguistics*, vol. 20, no. 1, pp. 44–70.

Rampton, B 2007, 'Neo-hymesian Linguistic ethnography in the United Kingdom', *Journal of Sociolinguistics*, vol. 11, no. 5, pp. 584–607.

Richardson, L 2000, 'Evaluating ethnography', *Qualitative Inquiry*, vol. 6, no. 2, pp. 253–255.

Sarangi, S & Roberts, C (eds), 1999, *Talk, Work and Institutional Order: Discourse in Medical, Mediation and Management Settings*, Mouton de Gruyter, Berlin.

Saville-Troike, M 1982, *The Ethnography of Communication*, Basil Blackwell, Oxford.

Scollon, R, Bhatia, V, Li, D & Yung, V 1999, 'Blurred genres and fuzzy identities in Hong Kong public discourse: Foundational ethnographic issues in the study of reading', *Applied Linguistics*, vol. 20, no. 1, pp. 23–43.

Slembrouck, S 2005, 'Discourse, critique and ethnography: class-oriented coding in accounts of child protection', *Language Sciences*, vol. 27, no. 6, pp. 619–650.

Starfield, S 2001, '"I'll go with the group": Rethinking discourse community in EAP', in J Flowerdew & M Peacock (eds), *Research Perspectives on English for Academic Purposes*, Cambridge University Press, Cambridge, pp. 132–147.

—— 2002, '"I'm a second-language English speaker": Negotiating writer identity and authority in Sociology One', *Language, Identity, and Education*, vol. 1, no. 2, pp. 121–140.

—— 2004, 'Wordpower: Negotiating success in a first-year sociology essay', in LJ Ravelli & RA Ellis (eds), *Analysing Academic Writing: Contextualised Frameworks*, Continuum, London, pp. 66–83.

—— 2011, 'Doing critical ethnographic research into academic writing: The theory of the methodology', in D Belcher, AM Johns & B Paltridge (eds), *New Directions in English for Specific Purposes Research*, University of Michigan Press, Ann Arbor, MI, pp. 174–196.

—— 2013, 'Researcher reflexivity', in CA Chappelle (ed.), *Encyclopedia of Applied Linguistics*, Wiley-Blackwell, Oxford, pp. 1–7.

Talmy, S 2013, 'Critical ethnography', in CA Chappelle (ed.), *Encyclopedia of Applied Linguistics*, Wiley-Blackwell, Oxford, pp. 1–6.

Van Maanen, J 1988, *Tales of the Field: On Writing Ethnography*, University of Chicago Press, Chicago, IL.

Watson-Gegeo, KA 1988, 'Ethnography in ESL: Defining the essentials', *TESOL Quarterly*, vol. 22, no. 4, pp. 575–592.

Willis, P 1980, 'On method', in S Hall, D Hobson, A Lowe & P Willis (eds), *Culture, Media, Language: Working Papers in Cultural Studies, 1972–79*, Routledge, London, pp. 88–95.

CHAPTER NINE

Critical Research in Applied Linguistics

Steven Talmy

Critical research in applied linguistics has become a productive area of empirical inquiry in recent years, generating studies on a range of topics and themes, in an array of settings and employing a variety of research methods. What unites this diverse stream of research is a general effort on the part of critical applied linguistics researchers to identify linkages, broadly construed, between local occasions of language learning and use to broader social processes, formations and discourses, that is, '[to draw] connections between classrooms, conversations, textbooks, tests, or translations and issues of gender, class, sexuality, race, ethnicity, culture, identity, politics' (Pennycook 2008, p. 169).

In this chapter, I provide a methodologically oriented overview of critical applied linguistics empirical inquiry. I begin with a brief discussion of certain assumptions and principles motivating the 'project' (Simon & Dippo 1986) of critical research. Afterwards, I describe some methodological options open to critical applied linguistics researchers, with particular emphasis on critical ethnography and critical discourse analysis. My purpose in selecting these two approaches is not only because they are commonly employed for empirical second language (L2) research, but because of the benefits that accrue when using both 'complementarily' (Miller & Fox 2004), particularly in terms of analytic accountability (how defensible or warranted an analysis is) and demonstrability of research claims (how warrants for research claims are shown to the reader). I then spend the remainder of the chapter elaborating the discussion by describing a critical ethnography I conducted in a high-school ESL program in Hawai'i.

Assumptions and principles of critical research in applied linguistics

The task of defining 'critical' is difficult, as there is a plurality of critical theories, based on the diverse work of a range of scholars, including Marx, the Frankfurt School, Volosinov, Gramsci, Freire, Althusser, Bernstein, Foucault and Bourdieu, among others. Just as critical theories are not monolithic, neither are they static, as they change and shift due to ongoing, 'synergistic' relationships among themselves, and with cultural studies, post-structuralism, postmodernism and postcolonialism (Kincheloe & McLaren 2000). To arrive at a settled-upon definition would be to deny a productive dissensus among critical scholars, who would prefer 'to avoid the production of blueprints of sociopolitical and epistemological beliefs' (Kincheloe & McLaren 2000, p. 281), since such a perspective would 'assume an epistemological stance in which the social world can be precisely defined – a position that is not very critical' (Quantz 1992, p. 448).

While there is no single agreed-upon definition of 'critical', there are certain principles and objectives shared in the critical 'project'. At the risk of producing the sort of 'blueprint' that Kincheloe and McLaren (2000) advocate against, these include a conception of *society* as stratified and marked by inequality, with differential structural access to material and symbolic resources, power, opportunity, mobility and education. Accordingly, society is characterized by asymmetries in *power* arrangements. Because '[p]ower operates not just on people but through them' (Simon & Dippo 1986, p. 197), there is a reciprocal, mutually constitutive relationship between social structures and human *agency*. That is, social structures shape or mediate social practices but do not determine them (Giddens 1979; also see Ahearn 2001). This means that *social reproduction* (i.e. the reproduction of unjust social relations) is never 'guaranteed' since power is not uni-directional or top/down. One consequence of this is a conception of *culture* as an 'ongoing political struggle around the meanings given to actions of people located within unbounded asymmetrical power relations' (Quantz 1992, p. 483). Further, society, power, agency and culture do not exist atemporally; they are *sociohistorically situated*. Historicization in critical research 'show[s] the conditions of possibility of a definite set of social forms and thus simultaneously establish[es] the historical limits of their existence' (Simon & Dippo 1986, p. 198). Relatedly, critical researchers are not content to simply 'describe' what they see; they attempt to promote change of inequality through sustained critique and direct action, or *praxis*. This 'emancipatory impulse' has garnered considerable criticism (see, for example, Ellsworth 1989), resulting in recent conceptions of praxis as more circumspect, situated, collaborative and *reflexive*. Finally, critical researchers dispute the contention that there is 'value-free' research, instead embracing their 'openly ideological' *values* (Lather 1986). It is ironic that because critical researchers are explicit about their values, they are susceptible to reproach regarding the so-called 'imposition' of them.

These general principles and objectives are shared and extended in critical research in applied linguistics, as evident in its increasingly diverse literature. Indeed, in many ways, the focus in critical applied linguistics on the conditions of language learning and use in everyday life uniquely positions researchers to examine in detail the role of language in producing, sustaining, challenging and transforming power asymmetries, discrimination, inequality, social injustice and hegemony as they pertain to race, ethnicity, class, gender, sexuality and more.

Research methods

The research methods most often employed in critical research in applied linguistics are qualitative, ranging from diary and/or interview studies (e.g. Benesch 2001; Motha 2006; Norton 2013), to critical pedagogical classroom research (e.g. Crookes & Lehner 1998; Morgan 1997), some form of critical discourse analysis (e.g. Blommaert 2005; Fairclough 2003; Van Dijk 2001) and critical ethnography (Heller 2011; Pérez-Milans 2011; Rojo 2010). In this review, I confine my remarks to the latter two approaches, particularly in terms of how the former can work to ground and elaborate findings generated in critical ethnography.

Critical ethnography developed as a response to more 'conventional' forms of ethnography (Anderson 1989; Masemann 1982). Canagarajah (1993), one of the first to have published a 'politically motivated ethnography' in applied linguistics, maintains that critical ethnography is 'an ideologically sensitive orientation to the study of culture that can penetrate the noncommittal objectivity and scientism [of] descriptive ethnography' (p. 605). May (1997, pp. 198–199) notes that this approach 'reject[s] the abrogation of a theoretical perspective for the "open-ended" collection of data' that is advanced in conventional ethnography; that it explicitly acknowledges its critical theoretical orientation and how it shapes interpretation; that 'reality' is conceived 'for what it is – a social and cultural *construction*, linked to wider power relations, which privileges some, and disadvantages other[s]' and that critical ethnography 'attempts to move beyond the accounts of participants … to examine the ideological premises and hegemonic practices which shape and constrain these accounts' (Foley & Valenzuela 2005; Heller 2011; Lave 2011).

Methodologically, critical ethnography maintains the conventional ethnographic requirements for persistent, prolonged engagement in the field, recurrent and iterative data analysis, and an emergent, recursive relationship between (critical) theory, data, research questions and interpretation (see Starfield this volume). A key distinction, however, is the above-mentioned commitment to the critical project. A critically located ethnographic methodology highlights the interplay between social structure, material relations and agency; addresses the ways that social structure is (or is not) instantiated, accommodated, resisted and/or transformed in the micropolitics of everyday life; contends with issues of ideology, hegemony and culture; critically addresses its own historically, materially and culturally specific interpretations; and works towards change, often with the collaboration of research participants (see, for example, Carspecken 1996; Thomas 1993).

Quality in critical discourse analysis and critical ethnography

What distinguishes critical ethnography from other forms of ethnography also presents it with one of its more enduring challenges: 'trustworthiness'. Verschueren (2001, p. 60) casts the challenge in particularly stark terms, arguing that

> [i]f critical approaches to language use in the context of social practices fail to be convincing as a result of a lack of theoretical and methodological rigour ... they destroy their own *raison d'être* and make the task all the more difficult for anyone who does observe the basic rules of documentation, argumentation and explicit presentation.

Lather (1986) has characterized the issue of quality in critical ethnography as being 'between a rock and a soft place', where the rock is 'the unquestionable need for trustworthiness' and the soft place 'is the positivist claim to neutrality and objectivity' (p. 65). She advocates adopting measures from conventional ethnography to ensure quality, including triangulation, member checks and systematized reflexivity, in addition to what she calls 'catalytic validity', that is, the extent to which the research promotes social change.

Another approach that can be enlisted in the pursuit of quality in critical ethnography is critical discourse analysis, which can work to generate, warrant and elaborate (critical) claims in demonstrable and data-near terms. There has been a significant upsurge in critical discourse research in recent years, much of which has been based in the quasi-systemic functional framework proposed by Fairclough (2003, *inter alia*; Mey 2001, p. 316; cf. Blommaert 2005). Despite the significance of Faircloughian 'CDA' (Critical Discourse Analysis) in critical research in applied linguistics, scholars have made several substantive critiques of it, ranging from its theoretical and methodological ambiguity, to a tendency to undertheorize context, to a problematic lack of reflexivity (see, for example, Slembrouck 2001; Verschueren 2001; also see Pennycook 2001, 2003). Further, Blommaert

(2005, p. 24) notes a propensity within Faircloughian CDA to 'identify itself as a "school"'. This 'create[s] an impression of closure and exclusiveness with respect to critique', and 'result[s] in suggestive divisions within discourse analysis – "critical" versus "non-critical" – that are [in fact] hard to sustain in reality.' Van Dijk (2013) concurs, arguing that CDA has become 'generally limited' to grammatical analysis: 'less of discourse structures, and even less of interactional, pragmatic, cognitive, social, political or cultural dimensions of power abuse', which require methods beyond those needed to analyse 'clause structures' (p. 3). Indeed, there are many different analytic methodologies that can be (and have been) used in critical discourse research, including interactional sociolinguistics, applied conversation analysis, membership categorization analysis and discursive psychology; it is these various approaches in general to which I refer below with the lower-case 'critical discourse analysis'.

Although discourse analysis has been used in conventional ethnographic research in applied linguistics for some time, critical discourse analysis has been notably underutilized in critical ethnography. Anderson (1989), for one, has lamented the tendency towards 'macro' cultural and social analysis in critical ethnography, arguing that it is imperative to include examination of what he calls 'microsocial interaction'. By neglecting analysis of social interaction, he maintains, critical ethnographers overlook the potential of critical discourse analysis 'to systematically explore how relations of domination' are produced, reproduced, contested and transformed in everyday conduct (Anderson 1989, pp. 262–263). Widdicombe (1995, p. 111) makes a similar point, stating that 'it is precisely in the mundane contexts of interaction that institutional power is exercised, social inequalities are experienced, and resistance [is] accomplished' (also see, e.g., Blommaert 2005; Wilkinson & Kitzinger 2008).

Techniques and instruments for critical research in applied linguistics

The techniques and instruments for empirical inquiry in critical applied linguistics depend on the particular method adopted, but generally tend not to be distinct from their 'descriptive' counterparts (Carspecken 1996; Heller 2011; Thomas 1993). In critical ethnography, for example, fieldwork techniques generally include participant-observation, fieldnotes, interviews, audio or video recordings of interaction and artefact analysis, while instruments can range from notebooks, research journals, interview protocols and survey questionnaires. Data analytic procedures can include thematic analysis, various coding schemes, memo-writing and graphic data-displays in addition to the use of computer-assisted qualitative data analysis software, a primary distinction being the theoretical framework motivating critical ethnography. Similarly, while critical discourse analysis is distinguished by its explanatory base(s) in critical theories, its techniques and instruments will similarly depend on the particular analytic approach(es) adopted, with objects of study ranging from textbooks, newspapers, magazines, site documents and pop-culture artefacts, to transcripts of recorded interactions, for example interviews, classroom talk or computer-mediated-communication (Van Dijk 2001).

A sample study

To elaborate the discussion above, I turn now to discuss briefly a 2.5-year-long critical ethnography that combined critical discourse analysis, which I conducted in the ESL program of Tradewinds High, a public high school in Hawai'i (Talmy 2008, 2009, 2010). Generally, the Tradewinds High study concerned the production of ESL as a stigmatized identity category at the high school, particularly among long-term or 'oldtimer' 'Local ESL' students in the ESL program, and the central role that linguicism (Phillipson 1988), or linguistic prejudice, played in this. As several applied linguistics studies of ESL in North American public schools attest, ESL in these settings is often considered a 'dummy program' (McKay & Wong 1996, p. 586), with ESL students cast in various ways as 'candidate[s] for cognitive overhaul and rescue' (p. 590). In the Tradewinds study, I observed the same sorts of stigma associated with ESL, and in contrast, positive attributes associated with the 'mainstream'. I characterized this as a pervasive 'mainstream/ESL' hierarchy that was in evidence throughout the wider Tradewinds context, with mainstream in the 'unmarked' superordinate position, and ESL in the 'marked' subordinate (cf. Bucholtz & Hall 2004). This hierarchy was constituted by and constitutive of normalized language ideologies and linguicism concerning immigrants, bi- and multilingualism and assimilationism in North America (see Figure 9.1). I used critical discourse analysis, particularly of old-timer Local ESL student interaction, to elaborate how these discriminatory language ideologies played out in everyday ESL classroom life.

Local ESL

'Local' is an identity category in wide circulation in Hawai'i and generally signifies someone (usually Asian/Pacific Islanders) who has been born and raised in the islands. 'Local ESL' is an 'etic' (see Starfield this volume) category that refers to students who were institutionally identified as ESL by Tradewinds, yet who displayed cultural knowledge of and affiliation with Local culture, cultural forms and social practices (including speaking

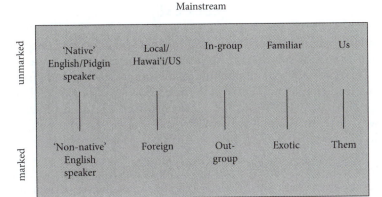

FIGURE 9.1 *Representing the 'mainstream/ESL' hierarchy at Tradewinds High*

Pidgin, or Hawai'i Creole, the Local language of Hawai'i);[1] difference from newcomer or low-L2-proficient classmates, who many Local ESL students characterized as 'FOBs' (fresh off the boat); and the L2 expertise and interactional competence necessary to participate in these practices.

Local ESL cultural productions of the ESL student

A primary argument from the Tradewinds study was that the knowledge, orientations and social practices of an 'institutionally disapproved interstitial community of practice' (Lave 1991, p. 78) comprised of old-timer Local ESL students came to assume varying degrees of prominence in each of the eight ESL classes I observed. Combining critical ethnography with critical discourse analysis, I examined Local ESL students' displays of resistant social practice in close detail. These practices included leaving assigned materials 'at home', not doing homework and completing assignments that required minimal effort (worksheets) but not others (writing activities). The more overt, interactionally mediated practices included bargaining for reduced requirements on classwork, refusal to participate in instructional activities and the often delicate negotiations with teachers that resulted. There was also a cluster of practices in which Local ESL students engaged in public displays of difference or 'distinction' (Irvine and Gal, 2000) from their low-L2-English and newcomer ESL classmates. This took form in many ways, including mobilization of the category 'FOB'. It was also evident in Local ESL students' targeted use of a mock language variety I call 'Mock ESL'.

Mock ESL

Mock language is a speech style that indexes some form of outgroup or 'foreign' status. It is a racializing discourse that can be characterized by hyper-'marked' syntax and phonology, lexical borrowing and displays of pragmatic incompetence. Perhaps the best known work on mock language is Jane Hill's (e.g. 1998), on the Mock Spanish (e.g. 'no problemo [*sic*]' 'no way, José' or Arnold Schwarzenegger's 'hasta la vista, baby' in the movie *Terminator 2*) used by non-Spanish-speaking whites in the US Southwest.

Mock ESL shares similar semiotics to other mock language varieties but indexes an archetypal, pan-ethnic Foreigner, rather than a particular racial or ethnolinguistic group. In my study, I used occasions of Mock ESL to ground and elaborate claims concerning the role of linguicism in producing the stigma of ESL; to demonstrate one means that Local ESL students produced 'distinction' from low-L2-proficient and newcomer classmates; and to illustrate how the 'mainstream/ESL' hierarchy evident outside the ESL program was projected *within* it in terms of a respecified 'Local ESL/FOB' hierarchy (see below).

Space constraints prohibit an extensive data display or analysis, but even brief consideration of two data fragments highlights how critical discourse analysis can work to elaborate and ground critical ethnographic claims. The first fragment involves China and Raven, two Local ESL students.[2] It is the beginning of their ESL class, and their teacher is giving instructions for an assignment and allotting the time to do it (15 minutes). China has been bargaining for twice that time. The fragment begins as China is mockingly justifying his need for this additional time: because he and Raven are ESL students (see the Appendix to this chapter for transcription conventions; transcripts are simplified).

```
01. China:  yeah [bu-
02. T:            [we (mu[st)
03. China:            [bu- [bu-
04. T:                      [we have to hurry
05. China:  ((higher pitch, light nasal tone)) but we E-S-L student!
                                        (([bʰʌ wi iɛsɛl studɛn]))
06. Raven:  ((Pidgin)) wi- wi so [dam!
                       we're- we're so dumb!
07. T:                           [that's okay!
08. China:  ((higher pitch, light nasal tone)) we no English!
                                        (([wi no ɪŋɡəlɪʃ:]))
09. Raven:  ((Pidgin)) haw du yu spel 'A'
                       how do you spell 'A'?
10. T:      ((to the class)) ten-thirty!
```

China's style shifts in lines 5 and 8 are examples of Mock ESL. In terms of prosody, both utterances are spoken in a higher pitch, with a light nasal tone, and both feature hyper-incorrect grammar. These features are in essence the embodied performance of the activity that China associates with the category 'ESL student' in line 8, 'we no English', and the attribute that Raven assigns it (in Pidgin) in line 6: 'so dumb'; this is expanded in line 9 with needing help to spell the letter 'A'. Thus, China animates a 'figure' (Goffman 1981) through Mock ESL: a low-L2-English-proficient, cognitively challenged newcomer, or 'FOB'. Although China has packaged his performance with several cues that he is mocking ESL, the teacher does not at first appear to realize this (line 7). She does moments later (line 10), however, orienting not only to the sardonic frame (Goffman 1974) keyed by China and Raven, but to their distinction from the 'FOB' category that they have indexed through this mocking performance.

The second fragment I consider involves Bush, a low-L2-proficient ESL student, and Mack Daddy, a Local ESL student of advanced English expertise. Bush has just volunteered to read to the class a sentence he has written for the vocabulary word 'moment'. However, his teacher has trouble understanding Bush, which provides Mack Daddy with an occasion to use Mock ESL.

```
01. Bush:        ((reading)) a cruel murderer have used a few
02.              moment to kill four little girl and buried her
03. T:           huh? used a what type of moment?
04. Bush:        a few moment
                 (([ə fɛu mowmɛ]))
05.              (2.7)((T goes to Bush's desk, looks at his paper))
06. Mack Daddy:  ((low pitch, nasal monotone)) I don't speak no English
                                   (([aI don spik now i:ŋlɪʃ]))
07. T:           excuse me Mack?
08.              (1.7)
```

Bush's style shift to Mock ESL, similar to China's in the previous fragment, features syntactic 'error', and exaggerated, marked phonology indexical of 'foreign' English. Also similar is the convergence of propositional content with embodied performance to iconize both the category of low-L2-English-proficient ESL student, or FOB, and Bush, as its archetypal incumbent. In contrast, Mack Daddy's style shift points to his awareness that L2 'problems' such as Bush's are resources for a Mock ESL performance, and also his L2-English expertise and interactional competence, which are required to carry it out. Mack Daddy has, in other words, indexed his distinctiveness from Bush and from the FOB category to which Bush has been ascribed membership. The teacher orients to this display of distinction and the ordering of categories it indexes: the marked 'FOB' in the subordinate position, and Mack Daddy's unmarked Local ESL counterpart in the superior. Although the teacher's line 7 utterance is a repair initiation, it is contextualized as a condemnation. This – and the fact that Mack Daddy does not respond (line 8) – suggests their orientations both to the sanctionability of this Mock ESL performance and to the stigmatized status of ESL that it connotes.

The local ESL/FOB hierarchy and fractal recursivity

I conceptualized displays of distinction such as those in which Mock ESL was used as in part constituting a 'fractally recursive' (Irvine & Gal 2000) projection *within* the ESL program of the mainstream/ESL hierarchy outside it, with 'Local ESL' in the unmarked position (in place of 'mainstream'), and 'FOB' in the marked subordinate (in place of 'ESL'). Fractal recursivity, a semiotic process proposed by Irvine and Gal (2000), 'involves the projection of [a language ideological] opposition, salient at some level of relationship, onto some another level' (p. 38). That is, the status asymmetry between ESL and mainstream students that was evident in the wider Tradewinds context was projected inward and respecified in the ESL classroom in practices such as those involving Mock ESL. However, just as the Local ESL/FOB hierarchy can be considered a fractally recursive projection of the mainstream/ESL hierarchy, the mainstream/ESL hierarchy can itself be considered a fractally recursive projection of oppositions ('American/Foreigner') in far more 'macro' (i.e. US) terms, that is, of *national* identities and *nationalist* language ideologies (cf. Lippi-Green 2012) (see Figure 9.2). In this respect, Local ESL students' displays of distinction were central to the reproduction in everyday ESL classroom conduct of the language ideologies and linguicism concerning immigrants, bi- and multilingualism and assimilationism at Tradewinds, and more broadly, in the supralocal US context.

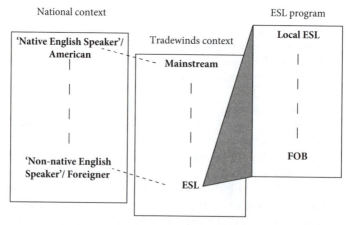

FIGURE 9.2 *Fractally recursive 'mainstream/ESL' and 'Local ESL/FOB' hierarchies*

Praxis

I should note that there was a critical pedagogical intervention concerning linguicism and the stigma of ESL that I was collaboratively planning with one of the teacher-participants from the first, piloting year of research. However, due to several reasons, including uncertainty surrounding a proposed 40 per cent budget reduction in ESL funding in Hawai'i, this teacher did not return to Tradewinds for the second year of the study. Although a much smaller-scale critical pedagogical 'unit' was planned instead, which connected ESL in the United States to the civil rights movement, and linguicism to other forms of discrimination, its implementation in the second year of the study was hastily planned, variably realized and, ultimately, unsuccessful. In this respect, praxis in the Tradewinds study primarily involved cultural critique, rather than some form of collaborative, pedagogically oriented direct action, with the study instead working 'to situate and understand local events in the context of broader structural relations of power, [in an effort] to direct such understanding toward more expansive efforts at structural change' (Levinson 2001, p. 363; cf. Foley & Valenzuela 2005; Lave 2011).

Conclusion

In this chapter, I have provided a brief discussion of empirical research in critical applied linguistics, focusing in particular on critical ethnography and critical discourse analysis. I have argued that using critical ethnography and critical discourse analysis complementarily can provide important benefits for the critical researcher: for example, critical ethnography allows critical discourse analyses to be more 'thickly described' (Geertz 1973) and deeply contextualized, and critical discourse analysis adds elements of rigour, analytic accountability and elaboration of ethnographic description to critical ethnography. I demonstrated these arguments in an overview of a study I conducted, using critical ethnography to sketch (altogether too briefly) the rationale for the study, aspects of its context and certain practices constituting the Local ESL community of practice, while using critical discourse analysis to explicate the communicative resources, interactional occasioning and implications of one of these practices: use of Mock ESL. Using critical discourse analysis helped to provide warrants for research claims; working in such data-near terms not only added an important dimension of demonstrability and accountability to my analysis, but it also wound up elaborating my arguments – brought them to life, as it were – in ways that a critical ethnographic thematic analysis would likely have precluded.

Notes

1 Utterances in Pidgin in this chapter are transcribed phonemically, accompanied by italicized English glosses.
2 Students selected their own pseudonyms.

Resources for further reading

Blommaert, J 2005, *Discourse: A Critical Introduction*, Cambridge University Press, Cambridge.

This introduction to critical discourse analysis introduces theoretical frameworks and attendant methodological options available for critical discourse analytic work that go beyond, for example, the approach proposed by Fairclough. Blommaert draws on several different traditions from sociolinguistics and linguistic anthropology to provide a rich theoretical rationale and extensive methodological toolkit for undertaking critical discourse analysis. He demonstrates the approach in several thematically arranged chapters that include engaging critical analyses of discourse.

Canagarajah, AS 1999, *Resisting Linguistic Imperialism in English Teaching*, Oxford University Press, Oxford.

This book-length critical ethnography, written by a leading scholar in critical applied linguistics, extends and elaborates his earlier (1993) study. The study is an important illustration of critical ethnography in applied linguistics and provides beginning scholars interested in conducting a critical ethnography with a helpful model for conceptualizing one.

Heller, M 2011, *Paths to Post-nationalism: A Critical Ethnography of Language and Identity*, Oxford University Press, Oxford.

This is a critical sociolinguistic ethnography of language ideologies concerning English and French in Canada. The book is comprised of 'a set of interlinked ethnographies' that Heller has undertaken in Francophone Canada over several decades, in addition to a helpful chapter that outlines her approach to theorizing critical ethnography and the methodology she employed.

Norton, B & Toohey, K (eds), 2004, *Critical Pedagogies and Language Learning*, Cambridge University Press, Cambridge.

This edited anthology is a comprehensive representation of the state of contemporary critical L2 pedagogical research, and thus, of a major area in critical applied linguistics. The studies are wide-ranging and diverse and are written by many well-known scholars. The book is theoretically engaging and includes several chapters that are methodologically oriented. The volume is particularly useful for students interested in gaining an understanding of the range of work represented in critical L2 pedagogy.

Pennycook, A 2001, *Critical Applied Linguistics: A Critical Introduction*, Lawrence Erlbaum, Mahwah, NJ.

This is an accessible introduction to critical applied linguistics, written by a leading scholar in the area. Pennycook discusses a wide range of topics in applied linguistics, critical social theories and critical applied linguistics and illuminates important complexities in these areas by contrasting different theoretical positions on them. The book, which is particularly helpful in its explication of theory, is also a model of critical reflexivity, subjecting its arguments to its own 'problematizing practice'.

Rojo, LM (ed.), 2010, *Constructing Inequality in Multilingual Classrooms*, Mouton de Gruyter, Berlin.

This is a comparative account of a major critical ethnographic research project undertaken by Rojo and several of her graduate students. The project, which involved longitudinal study of classrooms at four 'multicultural schools' in Madrid, Spain, sought to examine the consequences of increased immigration on schooling and pedagogical processes.

References

Ahearn, LM 2001, 'Language and agency', *Annual Review of Anthropology*, vol. 30, pp. 109–137.

Anderson, G 1989, 'Critical ethnography in education: Origins, current status, and new directions', *Review of Educational Research*, vol. 59, no. 3, pp. 249–270.

Benesch, S 2001, *Critical English for Academic Purposes: Theory, Politics, and Practice*, Lawrence Erlbaum, Mahwah, NJ.

Blommaert, J 2005, *Discourse: A Critical Introduction*, Cambridge University Press, Cambridge.

Bucholtz, M & Hall, K 2004, 'Language and identity', in A Duranti (ed.), *Companion to Linguistic Anthropology*, Blackwell, Malden, MA, pp. 369–394.

Canagarajah, AS 1993, 'Critical ethnography of a Sri Lankan classroom: Ambiguities in student opposition to reproduction through ESOL', *TESOL Quarterly*, vol. 27, no. 4, pp. 601–626.

Carspecken, F 1996, *Critical Ethnography in Educational Research: A Theoretical and Practical Guide*, Routledge, New York, NY.

Crookes, G & Lehner, A 1998, 'Aspects of process in an ESL critical pedagogy teacher education course', *TESOL Quarterly*, vol. 32, no. 2, pp. 319–328.

Ellsworth, E 1989, 'Why doesn't this feel empowering? Working through the repressive myths of critical pedagogy', *Harvard Educational Review*, vol. 59, no. 3, pp. 297–324.

Fairclough, N 2003, *Analysing Discourse: Textual Analysis for Social Research*, Routledge, London.

Foley, DE & Valenzuela, A 2005, 'Critical ethnography: The politics of collaboration', in NK Denzin and YS Lincoln (eds), *The Sage Handbook of Qualitative Research*, 3rd edn, Sage, Thousand Oaks, CA, pp. 217–234.

Geertz, C 1973, 'Thick description: toward an interpretive theory of culture', in C Geertz (ed.), *The Interpretation of Cultures: Selected Essays*, Basic Books, New York, NY, pp. 3–30.

Giddens, A 1979, *Central Problems in Social Theory: Action, Structure, and Contradiction in Social Analysis*, University of California Press, Berkeley, CA.

Goffman, E 1974, *Frame Analysis: An Essay on the Organization of Experience*, Harper & Row, New York, NY.

———— 1981, *Forms of Talk*, University of Pennsylvania Press, Philadelphia, PA.

Heller, M 2011, *Paths to Post-Nationalism: A Critical Ethnography of Language and Identity*, Oxford University Press, Oxford.

Hill, JH 1998, 'Language, race, and white public space', *American Anthropologist*, vol. 100, no. 3, pp. 680–689.

Irvine, JT & Gal, S 2000, 'Language ideology and linguistic differentiation', in PV Kroskrity (ed.), *Regimes of Language: Ideologies, Polities, and Identities*, School of American Research Press, Santa Fe, NM, pp. 35–83.

Kincheloe, JL & McLaren, P 2000, 'Rethinking critical theory and qualitative research', in NK Denzin & YS Lincoln (eds), *Handbook of Qualitative Research*, 2nd edn, Sage, Thousand Oaks, CA, pp. 279–313.

Lather, P 1986, 'Issues of validity in openly ideological research: Between a rock and a soft place', *Interchange*, vol. 17, no. 4, pp. 63–84.

Lave, J 1991, 'Situated learning in communities of practice', in LB Resnick, M Levine & SD Teasley (eds), *Perspectives on Socially Shared Cognition*, American Psychological Association, Washington, DC, pp. 63–82.

———— 2011, *Apprenticeship in Critical Ethnographic Practice*, University Of Chicago Press, Chicago, IL.

Levinson, BA 2001, *We Are All Equal: Student Culture and Identity at a Mexican Secondary School, 1988–1998*, Duke University Press, Durham, NC.

Lippi-Green, R 2012, *English with an Accent: Language, Ideology, and Discrimination in the United States*, 2nd edn, Routledge, London.

Masemann, VL 1982, 'Critical ethnography in the study of comparative education', *Comparative Education Review*, vol. 26, no. 1, pp. 1–15.

May, S 1997, 'Critical ethnography' in NH Hornberger & D Corson (eds), *Encyclopedia of Language and Education, Volume 8, Research Methods in Language and Education*, Kluwer Academic Publishers, Dordrecht, pp. 197–206.

McKay, SL & Wong, S-LC 1996, 'Multiple discourses, multiple identities: investment and agency in second-language learning among Chinese adolescent immigrant students', *Harvard Educational Review*, vol. 66, no. 3, pp. 577–608.

Mey, JL 2001, *Pragmatics: An Introduction*, Blackwell, Malden, MA.

Miller, G & Fox, KJ 2004, 'Building bridges: the possibility of analytic dialogue between ethnography, conversation analysis, and Foucault', in D Silverman (ed.), *Qualitative Research: Theory, Method, and Practice*, 2nd edn, Sage, London, pp. 35–55.

Morgan, B 1997, 'Identity and intonation: Linking dynamic processes in an ESL classroom', *TESOL Quarterly*, vol. 31, no. 3, pp. 431–450.

Motha, S 2006, 'Decolonizing ESOL: Negotiating linguistic power in US public school classrooms', *Critical Inquiry in Language Studies*, vol. 3, no. 2–3, pp. 75–100.

Norton, B 2013, *Identity and Language Learning: Extending the Conversation*, 2nd edn, Multilingual Matters, Bristol.

Pennycook, A 2001, *Critical Applied Linguistics: A Critical Introduction*, Lawrence Erlbaum, Mahwah, NJ.

——— 2003, 'Nostalgia for the real or refashioning futures: A response', *Discourse & Society*, vol. 14, no. 6, pp. 808–811.

——— 2008, 'Critical applied linguistics and language education', in S May and NH Hornberger (eds), *Encyclopedia of Language and Education: Volume 1, Language Policy and Political Issues in Education*, 2nd edn, Springer, Boston, MA, pp. 169–191.

Pérez-Milans, M 2011, 'Being a Chinese newcomer in Madrid compulsory education: Ideological constructions in language education practice', *Journal of Pragmatics*, vol. 43, no. 4, pp. 1005–1022.

Phillipson, R 1988, 'Linguicism: structures and ideologies in linguistic imperialism', in T Skutnabb-Kangas & J Cummins (eds), *Minority Education: From Shame to Struggle*, Multilingual Matters, Philadelphia, PA, pp. 339–358.

Quantz, RA 1992, 'On critical ethnography (with some postmodern considerations)', in MD LeCompte, WL Millroy & J Preissle (eds), *The Handbook of Qualitative Research in Education*, Academic Press, San Diego, CA, pp. 447–505.

Rojo, LM (ed.), 2010, *Constructing Inequality in Multilingual Classrooms*, Mouton de Gruyter, Berlin.

Simon, R & Dippo, D (1986), 'On critical ethnographic work', *Anthropology and Education Quarterly*, vol. 17, no. 4, pp. 195–202.

Slembrouck, S 2001, 'Explanation, interpretation and critique in the analysis of discourse', *Critique of Anthropology*, vol. 21, no. 1, pp. 33–57.

Talmy, S 2008, 'The cultural productions of the ESL student at Tradewinds High: Contingency, multidirectionality, and identity in L2 socialization', *Applied Linguistics*, vol. 29, no. 4, pp. 619–644.

——— 2009, 'Forever FOB?: Resisting and reproducing the Other in high school ESL', in A Reyes and A Lo (eds), *Beyond Yellow English: Toward a Linguistic Anthropology of Asian Pacific America*, Oxford University Press, New York, NY, pp. 347–365.

——— 2010, 'Resisting ESL: Categories and sequence in a critically 'motivated' analysis of classroom interaction', in H Nguyen and G Kasper (eds), *Talk-in-interaction: Multilingual Perspectives*, University of Hawai'i, National Foreign Language Resource Center, Honolulu, HI, pp. 181–213.

Thomas, J 1993, *Doing Critical Ethnography*, Sage, Newbury Park, CA.

Van Dijk, T 2001, 'Critical discourse analysis', in D Schiffrin, D Tannen & HE Hamilton (eds), *The Handbook of Discourse Analysis*, Blackwell, Oxford, pp. 352–371.

——— 2013, *CDA is NOT a method of critical discourse analysis*, Association for the Study on Discourse and Society, http://www.edisoportal.org/debate/115-cda-not-method-critical-discourse-analysis, viewed 13 March 2013.

Verschueren, J 2001, 'Predicaments of criticism', *Critique of Anthropology*, vol. 21, no. 1, pp. 59–80.

Widdicombe, S 1995, 'Identity, politics and talk: a case for the mundane and the everyday', in S Wilkinson & C Kitzinger (eds), *Feminism and Discourse, Psychological Perspectives*, Sage, London, pp. 106–127.

Wilkinson, S & Kitzinger, C 2008, 'Using conversation analysis in feminist and critical research', *Social and Personality Psychology Compass*, vol. 2, no. 2, pp. 555–573.

Appendix: Transcription conventions

–   abrupt sound stop
[overlapping talk
()   undecipherable/questionable transcription
(())   physical movement, characterizations of talk, coughing, etc.
(1.3)   pauses timed to tenths of a second

CHAPTER TEN

Narrative Inquiry

Gary Barkhuizen

Narrative inquiry is a way of doing research that focuses on the stories we tell about our lives. These stories are about our *experiences* of life – the meaning we make of the events we live or imagine in our future lives. Kramp (2004, p. 107) says that stories 'assist humans to make life experiences meaningful. Stories preserve our memories, prompt our reflections, connect us to our past and present, and assist us to envision our future'. In other words, stories are not merely a list of facts about the things we do, the people we do them with and where and when we do them, they also embody our understandings of those events as well as express our feelings about them. Read the following extract which comes from a larger written narrative – a teacher journal entry in which the teacher reflects on an encounter with a male colleague – and you will notice that she is not only writing about what happened but also about her emotional response to those events.

Extract 1

…Later that afternoon, I was in the photocopy room at work. I tried desperately to focus on my lesson preparation because I did not want my work performance to decline in any way due to sexist language. At some point, UB came into the room. He decided to make small-talk with me and asked me what I did over the weekend. I said that I went to the video shop and borrowed DVDs, but felt angry with the guy at the video shop because he called me 'love', as in 'Yes, love?' when I approached the desk to borrow DVDs. UB's response to me was a bewildered, 'Why?? I call my wife and daughter, love.' At this point, I felt very disgusted…

Experiences become narratives when we tell them to an audience and the narratives become part of narrative inquiry when they are investigated for research purposes. In this chapter, I begin by suggesting why narrative inquiry has recently gained legitimacy in applied linguistics and become more widely used, particularly in language teaching and learning research. I then outline some of the methodological options that have become available to narrative researchers in the field. I also give examples of various types of narrative data they have worked with. After a consideration of some of the ethical issues typically faced by narrative inquirers, I end with a sample narrative study which illustrates a number of the methods, assumptions and tensions discussed earlier in the chapter.

Underlying assumptions and methodology

A *narrative turn* in recent years has meant that in applied linguistics, researchers have begun to understand the importance of paying attention to how language teachers and learners use stories to make sense of their experience. Researchers learn about these experiences from the participants' own perspectives. Barkhuizen, Benson and Chik (2014), more specifically, suggest four explanations for this narrative turn. First, narrative inquiry has an intuitive appeal to researchers who have 'become weary of variables and the quantification of the positivistic approach' (Josselson 1993, p. xv). It is thus part of a broader turn towards qualitative research and away from the assumption that psychological, social and educational phenomena should be investigated in much the same way that scientists investigate natural phenomena. Second, interest in narratives reflects postmodern concerns with the self, identity and individuality, signalling a turn away from the quest for general social theories that would enable social scientists to predict human behaviour. Third, a related explanation is the importance that narrative has acquired as a resource that individuals draw upon in the construction of social identities. The stories they tell help researchers understand the ways in which they situate themselves and their activities in the world. Lastly, we point out that an interest in narrative has been linked to a turn towards the idea that research should both involve and empower the people whose experiences are the subject of research. Narrative inquiry expands the range of voices that are heard in research reports, often highlighting the experiences of marginalized groups (Hayes 2013). In the sections that follow, I outline some of the key assumptions and methodological issues associated with narrative inquiry.

Narrative epistemology

A *narrative epistemology* refers to the belief that we know about the world narratively. Bruner (1986, p. 116) refers to this way of knowing as narrative cognition: people make sense of the world by organizing experience temporally, seeking explications 'that are context sensitive and particular'. To put it simply, in order to understand their experiences, people construct stories out of them by synthesizing them into a unified whole. It would follow, then, that narrative researchers would want access to these stories, and in their endeavour to construct and analyse them for research purposes, a narrative epistemology would inform their 'philosophical approach to research, its theoretical underpinnings and its methodological procedures' (Barkhuizen 2013, p. 7). Narrative, therefore, as De Fina and Georgakopoulou (2012, p. 19) point out:

> becomes much more than a set of techniques and tools for collecting and analyzing data. It becomes a particular way of constructing knowledge requiring a particular commitment and even a bias from the researcher in addition to a political stance.

Narrative methods

The methods used by narrative researchers to collect and analyse data reflect the narrative epistemology to which they are oriented. Many of the methods are those typical of other forms of qualitative research, such as oral interviews, written diaries and online blogs. But what makes them *narrative* is their commitment to the meaning made by research participants of their lived experiences in particular spatiotemporal contexts. Data collection generates stories of experience; methods of analysis treat data as contextualized meaning making; and reporting of findings is handled with narrative awareness and ethical sensitivity. In the sections that follow, various forms of narrative data and approaches to data collection, analysis and reporting will be described.

Content

The *content* of narratives refers to *what* narratives are about, what was told and why, when, where and by whom. Research with aims of learning about the content of the experiences of the participants and their reflections on these focuses on the autobiographical 'big stories' of our lives, that 'entail a significant measure of reflection on either an event or an experience, a significant portion of a life, or the whole of it' (Freeman 2006, p. 131). Connelly and Clandinin (2006, p. 477) refer to narrative inquiry as 'the study of experience as story' and encourage inquirers to explore content in terms of three dimensions or commonplaces, relating to temporality (the times – past, present and future – in which experiences unfold), place (the place or sequence of places in which experiences are lived) and sociality (personal emotions and desires and interactions between people). A content or thematic analysis is typically conducted to examine systematically the content of narrative data (Barkhuizen, Benson & Chik 2014).

Narrative form

Narrative form refers to the way stories are constructed: the organization of ideas, the sequences of events, choice of words and textual coherence. William Labov's well-known early work in sociolinguistics (Labov 1972; Labov & Waletzky 1967) examined the spontaneous narratives we tell in everyday interactions. He identified basic elements or clauses that made up these narratives: abstract, orientation, complicating action, evaluation, resolution and coda. More recently, *small story* analysis has emerged as another kind of narrative analysis that pays very close attention to the form of narrative data. Small stories are snippets of often mundane talk in conversations (and sometimes in interviews) which tell of past, imagined or hypothetical events as opposed to 'big' narratives like life histories and those compiled from multiple interviews and other ethnographic data collected over an extended period of time (Bamberg & Georgakopoulou 2008). Close analysis of the text, similar to line-by-line conversation analysis (Wong & Waring 2010), examines turns at talk and other fine details of discourse, usually with the aim of discovering how the narrator's identity is co-constructed through talk-in-interaction with other participants in the conversation or interview. The following is a good example of a small story. It is an extract of an interview with a student teacher at a university in New Zealand. She is talking about a family member who is a migrant from Tonga also living in New Zealand and does not wish to take up ESL lessons because of her family responsibilities.

Extract 2

S (student teacher): Not interested in getting a whole lot more money, she's pretty much satisfied with just being at home, looking after the kids, not really interested, you know, when I asked her she said 'it's crossing my mind now but, no, I'm happy just staying home looking after the kids, making sure that they have their lunches, they go to school, they come back, there's someone at home, there's food there, 'cause if I go out and work or go and do a course, I'll have to send them off to other people to look after', and she doesn't quite trust that.

G (Gary): Ok, I see.

S: So her investment is more in motherhood, and she's quite happy with that.

G: And not really seeing going to some ESOL course as an alternative, yea, that makes sense.

S: And she doesn't mix on any sort of level with any other people, I mean, she just basically stays home with her kids. She goes out of the house in order to go shopping or go to church, so there's no other ethnic, people of different ethnicities that she really mixes with, so she doesn't feel it's really an essential part of her life to learn English.

Riessman (2008) suggests that combining both content and structural analyses enhances the quality of the analysis, generating insights beyond what a content analysis alone would achieve. Of course, any attempt at analysing the content of narratives must inevitably encounter and make sense of some narrative form along the way, even if it is just the way particular vocabulary items are used. However, the extent to which this happens can differ substantially from one study to the next.

Context

Riessman (2008, p. 105) says, 'Stories don't fall from the sky ... ; they are composed and received in contexts – interactional, historical, institutional, and discursive – to name a few.' This is an important message for narrative inquirers: context is important in the study of narrative. What is meant by *context*, however, differs considerably in different types of narrative research, and it is taken into account more or less by different narrative researchers. For those interested in examining the details of narrative form or text, the context of the talk-in-interaction (i.e. linguistic context) is their primary concern. At this level they focus on how the narrative unfolds in sequences of turns at talk. Who is talking, and when and what their roles are (including possibly that of researcher) at each moment of talk are examined in detail.

Another layer of context to which researchers pay attention is the local context of the narrative telling – for example, the physical setting, language choice, other present people, the purpose of talk and the conditions of interaction (e.g. time constraints, permission to talk). Some of these contexts can be more local than others, however. Barkhuizen (2008), when reporting on a study he conducted with two teachers participating in a graduate language teacher education course, suggested three interconnected levels of story (or contextual spaces) which not only help guide analysis but also encourage the researcher to look beyond the immediate contexts of the teacher and her classroom. The first level of story (all small letters) is personal and embodies the inner thoughts, emotions, ideas and theories of the teachers. It includes the social interactions in the teachers' immediate contexts, for example, during classroom lessons, during conversations with students and in teacher journals. The second level of Story (with a capital S) spreads wider than the immediate psychological and inter-personal context of teachers. Included here are consequences of decisions made typically by others in the work environment, as well as their attitudes, expectations and prescriptions – for example, a school's language-in-education policy and assessment practices. At this level of Story, teachers usually have less power to construct their practice and consequently their stories. Lastly, STORY (in capital letters) refers to the broader sociopolitical contexts in which teaching and learning takes place. Here, teachers have even less power to make decisions about conditions which influence their practice. Examples of STORIES include national language policies and curriculums imposed on schools by Ministries of Education. The use of capital letters to refer to this level of STORY merely signifies a wider, macro context and the power often associated with it. In no way does it diminish the worth of any individual teacher's story. Pavlenko (2007, pp. 176–177) recommends that narrative researchers should take into account the broader historical, political, social and economic contexts that both shape narratives and are reflected in them. They must also consider:

> language ideologies and discourses that have currency in narrators' communities and with regard to which they position themselves, and, last but not least, the setting where particular versions of narrative experience are produced and the audience they are produced for.

Narrative co-construction

Narrative data is always treated as co-constructed. In other words, stories are told to someone; they have an audience. During the process of data construction, the audience may or may not consist of the researcher and may even be the narrator, as is the case with autobiographical research. However, the extent of co-construction does vary depending on the nature of the data, the purpose for which it was gathered and the context in which it was collected. Ochs and Capps (2001) have placed narratives along a tellership continuum, with the extent and kind of involvement of those participating in their construction determining where on the continuum they lie. Towards one end of the continuum are those narratives which involve a high level of discursive collaboration. Here stories are told *with* another. These narratives are typically face-to-face or Skype conversations or unstructured life history interviews and are co-constructed through collaborative, negotiated performance (see also Extract 2 on page 172). Towards the other end of the tellership continuum are narratives told *to* others. The telling of stories becomes more of an individual activity with little or even no participation on the part of the audience. Long turns at interview talk in which experiences of past and imagined events are narrated are one example, and others are online language learning histories and written teacher journals which may be read later by a researcher or teacher educator as part of a professional development program (see also Extract on page 169).

Categorization and re-storying

Polkinghorne's (1995) distinction between *analysis of narratives* and *narrative analysis* is useful for conceptualizing two broad approaches to analysing and reporting narrative data. His two approaches correspond to the two ways of knowing (i.e. two kinds of cognition or ways of organizing experience) described by Bruner (1986), one of which has already been referred to above. According to Bruner's paradigmatic cognition, sense is made of the world by looking for similarities among things and then grouping them as members of the same category. Analyses of narrative content (Polkinghorne's *analysis of narratives*) follow the procedures of coding for themes, categorizing these and looking for patterns of association among them – what is called a content or thematic analysis. Bruner's second way of knowing, narrative cognition, organizes experience temporally, seeking meanings about phenomena within their particular contexts. Instead of pulling experiences apart, then, narrative thinking synthesizes them into a unified whole. What Polkinghorne's *narrative analysis* does is configure or re-story the various themes from the data into a coherent whole, that is, the outcome is a story. The distinction between these two broad analytical approaches is somewhat fuzzy, however. There is obviously some similarity in the analytical methods used and also in the later reporting of the findings (i.e. a coherent story or a discussion of separate, extracted themes). Some published research articles, for example, quote short extracts of data (often representing themes) and discuss these sometimes quite independently in their findings sections, whereas in others the entire findings section, if not most of the article, is presented as a coherent story of experience. The sample study included below (Giroir 2014) is an example of the latter (as is Casanave 2012).

Narrative as equitable

A number of researchers have emphasized the empowering, transformative nature of narrative inquiry and work within theoretical and methodological traditions that enable language learners, teachers and indeed themselves as researchers to (bring about) change. Hayes (2013), for instance, believes that narrative research has the potential to challenge the interests of more powerful academics and institutions in language education 'by foregrounding the voices of those who are traditionally seen as the objects of the research process' (p. 63). Enabling the sharing of their stories with others in different contexts may encourage those to reflect on and possibly change their practices. Several scholars have made the same point, including Nelson (2011) who suggests incorporating crafted narratives of classroom life (e.g. interview and observation data scripted into plays) into the applied linguistics research field, saying doing so may 'help to ameliorate the excluding effects of elitist scholarly discourse' (p. 470). What makes narrative inquiry potentially transformative, then, is its positioning of participants as equal contributors to the research process. It is *their* stories that are (co)constructed and shared and when listened to and reflected upon, either by themselves or others, bring about change. And this process, of course, includes researchers, who are intimately involved in all aspects of the study, from selecting the participants, co-constructing narrative data, analysing the data and then producing the research report. Yet, as Canagarajah (1996) says, they are often conspicuously absent from these reports, 'looming behind the text as an omniscient, transcendental, all knowing figure' (p. 324). Including a discussion of the researcher's positionality (or identity, see Norton & Early 2011) in the research report adds to the transparency and trustworthiness of the research process and shows how the researcher influenced the process along the way. It is also useful for others wishing to embark on their own narrative inquiry projects in the future.

Trustworthiness

Narrative inquiry is often accused of being 'soft' from a validity point of view because it deals with stories. I often hear: 'But what if participants don't tell you the truth?' My immediate answer is that the same could be asked of *any* type of research: responses to a survey questionnaire or structured interview or checks on a grammaticality judgement test could also elicit non-truths. But what is meant by *truth* here is important. One meaning is that participants are being deceptive – that is, they are lying. Well, as researchers we always hope that that is not the case. A second meaning relates to truth (what is told by participants) in the sense that it mirrors experience (what actually happened in reality). This is unlikely, and not only with narrative research, since as Polkinghorne (2007) points out, there are a number of constraints which make this compatibility impossible, including the limitations inherent in language when telling stories, the fact that stories are co-constructed with others and that narrators may not want to tell or be able to remember all details of the actual experience. Instead, narrative inquiry 'makes claims about the meaning life events hold for people. It makes claims about how people understand situations, others and themselves' (Polkinghorne 2007, p. 476). Narrative researchers do not aim to discover whether participants' stories are accurate reflections of their actual experiences (as I have just said, they cannot anyway) but to understand the meaning people attach to those experiences. In research on language teaching and learning, narrative inquiry can help us understand the particular, contextualized knowledge of those intimately involved in teaching and learning; in other words, the meaning they make of their practices in the particular contexts in which they experience their lives. To do this, our methods of data collection and analysis must necessarily be rigorous. As Riessman (2008) reminds us, researchers must present careful evidence for their claims from the narrative data they examine. The following section presents some examples of how this is done.

Techniques and instruments

The methods used to generate data in narrative inquiry are as varied as methods in qualitative research more generally, and many of them are very similar. However, the goal of methods in narrative inquiry is always to find stories of experience. As we have seen so far, these stories may be more or less co-constructed, they may be big or small and the focus of analysis may be on their form or their content, but what we want them to do ultimately is to tell us about the lived experiences of the narrators, from their perspective. In this section, I have listed in Table 10.1 some of the methods that have been used in narrative inquiry. For each type of method, I provide a brief description of some of that method's characteristics as well as a useful reference for further information and examples. Some of the key methods listed here are described in Barkhuizen, Benson and Chik (2014).

Table 10.1 Examples of data and methods used in narrative inquiry

Type	Characteristics	Study
Learner or teacher diaries	Autobiographical, introspective, written series of entries, typically longitudinal, reflective. Records learning or teaching in process. Could be about general topics, though may have a specific focus (e.g. learning strategies).	Casanave (2012)
Language learning histories	Retrospective written accounts of past learning. More recently online using Web.2 technologies. Often incorporated into lessons as classwork and used for research purposes.	Murphey, Chen and Chen (2005)
Narrative interviews	Typical semi- or un-structured. Narrators invited to 'Tell me about…' experiences related to research topic to elicit stories rather than target facts or specific research questions.	Chase (2003)
Teacher journals	Written reflections on teaching practice as well as broader school experiences. Often for professional development purposes. Analysed by teachers, researchers or both collaboratively.	Johnson and Golombek (2011)

(*continued*)

Type	Characteristics	Study
Narrative frames	Written story template consisting of a series of incomplete sentences and blank spaces of varying lengths. Structured as a story in skeletal form. Aim is to produce a coherent story by filling in the spaces according to writers' experiences and reflections on these.	Barkhuizen (2014)
Playscripts	Scripts for a play to be workshopped and performed. Constructed from data such as focus group discussions, interviews, classroom observations.	Nelson (2013)
Drawings	Drawings by language learners and teachers to represent their identities as learners and teachers. Self-portraits, often including others or objects in the same space, symbolizing particular meanings, identities or practices. Can be accompanied by other media, such as links to audio files, blogs, social media accounts.	Kalaja, Dufva and Alanen (2013)
Small stories	Snippets of talk-in-interaction, embedded in conversations and interviews. Analysed discursively, more or less taking into account local and broader context of construction and other ethnographic data, if available.	Bamberg and Georgakopoulou (2008)
Autoethnographies	A method that represents the perspective of the self. A focus on how culture shapes and is shaped by the personal. An emphasis on the creative resources of writing, especially narrative.	Canagarajah (2012)
Facebook stories	Use of Web.2 technologies. Mutual sharing of language learning histories, followed by commenting and collaborative narrative creation. Including use of photos and video/music links.	Chik and Breidbach (2011)

Ethical considerations

Like with all types of research, as other chapters in this volume point out, participants should be fully informed about the nature and purpose of a research project before they get involved. There are some aspects of narrative inquiry, however, which make this requirement even more significant. First, when we tell stories, spoken or written, we do so with an audience in mind. There are things we tell some people but not others. So, when participants are asked to write journals or language learning histories or tell stories in interviews, they should be informed in advance who the audience will be (e.g. their instructor (who may be the researcher)), an independent researcher, conference attendees or readers of published academic reports. Stories look different when produced for different audiences. Researchers should know this if they want to gather appropriate stories to meet their research purposes. But it is only fair to the participants that they too construct appropriate stories. Being fully informed of the research topic, purpose and processes will enable them to do so. Second, when working with language learners, it is sometimes the case that the narratives they construct for research purposes are also part of their classwork or assessment; that is, they have a dual purpose. If this is so, learners will need not only to be informed of this beforehand but also to be reminded throughout the project that their work will be used as data because they might get so caught up in the process of completing an assessment or a course requirement that they forget for the time being that what they are doing will later be used for research. Third, participants are encouraged by researchers to share personal details of their experiences, and they often do, especially when they get emotionally caught up in the topic and telling of their stories. Researchers need to tread very carefully when deciding how to manage the data, particularly with regard to representing the findings to another audience. One way to avoid ethical issues arising is to provide the draft report of the findings to participants for scrutiny once their data have been analysed. Another way is to use pseudonyms for participants (and places) so as to keep their identity anonymous. With narrative research, where studies may include only one or two participants, this can prove to be rather challenging, especially when some of the more personal aspects of the data are those that are more likely to give the identity of the participants away! In these cases, member checking or asking participants to scrutinize research reports for their approval before they are distributed to a wider audience is a good idea.

A sample study

In this section, I summarize a study which illustrates some of the typical characteristics of narrative inquiry. The study (Giroir 2014) is conceived as narrative, as is evident in the report, from the title through to the concluding statements. It addresses issues to do with participation, identity and positionality of two Saudi Arabian learners of English in the United States.

Background context and aim

The two cases reported in this study were part of a larger project which asked: 'How do L2 learners negotiate the periphery in order to achieve fuller participation in L2 communities?' (p. 40). Giroir, like others who are interested in how L2 learners form identities as they move from peripheral to full participation in social worlds, drew on Wenger's (1998) *communities of practice* framework. The two Saudi learners (males, aged 18 and 26) were particularly interesting to Giroir because they were Muslims of Arab descent. Her aim was to examine how, in the context of post-9/11 discourses, they were able to (re)negotiate their peripherality through their interactions in new, often racialized, L2 communities. Both participants were living and studying in the United States on scholarships from the Saudi government and at the time of the research were enrolled in ESL classes in an intensive English program at a large university.

Data collection

Data were collected over a full semester, during which time Giroir was a regular participant-observer in the students' classroom. She assisted the teacher at times and also interacted with students during class discussions. Although she was interested in the students' out-of-classroom community experiences, her involvement as an observer in the classroom gave her access to their 'narratives of experience' (p. 41), since the students were frequently offered opportunities to draw on personal experiences when interacting with each other to work on assigned course topics. Giroir was not granted permission to record class sessions but she kept detailed notes during observations. In addition to the observations, she conducted interviews of between one and two hours with each participant – these were digitally recorded and transcribed. Lastly, she observed, recorded and then transcribed a rather interesting photo narrative activity which involved the students using photography to document their experiences. They then, in class, gave a formal presentation in which they 'visually arranged and discussed photographs that represented their goals, inner thoughts, and views of themselves over time' (p. 41). Giroir held post-presentation interviews with the two students. In this exercise the participants constructed their own personal narratives from both visual artefacts (Riessman, 2008) and an accompanying oral commentary for the classroom audience, including the researcher. The presentation together with the following interview during which the researcher and student further explored relevant themes proved to be a very effective data gathering opportunity.

Data analysis

Giroir declares that her data were 'primarily narrative' (p. 41) and hence applying an analytical framework informed by narrative inquiry was most appropriate. In the description of her data analysis, she uses a number of key words, and I will briefly comment on some of these. The first is her position as a *co-constructor* of the participants' stories; they were mutually involved in 'meaning making, learning, and knowledge construction' about the participants' L2 community negotiations, what Barkhuizen (2011, p. 395) refers to as 'narrative knowledging'. In other words, sense was made of the phenomenon under study (the research topic) by the participants during their research activities, by the researcher during her research activities and by them all during the research activities they engaged in together. Specifically, narrative knowledging was achieved by the *interactional* nature of the stories told by the two students during the particular telling *contexts* of classroom activities with other students, their teacher and the researcher and also during the interviews. Across the full data set, Giroir identified broad categories of experience and then conducted a more detailed *thematic analysis* by coding for themes and *triangulating* across data sources. Giroir, in sum, approached the data as *discursive artefacts*. But this was not the end of the analytical process. In the report of her study, Girior presents two cohesive stories of the participants' experiences – she actually tells their stories in two separate sections in the written article reporting the study. The process of writing these stories, a process which Grior calls 'writing the findings', involved another layer of analysis: 'connecting and emplotting salient themes' (p. 42). This is the same analytical process I referred to above, described by Polkinghorne (1995) as *narrative analysis*. Benson (2013, p. 251) calls it narrative writing as method and argues:

> In my view, the findings of 'narrative analysis' studies are usually to be found in the narrative itself. We are more accustomed, perhaps, to expect findings to take the form of short statements that address research questions.

In Grior's article, she presents the two coherent stories as well as extensive discussion of them. In other words, she does not merely let the stories talk for themselves but adds a further layer of interpretation. As a final analytical step, member checking took place with one of the participants (that is, he read and commented on the written findings). This is particularly important with narrative research, where data and the interpretation thereof is typically very personal, may contain sensitive details and thus have ethical implications.

Reporting

I have already commented on one narrative feature of Giroir's report – the inclusion of two coherent and comprehensive stories of the two participants' experiences. The remainder of the article is fairly conventional, with sections covering the theoretical background, the context relevant to the topic and the methodology. It does include one further section worthy of mention, however. In this section, the researcher and author of the article positions herself within the study. She informs readers about aspects of her own identity that are relevant to the study, including those that might pose potential limitations on the collection of data and her interpretation of the data. For example, she describes her 'meaning-laden social identities' (p. 42) as a female native speaker of English who is a member of the mainstream target L2 community that is the focus of her study. She is also American, a woman and an outsider to the classroom community (she adds that she is of Lebanese descent and so shares physical features of the participants' ethnic group). She does not say much about these limitations except to point out that they undoubtedly shaped her interactions with the students and her interpretations of their experiences. However, she believes that these limitations were overcome by specific research strategies such as data triangulation, prolonged field engagement, member checks and peer debriefing, thus enhancing credibility and trustworthiness.

Implications

After a discussion in which Giroir examines how the two students negotiated their positionality and identities vis-à-vis the racialized and politicized L2 community in which they lived and studied, showing particularly how they engaged in discursive practices in order to achieve fuller participation in those L2 worlds, she presents implications for TESOL professionals inside classrooms. Her main suggestion is for teachers to adopt critical perspectives on pedagogy, which include making space in classroom discourse for learners to narrate, discuss and analyse authentic L2 experiences – in other words, to deconstruct these experiences to expose the power relations at play in interactions outside the classroom. Grior believes that narratives can do this because they 'mediate social practices that allow learners space to interpret conflicts and define their identities' (p. 54).

Resources for further reading

Barkhuizen, G (ed.), 2011b, 'Special-topic issue on *Narrative research in TESOL*', *TESOL Quarterly*, vol. 45, no. 3.

The introductory article in this special issue of *TESOL Quarterly* introduces the construct of narrative knowledging and locates narrative research in the field of TESOL. The following articles, both full-length and reflective pieces, illustrate narrative research in its various forms. Besides demonstrating research in practice, the articles focus on *issues* in narrative research in TESOL.

Barkhuizen, G (ed.), 2013b, *Narrative Research in Applied Linguistics*, Cambridge University Press, Cambridge.

This edited collection provides an overview of narrative research approaches and demonstrates how they work in actual studies conducted in varying contexts. Researchers pay particular attention to their methods of data collection and analysis. They frame their studies in narrative theory, briefly commenting on how this theory is relevant to their approach to narrative research. Each chapter includes a personal reflection by the researcher on their methods.

Barkhuizen, G, Benson, P & Chik, A 2014, *Narrative Inquiry in Language Teaching and Learning Research*. Routledge, New York, NY.

This book provides an accessible introduction to narrative inquiry. It discusses basic definitions and concepts; explains how and why narrative methods have been used in language teaching and learning research; and outlines the different approaches and topics covered by this research.

De Fina, A & Georgakopoulou, A 2012, *Analyzing Narrative: Discourse and Sociolinguistic Perspectives*, Cambridge University Press, Cambridge.

This book will be of interest to those wanting to learn more about sociolinguistic perspectives on narrative, including definitions and methods of analysis. The focus is very much on the discursive construction of narrative data with reference to particular ethnographic contexts.

Pavlenko, A 2007, Autobiographic narratives as data in applied linguistics. *Applied Linguistics*, vol. 28, no. 2, pp. 163–188.

This article offers a critical review of methods of analysing second language users' personal narratives. Strengths and weaknesses of these approaches are discussed and recommendations for systematic approaches are recommended. Although the focus is on second language users, the article is relevant and important for those working in applied linguistics more generally.

Riessman, CK 2008, *Narrative Methods for the Human Sciences*, Sage, Los Angeles, CA.

Although not specifically targeted for applied linguists, this book provides an excellent introduction to narrative methods in the human sciences, particularly sociology. The chapters are very readable with good examples. Major methods of analysis are covered, including thematic, structural and dialogic/performance.

References

Bamberg, M & Georgakopoulou, A 2008, 'Small stories as a new perspective in narrative and identity analysis', *Text & Talk*, vol. 28, no. 3, pp. 377–396.

Barkhuizen, G 2008, 'A narrative approach to exploring context in language teaching', *English Language Teaching Journal*, vol. 62, no. 3, pp. 231–239.

—— 2011, 'Narrative knowledging in TESOL', *TESOL Quarterly*, vol. 45, no. 3, pp. 391–414.

—— 2013, 'Introduction: Narrative research in applied linguistics', in G Barkhuizen (ed.), *Narrative Research in Applied Linguistics*, Cambridge University Press, Cambridge, pp. 1–16.

—— 2014, 'Revisiting narrative frames: An instrument for investigating language teaching and learning', *System*, vol. 47, pp. 12–27.

Barkhuizen, G, Benson, P & Chik, A 2014, *Narrative Inquiry in Language Teaching and Learning Research*. Routledge, New York, NY.

Benson, P 2013, 'Narrative writing as method: Second language identity development in study abroad', in G Barkhuizen (ed.), *Narrative Research in Applied Linguistics*, Cambridge University Press, Cambridge, pp. 244–263.

Bruner, J 1986, *Actual Minds, Possible Worlds*, Harvard University Press, Cambridge, MA.

—— 2012, *Analyzing Narrative: Discourse and Sociolinguistic Perspectives*, Cambridge University Press, Cambridge.

Canagarajah, AS 1996, 'From critical research practice to critical research reporting', *TESOL Quarterly*, vol. 30, no. 2, pp. 321–331.

—— 2012, 'Teacher development in a global profession: An autoethnography', *TESOL Quarterly*, vol. 46, no. 2, pp. 258–279.

Casanave, CP 2012, 'Diary of a dabbler: Ecological influences on an EFL teacher's efforts to study Japanese informally', *TESOL Quarterly*, vol. 46, no. 4, pp. 642–670.

Chase, SE 2003, 'Taking narrative seriously: Consequences for method and theory in interview studies', in YS Lincoln & NK Denzin (eds), *Turning Points in Qualitative Research: Tying Knots in a Handkerchief*, Altamira Press, Walnut Creek, CA, pp. 273–296.

Chik, A & Breidbach, S 2011, 'Online language learning histories exchange: Hong Kong and German perspectives', *TESOL Quarterly*, vol. 45, no. 3, pp. 553–564.

Connelly, FM & Clandinin, DJ 2006, 'Narrative inquiry', in JL Green, G Camilli & PB Elmore (eds), *Complementary Methods for Research in Education*, Lawrence Erlbaum, Mahwah, NJ, pp. 477–487.

Freeman, M 2006, 'Life 'on holiday'? In defense of big stories', *Narrative Inquiry*, vol. 16, no. 1, pp. 131–138.

Giroir, S 2014, 'Narratives of participation, identity, and positionality: Two cases of Saudi learners of English in the United States', *TESOL Quarterly*, vol. 48, no. 1, pp. 34–56.

Hayes, D 2013, 'Narratives of experience: Teaching English in Sri Lanka and Thailand', in G Barkhuizen (ed.), *Narrative Research in Applied Linguistics*, Cambridge University Press, Cambridge, pp. 62–82.

Johnson, KE & Golombek, PR 2011, 'The transformative power of narrative in second language teacher education', *TESOL Quarterly*, vol. 45, no. 3, pp. 486–509.

Josselson, R 1993, 'A narrative introduction', in R Josselson & A Lieblich (eds), *The Narrative Study of Lives*, Sage, Thousand Oaks, CA, pp. ix–xv.

Kalaja, P, Dufva, H & Alanen, R 2013, 'Experimenting with visual narratives', in G Barkhuizen (ed.), *Narrative Research in Applied Linguistics*, Cambridge University Press, Cambridge, pp. 105–131.

Kramp, MK 2004, 'Exploring life and experience through narrative inquiry', in K deMarrais & SD Lapan (eds), *Foundations for Research: Methods of Inquiry in Education and the Social Sciences*, Erlbaum, Mahwah, NJ, pp. 103–121.

Labov, W 1972, *Language in the Inner City: Studies in the Black Vernacular*. University of Pennsylvania Press, Philadelphia, PA.

Labov, W & Waletzky, J 1967, 'Narrative analysis: Oral versions of personal experience', in J Helm (ed.), *Essays on the Verbal and Visual Arts*, University of Washington Press, Seattle, WA, pp. 12–44.

Murphey, T, Chen, J & Chen, L-C 2005, 'Learner's constructions of identities and imagined communities', in P Benson & D Nunan (eds), *Learners' Stories: Difference and Diversity in Language Learning*, Cambridge University Press, Cambridge, pp. 83–100.

Nelson, CD 2011, 'Narratives of classroom life: Changing conceptions of knowledge', *TESOL Quarterly*, vol. 45, no. 3, pp. 463–485.

———— 2013, 'From transcript to playscript: Dramatising narrative research', in G Barkhuizen (ed.), *Narrative Research in Applied Linguistics*, Cambridge University Press, Cambridge, pp. 220–243.

Norton, B & Early, M 2011, 'Researcher identity, narrative inquiry, and language teaching research', *TESOL Quarterly*, vol. 45, no. 3, pp. 415–439.

Ochs, E & Capps, L 2001, *Living Narrative: Creating Lives in Everyday Storytelling*, Harvard University Press, Cambridge, MA.

Pavlenko, A 2007, 'Autobiographic narratives as data in applied linguistics', *Applied Linguistics*, vol. 28, no. 2, pp. 163–188.

Polkinghorne, DE 1995, 'Narrative configuration in qualitative analysis', *Qualitative Studies in Education*, vol. 8, no. 1, pp. 5–23.

———— 2007, 'Validity issues in narrative research', *Qualitative Inquiry*, vol. 13, no. 4, pp. 471–486.

Riessman, CK 2008, *Narrative Methods for the Human Sciences*, Sage, Los Angeles, CA.

Wenger, E 1998, *Communities of Practice: Learning, Meaning, and Identity*, Cambridge University Press, Cambridge.

Wong, J & Waring, HZ 2010, *Conversation Analysis and Second Language Pedagogy*, Routledge, New York, NY.

CHAPTER ELEVEN

Action Research

Anne Burns

Action research (AR) is gaining acceptance in applied linguistics studies as an empirical approach adaptable to higher degree and other research studies, as well as to engagement of practitioners in their personal professional growth through reflective practice and local practical inquiry. I describe the major philosophical and paradigmatic assumptions of AR, its origins and essential processes. Issues of validity and value, which remain contentious in AR, are then raised. I also outline briefly the main research techniques and tools, after which key ethical considerations are briefly discussed. Following the pattern of other contributions to this volume, the chapter ends with an illustrative example.

Underlying assumptions and methodology

What is action research?

AR is the superordinate term for a set of approaches to research which, at the same time, systematically investigate a given social situation and promote democratic change and collaborative participation. *Participatory action research* (PAR), *critical action research* (CAR), *action learning, participant inquiry, practitioner inquiry* and *cooperative inquiry* are all terms broadly underpinned by the assumptions and approaches embodied in AR. The common features they share are to: (a) undertake research to bring about positive change and improvement in the participants' social situation; (b) generate theoretical as well as practical knowledge about the situation; (c) enhance collegiality, collaboration and involvement of participants who are actors in the situation and most likely to be affected by changes; and (d) establish an attitudinal stance of continual change, self-development and growth. Those engaged in AR experience self-reflection on their behaviour, actions and interactions with others; deliberate interventions to question and enhance current practices; adaptation of research processes and methods to address issues that emerge directly; and unpredictability and openness to changes in research goals and questions as knowledge of the social situation expands and deepens. By way of summary:

> Action research involves a self-reflective, systematic and critical approach to enquiry by participants who are at the same time members of the research community. The aim is to identify problematic situations or issues considered by the participants to be worthy of investigation in order to bring about critically informed changes in practice. (Burns, cited in Cornwell 1999, p. 5)

Typically, the situations that participants wish to investigate are those they perceive to be 'problematic'. Rather than suggesting that the participants or their behaviours are the 'problems', the term *problematic* reflects a desire on the part of participants to 'problematize', that is question, clarify, understand and give meaning to the current situation. The impetus for the research is a perceived gap between what actually exists and what participants desire to see exist. In this sense, action researchers are change agents aiming 'to take a stand for a preferred future' (Atiti 2008) and interested in resolving, reformulating or refining dilemmas, predicaments or puzzles in their daily lives through systematic planning, data-gathering, reflection and further informed action.

In its historical applications within educational contexts, AR is typically depicted as three broad movements over the past sixty years (see Burns 2005, 2011 for detailed discussion): *technical-scientific* (a technically motivated, step-wise activity seeking basic improvements to practice), *practical-deliberative* (a solution-oriented approach to morally problematic situations) and *critical- emancipatory* (an empowering approach embedded in critical theory and addressing broader socially constituted educational structures at the local level). In 1993, Crookes argued that in language education contexts, critical-emancipatory approaches were uncommon and it could be said that this is still the case (although see Denos et al. 2009 for a recent example).

Processes in action research

In contrast to research approaches which follow more predictable, well-established procedures, AR is characterized by dynamic movement, flexibility, interchangeability and reiteration. Broad research phases are, however, discernible. Despite the large number of (contested) models in educational AR (Zuber-Skerritt, 1990, calculates that there are at least thirty), typical representations show spirals or cycles of (i) planning, (ii) action, (iii) observation and (iv) reflection (cf. Kemmis & McTaggart 1988). The spirals are interwoven, fluid and repeated throughout the investigation; thus, a researcher conducting AR should be prepared for unanticipated variations and reiterations in the process. For example, Burns (1999, p. 35) and the Australian practitioners she collaborated with experienced a 'series of interrelated experiences' involving numerous dynamic phases (Table 11.1).

Table 11.1 Interrelated experiences in action research phases

Phase	Focus of phase
Exploring	Identifying generalized areas for investigation
Identifying	Undertaking fact-finding to refine ideas
Planning	Developing a viable plan of action
Collecting data	Selecting and enacting initial data-gathering techniques
Analysing/reflecting	Simultaneously scrutinizing and reflecting on emerging data
'Hypothesising'/speculating	Developing initial predictions/explanations based on data
Intervening	Deliberately changing practices in response to predictions
Observing	Observing and evaluating outcomes of interventions
Reporting	Articulating processes formatively or summatively to others
Writing	Summarizing and disseminating written research accounts
Presenting	Summarizing and disseminating oral research accounts

One challenge for novice action researchers is to distinguish how AR differs from everyday educational practice. Everyday *action* and investigative processes of *research* are brought together in AR; the researcher must plan, act, observe and reflect 'more carefully, more systematically and more rigorously than one usually does in everyday life; and [to] use the relationships between these moments in the process as a source of both improvement and knowledge' (Kemmis & McTaggart 1988, p. 10).

In AR, the action in and on the social situation is deliberately interventionist; researchers are simultaneously critical participants *in* the action and researchers *of* the action. AR is essentially an exploratory and decision-generating process invoking key questions, actions and challenges. Table 11.2 presents the major phases and processes and suggests the kinds of actions and challenges that can arise.

Table 11.2 Typology of phases and processes in action research

Broad phases of AR	Key questions	Key actions	Key challenges
Plan	• What problematic areas for investigation and change can be identified in this social situation? • What changes to current practice are anticipated? • What outcomes are desired? • Who is involved in this situation? • What resources are needed?	• Develop statements /reflections/ questions • Identify, collaborate and dialogue with co-participants (colleagues, administrators, parents, students) • Outline initial action and research designs and processes • Identify scope, timing, resources	• Articulating implicit and explicit cultural and professional assumptions about status quo • Interrogating relationship of professional experience to research issues • Scanning political, social and educational constraints
Act	• What strategies and actions should be put in place? • What is distinctive in this action/ how will it lead to change? • What ethical issues are involved? • What evidence is emerging for renewed action?	• Initiate actions over critically selected time period • Observe deliberately, consciously and nonjudgmentally • Collaborate with co-participants • Adjust actions on basis of emerging observations	• Avoiding personal bias and interrogating preferred actions • Questioning preconceptions about outcomes • Maintaining openness to unpredictable or unwelcome outcomes
Observe	• What evidence about actions is required? • What types of data-gathering techniques should be used?	• Evaluate the nature of evidence required to document actions systematically • Identify/adapt/develop relevant data-collection tools and techniques	• Connecting data sources to research purpose and action • Selecting/reselecting data-collection tools • Ensuring triangulation of data techniques

(continued)

Broad phases of AR	Key questions	Key actions	Key challenges
	• What additional forms of data are needed? • What kinds of interim analyses are possible?	• Clarify range of perspectives required for adequate coverage • Identify roles of co-participants in data gathering	• Locating resources/materials required for data collection • Reviewing/readjusting actions on the basis of evidence • Maintaining rigour and thoroughness of procedures
Reflection	• What evidence is emerging and/ or re-merging from systematic observation? • What intended and unintended outcomes are identifiable as a consequence of the intervention? • What reformulations of the problem are required? • What ethical issues are arising from the research? • What balances in judgement need to be achieved?	• Adopt a formative approach to the emergence of findings • Maintain openness to possible revisions, redirections and new problems /questions • Interrogate personal and profession preconceptions/ assumptions • Ensure equitable and just consequences for all participants	• Rechecking and cross-checking evidence • Revising focus and aims of intervention and observation based on emerging evidence • Identifying and challenging preconceptions/assumptions • Informing research participants about progress and purpose • Involving participants in cross-checking judgements about evidence • Analysing evidence impartially • Maintaining awareness of the intersubjective nature of personal involvement

Validity and trustworthiness

Validity is a contested notion in AR. Criticisms about quality and validity have long been levelled against educational AR in relation to: methodological limitations (Ellis 2010) such as its lack of scientific rigour, replicability and generalizability; the tentativeness and unpredictability of the initial design and therefore its inability to set out validity measures in advance; the localized and therefore unreplicable nature of AR; the capacity of practitioners to design and conduct robust research (e.g. Jarvis 1983; Dörnyei 2007); and the level of rigour in research design (Brumfit & Mitchell 1989; Mackey & Gass 2005) and data analysis (Elliott & Sarland 1995; Winter 1987).

However, proponents argue that these criticisms misconstrue the nature and purpose of AR. Like the process of AR itself, validity in AR is highly dynamic and subject to variation, determined by the ongoing and changing aims of the research. Because of the complexity and contentions surrounding the term 'validity', as well as its strong associations with positivist and quantitative-experimental paradigms, AR commentators tend to avoid using it, instead preferring terms such as 'trustworthiness' (Zeichner & Noffke 2001), 'worthwhileness' (Bradbury & Reason 2001) or 'credibility' (Greenwood & Levin 2007). Trustworthiness refers to whether the data analyses, reports and interpretations constitute honest and authentic reconstruction of the research and of the knowledge that emerged in the social environment, while the value accruing to participants in undertaking the research contributes to its worthwhileness. Credibility relates to 'the arguments and the processes necessary for having someone trust research results' (Greenwood & Levin 2007, p. 67); internal credibility means that knowledge created is meaningful to the participants generating it, while external credibility is to do with convincing those uninvolved in the research that the outcomes are believable.

Fundamental to reconceptualizing validity in AR is the challenge of how to make judgements about the quality of the research. Altrichter et al. (1993, pp. 74–81) argue that four key questions should be considered when formulating criteria to evaluate AR quality:

- Have the understandings gained from research been cross-checked against the perspectives of all those concerned and/or against other researchers?
- Have the understandings gained from research been tested through practical action?
- Are the research aims compatible with both educational aims and democratic human values?
- Are the research design and data-collection methods compatible with the demands of teaching?

Taking these questions in turn, the following measures can enhance trustworthiness in AR (see Altrichter et al. 1993, pp. 74–81; Burns 1999, pp. 163–166).

Cross-checking perspectives

In line with qualitative research procedures more generally, this criterion concerns repetition and comparison of data in order to uncover discrepancies or alternative perspectives, typically sourced through:

Triangulation, a term derived from navigation where different bearings are taken to give accurate positioning on an object. In AR, triangulation means using more than one data-collection method (e.g. observations, followed by interviews, or surveys complemented by observations and focus groups) or making comparisons across different types of data (e.g. quantitative analyses compared with qualitative survey responses). Other procedures include investigator (using different researchers), theory (using multiple theoretical approaches) and environmental (using different locations) triangulation. By using different perspective sources, confidence that findings are not simply the result of using a particular method is increased.

Member-checks which involve taking the data to various participants and/or stakeholders for verification of the accuracy of the findings. The researcher's interpretations are cross-checked by those who supplied the data or by other 'members' of the social context in a position to provide views (e.g. principals, administrators, close colleagues). In some cases, *peer comparison*, using the perspectives of those relatively uninvolved, is also sought to test out the extent of the account's credibility (e.g. colleagues or administrators in other educational contexts, or parents).

Perspectives comparison which involves testing findings against research in comparable situations. Sources come from the literature, other action research accounts, presentations at professional workshops and conferences, or the researcher's deepening reflections. Failure to find rival explanations that show alternative data explanations, or *negative cases*, that confirm that patterns and trends identified in the data are accurate increases confidence in interpretations.

Cyclical iteration where the trustworthiness of findings and interpretations are compared with and tested against previous iterations of the AR cycle in order to build on previous evidence, expand the scope, purpose and central questions of the study, further triangulate the data and guard against researcher bias.

Testing through practical application

AR involves not just practical application but the development of empirical and theoretical insights about the social situation under investigation. Given the dynamic interaction between action and reflection, the strength of the theories that emerge rests on their ability to generate improvement in practice. Theory-testing is related to how the researcher demonstrates practical application for improvement, and critical reflection on the capacity of the intervention strategies to bring about changes and developments. This does not imply that intervention strategies will show immediate and clear-cut improvements in practice; but it does mean that the purpose and forward movement of the AR process is consistently focused on enhancing practical conditions within the social situation The knowledge generated is based not on received wisdom or 'grand theory', but on 'experiential knowing' (Heron 1996).

Compatibility with educational aims and democratic values

This criterion relates to ethical considerations (see below). As mentioned, AR is deliberatively interventionist, aimed at disturbing and unsettling the status quo. Consequently, participants may find themselves confronting surprising or even unpalatable realities or changing things in unanticipated ways. Despite disturbances to accepted practice, it is important that essential *educational* aims in the context are kept in mind. Also, methods should be compatible with research aims; if, for example, the aim is to work with novice teacher colleagues to understand and improve early teaching experiences, interviewing experienced colleagues about 'problems' in supporting novices is counterproductive to fostering good collegial relationships. Similarly, sharing these data with novices and asking for perspectives on their colleagues' views is only likely to increase feelings of alienation. AR strives to enhance cooperative participant relationships, and so showing how these relationships were treated within the research is relevant. Indicating explicitly how ethical principles were achieved and how participants' roles and these relationships were (re)negotiated through different research cycles is essential to ensuring research quality.

Compatibility with teaching demands

AR practitioners must be simultaneously researchers and actors in the social situation. Thus, the scope and aims of the research need to be realistic and justifiable within the constraints of the teaching context. The research should show how it builds upon, rather than detracts from, practitioners' major responsibilities for teaching. It should also show how it links to the notion of enhanced professionalism for educators and the personal and professional development of the participants. These criteria are closely tied to the notion of compatibility with educational aims and the concepts of reflexivity and praxis, in which theory and practice become mutually informing (e.g. Freire 1970).

Notwithstanding these considerations for enhancing the quality and rigour of AR, debates about what constitute underpinning validity criteria are very much at an evolutionary and contested point. And, as Greenwood and Levin note, in attempting to defend AR as a valid research approach, it would be unfortunate to assume 'transcendentally high standards' (2007, p. 113) that deter the very practitioners most likely to want to participate. Rather, '[t]he key in good AR practice is to design and sustain a process in which important reflections can emerge through communication and some good practical problem-solving can be done in as inclusive and fair a way as possible' (p. 113). If action researchers approach research in the spirit of providing fair and honest disclosure, and reflections on the contexts, the research issues, the cyclical phases and processes, the methods, the presentation and interpretation of the data, convincing 'validation' of the research (Heron 1996) is likely to ensue.

Techniques and instruments

Generally, action researchers employ qualitative techniques common in naturalistic exploratory research. There are essentially two main sources for data-gathering: observing and recording what people do; and asking people for their views and opinions. As in other forms of research, techniques should be closely aligned to the central questions or focus – it is pointless to try to understand what participants think about aspects of language learning by observing them undertake a particular task, for example. The techniques highlighted here do not imply, however, that AR data cannot be quantified through percentages, rankings, ratings and so on. However, using statistical calculations typical of quantitative approaches (see Phakiti this volume) is uncommon in AR. Burns (1999, Chapters 4 and 5) describes observational and non-observational techniques in detail.

Observing what participants do

Modes of observation include *other-observation* (researcher observations of other participants), *self-observation* (one's own behaviours, thoughts, actions, interactions) and *peer-observation* (observation by and with research colleagues, acting as mentors, influencers, critical friends, supervisors). Participant observation (where the researcher is part of the setting rather than a detached observer) is inevitable in AR; thus, peer-observation is a useful source of data triangulation to verify one's own observations. In some cases (more likely in formalized AR studies submitted as dissertations), *a priori* observational schemes developed for language acquisition research, such as FOCUS (Fanselow 1987) or Communicative Orientation to Language Teaching (COLT) (Spada & Fröhlich 1995) might be used, but more commonly, AR observations focus on specific issues under investigation. Richards (2003) suggests four main areas for focusing observations: (i) the *setting* (e.g. context, spaces, locations), (ii) the *systems* (e.g. typical routines and procedures), (iii) the *people* (e.g. roles, relationships, responses) and (iv) the *behaviours* (e.g. timing, activities, events).

Observation is accompanied by techniques for capturing the phenomena observed, so that the researcher can revisit the situation objectively. Classically, anthropological ethnographic observation uses fieldnotes made during (obtrusive to other participants) or immediately afterwards (unobtrusive to others) observation that record in an objective and factual style. Increasingly, fieldnotes include reflective commentary, questions for further consideration, evaluations, and self-observations, all relevant to the dynamic and evolving nature of AR. Another 'classic' of AR observation is the researcher journal or diary (see Perkins 2001 for an example), a self-reflective tool written for various purposes. Personal journals are often used to 'let off steam', ruminate on passing thoughts or insights and record hopes, anxieties or even confessions. Other kinds of journals are 'memoirs', more objective and factual reflections on events or people, or even 'logs', running records of what contacts and transactions occur during the day. In a variation on free-form journals, some AR practitioners use grids or tables with relevant headings, for instance dates/times, issues arising, actions taken, changes made, reflections, comments, reactions, literature references. Journals sometimes include drawings, sketches, diagrams, maps, illustrations of student work, and mindmaps. With the advent of technology, fieldnotes and journals can be shared creatively among researchers or set up as blogs (Weblogs, such as Blackboard) or vlogs (visual Weblogs, like Flikr) for running commentary between participants.

Audio or video recordings have the advantage of capturing observational data verbatim and are accurate and reliable sources of data. Audio recording is less intrusive, while video, although more intrusive, includes non-verbal behaviour. Accustoming participants to the presence of the recording device is likely to result in more authentic records of typical interaction. A challenge in AR observation is that the researcher is also an actor in the context. Thus, if peer observation is not readily available, other recording mechanisms are needed. Typical techniques include: hand-held recorders for short, rapid commentary; post-it notes for passing insights or reminders; 'jottings' on lesson-plans or class handouts; electronic whiteboard copies; focused observations by students acting as co-researchers; photographs by teacher or students using disposable, digital or mobile phone cameras; maps and diagrams; mindmaps linking key observations and insights; spoken and/or written debriefings with peer-observers immediately after observations. Undertaking and documenting observations are limited only by participants' creativity; the key consideration is making them focused, flexible, convenient and adaptable to preferences and circumstances.

Asking participants for views and opinions

Non-observational and introspective techniques involve seeking views, beliefs and opinions about issues under investigation. They also include collecting artefacts from the research site, such as documents (policies, curricula, lesson plans, student work, test results) providing a track record or paper trail that reflect people's activities. Two mainstays of non-observational data collection are interviews and surveys or questionnaires. Structured (pre-planned sets of questions posed in fixed order), semi-structured (sets of questions used flexibly) or unstructured (open-ended conversational interactions) interviews offer various ways to tailor this technique to a specific focus and purpose, as do different combinations of participants (individualized, paired, focus group–oriented). Interviews can easily double as classroom learning activities. A variation on formal interviews, well adapted to AR for example, is a class or group discussion angled towards the research topic. For greater reliability, interviews are frequently recorded, audio recording usually being sufficient to capture participants' introspections for later analysis.

Surveys or questionnaires eliciting written data through closed and/or open-ended questions are also well adapted to classroom activities. Closed questions involve selecting specified responses and lead to tabulation and quantification (percentages, averages, frequency), while open-ended questions elicit fill-in or short answers and offer qualitative data from which the researcher derives themes, patterns and trends. Questions focus typically on factual, behavioural or attitudinal information (Dörnyei 2003). A major challenge lies in question preparation so as to avoid lack of clarity, ambiguity, bias and 'leading-the-witness', and for this reason, piloting the questions is recommended. Decisions also need to be made about the language and literacy levels required and whether responses should be completed in the mother tongue or alternative language.

One problem that inevitably arises in using these techniques is teacher–student power-relationships. McKay (2006, p. 55) suggests minimizing this threat to authenticity by: (i) explaining the purpose of the interview, what will be done with the information and the benefits to participants; (ii) being sensitive to students' responses and any awkwardness or nervousness that might arise; (iii) providing feedback and reinforcement during the interview through thanks, praise and support. This advice applies equally to the preparation and distribution of questionnaires. Linked to the power-relation issue is the problem that 'self-report' data are notoriously unreliable; responses may be simplistic, aimed to please, impress or cover up actual opinions for fear of reprisal. Consequently, action researchers should critically evaluate data obtained in this way against other sources.

Finally, as in other research, AR data are 'traces' or representations of events that provide evidence for the researcher's findings and interpretations. Inevitably, what is highlighted from the data is selective, subject to researcher interpretation and ultimately represents dynamic situations statically. In AR, as perhaps in no other approach to research, to impact on practice, the evidence from the data must be supplemented and supported by what can be learned from and made meaningful about the practical social situation through deep reflection and experiential application.

Ethical considerations

As already noted, ethical considerations are tied up with the quality, value and democratic worth of the AR in changing and enhancing social situations for the participants. Thus, a fundamental ethical question is how the design of the research works towards educational improvement, more effective outcomes for students and the empowerment of teachers, professionally, educationally and politically. Underpinning AR goals are at least three important ethical issues (see also Burns, 2010).

Whose permission or consent is needed for the research?

It is vital to consider two types of permission. First, permission may need to be sought from the researcher's university, school board, district or school. Second, the researcher needs to obtain informed consent from other participants, such as colleagues and students. Even when written consent is not required, all stakeholders and participants have a right to information about the purpose, procedures, possible effects and how the research will be used, as well as assurances of anonymity, voluntary participation and withdrawal from the research without penalty. This is particularly important in an approach where researchers could be accused of 'experimenting' on their students and 'threatening' their educational achievement.

Who will be affected by the research?

Action researchers need to maintain vigilance about the possible consequences of the research on participants. No harm, risk or disadvantage should ensue, and again explanation and communication about the purpose of the research should be foregrounded. In AR, it is particularly important to be aware of the power differences inherent in the educational situation, and how they might affect participants' behaviours and reactions.

Who should be told about the research when it is completed?

Participants need to know that the outcomes of the research will be fed back to them for their input. Not only does the researcher do them the courtesy of sharing what comes out of the research but researcher interpretations are (re) affirmed. Information about how the research will be used and to whom it will be disseminated on completion also meets good ethical standards.

Conducting AR ethically involves confronting continual decisions, challenges and choices, which are not always self-evident because of the dynamic and shifting nature of the processes. Nevertheless, an ethical orientation is fundamental to the reflective and democratic spirit of AR and plays a central role in focusing and strengthening its quality, trustworthiness and credibility.

A sample study

The focus of Heather Denny's (2008) action research, conducted in a New Zealand (NZ) university over three semesters, was how to introduce her adult immigrant English as an additional language (EAL) learners to conversational skills and cultural norms of the local variety of English, as rapidly and efficiently as possible. The institutional curriculum required students to achieve criterion-based competencies in various spoken genres (e.g. *Is able to manage a conversation and keep it going for 6 minutes: opening, small talk, turn taking, responding to questions, remarks, etc., transitions, closing*). Perceiving that conversational models from available textbooks were inauthentic and non-reflective of local situations, she drew on work by Burns (2001), Butterworth (2000), Carter and McCarthy (1995), de Silva Joyce and Slade (2000) and Eggins and Slade (1997) to develop more realistic semi-scripted role-play dialogues. The approach involved 'giving native speakers a scenario based in real-life interactions…and asking them to role-play an exchange' which was recorded and transcribed (Denny 2008, p. 44). To facilitate and understand the development of her teaching practice using this approach, she undertook three cycles of AR with three different classes of mixed-age students at a level equivalent to 4.5 General on the International English Language Testing System (IELTS).

In the initial cycle, she used unscripted or semi-scripted conversations from published Australian materials (e.g. Delaruelle 2001), also experimenting by developing semi-scripted recordings and activities involving NZ native-speaker colleagues. Activities focused particularly on weaknesses identified in pre-tests; using formulaic expressions for conversational initiation and introducing discourse markers (*so, well, anyway*) to maintain interaction. Students conducted role-plays rated by peers using the institutional assessment criteria mentioned above.

The second cycle took the investigations further by focusing on the staging of conversational transitions from initiation, to requesting and giving advice and concluding the interaction. Three transitional strategies, identified from semi-scripted recordings and published material, provided data for class activities, including student demonstrations, discussion of strategies used and role-play of complete conversations, during which students self-assessed, using yes/no/sometimes responses against given criteria (e.g. Start a conversation; Speak fluently in conversation using discourse markers (e.g. well, anyway, so, listen, look, now); Find the right question to get information from my partner).

The final cycle extended skills by introducing more complex conversational negotiations, including strategies for gaining attention, introducing a situational problem such as with an employer, teacher and real-estate agent, and insisting. Students listened to models, which were from authentic or simulated sources compiled by Denny, and responded to questions about vocabulary, linguistic features, staging of the conversational genre, getting attention and stating the problem in general and in detail, and using discourse strategies such as introducing softeners, suggesting compromises and checking outcomes. Discussions about conversational models focused on context, participants, power relations, situations and politeness. Other activities involved paired practice, identification of relevant discourse transitions, strategies and markers, demonstration role-plays, peer-coaching and peer assessment.

During all three cycles, data were collected through teacher-created pre-tests and institutional post-tests, initial and final written self-assessments, a student survey and a reflective researcher journal. Pre- and post-tests consisted of role-plays observed and evaluated by Denny according to criteria. For pre-tests, Denny created her own set of criteria (e.g. Uses appropriate language to manage transition to discussion topic) designed to diagnose each student's learning needs. Post-tests utilized the institutional requirements mentioned earlier. After each teaching period, students completed self-assessment check-lists evaluating discourse competencies. In cycle three, self-assessment occurred before teacher assessment, so that responses were not influenced by results. Surveys were completed at the same time as post-teaching self-assessments and students were asked to identify various activities they found most effective:

(i)   direct activities using models;

(ii) more indirect activities such as practising with partners; and

(iii) most indirect activities such as practising outside class.

Denny's reflective journal recorded classroom activities, events and perceptions about effectiveness of activities, student progress and her own practices.

By comparing test results, she found that all students improved their weakest skills, but improvement across competencies was uneven. However, the self-assessments showed lower perceptions of individual improvement, particularly for activities in cycle two where students rated themselves higher on the pre-test. Surveys on preferred activities indicated that students found teacher information, practice in class, listening to tapes and studying transcripts the most useful across all cycles. Denny concluded that authentically oriented materials combined with classroom practice did contribute to student improvement. In relation to personal insights and skills development, she claimed that her professional learning about materials development as well as her knowledge about naturalistic data analysis increased: 'I have learned to trust the data in them and have progressively worked more directly with the tapes and transcripts, becoming gradually less worried that learners would find them too complex' (p. 55).

One area identified for future cycles was to investigate ways to enhance sociocultural knowledge of the discoursal features of naturalistic interaction. She also refined her research knowledge and skills realizing, particularly by the third cycle, the importance of recording student interaction for greater reliability in assessment and analysis, and wording surveys clearly and unambiguously. For further cycles, she saw follow-up student interviews as a way of triangulating data and increasing trustworthiness. She concluded: 'In all cycles I learned again that careful and trustworthy research takes more time than anticipated. However, I am convinced that the gathering of data facilitated more focused and rapid development of my teaching' (p. 56). Denny's research is a good example of a practitioner deepening her confidence in addressing a locally contextualized teaching issue and engendering self-reflective empirically based insights.

Resources for further reading

Altrichter, H, Posch, P & Somekh, B 1993, *Teachers Investigate Their Work. An Introduction to the Methods of Action Research*, Routledge, London.

While not focused on language teaching, this book is a classic for teachers, teacher educators and administrators wanting to understand and begin using action research alone or with professional colleagues. Organized as a handbook, it provides numerous practical methods and strategies.

Burnaford, G, Fischer, J & Hobson, D (eds), 2001, *Teachers Doing Research. The Power of Action Through Inquiry*, 2nd edn, Lawrence Erlbaum, Mahwah, NJ.

Using numerous examples from mainstream teacher action research projects in US schools and colleges, this book describes the processes of doing action research, discusses how technology can be integrated into methodology and explores the relationships between teacher research and the broader field of educational research.

Burns, A 2010, *Doing Action Research in English Language Teaching: A Guide for Practitioners*, Routledge, New York, NY.

This volume is a hands-on, practical guide for practitioners wishing to get started in action research. It introduces the main concepts and offers a step-by-step guide to the action research process. It includes numerous examples from language teacher action researchers internationally.

Edge, J (ed.), 2001, *Action Research*, TESOL, Alexandria.

This was one of the first books to provide chapter length examples of action research carried out in the field of language teaching internationally. The opening chapter offers an interesting synopsis of the history of action research, its developments within mainstream educational and applied linguistics/TESOL contexts and its relevance to teacher research and professional development.

Farrell, T (Series editor), *Language Teacher Research in… Series*, TESOL, Alexandria, VA.

This series of edited books is valuable in providing chapter length examples of research, including AR, carried out by language teachers in different international contexts – Asia (Farrell 2006), Europe (Borg 2006), the Americas (McGarrell 2007), the Middle East (Coombe & Barlow 2007), Australia and New Zealand (Burns & Burton 2008), Africa (Makalela 2009).

Griffee, D T 2012, *An introduction to second language research methods*, TESL-EJ Publications, E-book edition available at http://www.tesl-ej.org/pdf/ej60/sl_research_methods.pdf, viewed 13 May 2014.

Although this book is not specifically about designing and conducting action research, it is written very much in the spirit of encouraging teachers to become researchers so that their understanding of their beliefs and practices is expanded. One of the chapters deals specifically with AR design and is a useful introduction to the main processes and procedures.

Borg, S 2013, *Teacher Research in Language Teaching: A Critical Analysis*, Cambridge University Press, New York, NY.

This book reports on research investigating the extent to which teachers are engaged in research, both as consumers (or readers) and doers of research. It considers teachers' and academic managers' attitudes to teacher research and identifies factors that impede or promote engagement. It also reviews a number of projects conducted outside the context of formal study to examine how teacher research can be facilitated effectively.

References

Altrichter, H, Posch, P & Somekh, B 1993, *Teachers Investigate Their Work: An Introduction to the Methods of Action Research*, Routledge, London.

Atiti, A 2008, 'A critical action research on organisational learning and change for sustainability in Kenya', PhD thesis, Macquarie University, Sydney.

Bradbury, H & Reason, P 2001, 'Conclusion: Broadening the bandwidth of validity: Issues and choice-point for improving the quality of action research', in P Reason & H Bradbury (eds), *Handbook of Action Research*, Sage, London, pp. 447–455.

Brumfit, C & Mitchell, R 1989, 'The language classroom as a focus for research', in C Brumfit & R Mitchell (eds), *Research in the Language Classroom*, Modern English Publications and The British Council, London, pp. 3–15.

Burns, A 1999, *Collaborative Action Research for Language Teachers*, Cambridge University Press, Cambridge.

—— 2001, 'Analysing spoken discourse: Implications for TESOL', in A Burns & C Coffin (eds), *Analysing English in a Global Context*, Routledge, London, pp. 123–148.

—— 2005, 'Action research: An evolving paradigm?', *Language Teaching*, vol. 38, no. 2, pp. 57–74.

—— 2010, *Doing Action Research in English Language Teaching: A Guide for Practitioners*, Routledge, New York, NY.

—— 2011, 'Action research', in E Hinkel (ed.), *Handbook of Research in Second Language Teaching and Learning*, Volume II, Lawrence Erlbaum, Mahwah, NJ, pp. 237–253.

Butterworth, A 2000, 'Casual conversation texts in listening to Australia', in H de Silva Joyce (ed.), *Teachers' Voices 6: Teaching Casual Conversation*, National Centre for English Language Teaching and Research, Macquarie University, Sydney, pp. 3–10.

Carter, R & McCarthy, M 1995, 'Grammar and the spoken language', *Applied Linguistics*, vol. 16, no. 2, pp. 141–158.

Cornwell, S 1999, 'Interview with Anne Burns and Graham Crookes', *The Language Teacher*, vol. 23, no. 12, pp. 5–10.

Crookes, G 1993, 'Action research for second language teachers: Going beyond teacher research', *Applied Linguistics*, vol. 14, no. 2, pp. 130–144.

Delaruelle, S 2001, *Beach Street 2*, New South Wales Adult Migrant English Service, Sydney.

Denos, C, Toohey, K, Neilson, K & Waterstone, B 2009, *Collaborative Research in Multilingual Classrooms*, Multilingual Matters, Bristol.

Denny, H 2008, 'Teaching conversation and negotiation skills using teacher-made, semiscripted conversation models', in A Burns & J Burton (eds), *Language Teacher Research in Australia and New Zealand*, TESOL, Alexandria, VA, pp. 43–60.

de Silva Joyce, H & Slade, D 2000, 'The nature of casual conversation: Implications for teaching, in H de Silva Joyce (ed.), *Teachers' Voices 6: Teaching Casual Conversation*, National Centre for English Language Teaching and Research, Macquarie University, Sydney, pp. viii–xv.

Dörnyei, Z 2003, *Questionnaires in Second Language Research: Construction, Administration and Processing*, Lawrence Erlbaum, Mahwah, NJ.

———— 2007, *Research Methods in Applied Linguistics*, Oxford University Press, Oxford.

Eggins, S & Slade, D 1997, *Analysing Casual Conversation*, Cassell, London.

Elliott, J & Sarland, C 1995, 'A study of 'teachers as researchers' in the context of award-bearing courses and research degrees', *British Educational Research Journal*, vol. 21, no. 3, pp. 371–385.

Ellis, R 2010, 'Second language acquisition, teacher education and language pedagogy', *Language Teaching*, vol. 43, no. 2, pp. 182–201.

Fanselow, J 1987, *Breaking Rules: Generating and Exploring Alternatives in Language Education*, Longman, New York, NY.

Freire, P 1970, *The Pedagogy of the Oppressed*, Herder & Herder, New York, NY.

Greenwood, DJ & Levin, M 2007, *Introduction to Action Research. Social Research for Social Change*, 2nd edn, Sage, Thousand Oaks, CA.

Heron, J 1996, *Co-operative Inquiry: Research into the Human Condition*, Sage, London.

Jarvis, G 1983, 'Action research versus needed research for the 1980s', in L Lange (ed.), *Proceedings of the National Conference on Professional Priorities*, ACTFL, Materials Center, Hastings-on-Hudson, NY, pp. 59–63.

Kemmis, R & McTaggart, R 1988, *The Action Research Planner*, 3rd edn, Deakin University Press, Geelong.

McKay, S 2006, *Researching Second Language Classrooms*, Lawrence Erlbaum, Mahwah, NJ.

Mackey, A & Gass, S 2005, *Second Language Research: Methodology and Design*, Lawrence Erlbaum, Mahwah, NJ.

Perkins, A 2001, 'Here it is, rough though it may be: Basic computer for ESL', in J. Edge (ed.), *Action Research*, TESOL, Alexandria, VA, pp. 13–19.

Richards, K 2003, *Qualitative Inquiry in TESOL*, Palgrave, London.

Spada, N & Fröhlich, M 1995, *Communicative Orientation of Language Teaching Observation Scheme: Coding Conventions and Applications*, National Centre for English Language Teaching and Research, Macquarie University, Sydney.

Winter, R 1987, *Action-research and the Nature of Social Inquiry*, Gower Publishing, Aldershot.

Zeichner, KM & Noffke, SE 2001, 'Practitioner research', in V Richardson (ed.), *Handbook of Research on Teaching*, 4th edn, American Educational Research Association, Washington, DC, pp. 298–330.

Zuber-Skerritt, O 1990, *Action Research in Higher Education. Examples and Reflections*, Kogan Page, London.

CHAPTER TWELVE

Discourse Analysis

Brian Paltridge and Wei Wang

There are now many introductory books on linguistics. These books typically describe the sounds of a language, the ways that words are formed, the meanings of words and the sentence structure of a language. All of these are important in the description of languages. Many of these books, however, do not go beyond this and do not help us understand why we make particular language choices and what we mean by these choices. This is what discourse analysis aims to do. It can help us explain the relationship between what we say and what we mean in particular spoken and written contexts. It can also give us the tools to look at larger units of texts such as conversational and textual organizational patterns that are typical of particular uses of language or *genres*. Discourse analysis also looks at social and cultural settings of language use to help us understand how it is that people come to make particular choices in their use of language. This chapter will outline some of the ways in which spoken and written discourse may be examined. It will then present a sample study which looks at one particular aspect of discourse, the discourse structure of texts.

Approaches to analysing discourse

There are a number of ways in which discourse analysis might be carried out. Discourse analysts might, for example, examine paragraph structure, the organization of whole texts and typical patterns in conversational interactions such as the ways speakers open, close and take turns in a conversation. They might also look at vocabulary patterns across texts, words which link sections of texts together and the ways items such as *it* and *they* point backward or forward in a text; that is the use of *conjunction* and *reference* items (Halliday & Hasan 1976) in a text. Discourse analysts may also look at the broader social context of language use and how this impacts on what is said and how it is said in a written or spoken text. Discourse analysts also consider how the use of language both presents and constructs certain world views as well as how, through the use of language, we present who we are or how we want to be seen.

A number of aspects of language use considered under the heading of discourse analysis are also discussed in the area known as *pragmatics* (see e.g. Birner 2013; Cutting 2008; Huang 2007; Roever this volume). Pragmatics is especially interested in the relationship between language and the context in which it occurs. This includes the study of how the interpretation of language depends on knowledge of the world; how speakers understand the meaning of utterances; and how the use of language is influenced by relationships between speakers and hearers. Pragmatics, thus, is interested in what people mean by what they say rather than what words or phrases might, in their most literal sense, mean by themselves (Yule 1996). Pragmatics is sometimes contrasted with *semantics* which deals with literal or sentence meaning; that is, meaning without reference to users or purpose of communication.

Discourse analysis, then, in the sense we will be considering it here, focuses on:

- linguistic patterns which occur across stretches of spoken and written texts

- knowledge about language beyond the word, clause, phrase and sentence that is needed for successful communication

- what people mean by what they say and how they work out that understanding

- the relationship between language and the social and cultural contexts in which it is used

- the way in which language constructs different views of the world and different understandings.

Key areas of influence in discourse analysis

A number of different approaches to the analysis of discourse have had an influence in the area of applied linguistics. There are various ways in which these approaches could be described. One way is in terms of some of the people who have been influential in this area. The section that follows will give an overview of key researchers in the area of discourse analysis and what the particular approach to the analysis of discourse aims to do.

Speech act theory

A key person in the area of pragmatics and discourse analysis is the linguistic philosopher John Austin whose book *How to do Things with Words* (1962) laid the ground for what has come to be called *speech act theory*. Austin's work was further developed and systematized by the American philosopher John Searle (1969) who studied with Austin at Oxford University. Austin and Searle argued that in the same way that we perform physical acts, such as having a meal or closing a door, we can also perform acts by using language. We can use language, for example, to give orders, to make requests, to give warnings or to give advice. People, thus, 'do things with words' in much the same way as they perform physical actions (see Sadock 2004; Sbisà 2009 for reviews of speech theory; Paltridge 2015 for a sample study).

Cross-cultural pragmatics

The area of research which investigates the use of speech acts across cultures is commonly referred to as *cross-cultural pragmatics* (Rose & Kasper 2001). Researchers have observed that degrees of social distance and power between speakers are important factors in terms of how a particular speech act might be expressed. This varies, however, across cultures and may interact with other factors such as how much use of the particular speech act imposes on the other person, the age of participants involved in the interaction, the gender of the speaker or hearer and culture-specific hierarchies and roles particular to the interaction. An important contribution to cross-cultural pragmatics research is the work of Anna Wierzbicka (2003) who argues that differences in the use of language are due to differences in cultural norms and assumptions. In her view, to understand the use of language across cultures 'it is essential to not only know what the conventions of a given society are but also how they are related to cultural values' (Wierzbicka 2003, p. xv).

Conversational implicature

Another key figure in the area of pragmatics and discourse is the philosopher Paul Grice (1975) whose work on the way people cooperate with each other in conversational interactions has been extremely important. Grice introduced the term *conversational implicature* to describe the process by which we derive meanings from the situation in which language is used – that is, the way we work out what is meant by what someone says. Authors such as Chapman (2011) and LoCastro (2012) discuss practical implications of this view showing how crucial this notion is to understanding how conversational interactions work and the linguistic choices that people make as they interact with each other.

Politeness and face

Two further notions in the area of discourse analysis are *politeness* and *face*. An influential work in this area is Brown and Levinson's (1987) *Politeness: Some Universals in Language Usage*. In their view, politeness is based on the notions of *positive face* and *negative face*. Positive face refers to a person's need to be accepted or liked by others and to be treated as a member of a group knowing that their wants are shared by others. Negative face refers to a person's need to be independent and not imposed on by others. Other important work in this area includes Mills (2003) on gender and politeness and Watts (2003) who presents a view of politeness as politic or strategic, verbal behaviour. Recent research has also taken up the notion of *communities of practice* (Wenger 1998) in discussions of politeness – that is, the discourse expectations of the particular community or group and the local conditions in which the communication is taking place. Cross-cultural issues in politeness are discussed by Leech (2007) and Spencer-Oatey (2008).

Conversation analysis

There is also the important contribution of people working in the area of *conversation analysis* such as Sacks et al. (1974) who have explored conversational norms and recurring patterns in spoken interactions. Conversation analysts are interested, in particular, in how social worlds are jointly constructed and recognized by speakers as they take part in conversational discourse. Early work in conversation analysis looked mostly at everyday spoken interactions such as chat and casual conversation. This has since been extended, however, to include spoken discourse such as doctor-patient consultations, legal hearings, news interviews, psychiatric interviews, interactions in courtrooms and classrooms and gender and conversational interactions. For conversation analysts, ordinary conversation is the most basic form of talk and the main way in which people come together, exchange information and maintain social relations. It is, further, from this form of talk that all other talk-in-interaction is derived. A key feature of work in the area of conversation analysis is the tracing of how participants in a conversation 'interpret each others' actions and develop a shared understanding of the progress of the interaction' (Seedhouse 2005, p. 166); that is, how participants understand and respond to each other in their talk and how, from this understanding, sequences of talk develop (Hutchby & Wooffitt 2008). Researchers in the area of *discursive psychology* (Edwards 2005; Wetherell 2007) have extended this work by looking at issues such as discourse and identity (Benwell & Stokoe 2006), discourse and gender (Edley & Wetherell 2008; Speer 2005) and racial discourse (Stokoe & Edwards 2007; Wetherell & Potter 1992).

Genre analysis

Two linguists who have been especially influential in the area of discourse analysis are Michael Halliday and Ruqaiya Hasan. Halliday's notion of language as a system of choices and his views on the social functions of language (Halliday 1973; Halliday & Hasan 1989) are especially important in the area of discourse analysis. Their work has been extremely influential in the development of the *Sydney genre school* (Martin & Rose 2008; Rose 2012), a group of linguists and language educators who have examined a range of different texts and applied these analyses in various educational settings. Halliday and Hasan's (1976) work on *patterns of cohesion* – that is, the relationship between grammatical and lexical items in texts such as *reference items*, *conjunction* and *ellipsis* – has also made an important contribution to the area of discourse analysis. While the Sydney school genre studies have typically looked at written texts, the observations they have made are equally applicable to spoken texts. Thornbury and Slade (2006), for example, take a genre perspective on the grammar of conversation, as do Eggins and Slade (1997) in their work on the analysis of casual conversation.

Martin (1984, p. 25), from the Sydney genre school, describes genre as 'a staged, goal-oriented, purposeful activity in which speakers engage as members of our culture'. This view draws on Halliday's work and that of the anthropologist Malinowski and, in particular, the view that 'contexts both of situation and of culture [are] important if we are to fully interpret the meaning of a text' (Martin 1984, p. 25). Examples of genres examined in this perspective include service encounters, research reports, academic essays, casual conversations and *micro-genres* (Martin 1997; Martin & Rose 2008) such as descriptions, reports, recounts, procedures and expositions, described in terms of their discourse or *schematic structures* and genre-specific language features.

English for specific purposes genre studies are based largely on Swales' (1990, 2004) work on the discourse structure and linguistic features of texts. Swales uses the notion of *moves* to describe the discourse structure of texts. These studies have had a strong influence in the teaching of English for Specific Purposes and especially the teaching of academic writing to second language graduate students (see Paltridge 2014 for a review of this work). Genre studies in composition studies, and in what is often called the *rhetorical genre studies*, has been influenced in particular by a paper written by the speech communications specialist Carolyn Miller (1984) titled 'Genre as social action' and has been discussed, in particular, in relation to first-year undergraduate writing and professional communication in North American settings. Here, discussion is more on social and contextual aspects of genres rather than the language or discourse structures of texts (see Berkenkotter 2009; Devitt 2004; Schryer 2011 for reviews of rhetorical genre studies).

Critical discourse analysis

Researchers such as Fairclough (2003, 2010), Wodak (2011), Wodak and Meyer (2009), van Dijk (2001) and van Leeuwen (2008) have considered the use of language from a critical perspective, that is, how discourse is shaped by relations of power and ideology and the effects discourse has upon social identities, relations, knowledge and beliefs. This perspective, *critical discourse analysis*, starts with the assumption that language use is always social and that discourse both reflects and constructs the social world. A critical analysis might explore issues such as gender (see Sunderland this volume), ideology and identity (see Block this volume) and how these are reflected in particular texts. The analysis might commence with an analysis of the use of discourse and move from there to an explanation and interpretation of the discourse. From here, the analysis might proceed to deconstruct and challenge the texts, tracing ideologies and assumptions underlying the use of discourse and relating these to different views of the world, experiences and beliefs.

Contrastive rhetoric

The area of research known as *contrastive rhetoric* (Connor 1996) compares genres in different languages and cultures. Contrastive rhetoric has its origins in the work of Kaplan (1966) who examined different patterns in the academic essays written by students from a number of different languages and cultures. Although Kaplan has since revised his strong claim that differences in academic writing are the result of culturally different ways of thinking, many studies have found important differences in the ways in which texts are written in different languages and cultures. Other studies, however, have found important similarities in writing across cultures. Kubota (1992) and Kubota and Lehner (2004), for example, argue that just as Japanese expository writing has more than one rhetorical style, so too does English and that it is misleading to try to reduce rhetorical styles to the one single norm. Contrastive rhetoric has, in more recent years, moved to emphasize the social situation of writing rather than just discourse patterns across cultures. This has led to the area now known as *intercultural rhetoric* (Connor 2004, 2011) where writing is examined in relation to the intellectual history and social structures of different cultures.

Corpus approaches to discourse analysis

Important researchers in the area of corpus approaches to discourse analysis include Douglas Biber (1988, 1992) and his proposal for a multidimensional view of discourse and Ken Hyland (2009) who has analysed a range of academic genres from a corpus perspective. Corpus approaches to discourse analysis involves the collection of large sets of authentic or 'real word' texts and analysing features of language within them with the help of a computer. It is now a widely used methodology for doing discourse analysis and offers unique insights into the use of language. With the use of computers, researchers are able to explore patterns of language use (grammatical or lexical for instance) within texts. This use of modern technologies has greatly facilitated discourse-oriented research and dramatically reduced the time and resources needed to find particular linguistic patterns and collocations of words in texts.

Corpus-based discourse analyses can be categorized into three main approaches:

- Textual: approaches that focus on language choices, meanings and patterns in texts.

- Critical: an approach that draws on other research perspectives as well such as critical discourse analysis to explore underlying meanings and motivations of texts.

- Contextual: analyses where situational factors are also taken into consideration in the analysis and discussion of the texts (Hyland 2009).

There may be overlaps between each of these approaches, of course, as more than one approach may be used in the same study to answer the same research question. The core contribution of corpus approaches to discourse analysis, however, lies in their ability to make generalizable discoveries about patterns of language use across large samples of text (see Baker 2006; Flowerdew 2012 for further discussions of corpus assisted discourse analysis).

Classroom discourse analysis

John Sinclair and Malcolm Coulthard (1975) are two important early researchers in the area of classroom discourse analysis. By studying classroom discourse, researchers are able to gain insights into complex and dynamic relationships between discourse, learning and social practices. A key feature of classroom discourse analysis is the assumption that 'the task of systematically observing, analysing and understanding classroom aims and events is central to any serious educational enterprise' (Kumaravadivelu 1999, p. 454). There are, however, important differences as to how to observe and analyse classroom discourse. Edwards and Westgate (1994) make a distinction between approaches to the analysis of classroom talk where the focus is primarily on 'turns, sequences and meaning' and those where the focus is on a more linguistic analysis of rhetorical and lexico-grammatical patterns. Research within the 'turns, sequences, and meanings' tradition has been shaped by the theoretical perspectives of *conversation analysis* and *ethnomethodology* with a view to seeking insights into classroom aims and events through a detailed account of patterns of interactions within classrooms. Other research has taken a systemic functional orientation to looking at classroom discourse analysis with the aim of exploring relations between language structures and meanings that are made in the classroom (see Christie 2002; Hammond 2011; Walsh 2011, for further discussions of classroom discourse analysis).

Multimodal discourse analysis

Two key researchers in the area of multimodal discourse analysis are Gunther Kress and Theo van Leuuwen (see e.g. Kress 2010; Kress & van Leeuwen 2001, 2006). Multimodal discourse analysis examines how meaning is made through the use of modes of communication such as images, sounds, video, gestures and actions rather than just language. Multimodal discourse analysis has two main strands of research: one is the study of multimodality in texts such as internet webpages, comic books and magazines etc.; the other is the study of multimodality in spoken interactions such as interviews, classroom interactions and other face-to-face talk. Each area of research focus has drawn on different traditions in linguistic and social science research. While the work on the analysis of multimodality in texts has its roots in systemic functional linguistics, work on the analysis of spoken interactions has been more influenced by linguistic ethnography, anthropology and psychiatry. An influential work in this latter approach is Sigrid Norris's (2004) *Analysing Multimodal Interaction* which lays out a framework for analysing the multimodal nature of face-to-face interactions. These two lines of research sometimes interact, however, as texts on web pages become more interactive (e.g. Jewitt 2009; Kress 2003) and multimodal texts play an increasingly important role in classroom interactions (e.g. O'Halloran 2005; O'Halloran & Smith 2011).

In summary, each of these areas of research has given us insights into the organization and interpretation of spoken and written discourse. What each of these views reveals is, in part, a result of the perspective the researchers have taken and the questions they have asked. There are many ways, then, in which one could and can approach discourse analysis.

A sample study

The rest of this chapter discusses a discourse analysis project that drew on a number of research techniques to answer its set of questions. The study (Wang 2006, 2007, 2008a, b) examined newspaper commentaries on the events of September 11 that were published in China and Australia in the months that followed these events. The study aimed to explore how the texts were written from a discourse point of view as well as possible reasons for the ways in which they were written.

Research perspectives

The study drew on four research perspectives: intercultural rhetoric, rhetorical genre studies, the systemic functional view of genre and critical discourse analysis. The framework presented in Figure 12.1 summarizes the perspectives that were drawn on to examine the two sets of texts and the relationship between the texts and the sociocultural contexts in which they were produced.

Intercultural rhetoric was the major starting point for the study in that it explored similarities and differences in rhetorical patterns between the two sets of texts. The systemic functional view of genre was drawn on to examine textual features of genres. Work in the area of critical discourse

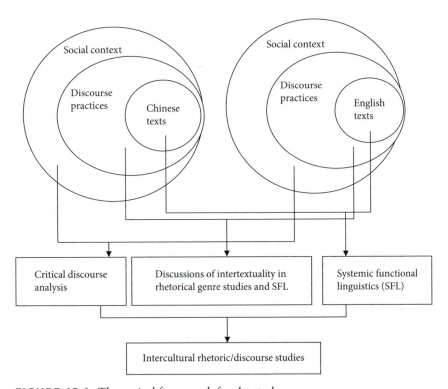

FIGURE 12.1 *Theoretical framework for the study*

analysis was drawn on to explore the social, political and contextual factors which contributed to the construction of the texts. The study, thus, aimed to describe not only linguistic characteristics of the texts but also considered how the texts had been produced and were consumed in the particular sociocultural context in which they had been written.

Data collection

Twenty-five Chinese newspaper commentaries published during the first three months after 11 September 2001 and twenty-five newspaper commentaries from Australian newspapers were the focus of the study. The criteria for selection were first, that the commentaries had to be close to the date of 11 September 2001; and second, that the commentaries focus on the issue of terrorism or the terrorist attacks of September 11. The total of fifty commentaries were considered both manageable and of sufficient range for both the linguistic and contextual analysis of the data.

An important feature of the data collection was the establishment of a *'tertium comparationis'* (a comparable platform) (Connor & Moreno 2005, p. 155; Moreno 2008) for the two sets of newspaper that were examined. Texts were chosen from Chinese and Australian newspapers, thus, taking into consideration geographic and demographic features that seemed to be comparable between the two countries. The newspapers were put into three broad groups: National General, National Specialist and State/Provincial. (The principal administrative division in China is a province, while in Australia it is a State.) Seven Australian and sixteen Chinese newspapers were matched to these categories. The number and sources of the texts are shown in the appendix.

Analysis of the data

The newspaper commentaries were examined at three levels of analysis, namely, textual, intertextual and contextual. At the textual level, the analysis aimed to identify similarities and differences in terms of macro- and micro-genres (Martin 1997; Martin & Rose 2008) in the two sets of texts. A *micro-genre* is a section of a text (or whole text) which represents a type of text such as exposition, discussion or problem-solution type text. The discourse structure of a micro-genre is described as its *schematic structure*. The discourse structures of the macro-genre newspaper commentaries (i.e. their *schematic stages*) were also analysed. Table 12.1 shows the typical structure of two of the key micro-genres found in the study, exposition (explanation) and exposition (argument).

Table 12.1 Examples of macro- and micro-genres and their discourse structures

Macro-genre	Schematic stages	Micro-genre	Schematic structures
Newspaper commentary	Heading ^ Name of author^ Introduction ^ Body ^ Conclusion ^	Exposition (Explanation)	Thesis ^ Orientation ^ Thesis Reiteration ^ Facts ^ Reasons ^ Solutions ^ Conclusion
Newspaper commentary	Heading ^ Name of author^ Introduction ^ Body ^ Conclusion ^	Exposition (Argument)	Thesis ^ Argument 1 ^ Argument 2 ^ Argument 3 ^ Conclusion 1 ^ Argument 1 ^ Argument 2 ^ Argument 3 ^ Conclusion 2

Note: ^ = followed by

At the intertextual level, the study examined how the writers employed outside sources to construct their texts by drawing on frameworks for analysis from rhetorical genre studies (Bazerman 2004) and systemic functional linguistics (White 2005). At the contextual level, the study investigated the role of the mass media and opinion discourses in the two sociocultural contexts and how this lead to different representations of terrorism in the texts (see Wang 2007, 2008a, b for further details on this).

Findings of the study

The study found that the Chinese writers frequently used explanatory expositions in their commentaries whereas the Australian writers used argumentative expositions. The study found, further, that the Chinese commentaries focused mainly on explaining terrorism, advocating an anti-terrorist battle under the leadership of the United Nations and discussing the possible impacts of the events of September 11 on the world economy. The Australian commentaries on terrorism debated the rhetoric of 'us' vs. 'them' and whether a humanitarian approach should be adopted to combat terrorism. These findings are very much in line with the role of the press in China as the public voice of the government and in Australia as a public forum for discussion, that is, the very different roles that newspaper commentaries play in the different social and cultural settings.

The study showed, then, that the newspaper commentaries on terrorism in the Chinese and Australian newspapers were constructed in different ways. It also showed that many of these differences can be traced back to the different sociocultural settings in which the texts were produced. It did this by drawing together textual and contextual views on the texts as a way of aiming to understand not only what the writers did but also why they did what they did.

Reliability and validity of the study

Taylor (2001) suggests a number of criteria by which discourse studies can be evaluated. These criteria, she argues, should be an integral part of any discourse analysis project. Key issues to consider in this are the *reliability* and *validity* of the project that has been carried out. The way in which each of these is taken up depends, of course, on whether the project is a quantitative, qualitative or mixed methods study (see Chapters 2, 3 and 4 where these research perspectives are discussed and how issues of reliability and validity are taken up in each of them).

In order to enhance the internal reliability of his study, Wang decided which newspapers would best represent the genre under investigation in terms of their circulation and which of them were most widely read in each of the social and cultural settings. Once he had decided which newspapers to select his texts from, he chose his texts from only these newspapers. He then analysed each of his texts in the same way. That is, he looked at the discourse structure of the macro- and micro-genres in each of the texts in the study. He looked for typical patterns in each of the sets of texts and considered the extent to which the use of the patterns he observed reflected particular sociocultural views of the relationship between the writers and their audience in the particular settings in which the texts were produced.

To ensure the external reliability of his study, Wang provided his sample texts and detailed analyses of each of the aspects he examined in the appendix to his study. In the methodology section of his study, he both explained and gave details of each of his categories of analysis so that his readers could then take these categories and re-analyse his data in the same way, if they wished to. In the presentation of his Chinese data, he provided English translations for each of his texts and glossed each of his Chinese examples in English so that a reader who cannot read Chinese would be able to follow his analysis and the arguments and claims he was making. That is, he provided sufficient information about the approach he used and his categories of analysis so that someone else approaching his data, in the same way, would come up with the same findings.

In terms of the validity of his study, Wang was careful to caution that his observations were limited to the set of texts that he had chosen for analysis. Even though his texts were chosen at random (although in a principled way), he was well aware that another set of twenty-five texts may reveal something different from what he observed, as indeed may an analysis of a larger set of texts. In terms of generalizability, then, he was well aware that this is not possible from the size of his sample. He did, however, provide sufficient details on the nature and source of his texts and his analyses of the texts, so that a reader could consider the extent to which his findings could be transferred or compared to what might be found in another, similar set of texts. By doing this, he aimed to provide *credibility*, *dependability* and *transferability* (Lincoln & Guba 1985) to the findings of his study. He, thus, left an *audit trail* that other people reading his research could follow by making as clear as possible what he had done and how he had reached his conclusions.

Ethical considerations in the study

Similarly, ethical considerations in discourse studies apply as they do to all other kinds of applied linguistics research (see Chapter 5 for an extended discussion of this). However, ethical considerations were not an issue for Wang's study as the texts that were chosen were publically available and no people were directly involved in the study. Notwithstanding, Wang took care to show respect for the traditions and customs of the countries and cultures involved in the study and the way in which he reported on these in his final project.

Resources for further reading

Gee, J & Handford M (eds), 2011, *The Routledge Handbook to Discourse Analysis*, Routledge, London.

This Handbook contains chapters on a wide range of areas including conversation analysis, genre analysis, corpus-based studies, multimodal discourse analysis and critical discourse analysis. Educational and institutional applications of discourse analysis are discussed as well as topics such as identity, power, ethnicity, intercultural communication, cognition and discourse.

Jaworski, A & Coupland, N 2006, 'Introduction: Perspectives on discourse analysis', in A Jaworski & N Coupland (eds), *The Discourse Reader*, 2nd edn, Routledge, London, pp. 1–37.

Jaworski and Coupland's introduction to the second edition of their book provides further details on a number of topics that have been presented in this chapter. This includes definitions of the term 'discourse', traditions in the analysis of discourse, speech act theory and pragmatics, conversation analysis and critical discourse analysis. Strengths and limitations of discourse studies are also discussed.

Paltridge, B 2012, *Discourse Analysis*, 2nd edn, Bloomsbury, London.

This book elaborates on many of the topics touched on in this chapter. There are chapters on discourse and society, discourse and pragmatics, discourse and genre, multimodal discourse analysis and conversation analysis. Grammar is considered from a discourse perspective as are corpus and critical approaches to the analysis of discourse.

Hyland, K & Paltridge, B (eds), 2011, *Continuum Companion to Discourse Analysis*, Continuum, London.

This set of chapters discusses a range of approaches and issues in researching discourse. Assumptions underlying methods and approaches are discussed as are research techniques and instruments appropriate to the goal and method of the research. The second part of the book provides an overview of key areas of discourse studies. In each chapter, the authors include a sample study which illustrates the points they are making and identify resources for further reading on the particular approach or issue under discussion.

References

Austin, JL 1962, *How to Do Things with Words*, Clarendon Press, Oxford.

Baker, P 2006, *Using Corpora in Discourse Analysis*, Continuum, London.

Bazerman, C 2004, 'Intertextuality: How texts rely on other texts', in C Bazerman & P Prior (eds), *What Writing Does and How It Does It: An Introduction to Analyzing Texts and Textual Practices*, Lawrence Erlbaum, Mahwah, NJ, pp. 83–96.

Benwell, B & Stokoe, E 2006, *Discourse and Identity*, Edinburgh University Press, Edinburgh.

Berkenkotter, C 2009, 'A case for historical "wide-angle" genre analysis: A personal retrospective', *Ibérica: Journal of the European Association of Language for Specific Purposes*, vol. 18, pp. 9–21, viewed 18 March 2014, http://www.aelfe .org/documents/02_18_Berkenkotter.pdf.

Biber, D 1988, *Variation Across Speech and Writing*, Cambridge University Press, Cambridge.

——— 1992, 'On the complexity of discourse complexity: A multidimensional analysis', *Discourse Processes*, vol. 15, no. 2, pp. 133–163.

Birner, B 2013, *Introduction to Pragmatics*, Wiley-Blackwell, Malden, MA.

Brown, G & Levinson, S 1987, *Politeness. Some Universals in Language Usage*, Cambridge University Press, Cambridge.

Chapman, S 2011, *Pragmatics*, Palgrave Macmillan, Basingstoke.

Christie, F 2002, *Classroom Discourse Analysis: A Functional Perspective*, Continuum, London.

Connor, U 1996, *Contrastive Rhetoric: Cross-Cultural Aspects of Second Language Writing*, Cambridge University Press, Cambridge.

——— 2004, 'Intercultural rhetoric research: Beyond texts', *Journal of English for Academic Purposes*, vol. 3, no. 4, pp. 291–304.

——— 2011, *Intercultural Rhetoric in the Writing Classroom*, University of Michigan Press, Ann Arbor, MI.

Connor, U & Moreno, A 2005, 'Tertium comparationis: A vital component in contrastive rhetoric research', in P Bruthiaux, D Atkinson, WG Eggington, W

Grabe & V Ramanathan (eds), *Directions in Applied Linguistics*, Multilingual Matters, Clevedon, pp. 153–164.

Cutting, J 2008, *Pragmatics and Discourse. A Resource Book for Students*, 2nd edn, Routledge, London.

Devitt, A 2004, *Writing Genres*, Southern Illinois University Press, Carbondale, IL.

Edley, N & Wetherell, M 2008, 'Discursive psychology and the study of gender: A contested space', in K Harrington, L Litosseliti, H Saunston & J Sunderland (eds), *Language and Gender Research Methodologies*, Palgrave Macmillan, London, pp. 119–138.

Edwards, D 2005, 'Discursive psychology', in KL Fitch & RE Sanders (eds), *Handbook of Language and Social Interaction*, Erlbaum, Mahwah, NJ, pp. 257–293.

Edwards, D & Westgate, DPG 1994, *Investigating Classroom Talk*, 2nd edn, Routledge, London.

Eggins, S & Slade, D 1997, *Analysing Casual Conversation*, Cassell, London, (republished 2005, Equinox Publishers, London).

Fairclough, N 2003, *Analyzing Discourse: Textual Analysis for Social Research*, Routledge, London.

———— 2010, *Critical Discourse Analysis: The Critical Study of Language*, 2nd edn, Longman, London.

Flowerdew, L 2012, *Corpora and Language Education*, Palgrave Macmillan, Basingstoke.

Grice, HP 1975, 'Logic and conversation', in P Cole & JL Morgan (eds), *Syntax and Semantics 3: Speech Acts*, Academic Press, New York, NY, reprinted in A Jaworski & N Coupland (eds), 1999, *The Discourse Reader*, Routledge, London, pp. 76–88.

Halliday, MAK 1973, *Explorations in the Functions of Language*, Edward Arnold, London.

Halliday, MAK & Hasan, R 1976, *Cohesion in English*, Longman, London.

———— 1989, *Language, Context and Text: Aspects of Language in a Social-Semiotic Perspective*, Oxford University Press, Oxford.

Hammond, J 2011, 'Classroom discourse', in K Hyland & B Paltridge (eds), *Continuum Companion to Discourse Analysis*, Continuum, London, pp. 291–305.

Huang, Y 2007, *Pragmatics*, Oxford University Press, Oxford.

Hutchby, I & Wooffitt, R 2008, *Conversation Analysis: Principles, Practices and Applications*, 2nd edn, Polity Press, Cambridge.

Hyland K 2009, *Academic Discourse: English in a Global Context*, Continuum, London.

Jewitt, C (ed.), 2009, *The Routledge Handbook of Multimodal Analysis*, Routledge, New York, NY.

Kaplan, RB 1966, 'Cultural thought patterns in intercultural education', *Language Learning*, vol. 16, no. 1, pp. 1–20.

Kress, G 2003, *Literacy in the New Media Age*, Routledge, London.

———— 2010, *Multimodality: A Social Semiotic Approach to Contemporary Communication*, Routledge, London.

Kress, G & van Leeuwen, T 2001, *Multimodal Discourse: The Modes and Media of Contemporary Communication*, Hodder, London.

——— 2006, *Reading Images: The Grammar of Visual Design*, 2nd edn, Routledge, London.

Kubota, R 1992, 'Contrastive rhetoric of Japanese and English: A critical approach', PhD thesis, Department of Education, University of Toronto.

Kubota, R & Lehner, A 2004, 'Toward critical contrastive rhetoric', *Journal of Second Language Writing*, vol. 13, no. 1, pp. 7–27.

Kumaravadivelu, B 1999, 'Critical classroom discourse analysis', *TESOL Quarterly*, vol. 33, no. 3, pp. 453–484.

Leech, G 2007, 'Politeness: Is there an East-West divide?', *Journal of Politeness Research*, vol. 3, no. 2, pp. 167–206.

Lincoln, YS & Guba, EG 1985, *Naturalistic Inquiry*, Sage, Beverly Hills, CA.

LoCastro, V 2012, *Pragmatics for Language Educators*, Routledge, London.

Martin, JR 1984, 'Language, register and genre', in F Christie (ed.), *Language Studies: Children's Writing: Reader*, Deakin University Press, Geelong, pp. 21–29, reprinted with revisions in C Coffin, T Lillis & K O'Halloran (eds), 2010, *Applied Linguistics Methods: A Reader*, Routledge, London, pp. 12–32.

——— 1997, 'Analysing genre: Functional parameters', in F Christie & JR Martin (eds), *Genre and Institutions: Social Processes in the Workplace and School*, Continuum, London, pp. 3–39.

Martin, JR & Rose, D 2008, *Genre Relations: Mapping Culture*, Equinox, London.

Miller, CR 1984, 'Genre as social action', *Quarterly Journal of Speech*, vol. 70, no. 2, pp. 151–167, reprinted in A Freedman & P Medway (eds) 1994, *Genre and the New Rhetoric*, Taylor and Francis, London, pp. 23–42.

Mills, S. 2003, *Gender and Politeness*, Cambridge University Press, Cambridge.

Moreno, A 2008, 'The importance of comparable corpora in cross-cultural studies', in U Connor, E Nagelhout & W Rozycki (eds), *Contrastive Rhetoric: Reaching to Intercultural Rhetoric*, John Benjamins, Amsterdam, pp. 25–41.

Norris, S 2004, *Analyzing Multimodal Interaction: A Methodological Framework*, Routledge, London.

O'Halloran, K 2005, *Mathematical Discourse: Language, Symbolism and Visual Images*, Continuum, London.

O'Halloran, K & Smith, BA (eds), 2011, *Multimodal Studies: Exploring Issues and Domains*, Routledge, New York, NY.

Paltridge, B 2014, 'Genre and second language academic writing', *Language Teaching*, vol. 47, no. 3, pp. 303–318.

——— 2015, 'Referees' comments on submissions to peer-reviewed journals: When is a suggestion not a suggestion?', *Studies in Higher Education*, vol. 40, no. 1, pp. 106–122.

Rose, D 2012, 'Genre in the Sydney school', in J Gee & M Handford (eds), *The Routledge Handbook to Discourse Analysis*, Routledge, London, pp. 209–225.

Rose, KR & Kasper, G 2001, *Pragmatics in Language Teaching*, Cambridge University Press, Cambridge.

Sacks, H, Schegloff, EA & Jefferson, G 1974, 'A simplest systematics for the organisation of turn taking for conversation', *Language*, vol. 50, no. 4, pp. 696–735.

Sadock, JM 2004, 'Speech acts' in LR Horn & G Ward (eds), *The Handbook of Pragmatics*, Wiley-Blackwell, Malden, MA, pp. 53–73.

Sbisà, M 2009, 'Speech act theory' in J Verschueren and J-O Östman (eds), *Key Notions for Pragmatics*, John Benjamins, Amsterdam, pp. 229–244.

Schryer, C 2011, 'Investigating texts in their social contexts: The promise and peril of rhetorical genre studies' in D Starke-Meyerring, A Paré, N Artemeva, M Horne & L Yousoubova (eds), *Writing in Knowledge Societies: Perspectives on Writing*, The WAC Clearinghouse and Parlor Press, Fort Collins, CO, pp. 31–52.

Searle, JR 1969, *Speech Acts*, Cambridge University Press, London.

Seedhouse, P 2005, 'Conversation analysis and language learning', *Language Teaching*, vol. 38, no. 4, pp. 165–187.

Sinclair, J & Coulthard, M 1975, *Towards an Analysis of Discourse*, Oxford University Press, Oxford.

Speer, SA 2005, *Gender Talk: Feminism, Discourse and Conversation Analysis*, Routledge, London.

Spencer-Oatey, H (ed.), 2008, *Culturally Speaking: Culture, Communication and Politeness Theory*, 2nd edn, Continuum, London.

Stokoe, E & Edwards, D 2007, '"Black this, black that": Racial insults and reported speech in neighbour complaints and police interrogations', *Discourse & Society*, vol. 18, no. 3, pp. 337–372.

Swales, JM 1990, *Genre Analysis: English in Academic and Research Settings*, Cambridge University Press, Cambridge.

——— 2004, *Research Genres: Explorations and Applications*, Cambridge University Press, Cambridge.

Taylor, S 2001, 'Evaluating and applying discourse analytic research', in M Wetherall, S Taylor & SJ Yates (eds), *Discourse as Data: A Guide for Analysis*, Sage, London, pp. 311–330.

Thornbury, S & Slade, D 2006, *Conversation: From Description to Pedagogy*, Cambridge University Press, Cambridge.

van Dijk, T 2001, 'Critical discourse analysis', in D Schiffrin, D Tannen & H Hamilton (eds), *The Handbook of Discourse Analysis*, Blackwell, Oxford, pp. 352–371.

van Leeuwen, T 2008, *Discourse and Practice: New Tools for Critical Discourse Analysis*, Oxford University Press, Oxford.

Walsh, S 2011, *Exploring Classroom Discourse: Language in Action*, Routledge, London.

Wang, W 2006, 'Newspaper commentaries on terrorism in china and Australia: A Contrastive genre study', PhD dissertation, University of Sydney.

——— 2007, *Genre across Languages and Cultures: Newspaper Commentaries in China and Australia*, VDM Verlag Dr. Müller, Saarbruecken.

——— 2008a, 'Intertextual aspects of Chinese newspaper commentaries on the events of 9/11', *Discourse Studies*, vol. 10, no. 3, pp. 361–381.

——— 2008b, 'Newspaper commentaries on terrorism in China and Australia: A contrastive genre study', in U Connor, E Nagelhout & W Rozycki (eds), *Contrastive Rhetoric: Reaching to Intercultural Rhetoric*, Benjamins, Amsterdam, pp. 169–191.

Watts, R 2003, *Politeness*, Cambridge University Press, Cambridge.

Wenger, E 1998, *Communities of Practice: Learning, Meaning and Identity*, Cambridge University Press, Cambridge.

Wetherell, M 2007, 'A step too far: Discursive psychology, linguistic ethnography and questions of identity', *Journal of Sociolinguistics*, vol. 11, no. 5, pp. 661–681.

Wetherell, M & Potter, J 1992, *Mapping the Language of Racism: Discourse and the Legitimation of Exploitation*, Harvester/Wheatsheaf, Brighton.

White, P 2005, 'The appraisal website', viewed 18 March 2014, http://www .grammatics.com/Appraisal/.

Wierzbicka, A 2003, *Cross-cultural Pragmatics: The Semantics of Human Interaction*, 2nd edn, Mouton de Gruyter, Berlin.

Wodak, R 2011, 'Critical discourse analysis', in K Hyland & B Paltridge (eds), *Continuum Companion to Discourse Analysis*, Continuum, London, pp. 38–53.

Wodak, R & Michael Meyer, M (eds), 2009, *Methods of Critical Discourse Analysis*, 2nd edn, Sage, London.

Yule, G 1996, *Pragmatics*, Oxford University Press, Oxford.

Appendix: Newspaper commentaries examined in the study (Wang 2006, p. 83)

Chinese Newspapers		No of texts	Australian Newspapers		No of texts
Chinese national general newspapers	*People Daily (Overseas edition)*	2	Australian national general newspaper	*The Australian*	10
	People Daily	3			
	Guangmin Daily	1			
	Xinhua Daily Telegraph	2			
	China Youth Daily	1			
	Economic Daily	1			
Chinese national specialist newspapers	*International Financial Daily*	1	Australian national specialist newspapers	*Australian Financial Review*	5
	Security Times	2			
	China's Economic Times	1			
	China's Defence Post	1			

(continued)

Chinese Newspapers		No of texts	Australian Newspapers		No of texts
Chinese provincial newspapers	*Hubei Daily*	1	Australian state newspapers	*Sydney Morning Herald*	2
	Wenhui Daily	2		*The Age*	2
	Hebei Daily	1		*The Courier Mail*	2
	Jiefang Daily	2		*Herald Sun*	2
	Huaxia Times	3		*Daily Telegraph*	2
	Study Times	1			

CHAPTER THIRTEEN

Research Synthesis

Lourdes Ortega

Research synthesis refers to a continuum of techniques and research procedures that have been developed by social scientists with the aim of reviewing past literature systematically. Simply put, the methodology produces contemporary literature reviews that differ from traditional literature reviews in taking an empirical perspective on the task of reviewing. Syntheses (also known as *systematic reviews* in some fields) investigate and evaluate past findings in a systematic fashion, always explicating the methodology followed in the review so as to enable replication by other reviewers. The approach began in the late 1970s in the fields of psychology, education and medicine and its use has been widespread across the social sciences since the late 1980s. In applied linguistics, the methodology was introduced in the mid 1990s and has witnessed a rapid development particularly since the late 2000s. Table 13.1 lists forty-five article-length syntheses published in the first twenty years of application of this method in our field.

Meta-analysis is probably the best-known technique for systematically synthesizing quantitative research. However, meta-analyses are a restricted form of synthesis that cannot always be conducted. For one, synthesists can engage in meta-analysis only when the body of research to be synthesized is clearly quantitative, that is, experimental, quasi-experimental or correlational. In addition, the methodology of meta-analysis is driven by questions about the magnitude of an effect or causal relationship and involves mathematical ways of summarizing past findings that demand the availability of a large number of studies.

Table 13.1 Article-length systematic research syntheses published in applied linguistics (1994 to February 2014)

Study	Key research question
Thomas (1994)*	How have SLA researchers measured proficiency for research purposes in their studies?
Ross (1998)**	How well does L2 self-assessment work?
Norris and Ortega (2000)**	How effective is L2 grammar instruction, and does type of instruction matter?
Goldschneider and DeKeyser (2001)**	How much of the L2 English morpheme accuracy order can be attributed to frequency and salience?
Masgoret and Gardner (2003)**	How well does amount of motivation predict L2 achievement in Garner's Attitude/Motivation Test Battery?
Ortega (2003)*	What is the relationship between syntactic complexity and L2 writing proficiency?
Roessingh (2004)**	What elements in the design and implementation of ESL programs support successful outcomes for ESL learners?
Dinsmore (2006)**	How different are native and non-native speaking performances in Universal Grammar studies?
Keck et al. (2006)**	How effective is task-based interaction in fostering L2 grammar and vocabulary gains?
Russell and Spada (2006)**	Is oral and written corrective feedback effective?
Jeon and Kaya (2006)**	How effective is L2 pragmatics instruction, and does type of instruction matter?
Taylor et al. (2006)**	How effective is explicit reading strategy instruction in improving L2 reading comprehension?
Téllez and Waxman (2006)†	What are best teaching practices to teach English Language Learners in k-12 schools in the U.S.?
Thomas (2006)*	How do SLA researchers measure proficiency for research purposes in their studies, twelve years after Thomas (1994)?
Indefrey (2006)**	Are L1 and L2 processed differently, according to hemodynamic research evidence?
Mackey and Goo (2007)**	How effective is task-based interaction in fostering L2 grammar and vocabulary gains?
Truscott (2007)**	Is written corrective feedback effective for improving L2 writers' accuracy in new writing?
Abraham (2008)**	How effective are computer glosses in supporting L2 reading comprehension and L2 vocabulary learning?
Lee and Huang (2008)**	How effective is typographical input enhancement as an L2 grammar implicit teaching technique?
Spada and Tomita (2008)**	Are L2 instructional gains moderated by whether structures are simple or complex?

(continued)

Study	Key research question
Wa-Mbaleka (2008)**	What is the strength of the relationship between reading and vocabulary learning and how do different reading conditions and factors moderate that relationship?
In'nami and Koizumi (2009)**	Do multiple-choice response formats (when compared to open-ended response formats) lead to measurement differences in tests of L1 reading, L2 reading, or L2 listening?
Taylor (2009)**	How effective are L1 or L2 glosses in supporting L2 reading comprehension during computer-mediated L2 reading versus traditional (paper) L2 reading?
Jun, Ramirez and Cumming (2010)**	What type, focus, and amount of tutoring is beneficial for supporting literacy among adolescents, at what ages and from what language background?
Li (2010)**	How effective is L2 oral corrective feedback in laboratory, classroom, and small group settings?
Lyster and Saito (2010)**	How effective is L2 oral corrective feedback in classroom settings?
Oswald and Plonsky (2010)*	What range of magnitudes is typically found in applied linguistic meta-analyses and what benchmarks can be derived from these empirically attested magnitudes?
Spada and Tomita (2010)**	Are L2 instructional gains moderated by whether structures are simple or complex?
Adesope et al. (2011)	How effective are different instructional interventions designed to teach reading or writing to English ESL immigrant students in kindergarten through grade 6?
Biber et al. (2011)	How effective is written error correction on the development of writing proficiency and revision skills?
Plonsky (2011)**	How effective is L2 strategy training?
Plonsky and Gass (2011)*	What is the quality of the research methods employed in the domain of L2 oral interaction research over the last three decades?
Sauro (2011)*	What do we know about the potential of synchronous computer-mediated communication CMC for additional language learning given the research trends, methods, and findings in this research domain over the last two decades?
Sebastian et al. (2011)	How different or similar are the brain activation patterns of bilingual speakers when compared to first-language activation patterns of monolingual, and to what extent does this depend on whether the bilinguals exhibit high, moderate, or low levels of L2 proficiency?
Yoon (2011)*	How promising are learner corpus concordancing activities in cultivating linguistic awareness in L2 writing and learner autonomy in L2 writers?

(continued)

Study	Key research question
Yun (2011)**	How effective are text-only and text-plus-visual glosses to promote L2 vocabulary acquisition during online reading?
Hulstijn (2012)*	In what ways has language proficiency been measured across 140 studies published between 1998 and 2011 in one of the top journals in bilingualism?
Chiu (2013)**	How educationally effective is supporting L2 vocabulary learning through computer technologies?
Grgurović et al. (2013)**	How effective are language learning pedagogies in bringing about language outcomes when they are supported by computer technology, as compared to without technology?
Jackson and Suethanapornkul (2013)**	How much evidence is there for the predictions of the Cognition Hypothesis regarding increases in complexity, accuracy, and fluency when tasks are made cognitively more demanding?
Plonsky (2013)*	What are the trends, strengths, and weaknesses in the designs, statistical analyses, and reporting practices observed across 606 primary quantitative studies published from 1990 to 2010 in two top journals in the field of SLA?
Shintani et al. (2013)**	How effective is L2 instruction when it is comprehension based versus production based?
Jeon and Yamashita (2014)**	What are the typical association strengths observed between passage-level L2 reading comprehension and ten key reading variables that have been often investigated?
Koo, Becker and Kim (2014)**	Are some large-scale reading assessment items more consistently difficult for English Language Learners than their mainstream peers in grade 3 and grade 10?
Plonsky (2014)*	How have trends evolved from 1990 to 2010 in the designs, statistical analyses, and reporting practices reported across 606 primary quantitative studies, and what do these changes suggest about needed future improvements in quantitative L2 methods?

Note: *Systematic quantitative synthesis. **Meta-analysis. †Systematic qualitative synthesis. Studies are listed in chronological order. Full citations are given in the references.

Other bodies of literature, however, offer descriptive, qualitative or mixed-methods data that cannot be appraised exclusively by notions of effect or causality or they are too small for meta-analytic quantification. In such cases, synthesists employ a number of empirically oriented methods in order to systematically review the literature, but they do not necessarily engage in all the formal quantitative procedures of meta-analysis. It is for this reason that we say all meta-analyses are also syntheses but not all syntheses are meta-analyses. It can be seen in Table 13.1 that in applied linguistics a good range of topics have been submitted to synthesis but mostly in the form of meta-analysis.

Underlying assumptions of the methodology

For a review to be considered a research synthesis, it must go beyond the collating and summarizing of individual study findings. Thus, none of the following summative techniques, in and of themselves, make a literature review into a synthesis: (a) presenting an authoritative narrative recount of past research activity in a given area, (b) summarizing many studies together in tabular form or (c) taking a count of how many studies yielded statistically significant findings in support of a given hypothesis. These are only traditional practices of good, traditional literature reviews. Research synthesists, on the other hand, must transcend such practices if they are to produce synthetic findings that are more than the sum of the parts and go beyond the individual results contained in any of the primary investigations synthesized (Norris & Ortega 2007).

Another trademark of many syntheses and meta-analyses (although not all) is a critical stance towards statistical significance. Many synthesists believe that while *probability* is an important dimension of quantitative research, *magnitude* is a distinct piece of information that is as important as probability and must be interpreted in conjunction with it (Kramer & Rosenthal 1999; Thompson 2006; for a recent discussion in L2 studies, see Plonsky 2014). When we pose questions about probability or statistical significance, we ask ourselves whether our observations are spurious (i.e., non-significant) or trustworthy (i.e., significant). This would only tell us whether the findings observed in a given study are likely to hold true if we carried out the same study again with a different sample drawn from the same population. Naturally, the issue of trustworthiness is very important in quantitative research paradigms, since it goes to the heart of generalizability. However, in the end, the questions of interest to experts – as well as to the public – are about magnitude. In applied linguistics, for example, an important question about the size of an effect would be: *How large or important* is the difference between providing instruction on an L2 grammar form or leaving it up to simple exposure to that form? And a central question about the strength of a relationship would be: If someone has below-average working memory capacity, *how severe or disadvantageous* can the consequences be for his or her potential to learn an L2 fast and well? By putting the emphasis on magnitude rather than probability or at least by always extracting and interpreting information about both probability and magnitude together, synthesists and meta-analysts seek to redress the many misuses and abuses of statistical significance that have been documented in all the social sciences (Harlow et al. 1997; Ziliak & McCloskey 2008), including applied linguistics (Lazaraton 2000; Plonsky 2013, 2014).

Finally, and as can be surmised from the discussion thus far, research synthesis typically has a positivist and quantitative orientation. This orientation is expected, given that the approach arose out of the desire to make sense of quantitative findings (Glass 1976). Nevertheless, some synthesists have recognized the need to explore appropriate methods for the systematic review of accumulated *qualitative* literatures. For example, over twenty years ago, educational sociologists George Noblit and Dwight Hare developed an approach for synthesizing ethnographic research that they called meta-ethnography (Noblit & Hare 1988) and more recently, a research team in medical sociology led by Mary Dixon-Woods at Leicester University has explored new principles for conducting critical interpretive syntheses of research (see Dixon-Woods et al. 2007). In applied linguistics, as indicated in Table 13.1, only one systematic synthesis of qualitative research exists (Téllez & Waxman 2006). In the future, and mirroring the evolution of research synthesis in the wider landscape of the social sciences, interest in qualitative forms of systematic reviewing may grow in our field (Norris & Ortega 2007). Suri and Clarke (2009) offer a cogent discussion of the tensions and possibilities that surround the application of systematic research synthesis to qualitative research in the educational and social sciences.

Validity and trustworthiness in research synthesis

Several key issues impinge on the validity and trustworthiness of a research synthesis. Reliability and validity can be weakened or strengthened at the point in the research process when effect sizes need to be calculated, aggregated and reported, as you will see when you read about *Techniques and instruments for research syntheses* in a later section. In this section, I discuss important validity considerations that arise during the sampling of the primary studies to be included in the review.

Apples and oranges or the problem of relevance

From the beginning of the research process, the synthesist faces two basic questions of relevance that can affect the validity of the review findings: How closely related to a given research question must a study be in order to be included in the synthesis? and How similar to each other must studies be in order for their findings to be combined meaningfully in the same synthesis? These questions can only be answered by carefully considering the purposes and research questions that guide a given synthesis. If we want to understand apples, it would be unwise to mix them with oranges in the same review. On the other hand, if we want to understand the two most popular fruits consumed daily in Western countries, then we may need to include precisely apples and oranges. If we want to understand fruit as a full category, moreover, we would want not only to mix apples and oranges but to include a wide palette of other types of fruit as well.

The apples and oranges question must be well justified in any synthesis and can only be satisfactorily answered if the synthesist has strong expert knowledge about the topic in question. In the end, therefore, substantive expertise in the research domain is as important as methodological expertise in the practice of research synthesis, and both are necessary to enhance the validity of the review. Coupled with the importance afforded to issues of coding, reliability and replicability, this is perhaps one of the reasons why research syntheses are often carried by teams rather than individuals (cf. Norris & Ortega 2006a).

Publication bias or the file-drawer problem

The problem of publication bias is little understood in the field of applied linguistics but well documented in all forms of quantitative research in the social sciences (Rothstein et al. 2005). First, studies that do not report at least some statistically significant result are likely to be rejected by journal referees. Secondly, authors are also inclined to give up on trying to publish a study which yielded no statistically significant outcomes, probably because they are well aware of the unspoken rejection bias of journals. In either case, the result is the same: studies that report statistically non-significant results are likely to be filed away in researchers' drawers and rarely make it into the public light. This means, in turn, that findings associated with a given research question are over-inflated if we only consider the universe of published studies, because statistically significant results are overrepresented (and statistically non-significant results underrepresented) in published literatures.

Therefore, good syntheses must always address the issue of publication bias. Among synthesists and meta-analysts, the preferred solution is to include unpublished or so-called fugitive literature in the synthesis. However, when including fugitive literature one must be doubly systematic and exhaustive in the sampling efforts. Particular care must be taken not to overrely on word-of-mouth knowledge of fugitive literature offered by immediate and far-away colleagues and their mentees and students. This knowledge, albeit valuable, is inevitably partial and most likely biased geographically and substantively. An arbitrary and incomplete sampling of unpublished studies can threaten the validity of the synthesis as much as an arbitrary and incomplete sampling of published studies would.

Whenever only published studies are included in a synthesis – unfortunately, the default case in applied linguistics thus far – the synthesist should assess the gravity of the publication bias at work. A wide range of sensitivity analyses has been developed specifically for this purpose (Rothstein et al. 2005). For example, Ross (1998) applied a mathematical estimation called the *fail-safe formula*; Norris and Ortega (2000) employed a visual technique called the *funnel plot*; and Li (2010) reported both the results of a funnel plot and a related technique called a *trim-and-fill analysis*. If both published and fugitive literatures are included in a synthesis, it is also informative to compare the main findings to the findings that obtain if published and fugitive studies are aggregated separately, as Taylor et al. (2006), Lee and Huang (2008), and Li (2010) did in our field.

Garbage in, garbage out or the problem of research quality

Ultimately, the quality of a synthesis is largely dependent on the quality of the primary evidence on which it is built. Some research synthesists follow the advice of educational psychologist Robert E. Slavin (1986), who advocated the *best evidence* approach to synthesizing. He proposed that only studies that meet the highest standards of methodological quality should be included in a synthesis. He was careful to warn that in the best evidence approach the task of determining what methodological rigour means must be explicitly rationalized anew by the synthesist for each research domain. It must also be justified for each study included in the synthesis, published or unpublished. A good illustration of these two points is offered in a meta-analysis by Slavin and Cheung (2005) that compared the effects of bilingual and English-only reading programs offered in elementary schools (and see also the online *Best Evidence Encyclopedia* of The Johns Hopkins University: http://www.bestevidence.org/, viewed 12 May 2014). Most synthesists, however, follow the broadly inclusive approach proposed by Gene Glass, the founder of meta- analysis (Glass 1976). As long as a study meets the set of inclusion criteria established at the onset of the synthesis, it will be included, so as to later perform sensitivity analyses that will help ascertain empirically whether, and in what ways, differences in research quality may have impacted the results of the review.

Norris and Ortega (2006b) argue, in agreement with most synthesists, that the inclusive approach serves well the field of applied linguistics. If the synthesist excludes certain studies a priori on grounds of poor research quality, this decision may always be contested, as methodological rigour is often in the eye of the beholder. Consider, for example, whether when carrying out a synthesis on effects of L2 instruction, intact classroom studies should be excluded because of their low internal validity due to lack of experimental control or whether laboratory studies should be excluded for their low ecological validity, despite their high internal validity. Either decision would always dissatisfy one or another sector of the research domain. On the other hand, if the reviewer is as inclusive as it is reasonable at the initial stage of study sampling, the accumulated evidence can be made sense of more fully in the synthesis, and any possible biases introduced by the varying research quality of the individual designs can be more closely inspected and appraised.

Techniques and instruments for research synthesis

A research synthesis will typically entail several steps, which derive from the empirical perspective on reviewing it embraces:

- *Problem specification*: As a first step, the research problem or question to be synthesized must be specified carefully and precisely; this is analogous to the step, necessary in any primary study, of formulating well-thought-out research questions.

- *Literature search and study eligibility criteria*: These two steps entail explicating how the primary studies will be located and which ones will be included or excluded in the synthesis and why; this parallels the need in any empirical study, quantitative or qualitative, to carefully plan the selection of participants and justify sampling procedures.

- *Coding book development*: At this step, a systematic coding scheme must be devised by which all variables under study in the synthesis will be extracted from each primary report; this is analogous to the design of an instrument (e.g. a test) or a procedure (e.g. an interview or an observation protocol) that will elicit the relevant evidence from each participant in as consistent and well-motivated a fashion as possible.

- *Coding of studies*: This step documents how the study coding was done and how the reliability of the coding process was safeguarded.

- *Data analysis and display*: This step is parallel to the processes involved in analysing and displaying results in primary research. The evidence reported in study after study must be extracted first by application of the coding scheme and then it must be processed and made sense of; and subsequently, the findings must be organized in numerical, visual and narrative displays.

- *Interpretation and dissemination*: As with all research activities, synthesizing ultimately is a process that demands interpretive and dialogic efforts within a disciplinary community; the results must be interpreted in a historical and disciplinary context and the findings disseminated in reports that others can read, judge, replicate and use for their own purposes.

Many research syntheses, and all meta-analyses, involve the calculation of what is known as *effect sizes*. An effect size is an index that captures numerically, and in a standardized form, the strength of a relationship or the magnitude of a difference. Effect sizes must be demystified. We all know *r*, or the correlation coefficient, and have learned to interpret it. This is, in fact, an effect size. It expresses the strength of a relationship between two variables represented by two sets of scores. The closer *r* is to positive 1 or negative 1, the stronger the relationship between the two variables is known to be (and this observed relationship may or may not be trustworthy, depending on the output we obtain for the probability value or *p* associated with each *r*; see Phakiti this volume). Correlations are always interpretable in this same way (from 0 to plus or minus 1), regardless of the variety of tests, instruments and methods by which the scores submitted to correlations are obtained. There are also many instances when researchers report their findings in natural units, such as words produced, hours studied or cigarettes smoked. Proportions and percentages are also effect sizes that everyone understands and uses in daily matters. When this is the case, the results do not need to be translated into a mathematical unit of some other kind but can be most meaningfully expressed in natural units and in proportions and percentages. For example, according to the famous report released by the US Department of Health, Education, and Welfare in 1967, cigarette smoking has been proven to increase mortality rates at different bands of magnitude: when compared to no smoking at all, smoking up to half a pack a day (or less than ten cigarettes) increases the chance of mortality by 40 per cent, and if we raise the consumption of cigarettes by four times, to two packs or more a day, the risk rate increases by three times (120 per cent). These are effect sizes that everyone understands.

But when a researcher reports mean performances of groups and subsequently compares mean group differences, the scores reported are specific to that study's instruments (e.g. a 42-point difference on the TOEFL in one study, a 3.68 difference on a 15-point test in another study, and so on). In order to compare mean results across many studies, therefore, each of the individual study results must first be converted into a common index, or an effect size, which can then be aggregated together in a total mean effect size. This effect size is typically *d* (Cohen 1988), which simply expresses the difference between two group means in standard deviation units. For example, a *d* of 1.45 indicates that the experimental group scored 1.45 deviation units above the control group on the post-test or that the advantage conferred by the treatment can be gauged to have had a magnitude of roughly one and a half deviation units in that study. Once we convert the results from each study into a d, we can average them and we will have the overall mean magnitude of a given treatment, based on however many studies we were able to combine. For example, a mean d of 1.45 indicates that, after inspecting study after study in our synthesis, we found that experimental groups had an average advantage over control groups of 1.45 deviation units in their favour.

It is important to emphasize that research synthesis, given its empirical take on the task of reviewing, adheres to the foundations of quantitative research in general. In order to enhance the reliability of the evidence and the validity of interpretations in primary quantitative research, it is important to consider the following issues against the context of the research questions and the design chosen: (a) sample size, (b) reliability of the instruments, (c) score distributions and (d) trustworthiness of the results. The same issues must also be considered by the synthesist, who will do well in thinking of each study as a 'participant' or 'informant' in the review. Thus, the synthesist must consider whether the number of accumulated studies is sufficient to carry out a full-blown meta-analysis or whether a synthesis using less powerful quantitative techniques is more appropriate in light of a small sample size. Furthermore, as with any elicitation instrument, the coding system employed to extract the same information consistently across all studies must be carefully developed and its reliable use enhanced and evaluated in the synthesis. In addition, if effect sizes are calculated, the synthesist should always make interpretations not only about the overall grand mean or average effect size but also about how spread out the results across individual studies are. Specifically, it is important to address the question: How representative of individual study results can a given average effect size be said to be? This can be achieved by reporting and inspecting the standard deviation associated with each mean effect size. Finally, whenever mean effect sizes are reported, confidence intervals that express the amount of error around the observed mean should also be calculated and reported. This information helps us determine how trustworthy the average findings really are, as it is equivalent to carrying out a statistical significance test.

Ethical considerations in research synthesis

Because synthesists only work with existing studies and previously reported results, they need not be concerned with norms for ethical conduct towards human participants. However, there are other ethical considerations worth mentioning. As with most quantitatively oriented research, syntheses and meta-analyses can be dangerously attractive and persuasive in their claim to take stock of accumulated evidence and in their aspiration to provide so-called final answers to important but elusive questions in a given domain of study. A related danger is what well-known meta-analyst Robert Rosenthal has called high-tech statistication (Rosenthal & DiMatteo 2001), which occurs when technical virtuosity in quantitative synthetic techniques is achieved at the expense of substantive quality and depth.

Being cognizant of these traps and knowing the limits of research syntheses is important (Norris & Ortega 2006b, 2007). No single synthesis can give a definitive answer to a research problem, because research is a human enterprise that is contingent on the time and space in which it is produced. Like all research, syntheses may be able to answer questions of now and here, but these questions will evolve. All knowledge will always be re-evaluated and re-calibrated, as human history and consciousness change. In addition, no dose of statistical or technical expertise can make up for lack of substantive expertise. Finally, research syntheses are always purely descriptive and correlational and cannot completely dispel debates surrounding causality, because the synthesist has no choice over the studies that make it into the review or over how individual researchers operationalized their variables and designed their investigations. In sum, syntheses can only produce evidence that is firmly rooted in the contexts in which the primary research has been carried out.

In the end, an ethical approach to practising research synthesis may come from 'a research ethic to think and act synthetically', and from 'a commitment to intelligible and respectful communication: between past and present studies, across theory and research and practice divides, between research contexts or camps, and among members of each research community' (Norris & Ortega 2006b, p. 36).

A sample study

I conclude this chapter with a quick tour of a meta-analysis that my colleague John Norris and I carried out (Norris & Ortega 2000) and which illustrates the methodology and its main concepts and procedures.

Problem specification

We set out to investigate the effectiveness of different types of L2 instruction. After examining the concepts most often discussed in this research domain, we decided against trying to gauge the effects of particular pedagogical techniques (e.g. recasts, grammar translation, input processing) because there were insufficient numbers of studies accumulated for any such technique. On the other hand, we adopted the theoretical notions of focus on form versus forms (Long 1991) and explicit versus implicit grammar teaching (DeKeyser 1995), because we reasoned they were workable characterizations of type of instruction that could be found in all specific techniques. We also decided to include as moderating variables the type of outcome measure (e.g. grammaticality judgement or free production task), the length of instruction (e.g. half an hour or 50 hours) and the durability of effects (i.e., whether any gains were maintained on delayed post-tests). The rationale was that these variables had been discussed in previous literature as important concerns when evaluating the effectiveness of L2 instruction and that information for at least the first two moderating variables could be extracted from each study (we expected that delayed post-tests would be present in only a subset of the studies).

Literature search and study eligibility criteria

Although we initially identified over 250 studies that were potentially relevant via electronic and manual searches, subsequently only seventy-seven study reports met the inclusion criteria for the synthesis that we had previously developed based on our knowledge of the research domain. Furthermore, we were able to include only a subset of these (specifically, forty-nine unique sample studies) in the meta-analysis part of the synthesis, because the remainder studies did not contain sufficient information to calculate effect sizes. The studies had been published between 1980 and 1998 and therefore represented the research domain as was practised in the 1980s and 1990s. The designs varied widely but all were (quasi-) experimental and involved instruction of a specific L2 form as the independent variable and measurement of performance on the same specific form as the dependent variable(s). After long deliberations, we decided to include only published studies and to inspect publication bias by means of a funnel plot. While we found no direct evidence of publication bias, we cautioned that this was most likely due to the fact that most individual researchers used complex multiple-treatment designs and therefore were able to report both statistically significant and non-significant results for different treatments within the same study. We also decided not to use methodological quality as a criterion for excluding studies and instead to adopt a broadly inclusive approach. That is, we decided to investigate research quality as an empirical matter, inspecting and synthesizing in full detail the research practices found across all seventy-seven studies.

Coding book development

An important and time-consuming step was to develop the coding book, which had to include a large number of categories in order to address each research question. For example, we decided that each study would be coded for methodological and background features such as learner characteristics, study design, sample size, length of treatment, timing of tests and statistical information reported. We also coded each study (and for multiple-treatment designs, each treatment group within each study) for substantive features, including: type of instruction (with five values: focus on form, focus on forms, focus on meaning, explicit and implicit), type of outcome measure (with four values: meta-linguistic judgement, selected response, constrained constructed response and free constructed response) and length of instruction (with four values: brief, short, medium and long; these categories were defined bottom-up, according to the range of observed instructional lengths in the seventy-seven studies).

Coding of studies

Both of us were involved as coders in the process of study coding. For most methodological, low-inference categories (e.g. year and type of publication) each coded a different half of the studies. Because we knew type of instruction and type of outcome measure would involve high-inference coding decisions, we decided to calculate and report reliability for these two categories only. Therefore, we set apart 20 per cent of the sample of studies and independently coded them for these substantive features. The reliability of the codings was satisfactory with values above 0.90 for both simple per cent agreement and *Cohen's kappa* (see Phakiti this volume).

Data analysis and display

We tallied all values for the coded methodological study features, aggregated them and presented them in tabular form (these results can be found in Tables 1–6 and Figures 1 and 2 in the original 2000 report). In order to answer the main research questions, we extracted effect sizes from the forty-nine unique sample studies for which sufficient information for this calculation was available. It is important to note that we calculated two distinct types of effect sizes, which we then aggregated and reported separately (as it should always be done if both types of effect sizes are used in the same meta-analysis): (a) standardized mean difference *d*s, which compared post-test performances of treatment versus control groups and (b) standardized mean gain *d*s, also called within-group pre-post contrasts, which expressed pre-to-post-test change for each group, including control or baseline groups. For each of the two effect size types, aggregations resulted in average effect sizes. We presented the information in the form of means, standard deviations and confidence intervals (which can be found in Tables 7–12 and Figures 3–8 in the original 2000 report).

Interpretation and dissemination

We found that L2 instruction overall was superior to simple L2 exposure or meaning-driven communication by nearly a full standard deviation unit on average ($d = 0.96$ based on forty-nine studies) and that explicit treatments were clearly superior to implicit treatments, in terms of both magnitude ($d = 1.13$ versus $d = 0.54$, based on sixty-nine and twenty-nine contrasts, respectively) and probability (the confidence intervals around these two means did not overlap, which amounts to saying that the two means were statistically significantly different from each other). On the other hand, the difference between focus on form and focus on forms treatments was small ($d = 1.00$ versus 0.93) and statistically not significant, indicating that both qualities of instruction were effective and neither one was superior to the other in the evidence examined (forty-three and fifty-five contrasts, respectively). We could offer no conclusive answers with regard to the influence of type of outcome measure or the varying lengths of instruction, due to insufficient sample size across categories for both variables. However, to our surprise, we found that the twenty-two studies which featured delayed post-tests yielded an average effect size of 1.02 and that the lower boundary of the associated confidence interval was 0.78, and from this we concluded that the effects of instruction were indeed durable for the participants involved in these twenty-two studies. Finally, we documented empirically a number of endemic methodological weaknesses typical of this domain, based on the full sample size of seventy-seven studies. We discussed these problems in detail and proposed some solutions.

It is important to stress that the main findings of this synthesis, as much as any other one, are contingent upon and grounded in the available accumulated evidence (Norris & Ortega 2006b). As authors of the synthesis, we have always felt readers of this study should not think of these results as directly generalizable to the abstract concept of 'L2 instruction'. This is simply because the real world of L2 instruction goes well beyond the world captured in those seventy-seven (or forty-nine) studies and offers a much richer kaleidoscope of contexts for the instruction of additional languages and much more varied approaches to the teaching of grammar than was possibly investigated in the particular studies synthesized. Moreover, the many methodological weaknesses uncovered and carefully documented also call for caution when extrapolating the findings beyond the concrete body of evidence synthesized. More modestly, we find value in the results of this meta-analysis because we hope they offer 'a useful empirical context within which future single-study findings from L2 type-of-instruction research can be more meaningfully interpreted' (Norris & Ortega 2000, pp. 499–500).

Resources for further reading

Cooper, H, Hedges, LV & Valentine, JC (eds), 2009, *The Handbook of Research Synthesis and Meta-Analysis*, 2nd edn, Russell Sage Foundation, New York, NY.

This edited collection constitutes the most comprehensive and encyclopedic treatment of meta-analysis to date. The utility (and difficulty) of chapters varies, but all have been written by international experts in specialized sub-areas of meta-analysis.

Hunt, M 1997, *How Science Takes Stock: The Story of Meta-Analysis*, Russell Sage Foundation, New York, NY.

This book offers a lively and accessible chronicle of the history of meta-analysis. Readers can learn a great deal of technical concepts in an intuitive fashion thanks to the variety of concrete examples offered from the fields of psychology, education and medicine.

Light, R & Pillemer, D 1984, *Summing Up: The Science of Reviewing Research*, Harvard University Press, Cambridge, MA.

This book is an unsurpassed classic treatise about research synthesis. It goes well beyond meta-analysis and offers many visual and descriptive techniques for synthesizing quantitative findings. For this reason, it is an invaluable tool to learn about the many options available in the methodology of synthesis.

Lipsey, MW & Wilson, DB 2001, *Practical Meta-Analysis*, Sage, Thousand Oaks, CA.

There are several textbook-like manuals about meta-analysis, but this one is particularly accessible and complete. It answers most technical questions that beginning meta-analysts will have about formulas for the calculation of different types of effect sizes, strategies for keeping track of study codings, and so on.

Cumming, G 2011. *Understanding the New Statistics: Effect Sizes, Confidence Intervals, and Meta-Analysis*, Routledge, New York, NY.

This statistics textbook requires advanced background knowledge in statistics and will not be easy to read for the average applied linguist. However, it is well worth the extra investment, as it can teach researchers in second language studies a great deal about how to think outside the box when it comes to inferential statistics and the relationships among numbers, research and meta-analysis.

Norris, JM & Ortega, L (eds), 2006, *Synthesizing Research on Language Learning and Teaching*, John Benjamins, Amsterdam.

This is the first and thus far only collection that exemplifies the methodology of research synthesis in applied linguistics. It includes applications of the methodology to universal grammar, interaction, negative feedback, pragmatics, reading strategies, the measurement of proficiency and best practices for English language learners in US schools. The variety of topics sampled in the empirical studies will help readers understand how synthesis can be applied to very diverse areas of research within applied linguistics. In the first chapter, the co-editors offer a critical, extensive overview of the principles and uses of synthesis.

References

Abraham, L 2008, 'Computer-mediated glosses in second language reading comprehension and vocabulary learning: A meta-analysis', *Computer Assisted Language Learning*, vol. 21, no. 3, pp. 199–226.

Adesope, OO, Lavin, T, Thompson, T & Ungerleider, C 2011, 'Pedagogical strategies for teaching literacy to ESL immigrant students: A meta-analysis', *British Journal of Educational Psychology*, vol. 81, no. 4, pp. 629–653.

Biber, D, Nekrasova, T & Horn, B 2011, 'The effectiveness of feedback for L1-English and L2-writing development: A meta-analysis' *TOEFL iBT™ Research Report*, 14, viewed 14 February 2014, http://www.ets.org/Media/Research/pdf/RR-11-05.pdf.

Chiu, Y-H 2013, 'Computer-assisted second language vocabulary instruction: A meta-analysis', *British Journal of Educational Technology*, vol. 44, no. 2, pp. E52–E56.

Cohen, J 1988, *Statistical Power Analysis for the Behavioral Sciences*, 2nd edn, Lawrence Erlbaum, Hillsdale, NJ.

DeKeyser, R 1995, 'Learning second language grammar rules: An experiment with a miniature linguistic system', *Studies in Second Language Acquisition*, vol. 17, no. 3, pp. 379–410.

Department of Health, Education, and Welfare 1967, *The Health Consequences of Smoking: A Public Health Service Review*, Public Health Service Publication No. 1696, Washington, DC.

Dinsmore, TH 2006, 'Principles, parameters, and SLA: A retrospective meta-analytic investigation into adult L2 learners' access to universal grammar', in J M Norris & L Ortega (eds), *Synthesizing Research on Language Learning and Teaching*, John Benjamins, Amsterdam, pp. 53–90.

Dixon-Woods, M, Booth, A & Sutton, AJ 2007, 'Synthesising qualitative research: A review of published reports', *Qualitative Research*, vol. 7, no. 3, pp. 375–422.

Glass, GV 1976, 'Primary, secondary, and meta-analysis of research', *Educational Researcher*, vol. 5, no. 10, pp. 3–8.

Goldschneider, J & DeKeyser, RM 2001, 'Explaining the "natural order of L2 morpheme acquisition" in English: A meta-analysis of multiple determinants', *Language Learning*, vol. 51, no. 1, pp. 1–50.

Grgurović, M, Chapelle, CA & Shelley, MC 2013. 'A meta-analysis of effectiveness studies on computer technology-supported language learning', *ReCALL*, vol. 25, no. 2, pp. 165–198.

Harlow, L, Mulaik, S & Steiger, J (eds), 1997, *What If There Were No Significant Tests?*, Lawrence Erlbaum, Mahwah, NJ.

Hulstijn, J. H. 2012. 'The construct of language proficiency in the study of bilingualism from a cognitive perspective', *Bilingualism: Language and Cognition*, vol. 15, no. 2, pp. 422–433.

In'nami, Y & Koizumi, R 2009, 'A meta-analysis of test format effects on reading and listening test performance: Focus on multiple-choice and open-ended formats', *Language Testing*, vol. 26, no. 2, pp. 219–244.

Indefrey, P 2006, 'A meta-analysis of hemodynamic studies on first and second language processing: Which suggested differences can we trust and what do they mean?', *Language Learning*, vol. 56, no. s1, pp. 279–304.

Jackson, D & Suethanapornkul, S 2013. 'The cognition hypothesis: A synthesis and meta-analysis of research on second language task complexity', *Language Learning*, vol. 63, no. 2, pp. 330–367.

Jeon, EH & Kaya, T 2006, 'Effects of L2 instruction on interlanguage pragmatic development: A meta-analysis', in JM Norris & L Ortega (eds), *Synthesizing Research on Language Learning and Teaching*, John Benjamins, Amsterdam, pp. 165–211.

Jeon, EH & Yamashita, J 2014, 'L2 reading comprehension and its correlates: A meta-analysis', *Language Learning*, vol. 64, no. 1, pp. 160–212.

Jun, SW, Ramirez, G & Cumming, A 2010. 'Tutoring adolescents in literacy: A meta-analysis', *McGill Journal of Education*, vol. 45, no. 2, pp. 219–238.

Keck, CM, Iberri-Shea, G, Tracy-Ventura, N & Wa-Mbaleka, S 2006, 'Investigating the empirical link between task-based interaction and acquisition: A meta-analysis', in JM Norris & L Ortega (eds), *Synthesizing Research on Language Learning and Teaching*, John Benjamins, Amsterdam, pp. 91–131.

Koo, J, Becker, BJ & Kim, Y-S 2014. 'Examining differential item functioning trends for English language learners in a reading test: A meta-analytical approach', *Language Testing*, vol. 31, no. 1, pp. 89–109.

Kramer, SH & Rosenthal, R 1999, 'Effect sizes and significance levels in small-sample research', in RH Hoyle (ed.), *Statistical Strategies for Small Sample Research*, Sage, Thousand Oaks, CA, pp. 59–79.

Lazaraton, A 2000, 'Current trends in research methodology and statistics in applied linguistics', *TESOL Quarterly*, vol. 34, no. 1, pp. 175–181.

Lee, S-K & Huang, HT 2008, 'Visual input enhancement and grammar learning: A meta-analytic review', *Studies in Second Language Acquisition*, vol. 30, no. 3, pp. 307–331.

Li, S 2010, 'The effectiveness of corrective feedback in SLA: A meta-analysis', *Language Learning*, vol. 60, no. 2, pp. 309–365.

Long, MH 1991, 'Focus on form: A design feature in language teaching methodology', in KD Bot, R Ginsberg & C Kramsch (eds), *Foreign Language Research in Cross-Cultural Perspective*, John Benjamins, Amsterdam, pp. 39–52.

Lyster, R & Saito, K 2010. 'Oral feedback in classroom SLA: A meta-analysis', *Studies in Second Language Acquisition*, vol. 32, no. 2, pp. 265–302.

Mackey, AV, Goo, JM 2007, 'Interaction research in SLA: A meta-analysis and research synthesis', in A Mackey (ed.), *Conversational Interaction in Second Language Acquisition*, Oxford University Press, New York, NY, pp. 379–452.

Masgoret, A-M & Gardner, RC 2003, 'Attitudes, motivation, and second language learning: A meta-analysis of studies conducted by Gardner and associates', *Language Learning*, vol. 53, no. s1, pp. 123–163.

Noblit, GW & Hare, RD 1988, *Meta-Ethnography: Synthesizing Qualitative Studies*, Sage, Newbury Park, CA.

Norris, JM & Ortega, L 2000, 'Effectiveness of L2 instruction: A research synthesis and quantitative meta-analysis', *Language Learning*, vol. 50, no. 3, pp. 417–528.

Norris, JM & Ortega, L (eds), 2006a, *Synthesizing Research on Language Learning and Teaching*, John Benjamins, Amsterdam.

—— 2006b, 'The value and practice of research synthesis for language learning and teaching', in JM Norris & L Ortega (eds), *Synthesizing Research on Language Learning and Teaching*, John Benjamins, Amsterdam, pp. 3–50.

———— 2007, 'The future of research synthesis in applied linguistics: Beyond art or science', *TESOL Quarterly*, vol. 41, no. 4, pp. 805–815.

Ortega, L 2003, 'Syntactic complexity measures and their relationship to L2 proficiency: A research synthesis of college-level L2 writing', *Applied Linguistics*, vol. 24, no. 4, pp. 492–518.

Oswald, FL & Plonsky, L 2010. 'Meta-analysis in second language research: Choices and challenges', *Annual Review of Applied Linguistics*, vol. 30, pp. 85–110.

Plonsky, L 2011. 'The effectiveness of second language strategy instruction: A meta-analysis', *Language Learning*, vol. 61, no. 4, pp. 993–1038.

———— 2013, 'Study quality in SLA: An assessment of designs, analyses, and reporting practices in quantitative L2 research', *Studies in Second Language Acquisition*, vol. 35, no. 4, pp. 655–687.

———— 2014, 'Study quality in quantitative L2 research (1990–2010): A methodological synthesis and call for reform', *The Modern Language Journal*, vol. 98, no. 1, pp. 450–470.

Plonsky, L & Gass, SM 2011, 'Quantitative research methods, study quality, and outcomes: The case of interaction research', *Language Learning*, vol. 61, no. 2, pp. 325–366.

Roessingh, H 2004, 'Effective high school ESL programs: A synthesis and meta-analysis', *Canadian Modern Language Review*, vol. 60, no. 5, pp. 611–636.

Rosenthal, R & DiMatteo, MR 2001, 'Meta-analysis: Recent developments in quantitative methods for literature reviews', *Annual Review of Psychology*, vol. 52, pp. 59–82.

Ross, S 1998, 'Self-assessment in second language testing: A meta-analysis and analysis of experiential factors', *Language Testing*, vol. 15, no.1, pp. 1–20.

Rothstein, HR, Sutton, AJ & Borenstein, M (eds), 2005, *Publication Bias in Meta-Analysis: Prevention, Assessment and Adjustments*, Wiley, Chichester.

Russell, J & Spada, N 2006, 'The effectiveness of corrective feedback for the acquisition of L2 grammar: A meta-analysis of the research', in JM Norris & L Ortega (eds), *Synthesizing Research on Language Learning and Teaching*, John Benjamins, Amsterdam, pp. 133–164.

Sauro, S 2011, 'SCMC for SLA: A research synthesis', *CALICO Journal*, vol. 28, no. 2, pp. 369–391.

Sebastian, R, Laird, AR & Kiran, S 2011, 'Meta-analysis of the neural representation of first language and second language', *Applied Psycholinguistics*, vol. 32, no. 4, pp. 799–819.

Shintani, N, Li, S & Ellis, R 2013, 'Comprehension-based versus production-based instruction: A meta-analysis of comparative studies', *Language Learning*, vol. 63, no. 2, pp. 296–329.

Slavin, RE 1986, 'Best evidence synthesis: An alternative to meta-analytic and traditional reviews', *Educational Researcher*, vol. 15, no. 9, pp. 5–11.

Slavin, RE & Cheung, A 2005, 'A synthesis of research on language of reading instruction for English language learners', *Review of Educational Research*, vol. 75, no. 2, pp. 247–284.

Spada, N & Tomita, Y 2008, 'The complexities of selecting complex (and simple) forms in instructed SLA research', in A Housen & F Kuiken (eds), *Proceedings of the Complexity, Accuracy and Fluency (CAF) Conference*, University of Brussels, Brussels, pp. 227–254.

———— 2010, 'Interactions between type of instruction and type of language feature: A meta-analysis', *Language Learning*, vol. 60, no. 2, pp. 263–308.

Suri, H & Clarke, D 2009, 'Advancements in research synthesis methods: From a methodologically inclusive perspective', *Review of Educational Research*, vol. 79, no. 1, pp. 395–430.

Taylor, A, Stevens, JR & Asher, JW 2006, 'The effects of explicit reading strategy training on L2 reading comprehension: A meta-analysis', in JM Norris & L Ortega (eds), *Synthesizing Research on Language Learning and Teaching*, John Benjamins, Amsterdam, pp. 213–244.

Taylor, AM 2009, 'CALL-based versus paper-based glosses: Is there a difference in reading comprehension?', *CALICO Journal*, vol. 27, no. 1, pp. 147–160.

Téllez, K & Waxman, HC 2006, 'A meta-synthesis of qualitative research on effective teaching practices for English Language Learners', in JM Norris & L Ortega (eds), *Synthesizing Research on Language Learning and Teaching*, John Benjamins, Amsterdam, pp. 245–277.

Thomas, M 1994, 'Assessment of L2 proficiency in second language acquisition research', *Language Learning*, vol. 44, no. 2, pp. 307–336.

———— 2006, 'Research synthesis and historiography: The case of assessment of second language proficiency', in JM Norris & L Ortega (eds), *Synthesizing Research on Language Learning and Teaching*, John Benjamins, Amsterdam, pp. 279–298.

Thompson, B 2006, *Foundations of Behavioral Statistics: An Insight-Based Approach*, Guilford, New York, NY.

Truscott, J 2007, 'The effect of error correction on learners' ability to write accurately', *Journal of Second Language Writing*, vol. 16, no. 4, pp. 255–272.

Wa-Mbaleka, S 2008, *A Meta-Analysis Investigating the Effects of Reading on Second Language Vocabulary Learning*, VDM Verlag, Saarbrücken.

Yoon, C 2011, 'Concordancing in L2 writing class: An overview of research and issues', *Journal of English for Academic Purposes*, vol. 10, no. 3, pp. 130–139.

Yun, J 2011, 'The effects of hypertext glosses on L2 vocabulary acquisition: A meta-analysis', *Computer Assisted Language Learning*, vol. 24, no. 1, pp. 39–58.

Ziliak, ST & McCloskey, DN 2008, *The Cult of Statistical Significance: How the Standard Error Costs Us Jobs, Justice, and Lives*, The University of Michigan Press, Ann Arbor, MI.

CHAPTER FOURTEEN

Ethics and Applied Linguistics Research

Peter De Costa

This chapter is situated within the larger and irreversible trend towards analysing ethical practices in applied linguistics, given the field's enduring commitment to addressing and resolving language-based problems in the real world (Bygate 2005). Indeed, most applied linguists would not disagree with the core principles of (1) respect for persons, (2) yielding optimal benefits while minimizing harm and (3) justice. Put simply, they are generally committed to an ethical protocol that averts harming research participants in any way. However, how applied linguists go about realizing these principles generally differ, and they are often influenced by the methodological paradigm they subscribe to, their training, the area of research in which they work, their individual personality and the macro and micro factors that shape their research process. Taking this constellation of factors into consideration, this chapter explores the distinction between macroethics and microethics before going on to address how ethical tensions can be addressed before, during and after the data-collection process.

Underlying assumptions

Ethics, according to Brown (2004), is 'an area where all research methods and techniques come together and tend to agree' (p. 498). Equally important to recognize is that what is considered ethical may vary from one researcher to the next. To some extent, what constitutes ethical research also depends on the research methods adopted, whether they are quantitative or qualitative, for example. As Kono (2013) puts it, 'if we consider the relationship between qualitative and quantitative research methods as a natural continuum, rather than an artificial dichotomy, we begin to see that each gradation of that continuum represents a different set of ethical questions' (p. 1). Looking at how ethics is interpreted from a paradigmatic perspective, however, Kubanyiova posits that a researcher working within the 'positivist paradigm tends to treat ethics in the same vein that is suggested in IRBs [Institutional Review Boards].[1] That is, ethical practice is ensured if rigorous procedures have been followed and ethical clearance obtained' (p. 2). By contrast, applied linguists working within a critical postmodernist paradigm would emphasize the values and ideologies of the researchers and issues of power surrounding the research process. On an ethical level, advocating for their participants and ensuring that social justice is served would be their primary objectives.

Admittedly, ethics can be examined from a variety of perspectives – quantitative versus qualitative (e.g. Kono 2013) – or along paradigmatic lines (Kubanyiova 2013; also Paltridge & Phakiti, this volume). A third way to explore ethics, while incorporating the first two approaches, is through a macroethical and microethical lens. Following Guillemin and Gillam (2004), Kubanyiova (2008) makes the distinction between *macroethics* and *microethics*. While the former refers to the 'procedural ethics of IRB protocols and ethical principles articulated in professional codes of conduct' (p. 505), the latter refers to 'everyday ethical dilemmas that arise from the specific roles and responsibilities that researchers and research participants adopt in specific research contexts' (p. 504). Building on this distinction, I have elected to use a macroethical/microethical lens to frame this chapter for two reasons. First, instruments used in applied linguistics straddle the qualitative/ quantitative divide because a data collection tool such as an interview is used in both quantitative and qualitative research. Similarly, from an ethical perspective, the division between paradigms has become increasingly blurred. As observed by Phakiti (this volume), the potential influence of personal bias or values on research outcomes is also acknowledged by researchers working within a postpositivist paradigm and is thus not the sole reserve of postmodernist researchers. Second, in adopting such a lens to examine ethics in applied linguistics, it is my intention to emphasize that both macroethical and microethical concerns need to be addressed in a concerted manner at the start, during and at the end of the research process.

Macroethics and microethics

Much of the ethics literature to date seems to be influenced by macroethical concerns in that it offers guidelines, often described as *best practices*. According to Brown (2011), such practices have come under the increasing scrutiny of university-wide IRB protocols, which are also often aimed at protecting the institution as much as the research participants (Duff 2008). Further, field-specific applied linguistics journals have tried to complement IRB protocols by providing guidelines for contributors. Among the journals, *TESOL Quarterly* probably offers the most detailed informed consent guidelines. Guidelines for reporting quantitative research and three types of qualitative research also appear in *TESOL Quarterly* (see Chapelle & Duff 2003).

Applied linguists have also turned to professional organizations with their various statements on ethics for direction. For example, The British Association for Applied Linguistics'(BAAL) *Recommendations on good practice in Applied Linguistics* delineates the teaching, administrative and research responsibilities applied linguists have to manage in relation to the field of applied linguistics, sponsors, their own institutions and the public (BAAL 2006). BAAL's ethical guidelines have been adopted by the Applied Linguistics Association of Australia (ALAA), who added an appendix to protect the linguistic rights of aboriginal and islander communities (ALAA 1998). In a similar vein, resolutions such as the *Resolution against Discrimination on the Basis of Accented Speech* (2011) passed by the membership of the American Association for Applied Linguistics (AAAL) have also afforded applied linguists macroethical guidance.

As helpful as these guidelines have been in articulating good practices that ought to be adopted by applied linguists, the guidelines also need to be complemented by microethical governance, that is, actual examples of how to negotiate ethical dilemmas in specific research contexts (De Costa 2014; Kubanyiova 2008; Ngo, Bigelow & Lee 2014). Such insights are also in keeping with the reflexive turn in applied linguistics as observed by Kramsch and Whiteside (2007), who called for researcher positioning 'to be explicitly and systematically accounted for and placed in its historical, political, and symbolic context' (p. 918).

Techniques and instruments: Enacting ethical practices

Drawing on Creswell's (2013) framework for addressing ethical issues, I discuss the conduct of macro- and microethical practices over three phases: (1) prior to conducting and at the start of the study, (2) during data collection and data analysis and (3) reporting the data and publishing the study. Underpinning these practices is the need to maintain rigour throughout the research process, which includes adopting sound techniques and instruments.

Prior to conducting and at the start of the study

On a macroethical level, the protocols of university ethical review boards need to be observed. As mentioned, the primary concern of most ethical review boards is that respect for persons and minimal harm are observed. To some extent, meeting expectations has become increasingly harder to achieve as more research is conducted in digital domains. As asserted by Wang and Heffernan (2010) in their investigation of computer-assisted language learning (CALL) classes, CALL settings in particular are susceptible to having online security and learners' personal data disclosure compromised. These concerns surrounding online research are echoed by Ortega (2007), who questioned researchers' loitering or lurking into chat rooms as such actions constituted an infringement of participant privacy. There is also a growing concern over whether participants' virtual or real anonymity is protected in corpus research. For example, McEnery and Hardie (2011) observed that despite procedural ethics, examples of poor practice in corpus building, particularly with regard to protection of participants' anonymity, can still be found even in well-known corpora. In short, efforts need to be made to protect participant's confidentiality, especially in research contexts involving participants who can face tangible consequences of what they write or say.

Researchers also play a vital role in educating IRBs because not all cultural settings require the same forms of consent; as noted by Holliday (see Chapter 3), different settings require different degrees of formality, informality and understanding. Similarly, co-principal investigators in different institutions, especially at institutions in cross-national contexts, may need to be informed about the ethical protocol observed by the researcher's home institution and academic discipline. The latter context is particularly important when collaborating with a researcher from a different discipline. Finally, when seeking participant's consent, consent forms need to be made accessible and understandable by simplifying the language, translating forms into multiple languages and creating the option for oral consent, so that such consent is in compliance with local cultural practices.

On a microethical level, rather than rehearsing a description of the techniques and instruments related to the earlier chapters in this volume, I would like to reinforce several issues raised by other contributors to this book next. First, and following Phakiti (this volume), it is important that the instruments used be valid and reliable. Given that participants give up their time to take part in studies even though they may be compensated for their participation, it is essential that researchers be cognizant of the time allocated to conduct interviews and experiments, and to administer questionnaires. As Holliday (this volume) rightly observes, 'people will very likely have far more important things to do and think about than taking part in your research project' (p. 56). Hence, sufficient thought should also be given to data reduction; put differently, only data which address the research questions should be collected as implementing this practice will also ensure responsible data management later.

However, data-collection corners should not be cut too hastily either. With regard to tests, for example, Spolsky (1997) reminds us that tests may also have ethical limitations that are difficult to avoid, thus making it necessary to conduct multiple tests and use alternative methods. Relatedly, when designing tests, translation directions or the use of dictionaries should be prepared, and glossaries or use of simplified English provided because high-stakes tests can have various negative consequences on learners (Solórzano 2008). Similarly, the language used in interviews or questionnaires needs to be translated or at least be simplified to a level comprehensible to the respondents (see Wagner this volume).

One way to avert teething problems in general is to conduct a pilot study and minimize the ethical impact on participants. Such an impact is further reduced if the needs of participants are served. Put differently, among other things, acting ethically entails taking into account elements of social justice (Hafernik et al. 2002) when, for example, working with an under-researched population such as immigrant learners and heritage speakers of a non-English language (Ortega 2005). Hence, the effects of the research project need to be considered before embarking on the project, and this includes weighing the potential negative impact of treatments on participants when conducting experiments (see Gass this volume).

During data collection and data analysis

While pre-emptive measures can be taken to ensure that ethical practices are in place, the researcher also needs to adopt a flexible approach when dealing with ethical problems that may emerge in specific research contexts. In other words, a fluid disposition, that is, one which is perceptive to emergent circumstances, needs to be cultivated. For example, when administering a survey (see Wagner this volume), research bias needs to be factored in. This includes being aware that participants may (1) give answers that enhance their own standing (prestige bias), (2) provide responses that reflect how they would like to think of themselves as acting, rather than how they really act (self-deception bias), and (3) respond according to how they think the researcher wants them to respond (acquiescence bias).

Similarly, as noted by Talmy (2010), researchers conducting interviews ought to view interviews as more than just an instrument to collect data. Rather, they also need to see interviews as a form of a social practice where both the interviewer and the interviewee engage in acts of discursive positioning as each evaluates the other during the interview process, thereby mutually shaping the type of information that is yielded during the interview. In essence, to ensure that ethical practices are in place, the researcher would need to work on developing a relationship with his or her participants and treat the exchange as being more than a transaction. Underscoring the importance of building relationships with immigrant communities with whom they worked, Ngo, Bigelow and Lee (2014) point out that researchers should not consider immigrants only as participants that would serve their academic interests (i.e. being a variable in research studies); instead, they should build trust and design research in a way that would also benefit these communities. While their observation is illuminating and is reminiscent of Ortega's (2005) point that research should bear social utility, such a decision is not without ethical repercussions and responsibilities. Holliday (this volume) reminds us that it may be unfair to develop relationships within a research setting which cannot be sustained in their own terms. This exhortation is borne out in Lee (2011), who describes an ethical bind she found herself in. Even though she found out about racializations faced by her research participant, Lee was reluctant to help by raising this issue with her participant's colleagues and the school authorities due to her ethical duties of keeping the confidentiality of her participant. Thus, even though Lee followed procedural (macro)ethics, she concluded that individual researchers need to make situated, (micro)ethical decisions that supersede professional ethical codes.

Analysing data is also fraught with ethical demands. When analysing quantitative data, researchers need to select appropriate statistical tests (e.g. parametric or non-parametric) to answer research questions (Phakiti this volume). Knowing and understanding the logic behind statistical analysis and the standards for a particular statistical test may mean having to consider alternate types of analyses. For example, Plonsky et al. (2014) highlight that parametric analyses may not be appropriate for small samples and/or non-normally distributed data and recommend instead bootstrapping (Davison & Hinkley 1997), a non-parametric procedure that produces a more stable and statistically accurate outcome.[2] Emphasizing the importance of managing subjectivity in qualitative research, Holliday (this volume) underlines the need for transparency of method and recommends keeping a research diary throughout the whole process as well as following a four-step data analytic process that includes coding, determining themes, constructing an argument and going back to the data. In short, transparent, rigorous and informed data analyses contribute towards preserving the ethical fibre of research.

Reporting the data and publishing the study

Writing from the perspective of action research, Burns (this volume) urges researchers to consider if the ends and outcomes contribute towards educational improvement and to factor in to whom research findings will be disseminated upon project completion. Relatedly, but referring specially to the (macro)ethical guidelines for quantitative and qualitative research published in *TESOL Quarterly* mentioned earlier, Shohamy (2004) noted that these guidelines (see Chapelle & Duff 2003) did not focus on researchers' responsibility regarding the uses and misuses of research results. As observed by Shohamy, researchers generally think their tasks are complete when their research report or article is turned in or published; however, she warns about the potential abuse of research results, which may be used inappropriately by consumers for immoral and unethical purposes.

Indeed, while there is no foolproof way for researchers to prevent their work from being misappropriated, one possible way to evade this problem on a microethical level is to foreground the statistical and practical significance of one's findings. If anything, there have been increasing calls for quantitative researchers to highlight the statistical as well as practical significance of their work (Norris & Ortega 2006; Plonsky & Gass 2011).[3] As noted by Plonsky (2013), researchers regularly omit findings because they fail to reach statistical significance or because they contradict the expectations of the researcher. These practices, he added, introduce bias in the available literature and therefore prevent research from accurately informing L2 theory, practice and future research. By the same token, Phakiti (this volume) alerts us to the importance of the practical significance of research findings. As he explains, sometimes it is useful to know that there is no statistical significance because a non-statistical finding may confirm a theory by illustrating that two variables are not related. Thus, acting ethically entails taking note of the statistical and practical significance of quantitative findings, especially in light of the growing interest in research synthesis, which takes stock of accumulated evidence and seeks to provide conclusive assertions in a given domain of study (see Ortega this volume). Consequently, researchers need to act ethically towards other members of the research community by being more transparent when reporting their data and making their work available to other applied linguists. Such efforts include engaging in replication work and publishing supplementary materials on the online space provided by journals such as *Applied Linguistics* and *Language Learning* (Plonsky et al. 2014).

Another growing ethical concern that applied linguists have to contend with is the 'publish or perish' culture engulfing the academy today. In the wake of mounting pressure to publish, due diligence needs to be paid to plagiarism in the field (Hamp-Lyon 2009; Wen & Gao 2007) as well as issues surrounding co-authorship. Student–faculty collaborative research, in particular, is prone to abuse because a deserving junior researcher may be excluded from the author list or given less prominence than they should be. Equally controversial are the phenomena of *ghost authors* (i.e. those who contribute substantially but are not acknowledged as they are often paid by commercial sponsors), *guest authors* (i.e. those who do not make substantial contributions but are included as authors with the hope of increasing the chances of publication) and *gift authors* (i.e. those who are included on the basis of a tenuous affiliation with a study) (Council of Science Editors 2012). To some extent, the macroethical guidelines provided by IRB protocols and by the American Psychological Association (2010) need to be recognized. While the former generally requires researchers to declare any conflicts of interests with commercial sponsors, the latter offers insights on collaborative authorship. In a similar vein, journal guidelines have also been helpful in providing authors with direction on ethical conduct. For example, *The Modern Language Journal* explicitly states that it allows for the publication of articles previously published in another (i.e. non-English) language, while *Language Learning* requires authors to submit a cover letter providing background to the submission and to disclose any special circumstances that may raise potential ethical considerations. Further, *TESOL Quarterly* clearly states that it is the author's responsibility to indicate to the editor the existence of any work already published, or under review elsewhere. In sum, it is crucial that authors balance these macroethical guidelines with reflexive microethical practices when it comes to publishing. Ultimately, authors need to be wary of taking on too many writing commitments and overextending themselves. Such a course of action could result in unnecessary delays to other collaborators and/or result in work of a compromised quality which, in turn, could result in a skewed representation of the author's participants. In the long run, hurried and sloppy scholarship only creates room for further misinterpretation by consumers of the research.

A sample study

De Costa (2014) illustrates the ethical problems encountered during a year-long ethnographic study in an English-medium school in Singapore. My study explored how a group of immigrant students was discursively positioned in the school and examined the impact their positioning had on their learning outcomes.

Prior to conducting and at the start of the study

After obtaining the approval of the Ministry of Education in Singapore, I approached the principal of a school, Orchid Girls' Secondary School (OGSS, a pseudonym). Upon securing her support and that of my teacher and student participants, I applied for IRB approval from the US university to which I was affiliated at the time of the study and distributed consent forms. My participants were also given the option to withdraw at any point of the study without penalty, if they desired. In reciprocation for their participation, I helped implement a lesson study professional development project for the teachers. For my student participants, I provided supplementary English lessons to my focal students, organized fieldtrips and furnished them with information about the Singapore education system. In short, I positioned myself as a 'researcher as resource' (Sarangi & Candlin 2003, p. 279).

During data collection and data analysis

I was on-site at OGSS for the entire school year, which allowed for a persistent and prolonged engagement with my participants. My enduring presence in the school earned me insider status within OGSS and helped offset any hasty and preliminary generalizations. Further, my holistic understanding of my research site was enhanced by having multiple data sources: observations, interviews, audio- and video-recorded classroom interactions and artefacts.

I was also reflexive about the need to exercise an *ethics of care* (Kubanyiova 2008), and to avoid taking advantage of the hospitality of teachers, who had punishing work schedules, I made it a point not to turn up for every lesson. Instead, lesson observations were staggered, and ample notice was given to participating teachers before turning up for their class. To ensure that a distancing stance from my participants was maintained, I took occasional timeouts (Emerson et al. 2011) from my research and participated in other activities at OGSS. Such timeouts insulated me from empathizing too much with my immigrant participants or becoming overly critical of their teachers.

Classroom interactions were also video-recorded. To reduce any tensions between my focal immigrant participants and their Singaporean peers, who viewed the immigrant students as the 'Other', I decided to only videotape the teacher and my focal students while they were delivering class presentations. To capture more interactions involving my focal learners and the teachers and their Singaporean peers, I switched to and purchased five audio recorders with a lapel microphone for my focal students. This decision was made to respect the wishes of some of the Singaporean students, who felt uncomfortable being videotaped.

In order to problematize the status and nature of the interview and consider how these interactions constitute relations of power (Talmy 2010), any mention of 'positioning' or 'identity' was omitted from the interview questions. There was thus a conscious attempt to maintain a difference between my research questions (which were related to positioning) and my interview questions. These interviews were also held at a time that was convenient for my participants. To preserve confidentiality, closed rooms were used for the interviews. Ethical care was also taken when collecting personal artefacts like student journals. For example, in order to accommodate a student's request to protect her privacy, I did not read certain sections of her journal, which she had stapled closed.

Given that data analysis was also conducted during the data-collection process, I cycled back and forth between all my different data sources to arrive at a logically coherent and rigorous analysis of how relations of power affected the students' language learning outcomes. Overall, a recursive handling of my data enabled me to avoid drawing a simplistic and skewed conclusion about how the school authorities influenced their language learning outcomes.

Reporting the data and publishing the study

Having collected the data, I subsequently had to decide how to choose and represent my data. In particular, I was cautious not to cast myself as 'researcher as expert' (Sarangi & Candlin 2003, p. 280). Thus, when reporting my findings to the principal and teachers of OGSS, I was selective in disclosing and brokering information to evade harming my student and teacher participants. Since completing my study, deliberate efforts have also been made to share my findings with a broader audience through journal publications and presentations at conferences organized by professional organizations. Disseminating my research findings through these various channels allowed me to honour the participants, who so graciously invited me into their lives for a year and whose language learning experiences are underrepresented in the applied linguistics literature (Ortega 2012).

The purpose of this example has been to illustrate the ethical problems encountered before, during and after an ethnographic case study. In general, when conducting applied linguistic research, some problems can be anticipated, while others need to be dealt with in an emergent manner. There is no silver bullet to dealing with ethical issues. One way is to equip and educate beginning applied linguists about the ethical dimensions of conducting research through research methodology courses taught in graduate programs (Loewen et al. 2014). On their part, journal editors can also provide leadership by offering readers more detailed ethical guidelines and examples of good practice. Another way is to have experienced applied linguists share narratives of their own experiences (De Costa forthcoming). Ultimately, however, researchers will need to engage in greater reflexivity to ensure that ethical practices are observed.

Notes

1 At US universities, the human ethics research committee is referred to as the Institutional Review Board (IRB). These committees often have different names in other parts of the world.
2 As noted by Phakiti (this volume), parametric tests are conducted for (1) data which are normally distributed, interval or continuous, and (2) independent data scores across all measures. By contrast, non-parametric tests are suitable for analysing (1) data that are not normally distributed, and (2) discrete variables or rank-order data.

3 By contrast, issues such as statistical significance and generalizability are not primary concerns of qualitative researchers, who instead emphasize the need for a thick description of data, especially in ethnographic and case study research.

Resources for further reading

BAAL 2006, 'The British Association for Applied Linguistics: Recommendations on good practice in Applied Linguistics', viewed 19 June 2010, http://www.baal. org.uk/dox/goodpractice_full.pdf.

This white paper provides useful recommendations on how to manage ethical responsibilities towards a range of stakeholders involved in research.

Duff, P 2008, *Case Study Research in Applied Linguistics*, Lawrence Erlbaum Associates, Mahwah, NJ.

This book explores ethics from a qualitative case study framework and underscores the importance of maintaining clear lines of communication with participants and reporting findings responsibly.

Mackey, A & Gass, S 2005, *Second Language Research: Methodology and Design*, Lawrence Erlbaum Associates, Mahwah, NJ.

This book covers ethics from primarily an experimental quantitative perspective and provides a sample consent form for an experimental study and advice on preparing an IRB protocol.

Richards, K, Ross, S & Seedhouse, P 2012, *Research Methods for Applied Language Studies*, Routledge, New York, NY.

This book helps beginning applied linguists establish an ethical protocol. It provides a checklist of important consideration, a guide to useful reading, and information on two valuable websites.

References

AAAL 2011, 'AAAL resolution against discrimination on the basis of accented speech', viewed 19 May 2014, http://www.aaal.org/displaycommon.cfm?an=1& subarticlenbr=15#Affirming_Commitment_to_Diversity

ALAA 1998, 'The Applied Linguistics Association of Australia: Recommendations on good practice in Applied Linguistics', viewed 20 February 2014, http://www. alaa.org.au/files/alaas_statement_of_good_practice.pdf

American Psychological Association 2010, *Publication Manual of the American Psychological Association*, 6th edn, American Psychological Association, Washington, DC.

BAAL 2006, 'The British Association for Applied Linguistics: Recommendations on good practice in Applied Linguistics', viewed 19 June 2010, http://www.baal. org.uk/dox/goodpractice_full.pdf

Brown, JD 2004, 'Research methods for applied linguistics: Scope, characteristics, and Standards' in A Davies & C Elder (eds), *The Handbook of Applied Linguistics*, Blackwell, Malden, MA, pp. 476–500.

——— 2011, 'Quantitative research in second language studies' in E Hinkel (ed.), *Handbook of Research in Second Language Teaching and Learning, Volume II*, Routledge, New York, NY, pp. 190–206

Bygate, M 2005, 'Applied linguistics: A pragmatic discipline, a generic discipline?', *Applied Linguistics*, vol. 26, no. 4, pp. 568–581.

Chapelle, C & Duff, P (eds), 2003, 'Some guidelines for conducting quantitative and qualitative research in TESOL', *TESOL Quarterly*, vol. 37, no. 1, pp. 157–178.

Council of Science Editors 2012, 'CSE's White paper on promoting integrity in scientific journal publications', viewed 6 December 2013, http://www.councilscienceeditors.org/files/public/entire_whitepaper.pdf

Creswell, JW 2013, *Qualitative Inquiry and Research Design*, 3rd edn, Sage, Thousand Oaks, CA.

Davison, AC & Hinkley, DV, 1997, *Bootstrap Methods and Their Applications*, Cambridge University Press, Cambridge.

De Costa, PI 2014, 'Making ethical decisions in an ethnographic study', *TESOL Quarterly*, vol. 48, no. 2, pp. 413–422.

De Costa, PI (ed.), forthcoming, *Exploring Ethical Issues from the Ground: Language Researcher Narratives*, Routledge, New York, NY.

Duff, P 2008, *Case Study Research in Applied Linguistics*, Lawrence Erlbaum Associates, Mahwah, NJ.

Emerson, RM, Fretz, RI & Shaw, LL 2011, *Writing Ethnographic Fieldnotes*. University of Chicago Press, Chicago, IL.

Guillemin M & Gillam, L, 2004, 'Ethics, reflexivity, and "ethically important moments" in research', *Qualitative Inquiry*, vol. 10, no. 2, pp. 261–280.

Hafernik JJ, Messerschmitt DS, & Vandrick S 2002, *Ethical Issues for ESL Faculty: Social Justice in Practice*, Lawrence Erlbaum Associates, Mahwah, NJ.

Hamp-Lyons, L 2009, 'Access, equity and ... plagiarism?', *TESOL Quarterly*, vol. 43, no. 4, pp. 690–693.

Kono, N 2013, 'Ethics in research', inCA Chapelle (ed.), *The Encyclopedia of Applied Linguistics*, Doi: 10.1002/9781405198431.wbeal0395.

Kramsch, C & Whiteside, A 2007, 'Three fundamental concepts in second language acquisition and their relevance in multilingual contexts', *The Modern Language Journal*, vol. 91, no. s.1, pp. 907–922.

Kubanyiova, M 2008, 'Rethinking research ethics in contemporary applied linguistics: the tension between macroethical and microethical perspectives in situated research', *Modern Language Journal*, vol. 92, no. 4, pp. 503–518.

——— 2013, 'Ethical debates in research on language and interaction', in CA Chapelle (ed.), *The Encyclopedia of Applied Linguistics*, Doi: 0.1002/9781405198431.wbeal0392

Lee, E 2011, 'Ethical issues in addressing inequity in/through ESL research', *TESL Canada Journal*, vol. 5, pp. 31–52.

Loewen, S, Lavolette, E, Spino, LA, Papi, M, Schmidtke, J, Sterling, S & Wolff, D 2014, 'Statistical literacy among applied linguists and second language acquisition researchers', *TESOL Quarterly*, vol. 42, no. 2, pp. 360–388.

McEnery, T & Hardie, A 2011, *Corpus Linguistics: Method, Theory and Practice*, Cambridge University Press, New York, NY.

Ngo, B, Bigelow, M & Lee, SJ 2014, 'Introduction to the special issue: what does it mean to do ethical and engaged research with immigrant communities?' *Diaspora, Indigenous, and Minority Education*, vol. 8, no. 1, pp. 1–6.

Norris, J & Ortega, L 2006, *Synthesizing Research on Language Learning and Teaching*, John Benjamins, Amsterdam.

Ortega, L 2005, 'For what and for whom is our research? The ethical as transformative lens in instructed SLA', *Modern Language Journal*, vol. 89, no. 3, pp. 427–443.

—— 2007, 'Online interactions and L2 learning: Some ethical challenges for teachers and researchers', invited speech presented at the University of Michigan, Ann Arbor, MI, 30 March.

—— 2012, 'Epistemological diversity and moral ends of research in instructed SLA', *Language Teaching Research*, vol. 16, no. 2, pp. 206–226.

Plonksy, L 2013, 'Study quality in SLA: An assessment of designs, analyses, and reporting practices in quantitative L2 research', *Studies in Second Language Acquisition*, vol. 35, no. 4, pp. 655–687.

Plonsky, L, Egbert J & Laflair, GT 2014, 'Bootstrapping in applied linguistics: Assessing its potential using shared data', *Applied Linguistics*, doi: 10.1093/applin/amu001

Plonsky, L & Gass, S 2011, 'Quantitative research methods, study quality, and outcomes: The case of interaction research', *Language Learning*, vol. 61, no. 2, pp. 325–366.

Sarangi, S & Candlin, C 2003, 'Trading between reflexivity and relevance: new challenges for applied linguistics', *Applied Linguistics*, vol. 24, no. 3, pp. 271–285.

Shohamy, E 2004, 'Reflections on research guidelines, categories, and responsibility', *TESOL Quarterly*, vol. 38, no. 4, pp. 728–731.

Solórzano, RW 2008, 'High stakes testing: issues, implications, and remedies for English language learners', *Review of Educational Research*, vol. 78, no. 2, pp. 260–329.

Spolsky, B 1997, 'The ethics of gatekeeping tests: what have we learned in a hundred years?', *Language Testing*, vol. 14, no. 3, pp. 242–247.

Talmy, S 2010, 'Qualitative interviews in applied linguistics: from research instrument to social practice', *Annual Review of Applied Linguistics*, vol. 30, pp. 128–148.

Wang, S & Hefferman, N 2010, 'Ethical issues in Computer-Assisted Language Learning: Perceptions of teachers and learners', *British Journal of Educational Technology*, vol. 41, no. 5, pp. 796–813.

Wen, Q & Gao, Y 2007, 'Dual publication and academic inequality', *International Journal of Applied Linguistics*, vol. 17, no. 2, pp. 221–225.

CHAPTER FIFTEEN

Developing a Research Project

Brian Paltridge and Aek Phakiti

This chapter concludes the first part of the volume by presenting an overview of key research processes as discussed in a number of the preceding chapters. Published research is used to exemplify each research process. The chapter then discusses the characteristics of a good research project, after which it outlines strategies for developing a successful research proposal. It then provides suggestions on how to choose and focus a research topic as well as how to refine a research question. Details to include in a research proposal are discussed as well as the specific areas that a research proposal needs to address. Questions to guide the design of a research proposal are also provided. The chapter concludes by providing criteria by which research projects are often judged.

Common research stages

This chapter first presents research processes that are common to most applied linguistics research. The research processes that are presented are applicable to quantitative, qualitative and mixed methods research. Figure 15.1 presents the stages typically involved in developing a research project. While the figure suggests a sequential model of research stages, in actual practice, these stages are often *iterative* and *cyclical* as one stage is likely to inform or influence other previous or later stages. Three published studies (Käänti et al. 2013; Moskovsky et al. 2013; Song 2012) are used to illustrate each of these research processes.

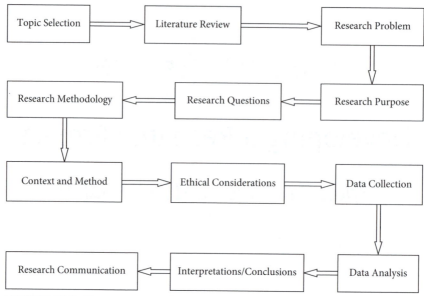

FIGURE 15.1 *Common research stages*

Researchers usually begin by choosing a topic that they would like to know more about. Topics can arise from a researcher's personal experience, or from a researcher's knowledge of existing theories or published research. The topic, however, often needs to be narrowed down, so that it is focused and its study is manageable within a given time frame. A topic can, for example, be refined from a review of the research literature on the particular topic. It is important, however, to distinguish a research topic from a research title. A topic is related to the construct or aspect of interest. A title, on the other hand, should give some indication of the topic(s) to be examined, the context in which the study will be carried out and/or the research methods to be employed. It is important to note that since a title cannot be very long (ideally fifteen to twenty words), it needs to be chosen with great care, so that it provides useful information about the study. The following are examples of research titles:

- Learning English through social interaction: The case of Big Brother 2006, Finland (Kääntä et al. 2013).

This title indicates the topic and context of the study. However, it does not tell us that the study adopted a conversation analytic framework to examine interactions among selected Big Brother (BB) contestants. This is something that could be usefully added to the title.

- The effects of teachers' motivational strategies on learners' motivation: A controlled investigation of second language acquisition (Moskovsky et al. 2013).

This study was a quasi-experimental study which examined the influence of motivational strategies by Saudi English as a foreign language (EFL) teachers on Saudi learners' learning motivation. The title does not suggest the research method but the word 'effects' implies that the study is somewhat experimental. Additionally, it does not tell us the specific context of the study. The use of the word 'controlled' implies that all aspects of the study were regulated whereas, in fact, the study used only a quasi-experimental design which did not employ random assignment, so it is not, in its fullest sense, controlled (see Gass this volume).

- Imagined communities and language socialization practices in transnational space: A case study of two Korean "study abroad" families in the United States (Song 2012).

The topics are presented clearly in this title (imagined communities (ICs) and [home] language socialization practices). It tells us the context and participants in the study (Korean families in the United States). The title also clearly suggests that this study was a case study. However, when we examine the actual study, we find that it was longitudinal and took about one year of data collection. It may have been helpful to have something about this feature of the study in its title.

Literature review

Doing a literature review is like conducting *library research*. What is involved in a literature review is, however, more than just finding relevant studies on a particular topic. We also need to consider theories relevant to the study as well as the history of research in that area. Understanding existing theories helps us set the direction of our research (e.g. this may determine whether it should employ quantitative or qualitative methods). It also helps us locate relevant studies. Identifying and locating previous research is essential for a successful research project. Studies can be identified and retrieved through databases, internet searches, academic journals and books. A review of the relevant literature involves defining the constructs or aspects under investigation and discussing how previous studies were conducted (e.g. aims, research questions, context and participants, research instruments, data analysis, findings, conclusions and implications).

Ary et al. (2006) identify seven benefits of doing a good literature review. First, it helps researchers see the frontiers of the particular research area, so the proposed study can go beyond these. Second, it helps put the original research questions in perspective. Third, it helps in limiting research questions and leads to a better definition of the concept(s) or construct(s) of interest. Fourth, it provides insights into the reasons for contradictory findings in previous studies. Fifth, it shows the research methodologies that were used in previous studies and may help researchers decide what methods will be useful, unpromising or can be improved upon in the proposed study. Sixth, it helps avoid unintentional replication of previous studies. Finally, it places the researcher in a better position to interpret the significance of research findings in light of the current status of the research area.

There are various structures a review of the literature might take depending on the research area and methodology to be adopted. For example, researchers may choose to write up their literature review using a *historical perspective approach* (theoretical developments, followed by research from the past to the present, leading to a statement of a research gap), a *contrastive approach* (comparing and contrasting competing perspectives/theories about a topic, leading to the rationale for the study) or an *aspect-by-aspect approach* (description and discussion of the various research aspects under investigation, which can then be integrated in the proposed study). See Evans, Gruba and Zobel (2011), Paltridge and Starfield (2007) and Punch (2007).

- Moskovsky et al.'s (2013) literature review illustrates the *historical perspective approach*. First, it discusses periods of L2 motivation research, adopting Dörnyei's (2001) definition of motivational strategies as '"the motivational influences that are consciously exerted to achieve some systematic and enduring positive effect"' (Moskovsky et al. 2013, p. 28). Relevant studies are mentioned as follows: 'The only three studies that we are aware of which have actually attempted to empirically test the effectiveness of motivational strategies are Dörnyei and Csizér (1998) in Hungary, Cheng and Dörnyei (2007) in Taiwan, and Guilloteaux and Dörnyei (2008) in South Korea' (Moskovsky et al. 2013, pp. 36–37).

- Käántä et al.'s (2013) review of the literature is an example of the *aspect-by-aspect approach*. It addresses English use and people's attitudes towards English in Finland. It then discusses recent development in conversation analytic approaches to second language (CA-SLA) research which take the view that language learning is socially 'co-constructed and jointly accomplished by interactants in situated, social interaction' (p. 97). Finally, it focuses on the case of BB, which is a reality TV show in which contestants are isolated from the outside world. The researchers then discuss previous research into BB.

- The literature in Song (2012) is structured in terms of the background and rationale for the study. It does not follow the literature review structure described above. The article starts off with a discussion of Asian families undertaking 'transnational migration to English speaking countries for their school-age children who could earn overseas education credentials and learn English through their experience' (p. 507). Song's literature examines research on study abroad families' transnational practices as a unique phenomenon and focuses on the topic of 'these families' future "imagined" membership of a particular community that they wish to enter upon return' (p. 508).

Research problem

After a comprehensive review of the literature, the research problem(s) or focus needs to be identified. A research problem may be suggested by previous researchers when they outline the limitations of their study and provide implications for further research or by carrying out an independent synthesis of previous research findings. A research problem may be seen as a research *gap* or *void* (what has not been addressed or explored thoroughly). There may be several gaps that can be addressed, but only one or two may be focused on due to time and budget constraints. The research gap may be identified in the relevant parts of the literature review or at the end of it.

- Määntä et al. (2013) review the literature, dealing with each area of research separately: learning and use of English in Finland, a conversational analytic approach to language learning as situated practice, and research on the BB TV programs. They identify research problems or gaps in the literature in each particular area as it is discussed. For example, they point out that in the context of Finland, where a close relationship between English and Finnish among young Finns exists, the BB show 'provides a special environment for examining multivalent and hybrid aspects of contemporary forms of communication' (p. 341). In the review of the CA-SLA framework, they state that 'most research in CA-SLA has so far focused on examining language learning in situations specifically designed for learning, such as classroom interaction, classroom dyads, and internship practices … or in such institutional situation of second language use as business phone calls …' (p. 342). They then state that 'The present study aligns itself with this emergent research interest in CA-SLA, focusing on language learning in non-pedagogical settings in three ways …' (p. 343). In relation to research on BB, they point out that 'To date, this research has mainly focused on the relationship between the audience(s) and the show … and on housemates' experiences of participating in the show … Only a few have examined the housemates' interaction in the house' (p. 343).

- Moskovsky et al. (2013) identify a gap in the literature at the end of their literature review by pointing out that 'Hence, to the best of our knowledge, there has not so far been a controlled (i.e., experimental and/or longitudinal) study that has addressed the issue of the effect of the implementation of motivational strategies in the language classroom' (pp. 38–39).

- In her article, Song (2012) discusses educational inequality and how parents' own trajectories (e.g. attendance at a prestigious high school) influence their children's learning goals and language learning practice. Song finally argues that 'transnational families' language learning practices should be considered not only from their involvement in the current, local community aspect, but also from their relationship to educational policies and practices of a prospective community that exists in their future and beyond national borders.' (p. 508)

Research purpose

In published articles, researchers typically present their research purpose or aim at the beginning of their paper. For example:

- Kääntä et al. (2013) aim to investigate 'how interactants can create language learning opportunities for themselves and others in and through social interaction'. (p. 340)

- Moskovsky et al. (2013) aim to 'assess the effects of motivational strategies used by Saudi EFL teachers ($N = 14$) on Saudi EFL learners' ($N = 296$) self-reported learning motivation' (p. 34).

- Song (2012) aims to 'explain the relationship between these families' future membership and current language learning practices' (p. 508).

Research questions

Research questions are asked to help researchers consider the most appropriate research methodology and design for their study. Some research questions require quantitative research designs (e.g. involving survey or experimental methods), whereas others suggest qualitative designs (e.g. using a case study or discourse analysis). Research questions should be congruent with the research problem or gap to be addressed. They should not be too broad or too specific. They should be capable of being answered given the method and techniques that are adopted to collect and analyse the data.

- Kääntä et al. (2013) do not explicitly describe their research questions but instead explore three research issues: the nature of 'extended repair sequence in meaning interaction' (pp. 345–347), 'a confirmation request as a way of entering a conversation' (pp. 347–349 and 'humor and mockery in group membership construction and maintenance' (pp. 349–354).

- Moskovsky et al. (2013) do not explicitly state their research questions, but, on the basis of the content of their result section, their two research questions are related to 'differential changes in learners' motivation over time as a function of treatment' (pp. 51–53) and 'group differences in learners' motivation at T2 [Time 2] due to treatment (and independent of preexisting group differences)' (pp. 53–56).

- Song (2012) asks two exploratory research questions: 'what are the mothers' ICs and how are these ICs related to their past and present membership and experiences?' and 'how do these ICs influence their view of their children's language learning goals and socialization practices? (p. 508).

Research methodology

A review of the literature can inform researchers of the research methods used by previous researchers as they may have investigated the same general topic. Through the review, we can gain a sense of what kinds of research methods or techniques are suitable for our own study. The choice of research methodology will lead to particular aspects of the research design: the procedures to follow, the data analysis involved, and the measures taken to ensure its validity and reliability. In terms of methodologies:

- Kääntä et al. (2013) employed the CA-SLA methodology to examine social interaction in the BB program. It can also be argued that this was also a case study as it focused on one contestant (i.e. Kaki) in particular.

- Moskovsky et al. (2013) adopted 'a quasi-experimental study with a pre-post intervention plus control design' (p. 38).

- Song (2012) utilized an ethnographic framework to examine two transnational Korean family cases in the United States.

Context and method

Context is related to the research setting or site where the study will be conducted. The research method of a particular study could be described as the operationalization of the research methodology that has been adopted. In a published research report, the methodology section typically describes this in detail (e.g. the choice of research setting and participants, the research instruments or techniques used, the data collection procedures (including any treatments or interventions), along with how the issues of reliability, validity/trustworthiness and ethics are to be addressed and how the data analysis was conducted in order to properly answer the research question).

- Kääntä et al. (2013) do not have an explicit section on the research method that they adopted. However, they provide detailed information about the empirical data being used for the study (e.g. 'The data analysed in this study come from the second BB season in Finland that started September 28, 2006 and draw from an average of 14 hours of recording live BB every day from a special BB 24/7 cable channel for two non-consecutive weeks' (p. 344)). They also describe how they selected the extracts to be analysed.

- Moskovsky et al. (2013) follow the traditional structure for the description of an experimental research method in which details on the following aspects are provided: participants, design and matching procedure, instruments (including a mention of a pilot study), intervention schedule and data collection.

- Song (2012) discusses her research method using the heading 'current study'. She presents information about the participants and the context of the study. She also adds that the study was 'part of an ethnographic investigation of Korean study abroad families and their children's language socialization practice in the US over one year between 2004-2006' (p. 511).

Ethical considerations

As discussed throughout this volume, ethical considerations are important in the conduct of research (see De Costa this volume). Participants should agree to participate in a study and be aware of any consequences of the study on them. Many journals nowadays ask authors to confirm that appropriate ethical procedures were followed as a requirement for submitting an article to the journal, so, while this may not be outlined in the published paper, this does not necessarily mean that these procedures were not followed.

- Kääntä et al. (2013) do not, for example, discuss the issues of ethics in their study as their data drew on publically available data. It could be argued that ethical clearance and consent from research subjects are not needed for this kind of data. It is not known, however, whether Kaki (and others) signed a consent form, or not, for their data to be used in the study.

● Moskovsky et al. (2013) discuss a number of ethical issues relevant to their study such as how potential participants were informed of the details of the study.

● Song (2012) does not explicitly mention ethical considerations in his paper. However, it is reasonable to assume that ethical clearance from the researcher's academic institution was given prior to the study and that all research participants consented to the study.

Data collection

The success of research depends on a successful data-collection stage. Appropriate data to serve the purpose of the research need to be identified. Then, tools appropriate to the type of research being conducting need to be developed. In quantitative research, research instruments or techniques might include a variety of tests (achievement, language proficiency, aptitude tests), questionnaires, structured observation schemes and think-aloud protocols. In qualitative research, research instruments or techniques may include fieldnotes, observations, diaries and journals, photographic records, interviews, written responses, student information, teacher records, teaching materials and information drawn from archival sources. The successful collection of data requires careful planning and needs to be reported on in subsequent papers derived from the study. For example, Kääntä et al. (2013) describe how their data were collected (pp. 344–345), Moskovsky et al. (2013) describe how they collected the data for the study (pp. 38–44) and Song (2012) provides a section which describes how the data were collected (pp. 511–512).

Data analysis

After the data have been collected, they are used to answer the research questions. Hence, the data need to be systematically analysed. The preparation of the data for analysis may include sorting the data into types, assigning identity codes to participants, inputting the data into a computer program, transcribing (or translating) the data, coding and reducing the data, carrying out reliability or credibility analysis and conducting further analysis of the data to address or answer the research questions. In quantitative research, data analysis can be done using various statistical procedures (e.g. correlational analysis, *t*-test, analysis of variance, etc, see Phakiti this volume). In qualitative research, the data analysis, for example, could be done through thematic analysis, content analysis, frequency counts, narrative inquiry (see Holliday this volume) or discourse analysis (see Paltridge & Wang this volume). In a mixed methods design, a combination of quantitative and qualitative analyses can be carried out (see Ivankova & Greer this volume). Here are some examples:

- Käntä et al. (2013) use extracts (employing conversation analysis conventions) to illustrate and interpret their data.

- Moskovsky et al. (2013) mainly perform statistical analysis including descriptive statistics, exploratory factor analysis, reliability analysis, and between-subject, mixed-model and repeated-measure analyses of variance (ANOVAs).

- Song (2012) discusses the inductive process of his data analysis which moves from the micro to the macro level (p. 512). She uses several excerpts to illustrate the data and then interprets the data that is relevant to the research issue under investigation.

Interpretations and conclusions

On the basis of the data analysis that has been conducted, researchers can begin to outline their research findings. The data and data analysis need to support any claims researchers wish to make. It is important to avoid claiming something that the data sets do not justify. A discussion of research findings (see the Discussion or Results and Discussion section of the report) needs to make reference to the theories and previous research that were considered in the review of the literature. For example:

- Käntä et al. (2013) present their findings using several extracts from video clips (with English translations) and interpret meanings and make inferences beyond the recorded interactions. In the Conclusion section, they summarize the key findings (p. 354), stating how their study illustrated the impact of English on young Finns' language use. They also connected the study to the previous literature.

- Moskovsky et al. (2013) present their research findings using several tables which contain statistical test outputs and interpret them in terms of statistical significance and effect sizes. They summarize the main findings and discuss the contributions of their study to the field. They conclude by noting the limitations of their research and the implications that had on their findings and for the direction of future research.

- Song (2012) uses several interview excerpts to illustrate each of the two family's cases, followed by an interpretation and an identification of other emerging issues. Commentary on previous literature is integrated into the discussion. There is also an implications section which draws on cases of children who have had transnational experiences and their language practices and which stresses the importance of this issue in language learning and teaching.

Research communication

It is important to share research findings with other people so as to contribute to the advancement of knowledge in the field. The communication of research can be done through presentations at conferences and seminars or in writing in the form of a dissertation, thesis, research report or journal article. It is important to understand the conventions of each channel of research communication and its audience. For example, the structure of a dissertation or thesis (e.g. Paltridge & Starfield 2007) can be different from that of a journal article (e.g. Chapelle & Duff 2003).

Essential features of a good research project

There are several important aspects that need to be considered when developing a research project. Therefore, it is important for any one researcher or research team to understand the desirable aspects of a research project.

Apart from a good understanding of the criteria by which to judge the quality of a study (e.g. adopted theoretical framework, validity/trustworthiness, ethics and research methods), the following three aspects need to be considered when developing a research project: *originality*, *worthiness* and *feasibility*. First, originality in the context of a research study means that it does not aim to find out something people in the field already know. Originality can be considered in terms of a new topic or aspect of research that has never been done before or has not been done as comprehensively as what is proposed. Originality can also be considered in terms of a new research context (e.g. new setting and participants) or new or revised research instruments or techniques (or a mixture of them). Finally, the discovery of knowledge or the development of fresh insights can also be considered original.

Second, the project needs to be *worth doing*. It is important to consider the value and relevance of the project because there are many things that might be done but are not worth doing. The worthiness of a research project can be determined by its likely yields and outcomes and the potential of the research to address the gap of knowledge in the existing research field. It will be considered worthwhile if it solves a particular outstanding research problem or resolves a prevalent misunderstanding, or finds new ways of doing some part of the research. Clearly, it must be of relevance and interest to people in the research field. The topic of the research should be of interest to a wide audience, such as the international readership of a journal. Connected to this is the question of whether the completed project is likely to lead to some kind of publication, such as a journal article or a book, so that the research is able to contribute to the development of the discipline in which it is located.

Third, a good research project needs to be *feasible* and *manageable* within the time frame available for it, with the resources that are available for it, and by the researcher(s) who will be carrying out the study. A project that may take three to four years, as with a doctoral project in the United Kingdom or Australia, will be much too ambitious if there is only a year available to carry out and complete it. We need to consider the financial resources required for the project, such as air fares and accommodation costs that, without which, the project may not be able to proceed. It is also important to consider whether the people who wish to carry out the project have the theoretical background and methodological skills that the proposed study requires. So, for example, if the study is a conversation-analysis project, the people carrying out the study need to know how to analyse conversational data from this perspective. Or, if the study requires some kind of statistical treatment, the researcher needs to be able to conduct statistical analysis. It is important to be realistic in this regard, and not, for example, live in the hope that someone will provide help when the time comes to the data analysis phase of the project.

It is important to stress that while appearing original and worthwhile, a project that aims to examine several complex aspects in one study using a variety of research instruments and techniques (e.g. tests, questionnaires, individual interviews, focus group interviews, observations, diaries and documents and data bases) may be unfeasible or unmanageable. Unless there is a team of several experienced researchers, each research aspect under study is likely to be investigated only superficially and the amount of data to analyse may be daunting, which will most likely result in a poor analysis being done. A good research project does not need to address everything one needs to know in a single study. Rather, it should thoroughly investigate a small number of aspects of a phenomenon. Even as part of a research degree, a thesis or dissertation is only a piece of research that prepares students to learn about research methods and methodologies and to do a manageable and meaningful research project. The acknowledgment of the limitations of the study, thus, is important because not only do they allow researchers to understand the validity and trustworthiness of the study, but they also allow the development of future research directions on the topic.

Developing a research proposal

There are a number of important steps to go through in developing a research proposal. We often tell students to start by drawing up a shortlist of topics and, from these, to choose one of them for investigation. It is often a good idea at this point to talk to someone who has had experience in carrying out research (e.g. a colleague, a professor or potential research supervisor) to get their advice on which of the topics, in their view, is the best one to proceed with. A general question needs to be formulated which can then be further focused. This stage of the process often causes new researchers the most trouble, so it is worth spending as much time as necessary to get the question right. In short, the question needs to be both *worth asking* and *capable of being answered*. There are many questions that are worth asking but which cannot, in any practical sense, be answered and there are questions that are capable of being answered but which are not necessarily worth doing. The study, thus, needs to strike a balance between the value of the research question and its answerability using the proposed methodology and within the researcher's ability to carry it out.

Once the research question has been decided on, researchers need to think about what data needs to be collected to answer the research question, where and how it might be collected, and how the data might be analysed. From this point, an initial research plan can be drawn up. At the same time, researchers need to read widely on the topic to determine whether they are on the right track. That is, they need to get an idea of what previous research has been done on the topic and to see how this research was carried out. After this has been successfully done, a detailed research proposal can be written. This proposal should include definitions of the key constructs mentioned in the proposal (such as 'negotiation of meaning' or 'willingness to communicate') that would enable someone reading the proposal (and in turn your completed research) to understand what exactly is meant when these terms are used. Also the ethical implications of the research need to be considered in terms of what permissions will be needed to carry out your research, and what guarantees of anonymity will be given to the people involved in the research project.

The structure of a research proposal

Table 15.1 shows the typical structure of a research proposal and the purpose of each of the sections of the proposal. Not every academic department will follow the same set of headings, of course, or ask researchers to cover each of these areas, so it is important to find out exactly what is needed in the particular context.

Table 15.1 The typical structure of a research proposal (adapted from Paltridge 1997)

Section	Purpose
Title	To summarize what the research will be about
Summary of the Proposed Study	To provide an overview of the whole research proposal (e.g. what the research aims to do, research methods adopted and key significant contributions of the proposed study). This section is similar to an abstract of a research article but does not have findings. Although it appears at the beginning, this section is often the last to be written.
Definitions of Terms	To provide the meaning of the key terms that readers will encounter in the relevant background literature or that are used in the research question/s
Background and Literature Review	To demonstrate the relationship between the proposed study and what has already been done in the particular area; that is, to indicate the research framework and the 'gap' or 'void' that the proposed study will address
Implications of the literature review	To consolidate a synthesis of the literature that eventually informs the focus of the proposed study in terms of a theoretical or methodological gap or research problem, leading to a specific study aim or research question (below)
Research Questions and/or Hypotheses	To provide an explicit statement of what the study will investigate, i.e. the questions the study will answer or the hypotheses it will test
Research Methodology	To provide an overview of the research approach that will be employed in the study, data that will be collected, how it will be analysed, etc. This section is similar to a 'Research Method' section in a research article, but the future tense is normally used instead of the past simple tense when it is about the proposed study.
Ethical Considerations	To provide a statement as to how participants will be advised of the overall nature of the study, and how informed consent will be obtained from them
Anticipated Problems and Limitations	To show awareness of the limitations of the study, what problems may be met in carrying it out and how they will be dealt with
Significance of the Proposed Study	To say why the study is worth carrying out. This can be discussed in terms of theoretical, methodological, pedagogical and/or policy-informed implications.
Resources and Budget Required	To say what resources the research will require and what costs may be anticipated in carrying out the study
Proposed Timetable	To give a working plan for carrying out, and completing, the study

(*continued*)

Section	Purpose
References	To provide detailed references and bibliographic support for the proposal
Appendices	To provide examples of materials, research instruments or data elicitation techniques that might be used, or adapted, in the study

Details to include in a research proposal

The expected length of the proposal will also vary from academic department to department, from degree to degree and across universities. Generally, though, it will be expected to provide a clearly focused research question or hypothesis that is both worth asking and capable of being answered. Precise definitions of the key terms in the research question/s or hypothesis should be included that will allow them to be clearly identified throughout the study. An awareness of key research which has already been carried out in the particular area should also be demonstrated. This includes a summary of what conclusions were reached in this previous research, by whom and when and whether these conclusions are in agreement or conflict with each other. An awareness of the main issues or controversies which surround the problem under investigation and the significant gaps in previous research in the particular area should also be shown. A description of how this previous research is relevant to the proposed study will also be expected.

It is also important that an appropriate research approach for the particular question or problem has been selected, and that a well-defined list of procedures that will be followed in the carrying out of the research has been included. The method of data collection and its analysis should be described. The proposal should also include, if appropriate, a description of any particular theoretical framework to be drawn on for the study and the reason/s for its use in the study. The proposal should indicate how the sample population (or data) will be selected for the study and the reason for this selection. It is also useful to plan for a pilot study in which the research instruments you will use are trialled and evaluated and an analysis of the trial data carried out.

The proposal should describe why the study is significant; that is, why the research question or hypothesis is worth investigating. Ethical issues, if there are any, need to be discussed. This will include a discussion of the question of whether informed consent needs to be obtained, and if so, how this will be done. It is also helpful to include a proposed timetable for the research as this will give an indication as to how realistic the proposal actually is. A budget statement is also important as this will give an indication of how realistic the proposal is in terms of financial requirements and whether the research might need to be adapted in the light of these.

Owing to the space limitations, we cannot include examples of a research proposal in this chapter. However, there are several examples of research proposals that can be found in the following online resource:

- http://www.bcps.org/offices/lis/researchcourse/develop_writing. html#planning, viewed 21 September 2014.

This website describes the steps involved in developing a research proposal (e.g. planning, writing drafts and evaluating them). It provides several examples of research proposals including examples from the fields of education and linguistics. It also offers practical advice in writing a thesis or a dissertation.

Criteria for judging a research study

The issues involved in judging and evaluating the quality of an empirical study are highly complex. Judging and evaluating a study involves an interaction between examiners' or reviewers' characteristics (e.g. areas of research, expertise, standing in the field), a researcher(s)'s written report and the context in which both the examiners/reviewers and the study interact. In most cases, an evaluation of an empirical study can be subjective, despite the use of criteria having been provided to judge it. For example, two examiners reading the same thesis or dissertation independently and using the same criteria may or may not agree with each other in terms of the thesis or dissertation quality. Bourke and Holbrook (2013) examined what thesis examiners look for in a thesis or dissertation.

Criteria for judging a thesis or dissertation

It is not straightforward to present a set of universal criteria for judging a thesis or a dissertation given that each educational institution will have its own developed standards. It nevertheless is useful and relevant, especially for research students to have a sense of how a thesis or a dissertation may be judged, so that they can be prepared to work towards the desired outcome. One can argue that writing a thesis or a dissertation without knowing how it will be assessed is an extremely difficult task to accomplish. Different educational institutes have their own criteria to grade a thesis or a dissertation. In this section, we introduce some key criteria that students should be aware of when they work on a thesis or dissertation (see e.g. Bourke & Holbrook 2013; Evans, Gruba & Zobel, 2011; Johnston 1997; Mullins & Kiley 2002).

Research problem and literature review

The thesis or dissertation effectively identifies, analyses and syntheses an issue, problem or research topic through reference to an up-to-date selection of research material. It establishes its significance in the field by using a suitable theoretical or conceptual framework and by considering relevant and significant previous research. The review of associated theories and previous research is accurate and critical. Key terminology is used precisely and consistently. The gap or need for the study is clearly identified from the existing research. The research questions and/or hypotheses to be investigated are important and relevant to the research issue or problem and connected closely to the review of literature.

Research methodology

The thesis or dissertation appropriately and adequately describes the methodology adopted, including the procedures used for the data gathering, ethical considerations and data analysis. It elaborates the rationale for the choice of the methodology for the research and, where appropriate, provides a connection between this methodology and the research methodology(ies) adopted in previous research on the topic. Overall, it demonstrates the researcher(s)'s strong command of the research methodology, including an understanding, recognition or awareness of both the strengths and weaknesses of the methodology that influence the validity or trustworthiness of the thesis.

Research procedures

The thesis or dissertation describes sufficiently the overall research procedures, including detailed descriptions and explanations of the research setting, the participants (if any), the ethical considerations, the research instruments, the data elicitation techniques, the specific stages of the data analysis and what care has been taken to ensure the data analysis is systematic and credible.

Findings and interpretation

The thesis or dissertation clearly and sufficiently presents and explains basic information on the findings in relation to the research aims, questions or hypothesis that are presented in the thesis. The presentation of the findings meets the expected conventions of the particular research design (e.g. experimental, survey, case study, narrative inquiry research). It takes an evidence-based approach to making inferences as well as offers a critical interpretation and discussion of the findings. The thesis does not attempt to overgeneralize its findings. It links the present findings to the relevant literature presented earlier (e.g. examining similarities or differences in research findings, new understanding or evidence).

Conclusion and implications

The originality and substantial level of the contribution of the thesis or dissertation may be considered in the conclusion section. In the conclusion chapter, the thesis clearly summarizes the key research findings, notes potential research limitations that affect the conclusions and recommends implications of the study for existing and future research. Implications can be discussed in regard to theoretical, methodological and/or pedagogical implications.

Writing quality

The thesis or dissertation is well-written, well-organized and coherent. It is free from grammatical or typological errors. It meets technical standards relevant to the field of research, including appropriate presentations of tables and figures, and accurate use of the reference style (e.g. APA Referencing Style).

Criteria for judging a journal manuscript

Academic journals also provide reviewers with criteria for assessing the quality of a submission. For the journal *TESOL Quarterly* (Mahboob & Paltridge 2014), these are:

- Does the manuscript contain new and significant information to justify publication?
- Is the problem significant and concisely stated?
- Are methodological and/or theoretical matters comprehensively described?
- Are the interpretations and conclusions justified by the results?
- Is adequate reference made to other work in the field?
- Does the manuscript appeal to the general interests of the *TESOL Quarterly* readership?
- Does the manuscript strengthen the relationship between theory and practice?

It is important, then, to consider the criteria by which a project will be judged when planning for as well as when carrying out the research, so that it meets particular quality expectations when it is completed.

Resources for further reading

Bell, J 2010, *Doing Your Research Project: A Guide for First-time Researchers in Education and Social Science*, 5th edn, Open University Press, Buckingham.

This is a practical book providing advice on how to develop a research project. Chapter 2 discusses planning a research project, selecting a topic, focusing the study and presenting a project outline.

Bourke, S & Holbrook AP 2013, 'Examining PhD and research masters theses', *Assessment & Evaluation in Higher Education*, vol. 38, no. 4, pp. 407–416.

This article analyses examiners' evaluation criteria such as literature review, methodology, contribution and presentation when they evaluate PhD and masters theses or dissertations.

Casanave, C 2014, *Before the Dissertation: A Textual Mentor for Doctoral Students at Early Stages of a Research Project*, Michigan University Press, Ann Arbor, MI.

This book presents critical, yet significant issues that students should consider before they start writing a dissertation or thesis (e.g. things to consider before deciding to pursue a doctoral degree, several types of writing that shapes a research project).

Chapelle, CA & Duff, PA 2003, 'Some guidelines for conducting quantitative and qualitative research in TESOL', *TESOL Quarterly*, vol. 37, no. 1, pp. 157–178.

This article provides guidelines for good research writing practice for both qualitative and quantitative research, particularly for a journal article.

Creswell, JW 2014, *Research Design: Qualitative, Quantitative, and Mixed Methods Approaches*, 4th edn, Sage, Thousand Oaks, CA.

This book presents approaches to designing qualitative, quantitative or mixed methods research. In this edition, Creswell includes the mixed methods approach. This book is useful for both developing a research proposal and writing up a research report.

Elphinstone, L & Schweitzer, R 1998, *How to Get a Research Degree: A Survival Guide*, Allen and Unwin, St Leonards.

The first chapter of this book ('Getting Started') is especially relevant to writing a research proposal. Section headings in this chapter include 'What is a thesis?', 'Distinction between a Master's and a Doctoral degree', 'Choosing a thesis topic', 'Defining your thesis topic', 'Methodology and research design', 'The research proposal', 'Criteria for assessing a research proposal' and 'Checklist of questions to be asked about a research proposal'.

Evans, D, Gruba, P & Zobel, J 2011, *How to Write a Better Thesis*, 3rd edn, Melbourne University Press, Melbourne.

This book introduces the nature of theses. It covers various issues involved in thesis writing (e.g. thesis structure, academic writing and content).

Griffee, DT 2012, *An Introduction to Second Language Research Methods: Design and Data*, TESL-EJ Publications, Berkeley, CA.

There are three parts to this e-book which is free to download from the TESL-EJ website: getting started, design and data. Chapter 2 presents in detail a typical structure of a research paper. It provides clear explanations of each section of a research report (e.g. title, introduction, literature review and research methods).

McIntosh, K & Ginther A (2014), 'Writing research reports', in AJ Kunnan (ed.), *The Companion to Language Assessment*, John Wiley & Sons, London.

While targeting at language assessment research, this chapter is useful to know more about what is involved in writing a research report. It provides tips and strategies for successful research reports.

Paltridge, B & Starfield, S 2007, *Thesis and Dissertation Writing in a Second Language: A Handbook for Supervisors*, Routledge, London.

This book provides a comprehensive treatment of and resources for thesis and dissertation writing. This book is useful for both research supervisors and students.

Punch, K 2007, *Developing Effective Research Proposals*, 2nd edn, Sage, London.

This book is a very good guide for writing research proposals. Chapter 8 contains sample quantitative and qualitative research proposals.

References

Ary, D, Jacobs, L, Razavieh, A & Sorensen, C 2006, *Introduction to Research in Education*, 7th edn, Thomson Wadsworth, Belmont, CA.

Bourke, S & Holbrook AP 2013, 'Examining PhD and research masters theses', *Assessment & Evaluation in Higher Education*, vol. 38, no. 4, pp. 407–416.

Evans, D, Gruba, P & Zobel, J 2011, *How to Write a Better Thesis*, 3rd edn, Melbourne University Press, Melbourne.

Johnston, S 1997, 'Examining the examiners: An analysis of examiners' reports on doctoral thesis', *Studies in Higher Education*, vol. 22, no. 3, pp. 333–347.

Käänta, L, Peuronen, S, Jauni, H, Paakkinen, T & Leppänen, S 2013, 'Learning English through social interaction: The case of *Big Brother* 2006, Finland', *The Modern Language Journal*, vol. 97, no. 2, pp. 340–359.

Mahboob, A & Paltridge, B 2014, 'In this issue', *TESOL Quarterly*, vol. 48, no. 4, pp. 651–654.

Moskovsky, C, Alrabi, F, Paolini, S & Ratcheva, S 2013, 'The effects of teachers' motivational strategies on learners' motivation: A controlled investigation of second language acquisition', *Language Learning*, vol. 63, no. 1, pp. 34–62.

Mullins, G & Kiley, M 2002, '"It's a PhD, not a Nobel Prize": How experienced examiners assess research theses', *Studies in Higher Education*, vol. 27, no. 4, pp. 369–386.

Paltridge, B. 1997, 'Thesis and dissertation writing: Preparing ESL students for research', *English for Specific Purposes*, vol. 16, no. 1, pp. 61–70.

Paltridge, B & Starfield, S 2007, *Thesis and Dissertation Writing in a Second Language*, Routledge, London.

Punch, K 2007, *Developing Effective Research Proposals*, 2nd edn, Sage, London.

Song, J 2012, 'Imagined communities and language socialization practices in transnational space: A case study of two Korean "study abroad" families in the United States', *The Modern Language Journal*, vol. 96, no. 4, pp. 507–524.

PART TWO

Areas of Research

Overview

This section of the book contains sixteen chapters. In each chapter, the authors provide a synthesis of current thinking and typical research processes, strategies and techniques in the area of research they are discussing. They also provide a sample study in their chapters in order to illustrate some of the methodological points they raise in their chapter. Resources for further reading on the particular research area are also provided.

- In *Chapter Sixteen* (Researching Speaking), Rebecca Hughes presents an overview of major approaches to research into spoken language and a brief summary of typical research methods used in this area of study.

- In *Chapter Seventeen* (Researching Listening), Larry Vandergrift provides a synopsis of recent research on listening in applied linguistics and discusses a range of research methods for examining the listening skill.

- In *Chapter Eighteen* (Researching Reading), Marie Stevenson examines key research areas in second language reading research (e.g. lexical, fluency, discourse, strategic, affective, intermodal and sociocultural) and explains research techniques frequently used in this area of study.

- In *Chapter Nineteen* (Researching Writing), Ken Hyland explores the complex and multifaceted nature of writing and introduces methods and techniques that reflect researchers' views of what writing is and how it should be studied.

- In *Chapter Twenty* (Researching Grammar), Neomy Storch addresses the questions of what constitutes knowledge of grammar and how we can assess that knowledge and whether and how best to teach grammar to second language learners.

- In *Chapter Twenty One* (Researching Vocabulary), David Hirsh presents the main lines of enquiry in vocabulary research, research stages and related test instruments and a discussion of key challenges facing vocabulary researchers.

- In *Chapter Twenty Two* (Researching Pragmatics), Carsten Roever examines areas of pragmatics studies that focus on the use of language in social contexts, specifically how speakers adjust their language use to different kinds of interlocutors and situations. He discusses common research instruments in pragmatics research including discourse completion tasks, role plays and metapragmatic judgement questionnaires.

- In *Chapter Twenty Three* (Researching Motivation), Lindy Woodrow provides a historical overview of second language motivation research and presents the major steps in structural equation modelling. She then focuses on the technique of confirmatory factor analysis which can be used to examine motivation.

- In *Chapter Twenty Four* (Researching Language Learning Strategies), Heath Rose presents key issues in conducting language learning strategy research, such as choosing appropriate research contexts and selecting the most appropriate research instruments to accurately examine strategy use.

- In *Chapter Twenty Five* (Researching Young Learners), Annamaria Pinter discusses what is distinctive about children as second and foreign language learners as compared to adults. She explores children's roles and status in research on the continuum of 'object-subject-active co-researcher'.

- In *Chapter Twenty Seven* (Researching Language Classrooms), Lesley Harbon and Huizhong Shen present recent trends in second language classroom research. In particular, they describe action research, classroom observation and narrative inquiry as some of the ways in which the language of the classroom might be researched.

- In *Chapter Twenty Seven* (Researching Language Testing and Assessment), John Read outlines key concepts and research procedures in research on language testing and assessment. He discusses how research studies can grow out of the process of test development to address issues that have an impact on the quality of assessment.

- In *Chapter Twenty Eight* (Researching Teachers' Beliefs), Simon Borg provides an overview of the development of research areas and methods on teachers' beliefs in education generally and considers some of the challenging definitional issues relevant to this research, such as the distinction between beliefs and knowledge.

- In *Chapter Twenty Nine* (Researching Language and Gender), Jane Sunderland presents six frequently adopted theoretical and methodological approaches to gender and language study (i.e. sociolinguistics, corpus linguistics, conversation analysis, discursive psychology, critical discourse analysis and feminist post-structuralist discourse analysis) and discusses the question of combining two or more of these for a given research project.

- In *Chapter Thirty* (Researching Language and Identity), David Block explores individuals' identities from two separate but often interlinked perspectives and methods. He focuses in detail on narrative research, identifying issues that arise in this approach to research.

- In *Chapter Thirty One* (Researching Language Teacher Education), Simon Borg presents major issues in the study of language teacher education, with specific reference to the professional learning of practising (as opposed to pre-service) teachers. He also highlights different areas of language teacher education that research can focus on.

CHAPTER SIXTEEN

Researching Speaking

Rebecca Hughes

Speaking is a capacity that human beings draw on almost as easily and unconsciously as we breathe, and yet it is one that is richly complex to research. Spoken discourse is at the heart of both the most sophisticated and the most mundane of human activities. Everyday conversation is the social glue which underpins all human relationships. By the age of three, a child who develops normally has gained a good day-to-day working vocabulary and by the age of five or six has grasped the basic linguistic and pragmatic skills required to develop their own identity and relationships within their family and the wider community (see Ochs & Sheifflin 2009 for a useful survey of child language acquisition embedded in social and cultural contexts).

At a more abstract level, the spoken language, from preliterate times to the present day, has been the originating and facilitating medium of a great deal of the creative, performative, political, educational and ideological developments through human history. Despite technological developments, face-to-face speech remains a primary medium by which all humans collaborate about information and tasks, develop organizational behaviour and express and comprehend emotional life with others.

Yet, despite (or perhaps because of) this pervasiveness and significance, research into spoken language remains a complex field to engage with and is the focus for much debate in applied linguistics theory and practice. This complexity arises in part from the fact that, depending on the aspect of the spoken form being researched, the central questions being investigated may relate to the narrowest aspect of speech – for example, investigating a particular phonetic feature (as in Levy & Strange 2008 'Perception of French vowels by American English adults with and without French language experience') or the broadest, such as understanding the effects of the development of a literate culture in an oral society (see, for example, the collection *The Making of Literate Societies*, Olson & Torrance 2001). The nature of the research techniques and strategies employed, and paradigms regarded as valid, will vary in line with the topic and outcomes of research which, as noted, may be extremely varied themselves.

In addition, the nature of the research will be strongly affected by the purposes for which it is undertaken and where it sits on the cline of theory and applications. One of the most tantalizing aspects of research into speech is that there is very little cross reference between areas with potentially overlapping interests. For example, the constraints on, and the nature of, lexical retrieval and articulation (how we come up with words and say them) have relevance to understanding the grammar of the spoken form. Speakers tend to construct utterances in predictably different ways from writers and this is in part due to the need to process the language being spoken in real time and with no potential for editing. However, many of the major advances in the understanding of spoken grammar have come from large studies of corpora (Biber et al. 1999; Carter & McCarthy 2006; Close & Aarts 2010; John & Brooks 2014; Leech 2000; Svartvik 1990), and there is little interplay between the insights of speech processing which shape these grammatical choices and speech captured as text in the form of a corpus. The work of scholars who take the 'emergent' nature of talk very seriously has gained ground somewhat in recent years. In the field known as 'interactional linguistics', Peter Auer, for instance, works at the intersection between grammar and conversation analysis (CA). Auer and Pfänder (2011) provide a useful set of perspectives and insights from those who follow this approach. More directly within the CA tradition, but with a strong focus on the temporality of speech, is the work of Elizabeth Couper-Kuhlen. Couper-Kuhlen (2012) shows how the work can sit between detailed analysis of emerging talk and some fundamental questions of linguistic theory. Many other influential researchers have adopted a similar approach. Fox et al. (2012) in *The Handbook of Conversation Analysis* published by Wiley provide an overview of the techniques involved.

Equally, the work in psycho- or neurolinguistics about unimpaired and impaired speech, or spoken-language recognition, is generally carried out in isolation from, for example, the needs of the second language learner or the norms of speech against which oral assessment is conducted. While these may seem distant areas from one another, taking an aspect of spoken language such as hesitations and reformulations (often listed in oral assessment criteria) and understanding the norms and constraints on spoken language in non-assessed contexts shows how there may be insights that have obvious relevance to each other.

Overall, therefore, in considering the focus of research into speaking, it has to be remembered that the individual speaker and the society in which they produce their discourse are inevitably difficult for the researcher into speaking to disentangle, and the exact nature of the object of study is not as clear-cut as it may seem at first glance. Much of the debate around approaches to researching speaking revolves around these issues, together with the fundamental issue of how to capture and analyse, without distortion, what is a transitory and dynamic medium.

Bearing in mind the necessary diversity of approaches to researching speaking outlined above, this chapter will aim to give an overview of some of the major approaches to research into speech and a brief summary of the typical methods by which investigations are undertaken.

Research strategies and techniques

Research into speaking is generally carried out via two main means: capturing and examining authentic speech data and capturing and examining elicited or non-authentic speech data. These areas are dealt with in more detail below, but, due to its centrality in a number of research methods, the section begins with some discussion of the role of transcription as a key tool in spoken language research.

A great number of approaches to spoken-language research depend on being able to access conversational or other forms of speech data and make it available through time for analysis. These range from discourse and CA to ethnographic approaches to large spoken corpora. In psycholinguistics and second language acquisition (SLA) studies, the role of transcription is less central, however, even though, in the former, there is often a role for elicited experimental data from subjects which needs to be captured in written form. This makes transcription one of the most key tools in spoken-language research and one which any new researcher needs to take into consideration in setting up their methodological framework.

Transcription of spoken data

Many types of research into spoken language depend on capturing the data via not only electronic recording but subsequently transcribing this into the static and more easily analysable written mode. Until the development of speech-recognition software which can assist the automation of transcription to some extent, the transfer of speech data into the written mode was an extremely time-consuming process and one that needed to be factored in to the research project framework design both practically (it can take at least six minutes to make an accurate, basic transcription of a single minute of talk) and from a theoretical perspective.

A primary question in spoken-language research is often therefore the type of transcription to be used. The decisions which a researcher needs to take about this can be regarded as relating to a basic process of materials gathering, and in some respect of developing an investigative tool. The reason for this is that writing down speech is not a neutral process, and decisions as to what features to capture and how best to represent these in the static, visual medium of writing relate closely to the overall purpose of the investigation. All transcription conventions attempt to represent the acoustic information in some way, but no system can capture the full breadth of linguistically salient information which even a short and apparently simple burst of speech contains.

The simplest conversation when transcribed and put under the microscope of analysis looks, to the untrained eye, chaotic. Here, for instance, is a two-person question and answer exchange transcribed for research into medical discourse and consulting skills (Ph = pharmacist, Pt = patient) (Salter et al. 2007, p. 4):

1 Ph 05. Yeah okay and you're happy with the box that you are using

2 Pt 09. Yeah I can manage them (0.2) they ain't all the same some of them have

3 Pt 09. got a slide but you have to watch you don't un uncover more than one

4 Pt 09. hole=

5 Ph 05. =Yes yeah I've actually brought some with me here

6 Pt 09. You see

7 Ph 05. I think the one you mean is (0.2) is it like that (0.3) is it like that so you

8 Ph 05. have to be careful when you pull the *slides out*

9 Pt 09. *That's right* yeah they're the ones

10 Ph 05. Yeah

11 Pt 09. Yeah (0.3) so that just pull one pull pull down to them morning

12 Ph 05. Pull down to the one you want

13 Pt 09. And then the next dinner time

14 Ph 05. Yeah and make sure you only go so far with them=

15 Pt 09. =That's right

16 Ph 05. Yeah

A variety of transcription conventions have emerged over the years, and the researcher using spoken data needs to familiarize themselves with these and decide on the level of detail and the salient features which are necessary to capture in the study in question.

The extract of talk between a pharmacist and patient above shows some of the very commonly used conventions in transcribing spoken language. For instance, you will see an 'equals' sign (=) at the end of the utterance at line 4 and another one at the start of the utterance at line 4. This indicates that the pharmacist interrupts, or overlaps with, the patient and that the word 'hole' and 'yes' are said simultaneously. You will also see numbers in brackets placed within an utterance: 'I think the one you mean is (0.2) is it like that (0.3) is it like that…'. These numbers indicate the length of pauses made by a speaker. In these examples, the pauses are 0.2 and 0.3 of a second respectively. Both pauses and overlapping talk can have significance in conversational analysis, and it is very common therefore to see this level of detail in a transcription.

A seminal chapter containing what has come to be known as *the Jefferson system* is shown in Sacks et al. (1978), and this has formed the basis of the transcription systems used in literally hundreds of other studies. Edwards and Lampert (1993) provide a thorough survey of transcription methods in relation to research frameworks. A good, and user friendly, summary of transcription conventions typically used in conversational analysis, discourse analysis and ethnographic studies can be found in ten Have (1999). Grundy (2013) provides a thoughtful introduction to transcription in the field of pragmatics for the novice researcher.

Parsing and tagging

A very specific kind of transcription is used in corpus linguistics and speech-recognition systems to capture not only acoustic information but also lexical and syntactic details. *Parsing* refers to the process by which spoken data is broken down into its grammatical constituents, and *tagging* is the means by which these constituents, often down to the level of individual words and parts of words (morphemes), are labelled so that a computer can aid the researcher in the process of analysis. The development of sophisticated search engines that can seek and analyse data on the World Wide Web is expanding the breadth and depth of this work (Kilgarrif & Grefenstette 2003; Kilgarriff et al. 2010). However, a further stage in the development of multimodal corpora and relevant tagging and searching devices is still needed for spoken-language research to be carried out on a par with the simplicity and directness of written word searches and tools which have been around for decades such as concordancers.

Elicited data and experimental approaches

As noted in the previous sections, for theoretical and methodological reasons, research into speech does not always or indeed necessarily take place directly on samples of spoken language as found in our daily lives. Those who do not use spontaneous spoken discourse fall broadly into two categories: those who seek to mimic authentic spoken data closely and elicit it in a more manageable way for analysis; those who step further away from contextualized speech data and construct experimental frameworks within which very precisely constrained samples of speech can be analysed.

An example of the former approach would be the well-known approach referred to as a *map task experiment*. This is a technique to elicit dialogue in ways that are predictable and constrained but, at the same time, create the need for explanation, clarification and convergence of understanding. Participants seek to share information of a route from A to B from two slightly different maps without showing them to each other. The maps are designed to have slight but important differences between them, and this leads to a rich, spontaneous, dialogue between the participants as they try to carry out the task of getting one or other of them to a specific destination. A corpus of these dialogues has been made publicly available at: http:// groups.inf.ed.ac.uk/maptask/index.html, viewed 16 March 2014.

Speech data are often gathered under much stricter experimental protocols, particularly when there is a very narrow research question being investigated. The approach involves, for example, a group of subjects who have a particular feature (dyslexic children, brain damaged patients, the elderly), a control group (children of similar age and background without dyslexia, etc.) and a set of carefully chosen prompts to elicit spoken data of the kind required by the investigator. Altmann et al. (2008), in the realm of health sciences and communication, investigated the oral performance of dyslexic children by means of a strictly experimental approach that elicited a narrow sample of responses required by the research design. The careful construction of the prompts by means of which samples of speech were gathered, and their relationship to the research questions, becomes clear in the following extract concerning their methods:

> In the current study, we presented participants with three-word stimuli that included a verb form and two nouns differing in animacy.[1] Noun stimuli consisted of a proper name and an inanimate noun chosen to be a good argument for a particular verb, so that a conceptual connection between the two could be easily established (e.g. kicked + football). Verb stimuli consisted of the past participles of three types of transitive verbs: control (CON) verbs comprised agent–patient verbs with regular morphology (e.g. stirred, kicked). Experimental verb types included agent–patient verbs with irregular (IRR) morphology (e.g. shaken, thrown) and theme–experiencer (TE) verbs with regular morphology (e.g. bored, confused). The two experimental verb types imposed different metalinguistic demands on participants. IRR verbs required participants to recognize that the past participle form could only be used in perfective sentences (e.g. had hidden), passive sentences (e.g. was hidden by), or in

adjectival structures (e.g. the hidden X). Thus, to succeed in using IRR verbs participants had to detect the small orthographic/phonological differences signalling the morphological form, and be explicitly aware of the grammatical constraints inherent in this morphological form (Altmann et al. 2008, pp. 58–59).

Disciplines in linguistics that value elicited/experimental speech data, or approach speech from a decontextualized perspective, and regard the norms of actual talk as less relevant include SLA, psycholinguistics and speech processing, among others.

Authentic data and CA approaches

The sharp contrast between the approach described above and that used by researchers who prioritize authentic data is clear when compared to the influential method or indeed whole school or sub-discipline of applied linguistics, known as *conversation analysis* or 'CA'. Those who use elicited data of one kind or another often argue that this is necessary because even large samples of authentic data simply may not show the feature that the investigators are interested in. Those who begin from authentic spoken interaction, however, turn this argument around and propose that even the apparently simplest and shortest example of a real exchange between situated interlocutors will provide a rich source of linguistic data. It is the starting point of such an approach to say that language is socially constructed, that meaning resides not so much in the words and clauses as in the understanding that emerges between speakers and that, on a moment-by-moment basis, speakers and hearers accommodate to one another in the achievement of conversational interaction. The detailed transcription, repeated hearings and interpretation by the researcher (often in discussion with others) of stretches of talk are the fundamental research tools of the CA tradition.

A guest editorial by Nielsen and Wagner (2007) in the *Journal of Pragmatics* provides an excellent overview and key references of the history of this influential approach from early studies situated in the field of sociology, through talk in institutional settings and what this reveals about individuals and organizations, to *interactional linguistics* and other newer branches. The role of authentic, situated, speech data is nicely summed up thus:

Although CA research has engaged in new topics, settings, and disciplines, it has kept its identity and has acted as a discipline in its own right with a well-defined methodology and a strong analytic tradition in which new studies are written. Studies are carefully crafted collections of cases, sometimes assembled over many years due to low frequency. The cases are the basis for and the proof of the description of the recipies [*sic*] for social actions described in the studies. Herein lies the core of CA: testable sequential description of social actions, carried out on the basis of data, which have not been elicited but collected in the field. (Nielsen & Wagner 2007, p. 442)

A useful and publicly available set of some of the seminal transcriptions used in the CA approach can be found at: http://www.talkbank.org/CABank/, viewed 16 March 2014).

Other research approaches that value actual spoken data at different levels of its production include: sociolinguistic and ethnographic approaches (which situate the research in a culture and a society and focus on interaction), corpus studies (which tend to focus more on word and clause level and the patterns that can be found in large bodies of speech data) and acoustic phonetics (which, at its most basic, deals with the stream of speech in terms of sounds as opposed to higher units such as words or clauses). The last two areas – particularly phonetic studies which have a very specialized set of measurement techniques, dedicated software and equipment – provide a warning not to confuse the using of actual instances of speech data with a particular set of research methods. It is not the case that using real-speech data equates to qualitative work. Samples of speech can be analysed in a number of ways, and approaches that value authentic data can be placed on a spectrum moving from situated/qualitative (such as CA or ethnographic work) to decontextualized/quantitative (such as acoustic phonetics, frequency studies from large corpora).

Synthesis of current thinking and research

Spoken-language research is rather unusual in that many of the debates surrounding questions of theory are intertwined with the very practical issues touched on above of what data are regarded as acceptable as a basis for investigation and how these are best approached. These issues go to the heart of a very fundamental question indeed for researching speaking: 'What is speaking and how do you analyse it?' In part, the question under debate is the need (or not) for wholly authentic speech data to be the basis of spoken-language research, and, in part, these conundrums relate to the much bigger question of the role of naturally occurring data in linguistic theory. A classic distinction in linguistics is that proposed by Noam Chomsky (1965) between *competence* (underlying aptitude in human beings for handling the language system) and *performance* (the tangible evidence of language used in the real world). This distinction set the tone of debates from the 1960s onwards and is still seen by many as relevant – in 2007 a whole issue of the *Modern Language Journal* was dedicated to questions arising from the basic distinction posed forty years earlier, and the conceptual distinction continued to have currency into the second decade of the twenty-first century (see, for instance, Neeleman

2013; Syrett & Lidz 2011). The reason for the longevity of the distinction is that it sits at the heart of a debate in linguistic inquiry that was neatly summed up by the editor of the *Modern Language Journal* special issue:

> Is acquiring a second language essentially a cognitive process situated in the mind of the individual learner? Or, is it, first and foremost, a social process because language learning necessarily occurs through interactive use with target language speakers? (Magnan 2007, p. 733)

Some of the complexities of research into spoken discourse therefore cross refer to ongoing debates in applied linguistics (for instance the interface between social and contextualized aspects of language and SLA theory) (Larsen-Freeman 2007) or the debates surrounding the role of culture on the grammar of an individual language (Everett 2005). An individual researcher's position in relation to this central debate will inform what evidence they regard as valid and useful in their approach to researching speaking. These issues, in turn, relate to the stance of the researcher and the general framework or paradigm they regard as most compelling. Therefore, as outlined in the previous section, the techniques and methods in spoken-language research are not only quite diverse, but they are also sometimes somewhat 'loaded' in terms of how they relate to competing views of language itself. All these points will influence a researcher's choices as to whether, for example, entirely natural or elicited speech data are preferable in a given study.

These methodological debates, in the same way as the theoretical ones outlined above, are not new and have been the locus of heated discussions since the 1960s and before. For instance, there is the well-known concept in applied linguistics called the *observer's paradox* which was first set out in a seminal chapter by William Labov (Labov 2006, first published 1966). This is based on the idea that when speech data is the object of study, it can be influenced by the presence of a researcher in significant ways. Put simply, all of us will tend to behave differently if we think we are being observed and that what we are saying is being recorded for future analysis. Labov himself solved this problem by designing an ingenious method for his data gathering. By asking various shop assistants quickly for a particular item, he elicited an unselfconscious answer ('fourth floor') that contained the particular spoken feature he was interested in.

There have been two major trends which are starting to bring spoken-language research firmly into the centre of debates in applied linguistics once more. The first is the acknowledgment in SLA and cognitive linguistics that the role of context and culture is difficult to exclude from theories that are to be meaningful rather than simply internally consistent. The role of the situated speaker or 'situated cognition' as it affects communicative outputs particularly in the realm of SLA is gaining more attention (Doehler 2010; Mori 2007). Influential applications of research such as work on oral assessment in large and high-stakes international examinations of second language use have also tended to push researchers to ask about the norms of spoken discourse in a variety or contexts (Hughes 2004; Pearce & Williams 2013).

The second area that is, and will continue to be, strongly influential is the role of new technologies on our capacity to capture, store and analyse large quantities of digitally recorded speech in audio and video formats. This trend is meeting up with two powerful drivers of change: the World Wide Web and commercial interests which require human–computer interactions to address spoken dialogue (currently mostly in restricted domains such as a call centre). Although essentially a text- and image-based medium, the web with its 'openness', data sharing potential and sheer size allows groups of users to draw on spoken data in quantities that were simply unthinkable five years ago. A search on the term 'conversation' in the popular video clip site YouTube (http://www.youtube.com/results?search_query=conversation&page=1, viewed 24 July 2014) generated over 90,000 hits in 2008 and about six-and-a-half-million returns in 2014. While some of these will include the mildly psychotic talking in monologue to their favourite tree, this is just one example of the richness of oral material which the web can provide. This trend for openly accessible multimodal data is changing the way that research into speaking is carried out in applied linguistics. For instance, the idea of the individual researcher recording data simply for a small, local, project and the data only being captured in the oral form seems quite old-fashioned as large archives or open access sites of video materials become readily available online. Second, the notion of a private corpus of speech will become less and less attractive as researchers understand the benefits of sharing the workload of capture, transcription and aligning sound files with transcriptions.

These changes will happen all the sooner if some of the commercial interests (for instance, gaming or automation of responses to human interlocutors via a call centre) that are encouraging practical approaches to analysing dialogue are able to link up with applied linguistic research. This will be particularly powerful for researchers in the field if a means is found to search and to model dialogues in ways that make them as accessible as text and meaningful to computers. Work in this field is already quite sophisticated, and in computational linguistics, an array of publications and platforms are being produced to deal with human–machine interactions via the spoken medium. Earlier versions included a site where a 'chatbot' learned to speak to you purely from the input you provided: http://www.jabberwacky.com/, viewed 19 April 2009 and these developed exponentially into highly diverse mobile applications such as the conversational puppy app 'Pupito' (https://itunes.apple.com/us/app/pupito!/id522091447?mt=8, viewed 16 March 2014) or the personalized language learning platform 'Duolingo' (https://www.duolingo.com/, viewed 16 March 2014). Some of these new approaches step outside the debates around the cognitive or cultural basis for language learning and are allowing a more sophisticated and data-driven set of theories to emerge about spoken language in context.

Sample studies

As has been noted throughout this chapter, speaking is a multifaceted human skill and there is no single research approach that can cover all the areas that interest the academic and wider community. Therefore, this section presents two contrasting studies that look at the same area of speaking – the details of interactive behaviour – in order to give a sense of the diversity of approaches and some examples of the typical stages to projects in the field of spoken discourse. Speaking is distinguished by its high potential for interactivity, and spontaneous conversational data is the hardest of all for linguistic theory and for human–computer systems to model. Within speaking, the mechanisms that allow smooth and seamless turn-taking have been an object of considerable attention. Both the studies presented here see turn taking as a key language resource in spoken language, but are carried out by sharply contrasting means.

Sample study 1: Durational aspects of turn-taking in spontaneous face-to-face and telephone dialogues (ten Bosch et al. 2004)

In this study, ten Bosch and colleagues wanted to look at the differences in turn-taking behaviour in two contexts: face to face and on the telephone. Their approach was corpus-based and rigorously quantitative. Using such a framework, it is crucial to match the data carefully and define the units that are being analysed extremely objectively. In part, this is simply the conventions of the quantitative approach and, in part, it is due to the need for researchers to include sufficient information for other researchers to carry out similar studies and compare or challenge results. The researchers took comparable examples of speech in the two contexts from a pre-existing corpus and analysed the duration of pauses between speaker turns. They defined a 'turn' in a way that lent itself to the quantitative approach: utterances between silences (see also e.g. Koiso et al. (1998) for an influential study on Japanese in this area which uses the same technique). They introduce their definition thus:

> A study by Weilhammer and Rabold (2003) on durational aspects of turn-taking, which was based on task-oriented dialogue data, has shown that the logarithm of the durations of pauses and overlaps can be modeled by a Gaussian distribution.[2] In their analysis, the definition of

turn was 'implicitly based' on the Verbmobil transcription conventions[3] (Burger 1997). Their definition of a turn states that 'a turn starts with the first word in the dialogue or with the first word breaking the silence that follows the previous turn'. Furthermore, 'the silence between two turns of one speaker is always overlaid by an utterance of the [interlocutor]'. The definition of a turn as used in the present study is very similar. (ten Bosch et al. 2004, p. 564)

In their discussion, the authors acknowledge the limitations of this approach, suggesting the need for a 'functional' definition of the turn. However, the benefit of this approach is that it does allow very rigorous and objective cross-genre (in this case, the telephone versus face-to-face mode) comparisons to be made. This is because the framework for the analysis is based on a unit that has been clearly defined and lends itself to measurement and to the analytical tools being used. One of their main findings was that pauses were of shorter duration in the telephone mode (see Figure 16.1).

The authors tentatively suggest that the lack of other cues to hold the floor (gaze and gesture, for instance), and the fact that the whole of the attention of the interlocutors is on the talk in hand, may account for this.

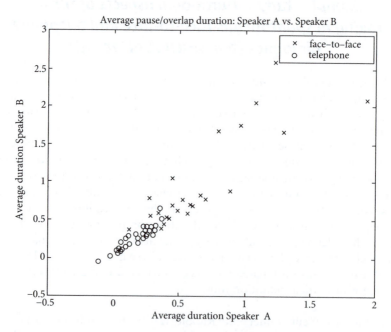

FIGURE 16.1 *Scatter plot of the average pause duration. Each dialogue is represented by a single point in the scatter diagram, of which the coordinates are determined by the average pause duration for each speaker (ten Bosch et al. 2004, p. 568)*

Sample study 2 – Negotiating negotiation:
The collaborative production of resolution in small
claims mediation hearings (Garcia 2000)

The second study shows the application of conversation analytical approaches to a real-world problem: mediation and negotiation. In particular, the study deals with the need for neutrality on the part of any mediator and the empowerment of the parties involved to reach a consensus for themselves. The CA approach is particularly useful in understanding how participants develop understanding between themselves in the process of interaction and was, therefore, seen as an appropriate paradigm by this researcher in contrast with earlier work on mediation which had tended to focus on outcomes rather than on the processes involved and how participants expressed consensus or resistance.

The analysis was based on fifteen examples taken from a larger videotaped collection of mediation encounters, transcribed using the *Jefferson method* (see Sacks et al. 1978), and closely analysed using CA methods to allow a better understanding of the emergence, or not, of consensus and the power relations holding between the various parties. The analyses showed, in detail, how the trained mediator retains neutrality and the strategies employed by them to empower the individuals involved to create their own resolutions to the issues.

In Excerpt 9, the mediator asks specifically for a price for the camera, rather than requesting 'a solution'. By soliciting a price for the camera, the mediator is supporting the idea that a possible solution would be for Disputant C ('Pete') to purchase the camera.

Excerpt 9
552 M: so: (0.4) so wha:t would it co:st fer pete t' =
553 *pur*chase *thuh* *cam*ra*?
554 (3.6)
555 A: i'm willing tuh negotiate that.
(Garcia 2000, p. 332)

In contrast to the first study, the interpretive role of the researcher is presented in relation to close analysis of specific instances of talk in context, rather than objective quantitative results that 'speak for themselves'. Discussing the benefits of using the CA approach to help produce a better understanding of key issues in this area, Garcia notes that it has tended to lack the interactional perspective and that the approach allows the research to show the specifics of how mediation works rather than dealing with abstractions.

These contrasting studies which end the chapter show something of the rich diversity of potential research on the spoken form and how it lends itself to a multiplicity of real-world questions as well as being at the heart of some of the most contentious areas of linguistic theory.

Notes

1 'Animacy' indicates the level of autonomous life the nouns showed. For example, 'dog' or 'bird' will score more highly on this than 'stone' or 'stick'.
2 Gaussian distribution is a term from statistics also known as the normal or the bell curve. It is applied to the tendency for the distribution of data points in many samples – for example, speech rates – to cluster around an average mid point with a small tail on each side of this peak showing higher or lower scores.
3 Verbmobil was a large artificial intelligence project in Germany looking at the automatic recognition of speech and translation into other languages.

Resources for further reading

Adolphs, S & Carter, R 2013, *Spoken Corpus Linguistics*, Routledge, New York, NY.

This book provides a useful summary and overview of the issues of building and analysing spoken corpora. It is particularly interesting in that it also incorporates 'multi-modal' aspects to provide a highly innovative framework suggesting ways in which researchers may begin to incorporate gesture and spoken language simultaneously in their analysis.

Chafe, W & Danielewicz, J 1987, 'Properties of spoken and written language', in Horowitz, R & Samuels, SJ (eds), *Comprehending Oral and Written Language*, Academic Press, San Diego, CA, pp. 83–113.

This remains one of the most accessible explanations of why speaking is different from writing and needs to be researched on its own merits.

Hughes, R 2010, *Teaching and Researching Speaking*, Longman, London.

This book offers an overview of research into spoken language that is particularly aimed at the English-language teaching community or those interested in the interface between teaching and research.

Jones, MJ & Knight, R 2013, *Bloomsbury Companion to Phonetics*, Bloomsbury Publishing, New York, NY.

This handbook covers the major aspects of phonetics that a novice researcher will need to become familiar with and also has some excellent material on new directions such as the perception of speech in social settings.

Sidnell, J & Stivers, T (eds), 2012, *The Handbook of Conversation Analysis*, Wiley-Blackwell, Malden, MA.

This extensive handbook brings together not only experts in the field of CA but also seeks to integrate their insights across into other related disciplines.

References

Altmann, LJP, Lombardino, LJ & Puranik, C 2008, 'Sentence production in students with dyslexia', *International Journal of Language & Communication Disorders*, vol. 43, no. 1, pp. 55–76.

Auer, P & Pfänder, S (eds), 2011, *Constructions: Emerging and Emergent* (Vol. 6). de Gruyter Mouton, Berlin.

Biber, D, Johansson, S, Leech, G, Conrad, S & Finegan, E 1999, *The Longman Grammar of Spoken and Written English*, Longman, London.

Carter, R & McCarthy, M 2006, *The Cambridge Grammar of English*, Cambridge University Press, Cambridge.

Chomsky, N 1965, *Aspects of the Theory of Syntax*, Massachusetts Institute of Technology Press, Cambridge, MA.

Close, J & Aarts, B 2010, 'Current change in the nodal system of English: A case study of must, have to and have got to', in H Sauer & G Waxenberger (eds), *The history of English Verbal and Nominal Constructions*, John Benjamins, Philadelphia, PA, pp. 165–182.

Couper-Kuhlen, E 2012, 'Turn continuation and clause combinations', *Discourse Processes*, vol. 49, no. 3–4, pp. 273–299.

Doehler, SP 2010, 'Conceptual changes and methodological challenges: On language and learning from a conversation analytic perspective on SLA', in P Seedhouse, S Walsh, C Jenks (eds), *Conceptualising Learning in Applied Linguistics*, Palgrave Macmillan, London, pp. 105–127.

Edwards, JA & Lampert, MD (eds), 1993, *Talking Data: Transcription and Coding in Discourse Research*, Lawrence Erlbaum Associates, Hillsdale, NJ.

Everett, DL 2005, 'Cultural constraints on grammar and cognition in Piraha', *Current Anthropology*, vol. 46, no. 4, pp. 621–646.

Fox, BA, Thompson, SA, Ford, CE & Couper-Kuhlen, E 2012, 'Conversation analysis and linguistics', in J Sidnell & T Stivers (eds), *The Handbook of Conversation Analysis*, John Wiley & Sons, Ltd, Chichester, pp.726–740.

Garcia, AC 2000, 'Negotiating negotiation: The collaborative production of resolution in small claims mediation hearings', *Discourse and Society*, vol. 11, no. 3, pp. 315–343.

Grundy, P 2013, *Doing Pragmatics*, Routledge, Abingdon.

Hughes, R 2004, 'Testing the visible: Literate biases in oral language testing', *Journal of Applied Linguistics*, vol. 1, no. 3, pp. 295–309.

John, P, & Brooks, B 2014, 'Lingua franca and its grammar footprint: Introducing an index for quantifying grammatical diversity in written and spoken language', *Journal of Quantitative Linguistics*, vol. 21, no. 1, pp. 22–35.

Kilgarrif, A & Grefenstette, G 2003, 'Introduction to the web as corpus', *Computational Linguistics*, vol. 29, no. 3, pp. 333–347.

Kilgarriff, A, Reddy, S, Pomikálek, J & Avinesh, PVS 2010, 'A corpus factory for many languages', *LREC2010*, pp. 904–10.

Koiso, H, Horiuchi, Y, Tutiya, S, Ichikawa, A & Ken, Y 1998, 'An analysis of turn-taking and backchannels based on prosodic and syntactic features in Japanese map task dialogs', *Language and Speech*, vol. 41, nos. 3–4, pp. 295–322.

Labov, W (2006), *The Social Stratification of English in New York city*, Cambridge University Press, New York, NY.

Larsen-Freeman, D 2007, 'Reflecting on the cognitive – social debate in second language acquisition', *The Modern Language Journal*, vol. 91, no. s1, pp. 773–787.

Leech, G 2000, 'Grammars of spoken English: New outcomes of corpus-oriented research', *Language Learning*, vol. 50, no. 4, 675–724.

Levy, ES & Strange, W 2008, 'Perception of French vowels by American English adults with and without French language experience', *Journal of Phonetics*, vol. 36, no. 1, pp. 141–157.

Magnan, SS 2007, 'Presenting the focus issue', *The Modern Language Journal*, vol. 91, Focus Issue, pp. 733–734.

Mori, J 2007, 'Border crossings? Exploring the intersection of second language acquisition, conversation analysis, and foreign language pedagogy', *The Modern Language Journal*, vol. 91, no. s1, pp. 849–862.

Neeleman, A 2013, 'Comments on Pullum', *Mind & Language*, vol. 28, no. 4, pp. 522–531.

Nielsen, MF & Wagner, J 2007, 'Continuity and diversity in conversation analysis', *Journal of Pragmatics*, vol. 39, no. 3, pp. 441–444.

Ochs, E & Sheifflin, BB 2009, 'Language acquisition and socialization: Three developmental stories and their implications', in A Duranti (ed.), *Linguistic Anthropology: A Reader*, Blackwell, Oxford, pp. 296–328.

Olson, D & Torrance, N 2001, *The Making of Literate Societies*, Blackwell, Oxford.

Pearce, WM & Williams, C 2013 'The cultural appropriateness and diagnostic usefulness of standardized language assessments for Indigenous Australian children', *International Journal of Speech-language Pathology*, vol. 15, no. 4, pp. 429–440.

Sacks, H, Schegloff, EA & Jefferson, G 1978, 'A simplest systematics for the organization of turn-taking of conversation', in Schenkein, J (ed.), *Studies in the Organization of Conversational Interaction*, Academic Press, New York, pp. 7–57.

Salter, C, Holland, R, Harvey, I & Henwood, K 2007, '"I haven't even phoned my doctor yet." The advice giving role of the pharmacist during consultations for medication review with patients aged 80 or more: Qualitative discourse analysis', *British Medical Journal*, vol. 334, no. 7603, p. 1101. doi: 10.1136/bmj.39171.577106.55, published 20 April 2007.

Svartvik, J. (ed.) 1990, *The London Corpus of Spoken English: Description and Research, Lund Studies in English 82*. Lund University Press, Lund.

Syrett, K & Lidz, J 2011, 'Competence, performance, and the locality of quantifier raising: Evidence from 4-year-old children', *Linguistic Inquiry*, vol. 42, no. 2, pp. 305–337.

ten Bosch, L, Oostdijk, N & de Ruiter, JP 2004, 'Durational aspects of turn-taking in spontaneous face-to-face and telephone dialogues', in I Habernal & V Matoušek (eds), *Text, Speech and Dialogue. (Lecture Notes in Computer Science)*. Springer, Berlin, pp. 563–570.

ten Have, P 1999, *Doing Conversation Analysis*, Sage Publications, London.

CHAPTER SEVENTEEN

Researching Listening

Larry Vandergrift

It is probably self-evident that, of the four foundational language skills, listening is the least understood and certainly the most difficult to investigate. The covert nature of the process and ephemeral nature of the input make the perceptual and interpretation processes involved in listening comprehension difficult to access. Research on listening in applied linguistics remains limited; however, recent studies have led to some new insights into the underlying cognitive processes, the teaching and the assessment of listening (see Vandergrift & Goh 2012). That being said, many questions still remain and, compared to the other skills, few theoretical models have emerged.

This chapter begins with a very brief synopsis of current research on listening in applied linguistics, followed by a critical overview of the range of methodologies that can be used to investigate the listening skill. It concludes with a sample study that illustrates the use of some of these research methodologies.

Brief overview of listening

Cognitive processes

A conceptual understanding of listening must acknowledge the interplay of physiological and cognitive processes at different levels, as well as the influence of contextual factors. Recent reviews of research on listening (e.g. Field 2008; Lynch 2009; Rost 2011; Vandergrift 2007; Vandergrift & Goh 2012) highlight two fundamental cognitive processes required for comprehension: bottom-up and top-down processes. Listeners use bottom-up processes when they construct meaning from the incoming sound stream by gradually combining increasingly larger units of meaning from the phoneme-level up to the discourse-level to build comprehension of an utterance or a text. On the other hand, listeners use top-down processes when they use context, prior knowledge (topic, genre, culture and other schema knowledge in long-term memory) and listener expectations to build a conceptual framework around the specific listening task. Individual units of meaning retained from bottom-up processing are slotted into the framework to eventually arrive at a reasonable interpretation of the message. Although these processes occur simultaneously and in parallel fashion, the degree to which listeners may use the one process more than the other will depend on the task or the purpose for listening.

Research on these cognitive processes suggests that listeners need to learn how to use both processes to their advantage, depending on the purpose for listening. Although the literature on listening instruction over the past years has tended to focus on the development of top-down processes, there is currently a renewed interest in the contribution of perceptual processing (bottom-up processes) to successful listening comprehension (Field 2008).

The speed and effectiveness of these cognitive processes depend on the degree to which listeners can efficiently process what is heard. Native language listeners do this automatically, with little conscious attention to individual words. Listeners learning a new language, on the other hand, have limited linguistic knowledge; therefore, less of what they hear can be automatically processed. Depending on their level of proficiency or the difficulty of the text or task, these listeners may need to consciously process some of the input and, given the limitations of working memory, comprehension either turns out to be incomplete or breaks down. To compensate for gaps in comprehension, skilled listeners can use their metacognitive knowledge about listening to orchestrate appropriate metacognitive and cognitive strategies, contextual cues and other relevant information available to them to inference what was not understood. Listeners also use metacognitive knowledge for successful comprehension when they (1) analyse task requirements; (2) activate appropriate listening processes for the task; (3) make appropriate predictions; (4) monitor their comprehension; (5) problem solve to figure out the meaning of what they do not understand; and (6) evaluate the success of their approach (Vandergrift 1999).

Variables that may influence comprehension

Listening involves more than cognitive processing, however. It can be constrained by affective factors such as motivation, self-efficacy and anxiety, which further limit how much information short-term memory can process at a given moment. Other learner variables that may impact comprehension include background knowledge of the topic of the text, proficiency level in the target language, age, metacognitive knowledge about listening, strategy use, native language listening ability, working memory capacity and auditory discrimination ability (see Vandergrift & Baker 2015). The listening task itself, that is, the type of information and level of detail required and what the listener is expected to do with that information, may also influence the outcome of listening (see Brunfaut & Revesz 2013). Text characteristics such as speed of delivery, frequency of pausing and hesitations, accent, and amount of informal language in the aural stream are further mitigating factors (see Bloomfield et al. 2011). In the case of texts that carry visual support, such as video, the speaker's actions and reactions as well as the degree of congruency between the spoken and the visual may also influence the level of comprehension (see Cross 2011). In the case of interaction with an interlocutor, the listener's sensitivity to paralinguistic cues (body language and non-verbal voice cues) as well as his/her power relationship to the interlocutor play a significant role in comprehension. Moreover, a correct literal understanding of a message does not necessarily ensure accurate comprehension. Successful comprehension also requires listeners to apply pragmatic knowledge (see Roever this volume) to interpret the speaker's implied meaning, which may go beyond the literal meaning of the utterance. An awareness of the processes and variables related to listening success, and their interaction, is fundamental to an understanding of the listening construct. Since space limitations preclude a more detailed discussion of the complexity of the listening construct and related variables, see Field (2008), Lynch (2009), Rost (2011) and Vandergrift and Goh (2012) for more detailed discussions.

Research methodologies for investigating listening

Rost (2011) suggests that two overlapping processes – learning to listen in a new language and listening to learn this new language – are involved in listening development. The distinction between product (listening to learn) and process (learning to listen) is a useful heuristic for the following discussion of the research methodologies for investigating listening. However, before exploring and discussing the different methodologies for investigating the product and the process of listening, I will briefly discuss the methods for measuring listening ability.

Measuring listening ability

Proficiency tests

Essential to product-oriented research, listening test scores provide baseline data from which to measure growth in listening ability over time and/or consequent to a pedagogical intervention. Test scores can also be used to assign a level of listening proficiency to participants in studies where proficiency in the target language is a variable under investigation. Test scores may provide a more objective criterion for assigning proficiency level than a grade, course level or teacher assessment. Their generalizability, however, is limited because they are either based on an in-house placement test instead of a more broad-based, standardized objective measure (Berne 2004) or they may be assessing only particular aspects of listening ability (Buck 2001). Listening research can be strengthened and more broadly generalized through the use of valid and reliable tests referenced to internationally understood benchmarks such as the ACTFL Proficiency Guidelines (ACTFL 1999) or the Common European Framework of Reference for Languages (Council of Europe 2001), for example.

The advantage of listening tests as a comprehension measure for research purposes is that they are not labour-intensive and can be easily administered to large groups. The major challenge for listening test development and listening research, however, is the measurement of pure listening comprehension ability – that is, assessing comprehension without introducing reading or writing as confounding variables. Pure listening comprehension is most appropriately measured through aural prompts and verification options that are limited to non-verbal evaluation techniques such as selecting among a choice of pictures or objects, sequencing pictures or other graphics, drawing a picture, tracing on a map or performing a physical response. On the other hand, when using aural prompts to assess listening comprehension, memory becomes a confounding variable.

Free written recall protocols

Free recall protocols (or comprehension restitution tasks, see Prince 2012) represent an alternative but more labour-intensive method for measuring aural comprehension of text content. Participants listen to a text and immediately afterwards write, in their native language or L2, as much information as possible about what they understood. For example, Guichon and McLornan (2008) used recall protocols to measure differences in comprehension when an aural text was presented in four different conditions (audio alone, video with audio, video with audio and target language subtitles and video with audio and native language subtitles) to different groups. After the first presentation of the text, students in each group wrote notes in the language of their choice, and after the second presentation, they prepared a detailed summary (recall protocols). The protocols were then analysed for the number of correct idea units, resulting in a score for each student and each group, to determine the level of listening success for each condition. Calculating a comprehension score is more labour-intensive than administering a listening test, especially if a second rater independently verifies a certain percentage of the protocols to ensure reliability of the scores. However, recall protocols have the capacity to assess comprehension without using question prompts. Memory will be a confounding variable here as well, but perhaps less so if note taking and approximate spellings are allowed. An additional advantage to recall protocols as a measure of comprehension is their capacity for providing insights into the comprehension process. In fact, Guichon and McLornan (2008) and Prince (2012) view free recall protocols (or comprehension restitution tasks) as tools to measure comprehension and to gain greater insight into comprehension processes.

Although listening test scores and recall protocols provide an objective measure for determining comprehension gains for research purposes, the reliability of the scores will be limited by the reliability of the test or, in the case of the written recall protocols, inter-rater reliability. In order for any measure of comprehension to be reliable for research purposes, scores may need to be controlled to account for any initial significant differences between groups, such as differences in listening ability or background knowledge of the text topic. Finally, although listening test scores may provide a product to identify a level of performance, they tell us nothing about the process, that is, how listeners arrive at the right answer or why comprehension breaks down.

Investigating the product of listening

Experimental research

Research on listening has traditionally focused on the outcome, or the product of listening. In this line of research, student performance on a listening test is used to measure the success of a particular intervention. Two groups complete a pre-test; the experimental group experiences a different condition (such as exposure to an alternative pre-listening activity) from the control group. After the intervention, which may be long or short term, both groups complete an immediate post-test to determine the effects of the experiment: did the intervention result in a statistically significant (see Phakiti this volume) higher score on the listening post-test by the experimental group over the control group? Sometimes, a delayed post-test is used to assess the long-term effects of the intervention, such as the retention of certain vocabulary items three months after the intervention. Generally, there is no interest in determining how the listeners used the experimental intervention to improve their comprehension.

Correlational research

Another line of product-oriented listening research involves determining the degree of relationship between different variables hypothesized to be related to listening success. In this case, listening test scores are correlated with the scores of an instrument that measures an individual variable in order to determine if there is a relationship between the two variables and the strength of that relationship. For example, student scores on a listening anxiety questionnaire or a sound discrimination test are correlated with listening achievement scores to determine any potentially significant relationship. It is important to note, however, that although positive or negative correlations may point to interesting relationships between a given variable and listening success, it is not possible to claim causality between that variable and listening success. Uncovering the nature of the relationship between the variables requires careful interpretation and may be elucidated by other quantitative methodologies (see below) such as regression analysis, serial equation modelling or path analysis or more qualitative research methodologies such as interviews or stimulated recalls (of questionnaire data) that explore the listening process.

If the sample size is large enough, one can also simultaneously examine the relationship of a number of learner variables with listening success through multiple regression analysis (see Phakiti this volume for further discussion of this statistical test) and determine the effect of these variables on listening success (Vandergrift 2006). By regressing the scores of a number of independent variables (e.g. sound discrimination ability, first language listening ability, metacognitive awareness of listening) on the dependent variable (listening test scores), it is possible to determine the approximate percentage of variance that each independent variable might contribute to listening success (the dependent variable). A path analysis goes beyond a simple correlational design to explore causality and observe how the variables might interact in leading to successful L2 listening comprehension (Vandergrift & Baker 2015). This line of research, although interesting for what it might reveal about the predictive validity of hypothesized variables on listening ability, must be based on scores from reliable instruments and statistically significant relationships that are carefully interpreted.

Investigating the process of listening

Although a product-oriented approach to investigating listening can yield useful information about level of listening proficiency or potentially interesting relationships between listening ability and other learner variables, this line of research is not interested in exploring the problems listeners may experience in comprehension or the reasons motivating a student response on questionnaires. A process-oriented approach, on the other hand, can provide potentially useful insights into the cognitive processes underlying listening comprehension. Process-oriented methodologies, such as questionnaires, interviews, stimulated recalls, think-alouds, observation, diaries, tracking software and aural perception processing responses provide opportunities for participants to reveal, or researchers to uncover, listener decision-making processes during comprehension.

Questionnaires

Questionnaires (open- or closed-response) administered immediately after a listening activity can provide insights into student awareness of the process of listening and, when used as a repeated measure, track any changes in awareness of the listening process or listening attitudes over time (e.g. Vandergrift et al. 2006). Closed-response questionnaires, or surveys, are particularly useful for collecting large amounts of data that can be compiled and analysed quickly. The reliability of this data, however, is dependent upon the reliability and validity of the instrument. Greater insights into the reason for student response to questionnaire items or to changes in item responses over time can be achieved with a stimulated recall, where the listener is asked to reflect on any changes in response patterns on the same questionnaire (see the sample study below).

Interviews

Interviews, a more personable oral version of the open-ended response questionnaire, represent a more flexible but time-consuming method for eliciting data about listening. Individual or group interviews afford an opportunity to gain greater insights from a representative group of participants on important themes emerging from a large-scale survey, such as the difficulties students experience with listening in learning another language (e.g. Graham 2006). In particular, a semi-structured interview allows the researcher to diverge from the interview protocol to explore listener responses in greater detail. Interview sessions must be recorded, transcribed, coded and analysed. The reliability and validity of interview responses are enhanced when the participant is given the opportunity to read the transcripts to validate or correct them and, in the case of coding, when inter-rater reliability is at an acceptable level (0.90 or higher).

Stimulated recall protocols

Stimulated recall is a version of the individual interview in which the researcher and the participant focus on another data set involving the participant, such as a video recording or questionnaire responses. In order to gain greater insight into listener behaviour or response, the researcher asks the participant to comment on a particular event in the video or an interesting pattern in questionnaire response. The reliability of the data, recorded and transcribed, will be directly proportional to the proximity of the event under discussion and the interview. Although time consuming, stimulated recalls can also provide insights into listener decision-making processes, such as navigating through support options while engaged in multimedia listening (Grgurović & Hegelheimer 2007).

Diaries

Diaries are, first of all, tools for language learners to reflect on their language learning; however, they are also a useful research tool for gaining insights into learner awareness of listening processes, strategy development, listener anxiety, listening goals and actions taken to improve listening performance. Diaries can be entirely open-ended or guided by the researcher through given prompts, and they can be particularly fruitful when used over time. For example, over a ten-week period, Goh (1997) was able to document the development of metacognitive knowledge about L2 listening. Classroom discussions based on reflection probes (e.g. Goh & Taib 2006) can also serve as the stimulus for subsequent diary writing. Although data gleaned from diaries, and any other kind of listening notes (e.g. Mareschal 2007), are constrained by ethical considerations (student permission) and lack of generalizability, they do provide helpful insights into metacognitive awareness about listening, strategy use and overall listening success.

Observation notes

Since listening is a covert process, observation is generally of limited value for investigating listening processes in uni-directional listening. However, observation of interviews, or other interactive situations, can provide some insights into listener behaviour in bi-directional listening. When recorded, these interviews can be reviewed by the researcher for evidence of the variable under investigation (e.g. number and type of clarification strategies used). Review of the video recording with the research participant, using stimulated recall immediately after the interview, provides an opportunity to discover how the participant either clarified meaning or helped the interlocutor to advance the conversation (Farrell & Mallard 2006).

Think-aloud protocols

The research methodologies discussed so far have been retrospective in nature, that is, listeners comment and reflect on listening events that have taken place in the recent or distant past. Introspective methodologies, on the other hand, attempt to tap the thought processes of listeners while they are actually engaged in the listening event. After some initial training in the process, participants 'think aloud' at predetermined intervals while listening to a recorded aural text. The resulting data, the listener's voiced thoughts on what he/she is doing to comprehend, are recorded simultaneously and later transcribed. Introspection is likely the closest researchers can come to tapping thought processes while information is still available to the listener in short-term memory. Think-aloud protocols can be useful for shedding light on where and how listeners experience difficulties as they are listening (Goh 2002), the development of strategy use over time (e.g.

Graham et al. 2008) or the differential use of visual and aural information to understand online academic lectures (e.g. Smidt & Hegelheimer 2004). The validity and reliability of think-aloud protocols depend heavily on how the listener is prompted by the researcher.

Tracking software

New technologies can provide further insights into the process of listening by tracking and analysing listener use of help functions while listening to a recorded academic lecture (e.g. Grgurović & Hegelheimer 2007) or listener use of pauses, rewinds and fast forwards while working on an MP3 player (e.g. Roussel 2011). Even greater insights into the motivation for listener behaviour can be gained, however, by complementing these methodologies with a stimulated recall as soon as possible after the listening event.

Auditory perception processing

Aural perceptual processing investigates phenomena associated with the bottom-up dimension of listening, such as word segmentation skills. In this line of research, listeners hear a stimulus, a word or a short sentence (presented with no contextual cues), and are then asked to choose from among several options, the word or phrase they thought they heard or write down what they thought they heard (recall protocol). The choice options are often built on potential error patterns (see Field 2004). Of interest are the errors made and what they might reveal about the listener's word segmentation strategies (e.g. influence of a native language segmentation strategy) and/or listener expectations. This line of research tends to be very micro in nature, excluding the macro-context of a text or communication that listeners generally use in real-life listening to support their interpretation of words in context.

Triangulation of data

Although all of the research methodologies outlined above provide greater insights into the process of listening, their generalizability is often limited. In order to overcome this limitation, researchers investigating a construct as covert as listening should try to use multi-method assessment to collect convergent data. Reliability and validity can be enhanced when data from more than one source are triangulated to provide a more complete picture of the listening construct; for example, videotaped data with a stimulated recall on the video recording can be complemented by a questionnaire (e.g. Cutrone 2005). In her doctoral thesis, Mareschal (2007) collected and analysed data from a listening questionnaire, stimulated recalls on the questionnaire responses, listening notebooks, think-alouds, observation and a summative, open-response questionnaire to document how a self-regulatory approach to listening instruction influenced the listeners' self-regulatory ability, strategy use, metacognitive knowledge and listening success. Although these methodologies may provide greater insight into the process of listening, they are more labour-intensive with regard to collection and analysis of the data and less conducive to parsimonious reporting in order to demonstrate the trustworthiness and credibility of the research.

A sample study

Background

The study I have chosen to illustrate some of the methodological considerations discussed in this chapter is a recent long-term, mixed methods study (Vandergrift & Tafaghodtari 2010) on metacognitive instruction in listening, using a pedagogical sequence grounded in metacognitive theory. My interest in conducting this study emerged from a number of observations in the research literature. First, the results of long-term listening strategy instruction appear inconclusive and instruction in individual strategies does not appear to lead to overall listening improvement (Field 2001). Second, a number of recent studies suggest that skilled listeners appear to orchestrate cognitive and metacognitive strategies in an interconnected fashion (Goh 2002; Graham & Macaro 2008; Vandergrift 2003). Third, the reading research literature is in general agreement that instruction in a repertoire of strategies is more effective than individual strategy instruction for teaching comprehension skills (Grabe 2009). Fourth, recent studies on listener metacognitive awareness suggest that systematically guiding language learners through the process of listening as part of regular listening practice (metacognitive instruction) can lead learners to practise the metacognitive processes involved in listening (see Vandergrift 2004). Finally, although the short-term effects of this process approach on student motivation and the development of metacognitive knowledge about listening have been demonstrated, the enduring effects of this approach on listening achievement still needed to be empirically demonstrated (Berne 2004; Vandergrift 2004).

Methodological considerations

The nature of this investigation led me, first of all, to design a carefully controlled quasi-experimental study to test the following hypotheses: (1) the experimental group receiving metacognitive instruction will outperform the control group; and (2) the less-skilled listeners in the experimental group would make greater gains in listening achievement than their more-skilled counterparts. This constituted the product focus of the study. Secondly, in order to track the hypothesized growth in metacognitive knowledge about listening throughout the study, and to gain greater insight into participant awareness of the process of listening, both groups completed a valid and reliable listening questionnaire (see Vandergrift et al. 2006, for information on the development and validation of this instrument). Finally, in an effort to gain an even deeper understanding of the development of listening processes, six participants from the experimental group were randomly selected to participate in a stimulated recall to explore any differences in their questionnaire responses at the mid- and end-points of the study. These last two methodologies constituted the process focus of the study.

Participants were university students from six intact French as a second language classes, randomly assigned by class to either a control or experimental group. Participants were identified as less- or more-skilled listeners on the basis of their score on a listening test (Cronbach's alpha = 0.90) also used as a post-test to measure growth in listening ability. Two instructors participated – one taught four different classes of low-intermediate learners and the other taught two different classes of high-beginners. To control for potentially confounding teaching variables, the same teacher taught both the control and the experimental group, and both groups listened to the same texts. All teaching sessions were observed by a research assistant to verify that the instructor respected the designated listening pedagogy for that group.

All participants completed the listening questionnaire at the beginning, mid- and end-points of the study, immediately after a listening activity. We hypothesized that the less-skilled listeners in the experimental group would demonstrate greater growth in the five factors related to metacognitive knowledge (i.e. Problem-Solving, Planning and Evaluation, Directed Attention, Mental Translation and Person Knowledge) than their more-skilled counterparts, and both the more- and less-skilled participants in the control group. Participants selected for the stimulated recall sessions met with a research assistant twice: after the mid-point and at the end of the study. At the first session, the research assistant presented the participant with his/her beginning and mid-point questionnaire responses and then discussed major discrepancies (two point differences) in responses with the participant. During the second session, the participant was asked to discuss possible reasons for further discrepancies in responses based on the final completed questionnaire. All stimulated recall sessions were audio-recorded, transcribed verbatim, coded and analysed for emerging themes using the QSR-N*Vivo7.[1]

The study took place over a 13-week term. Each week, the classes listened to a different authentic-type text related to the topic of the teaching unit. The pedagogical sequence experienced by the experimental group and the metacognitive processes underlying each step in the sequence are described in detail in Vandergrift and Tafaghodtari (2010). Participants in the control group listened to the same texts the same number of times: however, they did not engage in prediction; they were not given an opportunity to discuss, predict or monitor their comprehension with a classmate; and, they did not engage in any whole-class reflection on strategy use.

Results

In order to confirm the first two hypotheses, a 2-factor ANCOVA (analysis of co-variance) was performed. Independent variables consisted of group (treatment and control) and the level of listening ability (less- and more-skilled) factorially combined. To control for any initial differences in listening ability, pre-listening test scores were used as covariate in the analysis.

Results revealed that, overall, the experimental (metacognitive instruction) group outperformed the control group. Furthermore, the less-skilled listeners who received metacognitive instruction outperformed the less-skilled listeners in the control group. In addition, the less-skilled listeners in the experimental group showed greater improvement than their more-skilled counterparts (although the effect size was small). Evidence for the third hypothesis was not as clear in terms of demonstrated growth in metacognitive knowledge about listening. Although listeners in the experimental group evidenced greater growth in all areas of metacognitive knowledge about listening, only growth in Problem-Solving and Mental Translation was statistically significant. The surprising finding about translation was later elucidated through the stimulated recall where it became evident that students were misinterpreting the concept of translation. The recall protocols also provided additional evidence for growth in the five areas of metacognitive knowledge. This study is a good example of research that is both product- and process-oriented, using different research methodologies to explore the development of metacognitive knowledge for listening.

Conclusion

This chapter has presented an overview of methodologies for investigating listening in applied linguistics. The field is ripe for research. Emerging technologies and increased access to multi-modal online resources through high-speed internet and self-access centres, in particular, open up rich possibilities for teaching and researching listening (see Godwin-Jones 2012; Robin 2007). When researchers follow reliable guidelines for designing and conducting careful research, then small and large-scale studies, using various methodologies, can contribute to a growing body of evidence-based knowledge, developed by an engaged community of listening researchers and research-practitioners (see Cross & Vandergrift 2014). For more detailed information on areas for future research, see Rost (2006) and Vandergrift (2007).

Acknowledgements

The author wishes to thank the editors and Jeremy Cross for their comments and suggestions for revision.

Note

1　N*Vivo is a qualitative research tool for classifying, sorting and arranging data in order to analyse them for patterns and to identify themes.

Resources for further reading

Field, J 2008, *Listening in the Language Classroom*, Cambridge University Press, Cambridge.

This book is strong on bottom-up approaches to listening and provides plenty of ideas for the classroom. The research reported in this book generally uses psycholinguistic laboratory methods which can be helpful for the insights they offer into listener decoding processes; however, they lack ecological validity in that laboratory methods often rob listeners of the contextual supports that usually go along with real-life listening.

Lynch, T 2009, *Teaching Second Language Listening*, Oxford University Press, Oxford.

Lynch presents a good, readable overview of issues in second language listening. The book covers many important topics and is grounded in much of the author's own listening experiences.

Rost, M 2011, *Teaching and Researching Listening*, 2nd edn, Longman, London.

This comprehensive volume provides an overview of teaching and researching listening. The third section introduces a number of research methodologies and frameworks, as well as concrete topics for action research.

Vandergrift, L & Goh, CM 2012, *Teaching and Learning Second Language Listening: Metacognition in Action*, Routledge, New York, NY.

This book provides a thorough examination of many dimensions of listening comprehension, from theory to application to implementation, including descriptions of concrete class activities. Woven throughout is the informing thread of metacognition.

References

American Council for the Teaching of Foreign Languages (ACTFL) 1999, 'ACTFL proficiency guidelines', viewed 22 November 2013, http://www.actfl.org/sites/default/files/pdfs/public/ACTFLProficiencyGuidelines2012_FINAL.pdf

Berne, JE 2004, 'Listening comprehension strategies: A review of the literature', *Foreign Language Annals*, vol. 37, no. 4, pp. 521–531.

Bloomfield, A, Wayland, SC, Rhoades, E, Blodgett, A, Linck, J & Ross, S 2011, *What Makes Listening Difficult? Factors Affecting Second Language Listening Comprehension*, University of Maryland, College Park, MA.

Brunfaut, T & Revesz, A 2013, 'Text characteristics of task input and difficulty in second language listening comprehension', *Studies in Second Language Acquisition*, vol. 35, no. 1, pp. 31–65.

Buck, G 2001, *Assessing Listening*, Cambridge University Press, Cambridge.

Council of Europe (COE) 2001, *A Common European Framework of Reference for Languages: Learning, Teaching and Assessment*, Cambridge University Press, Cambridge.

Cross, J 2011, 'Comprehending news videotexts: The influence of the visual content', *Language Learning & Technology*, vol. 15, no. 2, pp. 44–68.

Cross, J & Vandergrift, L 2014, 'Guidelines for designing and conducting L2 listening studies', *ELT Journal*, vol. 69, no. 1, pp. 86–89.

Cutrone, P 2005, 'A case study examining backchannels in conversations between Japanese-British dyads', *Multilingua*, vol. 24, no. 3, pp. 237–274.

Farrell, TC & Mallard, C 2006, 'The use of reception strategies by learners of French as a foreign language', *The Modern Language Journal*, vol. 90, no. 3, pp. 338–352.

Field, J 2001, 'Finding one's way in the fog: Listening strategies and second-language learners', *Modern English Teacher*, vol. 9, no. 1, pp. 29–34.

——— 2004, 'An insight into listeners' problems: Too much bottom-up or too much top-down?', *System*, vol. 32, no. 3, pp. 363–377.

——— 2008, *Listening in the Language Classroom*, Cambridge University Press, Cambridge.

Godwin-Jones, R 2012, 'Digital video revisited: Storytelling, conferencing, remixing', *Language Learning and Technology*, vol. 16, no. 1, pp. 1–9.

Goh, C 1997, 'Metacognitive awareness and second language listeners', *ELT Journal*, vol. 51, no. 4. pp. 361–369.

——— 2002, 'Exploring listening comprehension tactics and their interaction patterns', *System*, vol. 30, no. 2, pp. 185–206.

Goh, C & Taib, Y 2006, 'Metacognitive instruction in listening for young learners', *ELT Journal*, vol. 60, no. 3, pp. 222–232.

Grabe, W 2009, *Reading in a Second Language*, Cambridge University Press, Cambridge.

Graham, S 2006, 'Listening comprehension: The learners' perspective', *System*, vol. 34, no. 2, pp. 165–182.

Graham, S & Macaro, E 2008, 'Strategy instruction in listening for lower-intermediate learners of French', *Language Learning*, vol. 58, no. 4, pp. 747–783.

Graham, S, Santos, D & Vanderplank, R 2008, 'Listening comprehension and strategy use: A longitudinal exploration', *System*, vol. 36, no. 1, pp. 52–68.

Grgurović, M & Hegelheimer, V 2007, 'Help options and multimedia listening: Students' use of subtitles and the transcript', *Language Learning and Technology*, vol. 11, no. 1, pp. 45–66.

Guichon, N & McLornan, S 2008, 'The effects of multimodality on L2 learners: Implications for CALL resource design', *System*, vol. 36, no. 1, pp. 85–93.

Lynch, T 2009, *Teaching Second Language Listening*, Oxford University Press, Oxford.

Mareschal, C 2007, 'Student Perceptions of a Self-Regulatory Approach to Second Language Listening Comprehension Development', PhD thesis. University of Ottawa.

Prince, P 2012. 'Writing it down: Issues relating to the use of restitution tasks in listening comprehension', *TESOL Journal*, vol. 3, no. 1, pp. 65–86.

Robin, R 2007, 'Learner-based listening and technological authenticity', *Language Learning and Technology*, vol. 11, no. 1, pp. 109–115.

Rost, M 2006, 'Areas of research that influence L2 listening instruction', in E Uso-Juan & A Martinez-Flor (eds), *Current Trends in the Development and Teaching of the Four Language Skills*, Mouton de Gruyter, Berlin, pp. 47–74.

———— 2011, *Teaching and Researching Listening*, 2nd edn, Longman, London.

Roussel, S 2011, 'A computer assisted method to track listening strategies in second language learning', *ReCALL*, vol. 23, no. 2, pp. 98–116.

Smidt, E & Hegelheimer, V 2004, 'Effects of online academic lectures on ESL listening comprehension, incidental vocabulary acquisition and strategy use', *Computer Assisted Language Learning*, vol. 17, no. 5, pp. 517–556.

Vandergrift, L 1999, 'Facilitating second language listening comprehension: Acquiring successful strategies', *ELT Journal*, vol. 53, no. 3, pp. 168–176.

———— 2003, 'Orchestrating strategy use: Toward a model of the skilled second language listener', *Language Learning*, vol. 53, no. 3, pp. 463–496.

———— 2004, 'Learning to listen or listening to learn?', *Annual Review of Applied Linguistics*, vol. 24, pp. 3–25.

———— 2006, 'Second language listening: Listening ability or language proficiency?', *The Modern Language Journal*, vol. 90, no. 1, pp. 3–17.

———— 2007, 'Recent developments in second and foreign language listening comprehension research', *Language Teaching*, vol. 40, no. 3, pp. 191–210.

Vandergrift, L & Baker, S forthcoming, 2015, 'Learner variables in second language listening comprehension: An exploratory path analysis', *Language Learning*, vol. 65, no. 2.

Vandergrift, L & Goh, C 2012, *Teaching and Learning Second Language Listening: Metacognition in Action*, Routledge, New York, NY.

Vandergrift, L, Goh, C, Mareschal, C & Tafaghodatari, MH 2006, 'The metacognitive awareness listening questionnaire (MALQ): Development and validation'. *Language Learning*, vol. 56, no. 3, pp. 431–462.

Vandergrift, L & Tafaghodtari, MH 2010, 'Teaching students how to listen does make a difference: An empirical study', *Language Learning*, vol. 60, no. 2, pp. 470–497.

CHAPTER EIGHTEEN

Researching Reading

Marie Stevenson

This chapter gives an overview of key issues and research areas in second language reading research, and describes research techniques frequently used in this field. It also describes a sample study that uses verbal protocol analysis as a data collection technique, in order to illustrate some of the methodological issues involved in collecting and analysing observational reading data.

Key issues

In contrast to writing, where the writer produces a text that can be examined and analysed, reading is essentially an internal activity, the relatively intangible product of which is a representation of the text that has been read in the mind of the reader. Probably for this reason, much reading research has traditionally been psycholinguistic in nature, focusing on gaining insight into the reader's internal cognitive processes. However, in recent decades reading research has broadened its focus by becoming more socially, culturally and multi-culturally oriented (Kamil et al. 2000). As a reflection of this, the more socioculturally oriented term 'literacy' is currently increasingly used alongside 'reading'. It needs, however, to be pointed out that many conceptualizations of literacy exist, many of which, at the very least, include both reading and writing and often also a variety of aspects of oral, aural and digital communication.

Within the field of applied linguistics, second language (L2) reading research has leaned heavily on first language (L1) reading research by echoing – and even amplifying – its cognitive focus. And like L1 reading research, L2 reading research is shifting its focus – albeit to a lesser extent – to incorporate other perspectives, particularly sociocultural ones. Reflecting this, the term 'multilingual literacy research' is sometimes used instead of 'second language reading research' (e.g. Fitzgerald 2003), and there is a growing trend that broader conceptualizations of literacy are being incorporated into second language reading research. Also similar to L1 reading research, the bulk of L2 reading research focuses on English – in this case as a second language, which has led to charges of Anglocentrism (e.g. Bernhardt 2003).

Although first language and second language reading research share commonalities, there are issues specific to second language reading, largely relating to the fact that L2 readers have access to more than one language and culture. An issue that has received considerable attention is the relationship between first and second language reading, sometimes referred to as '*transfer*'. Transfer refers to the extent to which knowledge and skills that readers possess in one language transfer to reading in another language. Numerous studies have investigated transfer from L1 to L2 (e.g. Bernhardt & Kamil 1995; Carrell 1991; Gottardo & Mueller 2009; Jared et al. 2011; Lee & Schallert 1997; Nikolov & Csapo 2010; Sparks et al. 2012; Taillefer 1996; van Gelderen et al. 2004, 2007; Yamashita 2002). An approach that has commonly been used to examine this issue is the component-skills approach, in which reading is viewed as being a set of sub-skills such as decoding, vocabulary knowledge, syntactic processing and metacognition (Jeon & Yamashita, 2014). This approach enables the identification of key predictors of L2 reading.

Some component-skills studies have focused on the interdependence between L1 and L2 reading (see interdependence hypothesis, Cummins 1979a, b). There is considerable evidence for the existence of strong relationships between various components of L1 and L2 reading, pointing towards some kind of common underlying proficiency. Other studies have focused on factors that impede the transfer of knowledge and skills between L1 and L2. It has been claimed that in L2 reading, below a certain threshold of language proficiency, readers are unable to fully transfer the strategic skills, such as guessing meaning from context or making inferences, which they possess in L1 reading. This hypothesis is sometimes referred to as the *threshold hypothesis* and is related to the more general threshold hypotheses formulated by Cummins (1979a) in relation to the educational development of bilingual children. This hypothesis also has its roots in the work of Alderson (1984) in which he raised the question of whether L2 reading problems were predominantly language problems or reading problems. Some studies investigating the notion of a threshold in L2 reading have emphasized the role of lack of L2 *language knowledge* in inhibiting transfer of reading ability from L1 to L2, while others have emphasized the role of lack of L2 *linguistic processing skills,* such as speed of word recognition and sentence parsing.

Despite assumptions that are sometimes made concerning the existence of an L2 reading threshold, the empirical evidence is by no means conclusive. For example, a meta-analysis by Jeon and Yamashita (2014) of research that examines the correlations between L2 reading comprehension and a variety of component skills found that language specific variables such as grammar and vocabulary correlated more strongly with L2 reading comprehension than did more general variables such as metacognition. This would indicate that L2 language proficiency may play a greater role in L2 reading than does general reading ability, although the role of general factors cannot be ignored, as these also correlate significantly with L2 reading comprehension. Moreover, this meta-analysis found little evidence for a transfer threshold as L2 language proficiency did not significantly affect the relationship between L1 and L2 reading comprehension.

A complicating factor in drawing overall conclusions from the research about the existence of a threshold is that studies differ in the methods they have used to investigate this issue and in the characteristics of participants. Factors such as proficiency level, age and characteristics of the readers' first language are likely to strongly influence the degree of transfer from L1 to L2.

Indeed, a second issue in L2 reading research is how the processing of words, sentences and texts in the second language is influenced by characteristics of the reader's first language, such as orthography, phonology and morphology. For instance, a number of studies have found that word identification processes in the second language are influenced by the characteristics of L1 writing systems, such as whether they are alphabetic or non-alphabetic (Nassaji 2014). Results of studies support the notion that word identification in an alphabetic L2, such as English, is easier for readers with an alphabetic L1 than for readers with a non-alphabetic L1, such as Chinese or Arabic (see Wang & Koda 2007). Investigating Chinese and Korean learners of Japanese, Horiba (2012) found that the development of second language word knowledge and its relationship to text comprehension was influenced by L1-related factors such as syntax. As Korean and Japanese are syntactically more similar than Chinese and Japanese, Korean learners appeared to find it easier to use syntactic knowledge to process Japanese sentences. At text level, the extent to which L1 and L2 share similar text structure properties (i.e. rhetorical distance) has been shown to influence textual processing, with greater similarities facilitating the processing of key ideas and semantic relations (Koda 2005).

A third issue that has emerged concerns the effects of bilingualism on reading and on the acquisition of literacy in the classroom. Psycholinguistic research has investigated how knowing two languages affects the electrical activity in the brain during reading (e.g. Perfetti et al. 2007). Other research has focused on the development of bilingual children's reading ability (e.g. Bialystok et al. 2005, 2007; Da Fontoura & Siegel 1995). One of the questions relating to this development is whether knowing two languages has a positive or a negative influence on the development of reading ability in either of the bilingual's languages.

Studies that compare monolingual and bilingual readers in terms of language knowledge and/or reading proficiency have typically found that monolinguals perform better than bilinguals (e.g. Silverman et al. 2013). For example, Silverman et al. (2013) found that monolinguals scored higher on both vocabulary and reading comprehension than bilinguals. However, some results from studies such as this may reflect that participants are not balanced bilinguals and/or are from disadvantaged minority contexts. There is also the issue of how bilingualism is defined: participants that one study may refer to as second language learners, another study may refer to as bilinguals. A case in point is the Silverman study, which makes a conscious choice to use the terms 'language learner' and 'bilingual' interchangeably.

Research that compares monolinguals and bilinguals in terms of metacognitive ability, rather than knowledge or processing speed, has tended to produce outcomes that are more favourable for bilingual readers. Studies have found that young bilinguals are more metalinguistically aware than monolingual children in areas that underpin reading development, although the evidence for this advantage has not been conclusive. In light of the mixed outcomes of studies, it has been suggested that it may be biliteracy, that is, the ability to read (and write) in two languages rather than bilingualism per se that is crucial in determining the course of the development of reading ability (Schwartz, Leikin & Share 2005). Schwarz et al. found that biliterate bilingual children outperformed both monoliterate bilingual children and monolingual children in terms of reading fluency and phonological awareness, but that there was little difference in terms of linguistic measures.

Reflecting the shift away from a psycholinguistic conceptualization of second language reading towards a sociocultural conceptualization, an issue that has come to the foreground in recent years is the relationship between literacy, literacy practices and identity. Literacy is increasingly viewed as being socially constructed, and as being understood in terms of practices not only engaged in by individuals but also embedded within the context of practices within the home, the school, the community and society as a whole (Norton 2010). These practices are instrumental in shaping learner identity. Research has demonstrated that if learners have a sense of ownership of meaning-making and are in a position of empowerment, they are able to engage in literacy practices that are meaningful and fruitful for their literacy development. Likewise, if learners do not have a sense of ownership or are disempowered, the literacy practices they engage in may not be very beneficial to the development of their literacy, and they may suffer (further) educational disadvantage. Research in this area has largely been carried out in second language contexts with learners from migrant or indigenous minority groups or foreign language learners in disadvantaged contexts (e.g. Medina 2010; Moore & McDonald 2013; Norton 2010; Owodally 2011).

Research areas

Figure 18.1 divides the field of second language reading research into seven areas: lexical, fluency, discoursal, strategic, affective, intermodal and sociocultural. For each area, one sample study is listed. The sample studies have been selected on the basis of recency and also for representativeness of the kind of research topics common in a particular area. The studies chosen also reflect some of the diversity in research methods in L2 reading research, ranging from qualitative research (e.g. case studies) to quantitative research (e.g. survey and experimental studies). It should be noted that many of the studies described below reflect the aforementioned cognitive orientation of much L2 reading research. It should also be noted that within most of the areas, studies can be found that have an instructional focus, as they examine the effectiveness of a particular form of reading instruction or evaluating the effectiveness of a program incorporating a particular form of instruction. Testing and assessment of reading has not been included as an area, as it is seen as falling within the field of language testing.

Research area	Examples	Sample study
Lexical	e.g. vocabulary; grammar	1. A quantitative study on the relationship between percentage of words known in a text and reading comprehension. (Schmitt, Jiang & Grabe 2011).
Fluency	e.g. reading speed; lexical access; syntactic parsing	2. A review of research on fluency in reading (Grabe 2010).
Discoursal	e.g. text structure; rhetorical features; background knowledge	3. A quantitative study on effects of text structure on L2 text recall (Chu, Swaffar & Charney 2002).
Strategic	e.g. knowledge of and use of reading strategies	4. A verbal protocol study of using L1 in L2 reading (Upton & Lee-Thompson 2001).
Affective	e.g. motivation; attitudes	5. A survey study on the effects of extensive reading on FL reading attitudes (Yamashita 2013).
Intermodal	e.g. relationship between reading & writing, listening or speaking	6. A verbal protocol study on hypermedia reading strategies (Akyel & Ercetin 2009).
Sociocultural	e.g. home literacy environment; educational context	7. A case study on literacy practices of two Puerto Rican families in the US (Compton-Lilly 2007).

FIGURE 18.1 *Research areas in L2 reading research*

Lexical

Research in this area focuses on various aspects of the relationship between vocabulary and reading comprehension. Some research has found that vocabulary knowledge is the language knowledge component that is most strongly related to reading comprehension (Koda 2005). Studies have focused on the role of reading in vocabulary development (e.g. Pulido 2007); on the effects of reading on incidental vocabulary acquisition (e.g. Brown, Waring & Donkaewbua 2008; Kweon & Kim 2008); and on the relationship between the words known in a text and reading comprehension (e.g. Schmitt, Jiang & Grabe 2011). A study by Schmitt, Jian and Grabe (2011) found no evidence that there is a threshold of knowledge of words in a text beyond which comprehension increases dramatically. Also, the study confirmed previous findings that readers need to know a very high percentage of words in a text as a pre-condition to being able comprehend the text.

Fluency

Fluency can be defined as 'the ability to read rapidly with ease and accuracy' (Grabe 2009, p. 291). Research in this area focuses on processing skills, such as reading speed, and speed of component measures, such as lexical access and syntactic parsing. Research in this area was pioneered by researchers such as Schmidt (1992) and Segalowitz (2000; Segalowitz & Segalotwitz, 1993). Literature reviews by Grabe (2010) and Nassaji (2014) indicate that studies by and large support the importance of fluency for second language reading. However, it should be noted that it is still unclear whether training to increase fluency can lead to improvements in text comprehension (see Fukkink, Hulstijn & Simis 2005).

Discoursal

Research in this area focuses on discoursal aspects of reading, such as text structure and background knowledge. Some studies look at the effects of such aspects on comprehension. For example, Chu, Swaffer and Charney (2002) found that when English texts were structured according to Chinese rhetorical conventions, L1 Chinese learners of L2 English had better recall than when texts were not structured in this way. Other studies look at online discourse processing, such as readers use of text structure information while actually reading texts (e.g. Chen & Donin 1997). Instructional studies look at the effects of discourse-oriented training on reading comprehension (e.g. Jiang 2012).

Strategic

Research in this area focuses on readers' knowledge and use of reading strategies. Reading strategies are activities and behaviours that readers engage in to assist them in comprehending a text, such as predicting text content or guessing meaning from context. Strategies are thought to be related to metacognition, which is readers' ability to reflect on and control their reading processes. Some studies have examined the effects of reading strategy instruction on reading comprehension. For example, Kern (1989) found that strategy training led to strong gains in reading comprehension. Other studies have focused on the role that metacognitive knowledge plays in reading comprehension. For example, Schoonen, Hulstijn and Bossers (1998) administered a questionnaire to Dutch high school readers on their knowledge of reading goals, text structure and reading strategies. They found that for children in higher grades, metacognitive knowledge played a greater role in both L1 (Dutch) and L2 (English) reading comprehension than at lower grades. Still other studies focus on the actual strategies that readers use, through online measurement of what readers do when they read in L1 and/or L2. For example, Upton and Lee-Thompson (2001) examined use of L1 when reading L2 texts for L1 Chinese and Japanese readers of L2 English. They found that L2 readers used L1 for a variety of strategic purposes, including predicting content and structure and monitoring their own reading behaviour.

Affective

Research in this area focuses on affective aspects of reading, such as motivation and attitudes. Until fairly recently, little L2 reading research had been carried out in this area (Mori 2002), and consequently the overall direction of the research is still taking shape. Topics that have recently been the subject of study are: the components of L2 reading motivation (Mori 2002); the relationship between motivation and reading comprehension (Kondo-Brown 2006); students' motivations for reading extensively (Takase 2007); the relationship between L1 and L2 reading attitudes (Yamashita 2004, 2007); and effects of extensive reading on reading attitudes (Yamashita 2013). For example, in a study of Japanese university students reading in English, Yamashita (2013) found that extensive reading had a positive effect on different aspects of FL reading attitudes. It should also be pointed out that extensive reading itself is a growing area of L2 reading research. See a recent meta-analysis by Nakanishi (2014).

Intermodal

Research in this area focuses on reading in relation to other traditional modalities (i.e. writing, listening and speaking), as well as in relation to digital modalities (e.g. hypertext, visual images). For traditional modalities, research has largely focused on reading-writing connections in academic writing and within this, on both reading to help writing and writing to help reading. Two publications that offer a good introduction to both theory and research on reading-writing relations are Hirvela and Belcher (2001) and Hirvela (2004).

For digital modalities, a few studies have been carried out about online reading for ESL readers (e.g. Esther & Noelia 2009; Tseng 2007). There is also a small but growing body of research on reading with hypertexts (e.g. Abdi 2013; Akyel & Ercetin 2009; Kasper 2003). For example, Akyel and Ercetin (2009) found that certain reading strategies common to print reading such as guessing meaning from context were not used in hypermedia reading and that strategies specific to utilizing annotations and navigating through the text were used. As yet, little work appears to have been done on visual literacy in a second language. However, a qualitative study by Petrie (2003) found that ESL teachers viewed graphics and images as being quite separate from texts rather than viewing them as visual language.

Sociocultural

Research in this area focuses on sociocultural aspects of reading, such as home, classroom and community literacy practices. This research, which is largely qualitative, has often been carried out from a social justice or educational policy perspective. It has sought to identify practices in the social, educational or home environment that may compromise children or adults in minority settings in acquiring literacy but has also sought to identify practices that these individuals engage in and resources they possess that are empowering and that can lead to positive gains in their literacy. For example, Compton-Lilly (2007) uses the notion of 'capital', taken from the sociologist, Bordieu, to examine the economic, social and cultural aspects of reading in the families of two elementary school children of Puerto-Rican background in the United States. She found that although the families did not possess much economic reading capital (e.g. computers, books), they were relatively rich in social capital (e.g. networks of relationships with family members, community and teachers) and that educators need to identify and utilize the unique funds of knowledge that children from various cultural backgrounds bring to classrooms.

There has been a call for more L2 reading research to incorporate a sociocultural perspective. Luke (2003) puts forward a multilingual literacy research agenda to examine issues such as how people use texts, discourses and literacies in homes, communities and schools and how the literacy resources that people have are recognized and incorporated into school-based literacy instruction. Fitzgerald (2003) makes a plea for a sociocognitive approach to L2 reading research in which social-cultural perspectives are combined with cognitive perspectives. As time goes by, it is likely that an increasing number of studies will examine both cognitive and sociocultural aspects of reading.

Research techniques

This section gives a brief description of some of the most commonly used techniques in reading research, which is organized around the distinction between process and product-oriented techniques. Process-oriented techniques provide information about the reading process, that is, about what readers do when they read. In contrast, product-oriented techniques provide information on the product of reading, that is, on comprehension or its components. The description of techniques does not include interviews, surveys, diaries and logbooks, which are used in reading research as well as in many other fields of applied linguistics research, as these are already discussed in other chapters of this book (see e.g. Vandergrift; Wagner).

Process-oriented techniques

Process-oriented techniques are used to infer readers' internal cognitive processes. Techniques may infer processes from observation (e.g. verbal protocols); from measurement of the time taken to respond to stimuli (e.g. speed measures); or from measurement of physiological responses, such as eye movements (i.e. eye-tracking) or the electrical activity of the brain (i.e. event-related potentials (ERPs)). Reading research has a strong tradition of using process measures in controlled, experimental settings, but there have also been abundant small-scale qualitative studies carried out, particularly using observational process measures. Below, three process-oriented techniques are described: verbal protocols, eye-tracking and speed measures.

Verbal protocols

Verbal protocols, also known as think-aloud protocols, are an observational technique that involve readers verbalizing thoughts about the text they are reading. Protocols may be directed towards gaining insight into a specific aspect of reading, such as deriving meaning from context, or they may be used to gain an overall picture of the strategies readers use in building a global representation of a text.

Verbal protocols can be collected either concurrently (i.e. while reading the text) or retrospectively (i.e. after reading the text). In concurrent collection, the thoughts that are verbalized are supposed to reflect the current content of short-term memory (Ericsson & Simon 1993). Although widely used, concurrent protocols have also been widely criticized for being disruptive to natural reading processes and for providing only a fragmentary representation of what actually goes on in a reader's mind when reading. While retrospective protocols are less potentially disruptive to reading processes, questions arise concerning the validity of the information obtained. Readers may not have accurate recall, and they are also more likely to provide explanations or interpretations rather than reporting what they actually did. Some researchers have sought a compromise by placing marks at various points in a text, with readers verbalizing their thoughts every time they reach a mark. For a study on the issue of disruptiveness in verbal protocols, the reader is referred to a study by Leow and Morgan-Short (2004).

Eye-tracking

Eye-tracking is a technique in which the reader wears a device that enables the measurement of eye movements made while reading. When reading, eyes make short, rapid, back or forth movements known as saccades and short stops, known as fixations. Fixation time is taken to provide an indication of the time taken to process the point in the text to which the reader is attending the most (Rayner 1998). However, an important methodological issue is that there is not necessarily a one-to-one relationship between processing time and fixation time. For example, readers sometimes make multiple fixations on the same word; words may also be processed when they are not directly fixated, such as words above or below the fixated word; and processing may also occur during saccades (Irwin 1996). For a detailed consideration of methodological issues involved in eye-tracking research, see Rayner (1998). The bulk of eye-tracking research has examined first language reading, and to date, only a handful of studies have examined second language reading (see Frenck-Mestre 2005). The use of eye-tracking in second language reading research is a field that is wide open for exploration in the coming years.

Speed measures

The speed with which processing is carried out is generally considered to be a reflection of readers' fluency. Common speed measures are the time taken to read the whole text (text level); speed of syntactic processing (sentence level); speed of word recognition (word level); and speed of letter recognition (letter level). In many cases, measures include sentences or words that are in some way anomalous (e.g. nonsense sentences), and the speed of processing these elements may be compared to the speed of processing elements that do not contain anomalies. Reaction times for such measures are generally measured using computers.

A methodological issue is whether the measures used are context-specific or non-context specific (Stevenson 2005). Context-specific measurements are made within a textual context. For example, speed of syntactic processing may be measured by registering the speed at which readers read each sentence of a text. In contrast, non-context specific measurements are made in an isolated context. For example, fluency of sentence-level processing may be measured by registering the speed reading of sentences presented as isolated items that together do not form a text. Non-context specific methods, which select items from a general sample of words that are not taken from a specific text, are able to provide a measure of general processing skills, whereas measures that use items taken from a specific text can only make more limited claims concerning processing as it relates to specific texts. However, on the other side of the coin, using non-context specific measures leaves the researcher open to the criticism that little can be said about real online textual processing.

Product-oriented techniques

Product-oriented techniques measure comprehension of reading or of a component of reading. Below, these techniques are divided into comprehension measures, which seek to gain insight into the quality of the readers' mental representation of a text, and knowledge component measures, which seek to gain insight into the level of knowledge that a reader possesses concerning a component that is relevant to reading, such as vocabulary or grammatical knowledge.

Comprehension measures

Broadly speaking, comprehension measures can be sub-categorized into measures that require short responses and measures that require extended responses, referred to by Bachman and Palmer (2010) as extended production responses.

The classic short response measure is the multiple-choice comprehension test, which though much maligned, remains popular due to the ease with which it can be administered and scored. A major criticism that has been levelled against this testing format is that it measures test-taking skills more than it measures reading ability, as readers who have developed good guessing strategies may score well regardless of whether they have a good understanding of the text.

Another common short response measure is the cloze test, in which the reader is required to restore words in the text that have been deleted. The underlying rationale is that the semantic and syntactic constraints to which the reader must be sensitive in order to provide correct responses are also constraints that guide textual processing (Koda 2005). Alderson (2000) points out that there is a difference between a 'cloze test' and 'gap-filling' test, although the terms are often used interchangeably. According to Alderson, cloze tests are tests in which every n-th word is deleted randomly, whereas in gap-filling tests the test constructor decides to delete certain words on the basis of criteria appropriate to the testing objective, thus giving the test constructor more control over what is measured. Both kinds of tests have been criticized for being more sensitive to linguistic constraints than to underlying meaning and for only being capable of measuring local rather than global comprehension. Many other kinds of short response formats exist, including short answer questions, yes/no questions, choosing from a heading bank for identified paragraphs and flow chart/diagram completion.

Extended response measures, such as recall and summarization, are said to tap more directly into the reader's comprehension of the text, without the intervention of test questions. In free recall, the reader is asked to recall everything they can about the text. In cued recall, questions are used to guide the reader to recall particular aspects of the text. In summarization, the reader is asked to summarize the main ideas, either with or without the possibility of consulting the text. The scoring of extended response measures is more time-consuming and less 'objective' than the scoring of short response measures, as the resulting recall or summarization protocols require intensive coding.

Knowledge component measures

Knowledge component measures are used to disentangle the knowledge components that contribute to reading ability. These measures typically focus on lower order linguistic aspects, such as vocabulary, grammar and spelling. However, they may also measure higher order conceptual aspects, such as topic knowledge, or metacognitive aspects, such as knowledge of reading strategies. Studies that use the component skills approach explained earlier in the chapter may incorporate a battery of knowledge measures as well as speed of processing measures and measures of global reading comprehension. Correlational statistical techniques, such as regression analysis, are frequently used to determine the strength of the relationship between the specific variables and reading comprehension measures.

A sample study

This section highlights methodological features of a verbal protocol study carried out by myself to compare first and second language reading strategies (see Stevenson, Schoonen & de Glopper 2007). I have chosen a verbal protocol study, as details of the use of this technique are notoriously scantily reported (Afflerbach 2000). Through this discussion, I hope to shed light on some of the methodological issues surrounding this widely used yet controversial technique. A brief description of the study will be given, followed by a discussion of methodological issues under the headings: texts; elicitation of verbalizations; modelling and instruction; and coding.

Description of the study

The study examined the extent to which readers' strategy use transfers from L1 to L2 by comparing the reading strategies of twenty-two Dutch junior high school students in L1 (Dutch) and a foreign language (English). I collected concurrent verbal protocols by recording each student thinking aloud while they read two texts in Dutch and two in English. In order to obtain more detailed information about strategy use than previous studies had been able to do, I classified the students' reading strategies in terms of three separate dimensions. The three dimensions in the coding scheme were: Orientation of Processing (i.e. whether strategies are directed towards content or language); Type of Processing (i.e. whether strategies involve regulating the reading process, processing the meaning of the text or rereading the text); and linguistic Domain of Processing (i.e. whether strategies are directed towards texts elements at below-clause level, clause level or above-clause level). The results showed that the readers focused more on the language in the text in FL and that they did this by, in particular, regulating their reading process and using language strategies at clause level and above (i.e. by translating and paraphrasing chunks of text they did not understand). Thus, in contradiction to claims made by the threshold hypothesis, the readers appeared to be able to make good use of reading strategies in FL reading. Moreover, the readers did not appear to be inhibited in FL in their use of strategies that focused on global text content.

Texts

If more than one text is to be read in a think-aloud study, for many research purposes it is desirable to match the characteristics of the texts. In my study, I matched the four texts (two Dutch, two English) in terms of text type: they were all argumentative texts. Topics were chosen that were similar but not overlapping (e.g. 'Children should wear school uniforms' (Dutch) and 'Boys and girls should be in separate classes some of the time' (English)). I also matched the texts in terms of the number of arguments and sub-arguments. For example, the Dutch and English texts mentioned above both contained one main argument, one counter argument and one refutation presented in six paragraphs. I also checked that there were no large discrepancies in the level of difficulty of the two texts by examining the mean sentence length, mean word length and the type token ratio. Lastly, I gave the texts to several teachers and educationalists to ascertain whether they felt that the topics and levels of the texts were suitable for the target students.

Elicitation of verbalizations

An important issue in verbal protocol studies is the manner in which verbalizations are elicited. I conducted an informal pilot study to determine the best way of doing this. I gave the two Dutch texts to be used in the study to a few students of the same age and grade as the students who would participate in the study. For one of the texts, students did not receive any prompting and were free to verbalize spontaneously. For the other text, dots were placed in the text after every five sentences, and students were instructed to think aloud when they reached each dot. It became apparent that prompting influenced the kinds of verbalizations made. Prompted verbalizations frequently consisted of a summary of what had just been read, whereas when readers verbalized spontaneously, they tended to voice the actual strategies they were using to help them understand the text. Therefore, I opted for spontaneous verbalization, but as a compromise I decided that if readers fell silent for more than five sentences they would be prompted verbally by asking 'what are you thinking about?' However, after the data was collected, it turned out that I had to exclude these prompted verbalizations from the data, as, just as with the dots, they nearly always resulted in the readers summarizing part of the text.

Modelling and instruction

It is necessary to provide modelling and instruction in thinking aloud. A pressing issue is weighing up the amount of instruction against any time constraints. In my study, there were considerable time constraints, given that the students could only absent themselves from normal classes for one 40-minute lesson at a time and that they needed to complete two reading tasks in this period. I decided to give each participant 15 minutes of instruction and practice immediately prior to reading the first text. I first modelled the technique myself, using a Dutch text similar to the texts in the study and then asked the participant to use the same text to practise thinking aloud. The same verbalizations were modelled for all participants, and the model provided examples of different kinds of reading strategies. The participants were instructed to read the texts aloud and to voice their thoughts consistently. They were told that they were free to voice their thoughts in Dutch or English. They were also told that the text did not have to be read in a linear fashion: they could reread or omit any part of the text.

Coding

Developing a workable coding scheme is a central issue in the analysis phase of any protocol study. Traditionally, the first step in doing this has been to make a word-for-word transcription of the protocol recordings. However, I was lucky to be able to skip this very time-consuming step by using a computer program called Observer 3.0 to code the protocols (Noldus Information Technology 1998). To develop my coding scheme – and thereafter code the data – I listened to the protocol recordings, stopped them at each point where a strategy ended, and typed codes into a format that I had set up in the computer program.

It is important to be able to demonstrate that the coding scheme that is developed is reliable, that is, that it can be used by different people in a consistent way. Thus, it is necessary to have all or part of the data coded by more than one coder and to use a statistical measure, such as Cohen's kappa, to calculate the inter-rater reliability. In my study, a research assistant and I independently encoded a quarter of the data. For a formula for determining how much of the data in a particular study needs to be coded by more than one coder, see Siegel and Castellan (1988).

Obtaining an acceptable level of reliability can be surprisingly difficult. I learnt from experience the importance of having a coding scheme that is not overly complicated. A balance needs to be struck between, on the one hand, obtaining sufficiently detailed information, and on the other, not making the categories in the coding scheme so finely grained that somebody else cannot distinguish between them. I also learnt that it was important for the coders to have an extended period of working and training together. The research assistant and I practised on protocols that would not be included in the reliability sample, adjusting categories in the coding scheme and discussing issues that arose as we went along. Discussing the coding scheme and practising coding turned out to be an invaluable step in developing a coding scheme that could be used reliably.

Resources for further reading

Grabe, W & Stoller, FL 2011, *Teaching and Researching Reading*, 2nd edn, Pearson Routledge, London.

In addition to an overview of L2 reading theory, this book provides an overview of cognitively oriented L2 reading research and a framework for researching reading in the classroom.

Koda, K 2005, *Insights into Second Language Reading; A Cross Linguistic Approach*, Cambridge University Press, Cambridge.

This book deals with the theoretical foundations of L2 reading and provides a detailed overview of components of reading, including relevant research.

Pressley, M & Afflerbach, P 1995, *Verbal Protocols of Reading*, Lawrence Erlbaum, Hillsdale, NJ.

This book provides a thorough overview of verbal protocol techniques, including the results of protocol studies and major methodological concerns.

Hulstijn, J, Schoonen, R & van Gelderen, A 2007, 'Unravelling the componential structure of second language skills', *TESOL Quarterly*, vol. 41, no. 1, pp. 186–192.

This article discusses some methodological features of three quantitative L2 research projects in which the component skills approach is used.

References

Abdi, R 2013, 'The effect of using hypertext materials on reading comprehension ability of EFL learners', *Procedia – Social and Behavioral Sciences*, vol. 83, no. 4, pp. 557–562.

Afflerbach, P 2000, 'Verbal reports and protocol analysis', in ML Kamil, PB Mosenthal, PD Pearson & R Barr (eds), *Handbook of Reading Research*, Volume III, Lawrence Erlbaum, Mahwah, NJ, pp. 163–179.

Akyel, A & Erçetin, G 2009, 'Hypermedia reading strategies employed by advanced learners of English', *System*, vol. 37, no. 1, pp. 136–152.

Alderson, JC 1984, 'Reading in a foreign language: A reading problem or a language problem?', In JC Alderson & AH Urquhart (eds), *Reading in a Foreign Language*, Longman, London.

—— 2000, *Assessing Reading*, Cambridge University Press, Cambridge.

Bachman, LF & Palmer, AS 2010, *Language Assessment in Practice*, Oxford University Press, Oxford.

Bernhardt, EB 2003, 'Challenges to reading research from a multilingual world', *Reading Research Quarterly*, vol. 38, no. 1, pp. 112–117.

Bernhardt, EB & Kamil, ML 1995, 'Interpreting relationships between L1 and L2 reading: Consolidating the linguistic threshold and the linguistic interdependence hypotheses', *Applied Linguistics*, vol. 16, no. 1, pp. 15–34.

Bialystok, E 2007, 'Acquisition of literacy in bilingual children: A framework for research', *Language Learning*, vol. 57, no. 1, pp. 45–77.

Bialystok, E, McBride-Chang, C & Luk, G 2005, 'Bilingualism, language proficiency, and learning to read in two writing systems', *Journal of Educational Psychology*, vol. 97, no. 4, pp. 580–590.

Brown, R, Waring, R & Donkaewbua, S 2008, 'Incidental vocabulary acquisition from reading, reading-while-listening, and listening to stories', *Reading in a Foreign Language*, vol. 20, no. 2, pp. 136–163.

Carrell, P 1991, 'Second language reading: Reading ability or language proficiency', *Applied Linguistics*, vol. 12, no. 2, pp. 159–179.

Chen, Q & Donin, J 1997, 'Discourse processing of first and second language biology texts: Effects of language proficiency and domain-specific knowledge', *The Modern Language Journal*, vol. 81, no. 2, pp. 209–226.

Chu, HJ, Swaffar, J & Charney, DH 2002, 'Cultural representations of rhetorical conventions: The effects on reading recall', *TESOL Quarterly*, vol. 36, no. 4, pp. 511–541.

Compton-Lilly, C 2007, 'The complexities of reading capital in two Puerto-Rican families', *Reading Research Quarterly*, vol. 42, no. 1, pp. 72–98.

Cummins, J 1979a, 'Linguistic interdependence and the educational development of bilingual children', *Review of Educational Research*, vol. 49, no. 2, pp. 222–251.

———— 1979b, 'Cognitive/academic language proficiency, linguistic interdependence, the optimum age question and some other matters', *Working Papers on Bilingualism*, vol. 19, pp. 197–205.

De Fontoura, H & Siegel, L 1995, 'Reading, syntactic and working memory skills of bilingual Portuguese-English Canadian children', *Reading and Writing: An Interdisciplinary Journal*, vol. 7, pp. 139–153.

Ericsson, KA & Simon, HA 1993, *Protocol Analysis: Verbal Reports as Data*, MIT press, Cambridge, MA.

Esther, UJ & Noelia, RM 2009, 'Reading printed versus online texts: A study of EFL Learners' strategic reading behavior', *International Journal of English Studies*, vol. 9, no. 2, pp. 59–79.

Fitzgerald, J 2003, 'Multilingual reading theory', *Reading Research Quarterly*, vol. 38, no. 1, pp. 118–122.

Frenck-Mestre, C 2005, 'Eye-tracking recording as a tool for studying syntactic processing in a second language: A review of methodologies and experimental findings', *Second Language Research*, vol. 21, no. 2, pp. 175–198.

Fukkink, RG, Hulstijn, J & Simis, A 2005, 'Does training in second language word recognition skills affect reading comprehension? An experimental study', *Modern Language Journal*, vol. 89, no. 1, pp. 54–75.

Gottardo, A & Mueller, J 2009, 'Are first- and second-language factors related in predicting second-language reading comprehension? A study of Spanish-speaking children acquiring English as a second language from first to second grade', *Journal of Educational Psychology*, vol. 101, no. 2, pp. 330–344.

Grabe, W 2009, *Reading in a Second Language: Moving from Theory to Practice*, Cambridge University Press, New York, NY.

———— 2010, 'Fluency in reading – Thirty-five years later', *Reading in a Foreign Language*, vol. 22, no. 1, pp. 71–83.

Hirvela, A 2004, *Connecting Reading and Writing in Second Language Writing Instruction*, University of Michigan Press, Ann Arbor, MI.

Hirvela, A & Belcher, D (eds) 2001, *Linking Literacies: Perspectives on L2 Reading-Writing Connections*, University of Michigan Press, Ann Arbor, MI.

Horiba, Y 2012, 'Word knowledge and its relation to text comprehension: A comparative study of Chinese- and Korean-speaking L2 learners and L1 speakers of Japanese', *The Modern Language Journal*, vol. 96, no. 1, pp. 108–121.

Irwin, DE 1996, 'Integrating information across saccadic eye movements', *Current Directions in Psychological Science*, vol. 5, no. 3, pp. 94–100.

Jared, D, Cormier, P, Levy, BA & Wade-Woolley, L 2011, 'Early predictors of biliteracy development in children in French immersion: A 4-year longitudinal study', *Journal of Educational Psychology*, vol. 103, no. 1, pp. 119–139.

Jeon, EU & Yamashita, J 2014, 'L2 reading comprehension and its correlates: A meta-analysis', *Language Learning*, vol. 64, no. 1, pp. 160–212.

Jiang, X 2012, 'Effects of discourse structure graphic organizers on EFL reading comprehension', *Reading in a Foreign Language*, vol. 24, no. 1, pp. 84–105.

Kamil, ML, Mosenthal, PB, Pearson, PD & Barr, R 2000, 'Preface', in ML Kamil, PB Mosenthal, PD Pearson & R Barr (eds), *Handbook of Reading Research: Volume III*. Lawrence Erlbaum Associates Publishers, Mahwah, NJ.

Kasper, FL 2003, 'Interactive hypertext and the development of ESL students' reading skills', *The Reading Matrix*, vol. 3, no. 3, viewed 22 March 2014, http://www.readingmatrix.com/articles/kasper/index2.html

Kern, RG 1989, 'Second language reading strategy instruction: Its effects on comprehension and word inference ability', *The Modern Language Journal*, vol. 73, no. 2, pp. 135–149.

Koda, K 2005, *Insights into Second Language Reading: A Cross-Linguistic Approach*. Cambridge University Press, Cambridge.

Kondo-Brown, K 2006, 'Affective variables and Japanese L2 reading ability', *Reading in a Foreign Language*, vol. 18, no. 1, pp. 55–71.

Kweon, S & Kim, H 2008, 'Beyond raw frequency: Incidental vocabulary acquisition in extensive reading', *Reading in a Foreign Language*, vol. 20, no. 2, pp. 191–215.

Lee, JW & Schallert, DL 1997, 'The relative contribution of L2 language proficiency and L1 reading ability to L2 reading performance: A test of the threshold hypothesis in an EFL context', *TESOL Quarterly*, vol. 31, no. 4, pp. 713–739.

Leow, RP & Morgan-Short, K 2004, 'To think aloud or not to think aloud: The issue of reactivity in SLA research methodology', *Studies in Second Language Acquisition*, vol. 26, no. 1, pp. 35–57.

Luke, A 2003, 'Literacy and the other: A sociological approach to literacy research and policy in multilingual societies', *Reading Research Quarterly*, vol. 38, no. 1, pp. 132–141.

Medina, C 2010, '"Reading across communities" in biliteracy practices: Examining translocal discourses and cultural flows in literature discussions', *Reading Research Quarterly*, vol. 45, no. 1, pp. 40–60.

Moore, D & MacDonald, M 2013, 'Language and literacy development in a Canadian native community: Halq'eme´ylem revitalization in a Stó:lō head start program in British Columbia', *The Modern Language Journal*, vol. 97, no. 3, pp. 702–719.

Mori, S 2002, 'Redefining motivation to read in a foreign language', *Reading in a Foreign Language*, vol. 14, no. 2, pp. 91–110.

Nakanishi, T 2014, 'A meta-analysis of extensive reading research', *TESOL Quarterly*, vol. 49, no. 1, pp. 6–37.

Nassaji, H 2014, 'The role and importance of lower-level processes in second language reading', *Language Teaching*, vol. 47, no. 1, pp. 1–37.

Nikolov, M & Csapó, B 2010, 'The relationship between reading skills in early English as a foreign language and Hungarian as a first language', *International Journal of Bilingualism*, vol. 14, no. 3, pp. 315–329.

Noldus Information Technology b.v. 1998, Observer (Version 3.0) [Computer software]. Noldus Information Technology b.v., Wageningen.

Norton, B. 2010, 'Identity, literacy, and English-language teaching', *TESL Canada Journal/Revue TESL du Canada*, vol. 28, no. 1, pp. 1–13.

Owodally, AMA 2011, 'Multilingual language and literacy practices and social identities in Sunni Madrassahs in Mauritius: A case study', *Reading Research Quarterly*, vol. 46, no. 2, pp. 134–155.

Perfetti, CA, Liu, Y, Fiez, J, Nelson, J, Bolger, DJ & Tan, L 2007, 'Reading in two writing systems: Accommodation and assimilation of the brain's reading network', *Bilingualism: Language and Cognition*, vol. 10, no. 2, pp. 131–146.

Petrie, GM 2003, ESL teachers' views on visual language: A grounded theory', *The Reading Matrix*, vol. 3, no. 3, pp. 137–168.

Pulido, D 2007, 'The relationship between text comprehension and second language incidental vocabulary acquisition: A matter of topic familiarity?', *Language Learning*, 57, no. 1, pp. 155–199.

Rayner, K 1998, 'Eye movements in reading and information processing: 20 years of research', *Psychological Bulletin*, vol. 124, no. 3, pp. 372–422.

Schmidt, R 1992, 'Psychological mechanisms underlying second language fluency', *Studies in Second Language Acquisition*, vol. 14, no. 4, pp. 357–385.

Schmitt, N, Jiang, X & Grabe, W 2011, 'The percentage of words known in a text and reading comprehension', *The Modern Language Journal*, vol. 95, no. 1, pp. 26–43.

Schoonen, R, Hulstijn, J & Bossers, B 1998, 'Language-dependent and language-independent knowledge in native and foreign language reading comprehension: An empirical study among Dutch students in grades 6, 8 and 10', *Language Learning*, vol. 48, no. 1, pp. 71–106.

Schwartz, M, Leikin, M & Share, DL 2005, 'Biliterate bilingualism versus mono-literate bilingualism', *Written Language and Literacy*, vol. 8, no. 2, pp. 179–205.

Segalowitz, NS 2000, 'Automaticity and attentional skill in fluent performance', in H Riggenbach (ed.), *Perspectives on Fluency*, University of Michigan Press, Ann Arbor, MI, pp. 200–219.

Segalowitz, NS & Segalowitz, SJ 1993, 'Skilled performance, practice, and the speed-up from automatization effects: Evidence from second language word recognition', *Applied Psycholinguistics*, vol. 14, no. 3, pp. 369–385.

Siegel, S & Castellan, NJ 1988, *Nonparametric Statistics for the Behavioral Sciences*, 2nd edn, McGraw-Hill, New York, NY.

Silverman, RD, Proctor, CP, Harring, JR, Doyle, B, Mitchell, MA & Meyer, AG 2013, 'Vocabulary and comprehension: An exploratory study with English monolingual and Spanish–English bilingual students in grades 3–5', *Reading Research Quarterly*, vol. 49, no. 1, pp. 31–60.

Sparks, RL, Patton, J, Ganschow, L & Humbach, N 2012, 'Do L1 reading achievement and L1 print exposure contribute to the prediction of L2 proficiency?', *Language Learning*, vol. 62, no. 2, pp. 473–505.

Stevenson, M 2005, 'Reading and writing in a foreign language: A comparison of conceptual and linguistic processes in Dutch and English', PhD thesis, University of Amsterdam, Amsterdam.

Stevenson, M, Schoonen, R & de Glopper, K 2007, 'Inhibition or compensation? A multidimensional comparison of reading processes in Dutch and English', *Language Learning*, vol. 57, no. 1, pp. 115–154.

Taillefer, G 1996, 'L2 reading ability: Further insight into the short-circuit hypothesis', *Modern Language Journal*, vol. 80, no. 4, pp. 461–477.

Takase, A 2007, 'Japanese high school students' motivation for extensive L2 reading', *Reading in a Foreign Language*, vol. 19, no. 1, pp. 1–18.

Tseng, MC 2007, 'An investigation of EFL learners' online reading skills', *Journal of Nanya Institute of Technology*, vol. 27, pp. 111–127.

Upton, TA & Lee-Thompson, LC 2001, 'The role of the first language in second language reading', *Studies in Second Language Acquisition*, vol. 23, no. 4, pp. 469–495.

van Gelderen, A, Schoonen, R, de Glopper, K, Hulstijn, J, Simis, A, Snellings, P & Stevenson, M 2004, 'Linguistic knowledge, processing speed and metacognitive knowledge in first and second language reading comprehension: A componential analysis', *Journal of Educational Psychology*, vol. 96, no. 1, pp. 19–30.

van Gelderen, A, Schoonen, R, Stoel, RD, De Glopper, K & Hulstijn, J 2007, 'Development of adolescent reading comprehension in language 1 and language 2: A longitudinal analysis of constituent components', *Journal of Educational Psychology*, vol. 99, no. 3, pp. 477–491.

Wang, M & Koda, K 2007, 'Commonalities and differences in word identification skills among learners of English as a second language', *Language Learning*, vol. 57, no. 1, pp. 201–222.

Yamashita, J 2002, 'Reading strategies in L1 and L2: Comparison of four groups of readers with different reading ability in L1 and L2', *ITL: Review of Applied Linguistics*, vol. 135–136, pp. 1–35.

———— 2004, 'Reading attitudes in L1 and L2, and their influence on extensive reading', *Reading in a Foreign Language*, vol. 16, no. 1, pp. 1–19.

———— 2007, 'The relationship of reading attitudes between L1 and L2: An investigation of adult EFL learners in Japan', *TESOL Quarterly*, vol. 41, no. 1, pp. 81–105.

———— 2013, 'Effects of extensive reading on reading attitudes in a foreign language', *Reading in a Foreign Language*, vol. 25, no. 2, pp. 248–263.

CHAPTER NINETEEN

Researching Writing

Ken Hyland

Writing is fundamental to modern societies and is of overarching significance in all our lives: central to our personal experiences, life chances and social identities. Its complex, multifaceted nature, however, is difficult to pin down and as a result, many research approaches have emerged to help clarify both how writing works and the purposes it is employed to achieve. Research, in fact, has taken philosophical, historical, empirical and critical directions and encompassed a wide range of different interpretive and quantitative methods. I briefly summarize and evaluate some of these and illustrate one through a sample study.

Assumptions, writing and research

First of all, it is important to recognize that writing research does not simply involve fitting suitable methods to particular questions. Methods are inseparable from theories and how we understand writing itself. For some people, writing is a product, an artefact of activity which can be studied independently of users by counting features and inferring rules. For others, it is a kind of cognitive performance which can be modelled by analogy with computer processing through observation and writers' on-task verbal reports. A third group sees it as the ways we make our social worlds and explore how writing connects us with readers and institutions in particular contexts. Different methods tell us different things about writing, but they always start with our preconceptions. Simplifying a complex picture, it is possible to group research methods according to their principal focus and whether they are concerned with illuminating our understanding of texts, writers or readers.

Text-oriented research

This views writing as an outcome of activity as words on a page or screen and can be descriptive (revealing what occurs), analytical (interpreting why it occurs) or critical (questioning the social relations which underlie and are reproduced by what occurs). Texts can also be examined in a variety of ways, looking at particular features or their themes, cohesive elements or move structures. We can examine a text in isolation or as a sample from a single genre, time period or writer, and we can collect a number of texts together as a corpus and aggregate those features as representative of other texts.

Traditionally, research into texts followed views inherited from structuralism and implicit in the Transformational Grammar of Noam Chomsky. Texts were seen as *langue* or a demonstration of the writer's knowledge of forms and grammatical rules rather than attempts to communicate, and methods were the means of revealing principles of writing independent of any actual contexts or users. From this perspective, writing improvement is measured by counting increases in features seen as important to successful writing and calculating the 'syntactic complexity' of texts by counting the number of words or clauses per T-unit and the number of T-units per sentence. There is, however, little evidence to show that syntactic complexity or grammatical accuracy are either the principal features of writing development or the best measures of good writing. Essentially, viewing texts in this way ignores their role as communicative acts and how they function as a writer's response to a particular communicative setting. Because all texts include what writers suppose their readers will know and how they will use the text, no text can be fully explicit or universally 'appropriate'. Rather, they need to balance what needs to be said against what can be assumed.

Writer-oriented research

This emphasizes the actions of writers rather than the features of texts. Champions of this approach believe that writing constitutes a process, or at least a complex of activities, from which all writing emerges and that this is generalizable across contexts of writing. Interest here is on what good writers do when they write, principally so that these strategies can be taught to students. Early work assumed that writing is more of a problem-solving activity than an act of communication and drew on the tools and models of cognitive psychology and artificial intelligence to reveal how people engage in a writing task to create and revise personal meanings. More recent work has given greater emphasis to the actual performance of writing in a particular context, exploring what Nystrand (1987) calls the *situation of expression*, to investigate the personal and social histories of individual writers as they write in specific contexts.

The goal is to describe the influence of this context on the ways writers represent their purposes in the kind of writing that is produced. As Prior (1998, p. xi) observes:

> Actually writing happens in moments that are richly equipped with tools (material and semiotic) and populated with others (past, present, and future). When seen as situated activity, writing does not stand alone as the discrete act of a writer, but emerges as a confluence of many streams of activity: reading, talking, observing, acting, making, thinking, and feeling as well as transcribing words on paper.

By using detailed observations of acts of writing, participant interviews, analyses of surrounding practices, and other techniques, researchers seek to develop more complete accounts of local writing contexts.

A range of methods have been employed to explore and elaborate the com posing process, moving beyond text analysis to the qualitative methods of the human and social sciences. Case study research has been particularly productive, focusing on 'natural scenes' rather than on experimental environments and often seeking to describe writing from an *emic* perspective, privileging the views of insiders or those participating in a situation. These studies have thus made considerable use of 'think-aloud protocols', or writers' verbal reports while composing (e.g. Smagorinsky 1994), retrospective interviews (e.g. Nelson & Carson 1998) and task observation (e.g. Bosher 1998), sometimes involving keystroke recording during composing (e.g. Sullivan & Lindgren 2006). Often research is longitudinal, following students over an extended period (e.g. Hyland 1998) and uses multiple techniques which may include recall protocols and analyses of several drafts.

However, while these descriptions give significant attention to the experiences of writers and to their understandings of the local features of the context they deal with as they write, concentrating on the local setting fails to capture the culture and event within which the action is embedded and which their writing must invoke. Texts do not function communicatively at the time they are composed but when they are read, as they anticipate particular readers and the responses of those readers to what is written. Texts evoke a social milieu which intrudes upon the writer and activates specific responses to recurring tasks and as a result most current writing research takes a more reader-oriented view to explore the ways writers see their audience and engage in cultural contexts.

Reader-oriented research

This looks beyond individual writers and the surface structures of products to see texts as examples of *discourse* or language in use. Discourse approaches recognize that texts are always a response to a particular communicative setting and seek to reveal the purposes and functions which linguistic forms serve in texts. Here, texts are not isolated examples of competence but the concrete expressions of social purposes, intended for particular audiences. The writer is seen as having certain goals and intentions, certain relationships to his or her readers and certain information to convey, and the forms a text takes are resources used to accomplish these. Writing is therefore seen as mediated by the institutions and cultures in which it occurs and every text is embedded in wider social practices which carry assumptions about writer-reader relationships and how these should be structured. These factors draw the analyst into a wider paradigm which locates texts in a world of communicative purposes, institutional power and social action, identifying the ways that texts actually work as communication.

One way writers are able to construct an audience is by drawing on their own knowledge of other texts and by exploiting readers' abilities to recognize intertextuality between texts. This perspective owes its origins to Bakhtin's (1986) view that language is fundamentally dialogic, that a conversation between writer and reader is an ongoing activity. Writing reflects traces of its social uses because it is multiply linked and aligned with other texts upon which it builds and which it anticipates. 'Each utterance refutes, affirms, supplements, and relies on the others, presupposes them to be known and somehow takes them into account' (Bakhtin 1986, p. 91). A key idea here is that of *genre*, a term for grouping texts together and referring to the repertoire of linguistic responses writers are able to call on to communicate in familiar situations. Genre reminds us that when we write, we follow conventions for organizing messages because we want our readers to recognize our purposes. Research into genres therefore seeks to show how language forms work as resources for accomplishing goals, describing the stages which help writers to set out their thoughts in ways readers can easily follow and identifying salient features of texts which allow them to engage effectively with their readers (e.g. Hyland 2008).

An overview of methods

While I have divided methods up according to the paradigms with which they are mainly associated, much writing research combines several methods, often both quantitative and qualitative, to gain a more complete picture of a complex reality. In fact, the concept of *triangulation*, or the use of multiple sources of data or approaches, can bring greater plausibility to the interpretation of results. It obviously makes sense to view research pragmatically, adopting whatever tools seem most effective and a researcher may, for example, gather student opinions about their writing practices through a questionnaire and supplement this with interview or diary data, and with the drafts of their essays, mixing methods to increase the validity of the eventual findings.

Another feature of writing research is that it tends to favour data gathered in naturalistic rather than controlled conditions. This is not to say that methods that elicit data through questionnaires, structured interviews or experiments are not employed or that they have nothing to tell us about writing. It is simply that there has been a strong preference for collecting data in authentic circumstances not specifically set up for the research, such as via classroom observations or analyses of naturally occurring texts. The main methods for researching writing are summarized in Figure 19.1 (Hyland 2003) and discussed briefly below.

Questionnaires:	Highly focused elicitations of respondent self reports about actions and attitudes.
Interviews:	Adaptable and interactive elicitations of respondent self reports.
Verbal reports:	Retrospective accounts and think-aloud reports of thoughts while composing.
Written reports:	Diary or log accounts of personal writing or learning experiences.
Observation:	Direct or recorded data of 'live' interactions or writing behaviour.
Texts:	Study of authentic examples of writing used for communication in a natural context.
Case studies:	A collection of techniques capturing the experiences of participants in a situation.

FIGURE 19.1 *Main data collection methods for researching writing*

Elicitation: Questionnaires and interviews

These are the main methods for eliciting information and attitudes from informants. *Questionnaires* are widely used for collecting large amounts of structured, often numerical, easily analysable self-report data, while interviews offer more flexibility and greater potential for elaboration and detail. Both allow researchers to tap people's views and experiences of writing, but interviews tend to be more qualitative and heuristic and questionnaires more quantitative and conclusive. Questionnaires are particularly useful for exploratory studies into writing attitudes and behaviours and for identifying issues that can be followed-up later by more in-depth methods. One major use of questionnaires in writing research has been to discover the kinds of writing target communities require from students. Rogerson-Revell (2007), for example, used a questionnaire to shed light on participants' use of English in business meetings in a European company and to identify some of the language difficulties that can result.

Interviews offer more interactive and less predetermined modes of eliciting information. Although sometimes little more than oral questionnaires, interviews generally represent a very different way of understanding human experience, regarding knowledge as generated between people rather than as objectified and external to them. Participants are able to discuss their interpretations and perspectives, sharing what writing means to them rather than responding to preconceived categories. This flexibility and responsiveness means that interviews are used widely in writing research to learn more about *writing practices* (to discover the genres people write and how they understand and go about writing); about *teaching and learning practices* (to discover people's beliefs and practices about teaching and learning); and about *discourse-features* (to discover how text users see and respond to particular features of writing). Interviews are particularly valuable as they can reveal issues that might be difficult to predict, such as how students interpret teacher written feedback (Hyland, 2013a) or the intentions of faculty tutors in marking undergraduate assignments (Hyland, 2013b).

Introspection: Verbal and written reports

The use of *verbal reports* as data reflects the idea that the process of writing requires conscious attention and that at least some of the thought process involved can be recovered, either as a retrospective written or spoken recall or simultaneously with writing as a think-aloud protocol.

Protocols involve participants writing in their normal way but instructed to verbalize all thinking at the same time so that information can be collected on their decisions, their strategies and their perceptions as they work. Think-aloud data have been criticized as offering an artificial and incomplete picture of the complex cognitive activities involved in writing. For one thing, many cognitive processes are routine and internalized operations and therefore not available to verbal description while, more seriously, the act of verbal reporting may itself slow task progress or distort the process being reported on. But despite these criticisms, the method has been widely used, partly because the alternative is to deduce cognitive processes solely from subjects' behaviour, and this would obviously be far less reliable. Think-aloud techniques have been extremely productive in revealing the strategies writers use when composing, particularly what students do when planning and revising texts. In one study, for example, de Larios et al. (1999) used the method to examine what students did when they were blocked by a language problem or wanted to express a different meaning, tracing the patterns they used in searching for an alternative syntactic plan.

Diaries offer an alternative way of gaining introspective data. These are first-person accounts of a language-using experience, documented through regular entries in a journal and then analysed for recurring patterns or significant events. Diarists can be asked to produce 'narrative' entries which freely introspect on their learning or writing experiences or set guidelines to restrict the issues addressed. These can be in the form of detailed points to note ('write about what you found most/least interesting about this class') or a loose framework for response ('note all the work you did to complete this task'). Alternatively, researchers may ask diarists to concentrate only on 'critical incidents' of personal significance or to simply record dates and times of writing. While some diarists may resent the time and intrusion involved, diaries provide a rich source of reflective data which can reveal social and psychological processes difficult to collect in other ways. Thus, Nelson (1993) used diaries to discover how her students went about writing a research paper, following their trail through the library, how they evaluated sources and took notes, the conversations they had with others, decisions they made and so on. This approach provided a rich account of writers' reflections, suggesting why they acted as they did and how they saw contextual influences.

Observations

While elicitation and introspective methods provide reports of what people *say* they think and do, observation methods offer actual evidence of it by systematic documentation of participants engaged in writing and learning to write. They are based on conscious noticing and precise recording of actions as a way of seeing these actions in a new light. Once again there are degrees of structure the researcher can impose on the data, from simply checking pre-defined boxes at fixed intervals or every time a type of behaviour occurs, to writing a full narrative of events. The most highly structured observations employ a prior coding scheme to highlight significant events from the mass of data that taped or live observation can produce (see Hyland 2003 for examples). All observation will necessarily privilege some behaviours and neglect others, as we only record what we think is important, but while a clear structure is easier to apply and yields more manageable data, such pre-selection may ignore relevant behaviour that wasn't predicted.

Observation is often combined with other methods, as in Camitta's (1993) 3-year study of vernacular writing among adolescents. She observed and interviewed writers of different races and genders between the ages of 14 and 18 outside school, in free school time when they clustered in groups to talk and write, and in writing surreptitiously in class. She found that these students produced a wide variety of genres and that when writing was free of school constraints it generated considerable interest and much oral sharing.

Text data

Finally, a major source of data for writing research is writing itself: the use of texts as objects of study. While texts can be approached in a variety of ways, most research now seeks to discover how people use language in specific contexts. The main approaches to studying written texts are currently genre and corpus analyses.

Genre analysis

This embraces a range of tools and attitudes to texts, from detailed qualitative analyses of a single text to more quantitative counts of language features. Sometimes researchers work with a single text, either because it is inherently interesting or because it seems representative of a larger set of texts or particular genre. A major policy speech, a newspaper editorial or an important scientific article can offer insights into forms of persuasion, particular syntactic or lexical choices, or the views of text writers. More generally, a sample essay may shed light on students' uses of particular forms or the assumptions underlying different choices. Bhatia (1993) suggests some basic steps for conducting a genre analysis which emphasize the importance of locating texts in their contexts as presented in Figure 19.2.

Such an approach forms a *case study*, but while this is a widely recognized method, it raises questions about how far a single text can be representative of a genre. Representativeness is strengthened if several texts are analysed, and corpus analyses, drawing on evidence from large databases of electronically encoded texts, are the main way of achieving this.

---

1   Select a text which seems representative of the genre you want to study.

2   Place the text in a situational context, that is, use your background knowledge and text clues to guess where the genre is used, by whom and why it is written the way it is.

3   Compare the text with other similar texts to ensure that it broadly represents the genre.

4   Study the institutional context in which the genre is used (through site visits, interviews, manuals, etc.) to better understand its conventions.

5   Select a focus for analysis (moves, lexis, cohesion, persuasion, etc.) and analyse it.

6   Check your analysis with a specialist informant to confirm your findings and insights.

FIGURE 19.2 *Steps in genre analysis (after Bhatia 1993, pp. 22–34)*

Corpus analysis

A *corpus* is simply a collection of naturally occurring language samples (often consisting of millions of words) which represent a speaker's experience of language in some restricted domain, thereby providing a more solid basis for genre descriptions. A corpus provides an alternative to intuition by offering both a resource against which intuitions can be tested and a mechanism for generating them. This enables analysts to depict what is usual in a genre, rather than what is simply grammatically possible, and helps to suggest explanations for why language is used as it is in particular contexts.

Corpus studies are therefore based on both qualitative and quantitative methods, using evidence of *frequency* and *association* as starting points for interpretation. *Frequency* is based on the idea that if a word, string or grammatical pattern occurs regularly in a particular genre or subset of language, then we can assume it is significant in how that genre is routinely constructed. *Association* refers to the ways features associate with each other in collocational patterns. A concordance program brings together all instances of a search word or phrase in the corpus as a list of unconnected lines of text and so allows the analyst to see regularities in its use that might otherwise be missed. In other words, we can see instances of language *use* when we read these lines horizontally and evidence of *system* when we read them vertically, pointing to common usage in this genre.

In a study of the acknowledgement sections from 240 masters and doctoral dissertations, for example, I found a strong tendency to use the noun *thanks* in preference to other expressions of gratitude (Hyland 2004). Sorting concordance lines on the word to the left of this search word revealed this noun was modified by only three adjectives: *special, sincere* and *deep* with *special* making up over two-thirds of all cases. Figure 19.3 is a screen shot from the program *MonoConc Pro* showing part of the results of this sorting.

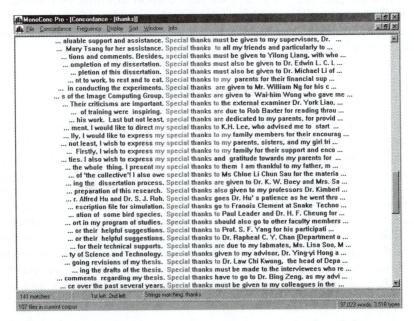

FIGURE 19.3 *Special thanks pattern in Masters/Doctoral acknowledgements*

A sample study

To illustrate some of these ideas and to show what one approach to writing research looks like in practice, the remainder of this chapter reports on a study of Hong Kong undergraduates' writing I conducted a few years ago (Hyland 2002). I will discuss the main stages under four headings: framing issues, selecting methods, collecting data and analysing data.

Framing the issue

The study emerged from a sense that my undergraduate students had considerable problems constructing a credible representation of themselves and their work in their research writing. They seemed reluctant to claim an appropriate degree of authoritativeness in their texts and to get behind their statements, making their work seem anonymous and disembodied. I decided to pursue these impressions by investigating how these students used authorial pronouns, framing the issue by relating the use of first person to rhetorical identity. This sees identity as less a phenomenon of private experience than a need for affiliation and recognition in particular social networks. When we write in particular genres, there is strong pressure to take on their forms and represent ourselves in a way valued by that community. This does not mean that writers simply slot into ready-made identities, but it limits individual manoeuvre. Newcomers, however, often find that the discourses of their disciplines support identities very different from those they bring with them from their home cultures, which prevent them from communicating appropriate commitments and undermine their relationship to readers.

Selecting methods

Framing pronoun use in terms of the constraints on rhetorical conventions of personality suggested two possible lines of inquiry. Basically, to adopt an ethnographic approach and focus on particular writers, investigating their personal and social histories and how these influenced their writing of academic assignments or to look for preferred choices of pronoun use in a representative collection of student writing and interview writers about their choices. I decided on the latter, partly because I was more comfortable with the methods involved and partly because I wanted a wider picture of how they saw the demands of the task and chose to represent themselves in this context. A corpus approach offers a starting point for analysis by providing quantitative information about the relative frequency and use of self-mention, pointing to systematic tendencies in students' choices of meanings. To understand why writers made the choices they did, I decided to support the text data with interviews, using focus groups as a way of reducing the threat to these L2 students.

Collecting data

To ensure that the text samples were representative of undergraduate research writing, I compiled a corpus of sixty-four final year project reports, a genre of 8,000–12,000 words and by far the most substantial piece of writing students do in their undergraduate careers. I obtained a broad cross-section of academic practice by collecting eight reports from each of eight different degree programs, including sciences, engineering, social sciences, technology and business. This involved getting agreement from writers and electronic copies of their reports. I then computer-searched the corpus for the first person uses *I, me, my, we, us, our, mine* and *ours* using a commercially available concordance program and checked all cases to ensure they were exclusive first person uses.

While corpus analyses are excellent for telling us what writers do, to stop here runs the danger of reifying conventions rather than explaining them. I therefore conducted interviews with a supervisor from each field and with student writers. The supervisors were asked about their own writing, that of their students and their impressions of disciplinary practices. The student interviews required more scaffolding and a more supportive environment and were conducted as focus groups of four or five students. All interviews had two parts. First, I asked participants to respond to features in selected texts as either writers or members of the readership for whom the texts were composed as a way of making explicit the tacit knowledge or strategies that they brought to acts of composing or reading. This was followed by more general observations of pronoun use to learn how respondents saw the practices of the cultures and communities that influenced their writing. All interviews were taped and written up as a summary immediately after the session and subsequently returned to several times, often with the assistance of the subjects.

Analysing data

The frequency counts showed 637 occurrences. In several sweeps of the data, I also noted the surrounding text of the target words to identify recurring pragmatic functions. Checking concordance lines is a recursive procedure which involves trying to narrow down, expand and combine initial categories. This recursion allowed me to classify each instance as performing one of five functions, either stating a goal, explaining a procedure, stating results or claims, expressing self-benefits or elaborating an argument. I validated the analysis by asking a colleague to independently code a sample of data.

In order to better understand student choices, I compared the findings with those of expert writers using an existing corpus of 240 published research articles in cognate disciplines. These papers were selected from journals on students' reading lists and totalled 1.3 million words, twice as large as the student corpus in order to strengthen observations about expert practices, as opposed to those about a specific student population. Analysis of the two corpora showed that first person pronouns were substantially more frequent in the published corpus and that the students generally sought to downplay their authorial identity by consciously avoiding its most authoritative functions such as making a commitment to an interpretation or claim. In other words, they sought to deny ownership and responsibility for their views. I set out to investigate these findings further through the interviews.

I also approached the interview data recursively using a form of *content analysis*, beginning with obvious or recurring topics and looking for themes. Subsequent passes through the data helped to generate and refine categories, identify core ideas, find links and gradually build a picture of the data. I attended to the frequency with which particular ideas occurred, the strength of their expression, their distribution across the informants and the rationale for the study. The data revealed a lot about beliefs and practices and raised issues concerning the students' intentions in using self-mention, their previous encounters with it in textbooks and class teaching and their sense of its meanings. It showed that the students were sensitive to the effects of author pronouns and reluctant to accept its clear connotations of authority and commitment. They viewed the use of *I* with misgivings as it seemed to imply an identity they did not want. Together, analysis of the corpus and interview material suggested that culture and context shape our communicative practices in significant ways, influencing our preferences for structuring information, the relationships we establish with our readers and how far we want to personally appear in our texts.

Conclusions

I have attempted to provide an overview of writing research approaches in this chapter. While space prevents elaboration, I hope to have shown that the questions we ask, the methods we adopt and the ways we interpret data are all products of the ways we understand what writing is. Explanation involves selecting texts and features through the filter of our theories and research interests and sifting out the ways that writers' interests, beliefs, affiliations, experiences, values and practices appear to influence their writing. Because these are not things that can be directly observed, the researcher must select from a repertoire of interpretations rather than hit on the truth, but by grounding these interpretations in written and oral data we help to ensure that they are not pure speculation either. Ultimately, all we can claim for our research is that our findings are a plausible interpretation of some aspect of a given context of communication.

Resources for further reading

Baker, P 2006, *Using Corpora in Discourse Analysis*, Continuum, London.

This is an accessible guide to creating and analysing written corpora. Topics covered include corpus building, concordancing, keyness, frequency and dispersion.

Hyland, K 2003, *Second Language Writing*, Cambridge University Press, New York, NY.

This is a teachers' guide to analysing and teaching L2 writing, with chapters on establishing students' needs, designing syllabuses, creating and sequencing tasks and feedback and assessment. It contains a chapter on different writing research methods with examples.

Hyland, K in press, 2016 *Teaching and Researching Writing*, 3rd edn, Routledge, London.

This book is an overview of writing with an up-to-date discussion of theories on writing together with methods for research and teaching. It also contains ideas for writing research projects together with example studies.

Bazerman, C, Krut, R, Lunsford, K, McLeod, S, Null, S, Rogers, P & Stansell, A (eds), 2010, *Traditions of Writing Research*, Routledge, London.

Chapters in this book reflect different approaches to writing research and addressing topics such as early childhood to academic writing and focusing on a range of different contexts.

There are also a number of free concordance tools on the web which allow you to search a range of academic, student, newspaper and literary corpora. The best of these are:

VLC Web Concordancer at: http://vlc.polyu.edu.hk/concordance/, viewed 14 January 2015.CobuildDirect site at: http://www.collins.co.uk/corpus/CorpusSearch.aspx, viewed 15 January 2015.

References

Bakhtin, M 1986, *Speech Genres and Other Late Essays*, University of Texas Press, Austin, TX.
Bhatia, VK 1993, *Analyzing Genre: Language Use in Professional Settings*, Longman, London.

Bosher, S 1998, 'The composing processes of three southeast Asian writers at the post-secondary level: An exploratory study', *Journal of Second Language Writing*, vol. 7, no. 2, pp. 205–233.

Camitta, M 1993, 'Vernacular writing: Varieties of literacy among Philadelphia high school students', in B Street (ed.), *Cross-Cultural Approaches to Literacy*, Cambridge University Press, Cambridge, pp. 228–246.

de Larios, J, Murphy, L & Manchon, R 1999, 'The use of restructuring strategies in EFL writing: A study of Spanish learners of English as a foreign language', *Journal of Second Language Writing*, vol. 8, no. 1, pp. 13–44.

Hyland, F 1998, 'The impact of teacher written feedback on individual writers', *Journal of Second Language Writing*, vol. 7, no. 3, pp. 255–286.

Hyland, K 2002, 'Authority and invisibility: Authorial identity in academic writing', *Journal of Pragmatics*, vol. 34, no. 8, pp. 1091–1112.

────── 2003, *Second Language Writing*, Cambridge University Press, New York, NY.

────── 2004, 'Graduates' gratitude: The generic structure of dissertation acknowledgements', *English for Specific Purposes*, vol. 3, no. 3, pp. 303–324.

────── 2008, 'Genre and academic writing in the disciplines', *Language Teaching*, vol. 41, no. 4, pp. 543–562.

────── 2013a, 'Student perceptions of hidden messages in teacher written feedback', *Studies in Educational Evaluation*, vol. 39, no. 3, pp. 180–187.

────── 2013b, 'Faculty feedback: Perceptions and practices in L2 disciplinary writing', *Journal of Second Language Writing*, vol. 22, no. 3, pp. 240–253.

Nelson, G & Carson, J 1998, 'ESL students' perceptions of effectiveness in peer response groups', *Journal of Second Language Writing*, vol. 7, no. 2, pp. 113–131.

Nelson, J 1993, 'The library revisited: Exploring students' research processes', in A Penrose & B Sitcoe (eds), *Hearing Ourselves Think: Cognitive Research in the College Writing Classroom*, Oxford University Press, New York, NY, pp. 60–80.

Nystrand, M 1987, 'The role of context in written communication', in R Horowitz and S J Samuels (eds), *Comprehending Oral and Written Language*, Academic Press, San Diego, CA, pp. 197–214.

Prior, P 1998, *Writing/Disciplinarity: A Sociohistoric Account of Literate Activity in the Academy*, Erlbaum, Mahwah, NJ.

Rogerson-Revell, P 2007, 'Using English for international business: A European case study', *English for Specific Purposes*, vol. 26, no. 1, pp. 103–120.

Smagorinsky, P (ed.), 1994, *Speaking about Writing: Reflections on Research Methodology*, Sage, Thousand Oaks, CA.

Sullivan, K & Lindgren, E (eds), 2006, *Computer Keystroke Logging and Writing*, Elsevier, London.

CHAPTER TWENTY

Researching Grammar

Neomy Storch

Grammar is a large and controversial topic in applied linguistics. In this chapter, I focus on two distinct areas related to this topic: (a) what constitutes knowledge of grammar and how we assess that knowledge and (b) grammar instruction in second language (L2) classes. The discussion of these two areas covers theoretical debates and empirical findings. This is then followed by a description of a study which attempted to address some of the shortcomings identified in current research on grammar instruction. I conclude with outlining what I consider to be areas of L2 grammar that require additional research.

L2 grammar knowledge: What is it and how do we measure it?

Knowledge of grammar is said to consist of two types: explicit and implicit knowledge. According to N. Ellis (2005), these two types of knowledge are distinct and exist in separate parts of the brain. R. Ellis (2005) lists seven criteria that can be used to distinguish between explicit and implicit grammar knowledge. These criteria include, among others: level of awareness, accessibility and whether learners can verbalize the knowledge.

Broadly speaking, *explicit knowledge* is conscious knowledge about a language (rules, conventions of use) that learners can often verbalize. Accessing this knowledge is slow because it requires controlled processing.

Implicit knowledge, on the other hand, is held unconsciously and can be accessed quickly and easily. It is the knowledge that learners draw on when comprehending or producing language in rapid, fluent communication. It is therefore implicit knowledge which is considered genuine knowledge of a language.

Thus when assessing grammatical knowledge or development in grammatical knowledge it is important to consider the kind of knowledge tested. According to Purpura (2004, 2012), tests which use constrained response type exercises (e.g. fill in the gap) test explicit knowledge. Implicit knowledge is tested via tasks requiring comprehension or production of language, in oral or written form. However, as R. Ellis (2005, 2009) points out, it is impossible to conclude with total certainty that when completing a particular test task the learner accesses only the type of knowledge that the test is designed to elicit. Rather, what researchers can do is attempt to design tests that will bias the use of one type of knowledge.

In designing grammar tests, scoring is also an important consideration (Purpura 2004, 2012). Whereas scoring constrained response type exercises is fairly straightforward, assessing extended oral and written output is more complex and requires measures not only of accuracy but also of syntactic complexity. This is because there may be a trade-off between accuracy and syntactic complexity. Some learners may achieve high scores of accuracy by using only simple sentences, whereas learners who use more complex sentences are perhaps more likely to make errors (Foster & Skehan 1996).

Extended written and oral output can be assessed using a qualitative or a quantitative approach. A qualitative approach employs a rating scale with discreet categories which describe the 'quality' of grammatical performance (Purpura 2004). The categories tend to describe global levels of accuracy (e.g. few errors overall) and syntactic complexity (e.g. a range of simple and complex sentences is evident). A quantitative approach to measuring accuracy is based on an error identification and count (Ellis & Barkhuizen 2005). Measures of accuracy are computed by dividing the total number of errors by the total number of words produced, or by computing the accuracy of production units, such as T-units or clauses. A T-unit, a common unit in the analysis of writing and speaking, is a main clause plus whatever subordinate clauses are attached to it or embedded in it (Hunt 1966). Thus the accuracy of a student's written or oral output can be represented in terms of the percentage of error-free T-units or the percentage of error-free clauses (Wolf-Quintero et al. 1998). Other measures of accuracy focus on the accurate use of a particular grammatical structure, such as verbs or articles. Measures of syntactic complexity include the proportion of clauses to T-units or the proportion of dependent clauses to all clauses (Wolf-Quintero et al. 1998).

L2 grammar instruction: Synthesis of current thinking and research

Although grammar is considered central to language learning and language use, the role of grammar in L2 teaching is very controversial. The main controversy centres on whether grammar should be taught in L2 classes explicitly. *Explicit grammar instruction* means presenting and explaining a predetermined set of grammar rules, usually but not necessarily followed by practice. Three distinct positions can be identified in the applied linguistics literature: a zero position, a focus on forms (FonFs) and a focus on form (FonF) position. These positions are based on assumptions concerning whether explicit knowledge can become implicit knowledge.

The first position, the zero position, is represented by scholars such as Krashen (1981, 1993) who see very little merit in teaching grammar explicitly. In his comprehensible input hypothesis, Krashen (1981) argued that to acquire an L2, learners simply need exposure to language input that they can understand (i.e. comprehensible input). The hypothesis was based on claims that the same processes underlie first and second language acquisition as well as research findings (e.g. Bailey et al. 1974) which showed that all learners, regardless of first language, age or whether they were instructed or naturalistic learners, proceeded along the same order and sequence in the acquisition of certain grammatical structures. Thus Krashen (1981, 1993) argues that grammar instruction serves very little purpose. It provides learners, in his view, with explicit knowledge which may enable them to monitor and edit their language output (assuming certain conditions are met), but this explicit knowledge does not become part of the learner's implicit knowledge system. Other supporters of this position are scholars who refer to Chomsky's (1976) Universal Grammar (UG) and who claim that second language acquisition is innate and has nothing to do with explicit knowledge (e.g. Schwartz 1993). The teaching implication of this position is that language classrooms should only focus on meaning; that is, language classes should provide learners with plentiful exposure to authentic and comprehensible L2 input, initially via listening and reading activities, and once the learner is ready, with authentic production opportunities.

The second position is that adopted by scholars such as DeKeyser (1998, 2007) who see merit in explicit grammar instruction. DeKeyser claims that when explicit grammar instruction is sustained and followed by appropriate meaning- based practice, it will contribute to the development of implicit knowledge. Lightbown (1991) suggests that explicit knowledge can act as a priming mechanism to help learners notice structures in the L2 input. Similarly, although N. Ellis (2005) argues that the bulk of language learning occurs through usage, he suggests that learning begins with an explicit representation of linguistic forms. Thus, the teaching implications of this position are that explicit grammar instruction should precede practice. This stance is often referred to as Focus on Forms (FonFs).

The third position is that adopted by scholars who see some merit in grammar instruction, but only when it is reactive rather than predetermined. This approach, proposed by Long (1991, 1996), is referred to as Focus on Form (FonF). It draws on Schmidt's (1990) noticing hypothesis which posits that only language which is attended to (i.e. noticed) is processed. Pedagogically, a focus on form means a spontaneous reaction to learners' language learning needs which occurs as learners engage in meaning-focused activities. These needs can be expressed as questions (e.g. clarification requests) or be evident in learners' errors. The teacher's role is to provide a brief explanation or correction which draws learners' attention to the problematic structure.

There are a few interesting points that should be noted about this debate. First, the three stances are largely theoretical rather than based on solid empirical research. Furthermore, the term FonF has been redefined and extended since its original formulation (Long 1991) and the distinction between FonF and FonFs has blurred. R. Ellis (2006), for example, distinguishes between incidental FonF and pre-emptive FonF. Incidental FonF, as in its original inception, is reactive and occurs spontaneously in response to a performance problem. Pre-emptive FonF, however, includes the use of tasks that are likely to elicit certain grammatical structures or predetermining the grammatical errors that will receive feedback (e.g. Doughty & Varela 1998), an approach which is closer to FonFs. Thus some authors (e.g. R. Ellis 2002; Garcia Mayo 2002; Lyster 2004) use the term form-focused instruction which seems to include elements of FonF and FonFs.

The available research evidence supports some form of grammar instruction. However, the evidence is largely indirect showing that in the absence of grammar instruction learners' grammatical accuracy may not develop. Perhaps the most convincing evidence comes from the French immersion programs in Canada, where researchers (e.g. Harley & Swain 1984) have shown that despite exposure to rich and plentiful L2 input (as advocated by Krashen), L2 learners may become fluent but not accurate in their use of the L2. My own small-scale study (Storch 2007) provides further support for this claim. The study examined the writing of learners at the beginning and end of a semester's study (12 weeks). The participants in the study ($n = 20$) were enrolled in degree programs. They were identified on an in-house diagnostic language test as needing further language support but, for a range of reasons, chose not to access the available language support services or enrol in ESL credit-bearing subjects. The study found that after a semester of study in an English medium university, the learners' writing improved in terms of organization and development of ideas but that there was little improvement in grammatical accuracy. A more recent and larger scale study (Knoch et al. 2014) shows that even after 1 year of studying in an English medium university, ESL learners' grammatical accuracy does not improve.

The other oft-cited study in support of grammar instruction is the large meta-analysis by Norris and Ortega (2000) which showed that explicit instruction led to more substantial and enduring gains in learning than implicit instruction (extended exposure to the target forms). It should be noted, however, that most of the studies included in the Norris and Ortega meta-analysis relied on tests of explicit knowledge to show gains.

The current orthodoxy on L2 grammar instruction is an acceptance that some form of grammar instruction is beneficial but that grammar should not be the sole focus of L2 classes as in traditional language pedagogy. Rather, a growing number of scholars (see Hinkel & Fotos 2002; Nassaji & Fotos 2011) advocate a communicative approach to L2 instruction which integrates a focus on meaning and on grammar. In such an approach, the primary focus is on relevant content material or tasks which provide learners with opportunities for exposure to and authentic practice in producing grammatical structures. Consequently, research on grammar instruction now focuses on how best to teach grammar within a communicative, task-based approach and on what are the most effective ways of responding to grammatical errors in learners' language.

Research on how to teach grammar: Research on tasks

Studies on how best to teach grammar attempt to investigate which communicative tasks and task conditions are most effective in drawing learners' attention to language. This research usually requires learners to work in pairs or small groups. Some researchers have focused on tasks which only require oral language output; others have investigated tasks which require learners to jointly produce written texts.

Studies on tasks requiring oral language output have, by and large, been informed by Long's interaction hypothesis (1991). This hypothesis (or interaction approach as it is now more commonly referred to) posits that certain interactional moves (e.g. clarification requests), which occur because of a perceived communication breakdown, not only serve to make input comprehensible but also draw learners' attention to linguistic problems and push them to modify their language, making it more grammatically accurate and appropriate. Thus, research from this theoretical perspective has attempted to identify tasks and task conditions which are likely to maximize learners' interactions. For example, Pica et al. (1993) argue that jigsaw tasks (where each learner holds information vital to the task completion and only one solution is possible) are the most effective because information exchange between the participants is obligatory.

In tasks which require learners to jointly produce written output, researchers audio record the learners' talk as they complete the tasks and the transcribed talk is then analysed for the amount of attention to grammatical structures that the tasks elicit. The unit of analysis that has often been employed in this kind of research is the *Language Related Episode* (LRE). This episode is defined as any part of a dialogue where learners talk about the language they are producing, question their language use, self and other correct (Swain & Lapkin 1998). Adopting a Vygotskian (1986) sociocultural theoretical perspective, Swain (2000) argues that these episodes are sites of language learning because learning arises in dialogue. From this theoretical perspective, speaking is perceived as a cognitive activity which externalizes thoughts. Once externalized, the thought can be analysed, questioned and reflected upon (Swain & Lapkin 2003). The term used to describe this activity of using language to deliberate about language is languaging (Swain 2010). Languaging can be self-directed or other-directed. The advantages of other-directed talk is that it affords learners opportunities to pool their linguistic resources and to resolve language problems that they may not have been able to resolve on their own (for a discussion of the benefits of other-directed talk during collaborative writing, see Storch 2013).

The following excerpt is taken from a study (Storch 2005) where learners composed a text in pairs. It provides an example of an LRE where learners engage in languaging; that is, externalizing their thoughts about the choice of a verb form. The learners offer suggestions (line 162), counter suggestions (lines 163, 164) and finally, by pooling their linguistic resources, reach a correct grammatical decision about the verb form required in this instance.

Excerpt	1:	Example of an LRE
162	M:	…the Vietnamese and the Laotian are
163	C:	improve
164	M:	have the, yeah, have, have improved yeah
165	C:	yes

A number of studies (e.g. Storch & Aldosari 2010; Swain & Lapkin 2001) have attempted to compare the effectiveness of various communicative written tasks in terms of the focus on language they generate. For example, Swain and Lapkin (2001) compared the efficacy of a dictogloss and a jigsaw task. The dictogloss task, originally designed by Wajnryb (1990), requires learners to reconstruct a text using notes taken from a dictation. The jigsaw in this study was based on a series of eight pictures. Each learner held four pictures and thus the task required the learners to arrange their pictures in a sequence and write out a story based on the pictures. The study found that both tasks were equally effective as they generated a similar number of LREs. Others (e.g. Garcia Mayo 2002; Storch 1998) found that a text reconstruction task, where learners are provided with content words but need to insert the necessary function words or change word forms, elicited more LREs than traditional grammar exercises (e.g. fill in the blanks) and more than the jigsaw and dictogloss (Alegría de La Colina & Garcia Mayo 2007).

A related area of research on tasks is how task implementation variables affect learners' attention to language. For example, Leeser (2004) examined how proficiency pairing affects learners' focus on grammar in the learning of Spanish. In his study, twenty-one pairs of learners completed a dictogloss task. The learners were grouped according to their L2 (Spanish) proficiency, forming eight pairs of high-high (H-H), nine pairs of high-low (H-L) and four pairs of low-low (L-L) learners. Leeser found that the H-H learners produced the highest number of LREs, followed by H-L and finally L-L dyads. The implications of these findings are that mixed proficiency pairing may be more conducive to learning than pairing low-proficiency learners (L-L). However, Storch and Aldosari (2013), in a study conducted in EFL classes in Saudi Arabia, found that it is not only proficiency grouping which determines the quantity of LREs but also the role relationship learners form when working in pairs. Employing a model of pair relationships (Storch 2002), the study found that pairs composed of similar proficiency learners (high-high and low-low) were more likely to form collaborative relationships where both learners were involved in deliberating over L2 choices. In mixed proficiency pairs (high-low), one learner was more likely to dominate the activity. In such dominant-passive pairs, there were fewer deliberations over language use and hence fewer LREs.

The assumption that underlies many studies investigating the effectiveness of various tasks is that those tasks or task conditions which elicit more interaction (e.g. more comprehension checks) or more deliberations about language (i.e. more LREs) are more effective for language development. However, as Nakahama et al. (2001) have pointed out, researchers also need to examine the language the learners produce during their interaction, to consider for example, the length, complexity and accuracy of the learners' utterances. There is also a need, as I have noted elsewhere (Storch 2008), to examine the quality of engagement with language evident in the LREs. An LRE may be short, composed only of one or two turns, or quite long and involve multiple turns. These qualitative differences in the level of engagement and their potential impact on language learning have not been sufficiently investigated. Another shortcoming of the research on the effectiveness of oral and written tasks is that there are very few studies which have investigated whether interactions or deliberations over language lead to development in implicit grammatical knowledge as measured by some form of a post-treatment test. The handful of studies that have attempted to address this gap in research have thus far either used constrained responses exercises such as multiple choice or true/false type exercises (e.g. Swain & Lapkin 2001) thus measuring explicit rather than implicit knowledge or have been small scale (e.g. Storch 2002).

Research on how to teach grammar: Feedback on errors

Another pedagogical intervention which aims to improve learners' grammatical accuracy is *corrective feedback (CF)*. Corrective feedback (feedback on errors) is pervasive in L2 classrooms. It is provided on both oral and written language production and can take a number of different forms. In the past 20 years or so, there has been extensive interest in CF as evident by the large number of articles and dissertations published on this topic.

Corrective feedback on oral production

Corrective feedback on oral language can be implicit or explicit. *Implicit CF* occurs when the corrective intent of the feedback is covert, as in the case of a *recast* or a clarification request (e.g. sorry?). A recast consists of a reformulation of the learner's incorrect utterance while maintaining the meaning of the original utterance. *Explicit corrective feedback* means an overt correction of erroneous utterances with or without explanations. The following examples illustrate the difference between implicit and explicit CF.

Example of implicit CF (recast)

Learner: Last night, I go to the movies.
Teacher: Oh, last night you went to the movies.

Example of explicit CF (overt correction with explanation)

Learner: Last night, I go to the movies.
Teacher: No, you say last night I went to the movies because last night means in the past.

Research on recasts has shown that it is perhaps the most prevalent form of teacher feedback (Ellis et al. 2001; Lyser & Ranta 1997), even in meaning-focused classes. However, there is a debate in the literature on whether recasts are the most effective forms of CF (see Goo & Mackey 2013 and the response by Lyster & Ranta 2013). Using *uptake* (learners repeating the correct model provided in the recast immediately after receiving the recast) as a measure of effectiveness, studies have shown that uptake is lower following recasts than following more explicit forms of feedback (Lyster 2004; Lyster & Ranta 1997; Lyster & Saito 2010). These findings and their implications are disputed by others (e.g. Goo & Mackey 2013; Mackey & Philp 1998) who question the use of immediate uptake as a measure of effectiveness. Uptake may occur in subsequent turns rather than in the immediate next turn or, as shown by Ohta (2000), the uptake may not be vocalized. However, perhaps the more important consideration in this discussion of uptake is whether uptake is necessarily evidence of noticing the CF or whether it does indeed lead to learning. Uptake is a repetition, and repetitions may be quite mechanical without much attention invested in the act (Panova & Lyster 2002).

Unlike descriptive studies of feedback, Loewen's (2005) study investigated the efficacy of recasts by using a post-test design. Following 17 hours of observation in twelve different ESL classes, Loewen developed individualized tests where learners were asked to recall the linguistic information provided to them in class. The study found a relatively high recall rate: 60 per cent in the short term (1–3 days after the feedback was provided) and 50 per cent 2 weeks later. However, it is questionable whether ability to recall translates into ability to use the structures correctly in free production (i.e. implicit knowledge).

Corrective feedback on written production

The debate about the efficacy of written CF resembles to some extent the debate about explicit grammar instruction. At one extreme are researchers who have argued that there is no merit whatsoever in feedback on grammar in L2 writing (e.g. Truscott 1996, 2007), whereas others (e.g. Ferris 1999, 2006) have argued that such feedback is beneficial. However, scholars on both sides of the debate agree that a more definitive stance on the merit of feedback requires additional research on written feedback (Ferris 2004; Truscott 1999).

Like CF on oral production, CF on writing can take different forms. It can range from indirect feedback, such as editing symbols in the margins (e.g. X) or underlining the erroneous structure, with or without a symbol indicating the type of error, to more direct forms such as writing the correct version above the incorrect one.

Research on written CF has tended to focus on the efficacy of different forms of the feedback (e.g. Bitchener & Knoch 2010a, b; Shintani & Ellis 2013; Van Beuningen et al. 2012), on whether it is better to provide targeted rather than comprehensive feedback (e.g. Ellis et al. 2008) as well as whether CF results in greater accuracy in writing (e.g. Bitchener et al. 2005; Bitchener & Knoch 2010a, b; Hartshorn et al. 2010; Storch &

Wigglesworth 2010a, b; Van Beuningen et al. 2012). For example, the study by Bitchener et al. (2005) compared the effectiveness of direct CF with and without a 5-minute individual conference and no feedback. Three errors were targeted in the feedback conditions: prepositions, simple past tense and use of definite articles. The study found that, although the combined feedback condition (written plus conference) was most effective, gains in accuracy did not show a linear upward trend. Furthermore, the structure targeted by the feedback was an important consideration, with prepositions showing least response to feedback.

The overwhelming conclusion that can be drawn about the efficacy of written CF is the complexity of this issue and the need for better designed studies. What scholars (e.g. Bitchener 2012; Ellis 2010; Ferris 2010; Storch 2010) on reflection now call for is for research which takes into consideration a host of individual learner factors (see Sheen 2011) such as L2 proficiency, language learning aptitude and attitudes as well as immediate (e.g. writing task) and larger (e.g. second versus foreign language classes) contextual factors. We also need longitudinal studies with clearly identified and defined measures of effectiveness and, above all, studies which collect qualitative data which could provide some insights into how learners process the feedback they receive. The following study attempted to incorporate some of the factors mentioned above.

A sample study

The sample study was part of a large-scale project which investigated the efficacy of different forms of written feedback in the short and long term and the impact of a number of individual learner variables including proficiency level and learners' attitudes as well as contextual factors such as task type and mode of composing (individually versus in pairs).[1]

The study examined the efficacy of two forms of feedback on writing: reformulation and editing. *Reformulation* is a technique whereby a native speaker rewrites the text produced by the learner correcting all grammatical errors while preserving the learner's ideas. Editing in this study involved providing learners with a symbol which located their error (e.g. underlining, insertion symbol) and an abbreviation which explained the type of error (e.g. C stood for word choice). All participants who received editing feedback were given a key to the symbols and abbreviations used.

The participants in this study were university students whose ESL proficiency was deemed to be advanced (based on IELTS scores). The participants (*n* = 48) formed two groups: one group of 12 pairs received feedback in the form of reformulations, the other group received feedback in the form of editing. All pairs were self-selected and students were paid for their participation. Both forms of feedback were given by the same research assistant, a native speaker who was an experienced ESL teacher.

The participants were required to attend on three different days. On each occasion, they were required to write a report (data commentary) based on a graphic stimulus, showing rainfall patterns in different cities in the world. On Days 1 and 5 (Session 1 and 2), they worked in pairs and their pair talk was audio recorded. On Day 28, they worked individually. Data collected on Day 28 enabled us to investigate the impact of feedback on writing completed beyond the immediate revision session (Day 5) and thus measured development in grammatical accuracy over time. Figure 20.1 summarizes what each session involved.

The following excerpts illustrate the original versions written by the participants and the form of feedback they received. Excerpt 2 provides an example of a reformulation. The reformulation contains two changes: deletion of an indefinite article (an) and changing the word rainfall to rainfalls.

Excerpt 2: Reformulations

Original:

This chart illustrates an average rainfall in each season in the year 2000.

Reformulated version:

This chart illustrates average rainfalls in each season in the year 2000.

Excerpt 3 illustrates the form of editing that participants received. In this example, three errors were identified in the original version: an omission (denoted by an insertion symbol), an error in choice of prepositions (C) and in word form (F).

Day	Duration	Task
Day 1	30 min	Students compose a short report in pairs.
Day 5, session 1	15 min	Pairs receive and discuss the feedback on their report.
Day 5, session 2	30 min	Version containing feedback removed. Pairs given an unmarked version of the text produced on Day 1 and are asked to rewrite it.
Day 28	20 min	Individual learners write a short report based on the same prompt as that used on Day 1.

FIGURE 20.1 *Study design*

Excerpt 3: Editing feedback

Original version:

The rainfall in Lagos city is 240 mm on average in summer, which the highest amongst the other season.

Edited version:

The rainfall in Lagos city is 240 mm on average in summer, which ∧ the

C   F

highest *amongst* the other *season*.

Analysis of the data

All written reports (produced by the pairs on Days 1 and 5 and by individual learners on Day 28) were analysed for fluency (length in words), grammatical accuracy and grammatical complexity. Grammatical accuracy measures included the percentage of error-free T-units and of error-free clauses. Complexity measures included clauses per T-unit ratios. The example below (Excerpt 4), taken from our data, shows a T-unit composed of two clauses separated by a slash. Only the first clause was coded as error-free.

Excerpt 4: an example of a T-unit, clauses and accuracy analysis

Beijing has about 160mm of rain in summer/which is around 16 times than that in winter (10mm)

Audio recorded and transcribed pair talk (collected on Day 5 in both sessions) were analysed for LREs. LREs were coded for the nature of engagement, distinguishing between single turn and multi-turn LREs, for their focus (lexis, grammar, mechanics) and for whether the decision reached in the deliberations was correct.

Findings

Analysis of the learners' writing showed that accuracy measures showed the most change over time. Reports written on Day 5 were more accurate than those written on Day 1. Both editing and reformulations led to similar gains in accuracy in the short term (see Table 20.1). However, when we compared accuracy scores on Day 5 with mean accuracy scores on Day 28, we found that the gains were more enduring for the students who received reformulations.

Table 20.1 Mean accuracy scores on Day 1, 5 and 28

	Day 1	Day 5	Day 28
Reformulation			
Error-free T units per T unit	51.47	66.43	61.46
Error-free clauses per clause	60.44	75.11	68.79
Editing			
Error-free T units per T unit	54.47	68.22	58.37
Error-free clauses per clause	64.02	74.74	66.84

Analysis of the pair talk transcripts showed that LREs dealt with a range of grammatical (and lexical) items, not limited to the items which received corrective feedback, and a large proportion (over 75%) of the LREs were resolved correctly. More importantly, editing seemed to generate a larger number of LREs than reformulations, particularly during the processing session on day 5, and these LREs tended to be longer (see Table 20.2).

Table 20.2 LREs generated on Day 5

	No. of LREs	Multi turn LREs	%
Reformulation			
Processing	134	98	73.13
Rewriting	225	187	83.11
Total	*359*	*285*	*79.38*
Editing			
Processing	190	159	83.68
Rewriting	220	206	93.64
Total	*410*	*365*	*89.02*

We were somewhat puzzled by our findings: editing generated greater attention to form (as evident by the larger number and lengthier LREs) than reformulations, yet the impact of reformulation on writing accuracy seemed longer lasting. A closer analysis of the learner talk provided a possible explanation. The analysis revealed that a number of pairs who received reformulations proceeded to memorize and reproduce the reformulated text. These findings suggest that we may need to re-examine the role of memorization in second language acquisition (see also Lantolf & Thorne 2006). Furthermore, these findings highlight the need to consider qualitative data very carefully.

Conclusion

For students interested in doing research on grammar, particularly those who are or plan to become language teachers, the most pressing research topics concern the most effective ways (in terms of tasks and feedback) of teaching grammar. Future studies on tasks need to consider not only how much attention to grammar different tasks generate but also the quality of students' language output (oral or written) when completing such tasks. We also need to investigate whether learners' interactions and engagement with grammar lead to improved grammatical ability by using tests of implicit grammatical knowledge. Such tests should require learners to produce extended speaking or writing, although admittedly when writing, learners are likely to draw on both their implicit and explicit knowledge (Williams 2012). Furthermore, future research on CF needs to investigate the impact of feedback on learners at different levels of L2 proficiency, whether CF may be more effective on some grammatical structures than on others, for some learners more so than for others and the effect of feedback on grammatical accuracy in the long term, as effects may not be apparent immediately. Given rapid developments in online technology, there is also a need to investigate the efficacy and impact of different forms of online delivery of CF (e.g. Sagarra & Abbuhl 2013).

In terms of research methodology, we need studies which collect different types of data (e.g. learners' output, interviews, think-aloud protocols) and analyse data using quantitative and qualitative analyses. Whereas quantitative analysis can employ various measures of grammatical and syntactic complexity, qualitative analysis should also consider learners' engagement with the feedback. Case studies (see Casanave this volume; Storch & Wigglesworth 2010a, b) may be particularly appropriate as they would enable researchers to collect rich, detailed data on the feedback provided, on how learners engage with the feedback and on learners' goals and attitudes to the feedback. Such studies could provide researchers and teachers with clearer insights and explanations about the efficacy of different forms of grammar instruction and corrective feedback. Furthermore, to date, studies on tasks and task implementation as well as on feedback have tended to be conducted largely in ESL and EFL contexts. There is clearly a need for research on grammar in classes that teach languages other than English.

Note

1   The study was funded by an Australian Research Council Discovery Grant # DP 0450422 awarded to Wigglesworth, G and Storch, N (2004–2006).

Resources for further reading

Bitchener, J & Ferris, D 2012, *Written Corrective Feedback in Second Language Acquisition and Writing*, Routledge, New York, NY.

The book addresses controversies regarding written CF by looking at two distinct strands of research into this topic: Second Language Acquisition (SLA) and L2 writing perspectives. The book discusses these perspectives under three overarching themes: theory, research and practice. It is relevant to both L2 researches and teachers. It provides clear directions for research and practical suggestions for implementing CF in the L2 classroom.

Ellis, R 2006, 'Current issues in the teaching of grammar: An SLA perspective', *TESOL Quarterly*, vol. 40, no. 1, pp. 83–107.

This article considers eight key questions relating to grammar pedagogy. These questions include, for example, what grammatical structures to teach, at what L2 proficiency grammar instruction should be introduced and whether to integrate grammar into communicative activities or to teach it separately. In discussing the questions, Ellis provides insights from theory and research and highlights issues which require further investigation.

Ellis, R & Barkhuizen, G 2005, *Analysing Learner Language*, Oxford University Press, Oxford.

This book is particularly useful for those wishing to analyse language output. It describes different types of analyses that can be undertaken, different measures that can be employed to assess grammatical accuracy and complexity and provides concrete examples of such analyses and measures.

Nassaji, H & Fotos, S 2011, *Teaching Grammar in Second Language Classrooms: Integrating Form-Focused Instruction in Communicative Contexts*, Routledge, New York, NY.

The book provides a very accessible discussion of various theories in SLA and their stance on grammar instruction as well as a summary of relevant empirical research. It also presents concrete examples of various classroom activities that integrate a focus on grammar and a focus on communication.

Purpura, J 2004, *Assessing Grammar*, Cambridge University Press, Cambridge.

This is a very accessible text which discusses factors which need to be taken into consideration in designing grammar tests. It provides clear examples of various grammar tests and response types.

References

Alegría de La Colina, AA & Garcia Mayo, MP 2007, 'Attention to form across collaborative tasks by low-proficiency learners in an EFL setting', in MP Garcia Mayo (ed.), *Investigating Tasks in Formal Language Learning*, Multilingual Matters, Clevedon, pp. 91–116.

Bailey, N, Madden, C & Krashen, S 1974, 'Is there a "natural sequence" in adult second language learning?', *Language Learning*, vol. 24, no. 2, pp. 235–243.

Bitchener, J 2012, 'A reflection on "the language learning potential" of written CF', *Journal of Second Language Writing*, vol. 21, no. 4, pp. 238–363.

Bitchener, J & Knoch, U 2010a, 'The contribution of written corrective feedback to language development: A ten months investigation', *Applied Linguistics*, vol. 31, no. 2, pp. 193–214.

—————— 2010b, 'Raising the linguistic accuracy levels of advanced L2 writers with written corrective feedback', *Journal of Second Language Writing*, vol. 19, no. 4, pp. 207–217.

Bitchener, J, Yong, S & Cameron, D 2005, 'The effects of different types of corrective feedback on ESL student writing', *Journal of Second Language Writing*, vol. 14, no. 3, pp. 191–205.

Chomsky, N 1976, *Reflections on Language*, Temple Smith, London.

DeKeyser, R 1998, 'Beyond focus on form: Cognitive perspectives on learning and practicing second language grammar', in C Doughty & J Williams (eds), *Focus on Form in Classroom Second Language Acquisition*, Cambridge University Press, New York, NY, pp. 42–63.

—————— 2007, 'Situating the concept of practice', in R DeKeyser (ed.), *Practice in Second Language*, Cambridge University Press, Cambridge, pp. 1–18.

Doughty, C & Varela, E 1998, 'Communicative focus on form', in C Doughty & J Williams (eds), *Focus on Form in Classroom Second Language Acquisition*, Cambridge University Press, Cambridge, pp. 114–138.

Ellis, N 2002, 'Does form-focused instruction affect the acquisition of implicit knowledge?', *Studies in Second Language Acquisition*, vol. 24, no. 2, pp. 223–236.

—————— 2005, 'At the interface: Dynamic interactions of explicit and implicit language knowledge', *Studies in Second Language Acquisition*, vol. 27, no. 2, pp. 305–352.

Ellis, R 2005, 'Measuring implicit and explicit knowledge of a second language: A psychometric study', *Studies in Second Language Acquisition*, vol. 27, no. 2, pp. 141–172.

—————— 2006, 'Current issues in the teaching of grammar: An SLA perspective', *TESOL Quarterly*, vol. 40, no. 1, pp. 83–107.

—————— 2009, 'Measuring implicit and explicit knowledge of a second language', in R Ellis, S Loewen, C Elder, J Philp & H Reinders (eds), *Implicit and Explicit Knowledge in Second Language Learning, Testing and Teaching*, Multilingual Matters, Bristol, pp. 31–64.

—————— 2010, 'A framework for investigating oral and written corrective feedback', *Studies in Second Language Acquisition*, vol. 32, no. s2, pp. 335–349.

Ellis, R & Barkhuizen, G 2005, *Analysing Learner Language*, Oxford University Press, Oxford.

Ellis, R, Basturkmen, H & Loewen, S 2001, 'Learner uptake in communicative ESL lessons', *Language Learning*, vol. 51, no. 2, pp. 281–318.

Ellis, R, Sheen, Y, Murakami, M & Takashima, H 2008, 'The effects of focused and unfocused written corrective feedback in an English as a foreign language context', *System*, vol. 36, no. 3, pp. 353–371.

Ferris, D 1999, 'The case for grammar correction in L2 writing classes: A response to Truscott (1996)', *Journal of Second Language Writing*, vol. 8, no. 1, pp. 1–10.

────── 2004, 'The "grammar correction" debate in L2 writing: Where are we, and where do we go from here? (and what do we do in the meantime ... ?)', *Journal of Second Language Writing*, vol. 13, no. 1, pp. 49–62.

────── 2006, 'Does error feedback help student writers? New evidence on the short- and long-term effects of written error corrections', in K Hyland & F Hyland (eds), *Feedback in Second Language Writing. Contexts and Issues*, Cambridge University Press, Cambridge, pp. 81–104.

────── 2010, 'Second language writing research and written corrective feedback in SLA', *Studies in Second Language Acquisition*, vol. 32, no. 2, pp. 181–201.

Foster, P & Skehan, P 1996, 'The influence of planning and task type on second language performance', *Studies in Second Language Acquisition*, vol. 18, no. 3, pp. 299–323.

Garcia Mayo, MP 2002, 'Interaction in advanced EFL pedagogy: A comparison of form-focused activities', *International Journal of Educational Research*, vol. 37, nos. 3–4, pp. 323–341.

Goo, J & Mackey, A 2013, 'The case against the case against recasts', *Studies in Second Language Acquisition*, vol. 35, no. 1, pp. 127–165.

Harley, B & Swain, M 1984, 'The interlanguage of immersion students and its implications for second language teaching', in A Davies, C Criper & H Howatt (eds), *Interlanguage*, Edinburgh University Press, Edinburgh, pp. 291–311.

Hartshorn, KJ, Evans, NW, Merrill, PF, Sudweeks, RR, Strong-Krause, D & Anderson, NJ 2010, 'Effects of dynamic corrective feedback on ESL writing accuracy', *TESOL Quarterly*, vol. 44, no. 1, pp. 84–109.

Hinkel, E & Fotos, S (eds), 2002, *New Perspectives on Grammar Teaching in Second Language Classrooms*, Lawrence Erlbaum, Mahwah, NJ.

Hunt, K 1966, 'Recent measures in syntactic development', *Elementary English*, vol. 43, no. 7, pp. 732–739.

Knoch, U, Rouhshad, A & Storch, N 2014, 'Does the writing of undergraduate ESL students develop after one year of study in an English-medium university?', *Assessing Writing*, vol. 21, no. 1, pp. 1–17.

Krashen, S 1981, *Second Language Acquisition and Second Language Learning*, Oxford University Press, Oxford.

────── 1993, 'The effects of grammar teaching: Still peripheral', *TESOL Quarterly*, vol. 27, no. 4, pp. 717–725.

Lantolf, JP & Thorne, SL 2006, *Sociocultural Theory and the Genesis of Second Language Development*, Oxford University Press, Oxford.

Leeser, MJ 2004, 'Learner proficiency and focus on form during collaborative dialogue', *Language Teaching Research*, vol. 8, no. 1, pp. 55–81.

Lightbown, P 1991, 'What have we here? Some observations on the influence of instruction on L2 learning', in R Philipson, E Kellerman, L Selinker, M Sharwood Smith & M Swain (eds), *Foreign Language Pedagogy Research: A Commemorative Volume for Claus Faerch*, Multilingual Matters, Clevedon, pp. 197–212.

Loewen, S 2005, 'Incidental focus on form and second language learning', *Studies in Second Language Acquisition*, vol. 27, no. 3, pp. 361–386.

Long, M 1991, 'Focus on form: A design feature in language teaching methodology', in K DeBot, R Ginsberg & C Kramsch (eds), *Foreign Language Research in Cross-Cultural Perspectives*, John Benjamins, Amsterdam, pp. 39–52.

——1996, 'The role of the linguistic environment in second language acquisition', in C Ritchie & TK Bhatia (eds), *Handbook of Language Acquisition: Second Language Acquisition*, Volume 2, Academic Press, New York, NY, pp. 413–468.

Lyster, R 2004, 'Differential effects of prompts and recasts in form-focused instruction', *Studies in Second Language Acquisition*, vol. 26, no. 3, pp. 399–432.

Lyster, R & Ranta, L 1997, 'Corrective feedback and learner uptake', *Studies in Second Language Acquisition*, vol. 19, no. 1, pp. 37–66.

—— 2013, 'Counterpoint piece: The case for variety in corrective feedback research', *Studies in Second Language Acquisition*, vol. 35, no. 1, pp. 167–184.

Lyster, R & Saito, K 2010, 'Oral feedback in classroom SLA: A meta-analysis', *Studies in Second Language Acquisition*, vol. 32, no. s2, pp. 265–302.

Mackey, A & Philp, J 1998, 'Conversational interaction and second language development: Recasts, responses and red herrings', *The Modern Language Journal*, vol. 82, no. 3, pp. 338–356.

Nakahama, Y, Tyler, A & Van Lier, L 2001, 'Negotiation of meaning in conversational and information gap activities: A comparative discourse analysis', *TESOL Quarterly*, vol. 35, no. 3, pp. 377–432.

Nassaji, H & Fotos, S 2011, *Teaching Grammar in Second Language Classrooms. Integrating Form-Focused Instruction in Communicative Contexts.* Routledge, New York, NY.

Norris, J & Ortega, L 2000, 'Effectiveness of L2 instruction: A research synthesis and quantitative meta-analysis', *Language Learning*, vol. 50, no. 3, pp. 417–428.

Ohta, A 2000, 'Rethinking recasts: A learner-centered examination of corrective feedback in the Japanese language classroom', in JK Hall & LS Verplaetse (eds), *Second and Foreign Learning Through Classroom Interaction.* Lawrence Erlbaum, Mahwah, NJ, pp. 47–72.

Panova, I & Lyster, R 2002, 'Patterns of corrective feedback and uptake in an adult ESL classroom', *TESOL Quarterly*, vol. 36, no. 4, pp. 573–595.

Pica, T, Kanagy, R & Falodun, J 1993, 'Choosing and using communication tasks for second language instruction and research', in G Crookes & S Gass (eds), *Task and Language Learning*, Multilingual Matters, Clevedon, pp. 9–34.

Purpura, J 2004, *Assessing Grammar*, Cambridge University Press, Cambridge.

—— 2012, 'Assessment of grammar', in C Chapelle (ed.), *The Encyclopaedia of Applied Linguistics*, Wiley-Blackwell, Malden, MA.

Sagarra, N & Abbuhl, R 2013, 'Optimizing the noticing of recasts via computer-delivered feedback: Evidence that oral input enhancement and working memory help second language learning', *The Modern Language Journal*, vol. 97, no. 1, pp. 196–216.

Schmidt, R 1990, 'The role of consciousness in second language learning', *Applied Linguistics*, vol. 11, no. 2, pp. 129–158.

Schwartz, B 1993, 'On explicit and negative data effecting and affecting competence and linguistic behaviour', *Studies in Second Language Acquisition*, vol. 15, no. 2, pp. 147–163.

Sheen, Y 2011, *Corrective Feedback, Individual Differences and Second Language Learning*, Springer, New York, NY.

Shintani, N & Ellis, R 2013, 'The comparative effect of direct written corrective feedback and metalinguistic explanation on learners' explicit and implicit knowledge of the English indefinite article', *Journal of Second Language Writing*, vol. 22, no. 3, pp. 286–306.

Storch, N 1998, 'Comparing second language learners' attention to form across tasks', *Language Awareness*, vol. 7, no. 4, pp. 176–191.

—— 2002, 'Patterns of interaction in ESL pair work', *Language Learning*, vol. 52, no. 1, pp. 119–158.

—— 2005, 'Collaborative writing: Product, process and students' reflections', *Journal of Second Language Writing*, vol. 14, no. 3, pp. 153–173.

—— 2007, 'Development of L2 writing after a semester of study in an Australian University', *Indonesian Journal of English Language Teaching*, vol. 2, no. 2, pp. 173–189.

—— 2008, 'Metatalk in a pair work activity: Level of engagement and implications for language development', *Language Awareness*, vol. 17, no. 2, pp. 97–114.

—— 2010, 'Critical feedback on written corrective feedback,' *International Journal of English Studies*, vol. 10, no. 2, pp. 29–46.

—— 2013, *Collaborative Writing in L2 Classrooms*, Multilingual Matters, Bristol.

Storch, N & Aldosari, A 2010, 'Learners' use of L1 (Arabic) in pair work activity in an EFL class', *Language Teaching Research*, vol. 14, no. 4, pp. 355–376.

—— 2013,'Pairing learners in pair-work activity', *Language Teaching Research*, vol. 17, no. 1, pp. 31–48.

Storch, N & Wigglesworth, G 2010a, 'Learners' processing, uptake, and retention of corrective feedback on writing. Case studies', *Studies in Second Language Acquisition*, vol. 32, no. s2, pp. 303–334.

—— 2010b, 'Students' engagement with feedback on writing: The role of learner agency/beliefs', in R Batstone (ed.), *Sociocognitive Perspectives on Language Use and Language Learning*, Oxford University Press, Oxford, pp. 166–185.

Swain, M (2000), 'The output hypothesis and beyond: Mediating acquisition through collaborative dialogue', in JP Lantolf (ed.), *Sociocultural Theory and Second Language Learning*, Oxford University Press, Oxford, pp. 97–114.

—— (2010), 'Talking it through': Languaging as a source of learning', in R Batstone (ed.), *Sociocognitive Perspectives on Language Use and Language Learning*, Oxford University Press, Oxford, pp. 112–130.

Swain, M & Lapkin, S 1998, 'Interaction and second language learning: Two adolescent French immersion students working together', *The Modern Language Journal*, vol. 82, no. 3, pp. 320–337.

—— 2001, 'Focus on form through collaborative dialogue: Exploring task effects', in M Bygate, P Skehan & M Swain (eds), *Researching Pedagogic Tasks: Second Language Learning, Teaching and Testing*, Longman, London, pp. 99–118.

—— 2003, 'Talking it through: Two French immersion learners' response to reformulation', *International Journal of Educational Research*, vol. 37, nos. 3–4, pp. 285–304.

Truscott, J 1996, 'The case against grammar correction in L2 writing classes', *Language Learning*, vol. 46, no. 2, pp. 327–369.

———— 1999, 'The case for "the case against grammar correction in L2 classes": A response to Ferris', *Journal of Second Language Writing*, vol. 8, no. 2, pp. 111–122.

———— 2007, 'The effect of error correction on learners' ability to write accurately', *Journal of Second Language Writing*, vol. 16, no. 4, pp. 255–272.

Van Beuningen, CG, De Jong, NH & Kuiken, F 2012, 'Evidence on the effectiveness of comprehensive error correction in second language writing', *Language Learning*, vol. 62, no. 1, pp. 1–41.

Vygotsky, LS 1986, *Thought and Language*, MIT Press, Cambridge, MA.

Wajnryb, R 1990, *Grammar Dictation*, Oxford University Press, Oxford.

Williams, J 2012, 'The potential role(s) of writing in second language development', *Journal of Second Language Writing*, vol. 21, no. 4, pp. 321–331.

Wolf-Quintero, K, Inagaki, S & Kim, H 1998, *Second Language Development in Writing: Measures of Fluency, Accuracy and Complexity*, University of Hawai'i at Manoa, Honolulu.

CHAPTER TWENTY ONE

Researching Vocabulary

David Hirsh

Vocabulary has become a well-researched area within second language studies, with particular research interest in investigating key questions which could inform the vocabulary learning and teaching process. This chapter will highlight the main lines of inquiry which vocabulary research has to take account of, present research methods and tools associated with good vocabulary research, discuss some key challenges facing vocabulary researchers and conclude by presenting a study which aimed to take account of some of these issues.

Current thinking and related research

This section looks at some of the dominant themes and related studies associated with current thinking in researching vocabulary.

Determining what a word is

A suitable place to begin a discussion of important thinking and research in vocabulary studies is to look at what is a *word*. The current thinking is that words are, from a teaching and learning perspective, most suitably treated as *word families*. A word family is a group of word forms derived from a core word and conveying a core meaning or meanings. Researchers need to deal objectively with what constitutes a word family. Bauer and Nation (1993) provide guidelines for determining word family membership in the form of commonly occurring, productive and regular inflexed and derived forms which a language learner could reasonably be expected to recognize when applied to a word they already know. The guidelines would group *contribute*, *contributes*, *contributed*, *contributing*, *contribution*, *contributions*, *contributor* and *contributors* into one word family. Examples of some commonly used inflexed and derived forms appear in Figure 21.1.

Inflexed forms	Derived forms	
-- s	un --	-- ity
-- ed	pre --	-- ness
-- ing	anti --	-- ful

FIGURE 21.1 *Common inflexed and derived forms (Bauer & Nation 1993, pp. 253–279)*

Schmitt and Zimmerman (2002) tested the extent to which knowledge of one member of a word family facilitates easy recognition of other members of the family, with a particular interest in productive uses of words. They found that knowledge of other word family members was linked to familiarity with derived forms and that knowledge of derived forms increased with general language proficiency. Mochizuki and Aizawa (2000) were similarly interested in knowledge of affixes (synonymous with derived forms here) and found moderate correlations between the vocabulary size of second language learners and their knowledge of prefixes (0.58) and suffixes (0.54).

Conditions for vocabulary learning

Another major issue for vocabulary researchers is how words are learnt. There is some contention regarding the merits of direct learning of vocabulary as opposed to incidental learning, where the learning is not deliberate but rather through exposure to and use of language. The backdrop for this debate is studies which have examined conditions which promote vocabulary learning and strategies that enhance vocabulary learning and retention (see Laufer & Hulstijn 2001). The debate over the merits of direct learning will continue, with recent research indicating that direct vocabulary learning can be an effective means of vocabulary learning (see Elgort 2013). Nation (2001) sees an important role for both incidental learning and direct learning of vocabulary in second language programs and makes the important point that, in both cases, the quality of learning is dependent upon what happens when a new word is met.

Nation (2001) has identified three key conditions which increase the quality of vocabulary learning in the case of direct learning. These are *noticing, spaced retrieval* and *generative use. Noticing* highlights the need for the learner to focus on a new word as a specific language learning goal; *spaced retrieval* highlights the value of recalling the new word's meaning at a later time; and *generative use* highlights the importance of using a newly learned word productively in writing or speaking. Following this line of inquiry, Godfroid, Boers and Housen (2013), using head-mounted eye-tracking equipment with twenty-eight female Dutch-speaking participants, showed that unknown words received more attention than known words.

The quality of both incidental and direct vocabulary learning are conditional on the amount of learner involvement while processing words. Laufer and Hulstijn (2001) have identified three key dimensions which have been linked to learner involvement during incidental vocabulary learning. They are *need* (motivational need to use a new word), *search* (attempt to find the word meaning or form) and *evaluation* (comparison of the new word with known words). The themes of *learner involvement* and *deep processing* are frequent in studies of vocabulary learning and are evident in Laufer and Hulstijn's (2001) *Involvement Load Hypothesis*, which states that the effectiveness of word retention is dependent upon the amount of motivation and cognitive loading associated with the task in which words are learnt. The hypothesis builds on studies such as Newton (1995) which investigated the effect of negotiation of word meaning in group interactive tasks; finding negotiated words were retained better than words not negotiated; and Joe (1995) who investigated the effect of generated use of new words in learner language, finding that generated words were retained better than words not generated.

In related research, Kim (2008) investigated the effect of different levels of task- induced involvement on initial word learning and subsequent word retention and found that tasks which had higher levels of learner involvement resulted in improved initial word learning and improved word retention. Following a similar line of inquiry, Min (2008) investigated the impact of reading and vocabulary-focused activities on vocabulary learning and retention, finding that tasks that induced higher involvement loads resulted in enhanced vocabulary learning and thus greater vocabulary gains over time. More recently, Lee and Hirsh (2012) provided scientific evidence that tasks seen as inducing lower involvement load (such as multiple-choice questions) can result in more effective vocabulary learning and vocabulary retention than tasks seen as inducing higher involvement load (such as sentence writing) in certain learning contexts. This particular study was carried out in a university setting in Taiwan.

Categories of words

Another major issue in vocabulary research is how words are categorized into groups. Not all words are equal when it comes to language use, with common distinctions made between *high frequency* words, *academic* words, *technical* words and *low frequency* words. The 2,000 most frequently occurring words in English, termed high frequency vocabulary, are regarded as critical for communication in English. They provide 90 per cent lexical coverage (the percentage of word occurrences used from this list) of conversation (Nation 2001); up to 90 per cent coverage of fiction (Hirsh & Nation 1992) and about 80 per cent coverage of newspapers (Hwang & Nation 1989); and are widely accepted as the starting point for second language vocabulary learning.

Beyond high frequency words, research has focused on specialized groups of words. Academic vocabulary occurs frequently in academic texts across a range of subject areas. Technical words are associated with specific subject areas. A further category, low frequency words, is a default term describing words which do not appear frequently in a text or sample of language being looked at. Many specialized technical terms would be regarded as low frequency when occurring in contexts outside their subject area. Technical vocabulary is a relatively under-researched area in light of its important role in specialized reading (see Chung & Nation 2003).

Vocabulary size

A further important issue for vocabulary researchers is counting and grouping words: the number of words in English, the most useful words for different communicative tasks and the vocabulary size of groups of users. This has identified thresholds for effective language use and has given rise to the concept of a vocabulary gap in second language learning.

One line of inquiry has examined vocabulary size for first and second language users. Goulden et al. (1990) estimate that there are 117,000 word families in English, of which their participant group of English as a first language university students knew on average 17,200, suggesting acquisition of 1,000 new words during each year of schooling and a very large number of words never learnt and in many cases never met in spoken or written language. A considerably lower vocabulary size of 1,200 word families was determined by Nurweni and Read (1999) for a group of second language college students in Indonesia.

Another line of inquiry has examined the vocabulary size required for specific uses of language. Studies of this type have assumed that, although a language user needs to be familiar with 95 per cent of the words in a spoken or written text (i.e. nineteen out of twenty word occurrences) for satisfactory comprehension (Laufer 1989), closer to 98 per cent of the words (i.e., forty-nine out of fifty) is required for more pleasurable and effective language use (Hu & Nation 2000). Below the 95 per cent threshold, there is likely to be inadequate familiar language for the meaning of unknown words to be determined based on contextual clues. Laufer (1992) identified a turning point in second language reading comprehension occurring at the 3,000 word level, suggesting this as a minimum threshold for reading. Nation (2006), aiming for 98 per cent lexical coverage, estimated 6,000–7,000 word families required for listening to movies and discussions and 8,000–9,000 word families required for reading novels and newspapers. A middle-ground benchmark of 4,000 word families has been suggested (see Alderson 2007).

Researchers have sought to identify stages of vocabulary knowledge beyond the 2,000 word list to address the vocabulary gap between second language vocabulary size and the vocabulary required for effective use of English in different contexts. The focus has largely been on prioritizing, that is to identify the words that provide the best return in terms of comprehension and communicative quality. Studies of this type have examined word occurrence in specific uses of English to identify core vocabularies.

A series of studies have focused on the vocabulary of academic study as one area of language learning. One approach has been to identify commonly used academic words. Coxhead (2000) identified 570 candidates for an Academic Word List, representing words occurring frequently in first-year undergraduate reading in a broad range of subject areas. Another approach has been to identify the vocabulary for specific areas of study. Ward (1999) followed this approach to identify the most useful vocabulary for reading undergraduate engineering texts, Coxhead and Hirsh (2007) developed a word list for science students, and, more recently, Hsu (2013) constructed a Medical Word List designed to bridge the gap between non-technical and technical vocabulary. These approaches represent targeted vocabulary lists which would provide good return for learning effort for specific groups of learners.

Aside from interest in vocabulary gaps and growth, there is research interest in vocabulary loss (or attrition). The study of vocabulary attrition for participants no longer using a language draws on data collected at intervals of months or even years to chart a pattern of lexical loss over time. Min (2008) found significant vocabulary loss three months after language instruction ended, with indications that most receptive and productive word knowledge became partially known words, suggesting that only formal knowledge of most target vocabulary is retained. Related to this line of inquiry is interest in how words are stored in memory, and the impact loss of one word has on the recall and use of other words (see Meara 2004) and mirrors interest in how knowledge of one word impacts on the learning of others (see Laufer 1990). This view of vocabulary knowledge as interrelated challenges the more simplistic methodologies based on the counting of isolated word items.

Receptive and productive knowledge

There are two remaining issues to be highlighted here for vocabulary researchers. The first concerns the widely accepted view that people know more words than they use. A clear distinction is made in vocabulary research between receptive and productive vocabulary knowledge (see Laufer 1998). Receptive knowledge of words relates to word recognition in written and spoken texts, and tests of receptive vocabulary knowledge assess the ability to attach a meaning to a word in written form or to transcribe words presented in oral language. Productive knowledge of words relates to word use in meaningful contexts, either written or spoken.

Tests of receptive and productive vocabulary knowledge measure different forms of word knowledge and require different units of measurement (Nation, personal communication, 18 April 2008). It can be assumed that receptive knowledge of a word form or type (e.g. *succeed*) indicates receptive knowledge of other members of the word family (i.e. *succeeds, success, successes, succeeding, succeeded, successfully, unsuccessful, unsuccessfully*). Productive knowledge, on the other hand, concerns retrieval from memory of a single word type (or *lemma*). It cannot be assumed that productive knowledge of one word form indicates productive knowledge of other word forms in the word family. This is because people do not productively use all the words they know. Thus, while measures of receptive knowledge should count and report in *word family* units, productive knowledge measures should count and report in *word type* units.

The company words keep

The final issue to be discussed here regarding vocabulary research is how words appear in the language. Vocabulary lists present words in isolation, detached from meaningful contexts and the words they appear commonly with in spoken or written language. In contrast, concordance data displays words in context, with scope through use of corpora to focus on a word's use in specific contexts. A researcher could examine how a word is commonly used in a particular kind of text (e.g. newspapers) or in a particular subject area (e.g. nursing). Differences between spoken and written uses of a word can be examined, as can differences in word use between groups of language users. The range of data available depends on the nature of the corpus and the complexity of the word analysis programs used. One line of inquiry in this area is the investigation of *lexical bundles*, or recurring multiword sequences, also referred to as *lexical phrases* and *lexical chunking*. Lexical bundles are frequently occurring sequences of words such as *has to do with, one of the things* and *you're never going to believe this*, differing from idiomatic expressions such as *in a nutshell*, and assuming important discourse functions in the language (see Biber & Barbieri 2007).

Research stages and related test instruments

This section looks at a sample of research tools and test instruments associated with some of the main lines of inquiry in vocabulary research.

Investigating depth of vocabulary knowledge

One test instrument draws on elements of Nation's (2001) well-established model of word knowledge at three levels: *form* (spelling, sound, word parts), *meaning* (associations) and *use* (grammar, collocations, constraints on use). Read (1998) developed a word associates test to allow investigation of the semantic associations between words, as an indicator of depth of word knowledge. This tool focuses on identifying words with a meaning associated with a target word item, and requires test-takers to select suitable responses from those provided. Distractor items which have no association with the target word are included in the possible choices. An example of this test format is provided in Figure 21.2.

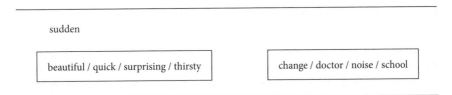

sudden

| beautiful / quick / surprising / thirsty | | change / doctor / noise / school |

FIGURE 21.2 *Sample item from the word associates test (adapted from Read 1998, p. 46)*

In the example given in Figure 21.2, knowledge of word associations for the target word *sudden* is being tested. In this test format, the group of four adjectives in the left hand box includes two words which are synonyms of the target word or represent one aspect of the target word meaning (e.g. *sudden-quick*; *sudden-surprising*), and two distractor items. The group of four nouns in the right hand box includes two collocates of the target word, meaning that the two words occur together frequently in the language (e.g. *sudden change*; *sudden noise*), and two distractor items.

Investigating vocabulary demands for specific uses

Computer-based programs can be used to examine the lexical demands of communicative tasks such as reading, writing or listening, by determining how many words are required for the task. Research in this area involves preparing an electronic version of a text, spoken or written, to be analysed, and examining word occurrence in the text using a computer program. *Range* (Heatley & Nation 1998) is a program designed to list words and their frequency of occurrence in a text according to word family lists: the 1,000 most frequently occurring words in English; the second 1,000 most frequently occurring words; and academic words. Words occurring in a text which are not from these three word lists are reported as *other words*. An example of a results summary for a sample of text produced by a second language writer using Range appears in Figure 21.3.

Word list	Percentage coverage
one (first 1,000 words)	72
two (second 1,000 words)	4
three (academic words)	10
other words	14
Total	100

FIGURE 21.3 *Lexical profile of a sample of second language writing*

Figure 21.3 shows how Range has been used to statistically present word use in the text, indicating that 72 per cent of all words in the text were words from the first 1,000 word level, while 4 per cent of words were from the second 1,000 word level and 10 per cent of words in the text were academic words. The combined lexical coverage of high frequency (the first and second thousand words) and academic vocabulary for a text is the added values for these three levels, in this case 86 per cent. The remaining 14 per cent of words shown in Figure 21.3 as *other words* could be misspelt words, proper nouns, technical words related to the subject area of the text or low frequency words.

Investigating vocabulary size

A series of test instruments have been developed to enable researchers to reliably investigate how many words a group of language users know. Tests tend to distinguish between receptive vocabulary knowledge and productive vocabulary knowledge, with tests developed to measure productive vocabulary knowledge in both controlled (measurement of correct elicitation of target items) and free (no specific target items being elicited) formats. This gives rise to three widely used formats for vocabulary size measurement: receptive, controlled productive and free productive (see Laufer 1998) as presented in Figure 21.4.

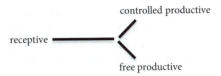

FIGURE 21.4 *Types of vocabulary knowledge (adapted from Zhong 2008, p. 13)*

A test instrument designed to measure receptive vocabulary size is the *Vocabulary Levels Test* (Nation 1983). This employs a word-meaning format to assess word meaning recognition at five word levels: 2,000, 3,000, 5,000, 10,000 and academic words. An example of a test item from the 2,000 word section of a version of this test format appears in Figure 21.5.

Choose the right word to go with each meaning. Write the number of that word next to its meaning.

    1. copy

    2. event   ___ end or highest point

    3. motor   ___ this moves a car

    4. pity   ___ thing made to be like another

    5. profit

    6. tip

FIGURE 21.5 *Sample of the 2,000 word section of the Vocabulary Levels Test (adapted from Schmitt, Schmitt & Clapham 2001, p. 82)*

A test instrument designed to measure productive vocabulary knowledge in a controlled format is the *Controlled Productive Vocabulary Levels Test* (Laufer & Nation 1999). This assesses the ability to complete the missing letters in a target word presented in a sentence at five word levels: 2,000, 3,000, 5,000, 10,000 and academic vocabulary. An example of a test item from the 2,000 word section appears in Figure 21.6.

Complete the underlined words.

1. I'm glad we had this opp_____ to talk.

FIGURE 21.6 *Sample of the 2,000 word section of the Controlled Productive Vocabulary Levels Test (adapted from Laufer & Nation 1999, p. 46)*

A tool designed to measure lexical richness in a student's writing is the *Lexical Frequency Profile* (Laufer & Nation 1995). This instrument statistically compares the proportion of high frequency words and academic words in a sample of writing through computer analysis of word use in the text.

Another test instrument designed to measure productive vocabulary knowledge in a free way is Lex30 (Meara & Fitzpatrick 2000). In this test, participants are instructed to list words associated with a high frequency prompt word. All the words produced by an individual test-taker are examined in terms of word frequency, that is, the proportion of words within and outside the 2,000 word list, to indicate lexical richness. An example of words listed by a test-taker which are associated with the target word *attack* are indicated in Figure 21.7. These words are *war, castle, guns* and *armour*, indicating that the test-taker thought of these words when prompted by the target word.

---

1. attack: war, castle, guns, armour

FIGURE 21.7 *Lex30 test item and sample answers (adapted from Meara & Fitzpatrick 2000, p. 28)*

New methodologies in vocabulary size assessment will continue to be developed in the search for more robust reporting.

Investigating vocabulary growth

Methodologies have been developed to allow researchers to investigate how many words are learnt or acquired during a certain period, such as a semester or a year of study. Two main approaches have been used. One approach is to compare the vocabulary size of groups of learners representing different stages of learning, such as the fifth (grade 5) and sixth (grade 6) years of schooling, in the same learning environment. Laufer (1998) used this approach in a study of the productive vocabulary knowledge growth of grade 10 (aged 16 years) and grade 11 (aged 17 years) second language high school students in Israel. Another approach is to collect data from one group of learners at two different stages of learning (e.g. 12 weeks apart) using a pre-test and post-test format. Horst and Collins (2006) used this approach at intervals of 100 hours of instruction with second language elementary school students in Quebec. In either approach, decisions need to be made on which vocabulary knowledge test instruments (receptive, controlled productive or free productive) to employ.

Investigating strategies in vocabulary learning and vocabulary use

An area of vocabulary research which has involved rich data collection is strategy use, with the focus largely on determining which vocabulary learning strategies are associated with effective vocabulary learning and effective vocabulary use. Methodologies used in such studies include *participant questionnaires*, focusing on strategies used and their effectiveness, *student logs*, comprising written reflections of strategy use while reading and *think-aloud protocols*, where participants explain processes as they use the language.

Gu (2003) investigated vocabulary strategy use of two successful adult English as a foreign language learners at three stages of an intensive reading task: meeting new words, committing words to memory and use of new words. The study was designed to determine which strategies were used by participants as they encountered new words in a text on pollution in Athens which, it was estimated by the researcher, contained about one new word in fifty (i.e. the participants would know 98 per cent of the words in the text). Think-aloud protocols and follow-up interviews were used to focus on task-specific as well as more general vocabulary learning strategy use. The findings indicated that both learners displayed high levels of motivation to learn new words and employed a wide range of metacognitive and cognitive strategies. Metacognitive strategy use included self-initiation to learn beyond what was required, conscious selection of strategy use and applying criteria such as relevance, interest and importance in selecting words to learn. Cognitive strategy use included using contextual clues, negotiating between dictionary meaning and contextual meaning and using newly learnt words productively.

Analysis of lexical bundles

The last type of research tool discussed here is concerned with studies of how individual words are used in different linguistic contexts. While vocabulary lists present words in isolation, research on lexical bundles explores the way words are used in the language, with particular interest in identifying recurring groups of words which could be used as a model for language learners and language assessment. Research of this type requires access to a corpus of language and appropriate software. The focus for the research will indicate the type of corpus and program required and the parameters of the analysis. Oxford Wordsmith Tools (Oxford University Press 2008) is one program available to researchers which reports concordance data from which recurring lexical bundles could be identified. An example of data from a concordance results file for *issue* appears in Figure 21.8.

social and economic issues
public moral issues
environmental issues
the key issues

FIGURE 21.8 *Concordance data on the word issue (adapted from Thurstun & Candlin 1997, p. 2)*

Challenges associated with vocabulary research

Vocabulary researchers are faced with some predictable challenges, each with appropriate responses. One challenge inherent in research involving participants is minimizing the effect of participant reorientation to suit the study focus or goals. Reorientation, in this sense, describes the process of study participants temporarily changing their behaviour because of the study. This is called the *Hawthorne Effect* (Landsberger 1958) and can occur if information about the study is shared with learners prior to or during collection of data. Studies of vocabulary learning strategy use and classroom vocabulary learning would be particularly susceptible to reorientation on the part of language learners and their teachers. There is an ethical requirement for informed and voluntary participation in studies of this type. Careful consideration should thus be placed to the information being shared with the participants (e.g. learners) and their teachers and the timing of this.

When using parallel pre-tests and post-tests, preventive measures to minimize the impact of the pre-test on subsequent vocabulary learning can include: collection of all copies of pre-tests; not communicating test results with participants or teachers during the survey period between the two sets of tests (pre and post); and not indicating to participants or teachers the relationship between the pre-tests and post-tests.

Another challenge in studies of participant vocabulary knowledge relates to the use of test instruments and the data they generate. Researchers face dual concerns of sampling a sufficient number of vocabulary items to address reliability and validity needs while minimizing the effect of participant test fatigue. Vocabulary levels tests sampling receptive knowledge at five levels of vocabulary (2,000, 3,000, 5,000, 10,000 and academic vocabulary) and including thirty test items per vocabulary level can be completed within 30 minutes. This test format represents a response to these dual concerns.

A further challenge in vocabulary research can occur in the measurement of vocabulary growth. Such studies use pre-tests and post-tests to indicate changes in performance on the test instruments. These tests need to be comparable in what they test and how they test it, in order for meaningful comparisons to be made. Use of test instruments in longitudinal studies of vocabulary growth should be subject to reliability assessment, particularly where multiple versions of a test format are used on the assumption that the test versions are parallel – that is, that they measure similar aspects of knowledge at a similar level. Xing and Fulcher (2007) have indicated that the 2,000, 3,000 and academic vocabulary levels of two different versions of the receptive vocabulary levels test are highly correlated – that is they can be used reliably in a parallel format but that the 5,000 word-level versions are not parallel (i.e. one version is more difficult) and thus are in need of revision.

A sample study

I have selected a vocabulary study to show how it took account of a number of issues, methods and challenges in the research design. The study (Zhong 2008) was conducted by one of my research students, Hua Zhong. She was interested in investigating vocabulary learning in a high school setting in China, employing pre-tests and post-tests for a single group of participants. The constraints of the study period restricted the duration of the study period to 10 weeks. She was interested in both receptive and productive knowledge of words at four word levels (2,000, 3,000, 5,000 and academic vocabulary). The study built on earlier findings that receptive and productive vocabulary knowledge grows at different rates (see Laufer 1998).

The study dealt with a series of methodological issues. It employed the use of identical pre-tests and post-tests, and thus one key concern was to ensure that the pre-tests had minimal impact on the English language learning program during the 10-week study period. The test instruments used were the receptive vocabulary levels test (Nation 1983) and controlled productive vocabulary levels test (Laufer & Nation 1999). A pilot test was conducted to determine which test items in these two test instruments would be suitable for the selected group of learners in terms of content and language level. Marking criteria were developed to ensure reliability and objectivity in making decisions on whether partial words were satisfactorily completed in the controlled productive vocabulary levels test. Procedures for data analysis were developed and pilot tested to ensure findings were empirically sound. Each of these issues is discussed.

One feature of the study was its longitudinal nature, conducted during 10 weeks of the school semester. It was decided that vocabulary learning during this 10-week period could be measured most accurately if the pre-tests and post-tests were the same, and analysis was made of one group of learners at two stages of their learning. The thinking was that if data from the pre-tests and post-tests were fully comparable, then differences between the test scores could be used as indicators of vocabulary learning.

It was realized that the study participants and their teacher could not be told about the relationship between the pre-tests and post-tests until the completion of the study, for fear of the pre-tests being regarded as a vocabulary learning goal for the subsequent 10 weeks. As preventive measures, the researcher ensured that all copies of the pre-tests were collected and that no pre-test results were passed on to the teacher or research participants until completion of the study.

Another feature of the study was its focus on a homogenous study population of high school students learning English as a foreign language in China. The study employed a pilot test with a small number of Chinese background participants who had a similar language proficiency to the main participant group. The pilot test was designed to check that the test instruments were appropriate for this participant group in terms of content and language level. The pilot test indicated which test items were unsuitable, and which word levels of the existing test instruments (2,000, 3,000, 5,000, 10,000 and academic words) would be applicable to the study and in particular whether the 10,000 word level should be used. It became clear that the 10,000 level would be unlikely to generate any useful data due to anticipated low levels of both initial vocabulary knowledge and subsequent vocabulary learning over 10 weeks for this participant group.

The pilot test was also used to generate a small amount of raw data which the researcher used to refine procedures for ensuring objectivity in marking decisions in the case of the controlled productive vocabulary levels test where variable answers were possible for each test item. Guidelines were developed and tested to standardize marking decisions to take account of differences in the spelling and grammatical form (e.g. singular or plural noun forms) of target vocabulary items. Minor spelling mistakes and grammatical errors were ignored on this basis: for spelling, one missing, added or wrong letter per word or two adjacent letters in the wrong order were ignored; for grammar, errors in suffix endings involving –ed, –s and –ing were ignored. The intention of the marking guidelines was to focus on vocabulary knowledge while dealing objectively with variations in form and accuracy of productive use.

Another feature of the study was its small participant size for quantitative research. From eighty-three students approached, sixty-four gave their consent to participate in the study indicating a 77.1 per cent participation rate. From this, forty-one participants completed all the required tests allowing their data to be utilized in the study. This indicated a 35.9 per cent attrition rate. The number of participants in the study impacted on the statistical tools to be used in the data analysis. Taking account of the small number of participants, the researcher employed descriptive statistics to describe the trends and patterns evident in the data, in the form of mean scores and ratios. Parametric techniques, widely used to enable generalizations to be made regarding the data, were not used in the study due to the small sample size and to the abnormal distribution of data indicated through descriptive statistics to compare scores for mean, median and mode.

The adjustment of the methodology to suit the study enabled meaningful findings to be generated. They indicated significant levels of useful vocabulary growth, particularly of academic vocabulary, as well as overall higher levels of growth for productive vocabulary knowledge than for receptive vocabulary knowledge during the 10 weeks. The researcher was able to relate the study findings to previous research in the area, having employed similar principles and methodologies to earlier studies of this type while having ensured that issues of reliability and validity were built into the research model.

Resources for further reading

Bogaards, P & Laufer, B (eds), 2004, *Vocabulary in a Second Language*, John Benjamins, Amsterdam.

The editors of this book have assembled eleven chapters, primarily from papers presented at the Second Language Vocabulary Acquisition Colloquium held at Leiden University in 2002. The volume provides a host of new insights into experimental research covering the areas of selection, acquisition and testing of vocabulary.

Nation, ISP 2001, *Learning Vocabulary in Another Language*, Cambridge University Press, Cambridge.

Paul Nation provides a thorough overview of research on vocabulary spanning decades, providing insights on theory and practice, case studies and large-scale empirical studies, which inform contemporary approaches to the teaching and learning of vocabulary.

Read, J 2000, *Assessing Vocabulary*, Cambridge University Press, Cambridge.

This book focuses on a broad range of assessment tools and procedures for investigating vocabulary learning, knowledge and use. The book highlights and evaluates key studies, examines the role of corpus analysis and identifies areas for future research in vocabulary assessment.

Read, J 2013, 'Second language vocabulary assessment', *Language Teaching*, vol. 46, no. 1, pp. 41–52.

This article written by John Read provides a comprehensive timeline spanning 1935 to 2012 of the development and validation of measures to assess the vocabulary knowledge and ability of second language learners.

Nation, ISP & Webb, S 2011, *Researching and Analyzing Vocabulary*, Heinle Cengage Learning, Boston, MA.

Paul Nation and Stuart Webb have provided a comprehensive overview of major areas of research in the field of vocabulary studies, incorporating guidance on carrying out research with particular attention given to classroom learning and teaching.

Schmitt, N 2010, *Researching Vocabulary: A Vocabulary Research Manual*, Palgrave Macmillan, Basingstoke.

In this book, Norbert Schmitt has assembled a comprehensive literature review and how-to guide for researchers in the area of vocabulary studies, including example research projects and vocabulary resources.

Schmitt, N & McCarthy, M (eds), 1997, *Vocabulary: Description, Acquisition and Pedagogy*, Cambridge University Press, Cambridge.

This edited volume presents fifteen papers covering the theory and practice of vocabulary teaching and learning, with relevant chapters on approaches to research in key areas of vocabulary studies such as word knowledge and lexical chunks.

Online resources

Compleat Lexical Tutor, www.lextutor.ca, viewed 2 July 2014.

Tom Cobb has assembled a range of online tools and resources with open access for language researchers, teachers and learners. The site includes vocabulary levels tests, lexical profile software, concordance software with accompanying corpora and information on word lists.

Range, http://www.victoria.ac.nz/lals/about/staff/paul-nation, viewed 2 July 2014.

Range is a computer-based program designed to report on word occurrence in written texts at set vocabulary levels. Paul Nation has provided on his web-page an open-access link to two downloadable versions of Range, each with corresponding word lists and instruction files, including word lists developed from the British National Corpus.

References

Alderson, JC 2007, 'Judging the frequency of English words', *Applied Linguistics*, vol. 26, no. 3, pp. 383–409.

Bauer, L & Nation, P 1993, 'Word families', *International Journal of Lexicography*, vol. 6, no. 4, pp. 253–279.

Biber, D & Barbieri, F 2007, 'Lexical bundles in university spoken and written registers', *English for Specific Purposes*, vol. 26, no. 3, pp. 263–286.

Chung, T & Nation, P 2003, 'Technical vocabulary in specialized texts', *Reading in a Foreign Language*, vol. 15, no. 2, pp. 103–116.

Coxhead, A 2000, 'A new academic word list', *TESOL Quarterly*, vol. 34, no. 2, pp. 213–238.

Coxhead, A & Hirsh, D 2007, 'A pilot science-specific word list', *Revue Française de Linguistique Appliqueé*, vol. 7, no. 2, pp. 65–78.

Elgort, I 2013, 'Deliberate learning and vocabulary acquisition in a second language', *Language Learning*, vol. 61, no. 2, pp. 367–413.

Godfroid, A, Boers, F & Housen, A 2013, 'An eye for words: Gauging the role of attention in incidental L2 vocabulary acquisition by means of eye-tracking', *Studies in Second Language Acquisition*, vol. 35, no. 3, pp. 483–517.

Goulden, R, Nation, P & Read, J 1990, 'How large can a receptive vocabulary be?', *Applied Linguistics*, vol. 11, no. 4, pp. 341–363.

Gu, P 2003, 'Fine brush and freehand: The vocabulary-learning art of two successful Chinese EFL learners', *TESOL Quarterly*, vol. 37, no. 1, pp. 73–104.

Heatley, A & Nation, P 1998, Range, School of Linguistics and Applied Language Studies, Victoria University of Wellington, Wellington, viewed 2 July 2014, http://www.victoria.ac.nz/lals/about/staff/paul-nation

Hirsh, D & Nation, P 1992, 'What vocabulary size is needed to read unsimplified texts for pleasure?', *Reading in a Foreign Language*, vol. 8, no. 2, pp. 689–696.

Horst, M & Collins, L 2006, 'From *faible* to strong: How does their vocabulary grow?', *Canadian Modern Language Review*, vol. 63, no. 1, pp. 83–106.

Hsu, W 2013, 'Bridging the vocabulary gap for EFL medical undergraduates: The establishment of a medical word list', *Language Teaching Research*, vol. 17, no. 4, pp. 454–484.

Hu, M & Nation, P 2000, 'Unknown vocabulary density and reading comprehension', *Reading in a Foreign Language*, vol. 13, no. 1, pp. 403–430.

Hwang, K & Nation, P 1989, 'Reducing the vocabulary load and encouraging vocabulary learning through reading newspapers', *Reading in a Foreign Language*, vol. 6, no. 1, pp. 323–335.

Joe, A 1995, 'Text-based tasks and incidental vocabulary learning', *Second Language Research*, vol. 11, no. 2, pp. 149–158.

Kim, Y 2008, 'The role of task-induced involvement and learner proficiency in L2 vocabulary acquisition', *Language Learning*, vol. 58, no. s1, pp. 285–325.

Landsberger, H 1958, *Hawthorne Revisited: Management and the Worker, Its Critics, and Developments in Human Relations in Industry*, Cornell University, Ithaca, NY.

Laufer, B 1989, 'What percentage of text-lexis is essential for comprehension?', in C Lauren & M Nordman (eds), *Special Language: From Humans Thinking to Thinking Machines*, Multilingual Matters, Clevedon, pp. 316–323.

—— 1990, 'Words you know: How they affect the words you learn', in J Fisiak (ed.), *Further Insights into Contrastive Analysis*, John Benjamins, Amsterdam, pp. 573–593.

—— 1992, 'How much lexis is necessary for reading comprehension?', in P Arnaud & H Bejoint (eds), *Vocabulary and Applied Linguistics*, Macmillan, London, pp. 126–132.

—— 1998, 'The development of passive and active vocabulary in a second language: Same or different?', *Applied Linguistics*, vol. 19, no. 2, pp. 255–271.

Laufer, B & Hulstijn, J 2001, 'Incidental vocabulary acquisition in a second language: The effect of task-induced involvement load', *Applied Linguistics*, vol. 22, no. 3, pp. 1–26.

Laufer, B & Nation, P 1995, 'Vocabulary size and use: Lexical richness in L2 written production', *Applied Linguistics*, vol. 16, no. 3, pp. 307–322.

———— 1999, 'A vocabulary size test of controlled productive ability', *Language Testing*, vol. 16, no. 1, pp. 33–51.

Lee, Y & Hirsh, D 2012, 'Quality and quantity of exposure in L2 vocabulary learning', in D Hirsh (ed.), *Current Perspectives in Second Language Vocabulary Research*, Peter Lang, Bern, pp. 79–116.

Meara, P 2004, 'Modelling vocabulary loss', *Applied Linguistics*, vol. 25, no. 2, pp. 137–155.

Meara, P & Fitzpatrick, T 2000, 'Lex30: An improved method of assessing productive vocabulary in an L2', *System*, vol. 28, no. 1, pp. 19–30.

Min, H 2008, 'EFL vocabulary acquisition and retention: Reading plus vocabulary enhancement activities and narrow reading', *Language Learning*, vol. 58, no. 1, pp. 73–115.

Mochizuki, M & Aizawa, K 2000, 'An affix acquisition order for EFL learners: An exploratory study', *System*, vol. 28, no. 2, pp. 291–304.

Nation, P 1983, 'Testing and teaching vocabulary', *Guidelines*, vol. 5, no. 1, pp. 12–25.

———— 2001, *Learning Vocabulary in Another Language*, Cambridge University Press, Cambridge.

———— 2006, 'How large a vocabulary is needed for reading and listening?', *Canadian Modern Language Review*, vol. 63, no. 1, pp. 59–82.

Newton, J 1995, 'Task-based interaction and incidental vocabulary learning: A case study', *Second Language Research*, vol. 11, no. 2, pp. 159–177.

Nurweni, A & Read, J 1999, 'The English vocabulary knowledge of Indonesian university students', *English for Specific Purposes*, vol. 18, no. 2, pp. 161–175.

Oxford University Press 2008, Oxford Wordsmith Tools 4.0, viewed 2 July 2014, http://www.lexically.net/wordsmith/

Read, J 1998, 'Validating a test to measure depth of vocabulary knowledge', in A Kunnan (ed.), *Validation in Language Assessment*, Erlbaum, Mahwah, NJ, pp. 41–60.

Schmitt, N, Schmitt, D & Clapham, C 2001, 'Developing and exploring the behaviour of two new versions of the Vocabulary Levels Test', *Language Testing*, vol. 18, no. 1, pp. 55–88.

Schmitt, N & Zimmerman, C 2002, 'Derivative word forms: What do learners know?', *TESOL Quarterly*, vol. 36, no. 2, pp. 145–171.

Thurstun, J & Candlin, C 1997, *Exploring Academic English: A Workbook for Student Essay Writing*, National Centre for English Language Teaching and Research, Sydney.

Ward, J 1999, 'How large a vocabulary do EAP engineering students need?', *Reading in a Foreign Language*, vol. 12, no. 2, pp. 309–324.

Xing, P & Fulcher, G 2007, 'Reliability assessment for two versions of vocabulary levels tests', *System*, vol. 35, no. 2, pp. 182–191.

Zhong, H 2008, 'Vocabulary size development: A study of Chinese high school students', MEd TESOL dissertation, University of Sydney, Sydney.

CHAPTER TWENTY TWO

Researching Pragmatics

Carsten Roever

Pragmatics as a field is a broad area and is investigated through an equally wide range of research approaches. The study of pragmatics traditionally focuses on the relationship between language use and context, that is, how features of the external, real-world context are reflected in the language used. Such context incorporates the physical context, which is reflected through deictic expressions (this, there, mine); the interpersonal context, including the interlocutors' shared history and their relationship in terms of acquaintanceship and power differential; and the social context with its rules of appropriate conduct.

Pragmatics research in applied linguistics is mostly concerned with the relationship between language use on the one hand and the social and interpersonal context of interaction on the other. Specifically, the field of cross-cultural pragmatics investigates differences in pragmatics based on first language background, whereas interlanguage pragmatics investigates how second language learners' knowledge and ability for use of target language pragmatics develops.

Research approaches in pragmatics range from the recording of authentic, unelicited discourse, via elicitation of extended discourse or individual utterances to elicitation of metapragmatic knowledge. Some psycholinguistic research has also appeared (Edmonds 2014; Holtgraves 2012; Taguchi 2011, 2013) but it remains a secondary concern.

Typical stages in this research

Stage 1: Which aspect of pragmatics is to be investigated?

The first decision to be made in this research is what aspect of pragmatics to investigate. Traditionally, the major focus has been on speech acts, and of the speech acts investigated, requests (Li 2013; Nguyen & Basturkmen 2013; Salgado 2011; Shively 2011; Takimoto 2012; Wang 2011) and apologies (Adrefiza & Jones 2013; Ho 2013; Sykes 2013) have been the most frequently researched ones. Other speech acts include refusals (Hong 2011; Ren 2012; Taguchi 2011), compliments and compliment responses (Bhatti & Zegarac 2012; Cheng 2011; Maiz-Arevalo 2012), suggestions/ advice (Lee 2010; Li 2010; Park 2012), agreement and disagreement (Houck & Fuji 2013; Malamed 2010), complaints (Chen, Chen & Chang 2011; Do 2013; Ho, Henry & Alkaff, 2012), criticism (Nguyen 2013a, b) and some others.

Of course, pragmatics does not only consist of speech acts but research into other aspects of pragmatics is less common. Politeness has been investigated with and without regard to specific speech acts (Bardovi-Harlig & Dörnyei 1998; Bella 2012; Schauer 2006), and implicature, which describes indirect, implied language use, has also received some attention (Bouton 1988; Roever 2013; Taguchi 2011, 2012). Routine formulae have been more widely investigated (Bardovi-Harlig 2009, 2013; Bardovi-Harlig & Bastos 2011; Roever 2012).

Following critiques of the speech act approach (Kasper 2006; Meier 1998), there has recently been a move away from research on isolated utterances and increasing interest in discursive approach to pragmatics research, influenced by Conversation Analysis (CA; for an introduction, see Sidnell 2010). Rather than focus on head acts of speech acts, this discursive orientation sees requesting, apologizing, disagreeing etc., as social actions that unfold over longer discourse sequences and are co-constructed between interlocutors. This research approach encompasses longitudinal studies as well as cross-sectional work and has looked at requests (Al-Gahtani & Roever 2012, 2013, 2014), disagreement (Dippold 2011; Pochon-Berger & Pekarek Doehler 2011), topic management in discussions (Galaczi 2013) and displaying participantship (Ishida 2011).

Stage 2: What independent variables are to be investigated?

Pragmatics research in applied linguistics can be divided into two large camps and a smaller cluster of other studies. The large research areas concern *cross-cultural pragmatics* and *interlanguage pragmatics*. Cross-cultural pragmatics typically makes membership in a cultural group, usually defined as an L1 group, the independent variable[1] and compares differences between the groups. Acquisition of second language pragmatics is not a concern in these studies. The largest study in cross-cultural pragmatics was the Cross-Cultural Speech Act Realization Patterns (CCSARP) project (Blum-Kulka et al. 1989), which collected L1 and L2 request and apology data from 1,946 participants with Discourse Completion Tasks (DCTs), covering seven native and three target languages. One problem with cross-cultural pragmatics research is the type of conclusions to be drawn from findings. A difference between two cultural groups in their speech act realization or the cultural norms underlying their pragmatic performance does not necessarily mean that communication between them will be problematic or flawed. It simply means that a difference exists which may or may not impact communication.

The second major type of research is interlanguage pragmatics research, also known as acquisitional or developmental pragmatics research. In this research tradition, the focus is on the acquisition of pragmatic competence in a target language, so the independent variable in such studies is a factor that is hypothesized to affect L2 pragmatic competence, most commonly L2 proficiency or exposure to the L2 environment. The independent variable can simply be native-speaker status and would then involve a comparison between learners' and native speakers' performance on the research instrument. Alternatively, the independent variable can have various levels, for example, low-proficiency, mid-proficiency and high-proficiency learners can be compared in a 'pseudo-longitudinal' design, which hopes to predict developmental trajectories. Similarly, learners with different levels of exposure can be compared, for example, no exposure, 5 months in the L2 country and 10 months in the L2 country (e.g. Grieve 2013). Often, there is also a native speaker comparison group to establish a baseline of native speaker performance with which learners are then contrasted.

Stage 3: What research instrument is to be used?

The most commonly used research instruments in pragmatics research are DCTs, role plays, metapragmatic judgements and multiple choice instruments. Other less commonly used research approaches include interviews, observations and the collection of natural data. In this section, the two most frequently used research tools will be discussed: DCTs and role plays (for discussion of other possible instruments, see Golato & Golato 2013; Martinez-Flor & Uso-Juan 2010).

Discourse completion tasks

DCTs used to be the standard way of collecting data in interlanguage and cross-cultural pragmatics research because they allow rapid and targeted collection of a large amount of data. However, critiques of DCT research (Golato 2003; Kasper 2006; Meier 1998) have made the uncritical use of DCTs impossible, and researchers must now make a case for the use of a DCT as a research instrument.

A DCT traditionally consists of a situational prompt, which is followed by a gap for the participant to enter their response. The prompt is a situation description that provides background on the setting that the imaginary interaction occurs in as well as on the imaginary interlocutor. Prompts can be more or less detailed, and their level of detail has been found to influence participants' responses (Billmyer & Varghese 2000). It is very important in the design of the prompt to assign the participants roles that they can identify with and describe situations that are familiar to them. In addition to the prompt, the gap can be preceded by an opening utterance of the imaginary interlocutor and followed by a rejoinder. A DCT item might therefore look as in Figure 22.1 (the parts in brackets are optional).

You need to print out a letter but your printer is not working. You decide to ask your housemate Jack if you can use his printer. Jack is in his room reading a book as you walk in.

[Jack: Hey, how are you?]

You: _____

[Jack: Sure, go for it.]

FIGURE 22.1 *Example of DCT item*

The relationship with the imaginary interlocutor is crucial, and DCT situations are usually constructed to incorporate some of the context variables identified (Brown & Levinson 1987) as influencing politeness in conversation: *power*, *social distance* and *degree of imposition*.

Power concerns the relative power difference between the participant and the imaginary interlocutor and can have three basic settings: high power (of the imaginary interlocutor), equal power and low power. In the example shown in Figure 22.1, power would be equal. Examples of high power interlocutors for student participants are professors, landlords, employers or police officers, but it can be difficult to find lower-power interlocutors if participants are students and do not have much experience being in positions of power. Possibilities include casting the participant as an assistant manager of a small shop who is talking to an employee or as a graduate assistant/ tutor talking to a student. Depending on the target culture, they could also be cast as talking to a younger relative.

Social distance is the degree of shared group membership and/or acquaintanceship. In the DCT example in Figure 22.1, social distance would be considered low as housemates tend to know each other fairly well. High social distance pertains to interlocutors that the participant does not know and has little in common with, for example, strangers on the bus, customers in a shop, a professor they do not know. Medium social distance might apply to interlocutors who are vaguely but not well known or who share group membership with the participant without much personal knowledge, for example, a colleague in another department, a fellow student of the same age that the participant has never talked to or a distant relative.

Imposition differs somewhat by speech act. In a request, like the example in Figure 22.1, it is the cost to the imaginary interlocutor of complying with the participant's request. Such cost can be in terms of time, money, effort or inconvenience. The example above would be considered a low-imposition situation, with high-imposition examples including borrowing a large amount of money, asking for a ride to a distant airport, borrowing a laptop that the interlocutor also urgently needs or asking for help with a difficult and time consuming move. In apologies, imposition is the severity of offence, that is, the cost of the damage to the interlocutor caused by the participant's (imaginary) action or the severity of violation of a norm. Low-imposition apology situations include almost but not actually breaking an item, losing or destroying something cheap that belongs to the interlocutor (a magazine, a pencil) or bumping into somebody without causing any damage. In high imposition apology situations, the participant might be cast as destroying a valuable possession of the interlocutor's (a camera, a laptop), spilling red wine on a light carpet or bumping into the interlocutor and knocking them over.

All three context variables (power, social distance and degree of imposition) are measured on a continuum, and they are not all-or-nothing propositions. In addition, there may be culture-specific variables, such as age or gender that may affect responses. It is recommended that researchers check prior to data collection whether their own intuitions about context variables and other variables match the target participants' views.

DCTs are usually designed so that they systematically incorporate combinations of contextual variables (and other variables, where applicable). However, researchers frequently have to make choices as to which context variables they will focus on in their study because even if the three context variables identified by Brown and Levinson were only varied dichotomously, this would lead to eight possible variable combinations, as shown in Table 22.1.

Table 22.1 Combinations of power, imposition and social distance if varied dichotomously

	Power (P)	Imposition (I)	Social distance (D)
1	High (+)	High (+)	High (+)
2	High (+)	High (+)	Low (−)
3	High (+)	Low (−)	High (+)
4	High (+)	Low (−)	Low (−)
5	Equal (+/−)	High (+)	High (+)
6	Equal (+/−)	High (+)	Low (−)
7	Equal (+/−)	Low (−)	High (+)
8	Equal (+/−)	Low (−)	Low (−)

If some variables are considered to have multiple levels, the number of possible combinations would increase according to the following formula:

number of combinations = levels of power * levels of imposition * levels of social distance * levels of additional variable x * levels of additional variable y etc.

So, in a study that incorporates a medium social distance setting in addition to varying power and imposition dichotomously and also looks at gender of the imaginary interlocutor as a variable (male/female), eight different combinations would result. Given that each combination of context variables should be represented by at least two DCT items (better three or four), it is often not possible to vary more than two variables (either two context variables or a context variable and another variable) in a given study. To avoid fatigue and inauthentic responses, participants should not be expected to complete more than twenty DCT situations, preferably no more than twelve. Care must be taken to ensure that the other context variables and possible other variables are controlled and kept equal for all situations. So if power and imposition are varied, social distance needs to be kept constant for all situations (usually low), and there must be reason to assume that other possible variables do not have much of an influence, or they must be systematically controlled as well. Keeping variables constant limits the range of conclusions that can be drawn from the study, but this trade-off between practicality and external validity is common and unavoidable.

Role plays

Design considerations for role plays are similar to DCTs in terms of the context variables of power, social distance and degree of imposition. For role plays as well, researchers vary one or more of these context variables and design role play situations so as to include different combinations of them. However, since role plays are much more resource intensive, time consuming and tiring for researcher and participants alike, the number of situations will generally be smaller and not exceed six. The major obvious difference between role plays and DCTs is that role plays involve extended conversations between the interlocutor and the participant. This allows speech acts to unfold over several turns and data resembles authentic conversation more than in a DCT. Also, role plays elicit ability for use rather than knowledge like DCTs, because participants have to produce language under the pressures and constraints of a communicative situation.

However, it is important to note that role plays are not the same as authentic conversations. Most importantly, participants are aware of the simulated nature of role plays, which have no stakes attached, unlike authentic conversation, and role plays do not impact real-world outcomes and/or relationships. Participants therefore do not have the same motivations as they would in authentic interactions, and they simultaneously orient to two social situations – the role played scenario as well as the role play setting itself. In addition, role plays tend to be conducted in controlled environments to enable recording, so facilitative and inhibiting effects of the natural environment, such as background noise, visual cues or model interactions by others, are lacking.

Another consideration in role plays concerns interlocutor effects. While interactions in role plays develop more naturally than they ever could in DCTs, comparability between different interactions is limited due to the co-constructed nature of conversation. However, interlocutors can try to keep their conversations with participants fairly similar by following broad guidelines. For example, in exchanges where participants are meant to make a request, interlocutors might follow a strategy of not immediately acceding to the request but introducing a complication, which then leads to a successful solution having to be negotiated. Such complicating strategies lengthen the interaction and thereby force participants to display more of their pragmatic competence, but at the same time, they may not be feasible for low-proficiency learners, whose L2 proficiency may be too limited to support lengthy negotiations.

Another possible interlocutor effect relates to the plausibility of the role taken on by the interlocutor. Interlocutors frequently perform a variety of very different roles to accommodate different context variable settings. For example, if the variable 'power' is varied and the participant is a graduate student, the interlocutor might play a professor (P+), a fellow graduate student (P=) and an employee in the video store where the participant is cast as the manager (P–).[2] Participants have to suspend disbelief to imagine the interlocutor's portrayed persona as real, and this increases their awareness of the simulated and non-authentic nature of role plays.

Besides these caveats, role plays also have logistical limitations. Unlike DCTs, which can be administered to large groups of participants in far-flung locations, role play data has to be collected in individual sessions between participants and researcher/confederate, which increases time and costs.

The eventual decision as to whether a DCT or a role play is more suitable for a given study depends primarily on the types of conclusions to be drawn from the study. If researchers are interested in isolated pieces of participants' knowledge that do not require discourse unfolding over various turns, DCTs are appropriate. For example, studies on address terms, formulaic expressions or investigations of the repertoire of semantic formulae participants know can rely on DCTs. However, if ability for use or complex speech acts are to be investigated or participants' ability to construct extended discourse, role plays are preferable. For example, investigations of how participants realize speech acts in discourse need to employ role plays rather than DCTs.

Stage 4: How will the data be analysed?

Data analysis of the most frequently investigated speech acts, request and apology, traditionally follows the coding scheme developed originally in the CCSARP project (Blum-Kulka et al. 1989) and later modified by several authors (Hudson et al. 1995; Trosborg 1995). The CCSARP coding scheme and its derivatives atomize speech acts into head acts and supportive moves and can code for modifications within both. The unit of coding is 'strategy' and as an example, take the following apology situation and participant response (from Roever 2000):

> *Rushing to get to class on time, you run around the corner and bump into another student almost knocking him down. The other student is male, about your age, but you don't know him.*
>
> Oh my gosh! I'm so sorry. Are you okay? I'm late and I guess I wasn't watching where I was going. Are you sure you're okay?

According to CCSARP, this utterance would be segmented and coded as follows:

'Oh my gosh!' = Alerter

'I'm so sorry.' = Illocutionary force indicating device (IFID) with intensifying adverbial

'Are you okay?' = Concern for the hearer

'I'm late and I guess I wasn't watching where I was going.' = Taking on responsibility

'Are you sure you're okay?' = Concern for the hearer

The frequency of strategies is counted and compared between the groups of interest, for example, native speakers and L2 learners. Such comparisons can be done simply by contrasting different frequency counts or using an inferential statistical procedure such as chi-square, which indicates a relationship between group membership and the frequency of use of a certain strategy.

There has, however, recently been increasing criticism of the atomistic CCSARP approach because it does not handle extended interactions well and because the categories are not always well-defined (Kasper 2006; Meier 1998). An alternative is an approach that considers how linguistic and social actions are accomplished not just through individual utterances but through the larger organization and sequencing of discourse. CA has amassed a large amount of research on the analysis of extended discourse over the fifty years of its existence, taking the turn as the fundamental unit as analysis and describing how interactions are structured around a central exchange (e.g. request followed by acceptance/refusal) with pre-expansion sequences recognizably preceding and foreshadowing this exchange, insert expansion sequences occurring between the two components of the central exchange and post-expansion sequences following it (Schegloff 2007). Fundamentally, CA prefers a bottom-up approach to the analysis of discourse, frowning on analysts imposing pre-existing categories or research questions on the data.

The ultimate goal of any analysis is to compare the different levels of the independent variable, for example, NS versus NNS or NNS of different proficiency or exposure levels. Different combinations of context variables and their effect also need to be explored, possibly nested within the other independent variable. Quantitative approaches to this are more common in traditional speech act research than in CA-inspired discursive research, which uses qualitative analysis of coding and categorization. Finally, differences between groups and context variables are described and interpreted.

A sample study

An interlanguage pragmatics study (Byon 2004) investigated knowledge of Korean requests by native English speaking Korean as a foreign language (KFL) learners in the United States and compared their responses with Korean native speaker and American English native speaker data. While the focus of his paper was on the learners, Byon included native speakers of both languages to facilitate the identification of transfer effects. He used a DCT, which does not allow conclusions as to actual, real-world realizations of requests in conversation, but his focus on cataloguing learners' repertoire of request strategies and detecting the effect of sociopragmatic variables justifies his choice of research instrument. He systematically varied the context variables Power (higher/equal/lower) and

Social Distance (high/low). This generated six possible combinations of context variables, and he used two items per combination, leading to a 12-item DCT. He validated his DCT by having a small sample of native Korean and native English speakers evaluate the plausibility of the situations and the degree of imposition. He found that the situations were plausible and that imposition was rated similarly in both speech communities, although he does not provide these ratings in the paper.

It is worth noting that Byon did not keep imposition constant (i.e. always low or always high) for his situations nor did he claim that he did. For example, both his +P/+D situations are clearly not low imposition, requiring participants to ask a professor to allow them into a class where registration has already closed or to ask a professor to schedule a special exam sitting for them so they can attend a relative's wedding. In contrast, his =P/+D situations are certainly low imposition, requiring participants to ask a passing student for a dorm location or to ask a passing student to take a picture of the participant and a visiting friend. The imposition of another situation depends on (unmentioned) context variables when the participant needs to ask a roommate to borrow his/her computer for an evening to complete an assignment. If the roommate also needs the computer, this is a high-imposition situation, but if the roommate is going to be out for the evening and does not need it, it is much lower imposition. However, no such background information is given. These inconstant imposition settings do not matter much if only groups are compared and context variable effects are not investigated, but since Byon does investigate them, not keeping imposition constant introduces an intervening variable and makes the results and any conclusions drawn from them less defensible.

Byon investigated two independent variables:

- language background, with three levels: native Korean speaker, learner of Korean, native English speaker

- context variables, with six levels: +P/+D, =P/+D, –P/+D, +P/–D, =P/–D, –P/–D

His dependent variable was use of request strategies.

Byon recruited fifty female participants for each of his three groups. He screened his KFL participants to make sure they had sufficient Korean proficiency to answer the questionnaire but he eliminated potential participants who had spent extended periods in Korea to keep the sample homogenous. He further limited his sample to female participants in order to avoid gender effects but did not specify what these gender effects might be. While such limitations of the sample group are legitimate and often necessary to avoid having to consider too many variables for too small a sample, limiting the sample to a subset of the target population reduces the range of conclusions that can be drawn from the study. Strictly speaking,

Byon's conclusions should be limited to female language users and for learners of Korean, they should be limited to learners in a foreign language situation.

Byon administered his DCT to his participants and then analysed the data in a series of steps. He started out using the CCSARP and the coding scheme developed by Hudson et al. (1995) and adapted these existing schemes for his data. Such adaptation is commonly necessary because pre-existing coding schemes often do not represent a new data set well and need even more revision if the data set consists of a target language different from the one used in the creation of the prior coding schemes. In adapting the scheme, the original scheme is first applied to the data and exemplars that do not fit are identified and new categories are created to accommodate them while deleting categories that do not occur in the data set.

Byon reports his results by first providing an inventory of the strategies used with examples and then shows total frequencies for each strategy across all situations by group. In the next section, he compares the most frequent supportive moves for the three groups and discusses selected differences that are particularly striking or pedagogically relevant. It is often impossible and unnecessary to discuss all differences and similarities, so researchers need to focus on the ones that are of most theoretical or practical interest.

Next, Byon analyses the effect of the context variables Power and Distance to understand the level of sociopragmatic awareness (sensitivity to contextual features) learners have attained. He finds, for example, that the native speakers used more indirect strategies when talking to someone higher in power but more direct strategies when talking to someone lower in power. The KFL learners on the other hand used indirect strategies in both cases. This can indicate that the KFL learners do not understand the sociopragmatic rules of Korean conversation about using directness/indirectness, in other words, their sociopragmatic knowledge is not adequately mapped to their pragmalinguistic knowledge. It can, however, also indicate that the learners construed the social relationships in a non-Korean way and did not consider a junior student club member or younger roommate as less powerful than themselves. This shows that they do not have a comprehensive understanding of social relationship structures in Korean society but does not allow the researcher to draw conclusions about the relationship between their sociopragmatic and pragmalinguistic knowledge. To ensure that effects of social variables are due to sociopragmatic-pragmalinguistic mapping rather than differences in knowledge about social structures and relationships, researchers should ask a pilot sample of participants from both speech communities to rate power and distance, just as Byon did.

In the final section of his presentation and discussion of results, Byon compares the use of request head acts between groups and under different context conditions and explains findings in terms of transfer effects.

Byon's study is a fairly typical interlanguage pragmatics study conducted in a traditional, speech act oriented way. Among its major strengths is Byon's focus on Korean as a target language, which adds to the still very spotty knowledge base of the acquisition of pragmatics in languages other than English. Byon's careful checking of the plausibility of his situations and his development of a coding scheme that is based on previous work but fits his own data set are also strong points of his study. One of the major methodological issues in Byon's paper is the impact of imposition, which was not kept constant for all situations. This makes findings on the effect of context variables somewhat questionable. Similarly, he did not ensure that all groups had similar perceptions of power and distance, so he cannot draw conclusions about the structure of learners' pragmatic knowledge. Finally, the use of DCTs imposes limitations on the type of data to be collected, and Byon's conclusions must be seen as limited to pragmatic knowledge about speech act formulae rather than ability for use in discourse.

The methodological shortcoming of much traditional interlanguage and cross-cultural pragmatics research has led to a shift in focus towards collecting interactive data, with researchers increasingly collecting and analysing extended discourse. This does not mean that DCT research no longer has a place in pragmatics work, but the challenges and opportunities inherent in investigating longer stretches of discourse, be they real or role played, are becoming foregrounded in this research area.

Notes

1   The independent variable is a factor that distinguishes groups of participants or tasks from each other and is hypothesized to cause the outcome.

2   There is some confusion in the literature with regard to the meaning of P–. It can mean that the interlocutor is in the lower power position or it can mean that there is no power differential. In this paper, P– means that the interlocutor is in the lower power position and P = means that there is no power differential. P+ always indicates that the interlocutor is higher in power.

Resources for further reading

Blum-Kulka, S, House, J & Kasper, G (eds), 1989, *Cross-Cultural Pragmatics: Requests and Apologies*. Ablex, Norwood, NJ.

Though a bit outdated, this is still the 'grandfather' of the cross-cultural pragmatics research literature. The use of DCTs limits this study a bit, and Kasper herself is now critical of some of the categorizations used (Kasper 2006), but the CCSARP manual is still an invaluable and highly influential tool.

Golato, A 2003, 'Studying compliment responses: A comparison of DCTs and recordings of naturally occurring talk', *Applied Linguistics*, vol. 24, no. 1, pp. 90–121.

Golato's paper was extremely influential in showing the limits of the DCT research by contrasting DCT data with authentic real-world data. It illustrates very well how cautious researchers have to be in interpreting data and how the use of certain research instruments shapes the data we obtain.

Bardovi-Harlig, K, Felix-Brasdefer, JC & Omar, AS (eds), 2006, *Pragmatics and Language Learning*, vol. 11 and Greer, T, Tatsuki, D & Roever, C (eds), 2013, *Pragmatics and Language Learning*, vol. 13, National Foreign Language Resource Center, University of Hawai'i at Manoa, Honolulu, HI.

These edited volumes contain selected papers from the Pragmatics and Language Learning conferences in 2005 and 2010 and illustrate the breadth of pragmatics research as well as the increasing importance of discursive approaches to pragmatic analysis.

Martinez-Flor, A & Uso-Juan, E (eds), 2010, *Speech Act Performance*, John Benjamins, Amsterdam.

This edited volume discusses the main research instruments used in pragmatics research as well as the main speech acts that have been investigated. It provides a comprehensive overview of pragmatics research with a methodological focus.

References

Adrefiza & Jones, JF 2013, 'Investigating apology response strategies in Australian English and Bahasa Indonesia: Gender and cultural perspectives', *Australian Review of Applied Linguistics*, vol. 36, no. 1, pp. 71–101.

Al-Gahtani, S & Roever, C 2012, 'Proficiency and sequential organization of L2 requests', *Applied Linguistics*, vol. 33, no. 1, pp. 42–65.

—— 2013, '"Hi doctor, give me handouts": Low-proficiency learners and requests', *ELT Journal*, vol. 67, no. 4, pp. 413–424.

—— 2014, 'Insert and post-expansion in L2 Arabic requests', *System*, vol. 42, no.1, pp. 189–206.

Bardovi-Harlig, K 2009, 'Conventional expressions as a pragmalinguistic resource: Recognition and production of conventional expressions in L2 Pragmatics', *Language Learning*, vol. 59, no. 4, pp. 755–795.

—— 2013, 'On saying the same thing: Issues in the analysis of conventional expressions in L2 pragmatics', in T Greer, D Tatsuki & C Roever (eds), *Pragmatics and Language Learning*, vol. 13, National Foreign Language Resource Center, University of Hawai'i at Manoa, Honolulu, HI, pp. 191–212.

Bardovi-Harlig, K & Bastos, M 2011, 'Proficiency, length of stay, and intensity of interaction and the acquisition of conventional expressions in L2 pragmatics', *Intercultural Pragmatics*, vol. 8, no. 3, pp. 347–384.

Bardovi-Harlig, K & Dörnyei, Z 1998, 'Do language learners recognize pragmatic violations? Pragmatic vs. grammatical awareness in instructed L2 learning', *TESOL Quarterly*, vol. 32, no. 2, pp. 233–259.

Bella, S 2012, 'Pragmatic awareness in a second language setting: The case of L2 learners of Greek', *Multilingua*, vol. 31, no. 1, pp. 1–33.

Bhatti, J & Zegarac, V 2012, 'Compliments and refusals in Poland and England', *Research in Language*, vol. 10, no. 3, pp. 279–297.

Billmyer, K & Varghese, M 2000, 'Investigating instrument-based pragmatic variability: Effects of enhancing discourse completion tasks', *Applied Linguistics*, vol. 21, no. 4, pp. 517–552.

Blum-Kulka, S, House, J & Kasper G (eds), 1989, *Cross-Cultural Pragmatics: Requests and Apologies*, Ablex, Norwood, NJ.

Bouton, L 1988, 'A cross-cultural study of ability to interpret implicatures in English', *World Englishes*, vol. 7, no. 2, pp. 183–196.

Brown, P & Levinson, SD 1987, *Politeness: Some Universals in Language Usage*, Cambridge University Press, New York, NY.

Byon, AS 2004, 'Sociopragmatic analysis of Korean requests: Pedagogical settings', *Journal of Pragmatics*, vol. 36, no. 9, pp. 1673–1704.

Chen, Y, Chen, CD & Chang, M 2011, 'American and Chinese complaints: Strategy use from a cross-cultural perspective', *Intercultural Pragmatics*, vol. 8, no. 2, pp. 253–275.

Cheng, D 2011, 'New insights on compliment responses: A comparison between native English speakers and Chinese L2 speakers', *Journal of Pragmatics*, vol. 43, no. 8, pp. 2204–2214.

Dippold, D 2011, 'Argumentative discourse in L2 German: A sociocognitive perspective on the development of facework strategies', *The Modern Language Journal*, vol. 95, no. 2, pp. 171–187.

Do, HTT 2013, 'Complaints in Vietnamese by native and non-native speakers', in C Roever & HT Nguyen (eds), *Pragmatics of Vietnamese as Native and Target Language*, National Foreign Language Resource Center, University of Hawai'i, Honolulu, HI, pp. 111–134.

Edmonds, A 2014, 'Conventional expressions', *Studies in Second Language Acquisition*, vol. 36, no. 1, pp. 69–99.

Galaczi, E 2013, 'Interactional competence across proficiency levels: How do learners manage interaction in paired speaking tests?', *Applied Linguistics*, doi: 10.1093/applin/amt017.

Golato, A & Golato, P (2013), 'Pragmatics research methods', in C Chapelle (ed.), *The Encyclopedia of Applied Linguistics*, Wiley-Blackwell, Oxford.

Grieve, A 2013, 'Acquisition of the pragmatic marker "Like" by German study abroad adolescents', in T Greer, D Tatsuki & C Roever (eds), *Pragmatics and Language Learning*, vol. 13, National Foreign Language Resource Center, University of Hawai'i at Manoa, Honolulu, HI, pp. 161–190.

Ho, DGE, Henry, A & Alkaff, SNH 2012, '"You don't seem to know how to work": Malay and English spoken complaints in Brunei', *Pragmatics*, vol. 22, no. 3, pp. 391–416.

Ho, LGA 2013, 'Apologizing in Vietnamese as a native and a target language', in C Roever & HT Nguyen (eds), *Pragmatics of Vietnamese as Native and Target Language*, National Foreign Language Resource Center, University of Hawai'i at Manoa, Honolulu, HI, pp. 77–110.

Holtgraves, T 2012, 'The role of the right hemisphere in speech act comprehension', *Brain and Language*, vol. 121, no. 1, pp. 58–64.

Hong, W 2011, 'Refusals in Chinese: How do L1 and L2 differ?', *Foreign Language Annals*, vol. 44, no. 1, pp. 122–136.

Houck, N & Fuji, S 2013, 'Working through disagreement in English academic discussions between L1 speakers of Japanese and L1 speakers of English', in T Greer, D Tatsuki & C Roever (eds), *Pragmatics and Language Learning*, vol. 13,

National Foreign Language Resource Center, University of Hawai'i at Manoa, Honolulu, HI, pp. 103–132.

Hudson, T, Detmer, E & Brown, JD 1995, *Developing Prototypic Measures of Cross-Cultural Pragmatics* (Technical Report #7), Second Language Teaching and Curriculum Center, University of Hawaii, Honolulu, HI.

────── 2011, 'Engaging in another person's telling as a recipient in L2 Japanese: Development of interactional competence during one-year study abroad', in G Palotti & J Wagner (eds), *L2 Learning as Social Practice: Conversation-Analytic Perspectives*, National Foreign Language Resource Center, Honolulu, HI, pp. 17–44.

Kasper, G 2006, 'Speech acts in interaction: Towards discursive pragmatics', in Bardovi-Harlig, JC Felix-Brasdefer & AS Omar (eds), *Pragmatics and Language Learning*, vol. 11, National Foreign Language Resource Center, University of Hawai'i at Manoa, Honolulu, HI, pp. 281–314.

Lee, C 2010, 'An exploratory study of the interlanguage pragmatic comprehension of young learners of English', *Pragmatics*, vol. 20, no. 3, pp. 343–373.

Li, ES 2010, 'Making suggestions: A contrastive study of young Hong Kong and Australian students', *Journal of Pragmatics*, vol. 42, no. 3, pp. 598–616.

Li, S 2013, 'Amount of practice and pragmatic development of request-making in L2 Chinese', in N Taguchi & J Sykes (eds), *Technology in Interlanguage Pragmatics Research and Teaching*, John Benjamins, Amsterdam, pp. 43–69.

Maiz-Arevalo, C 2012, '"Was that a compliment?" Implicit compliments in English and Spanish', *Journal of Pragmatics*, vol. 44, no. 8, pp. 980–996.

Malamed, LH 2010, 'Disagreement: How to disagree agreeably', in A Martinez-Flor & E Uso-Juan (eds), *Speech Act Performance: Theoretical, Empirical and Methodological Issues*, John Benjamins, Amsterdam, pp. 199–216.

Martinez-Flor, A & Uso-Juan, E 2010, *Speech Act Performance: Theoretical, Empirical and Methodological Issues*, John Benjamins, Amsterdam.

Meier, AJ 1998, 'Apologies: What do we know?', *International Journal of Applied Linguistics*, vol. 8, no. 2, pp. 215–231.

Nguyen, TTM 2013a, 'An exploratory study of criticism realization strategies used by NS and NNS of New Zealand English', *Multilingua*, vol. 32, no. 1, pp. 103–130.

────── 2013b, 'Instructional effects on the acquisition of modifiers in constructive criticism by EFL learners', *Language Awareness*, vol. 22, no. 1, pp. 76–94.

Nguyen, TTM & Basturkmen, H 2013, 'Requesting in Vietnamese as a second language', in C Roever & HT Nguyen (eds), *Pragmatics of Vietnamese as Native and Target Language*, National Foreign Language Resource Center, University of Hawai'i at Manoa, Honolulu, HI, pp. 77–110

Park, I 2012, 'Seeking advice: Epistemic asymmetry and learner autonomy in writing conferences', *Journal of Pragmatics*, vol. 44, no. 14, pp. 2004–2021.

Pochon-Berger, E & Pekarek Doehler, S 2011, 'Developing "methods" for interaction: A cross-sectional study of disagreement sequences in French L2', in JK Hall, J Hellermann & S Pekarek Doehler (eds), *L2 Interactional Competence and Development*, Multilingual Matters, Clevedon, pp. 206–243.

Ren, W 2012, 'Pragmatic development in Chinese speakers' L2 English refusals', *EUROSLA Yearbook*, vol. 12, no. 1, pp. 63–87.

Roever, C 2000, 'Rejoinders in production questionnaires revisited', Unpublished manuscript, University of Hawai'i at Manoa, Honolulu, HI.

———— 2012, 'What learners get for free: Learning of routine formulae in ESL and EFL environments', *ELT Journal*, vol. 66, no. 1, pp. 10–21.

———— 2013, 'Testing implicature under operational conditions', in G Kasper & S Ross (eds), *Assessing Second Language Pragmatics*, Palgrave Macmillan, New York, NY, pp. 43–64.

Salgado, EF 2011, *The Pragmatics of Requests and Apologies*, John Benjamins, Amsterdam.

Schauer, GA 2006, 'Pragmatic awareness in ESL and EFL contexts: Contrast and development', *Language Learning*, vol. 56, no. 2, pp. 269–318.

Schegloff, EA 2007, *Sequence Organization in Interaction*, Cambridge University Press, Cambridge.

Shively, RL 2011, 'L2 pragmatic development in study abroad: A longitudinal study of Spanish service encounters', *Journal of Pragmatics*, vol. 43, no. 6, pp. 1818–1835.

Sidnell, J 2010, *Conversation Analysis: An Introduction*, Wiley-Blackwell, Oxford.

Sykes, J 2013, 'Multiuser virtual environments: Learner apologies in Spanish', in N Taguchi & J Sykes (eds), *Technology in Interlanguage Pragmatics Research and Teaching*, John Benjamins, Amsterdam, pp. 71–100.

Taguchi, N 2011, 'The effect of L2 proficiency and study-abroad experience on pragmatic comprehension', *Language Learning*, vol. 61, no. 3, pp. 904–939.

———— 2012, *Context, Individual Differences and Pragmatic Competence*, Multilingual Matters, Bristol.

———— 2013, 'Comprehension of conversational implicature: What response times tell us', in N Taguchi & J Sykes (eds), *Technology in Interlanguage Pragmatics Research and Teaching*, John Benjamins, Amsterdam, pp. 19–41.

Takimoto, M 2012, 'Assessing the effects of identical task repetition and task-type repetition on learners' recognition and production of second language request downgraders', *Intercultural Pragmatics*, vol. 9, no. 1, pp. 71–96.

Trosborg, A 1995, *Interlanguage Pragmatics: Requests, Complaints, and Apologies*, Mouton de Gruyter, Berlin.

Wang, VX 2011, *Making Requests by Chinese EFL Learners*, John Benjamins, Amsterdam.

CHAPTER TWENTY THREE

Researching Motivation

Lindy Woodrow

Research into language learning motivation is relatively recent, with studies dating back to the mid-twentieth century. This chapter will provide an overview of the major thinking and research in motivation. Early research focused on the work of Robert Gardner and colleagues (e.g. Gardner 1985; Gardner & Lambert 1972). Their research was located within a *social-psychological paradigm* which dominated research into language learning motivation until the 1990s. In the 1990s, major academic journals called for a diversification of theorizing in motivation informed by other disciplines, notably education. This resulted in a number of new studies into language learning motivation that did not use the Gardnerian paradigm. In this chapter, four areas of motivational research will be discussed. First, the Gardnerian socio-educational model of language learning will be briefly presented. Research since the 1990s will then be considered: self-determination theory (Deci & Ryan 1980, 1985), a process model of motivation (Dörnyei & Otto 1998) and goal orientation theory (Ames & Archer 1988). The section on goal orientation theory uses Woodrow's (2006) study to highlight confirmatory factor analysis as a technique that may be used to investigate latent constructs.

Gardner's socio-educational model of language learning

The work of Gardner and colleagues into language learning motivation was the most significant contribution to research in the area in the twentieth century. Gardner's research into second language motivation was developed in bilingual Canada and resulted in the socio-educational model of second language learning. The model is based on the belief that the social and cultural setting can influence motivation which influences the formal and informal contexts of language learning which, in turn, results in linguistic and non-linguistic outcomes (Gardner 1985, 2006). The model has four distinct areas: *antecedent factors*, *individual difference variables*, *language acquisition contexts* and *outcomes*. In the model, goal orientations are viewed as antecedents of motivation. Motivation comprises the desire to learn the second language, motivational intensity and attitudes towards learning a language. It is the notion of goal orientations that captured the attention of the research world when the model was introduced. This was a very influential view of second language motivation for many years. Gardner referred to two orientations: *instrumental* and *integrative motivation*. An instrumental orientation refers to a situation whereby the learner is motivated to learn the language for extrinsic reasons, such as for financial gain or job promotion. An integrative orientation refers to the situation whereby the learner is motivated to learn the language because they identify with the target culture. In Gardner's theory, these orientations do not appear in the core construct of motivation. However, in many research projects in the twentieth century, these orientations replace the motivation construct itself, thus, according to Gardner, over-simplifying the theory (Gardner 1988). Masgoret and Gardner (2003) conducted a meta-analysis of studies using Gardner's model of language learning.

In the 1990s, there was considerable debate through a series of journal articles that questioned the relevance of the Gardnerian model of motivation to contexts other than bilingual Canada where the research had originated (Crookes & Schmidt 1991; Dörnyei 1990, 1994; Oxford 1994; Oxford & Shearin 1994; Tremblay & Gardner 1995). For example, how relevant is an integrative orientation that focuses on the extent to which a learner wishes to identify with the target culture to Chinese students studying English as a subject in Chinese schools? As a result of this discussion, a number of studies emerged that focused on conceptualizations of motivation from research in areas other than language learning, notably, workplace and education motivation. Some of these research studies are presented in papers on language learning motivation published in the 1990s. Oxford's (1996) volume, for example, includes articles on a range of motivational issues, for example, goals and expectancy (Schmidt et al. 1996) and linguistic self-confidence and contextual influences (Dörnyei 1996). A further volume of research into motivation was published in 2001 (Dörnyei & Schmidt 2001) as a result of a state-of-the-art colloquium on second language motivation at the annual meeting of the American Association of Applied Linguistics held in Vancouver.

Self-determination theory

Self-determination theory (Deci & Ryan 1980, 1985; Ryan & Deci 2000) focuses on the extent to which individuals can exert control over their environment. This has been applied to language learning (McIntosh & Noels 2004; Noels 2001; Noels et al. 2000). Central to this theory is the conceptualization of motivation as *intrinsic* and *extrinsic*. Intrinsic motivation reflects a willingness to engage in a given task for the inherent interest or pleasure gained from the task. Three types of intrinsic orientations have been suggested: intrinsic knowledge, where an individual is motivated by a quest for knowledge; intrinsic accomplishment, which refers to the satisfaction experienced by accomplishing a challenging task and intrinsic stimulation, which refers to the enjoyment of the given task (Noels 2001; Vallerand 1997). Extrinsic motivation reflects a willingness to engage with tasks to achieve a specific outcome. Deci and Ryan classify extrinsic motivation according to level of internalization. Thus, an external regulation could refer to passing an examination or to getting a good job while internal or integrated regulation could refer to improving an individual's opinion of their capability (Ryan & Deci 2000).

Noels and colleagues investigated extrinsic and intrinsic motivation in relation to the Gardnerian model of motivation. Their research indicated that the intrinsic and extrinsic conceptualization was applicable to language learners and suggested a model of motivation that integrated self-determination theory and the Gardnerian model of motivation. In particular, they examined social contact, needs, orientations, second language use and linguistic and non-linguistic outcomes (Noels 2001; Noels et al. 1999, 2000; Pae 2008). More current research using the self-determination theory framework seeks to integrate motivation into a more complex model of variables, such as learning strategies (McIntosh & Noels 2004) and self-efficacy (Busse & Walter 2013).

A process model of motivation

Dörnyei and Otto (Dörnyei 2000; Dörnyei & Otto 1998) proposed a *process model* of motivation which reflects dynamic and contextual aspects of second and foreign language motivation. This model includes a temporal dimension of motivation designed to account for changes in motivation over time. This, Dörnyei argues, is logical since language learning is a lengthy process and success is based on sustained learning over a period of years (Dörnyei 2001). The process model of motivation is complex. It is based on Heckhausen and Kuhl's action control theory (Heckhausen 1991; Heckhausen & Kuhl 1985). This model considers the stages of motivation from before engaging in a given task to after task completion. Three stages are hypothesized: the preactional stage that reflects desire and goal setting; the actional stage that reflects engagement and appraisal; and the postactional stage that reflects causal attributions and further planning.

Current thinking in motivation higlights the importance of the social and the dynamic nature of motivation (Dörnyei & Ushoida 2011). This conceptualization includes the notion of the perception of self, for example, future self and vision as motivational force (Dörnyei & Kubanyiova 2014; Ryan 2009); contextual influences such as teacher motivational strategies (Guilloteaux & Dörnyei 2008; Moskovsky et al. 2013); and an emphasis on the temporal dimension of motivation – how motivation fluctuates (Dörnyei & Ushoida 2011; Lamb 2004).

Research strategies and techniques

The strategies used in second language motivation research are governed by the nature of motivation. Since motivation is a latent construct, it cannot be observed directly and so depends upon self-report measures such as questionnaires and interviews. Usually motivation is not considered in isolation and often models are hypothesized as comprising a number of motivational variables. These variables are usually examined in relationship to a language variable such as achievement as measured by a language test.

The most common design in motivational research is a cross-sectional study which typically aims to provide a snapshot of a given aspect on a single occasion, for example, Dörnyei et al. (2006) conducted a large-scale study into language learning motivation in Hungary. Cross-sectional studies involve collecting data on one occasion and often involve questionnaires. For example, a researcher can collect data about the motivational profile at the time of data collection. Cross-sectional studies enable the researcher to examine relationships between variables. For example, such a design might measure motivation and compare this to language proficiency. The advantage in using a cross-sectional design is that it is easy to collect data from a large number of participants. Cross-sectional research can be contrasted with longitudinal research, which involves collecting data on a number of occasions over a period of time, such as Ushoida's (2001) study that collected qualitative data about motivation of language learners at university over a 2-year period.

Second language research typically uses quantitative measures where the latent variable of motivation is operationalized by *observed variables*. To operationalize a variable means to make the variable measurable. In research into latent constructs, this is usually done by asking questions of individuals, most frequently by constructing questionnaire items. Questionnaire items typically use some form of rating scale, such as a *Likert scale* or a *semantic differential* scale. These are closed questions that can be assigned a numerical value. A Likert-scale item requires the respondent to indicate the extent to

---

Example of a Likert-scale item

Fill in the circle that best expresses your view

My teacher is efficient

Strongly agree   Agree   Neutral   Disagree   Strongly disagree

O   O   O   O   O

Semantic differential scale

Rate the efficiency of your English teacher by marking an X on the scale.

My English teacher is efficient __: __: __: __: __: __: inefficient.

FIGURE 23.1 *Examples of questionnaire items*

which they agree or disagree according to a numerical scale. For example, a five-point Likert scale ranges from 1 (strongly disagree) to 5 (strongly agree). In a similar manner, semantic differential scales ask for a rating on a line based on a statement.

These are then assigned a numerical value in a similar way to a Likert scale. Figure 23.1 shows examples of a Likert type scale item and a semantic differential type item.

Questionnaires rely upon self-report, that is, the data come from the respondent's own account of their experiences or views. One issue concerning this is that participants may provide responses that reflect how they would like to be viewed (Oller 1982). For this reason, it is important that questionnaires are worded very carefully avoiding obvious desirable answers. It is also important that confidentiality is ensured.

The resulting data from questionnaires is typically analysed using inferential statistics (see Phakiti this volume). Inferential statistics refer to statistical techniques that can be used to make inferences from data from a small group of respondents to a larger population thus enabling findings to be generalized. Motivational research typically uses inferential statistical analysis on data provided by questionnaires. The relationship between variables, often presented in the form of a motivational model, is frequently the main concern of motivation research. Typical analyses are often based on correlations between variables.

Instrumentation and data analysis

The most widely used questionnaire or instrumentation to measure motivation and related variables is Gardner's (1985) *Attitudes/Motivation Test Battery*. This instrument operationalizes the variables proposed in his socio-educational model of language learning. These variables include attitudes towards target language speakers, teachers and learning situations; motivational orientations, desire and intensity; anxiety and parental encouragement. The scale uses three types of questionnaire items: Likert scale, multiple choice and semantic differential scale. The *Attitudes/Motivation Test Battery* instrument is a published standardized test of language learning motivation. It has sound psychometric properties (Gardner & MacIntyre 1993) and has been widely used and adapted. The instrumentation and instructions on how to use this are available from Gardner (1985).

Noels and colleagues devised the *Language Learning Orientations Scale* to measure motivation which comprised amotivation (lack of or passive engagement), external regulation, interjected regulation, indentified regulation, intrinsic motivation knowledge, intrinsic motivation, accomplishment and intrinsic motivation stimulation (Noels et al. 2001, 2003). It uses 7-point Likert scales to assess these motivational variables. The scale asks respondents to rate the extent to which they agree or disagree with a series of statements from 1 (disagree completely) to 7 (agree completely).

When considering motivation from a broader sociodynamic perspective, it is becoming common to use mixed-methods. In this way, complex models that reflect contextual influences, multi variable models and the fluctuation of motivation over time can be investigated (Ushioda 2013).

Data analysis

In motivation research, data are frequently analysed using statistical procedures using correlations. These include basic techniques such as *bivariate correlations* (see Phakiti this volume) that examine the linear relationship between two variables. More complicated procedures include *exploratory factor analysis*. This technique is used to investigate the extent to which observed variables are indicative of underlying latent variables or factors. Further complex analyses include *structural equation modeling* which involves testing hypotheses about relationships between variables. Studies using structural equation modeling have increased in recent years. This is probably due to the development of powerful statistical analysis software that reduces the burden on the researcher who wishes to employ this kind of analysis.

There are two types of factor analysis: *exploratory factor analysis* and *confirmatory factor analysis*. Exploratory factor analysis is used in early stages of researching motivation. A large number of observed variables (questionnaire items) are analysed to examine the extent to which these correlate, which may provide evidence for the composition of a latent variable. The analysis produces a more manageable set of factors. Exploratory factor analysis is calculated using computer software such as the Statistical Package for the Social Sciences (SPSS Inc. 2007). This software generates output in the form of a table that includes *factor loadings*. A factor loading is a correlation coefficient. This is a number less than 1.00 that reflects the magnitude of the relationship between the variable and the factor. For example, a factor loading of 0.90 indicates a strong relationship while a loading of 0.2 indicates little relationship. Exploratory factor analysis is used a great deal in the preparatory stages of research where evidence is required of the make-up of a given variable. A great deal of Gardner's research used this technique (Gardner 1985; Gardner & Lambert 1959, 1972).

There are a number of issues researchers need to be aware of when using exploratory factor analysis. The most important is deciding how many factors to extract and how the factors should be labelled. Two main methods are used for deciding how many factors should be extracted. First, Cattell's *scree test* may be used to provide a visual representation of the data. This is a visual representation of the variables in the data set. The scree plot should indicate a line that sharply increases at a given point on a graph. Where this happens will indicate whether, for example, three or four factors be selected. The second method, known as *Kaiser's criterion* (Kaiser 1960), uses *eigenvalues* to determine factors. An eigenvalue represents the total variance explained by the factor. Only factors with eigenvalues higher than 1.00 are then considered for inclusion in the factor.

Once the number of factors is decided, they need to be labelled. The choice of label should be evident from the *indicator variables* – that is, those variables within the factor that have the highest loadings. Consideration is also given to the common features of variables loading on that factor. Of course, this is can be quite controversial because it is based on the researcher's personal judgement.

Confirmatory factor analysis is conceptually similar to exploratory factor analysis but uses structural equation modeling to confirm rather than explore a latent model. Structural equation modeling is discussed below.

Structural equation modeling

Structural equation modeling is a relatively new development in data analysis. This technique has gained in popularity in recent second language motivation studies (Dörnyei et al. 2006; Gardner et al. 1997). This is because structural equation modeling is very useful when considering the nature of latent variables and for testing hypothesized models. Structural equation modeling can be used to identify relationships between variables. It is sometimes referred to as causal modeling, although this is not strictly true. Causality cannot be claimed based on statistical evidence alone but needs substantial theoretical evidence. When using structural equation modeling, a model is proposed and then tested to examine how the data fit the model. Thus, a clear conceptual model is hypothesized based on theorizing and/or previous empirical evidence. The variables in the hypothesized model then need to be operationlized or measured by some form of research instrument. The data collected are then examined to determine to what extent the data fit the model. The following steps are usually followed in a research project using structural equation modeling (adapted from Blunch 2008, pp. 75–78):

1 Statement of research questions.
2 Design of a hypothetical model including directional paths.
3 Decide how concepts will be measured.
4 Collect data.
5 Test model fit using computer software.
6 Examine computer output for model fit.
7 If necessary, modify model.
8 Accept or reject model.

When specifying a structural model, rectangles are used to indicate an observed variable, an oval is used to indicate a latent variable, a small circle indicates the error associated with the variable and an arc is used to indicate a correlation. Figure 23.2 illustrates this.

Structural equation modeling requires the researcher to hypothesize a model with directional relationships between several variables – latent and observed. This model is then confirmed or rejected by using *goodness-of-fit-indices* that compare the hypothesized model with the data. There are a large number of fit indices that can be used to help researchers evaluate the extent to which the model is likely to be supported by the data. Because the indices reflect different views of model building, researchers usually use several fit indices to provide evidence to accept or reject the proposed model. Most structural equation modeling studies use the Chi square (χ^2) statistic. In structural equation modeling, this statistic reflects the null hypothesis that is known to be false *a priori*, thus the null hypothesis states that the model is 100 per cent correct. So, a non-significant value indicates a good fit to the data. However, since structural equation modeling is very sensitive to sample size chi squared normed (χ^2/df), (chi square divided by the degrees of freedom) is often used as well.

In addition to this, other fit indices are also used. Table 23.1 presents some of these fit indices. Views on acceptable values associated with fit indices vary slightly in reported research. Table 23.1 shows those recommended by Holmes-Smith (2000) since these were used in the sample study.

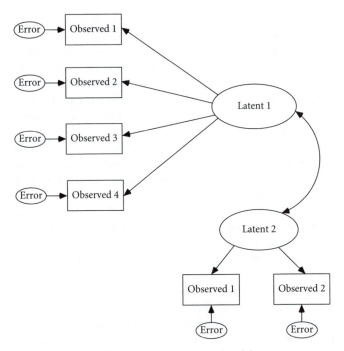

FIGURE 23.2 *Symbols used in structural equation models*

Table 23.1 Fit indices for structural equation models (based on Holmes-Smith 2000)

Index	Symbol	
Chi-square	χ^2	Non-significant
Normed Chi-square (Chi-square divided by degrees of freedom)	$\chi^{2/df}$	1.00 – 3.00
Goodness-of-Fit Index	GFI	0.90 or higher
Adjusted Goodness-of-Fit Index	AGFI	0.90 or higher
Root Mean Square Residual	RMR	Region of 0.05
Root Mean Square Error of Approximation	RMSEA	Region of 0.05
Normed Fit Index	NFI	0.90 or higher
Nonnormed Fit Index	NNFI	0.90 or higher
Comparative Fit Index	CFI	0.90 or higher

There are a number of issues that a researcher needs to be aware of when using structural equation modeling. First, a proposed model may not be the best model to fit the data. The fit indices can only provide evidence on adequate versus inadequate models. Another issue is that it requires a large sample size which increases with the number of variables or model parameters. A minimum sample size would be 150 cases (participants) but some researchers recommend a ratio of 5–10 cases per variable (Tabachnick & Fidell 2012). As mentioned, structural equation modeling is sometimes referred to as causal modeling; however, in models where causality is addressed, this is inferred from the model rather than 'proved'. The model can only tell the researcher that a cause and effect relationship is feasible based on the data.

There are a number of data analysis techniques that can be facilitated using structural equation modeling. *Confirmatory factor analysis* is one such technique. Confirmatory factor analysis is similar to exploratory factor analysis described above except in that the model is first hypothesized and then tested rather than the data being explored first and then a model emerging. So, the researcher makes decisions before the analysis, based on theory and empirical research. The researcher follows the same steps for structural equation modeling outlined above. First, the hypothesized model of relationships between variables is designed. These constructs need to be operationalized. This means items are designed that will measure the underlying construct. A questionnaire is often used for this. The data is then collected and put into a software program such as Analysis of Moment Structures 21 (Arbuckle 2012). This can test the fit of the data to the model. This model is then accepted, adjusted or rejected.

In confirmatory factor analysis, a model is proposed where one or more latent variables are hypothesized to be made up of particular observed variables. This model is then tested and may be modified. In confirmatory factor analysis, unlike exploratory factor analysis, observed variables can be removed from the model. As such, confirmatory factor analysis is very useful for the development of questionnaires focusing on latent variables. The researcher would start with a large bank of items (observed variables) and remove those that are not indicative of the latent variables.

A sample study

The study described in this section is Woodrow's (2006) examination of the notion of *adaptive language learning in a second language setting*. This study proposed and tested a model of adaptive learning that comprises several related variables: motivation, self-efficacy, anxiety and language learning strategies. Part of the study involved applying a goal orientation conceptualization of motivation as used in education (Ames 1992) to English language learners. This fitted in with the move in the 1990s to consider second language motivation from a broader perspective informed by theorizing outside of language learning. The research used a questionnaire to measure goal orientations of English for academic purposes (EAP) students. Based on theorizing and empirical evidence, a three factor latent model was proposed and tested using confirmatory factor analysis. The study indicated that goal orientations were applicable to EAP learners. This has implications for classroom practice in terms of motivating EAP language learners.

Background to the study

The study used goal orientation theory from education research (Ames 1992; Ames & Archer 1988) as a conceptualization for second language motivation relevant to adult EAP students studying in an ESL environment. Gardner's proposed model of language learning included integrative and instrumental orientations. However, these are not central to the model and reflect a socio-cultural perspective whereby the learner has the assumed goal of integrating into the target culture. In contrast, goal orientation theory reflects a sociocognitive perspective with a focus on the learning process. In goal orientation theory, goals are typically classified as being task or performance (Ames & Archer 1988). A task goal (also known as a learning or mastery goal) is viewed as being desirable and most likely to result in positive learning outcomes. A learner adopting this goal would be motivated by learning tasks and achievement for its own sake; they would view competence as being related to effort and have a positive view of errors as contributing to the learning process. A performance goal (also known as an ego or ability goal) reflects a focus on ego or self rather than on achievement for its own sake. While a task goal is concerned with developing competence, a performance goal is concerned with displaying competence (Urdan et al. 2002). In recent years performance goals have been re-conceptualized as approach and avoid goals (Smith et al. 2002). A performance approach goal reflects a desire to demonstrate high ability while a performance avoid goal reflects the desire to avoid demonstrating low ability (Elliot & Church 1997; Elliot et al. 1999; Middleton & Midgely 1997; Midgley et al. 1998).

The study

The study involved a sample of EAP learners. The learners were given a questionnaire to measure their goal orientations. A model of goal orientations was proposed and tested using confirmatory factor analysis. The results indicated a good fit to the data. Based on these results, it was evident that this conceptualization of motivation is relevant to EAP learners. The participants in this study were 275 students (male, $n = 139$; female, $n = 136$) taking EAP courses at intensive language centres in Australia prior to university entry. The students completed a 5-point Likert type questionnaire on goal orientations. The goal orientations were measured using sub-scales taken from the Patterns of Adaptive Learning Survey (PALS) (Midgley et al. 1997). The items were adapted for use with adult second language learners. The questionnaire comprised three sub-scales to measure task, performance approach and performance avoid goal orientations. An example of a task goal item is: *I like English language learning tasks that I'll learn from even if I make a lot of mistakes.* An example of a performance approach goal item is: *Doing better than other students in this class is important to me.* An example of a performance avoid goal is: *It's very important to me that I don't look as though I can't speak English in my class.* The questionnaire used a 5-point Likert scale ranging from 1 – *not at all true of me* to 5 – *very true of me.* Each sub-scale comprised five items.

Confirmatory factor analysis was chosen as the most applicable method of data analysis because the research concerned a latent structure specified *a priori.* A model of motivation orientations comprising task, performance approach and performance avoid was specified using *Linear Structural Relations* (LISREL) computer software (Jöreskog & Sörbom 1996). While exploratory factor analysis can be computed using SPSS, confirmatory factor analysis needs structural equation modeling – specific software such as LISREL or the SPSS supported package Arbuckle (2012). The confirmatory factor model was specified using a covariance matrix as data for the model. The model was then tested for fit using various fit indices (see Table 23.1).

The proposed *confirmatory factor* model of motivation indicated a moderate to good fit to the data according to the fit indices and the factor loadings. The factor loadings are interpreted as in exploratory factor analysis. High loadings indicate a strong relationship between the latent variable and the observed variable. The model confirmed three latent variables: task, performance approach and performance avoid goal orientations. The model includes error for each observed variable. Correlations between the latent variables are also illustrated. Thus, performance goals were highly correlated, probably because both are informed by self-referent perspectives. There was a small correlation between task and performance approach goals, which is in keeping with other researchers (Midgley et al. 1998). There was also a moderate correlation between a task goal and a performance avoid goal. This result indicates that for this sample, participants could feasibly have both orientations. Figure 23.3 illustrates the model and Table 23.2 provides the fit indices.

Conclusions reached in the study

This study made a contribution to second language motivation research because it applied goal orientation theory to English language learning. It used this conceptualization of motivation for EAP learners. It seems reasonable to adopt an educational perspective with such a sample since the learners have both language and educational goals. The participants all intended to continue to study in a tertiary institution. The results from the confirmatory factor model indicated that goal orientation theory is applicable to EAP learners. The results also confirmed that a task goal is a variable of adaptive learning and that it was related to high achievement in language learning.

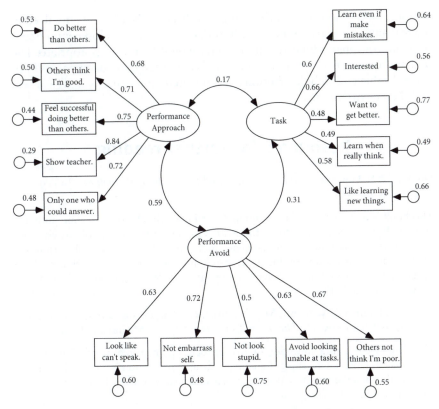

FIGURE 23.3 *Confirmatory factor analysis for motivational goals*

Table 23.2 Fit Indices for confirmatory factor analysis of second language motivation goal orientations

	χ^2	p	χ^2/df	RMR	RMSEA	GFI	AGFI	CFI	NFI	NNFI
Motivation Goals	194.96	0.000	2.22	0.06	0.07	0.91	0.87	0.90	0.84	0.88

This project examined a new way of thinking about motivation in language learning but like most research into motivation, it used a cross-sectional design which provided a snapshot of the motivation of the sample. However, second language motivation may change over time as the second language develops and is influenced by many teaching and learning contexts (Ushioda 2001). So, there is a need for more research that can reflect these contextual and temporal aspects of second language motivation. It would be valuable for such research to be qualitative, thus making it possible to examine motivation from various angles, reflecting the elements involved in the teaching and learning process. In order to capture developmental issues over time, a longitudinal research design would be most appropriate. The best approach is perhaps a mixed methods approach that encompasses both generalizable and rich descriptions of motivated (and demotivated) learners and their environments.

Resources for further reading

Dörnyei, Z & Ushioda, E 2011, *Teaching and Researching Motivation*, 2nd edn, Pearson, Harlow.

This book is in its second edition and includes Ema Ushioda as the second author. Ushioda brings a qualitative focus to research in motivation. The book provides an overview of research into second language motivation. There is a useful section on sources and resources for conducting research into motivation. This includes advice for developing research projects focusing on language learning motivation and the methods used to do this.

Mercer, S, Ryan, S & Williams, M (eds), 2013, *Psychology for Language Learning: Insights from Research, Theory and Practice*, Palgrave Macmillan, London.

This volume contains a collection of articles focusing on current psychological constructs in language learning. Language learning motivation is a central theme running through the volume. As such, it provides a state of the art view of motivation research.

Dörnyei, Z & Ushioda, E (eds), 2009, *Motivation, Language, Identity and the L2 Self*, Multilingual Matters, Clevedon.

Dörnyei is arguably the most prominent researcher and scholar in second language motivation today. This collection of research papers into second language motivation is a valuable contribution to the literature in the field. The collection includes qualitative studies into motivation.

Midgley, C (ed.), 2002, *Goals, Goal Structures and Patterns of Adaptive Learning*, Lawrence Erlbaum, Mahwah, NJ.

This is a selection of papers based on a long-term study using the PALS into motivation in a school setting. It includes a methodological focus and a chapter on methods to investigate motivation.

Murray, G, Gao, X & Lamb, T 2011, *Identity, Motivation and Autonomy in Language Learning*, Multilingual Matters, Bristol.

The current trend in motivation research is to examine its relationship to other related variables. This volume of articles brings together a number of contemporary studies focusing on identity, motivation and autonomy in a wide range of research settings and using various research methodologies.

Ushioda, E 2013, *International Perspectives on Motivation: Language Learning and Professional Challenges*, Palgrave Macmillan, London.

This edited volume focuses on motivation and the learning of English. It features articles based on research conducted in different regions and educational settings. It includes a chapter on goal orientations by this author.

Schunk, DH, Meece, PR & Pintrich, PR 2013, *Motivation in Education: Theory, Research and Applications*, 4th edn, Pearson, Upper Saddle River, NJ.

This book provides an overview of the major theories of motivation in education research. It describes how these perspectives on motivation may be implemented in classrooms.

Woodrow, LJ 2006, 'A model of adaptive second language learning', *Modern Language Journal*, vol. 90, no. 3, pp. 297–319.

This article presents the research that resulted in the motivation model of adaptive second language learning referred to in this chapter. The model comprises self-efficacy, anxiety, motivation and language learning in relation to English language proficiency.

References

Ames, C 1992, 'Classrooms: Goals and structures and student motivation', *Journal of Educational Psychology*, vol. 84, no. 3, pp. 261–271.

Ames, C & Archer, J 1988, 'Achievement goals in the classroom: Students learning strategies and motivational processes', *Journal of Educational Psychology*, vol. 80, no. 3, pp. 260–267.

Arbuckle, JL 2012, *AMOS (version 21)*, SPSS, Chicago, IL.

Blunch, NJ 2008, *Introduction to Structural Equation Modeling Using SPSS and AMOS*, Sage, London.

Busse, V & Walter, C 2013, 'Foreign language motivation in higher education: A longitudinal study of motivational changes and their causes', *Modern Language Journal*, vol. 97, no. 2, pp. 435–456.

Crookes, G & Schmidt, RW 1991, 'Motivation: Reopening the research agenda', *Language Learning*, vol. 41, no. 4, pp. 469–512.

Deci, EL & Ryan, RM 1980, 'The empirical exploration of intrinsic motivational processes', in L Berkowitz (ed.), *Advances in Experimental Social Psychology*, vol. 13, Pergamon Press, New York, NY, pp. 39–80.

——— 1985, *Intrinsic Motivation and Self-Determination in Human Behaviour*, Plenum, New York, NY.

Dörnyei, Z 1990, 'Conceptualizing motivation in foreign language learning', *Language Learning*, vol. 40, no. 1, pp. 45–78.

——— 1994, 'Understanding L2 motivation: On with the challenge', *The Modern Language Journal*, vol. 78, no. 4, pp. 515–523.

——— 1996, 'Moving language learning motivation to a larger platform for theory and practice', in R Oxford (ed.), *Language Learning Motivation: Pathways to the New Century* (Technical report vol. 11), University of Hawai'i at Manoa, Honolulu,, HI, pp. 71–80.

———— 2000, 'Motivation in action: Towards a process-oriented conceptualization of student motivation', *British Journal of Educational Psychology*, vol. 70, no. 4, pp. 519–538.

———— 2001, 'New themes and approaches in second language motivation research', *Annual Review of Applied Linguistics*, vol. 21, pp. 43–59.

Dörnyei, Z, Csizer, K & Nemeth, N 2006, *Motivation, Language Attitudes and Globalisation: A Hungarian Perspective*, Multilingual Matters, Clevedon.

Dörnyei, Z & Kubanyiova, M 2014, *Motivating Learners, Motivating Teachers: Building Vision in the Language Classroom*, Cambridge University Press, Cambridge.

Dörnyei, Z & Otto, I 1998, 'Motivation in action: A process model of L2 motivation', *Working Papers in Applied Linguistics*, vol. 4, pp. 43–69.

Dörnyei, Z & Schmidt, RW (eds), 2001, *Motivation and Second Language Acquisition*, University of Hawai'i at Manoa, Honolulu, HI.

Dörnyei, Z & Ushioda, E 2011, *Teaching and Researching Motivation*, 2nd edn, Pearson, Harlow.

Elliot, A & Church, M 1997, 'A hierarchical model of approach and avoidance', *Journal of Personality and Social Psychology*, vol. 72, no. 1, pp. 218–232.

Elliot, A, McGregor, HA & Gable, S 1999, 'Achievement goals, study strategies and exam performance: A mediational analysis', *Journal of Educational Psychology*, vol. 91, no. 3, pp. 549–563.

Gardner, RC 1985, *Social Psychology and Language Learning*, Edward Arnold, London.

———— 1988, 'The socio-educational model of second language learning: Assumptions, findings and issues', *Language Learning*, vol. 38, no. 1, pp. 101–126.

———— 2006, 'The socio-educational model of second language acquisition', *EUROSLA Yearbook*, vol. 6, no. 1, pp. 237–260.

Gardner, RC & Lambert, W 1959, 'Motivational variables in second language acquisition', *Canadian Journal of Psychology*, vol. 13, no. 4, pp. 266–272.

———— 1972, *Attitude and Motivation*, Newbury House, Rowley, MA.

Gardner, RC & MacIntyre, PD 1993, 'On the measurement of affective variables', *Language Learning*, vol. 43, no. 2, pp. 157–194.

Gardner, RC, Tremblay, P & Masgoret, A 1997, 'Towards a full model of second language learning: An empirical investigation', *The Modern Language Journal*, vol. 81, no. 3, pp. 344–362.

Guilloteaux, MJ & Dörnyei, Z 2008, 'Motivating language learners: A classroom-oriented investigation of the effects of motivational strategies on student motivation', *TESOL Quarterly*, vol. 42, no. 1, pp. 55–77.

Heckhausen, H 1991, *Motivation and Action*, Springer, New York, NY.

Heckhausen, H & Kuhl, J 1985, 'From wishes to action: The dead ends and short cuts on the long way to action', in M Frese & J Sabini (eds), *Goal Directed Behaviour: The Concept of Action in Psychology*, Lawrence Erlbaum, Hillsdale, NJ, pp. 134–160.

Holmes-Smith, P 2000, *Introduction to Structural Equation Modeling Using LISREL*, School Research, Evaluation and Measurement Services, Melbourne.

Jöreskog, KG & Sörbom, D 1996, *LISREL 8: User's Reference Guide*, Scientific Software International, Chicago, IL.

Kaiser, HF 1960, 'The application of electronic computers to factor analysis', *Educational and Psychological Measurement*, vol. 20, no. 1, pp. 141–151.

Lamb, M 2004, 'Integrative motivation in a globalizing world', *System*, vol. 32, no. 1, pp. 3–19.

Masgoret, A & Gardner, R 2003, 'Attitudes, motivation, and second language learning: A meta–analysis of studies conducted by Gardner and associates', *Language Learning*, vol. 53, no. 1, pp. 123–163.

McIntosh, CN & Noels, KA 2004, 'Self-determined motivation for language learning: The role of need for cognition and language learning strategies', *Zeitschrift für Interkulturellen Fremdsprachenunterricht*, Online, vol. 9, no. 2, p. 28, viewed 19 August 2014, https://zif.spz.tu-darmstadt.de/jg-09-2/beitrag/Mcintosh2.htm

Middleton, M & Midgley, C 1997, 'Avoiding the demonstration of lack of ability: An underexplored aspect of goal theory', *Journal of Educational Psychology*, vol. 89, no. 4, pp. 710–718.

Midgley, C, Kaplan, A, Middleton, M, Maehr, M, Urdan, T, Anderman, L, Anderman, E & Roeser, R 1998, 'The development and validation of scales assessing students' achievement goal orientations', *Contemporary Educational Psychology*, vol. 23, no. 2, pp. 113–131.

Midgley, C, Maehr, M, Hicks, L, Roeser, R, Urdan, T, Anderman, E, Kaplan, A, Arunkumar, R & Middleton, M 1997, *Patterns of Adaptive Learning Survey*, University of Michigan, Ann Arbor, MI.

Moskovsky, C, Alrabai, F, Paolini, S & Racheva, S 2013, The effects of teachers' motivational strategies on learners' motivation: A controlled investigation of second language acquisition', *Language Learning*, vol. 63, no. 1, pp. 34–62.

Noels, KA 2001, 'New orientations in language learning motivation: Towards a model of intrinsic, extrinsic and integrative orientations and motivation', in Z Dörnyei & RW Schmidt (eds), *Motivation and Second Language Learning*, University of Hawai' i Press, Honolulu, HI, pp. 43–68.

Noels, KA, Clement, R & Pelletier, LC 1999, 'Perceptions of teachers' communicative style and students' intrinsic and extrinsic motivation', *The Modern Language Journal*, vol. 83, no. 1, pp. 23–34.

—— (2001), 'Intrinsic, extrinsic and integrative orientations of French Canadian learners of English', *Canadian Modern Language Review*, vol. 57, no. 3, pp. 424–442.

Noels, KA, Pelletier, LC, Clement, R & Vallerand, RJ 2000 'Why are you learning a second language? Motivational orientations and self-determination theory', *Language Learning*, vol. 50, no. 1, pp. 57–85.

—— (2003), 'Why are you learning a second language? Motivational orientations and self-determination theory', *Language Learning*, vol. 53, no. 1, pp. 33–64.

Oller, JW 1982, 'Gardner on affect: A reply to Gardner', *Language Learning*, vol. 32, no. 1, pp. 183–189.

Oxford, R 1994, 'Where are we regarding language learning motivation?' *The Modern Language Journal*, vol. 78, no. 4, pp. 512–514.

Oxford, R & Shearin, J 1994, 'Language learning motivation: Expanding the theoretical framework', *The Modern Language Journal*, vol. 78, no. 1, pp. 12–28.

Oxford, RL (ed.), 1996, *Language Learning Motivation: Pathways to the New Century* (Technical report vol. 11), University of Hawai'i at Manoa, Honolulu, HI.

Pae, TI 2008, 'Analysis of the factors affecting second language achievement', *Journal of Language and Social Psychology*, vol. 27, no. 5, pp. 5–27.

Ryan, RM & Deci, EL 2000, 'Intrinsic and extrinsic motivations: Classic definitions and new directions', *Contemporary Educational Psychology*, vol. 25, no. 1, pp. 54–67.

Ryan, S 2009, 'Self and identity in L2 motivation in Japan: The ideal L2 self and Japanese learners of English', in Z Dornyei & E Ushioda (eds), *Motivation, Language Identity and the L2 Self*, Multilingual Matters, Bristol, pp. 120–143.

Schmidt, RW, Boraie, D & Kassabgy, O 1996, 'Foreign language motivation: Internal structure and external connections', in R Oxford (ed.), *Language Learning Motivation: Pathways to the New Century* (Technical report vol. 11), University of Hawai'i at Manoa, Honolulu, HI, pp. 9–70.

Smith, M, Duda, J, Allen, J & Hall, H 2002, 'Contemporary measures of approach and avoidance goal orientations: Similarities and differences', *British Journal of Educational Psychology*, vol. 72, no. 2, pp. 155–190.

Tabachnick, BG & Fidell, LS 2012, *Using Multivariate Statistics*, 6th edn, Pearson, Boston, MA.

Tremblay, P & Gardner, R 1995, 'Expanding the motivation construct in language learning', *The Modern Language Journal*, vol. 79, no. 4, pp. 505–520.

Urdan, T, Ryan, RM, Anderman, E & Gheen, MH 2002, 'Goals, goal structures and avoidance behaviors', in C Midgley (ed.), *Goals, Goal Structures and Patterns of Adaptive Learning*, Lawrence Erlbaum, Mahwah, NJ, pp. 55–84.

Ushioda, E 2001, 'Language learning at university: Exploring the role of motivational thinking', in Z Dörnyei & RW Schmidt (eds), *Motivation and Second Language Acquisition* (Technical report vol. 23), University of Hawai'i at Manoa, Honolulu, HI, pp. 93–125.

―――― 2012, 'Motivation: L2 learning as a special case?', in S Mercer, S Ryan & M Williams (eds), *Psychology for Language Learning: Insights from Research, Theory and Practice*, Palgrave-Macmillan, London.

―――― 2013, *International Perspectives on Motivation: Language Learning and Professional Challenges*, Palgrave Macmillan, London.

Vallerand, RJ (1997), 'Toward a hierarchical model of intrinsic and extrinsic motivation', in MP Zanna (ed.), *Advances in Experimental Social Psychology*, Academic Press, New York, NY, pp 271–360.

Woodrow, LJ 2006, 'A model of adaptive language learning', *The Modern Language Journal*, vol. 90, no. 3, pp. 297–319.

CHAPTER TWENTY FOUR

Researching Language Learner Strategies

Heath Rose

A large area of interest within the field of applied linguistics is the investigation of why certain individuals are able to learn languages more effectively than others. This area of research, called *individual differences in second language acquisition* (see Dörnyei 2005), has become an important field in applied linguistics, incorporating diverse notions such as age, motivation (see also Woodrow this volume) and the exploration of the strategies that language learners use to support their language's own development. While early research into learner strategies in the 1970s (e.g. Rubin 1975) had the intent of highlighting strategies of 'good' language learners, the area of language learner strategies has blossomed into a research field in its own right. Because strategies are learner-driven, the field has naturally strong ties to the fields of self-regulation (see Tseng et al. 2006), learner autonomy (see Benson 2013) and agency (see Gao 2010). This chapter aims to provide an overview of language learner strategy research and to outline the typical stages in conducting research in this field. It, then, discusses issues involved with choosing the right data collection instruments and theoretical framework for research. Finally, it discusses problems in the field.

A synthesis of current thinking and research on language learner strategies

Language Learner Strategies are processes and actions that are consciously deployed by language learners to help them to learn or use a language more effectively. A more specific definition is the '[t]houghts and actions, consciously chosen and operationalized by language learners, to assist them in carrying out a multiplicity of tasks from the very outset of learning to the most advanced levels of target language performance' (Cohen 2011, p. 7). There is considerable debate over what these 'thoughts and actions' include, and also over the relationship strategies have with language learning success. One central problem in the study of any individual difference in second language acquisition (SLA) is how to measure success, which is an issue that remains severely underdeveloped (see Macaro 2010 for further discussion).

In general, learner strategies can be divided into those applied for language learning, those applied for language use and those applied to language testing (Cohen 2011). Language *learning* strategies encompass the cognitive strategies (e.g. memorization and recollection techniques) and metacognitive strategies (e.g. the preplanning, monitoring and evaluation of one's learning) used by a learner when learning a language. Under many conceptualizations, the definition also encompasses the affective and sociocultural strategies used to regulate external factors in the learning process. For example, a sociocultural strategy might involve how the learner engages and learns with others in the environment around them; an affective strategy refers to how a learner regulates their emotions and attitude towards learning. A language *use* strategy encompasses the strategies deployed when a learner is using the language and includes different foci such as coping strategies (e.g. compensating for lacks in language knowledge) and more general communication strategies (e.g. accommodating and adjusting language to different speakers and contexts). While the distinction between language learning and language use is useful to compartmentalize and focus a research topic, some researchers prefer not to emphasize the difference because 'it does not acknowledge the fact that every instance of language use offers the potential for language learning' (Oxford et al. 2014, p. 32). Test-taking strategies offer a further dimension to strategic behaviour due to the fact that learners often apply a very different set of strategies in the high-stakes context of language examinations. Often, test-taking strategies have a clear purpose to navigate and manage a test; a learner, for example, will read a passage in a test very differently to how they would engage with the same text for the purposes of extracting meaning (language use), or study (in the sense of language learning). In the application of test-taking strategies, a learner may read the questions first and engage with the text for the sole purposes of finding the answers to the questions. Studies such as Phakiti (2003) have found the use of cognitive and metacognitive strategies to have a positive relationship to reading test performance; that is, more successful test-takers report using significantly more strategies than less successful test-takers.

In addition to focussing strategy research on certain functions of language learning (such as cognitive strategies, metacognitive strategies, affective strategies and sociocultural strategies), it is also possible to examine learner strategies used in the development of a particular language skill (such as reading, listening, speaking and writing), or in a refined segment of acquisition (e.g. vocabulary or grammar). In the 1970s, 1980s and early 1990s, researchers aimed to research strategies across the multiple functions and skills involved when learning and using a second language (O'Malley & Chamot 1990; Oxford 1990; Rubin 1975, 1987). Vast inventories such as Oxford's (1990) Strategy Inventory of Language Learning (SILL) were widely used by researchers and teachers to measure general strategy use. These inventories were influential in the establishment of language learner strategies as a legitimate field of study in applied linguistics. However, conflicting research findings and difficulties in categorizing strategies within such inventories opened the field up to much criticism. Since the late 1990s and early 2000s, current thinking in the field is moving away from broad definitions and 'catch-all' terms that simplify the complexity of language learning. Researchers generally agree that the days of casting a wide net over defining 'good' and 'bad' language learners is a research practice of the past. Researchers nowadays are more concerned with the intricacies of how learners make use of strategies in more finely focused areas of the learning process, rather than making broad assumptions of strategy use across a range of functions, skills and contexts.

Typical stages in language learner strategy research

Typical steps taken by researchers in the area of learner strategies involve, first, choosing a focus of strategy research in order to avoid the pitfalls of the catch-all studies of the past. Second, choosing the correct instruments to measure strategy use is especially important in order to collect valid data, which may not be immediately apparent to the researcher. Finally, in the data analysis stage, it is essential that researchers evaluate the validity of learner-reported strategy use against actual strategic behaviour. Each of these three stages will be discussed in turn.

Choosing a focus of strategy research

Researchers of learner strategies in recent years highlight the importance of focussing on situated contexts. Takeuchi et al. (2007, p. 92), for example, state that the 'individual and situational context in which a learner operates is complex'. For example, a participant could well deploy a completely different cluster of strategies to the task of vocabulary learning compared with those applied to the study of speaking and communication. Likewise, those deployed by high-school learners of language might differ greatly to those deployed by the same learners when learning the same language during a language exchange, or at university. Thus, a researcher must embrace this complexity when setting up a study to ensure findings are situated in the context being studied.

A researcher will need to decide what dimension of learner strategies to focus on, whether it be a particular language learning skill, such as the investigation of reading strategies, listening strategies and vocabulary-acquisition strategies, or a functional dimension of language learning strategies, such as looking at the cognitive strategies and metacognitive strategies in a broader scope of second language learning. The focus of strategy research could be refined even further by looking at a function within a skill, such as the cognitive strategies deployed when listening to lectures in a second language. Without such a focus, the researcher is in danger of drawing sweeping conclusions of language learning that may extend beyond the sample used for the study.

Instrumentation and data collection

The selection of appropriate instruments to measure a learner's strategic thoughts and actions is one of the most important challenges faced by researchers in the field. Historically, researchers have used questionnaires based on inventories of reported strategy use, but due to the problems outlined later in this chapter, there have been calls for researchers to use more qualitative data collection techniques (e.g. Rose 2012a; Woodrow 2005). A researcher will have to weigh up the importance of thin data obtained from a larger number of participants in quantitative approaches against the benefits of thick data obtained from a smaller number of participants using qualitative approaches. Generally speaking, a quantitative approach might be a good fit to investigate *what* strategies are deployed, and a qualitative approach might be a better fit to answer *how* strategies are deployed. Furthermore, quantitative approaches may be more appropriate in a field where a lot of research has been done (e.g. ESL reading strategies), but a qualitative approach will provide more valuable data for lesser-researched areas (e.g. Chinese as a foreign language reading strategies), because a questionnaire could potentially miss unexpected intricacies in the learning process.

Data analysis

Data analysis will largely depend on the instruments chosen by the researcher: see Phakiti (this volume) for an overview of quantitative data analysis and Holliday (this volume) for an overview of qualitative data analysis. However, there are a few issues particular to learner strategy research that researchers should consider when analysing data. First, strategy research has come under criticism for studies that compute mean scores of strategy inventories (Dörnyei 2005; Tseng et al. 2006). Dörnyei (2005, p. 182) has been particularly vocal in his criticism of the SILL, arguing that 'the scales in the SILL are not cumulative and computing mean scores is psychometrically not justifiable'. This argument is based on the fact that the SILL frequency scales are not linear in relationship, and that the SILL items connect to specific (and separate) behaviours rather than general trends and shared inclinations that can be pooled together as part of the same scale. Other inventories such as those listed later in this chapter are less susceptible to criticism, but a researcher will have to consider the most appropriate statistical tests to run based on the nature of the questionnaire used.

Inventories can be extremely useful when coding qualitative data as they identify known learner strategies based on decades of research. Once again, in a well-established field like ESL reading strategies, the researcher can begin coding with a 'start list' of codes based on such inventories, but in a lesser researched area, these codes might emerge from the data as researchers become more familiar with the processes at hand. This decision of whether coding is a bottom-up or top-down, inductive or deductive, or emic or etic process is an important one to be made by the researcher in the data-analysis stage – and is a topic discussed at length by Gu (2014).

Research strategies and techniques

As strategies are learner-internal and not immediately observable, research techniques employed by researchers tend towards those that rely on self-report of the learners themselves. This section will explore the issues involved in the application of commonly used techniques of questionnaires, interviews, introspective and retrospective learning tasks and diaries.

Questionnaires

Questionnaires were one of the most widely used instruments of learner strategy research in the 1990s, which was a decade of booming research in the field. Thus, novice researchers are often tempted to replicate research from this time, which can be dangerous, considering that some of these questionnaires are no longer compatible with current thinking in the field. To help researchers decide on an appropriate instrument, an outline of commonly used measures is provided:

- *Strategy Inventory of Language Learning* (SILL). Oxford's (1990) SILL is 'the most widely used instrument in language learner strategy research' (White et al. 2007, p. 95). However, in modern times, the questionnaire is seen as quite problematic. Because each item is directly connected with a specific strategy, students who use many strategies in an ineffective way can be measured as more strategic than students who apply a smaller number of strategies in a more effective fashion – a problem not unnoticed by Oxford herself (Yamamori et al. 2003). This, coupled with issues of validity outlined by Dörnyei (2005), means novice researchers in the area of learner strategies should avoid using the SILL as their main instrument.

- *Motivated Strategies for Learning Questionnaire* (MSLQ). The MSLQ was developed by a team of researchers (Pintrich et al. 1991) about the same time as the SILL. Although the scale was the result of three years of development and testing, it was not as widely used as the SILL, perhaps due to the creators' later cautiousness in claiming it to only have relatively good reliability (Pintrich et al. 1993). In his critique of the SILL, Dörnyei (2005) has a more favourable position towards the MSLQ, arguing it to be the most widely known data collection instrument in the field of educational psychology.

- *Language Strategy Use Inventory* (Cohen et al. 2006), sometimes referred to as the Language Strategy Use Survey, was developed to have a more practical focus. The authors acknowledge that its validity is fair, but not strong (Cohen 2011).

- *Survey of Reading Strategies* (SORS) (Mokharti & Sheorey 2002) was developed from the *Metacognitive Awareness Of Reading Strategies Inventory* (Mokhtari & Reichard 2002). The SORS is considered to have good overall reliability and is still used widely today. This survey is an example of an attempt to move away from a one-size-fits-all questionnaire, and tailor strategy research to specific skills.

- *Metacognitive Awareness Listening Questionnaire* (MALQ). This questionnaire, developed by Vandergrift et al. (2006), specifically measures strategies deployed in listening tasks. While the instrument does not include all possible listening strategies, it is considered to have good internal validity (White et al. 2007, p. 96).

While the above is an outline of popular questionnaires in strategy research, it is not an exhaustive list. In fact, many other questionnaires have been developed for niche areas of strategy research, so it is important for researchers to familiarize themselves with the instruments used in their chosen field. For example, Zhang et al. (2014) constructed their own forty-item writing strategy survey for use in primary classrooms in Singapore, which showed robust reliability and would serve as a useful base for similar studies into writing strategies.

The use of such inventories calls into question issues of validity surrounding self-report measures, which are particularly problematic seeing as much learner strategy research centres on cognitive and metacognitive processes of which the learner might not be accurately able to describe. Moreover, in any longitudinal study, the use of questionnaires can influence the very strategies being measured. Rubin et al. (2007, p. 151), for example, state that the act of reading a questionnaire that lists known strategies can raise awareness for older learners. For these reasons, researchers must be cautious of the impact of using such measures on the validity of the study.

Introspective tasks

For those studies where cognitive and metacognitive strategies are a key focus, a range of introspective methods such as think-aloud techniques, where participants voice their thoughts while completing a task, can be useful for collecting data. Gu (2014, p. 74) claims that it is 'widely agreed that various versions of thinking aloud are the most direct and therefore best tools available in examining the on-going processes and intentions as and when learning happens'. Hyland (2010, p. 197) supports this notion in his assertion that think-aloud techniques have been extremely productive in the investigation of the writing strategies that students deploy when composing, planning and revising texts. Hyland's claim is also supported in recent research (e.g. Alnufaie & Grenfell 2012) that examines, via a think-aloud task, the writing strategies used in examination writing tasks by ESL students in Saudi Arabia.

Retrospective interviews

While think-aloud tasks can be useful in the study of silent learning activities, they have obvious interference in language learning tasks where the act of voicing thoughts aloud would interfere with the learning process and language use. For this reason, researchers often have to turn to retrospective methods, such as interviewing participants after the event being studied. Takeuchi et al. (2007, p. 94) make the following observation:

> As the field moves towards a deeper understanding of strategy use influenced by particular cultural, contextual, and individual factors, retrospective interviews re-emerge as an important tool providing opportunities for exploration and elaboration of aspects of strategy use.

Nevertheless, retrospective interviews are sometimes seen as problematic due to the time between completion of a task (in this case a learning event) and the reporting of it in a retrospective interview.

Stimulated recall

Stimulated recall is a data collection technique that aims to strengthen reliability of retrospection through the use of stimuli to prompt memory of the processes and behaviours associated with completing a task. In language studies research, stimuli are often in the form of audio or video recordings of the task being studied but can include a number of other artefacts such as a test when examining test-taking strategies, a textbook when examining learning strategies and a recording of a lecture with a student's handwritten notes when examining language use strategies. In discussing the usefulness of stimulated recall in researching learner processes, Tseng et al. (2006), observe that the method is a highly promising but yet underutilized data collection technique. Stimulated recall, however, has potential problems related to issues of mistaken memory and retrieval, ill-timing and poor instructions (Mackey & Gass 2005), and thus the researcher must design the task carefully to ensure the use of strong stimuli to activate memory structures. According to Vandergrift (2010), the reliability of stimulated recall protocols is clearly connected to the amount of time between the stimulated recall session and the event being discussed. Thus, stimulated recall tasks work best when applied immediately after the event being researched (Mackey & Gass 2005). Rose (2012b; 2013) has found that, when used effectively, stimulated recall data are more revealing and more reliable than other self-report instruments, such as questionnaires and interviews.

Diary studies

One underutilized data collection technique in the field of language learner strategies is the use of learner journals or diaries. Journals can be a powerful research method to gain insight into learner practices and thoughts that may be impossible to elicit using other data collection methods, because the participants help the researcher keep records of a learner's own thoughts, emotions and actions (Dörnyei 2007). In some learner strategy studies (e.g. Ma & Oxford 2014), diaries have been used to provide a less structured narrative-like account of strategy use. Bolger et al. (2003) outline a number of structured diary formats, of which an 'event-based design' is probably of most relevance to learner strategy research. Here, participants are asked to answer questions in the diary directly after the learning event being studied. This format helps to minimize the time between the event and the report, thus avoiding the problems of other retrospective data collection methods, but adds structure to a research project more so than a narrative account.

Problems associated with researching language learner strategies

Problems faced by researchers of language learner strategies tend to fall into two categories: those of a methodological nature and those of a definitional nature. As such, both of these will be discussed in turn.

Methodological problems

The largest challenge faced by researchers of language learner strategies is the issue of how to measure them. The bulk of research into language learner strategies centres on the use of questionnaires and learner introspection. Putting aside the issues of validity of questionnaires already discussed, researchers must also contend with the reliability of self-report measures. Triangulation of data through use of multiple methods is paramount to researching language learner strategies in order to highlight potential inconsistencies in reported strategy use. In general, there is a trend in current research to move towards more context-specific research approaches using in-depth qualitative methods which provide a richer and more reliable picture of strategy use. Therefore, if a quantitative approach is pursued, it should generally be supplemented with some degree of qualitative data in order to substantiate findings.

Definitional problems

A second problem associated with researching language learner strategies is the definitional fuzziness of major concepts in the field. Macaro (2006, p. 325) summarizes these problems as a lack of consensus of:

1 Whether strategies occur inside or outside of the brain.
2 Whether learner strategies consist of knowledge, intention, action or all three.
3 Whether to classify strategies in frameworks, hierarchies [or clusters].
4 Whether strategies survive across all learning situations, tasks and contexts.
5 Whether they are integral or additive to language processing.

Macaro (2006) also points to a lack of consensus in the field of what strategies consist of, how they should be defined, their relationship to skills and processes and their effect on language development in the long term.

Owing to definitional problems, there has been mounting criticism over learning strategy research since its very inception, including the following observations:

1   There are conflicting results and methodologies (Skehan 1989).

2   Definitions of learning strategies are 'ad hoc and atheoretical' (Ellis 1994, p. 533).

3   Past studies have attempted to describe and quantify strategies rather than to incorporate them into a model of psycholinguistic processing (Ellis 1997).

4   The conceptualization of learning strategies is 'rather inconsistent and elusive' (Dörnyei & Skehan 2003, p. 608).

5   The 'term has been used in far too broad a sense, including a number of different things that do not necessarily belong together' (Dörnyei & Skehan 2003, p. 610).

6   The construct of learning strategies, while useful for researchers, is less helpful when conducting in-depth analyses of what it consists of (Dörnyei 2005).

7   There has been no coherent agreement on the defining criteria for a language learning strategy (Tseng et al. 2006).

Dörnyei and his collaborators have been particularly vocal on several occasions that the problematic concept of strategies be abandoned in place of self-regulation, which they argue is a more stable field (Dörnyei 2005; Dörnyei & Skehan 2003; Tseng et al. 2006). Self-regulation is argued to examine underlying intentions that manifest in strategy use, rather than examining the actual strategies themselves. In response to this argument, Grenfell and Macaro (2007, p. 27) have argued that Dörnyei has made 'a straw man in order to knock him down' indicating that Dörnyei's criticisms were based on weaker aspects of strategy research which were not representative of current trends in the field. I have argued previously that replacing strategy research with self-regulation would be a case of throwing the baby out with the bathwater, in that it throws out decades of research because of definitional issues. Indeed, self-regulation and learner strategies are not incompatible but examine different parts of the learning process – a sentiment shared by Gao (2006). More recently, Gu (2012, p. 331) has argued that 'conceptual fuzziness should not be a problem serious enough to overthrow forty years of research on language learning strategies' and 'the proposed alternative term "self- regulation" or even a more general and key term "learning" fall into the same fuzziness trap', indicating 'that the find-another-term solution is not viable'.

Definitional fuzziness is often a concern for fields of study in SLA, where the process of learning is not easily definable, nor easily categorized into neat boxes. Larsen-Freeman and Cameron (2008) prefer to view language acquisition as a complex adaptive system, in order to move away from an ideology that clearly defined lines can be drawn around something as complex as language learning. They argue that while linguists treat language as a stable system, applied linguists need a very different theory of language: 'complex systems are at one and the same time both stable and variable' (Freeman & Cameron 2008, p. 79). By taking a more complex view of language, issues such as definitional fuzziness in learner strategies are seen as a natural occurrence, rather than a reason to dismiss them outright.

Nevertheless, the early to mid-2000s mark a watershed in language learner strategy research, when in light of criticism of definitional fuzziness, the field shifted focus (see Macaro 2010 for a list of published research over time). Some researchers repositioned language learner strategy research within a theoretical framework of self-regulation (e.g. Tseng et al. 2006). Oxford (2011) later integrated self-regulation into her positioning of strategic learning in the 'strategic self-regulation (S2R) model', although this model has not gained the same traction in the field as her more widely known 1990 taxonomy. In general, the field has moved closer to others around it, including self-regulation, cognitive science, learner autonomy, and more recently, agency.

A sample study

To illustrate research into language learner strategies, I will draw on a multifaceted study into the learning strategies deployed by students learning Japanese as a foreign language, which has been disseminated in a number of research articles (Rose 2012a, b, 2013; Rose & Harbon 2013). The study involved the examination of learning strategies and self-regulatory mechanisms deployed by learners of Japanese as a foreign language when studying written Japanese characters called *kanji*. The study focused on kanji learning because the learning of this script is a major obstacle for foreign language learners to attain literacy in Japanese. Additionally, a focus on kanji learning allowed the researcher to examine multiple functions of strategic behaviour in a specific learning context.

The study took a qualitative approach in line with recommendations at the time for this kind of research (Tseng et al. 2006; Woodrow 2005). Data collection tools included stimulated recall tasks, semi-structured retrospective interviews, and a strategy inventory for kanji learning, which was developed from previous work in the field (Bourke 1996; Rose 2003). The study took a multiple case study approach in order to obtain a richer picture of strategy use over a longer period of time. Participants for the study were selected based on criteria that aimed to sample typical, extreme and deviant cases of strategy use. This decision was based on limitations of previous research, which tended to focus on the good language learner and neglected other cases.

Participants were interviewed bi-weekly in conjunction with regular kanji tests to investigate the types of learning activities they were engaged in. Stimulated recall tasks were built into the interviews, where the students would retake their classroom-based kanji tests in front of the researcher while talking-aloud their cognitive processes when recalling each kanji. Thus, when provided with the stimuli of the test, the participants could more accurately voice in detail how they recalled (and had learned) each item on the test, bringing the retrospection closer to introspection and improving the validity of the data yielded.

Data from the stimulated recall were analysed qualitatively by coding responses according to known strategy inventories – in this case an inventory of kanji learning strategies compiled by Bourke (1996) and later adapted by Rose (2003). Qualitative data provided a rich window into the cognitive strategies students deployed when learning kanji such as:

> The verb *taberu* [*eat*]. Yeah. It looks like a house. So, for me, I eat in a house, or I eat in a restaurant, which is like a building. So I would always think of it as the building. (Participant E, Interview 4)

In this instance, the data show that the learner used a pictorial association strategy when linking the kanji 食 [*eat*] with her existing understanding of the shape of a building. The participant then related this picture with the meaning of the kanji through a mnemonic strategy of 'eating in a restaurant, which is like a building' (Rose 2013, p. 985). While qualitative data show how second language learners learn individual, and often isolated, kanji, they can form a bank of examples which further provide a broader picture of the learner strategies employed.

As part of this study, twelve participants were given twenty different kanji, each in ten separate stimulated recall tasks, resulting in 200 items per participant and 2400 in total. With this volume of data, there was some scope to quantify the qualitative data yielded, in order to illustrate the patterns and differences in strategy choice across cases. By analysing data in this way, the study was able to draw conclusions of not only how learning strategies were deployed, but also patterns of learning strategies over time, and across cases. Examining patterns within and across cases, conclusions could be drawn within this cohort of learners, such as the necessity for advanced learners to break a kanji into its smaller components rather than memorize them in a more holistic fashion.

A methodological finding of the study highlighted the inaccuracies of questionnaires in this type of research (Rose 2012b). For example, questionnaire data indicated that students self-reported that they applied pictorial association strategies when learning kanji (such as in the example of kanji 食 [*eat*], above). However, stimulated recall sessions showed that application of pictorial strategies was quite rare, and, in fact, almost non-existent in the advanced learners. Such disconnect between reported strategy usage and observed strategy usage highlights the inherent dangers of self-report measures. While the stimulated recall task aimed to validate self-report, the researcher was still reliant on participants to be consciously aware of their cognitive processes and behaviours to an extent that they could articulate them accurately. In a subsequent four-year funded project that was based on this study, eye-tracking methodologies were utilized as an additional data collection technique to further enhance understanding of how learners study kanji. Such decisions were in light of recent studies that showed very encouraging evidence supporting the usefulness of eye-tracking methodologies to support introspective, self-report data collection techniques (Gu 2014).

Resources for further reading

Cohen, AD & Macaro, E (eds), 2007, *Language Learner Strategies: Thirty Years of Research and Practice*, Oxford University Press, Oxford.

This edited volume provides a wide overview of strategy research from key authors in the field. The first half of the book addresses many important issues faced by researchers. The second half summarizes research in numerous sub-fields, such as writing strategies, reading strategies and vocabulary learning strategies.

Cohen, AD 2011, *Strategies in Learning and Using a Second Language*, Pearson Education, Harlow.

This is one of the more thorough and balanced introductions to language learner strategies of the recent publications. Rather than being driven by a personal agenda, its purpose is to provide a comprehensive resource of current trends in the field. It explores the nature of strategies on a number of key dimensions, provides an outline of methods suitable for strategy research and delves into issues surrounding strategy instruction.

Dörnyei, Z 2005, *The Psychology of the Language Learner: Individual Differences in Second Language Acquisition*, Lawrence Erlbaum, Mahwah, NJ.

In Chapter 6 of his book (pp. 162–195), Dörnyei critically evaluates language learning strategy research. It is essential reading for novice researchers, as it questions many problematic facets of the field, including commonly used conceptualizations and data collection tools. Much of this content also appears in an earlier co-authored work (Dörnyei & Skehan, 2003).

Oxford, RL 2011, *Teaching and Researching Language Learning Strategies*, Pearson Education, Harlow.

In this book, Oxford introduces her Strategic Self-Regulation (S2R) Model. The impact of criticisms of the mid-2000s is clear, with links to self-regulation theory throughout the book. While this model has not gained as much traction as her 1990s taxonomy of learning strategies, the book remains an important read.

Rose, H 2012a, 'Reconceptualizing strategic learning in the face of self-regulation: Throwing language learning strategies out with the bathwater', *Applied Linguistics*, vol. 33, no. 1, pp. 92–98.

This article weighs up the arguments to discard language learning strategies in place of self-regulation and acts as a good counterpoint to the claims made by Dörnyei (2005). The article acknowledges that self-regulation is an important emerging field but is an inadequate replacement for strategy research. A similar perspective can be found in Grenfell and Macaro (2007), Gao (2006) and Gu (2012).

Macaro, E 2010, 'The relationship between strategic behaviour and language learning success', in E Macaro (ed.), *Continuum Companion to Second Language Acquisition*, Continuum, London.

In this chapter, Ernesto Macaro takes a critical look at language learner strategy research over the previous thirty-five years. The chapter includes a useful table of published strategy research over time that aimed to correlate strategies with language learning success. Of further interest is a previous journal article by Macaro (2006) that explores the issues surrounding the theoretical challenges of learner strategy research at a critical juncture in its history.

References

Alnufaie, M & Grenfell, M 2012, 'EFL students' writing strategies in Saudi Arabian ESP writing classes: Perspectives on learning strategies in self-access language learning', *Studies in Self-Access Learning Journal*, vol. 3, no. 4, pp. 407–422.

Benson, P 2013, *Teaching and Researching Autonomy*, Routledge, New York, NY.

Bolger, N, Davis, A & Rafaeli, E 2003, 'Diary methods: Capturing life as it is lived',*Annual Review of Psychology*, vol. 54, pp. 579–616.

Bourke, B 1996, *Maximising efficiency in the kanji learning task*, PhD thesis, University of Queensland, Brisbane.

Cohen, AD 2011, *Strategies in Learning and Using a Second Language*, Longman/ Pearson Education, Harlow.

Cohen, AD, Oxford, RL & Chi, JC 2006, 'Language strategy use survey', in AD Cohen & SJ Weaver (eds), *Styles and Strategies-based Instruction: A Teachers' Guide*, Center for Advanced Research on Language Acquisition, University of Minnesota, Minneapolis, MN, pp. 68–75.

Dörnyei, Z 2005, *The Psychology of the Language Learner: Individual Differences in Second Language Acquisition*, Lawrence Erlbaum Associates, Mahwah, NJ.

—— 2007, *Research Methods in Applied Linguistics: Quantitative, Qualitative, and Mixed Methodologics*, Oxford University Press, Oxford.

Dörnyei, Z & Skehan, P 2003, 'Individual differences in second language learning', in CJ Doughty & MH Long (eds), *The handbook of second Language Acquisition*, Blackwell, Oxford, pp. 589–630.

Ellis, R 1994, *The Study of Second Language Acquisition*, Oxford University Press, Oxford.

————— 1997, *Second Language acquisition*, Oxford University Press, Oxford.

Gao, X 2006, 'Has language learning strategy research come to an end? A response to Tseng, Dörnyei', *Applied Linguistics*, vol. 28, no. 4, pp. 615–620.

————— 2010, *Strategic Language Learning: The Roles of Agency and Context*, Multilingual Matters, Bristol.

Grenfell, M & Macaro, E 2007, 'Claims and critiques', in AD Cohen & E Macaro (eds), *Language Learner Strategies: Thirty Years of Research and Practice*, Oxford University Press, Oxford, pp. 9–28.

Gu, Y 2012, 'Learning strategies: Prototypical core and dimensions of variation', *Studies in Self-Access Learning Journal*, vol. 3, no. 4, pp. 330–356.

————— 2014, 'To code or not to code: Dilemmas in analysing think-aloud protocols in learning strategies research', *System*, vol. 43, pp. 74–81.

Hyland, K 2010, 'Researching writing', in B Paltridge & A Phakiti (eds), *Companion to Research Methods in Applied Linguistics*, Continuum, London, pp. 191–204.

Larsen-Freeman, D & Cameron, L 2008, *Complex Systems and Applied Linguistics*, Oxford University Press, Oxford.

Ma, R & Oxford, RL 2014, 'A diary study focusing on listening and speaking: The evolving interaction of learning styles and learning strategies in a motivated, advanced ESL learner', *System*, vol. 43, pp. 101–113.

Macaro, E 2006, 'Strategies for language learning and for language use: Revising the theoretical framework', The *Modern Language Journal*, vol. 90, no. 3, pp. 320–337.

————— 2010, 'The relationship between strategic behaviour and language learning success', in E Macaro (ed.), *Continuum Companion to Second Language Acquisition*, Continuum, London, pp. 268–299.

Mackey, A & Gass, SM 2005, *Second Language Research: Methodology and Design*, Lawrence Erlbaum Associates, Mahwah, NJ.

Mokharti, K & Sheorey, R 2002, 'Measuring ESL students' awareness of reading strategies', *Journal of Developmental Education*, vol. 25, no. 3, pp. 2–10.

Mokhtari, K & Reichard, CA 2002, 'Assessing students' metacognitive awareness of reading strategies', *Journal of Educational Psychology*, vol. 94, no. 2, pp. 249–259.

O'Malley, JM & Chamot, AU 1990, *Learning Strategies in Second Language Acquisition*, Cambridge University Press, New York, NY.

Oxford, RL 1990, *Language Learning Strategies: What Every Teacher Should Know*, Newbury House Publisher, New York, NY.

————— 2011, *Teaching and Researching Language Learning Strategies*, Pearson Education, Harlow.

Oxford, RL, Rubin, J, Chamot, AU, Schramm, K, Lavine, R, Gunning, P & Nel, C 2014, 'The learning strategy prism: Perspectives of learning strategy experts', *System*, vol. 43, pp. 30–49.

Phakiti, A 2003, 'A closer look at the relationship of cognitive and metacognitive strategy use to EFL reading comprehension test performance', *Language Testing*, vol. 20, no. 1, pp. 26–56.

Pintrich, PR, Smith, DAF, Garcia, T & McKeachie, WJ 1991, *A manual for the Use of the Motivated Strategies for Learning Questionnaire (MSLQ)*, National

Center for Research to Improve Post secondary Teaching and Learning, Ann Arbor, MI.

———— 1993, 'Reliability and predictive validity of the motivated strategies for learning questionnaire (MSLQ)', *Educational and Psychological Measurement*, vol. 53, no. 3, pp. 801–813.

Rose, H 2003, 'Teaching learning strategies for learner success', *BABEL: Journal of Modern Language Teaching Association Australia*, vol. 38, no. 2, pp. 32–38.

———— 2012a, 'Reconceptualizing strategic learning in the face of self-regulation: Throwing language learning strategies out with the bathwater', *Applied Linguistics*, vol. 33, no. 1, pp. 92–98.

———— 2012b, 'Language learning strategy research: Where do we go from here?', *Studies in Self Access Learning*, vol. 3, no. 2, pp. 137–148.

———— 2013, 'L2 learners' attitudes toward, and use of, mnemonic strategies when learning Japanese kanji', *The Modern Language Journal*, vol. 97, no. 4, pp. 981–992.

Rose, H & Harbon, L 2013, 'Self-regulation in second language learning: An investigation of the kanji learning task', *Foreign Language Annals*, vol. 46, no. 1, pp. 96–107.

Rubin, J 1975, 'What the good language learner can teach us', *TESOL Quarterly*, vol. 9, no. 1, pp. 41–51.

———— 1987, 'Learner strategies: Theoretical assumptions, research history and typology', in A Wenden & J Rubin (eds), *Learner Strategies in Language Learning*, Prentice Hall, Upper Saddle River, NJ, pp. 15–30.

Rubin, J, Chamot, AU, Harris, V & Anderson, NJ 2007, 'Intervening in the use of strategies', in AD Cohen & E Macaro (eds), *Language Learner Strategies*, Oxford University Press, Oxford, pp. 15–30.

Skehan, P 1989, *Individual Differences in Second Language Learning*, Edward Arnold, London.

Takeuchi, O, Griffiths, C & Coyle, D 2007, 'Applying strategies: The role of individual, situational, and group differences', in AD Cohen & E Macaro (eds), *Language Learner Strategies*, Oxford University Press, Oxford, pp. 69–92.

Tseng, WT, Dörnyei, Z & Schmitt, N 2006, 'A new approach to assessing strategic learning: The case of self-regulation in vocabulary acquisition', *Applied Linguistics*, vol. 27, no. 1, pp. 78–102.

Vandergrift, L 2010, 'Researching listening', in B Paltridge & A Phakiti (eds), *Companion to Research Methods in Applied Linguistics*, Continuum, London, pp. 431–462.

Vandergrift, L, Goh, CCM, Mareschal, CJ & Tafaghodtari MH 2006, 'The metacognitive awareness listening questionnaire: Development and validation', *Language Learning*, vol. 56, no. 3, pp. 431–462.

White, C, Schramm, K & Chamot, AU 2007, 'Research methods in strategy research', in AD Cohen & E Macaro (eds), *Language Learner Strategies: Thirty Years of Research and Practice*, Oxford University Press, Oxford, pp. 93–116.

Woodrow, L 2005, 'The challenge of measuring language learning strategies', *Foreign Language Annals*, vol. 38, no. 1, pp. 90–100.

Yamamori, K, Isoda, T, Hiromori, T & Oxford, RL 2003, 'Using cluster analysis to uncover L2 learner differences in strategy use, will to learn, and achievement over time', *International Review of Applied Linguistics*, vol. 41, no. 4, pp. 381–409.

Zhang, L, Aryadoust, V & Zhang, DL 2014, 'Taking stock of the effects of strategies-based instruction on writing in Chinese and English in Singapore primary schools', in RE Silver & W Bokhorst-Heng (eds), *Quadrilingual Education in Singapore: Pedagogical Innovation in Language Education*, Springer, Boston, MA.

CHAPTER TWENTY FIVE

Researching Young Learners

Annamaria Pinter

This chapter will endeavour to give just a brief account of the developments in the 'Age factor' literature and their implications, and then it will outline some current trends in research within applied linguistics with a focus on younger language learners (as opposed to adults) highlighting what emerges as distinctive about children. Finally, and perhaps most importantly, the chapter will devote a substantial section to discussing the status of children in current second language acquisition (SLA)/applied linguistics research. I will suggest that there are three ways in which children can be conceptualized in research (object, subject and active participant/co-researcher), and all studies sit somewhere on this continuum. Two examples from different ends of the continuum will be exemplified in some detail to illustrate methodological, ethical and procedural differences. Finally, resources will be listed for further study and exploration.

When writing a chapter about young learners, it is important to define what the term means. Definitions of 'young learners' and 'children' are notoriously difficult to pin down, and the use of these concepts has been inconsistent both within and outside applied linguistics. While some scholars use terms such as 'early childhood', 'middle childhood' and 'adolescence' or 'youth', there is no firm agreement about the exact age brackets implied by these terms (see e.g. Ellis 2014). In this chapter, I will refer to children learning L2 English formally in both primary and pre-primary education and also in informal contexts (roughly between the ages of 4/5 and 12/13).

Young learners and the 'age factor'

In applied linguistics, one key area of research for the last thirty years has been the effect of age, and despite the huge amount of research devoted to the age factor, outcomes are still inconclusive. Dörnyei (2009, p. 233) comments that 'while everybody agrees that the learner's age does influence the SLA process, scholars have not been able to establish the exact pattern or nature of age related change, let alone identify the specific causes and mediators of the process.'

On the face of it, it seems that younger children have clear advantages over adult learners because in ESL contexts, they end up as fluent and competent speakers, very similar to their native-speaking counterparts. Adults or those who start an L2 later in life are typically less successful in their attempts to master the L2. However, these anecdotal observations in ESL contexts about children as more successful language learners have not been fully backed up by clear empirical evidence.

To explain the age-related effects on language learning, the 'Critical Period Hypothesis' (CPH) (Lenneberg 1967) was proposed some time ago. The CPH is based on biological principles, and it refers to a declining learning ability once a specific window of opportunity has closed. A critical period for L1 has been largely accepted, based on studies such as those by Mayberry, Lock and Kazmi (2002) with deaf children. This body of work shows that deaf children who had no access to early language input were unable to acquire English grammar well enough even after several years of effortful learning. Delayed linguistic input (i.e. missing an early window of opportunity) was indeed the cause of their problems. For L2 learning, the link between biology, that is, the CPH and language acquisition, is much less clear.

DeKeyser's (2012) meta-analysis of age factor studies suggests that there is indeed some empirical evidence for an upper age limit to the decline at least for some linguistic features. Studies that explored correlations between age of arrival (AOA) using grammaticality judgment tests (GJT) found non-continuity of decline in implicit language learning ability. Those studies that looked at the correlation between AOA and L2 proficiency of morpho-syntax as measured by other tests (not GJT) also showed that learners older than 15–16 years of age were simply not as good as younger learners. Looking at studies which examined the correlations between AOA and phonological ratings indicates that younger learners are consistently rated better. DeKeyser (2012) comments that not all aspects of language are effected in the same way, for example, different morpho-syntactic structures show different degrees of decline (DeKeyser 2000; Johnson & Newport 1989), and there are some areas of language learning (such as vocabulary learning) which might be less effected or not effected at all.

Krashen et al. (1979) suggested that CPH studies should be categorized into two main types: those exploring the 'speed of learning' and those exploring 'ultimate attainment'. Younger children are good at achieving more native-like levels ultimately, but they are certainly not faster learners than adults. Studies that have analysed data from the same learners tend to show that after a limited exposure, older learners will do better, but after a longer period of time (several years), younger learners tend to overtake older ones (Jia & Fuse 2007; Larson-Hall 2008; Snow & Höfnagel-Höhle 1978).

The 'younger the better' hypothesis however applies only in naturalistic environments where children are immersed in the language environment and have plenty of opportunities to interact with a variety of native speakers. Jia and Fuse (2007) talk about at least three factors working together in the case of young immigrant children: a sensitive time window, a richer L2 environment and experience with less interference with their L1. In English as a foreign language (EFL) contexts, however, such advantages simply do not apply. In these contexts, where children are learning English as a school subject, 'the older the better' seems to be true because older learners rely on more efficient learning strategies, larger memory stores and can focus on the learning task with intensity. Even if younger children were better in the long run, the time spent on learning the second language in most formal EFL contexts is so minimal (often just 2 × 45 minutes a week) that younger learners simply do not have the chance to overtake older ones (Singleton & Ryan 2004). Muñoz (2006) also reports that older learners in Spanish schools progress faster than younger learners, and even after longer periods of time, younger learners do not outperform later starters, except perhaps in pronunciation (Muñoz 2008). This early ability to acquire good pronunciation is a common observation across many studies. As Dörnyei (2009) points out:

> Indeed, some linguistic areas such as pragmatic knowledge and vocabulary size might show a continuous growth throughout the lifespan, whereas the hierarchy of neural circuits that underlies phonetic skills appears to be subject to CP [Critical Period] effects. (p. 245)

More recently, longitudinal studies have been suggesting that language learning in childhood may be complex and unique to different learner trajectories. Jia and Aaronson's (2003) longitudinal study of Chinese immigrant children in the United States indicates that there is quite a high variability of acquisition rates across the participating children. Cognitive, social and cultural variables all interact with each other.

Different methodological shortcomings make it difficult for us to interpret the results of the age factor studies. For example, many studies compare L2 learners with native speakers. These comparisons with native speakers are problematic because 'native-ness' is a difficult concept and the boundaries of 'nativeness' are hard to define. In addition, if younger learners are tested using the same test tools as older learners, this may put them at a disadvantage. If they are less adept at taking tests, their results will come across as worse than their actual ability.

Much hope therefore rests with the technological enhancements offered by neuroscience, although currently evidence from neuroscience is ambiguous. Overall, according to DeKeyser (2012) evidence in the literature definitely supports some non-continuous age effects. This is contrasted with evidence from self-rating and census data (e.g. Bialystok & Hakuta 1994; Chiswick & Miller 2008; Hakuta et al. 2003) which suggests that there is a continuous life-long decline in one's ability to learn a second language. There are also many studies that claim that adults can hold up under scrutiny and achieve native-like or near native-like levels even in the area of pronunciation (e.g. Birdsong 2007; Bongaerts, Mennen and van der Slik 2000). Typically, these adults are exposed to good quality input, have appropriate training and are highly motivated learners. They are also high achievers, score high levels on aptitude tests and are often highly educated language professionals with a huge amount of practice, reflection and training. Nonetheless, these studies go some way of refuting the existence of the CPH and instead emphasize the importance of social and psychological variables in the context, such as the learners' personal commitment and motivation, and general 'favourable circumstances' in the case of young learners (Marionova-Todd et al. 2000).

The age factor literature continues to be one of the most researched areas in SLA despite, or, perhaps, because of the lack of consensus. In the future, studies that have a longitudinal design to track learners using different tasks and measures and studies in neuroscience hold promise to understand better aspects of the age effect.

Young learners and L2 learning: Extension of adult studies in applied linguistics

Almost everywhere in the world English is being introduced to ever younger generations of children in preschools and primary schools (Rixon 2013). Immersion programs, cram schools and private institutions are on the rise attracting the attention of parents, promising a better future for their children through learning English early in life. Since more and more programs are run for young learners, more and more research is generated in these contexts with children as research objects/subjects. Studies often compare children to adults, and whatever aspects of L2 learning is focused on, the findings are always interpreted against the backdrop of the more established adult literature in SLA and applied linguistics.

Processes of L2 acquisition in childhood are in some ways similar but not the same as adult processes for two main reasons, which are cognitive and social (Paradis, 2007). According to Philp et al. (2008), children's SLA is different from adults in that they learn from both adults and peers and these different relationships actively shape their learning experiences. Teachers provide more formal input while peers serve as a source of informal input and provide opportunities for enjoyable practice. Siblings can also be sources of useful language learning through playing together informally at home (e.g. Mitchell & Lee 2008). Nicholas and Lightbown (2008) claim that young learners (aged between 2 and 7 years) go through what we refer to as a 'substantial silent period', and they also engage in specific patterns of code-mixing and extensive language play. Language play has been studied particularly extensively, and research shows that it supports affiliation, it is fun and engaging, children can assume new roles and this gives them low-anxiety opportunities for practice and confidence growth (e.g. DaSilva & McCafferty 2007). Language play might involve not only the manipulation of form as well as meaning, a great deal of imitation and repetition but also deeper processing (e.g. Cekaite & Aronson 2005; Cook 2000; Sullivan 2000). Older learners, on the other hand, tend to benefit from more formal teaching, rely more on their developing cognitive and metacognitive skills and can usefully reflect on their learning processes.

Studies with child participants often compare different groups of children to extend the findings of the adult literature in an area, such as task-based learning (e.g. Mackey et al. 2003; Oliver & Mackey 2003) to children. The task-based approach with children has been a particularly exciting area of research (e.g. Mackey et al. 2007; Mackey, Oliver & Leeman 2003; Oliver 2002; Oliver & Mackey 2003), as well as classrooms and corrective feedback (Lyster & Ranta 1997; Spada & Lightbown 1993). In addition, research has also focused on interactional opportunities provided by peers (e.g. Miller 2003; Willett 1995). A large majority of these studies are experimental and fall into a quantitative tradition, but qualitative studies have also contributed to our understanding of L2 child learning thanks to classics such as Wong Fillmore (1976). Longitudinal qualitative approaches help us understand language acquisition over time (e.g. Hawkins 2005; Jia & Aaronson 2003; Toohey 2000), and they shed light on individual differences and unique pathways of learning.

EFL and ESL contexts are still substantially different, although the distinction is not as clear-cut as it used to be due to the availability of the internet and global travel. Many children move in and out of EFL and ESL contexts and/or have access to a variety of virtual language learning opportunities that go well beyond the walls of the classrooms. Overall, much less research has targeted EFL than ESL but see Nikolov (2009) or Edelenbos and Kubanek (2009). Edelenbos and Kubanek (2009) summarize features of good practice in EFL contexts based on some empirical research in Europe and beyond. They suggest that in EFL contexts, children need frequent exposure to English in the primary years, they benefit from holistic learning and contextualized themes and the teaching needs to be multisensory. Children can achieve more comprehension than production, and they need to be learning the L2 in an active way. In addition to linguistic goals, most primary programs promote tolerance and understanding of other cultures.

Young learners and their status in applied linguistics research

According to Kellett (2010), children are portrayed as either objects or subjects in the majority of research where they are participants. When they are portrayed as objects, typically, children are passive and unaware, and their own consents are rarely sought. As objects of the research, they have no control whatsoever over the research process and often do not understand what is going on and why. Research like this is typically of large scale, involving large numbers of learners, and indeed, individual differences and unique characteristics of children do not matter. When children are portrayed as subjects, their characteristics are more in the focus, and the qualitative and longitudinal research designs tend to allow for a closer tracking of unique features of child learners. As subjects, children are also more likely to be aware of the research project, their comments might be sought and the adult researchers might make conscious efforts to get to know them. However, even in the subject role, they have no control over the research process which is still entirely adult-motivated, adult-initiated and adult-dominated.

In some applied linguistics research, children are not treated differently from adults. However, researchers, often retrospectively, flag up methodological difficulties such as the particular tools used did not actually suit the children's needs (e.g. Macaro & Erler 2008, or Gue et al. 2005). In other studies, there is a clear acknowledgement from the start that the child participants need to be treated differently from adults. For example, Mackey and Gass (2005) in their research methods manual comment that child subjects are different from adults, and thus, researchers need to explain their study carefully, so that it is comprehensible and meaningful to the child. This suggests that tools, tasks and tests need to be tailored to children's cognitive and social needs and made more child-friendly. Adult instruments such as questionnaires can be reworked and simplified, interview schedules can be embedded in familiar contexts (Eder & Fingerson 2002) and alternative methods (e.g. drama, or role plays, drawings) that adults judge to be appropriate based on their experience might be used with children. However, all these 'child-friendly' approaches and adjustments, although consistent with a 'subject' rather than an 'object' status, ultimately come from our adult perspectives and understandings about what might be appropriate for certain age groups.

More recently, with the rise of the concept of the 'social child' (Christensen & James 2008; Christensen & Prout 2002), following the political legacy of the UN resolution (Declaration of Children's Rights by the United Nations 1989), some child researchers have come to reject research where children are objects (unknowing, passive receivers of the research) or even subjects (participants defined by adult criteria) in favour of working with children as social actors/active research participants or even co-researchers. This means that children are placed right in the centre of the research process, and the adult researcher makes a conscious effort to include the children in the research in a way that they can shape it and influence it ideally at every step of the way. According to Scott (2008, p. 88), 'the best people to provide information on the child's perspective, actions, and attributes are the children themselves'.

A substantial body of research in sociology and anthropology suggests that there are many potential benefits of working with children in this way. They commit to the research project fully which leads to rising levels of self-esteem and to taking ownership of the project. They also acquire useful transferable skills and have fun at the same time. Children can offer insights that are drastically different from adults' views and even challenge those. Working with children as co-researchers is an area that is currently almost totally absent from applied linguistics (Pinter 2014), even though, in addition to the studies that conceptualize children as objects or subjects, we do need studies that extend children's roles and elevate their status.

How can such a perspective be possible? The first step is to begin work with a group of children who are aware of and interested in contributing to a project proposed by the adult researcher. When these children have spent some time working alongside the adult researcher taking responsibility for various aspects of the research process on a voluntary basis, they might be interested to be involved more. At some point, some children may become fully-fledged researchers themselves who are able to take full control of the process. However, this should be seen as a continuum where any move towards more responsibility will help engage the children more meaningfully, but where the goal is not necessarily to achieve full control. Children taking full control over the research process will in fact be impossible and undesirable in some contexts. Small steps might be more appropriate especially at the start. For example, children might usefully feed ideas into the research tool designed by an adult researcher for other children, or they may take spontaneous interest in the research process, ask questions and make comments that are meaningful to them (e.g. Kuchah & Pinter 2012; Pinter & Zandian 2012, 2014).

Working with children as social actors/co-researchers, of course, will mean that ethical and methodological dilemmas intensify and take on new shapes and guises. Relationship building between the adult researcher and the children becomes crucially important. Time and effort need to be devoted to rapport building and revisiting agreements, understandings and shared ideas. Reflexivity, which entails checking and double-checking the adult's own and the children's interpretations of the research process and everyone's roles in it, is time-consuming but essential. Dilemmas regarding how much of the children's time is ethical to take and where the line falls between facilitating their progress towards ownership of the research as opposed to just exposing them to adult concepts of research are difficult to solve. There is also a great deal of peer pressure and a culture of adult dominance in schools, so how the children are to be persuaded that there is no right answer and their opinions and views are not being evaluated are also important issues to tackle. Some researchers recommend conducting research outside school premises, but in many cases, this is neither feasible nor necessary. Children need to be able to give their own consent when it comes to the research project, and the adult researchers need to take steps to make sure that the children understand what this means.

All research is representation, and ultimately, it is still the adult researcher who writes up the research and makes sense of it. Gallacher and Gallagher (2008) in their discussion of participatory research claim that involving children as active participants is just another adult-controlled tool. While these critical comments are undeniably relevant, this does not mean that we must abandon our quest of exploring opportunities for research in applied linguistics where children can take more of a central stage.

What type of research one ends up doing with children within applied linguistics will depend on a number of considerations, such as one's experience, one's interest and the research question, but also it crucially depends on the researcher's own conceptions of childhood (e.g. Alderson 2005). What do we believe about children? Are they unreliable, vulnerable and helpless, needing control, or are they in fact responsible and capable to make decisions for themselves? Whatever our deep-rooted beliefs may be, they will inevitably influence how we will proceed in any research project.

Sample studies

According to how the children are perceived by the researchers, that is, as objects, subjects or active participants/co-researchers, there is a continuum of methodological decisions from the passive object to the active participant co-researcher status. Here, I contrast two studies (namely Kuchah & Pinter 2012; Mackey et al. 2003) that show very different methodological decisions reflecting different researcher priorities regarding the status of children in the research but also reflecting very different topics and research questions. There is no suggestion that one study is 'better' than the other, though. Instead, Table 25.1 is intended to contrast two different ways of researching young learners and the consequences of one's choices. But, the intention is also to suggest that once we are familiar with the different possibilities, we can make informed decisions about combining aspects of different approaches.

Table 25.1 Different ways of researching children: two examples

	Mackey et al. 2003	Kuchah and Pinter 2012
Source	Journal article	Journal article
Design	Experimental	Exploratory
Aims	Comparison between adult and child participants' L2 output	Children's views are sought without reference to adults
Analysis	Quantitative	Qualitative
Researcher intention/ explicit/implicit belief about status of child participants:	An implicit assumption that children's output will be different from that of the adults because of their less-developed cognitive and social skills	An explicit intention to explore what good teaching is from the children's point of view
Focus	Eliciting L2 language output: task-based research (immigrant children in Australia)	Eliciting views and perspectives: interview study with children about their views about good teachers and good English teaching (Children in a French-medium school in Cameroon)
Participants	96 participants, children and adults in equal numbers Adults: university students Children: 8–12 years old Randomly matched into NS/NNS and NNS/NNS adult and child pairs (12 pairs of each type of pairing)	2 groups of learners (5–6 in each group; 1 group of girls and 1 group of boys; open-ended questions and prompts
Tools	Tasks: 2 tasks: describe and draw (one way task) and complete a picture together (two way tasks)	Different tools: drawings, sentence completion, free-flowing discussion
Data	All pairs did both tasks and were recorded talking; the first 100 utterances were analysed for target like/non-target like utterances and feedback; modified input was also coded	Variety of data from a variety of sources: negotiation of interpretations; focus on unique views and interpretations; attention paid to what is 'raw and spontaneous' as opposed to what is a standard answer to an adult question
Results	Expressed in statistics; statistically significant correlations are reported and the findings are explained with reference to adult studies	Expressed qualitatively, by analysing the flow of the discussion between adult researcher and the children
Ethics	No specific discussion	Dilemmas and complexities are fully discussed

These two are very different studies, asking very different questions. Mackey et al. (2003) is representative of the traditional approach within applied linguistics where the children are compared to adults. In a large group, individuals fade into insignificance, and children certainly do not need to know too much about why the research is undertaken. Of course, this is perfectly understandable with these procedures, within this tradition and with these research questions. Kuchah and Pinter (2012), although do not go very far on the continuum from object status to fully-fledged co-researcher status, do indicate that it is possible to incorporate procedures into the design that help children to take at least some ownership of the research and bring their own perspectives to the research. In this case, the children actually convinced the adult researcher to change his research design by including a teacher in the study that they recommended. Not only did they voice their opinions and views about good English teaching, they also influenced the shape of the adult study in a significant way.

Table 25.2 contains some key questions researchers working with children should consult.

Table 25.2 Key questions to ask when working with child research participants

Questions	Comments
What are my underlying beliefs about children and childhood? How are these beliefs influencing the type of project I am planning to engage in?	Every researcher working with children needs to ask this question, even though there is no 'right' answer.
What are my research questions? What is the relationship between the questions, the type of tools required to probe into these questions and the age of the children?	It is important to make sure that the types of tools will be appropriate for the group of children they are intended for. Some initial observation of the children is recommended, even the children's opinions or views are not the focus of the study.
What are the implications of my status as a researcher in the given context? What is the level of researchers' knowledge and experience in child research?	You might be conducting a large-scale study where your identity and status as a researcher is less important. It is important to think about the power gap between any adult and child in a project and how such a gap might be an influencing factor that needs to be considered.

(continued)

Questions	Comments
What is the time allocated for the project?	If you want to work with the children more closely and want to involve them more actively, perhaps as co-researchers in the study, relationship building can take a lot of time. It is important to think about the time frame realistically.
What research ethics apply in my context?	Schools, local authorities in different contexts as well as your university (if you are doing research as part of your PG studies) will all have ethical guidelines to follow, in addition to your own personal concerns and views. It is important to engage with all of these, revisit them during the study and work out some compromises which are recorded in writing.
How will I negotiate access? Whose consent will I need?	Parents' consent? Head-teacher's consent? The children's consent? All of the above? What if there is a conflict?
How will I make sure that the children understand the focus of the research?	In some studies, this is less important than others. You need to think about how important it is in your study for the children to have a full understanding of the research. Often, this requires time and talking things through several times. Also, children's spontaneous comments reveal a great deal about their perspectives.
How will the children participate in the study? Why? Is there another way?	Have you thought about alternative ways the children may usefully contribute to the study? Is it meaningful/ feasible to discuss options with them? Have you got additional ideas just in case something planned does not work out? Have you thought about showing your initial plan for the study to some children (other than the ones you will be working with) and ask for their feedback?
Where is the project going to run?	If possible, organize a safe, quiet and friendly venue; sometimes, it is not possible to take children out of school, but a library corner is much better than the teachers' staffroom.

(continued)

Questions	Comments
How will I monitor their participation?	During the study, children may lose interest or change their minds, so you need to think of monitoring their participation and revisit the goals of the study and their consent.
Whose interests does this study serve?	This is an ethical question which makes you think about the outcomes of the study. How can you give something back to the children? What is their benefit?
How will the results be analysed and disseminated?	Can the children feed into these stages of the research? It might not be appropriate at all for some research questions, but if it is, how can you involve them? Children's own written summaries might be included in the adult's report.

Conclusion

This chapter has tried to illustrate just how rich the 'young learners' field is within applied linguistics. Researchers continue to investigate how age affects the L2 learning process in childhood, what research comes out of classrooms and other learning contexts with children as research participants and what roles children can take in research. Future research in applied linguistic needs to pay more attention to EFL contexts, engage more in longitudinal research that unpacks the complexities of learning and, to add to the traditional body of evidence, needs to involve children as more active and more equal participants in research.

Resources for further reading

Books

Murphy, V 2014, Second Language Learning in the Early School Years: Trends and Contexts: An Overview, Oxford University Press, Oxford.

This is an up-to-date volume that examines past and present research evidence on bilingualism, second language and foreign language learning in childhood, making links between different contexts and highlighting the similarities and differences in child L2 learning across these contexts. The discussion focuses on learning contexts that intersect with educational provision in the early school years and explores current trends towards a younger starting age for foreign language learning. The book provides a broad overview of research findings across a range of different contexts.

Pinter, A 2011, *Children Learning Second Languages: Research and Practice in Applied Linguistics*, Palgrave, Macmillan, Basingstoke.

This volume covers child development, L1 and L2 language learning processes in childhood and offers a guide to contexts from foreign language learning at school to immersion education and bilingual/trilingual acquisition at home. It also gives an overview of current research in the area of child SLA and pedagogy, highlighting the strengths and weaknesses of different traditions and types of research. This is followed by a close examination of eight case studies and some suggestions for future research. Resources are also listed, including hands-on teaching materials, handbooks, theoretical books, details of organizations and projects in the broad area of child second language learning.

Philp J, Oliver, R & Mackey, A (eds), 2008, *Second Language Acquisition and the Younger Learner – Child's Play?*, John Benjamins, Amsterdam.

This book highlights the distinctiveness of child SLA through a collection of different types of empirical research all focused on younger learners. Child SLA is often thought of as simple (and often enjoyable and universally effortless), in other words, as 'child's play'; the learning paths which emerge in the sixteen papers in this book invite the reader to reconsider the reality and the complex processes for many younger learners. Chapters describe second and foreign language learning by children ranging from preschoolers to young adolescents, in home and school contexts, with caregivers, peers and teachers as interlocutors.

Sergeant, J & Harcourt, D 2012, *Doing Ethical Research with Children*, Open University Press, McGraw Hill, Maidenhead.

This is a step-by-step guide to planning, undertaking and disseminating research with children focusing on ethical questions and dilemmas. The book presents an overview of different traditions of research with children and the discussion combines both theoretical and practical concerns. The authors emphasize the importance of research that gives agency and voice to children. There are regular reflection tasks and case studies highlighting important aspects of research procedures involving child participants.

Singleton, D & Ryan, L 2004, *Language Acquisition: The Age Factor*, Multilingual Matters, Clevedon.

This is a comprehensive overview of the CPH both in first and second language development. It addresses key theoretical perspectives as well as educational dimensions and offers a balanced discussion of this complex area of research. The authors also discuss what the research results mean for practice and policy. This is an excellent resource for all those interested in the CPH.

Projects

Enever, J (ed.), 2011, *ELLIE: Early Language Learning in Europe*, British Council, London.

This project reports on the challenges and achievements of introducing English as foreign language to 6–7-year-olds in seven European countries. Data was drawn from 1400 children across different context in a large-scale longitudinal research study. The breadth and the depth of the research provides sound basis for future policy development in Europe and beyond. See <http://www.ellieresearch.eu>, viewed 24 July 2014.

Rixon, S 2013, *British Council Survey of Policy and Practice in Primary English Language Teaching Worldwide*, British Council, London.

This is a very large database containing information about global practices in relation to English-language teaching in primary contexts. The current survey represents sixty-four countries. Information drawn from questionnaires filled in by primary sector experts in ELT/ESL covers topics, such as policy, age of starting English, teacher supply, curriculum and syllabus, target levels and assessment, transition from primary to secondary and public-/private-sector relationships. This is an invaluable source of information (downloadable at <www.britishcouncil.org>, viewed 24 July 2014).

Websites

BRITISH COUNCIL English for kids and teens: http://learnenglishkids. britishcouncil.org/en/, viewed 29 January 2015.

ESL kids world: http://www.eslkidsworld.com/, viewed 24 July 2014.

International Children's Digital Library: http://en.childrenslibrary.org/, viewed 24 July 2014.

IATEFL Young Learners SIG: https://www.yltsig.org, viewed 24 July 2014.

TESOL-K12: http://www.tesol.org/advance-the-field/standards/prek-12-english-language-proficiency-standards, viewed 24 July 2014.

References

Alderson, P 2005, 'Designing ethical research with children', in A Farrell (ed.), *Ethical Research with Children*, Open University Press, Maidenhead, pp. 27–36.

Bialystok, E & Hakuta, K 1994, *In Other Words: The Science and Psychology of Second Language Acquisition*, Basic books, New York, NY.

Birdsong, D 2007, 'Native-like pronunciation among late learners of French as a second language', in OS Bohn & MJ Munro (eds), *Language Experience in Second Language Learning*, Benjamins, Philadelphia, PA, pp. 99–116.

Bongaerts, T, Mennen, S & van der Slik, F 2000, 'Authenticity of pronunciation in naturalistic second language acquisition: The case of very advanced late learners of Dutch as a second language', *Studia Linguistica*, vol. 54, no. 2, pp. 298–308.

Cekaite, A & Aronsson, K 2005, 'Language play, a collaborative resource in children's L2 learning', *Applied Linguistics*, vol. 26, no. 2, pp. 169–191.

Christensen, P & James, A 2008, 'Researching children and childhood cultures of communication: Introduction', in P Christensen & A James (eds), *Research with Children: Perspectives and Practices*, Routledge, London, pp. 1–9.

Christensen, P & Prout, A 2002, 'Working with ethical symmetry in social research with children', *Childhood*, vol. 9, no. 4, pp. 477–497.

Chiswick, BR & Miller, PW 2008, 'A test of the critical period hypothesis for language learning', *Journal of Multilingual and Multicultural Development*, vol. 29, no. 1, pp. 16–29.

Cook, G 2000, *Language Play, Language Learning*. Oxford University Press, Oxford.

Dasilva Iddings, A & McCafferty S 2007, 'Carnival in the mainstream kindergarten classroom: A Bakhtinian analysis of L2 learners' off -task behaviours', *The Modern Language Journal*, vol. 91, pp. 31–44.

DeKeyser, R 2000, 'The robustness of critical period effects in second language acquisition', *Studies in Second Language Acquisition*, vol. 22, pp. 499–533.

—— 2012, 'Age effects and second language learning', in S Gass & A Mackey (eds), *The Routledge Handbook of Second Language Acquisition*, Routledge, London, pp. 442–460.

Dörnyei, Z 2009, *The Psychology of Second Language Acquisition*, Oxford University Press, Oxford.

Edelenbos, P & Kubanek, A 2009, 'Early foreign language learning: Published research, good practice and main principles', in M Nikolov (ed.), *The Age Factor and Early Language Learning*, Mouton de Gruyter, Berlin, pp. 39–58.

Eder, D & Fingerson, L 2002, 'Interviewing children and adolescents', in JB Gubrium & JA Holstein (eds), *Handbook of Interview Research*, Sage, Thousand Oaks, CA and London, pp. 181–202.

Ellis, G 2014, 'Young learners: Clarifying our terms', *ELT Journal*, vol. 68, no. 1, pp. 75–78.

Gallacher, LA & Gallagher, M 2008, 'Methodological immaturity in childhood research?', *Childhood*, vol. 15, no. 4, pp. 499–516.

Gue, PY, Hu, G & Zhang, LJ 2005, 'Investigating language learners' strategies among lower primary school pupils in Singapore', *Language and Education*, vol. 19, no. 4, pp. 281–303.

Hakuta, K, Bialystok, E & Wiley, E 2003, 'Critical evidence: A test of the critical period hypothesis for second language acquisition', *Psychological Science*, vol. 14, no. 1, pp. 31–38.

Hawkins, M 2005, 'Becoming a student: Identity work and academic literacies in early schooling', *TESOL Quarterly*, vol. 39, no. 1, pp. 59–82.

Jia, G & Aaronson, D 2003, 'A longitudinal study of Chinese children and adolescents learning English in the United States', *Applied Psycholinguistics*, vol. 24, no. 1, pp. 131–61.

Jia, G & Fuse, A 2007, 'Acquisition of English grammatical morphology by native Mandarin-speaking children and adolescents: Age-related differences', *Journal of Speech, Language and Hearing Research*, vol. 50, no. 5, pp. 1280–1299.

Johnson, JS & Newport, EL 1989, 'Critical period effects in second language learning: The influence of maturational state on the acquisition of English as a second language', *Cognitive Psychology*, vol. 21, no. 1, pp. 60–99.

Kellett, M 2010, *Rethinking Children and Research: Attitudes in Contemporary Society*, Continuum, London.

Krashen, SD, Long, MA & Scarcella, RC 1979, 'Age, rate and eventual attainment in second language acquisition', *TESOL Quarterly*, vol. 13, no. 4, pp. 573–582.

Kuchah Kuchah, H & Pinter, A 2012, 'Was this an interview? Breaking the power barrier in adult-child interviews in an African context', *Issues in Educational Research*, vol. 22, no. 3, pp. 283–297.

Larson-Hall, J 2008, 'Weighing the benefits of studying a foreign language at a younger starting age in a minimal input', *Second Language Research*, vol. 24, no. 1, pp. 35–63.

Lenneberg, EH 1967, *Biological Foundations of Language*, Wiley, New York, NY.

Lyster, R & Ranta, L 1997, 'Corrective feedback and learner uptake: Negotiation of form in communicative classrooms', *Studies in Second Language Acquisition*, vol. 19, no. 1, pp. 37–61.

Macaro, E & Erler, L 2008, 'Raising the achievement of young beginner readers of French through strategy instruction', *Applied Linguistics*, vol. 29, no. 1, pp. 90–119.

Mackey, A, Kanganas, AP & Oliver, R 2007, 'Task familiarity and interactional feedback in child ESL classrooms', *TESOL Quarterly*, vol. 41, no. 2, pp. 285–312.

Mackey, A, Oliver, R & Leeman, J 2003, 'Interactional input and the incorporation of feedback: An exploration of NS-NNS and NNS-NNS adult and child dyads', *Language Learning*, vol. 53, no. 1, pp. 35–66.

Mackey, A & Gass, SM 2005, *Second Language Research: Methodology and Design*, Routledge, New York, NY.

Marinova-Todd, S, Bradford Marshall, HD & Snow, C 2000, 'Three misconceptions about age and L2 learning', *TESOL Quarterly*, vol. 34, no. 1, pp. 9–34.

Mayberry, RI, Lock, E & Kazmi, L 2002, 'Development: Linguistic ability and early language exposure', *Nature*, 417, p. 38.

Miller, J 2003, *Audible Differences: ESL and Social Identity in Schools*, Multilingual Matters, Clevedon.

Mitchell, R & Lee, CN 2008, 'Learning a second language in the family' in J Philp, R Oliver & A Mackey (eds), *Second Language Acquisition and the Young Learner: Child's Play?*, John Benjamins, Amsterdam, pp. 255–278.

Muñoz, C 2006, 'The effects of age on foreign language learning: The BAF project', in C Muñoz (ed.), *Age and the Rate of Foreign Language Learning*, Multilingual Matters, Clevedon, pp. 1–40.

—— 2008, 'Symmetries and asymmetries of age effects in naturalistic and instructed L2 learning', *Applied Linguistics*, vol. 29, no. 4, pp. 578–596.

Nicholas, H & Lightbown, PM 2008, 'Defining child second language acquisition, defining roles for L2 instruction', in J Philp, R Oliver & A Mackey (eds), *Second Language Acquisition and the Young Learner: Child's Play?*, John Benjamins, Amsterdam, pp. 27–52.

Nikolov, M (ed.), 2009, *The 'Age Factor' and Early Language Learning: Studies on Language Acquisition*, Mouton de Gruyter, Berlin.

Oliver, R 2002, 'Age differences in negotiation and feedback in classroom and pairwork', *Language Learning*, vol. 50, no. 1, pp. 119–151.

Oliver, R & Mackey, A 2003, 'Interactional context and feedback in child ESL classrooms', *The Modern Language Journal*, vol. 87, no. 4, pp. 519–533.

Paradis, J 2007, 'Second language acquisition in childhood', in E Hoff & M Shatz (eds), *Blackwell Handbook of Language Development*, Blackwell Publishers, Oxford, pp. 387–405.

Philp, J, Oliver, R & Mackey, A (eds), 2008, *Second Language Acquisition and the Young Learner: Child's Play?* John Benjamins, Amsterdam.

Pinter, A 2014, 'Child participant roles in applied linguistics research', *Applied Linguistics*, vol. 35, no. 2, pp. 168–183.

Pinter, A & Zandian, S 2012, 'I thought it would be tiny little one phrase that we said, in a huge big pile of papers: Children's reflections on their involvement in participatory research', *Qualitative Research*, doi: 10.1177/1468794112465637

―――― 2014, 'I don't ever want to leave this room' – researching with children', *ELT Journal*, vol. 68, no. 1, pp. 64–74.

Scott, J 2008, 'Children as respondents: The challenge for quantitative methods', in P. Christiansen & A James (eds), *Research with Children: Perspective and Practices*, Routledge, London, pp. 87–108.

Singleton, D & Ryan, L 2004, *Language Acquisition: The Age Factor*, Multilingual Matters, Clevedon.

Snow, C & Höfnagel-Höhle, M 1978, 'Age differences in second language acquisition' in E Hatch (ed.), *Second Language Acquisition: A Book of Readings*, Newbury House, Powley, MA, pp. 333–346.

Spada, N & Lightbown, P 1993, 'Instruction and the development of questions in L2 classrooms', *Studies in Second Language Acquisition*, vol. 15, no. 2, pp. 205–224.

Sullivan, P 2000, 'Language play and communicative language teaching in a Vietnamese classroom', in JP Lantolf (ed.), *Sociocultural Theory and Second Language Learning*, Oxford University Press, Oxford, pp. 115–131.

Toohey, K 2000, *Learning English at School: Identity, Social Relations and Classroom Practice*, Multilingual Matters, Clevedon.

United Nations, 1989, *United Nations Convention on the Right of the Child*, United Nations, New York, NY.

Willet, J 1995, 'Becoming first graders in an L2: An ethnographic study of L2 socialisation', *TESOL Quarterly*, vol. 29, no. 3, pp. 473–503.

Wong-Fillmore, L 1976, 'The language learner as an individual: Implications of research on individual differences for the ESL teacher', in MA Clarke & J Handscombe (eds), *On TESOL '82: Pacific Perspectives on Language Learning and Teaching*, TESOL, Washington, DC, pp. 157–171.

CHAPTER TWENTY SIX

Researching Language Classrooms

Lesley Harbon and Huizhong Shen

Research into what happens in language classrooms is an important area of applied linguistics research. Second language classroom research is in many ways the link between theory and practice (Lightbown 2000; Nunan & Bailey 2009). Well-planned and well-designed language classroom research can help us examine our theoretical assumptions as well as what happens in actual practice. There is also a wide range of aspects of language learning and teaching that might be examined in this research. This might include a focus on speaking, listening, reading or writing. It might examine the teaching and learning of grammar and vocabulary, or it might focus on issues in the area of pragmatics, motivation or identity development, to name just a few. Students and/or aspects of the teaching context itself can also become the focus of the classroom research. This chapter outlines current trends in classroom research. It will then discuss classroom observation and narrative inquiry as ways in which what goes on in the classroom might be examined. Finally, a sample study is described which employs classroom observation as its key research technique.

Much classroom research has come about because teachers are seeking to solve problems or answer pressing questions about their current teaching practices (Mackay 2006). The teachers themselves may undertake the research, as is the case with action research (see Burns this volume), or they can become the subject studied by a researcher who is not from the teaching context. Classroom research can aim to test a hypothesis, test a theory or even replicate an earlier study. Some researchers explore hunches they have about their own teaching or student learning. Other researchers conduct research where funding has been granted for a specific purpose, so the focus of the research has already been established. Both quantitative (Phakiti this volume) and qualitative (Holliday this volume) methodologies can be employed in second language classroom research.

Often, classroom research requires the researcher to work closely with the language teacher. Arrangements need to be made about observation times and places. The researcher's presence should not impose on what is happening in the classroom and needs to be considered in any arrangements for data collection that will take place. Classroom teacher/researcher collaborations can be extremely fruitful (Lightbown 2000), and teachers will trust the researcher if all purposes and processes are made explicit to them through the period of the research (Nunan & Choi 2011).

Important considerations in second language classroom research

A glance through the contents pages of any of the current general research textbooks would see that there are often common stages in undertaking classroom research. Important reference manuals for this type of research include Denzin and Lincoln's (2005) *Handbook of Qualitative Research*, Cohen et al.'s (2007) *Research Methods in Education*, Arthur et al.'s (2012) *Research Methods and Methodologies in Education*, Cresswell's (2012) *Educational Research: Planning, Conducting, and Evaluating Quantitative and Qualitative Research* and Lodico et al.'s (2006) *Methods in Educational Research*. Books that focus on classroom-based research, in particular, include Allwright and Bailey's (1989) *Focus on the Language Classroom*, Nunan's (1989) *Understanding Language Classrooms*, Nunan and Bailey's (2009) *Exploring second language classroom research: A comprehensive guide* and Wallace's (1998) *Action Research for Language Teachers* (see also Burns this volume).

In the early stages of the project, researchers need to consider their own beliefs and understandings of the topic. Researchers need to review the literature (primary sources especially) not only about the research problem itself, but also the research available on the method chosen for the project. The researcher then decides on the design, method, sampling and population, examines data collection instrumentation (and adapts or devises new versions), conducts the research and then analyses the data, reducing the data to smaller chunks of information, in order to link, compare and make meaningful findings from their study.

Researchers are obliged to conduct classroom research in an ethical manner. Much research is conducted under the auspices of higher education institutions, and such institutions have committees especially set up for examining ethical procedures of the research undertaken in its name. Researchers need to follow research approval guidelines for ethical purposes. Research conducted with permissions and checks on ethical processes should guarantee anonymity and safety to participants.

From the time the research project is first conceived, right through to the point where the results are published, the researcher needs to aim for a positive, professional relationship with their participants. The researcher should never forget the human side of conducting classroom research. In the midst of all of classroom language learning and teaching, people are involved. The researcher, thus, must seek to develop good working relationships with the people involved in their project.

Research techniques and methods

Researchers can utilize a range of research techniques to gather data for language classroom research. For instance, introspective techniques such as think-aloud protocols and retrospective techniques such as interviews carried out after a classroom event has taken place have made an important contribution to classroom-based research. These techniques can be used to ask teachers and students to explain their thinking, beliefs and perceptions of what goes on in the language learning classroom (Mckay 2006). Researchers can also use diaries as a source of data. Studies of this kind, in which teachers or students write what they think about their teaching and learning, are another useful way of carrying out classroom-based research. Also, through the analysis of interactional patterns, researchers can examine teacher–student discourse in order to uncover patterns that may, in some way, impact on language teaching and learning (Duff 2007). Two further research strategies, classroom observation and narrative inquiry, are discussed below as ways of conducting language classroom research.

Classroom observation

Classroom observation is defined by Gebhard and Oprandy (1999, p. 35) as 'non-judgmental description of classroom events that can be analyzed and given interpretation'. Mackey and Gass (2005) describe how observations allow researchers to collect comprehensive information about types of language, activities, interactions, instruction and other notable events, most importantly, at close range. The researcher will choose to take observations of either the whole language classroom or aspects of it, or activities within it. Observations may be taken of the teacher, a student or students. With a teacher focus, these aspects may range from the amount of teacher use of the target language, teacher use of materials, their handling of critical incidents, through to the type of praise given by teachers to student responses. With a student focus, the exploration can be anything from student questioning, to student eye contact with the teacher, to student participation in group work and more. As well, there are a multitude of aspects of the classroom context which can be examined, for example, gender and its impact on classroom processes, or issues of race. The number of research questions possible for language classrooms, thus, is considerable.

Researchers are also able to include *participant observation* or *non-participant observation* in their research design. In participant observation, the researchers take part in the classroom processes they are investigating, taking notes on what they observe. In non-participant observation, the researchers are present but do not participate in the classroom processes. Researchers are therefore free to take notes and work with any devices they need to help them record what is happening in the classroom.

The terms *emic* and *etic* are very often mentioned in relation to classroom research due to an adopted role of the researcher in classroom observations. Researchers who try to get an inside view of what is happening in the classroom take an emic perspective in their research, whereas researchers who take more of an outside view on the event take an etic view of this (see Starfield this volume).

The researcher can carry out observations of the language classrooms very simply. By that, we mean that all a researcher needs is a pen and paper to be able to take fieldnotes about what they observe at a certain point in time. Fieldnotes can provide detailed descriptions of people, places, activities and events and are taken in conventional notation (as fast as the researcher can write or type). Sometimes, however, there are more complex and structured approaches to observing language classrooms that might be used. Over the years, various observation schedules and schemes have been devised to take data from language classrooms.

Observational work came to the fore with the first well-documented scheme, known as the Flanders Interaction Analysis Category observation system (Flanders 1970) that allowed researchers to examine and interpret observable classroom verbal behaviours such as teacher praise, questioning, lecturing, giving directions and student talk or silence. The language teacher's classroom talk was divided into discrete categories which allowed the observing researcher to note down occurrences of the different categories of talk measured at fixed intervals and to assign numerical values to each of these. There was also describing, tracking of students' verbal behaviours in set of observational categories. Flanders' work led to many classroom studies applying using this system, or adaptations of it, to their own classroom research (see e.g. Harbon 2000; Harbon & Horton-Stephens 1997).

Critics of such structured systems claim, among other things, that the communicative language classroom is far too complex for all notions to be labelled and captured in this manner, and that the essential communicative nature of the language classroom is lost. In response to those criticisms, more sophisticated observation schedules such as the COLT (Communicative Orientation of Language Teaching) scheme have been designed (Allen et al. 1984) and implemented according to a detailed coding manual (Spada & Fröhlich 1995). The Spada and Fröhlich manual (1995) has allowed users to capture more of the communicative aspects of the classroom than did the earlier Flanders's (1970) scheme. The COLT scheme is one, however, that requires the user to be trained in its methods to be true to the scheme's intentions.

Whichever strategies and techniques are chosen for classroom observation research, it is important that the researcher has a tightly structured and systematic data gathering instrumentation. It is important that the instrument could be used by another researcher in a replication study, and the same types of findings emerge.

Narrative inquiry

Early observational classroom studies quantified teacher–student interaction (Duff 2007). In the past twenty years, however, scholars have recognized that classrooms can be more fully understood from the views of participants. Narrative inquiry has come to the fore as one of the ways that second language classroom practices and processes can be explored and understood in this way (Barkhuizen 2011). As teachers' personal and professional narratives embody their knowledge, values and understandings of the classroom, narrative inquiry is increasingly common in second language classroom research. Narrative inquiry allows researchers to investigate educational practices and explore different phenomena through the teachers' or their students' personal life stories (Zhao & Poulson 2006).

There are no specific steps for conducting narrative inquiry; however, the end point must be the formulation of narratives. Barkhuizen's (2011, p. 398) reminder is that 'narratives are discursive artifacts, and, whether written, spoken, or visual (e.g. drawings, drama), are constructed in particular contexts'. Zhao and Poulson (2006) describe biographical narrative inquiry and their suggested strategy to elicit teacher narratives. First, they suggest undertaking an initial interview and then require their informants to narrate their personal and professional timelines and career paths, such as might be found in an oral history. After recording and transcribing this material, the accuracy of transcription is established by presenting informants with hard copies of the data to read and check.

A narrative analysis then follows. The researcher places together the larger narrative accounts which have been gathered during the initial interview phase. These may be accounts of classroom phenomena, actions, moments, metaphors and people. The accounts are then synthesized or condensed to create focused episodes or stories. They are matched with and give further insight into the biographical data gathered earlier. What is key with narrative inquiry is that metaphors are identified and stories are constructed to produce narrative episodes.

Researchers are wise to heed Barkhuizen's (2011, p. 393) reminder that 'narrative researchers are intimately implicated in their research activities'. As researchers become closer to the storytellers, they cannot help but become close to the storyteller and the stories. Acknowledgement of this relationship is essential.

The stories of three teachers in Golombek and Johnson's (2004) narrative inquiry study are an example of this. The reader of the research report meets the three teachers, Jenn, Michael and Lynne and their teacher-authored narratives as they make links between their teaching and their students' learning. Jenn's narrative of her practice is told through her story depicted as one of 'forgiveness and power in the classroom'. Michael's teacher narrative is told through the story of 'giving children quiet space'. Lynne's teacher narrative is told through the story of her 'letting ... students read'. According to Golombek and Johnson (2004), the strength in such a narrative inquiry is how they are able to show, through teachers' own voices, how teachers come to know about their work, as well as what they come to know.

This type of narrative research, then, allows 'fuller, more textured, humanized, and grounded accounts of the experiences of teachers and learners in contemporary classrooms' (Duff 2007, p. 983) than might be obtained with other research methods which take a more distanced view of what is happening in the language learning classroom.

Validity and reliability in classroom-based research

It is important for researchers in language classrooms to consider the validity and reliability of any data collection instruments they employ. A simple set of questions can provide useful assistance to guide the researcher from the conceptualization stage right through to the final reporting. Such questions may be about whether the instruments:

- provide the data which the researcher intended to gather;
- capture all that is required about the people, classroom context, interactions and activities that are being examined; and
- were familiar enough to participants to cause as little disruption to the regular processes of the classroom as possible.

With observation instruments, the researcher must ensure that all those who will use the instruments are thoroughly trained and given sufficient opportunity to gain experience in its use in a number of situations, or pilot studies, prior to the main study. The same goes for the interpretation of observations. It is useful to work with other researchers in this so as to avoid the misinterpretation of events.

Problems associated with researching language classrooms

Researchers need to consider the problems they might encounter in undertaking classroom research. Both in observational research and in narrative inquiry, there are a number of limitations that need to be acknowledged. With classroom observation, the data collected really just portray snapshots of limited periods of time. The conclusions drawn are thus tentative and at best can be taken as indicative rather than conclusive. Other problems with gathering classroom observation data are concerned with issues of consistency in the data gathering. The researcher must ensure the research questions are tightly linked to the data collection and analysis, so that the research can truly be considered to be a reflection of what it aims to research. The researcher's tight control of the relatedness of research questions, method, analysis and interpretation underpin the strength of the validity and reliability of the research findings.

The phenomenon of a researcher observing classrooms brings in the issue of having an outside observer, or possibly a participant observer taking part in classroom activities. Cameras pointing at the teacher or students, audio recording devices placed near classroom members, all add to creating the impression that the classroom is 'on display'. The fear is that data collected if participants are 'playing to the camera' may not be as real a picture as possible. The researcher thus needs to ensure that the participants do not act or behave in a way that will impact on the researcher's attempt to obtain a 'real' or 'natural' view of the classroom processes under interrogation.

A sample study

The sample study chosen here as an example of second language classroom research is the paper, 'Where is the technology-induced pedagogy? Snapshots from two multimedia EFL classrooms' reported in the *British Journal of Educational Technology* (Zhong & Shen 2002). The research primarily employed classroom observation focusing on three aspects of the teachers' language pedagogy: the approach of the teacher towards teaching, the design of the course taught and procedures chosen for language teaching and learning in two multimedia English as a foreign language (EFL) classrooms.

The paper reports on a study set in a school in China where the language curriculum was becoming increasingly oriented towards and linked to information and communication technologies (ICT). The study was conducted in two ICT-supported EFL classrooms. With a school ICT integration orientation, there was an assumption that there would be technology-induced pedagogical changes in the EFL classroom. The researchers set out to test the hypothesis that 'there is no technology-induced pedagogy', which is implied in the title of the research paper: 'Where is the technology pedagogy?' The subtitle 'Snapshots from two multimedia EFL classrooms' defines the nature and scope of the study. The study was a classroom-based project that used observation as its key research strategy.

After defining the study, three research questions were framed which were closely related to the research purpose and issues under examination. The research questions were: (1) What pedagogical models do teachers use in the multimedia classroom? (2) How does the multimedia classroom differ from the pre-multimedia classroom in classroom interaction? (3) What is the role of the teacher and the student in the technology-enhanced learning environment?

In the early sections of the paper, the researchers provide a simple outline of the key notions they found in the literature review which informed their decisions to undertake the project as they did. They note other studies which examined similar issues and the conclusions that had been reached in those studies.

Classroom observation was used as a key research strategy. The collection of the data, however, went beyond one single method. Based on the understanding that qualitative language classroom research is holistic in nature, the researchers saw no reason why research into the language classroom could not include elements of other research methods. The researchers examined teachers' detailed lesson plans as well as the courseware they had designed as an added way of collecting and validating the data gathered from in-class observation and videotaping. This allowed the researchers to cross-check the findings which contributed to establishing validity within the research.

Video recording of the classroom processes was effective in that it captured precisely what was happening in the multimedia language classrooms in teaching and learning, the context in which learning was taking place as well as many of the less-observable aspects of the classroom dynamics such as participants' general demeanours and other non-verbal actions in the process of classroom interaction.

Much of the data gathered from these instruments, however, was not used in this study. This is common practice, especially when researchers undertake a study with a very clear purpose in mind such as writing a paper for a specific academic journal. In this study, the researchers examined and analysed only the most salient data which enabled them to provide an account or interpretations of what they believed to be the realities of instructional practices and processes in the two Chinese English-language classrooms.

The qualitative exploration of the instructional procedures aimed to capture the classroom culture in a holistic way. However, the researchers claimed to be aware that they may not have observed everything, as what they observed was only the tangible part of the classroom processes and interactions. As non-participant classroom researchers, they were only exposed to what was occurring around them in the classroom at one point in time. The researchers did not claim to be inside the thinking of the teachers and students concerning the research focus.

The less-easily-observable elements of a second language classroom like this could, nevertheless, be reconstructed utilizing other research methods such as narrative inquiry, discussed earlier in this chapter. By interviewing the participants and inviting them to talk about their life histories, particularly critical incidents that happened in different points in time in their life, linking to images and metaphors of classroom incidents, the researchers may have been able to better understand the hidden factors such as traditional Chinese cultural and educational assumptions and practices, which may have contributed to who the participants are and what they believe and do in the classroom.

When designing a qualitative research into a language classroom, it is crucial to take into consideration the physical context in which the research is conducted. It often helps to establish a profile of the research site, including a brief description of the institution, its vision and expectations, the detail of the sample, specific techniques for ensuring a non-obtrusive approach to the classroom, research constraints and ethical considerations. These are included in detail on pages 40–43 in the published study (Zhong & Shen 2002).

The research questions were addressed by examination of the videotaped observations and examination of teachers' lesson plans. The focus of the observation was on the teacher and aspects of the context of teaching and learning in the two multimedia language classrooms. It was anticipated that this could be best addressed by observing how the teachers taught. A comparative study of the approaches the teachers employed, as well as the materials and tasks they designed for classroom interaction in the two multimedia EFL classrooms, may provide empirical evidence to show how a multimedia English class differs (or not) from a traditional language class through a qualitative analysis of the learning events and instructional sequence recorded during classroom observation.

In the sample study, the researchers chose two schools, a government school and a private school in China. The government school was a selective school with good computer networks and an innovative language curriculum. The private school was well-resourced and keen to integrate

ICT into the teaching and learning at the school. This was followed up with a description of the classes to be observed as well as the teachers and the materials they would use for teaching in the two multimedia EFL classes. Pseudonyms were used for the two institutions and the teachers involved in the research project to protect their privacy.

Prior to the commencement of the actual research, permission was obtained in which the nature, scope and involvement of the school and participants were clearly outlined. The schools and the participants were also made aware of, and agreed to, the procedures of data collecting, validating and reporting.

As discussed above, data collection for this study involved classroom observation, video recording and examination of teachers' lesson plans. Once data were collected from the classes, they were then analysed. The researchers also cross-checked the data from classroom observations against the teachers' lesson plans to identify the structure of the lessons. The researchers found that the two multimedia lessons were sequenced in a similar way, consisting of five phases: *revision, presentation, reading, practice* and *consolidation/homework*. The basic structure of the two lessons is shown in Figure 26.1.

Figure 26.1 is a graphic representation of the lesson construction showing the various phases and their relationships in the classroom instruction. The figure shows how the researchers reduced the whole gamut of classroom practices to meaningful data. The analysis of the events and tasks for different phases highlighted the role of the teacher and the students in the classroom as well as the function of the computer in each of the five phases. The computer was used in class not as a medium for interactive learning but an electronic tool for the teacher to present lesson materials in a teacher-led manner.

In the qualitative analysis, the researchers also examined in detail a range of lesson elements. It was found that new technologies were used

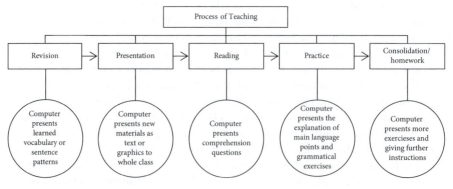

FIGURE 26.1 *Structure of two lessons and the use of computers (Zhong & Shen 2002, p. 41)*

as accessories and classroom procedures and were predominantly teacher-driven. A linear sequence tended to be followed with a focus largely on language forms. The use of computers in the language class did not bring about any pedagogical changes, as teachers simply used their traditional method of language teaching in the multimedia classroom. There was very little difference between the traditional English classroom and the multimedia classroom, and teachers retained a dominant role in knowledge transmission with students still on the receptive end of the continuum, something that neither of the researchers had anticipated. With this and other related findings, the researchers concluded their research.

Resources for further reading

Barkhuizen, G 2011, 'Narrative knowledging in TESOL', *TESOL Quarterly*, vol. 45, no. 3, pp. 391–414.

Barkhuizen, G (ed.), 2013, *Narrative Research in Applied Linguistics*. Cambridge University Press, Cambridge.

This book is for researchers wishing to confirm definitions, dimensions and methodological aspects of narrative research. Readers can essentially explore what narrative research is all about, its theoretical base, how narratives are constructed and how they are co-constructed. The general structure of the chapters allows easy navigation.

Barkhuizen is guest editor of this special issue of *TESOL Quarterly* and provides not only information about processes involved in narrative inquiry, but also introduces the paper authors thoroughly, seeing the synergies between each paper for better understanding of this research strategy.

Barkhuizen, G, Benson, P & Chik, A (eds), 2014, *Narrative Inquiry in Language Teaching and Learning Research*. Taylor & Francis, New York, NY.

Readers are guided through key aspects and published research on oral, written and multimodal narrative, as well as data analysis and reporting issues. There is advice given about all aspects of narrative inquiry research. The authors state their awareness of both investigating and writing narratives, and that the information provided becomes a 'map' rather than a 'set of guidelines'.

Duff, PA 2007, 'Qualitative approaches to classroom research with English language learners', in J Cummins & C Davison (eds), *International Handbook of English Language Teaching*, Springer, New York, NY, pp. 973–986.

Duff's chapter in this handbook is an all-important read in any preparation to undertake language classroom research. As well as outlining the features of qualitative classroom research, she considers some properties of qualitative research, paradigm debates, the role of triangulation, emic perspectives, collection methods in qualitative research, combining macro-level and micro-level ethical issues and criteria for evaluating qualitative research.

Gass, SM & Mackey, A 2011, *Data Elicitation for Second and Foreign Language Research*, Routledge, New York, NY.

Chapter 8 in this volume is titled 'Classroom-based research', and after discussing naturalistic classroom research, the authors concentrate chiefly on observational research in language classrooms, deconstructing observation schemes and the steps, stages, processes and 'etiquette' of undertaking observational classroom research.

Holliday, AR 2007, *Doing and Writing Qualitative Research*, 2nd edn, Sage, London.

Holliday's volume is an easy-to-read text that deals with various aspects of qualitative research, from the basics of starting out, deciding on the question and project, right through to data collection strategies, and writing up findings, much of which is relevant to classroom research.

Hopkins, D 2008, *A Teacher's Guide to Classroom Research*, 4th edn, McGraw-Hill, Maidenhead.

This very practical guide, now in its 4th edition, encourages classroom teachers to undertake classroom research. With very solid arguments in the first and last chapters outlining reasons why classroom teachers *can* and *should* undertake classroom research, the remaining chapters help teachers to refine a research focus, to plan for observations and to gather, analyse and report on research findings. It is written in an easy-to-read style, so as to instil confidence in teachers considering taking up the research challenge. Although not specifically written for language teachers, it is still very applicable to second language classroom research.

Nunan, D & Bailey, KM 2009, *Exploring Second Language Classroom Research: A Comprehensive Guide*, Heinle, Cengage Learning, Boston, MA.

This volume is certainly comprehensive, as the title suggests. Part I introduces second language classroom research, defines key concepts and guides researchers to start their projects. Part II covers experimental classroom research, survey, case study, ethnography and action research. Part III has closest links with this chapter, because of its focus on classroom observation. Covered also in the remainder of the volume are introspective methods, elicitation and analysis.

References

Allen, JPB, Fröhlich, M & Spada, N 1984, 'The communicative orientation of second language teaching: An observation scheme', in J Handscombe, A Orem & BP Taylor (eds), *On TESOL '83: The Question of Control*, TESOL, Washington, DC, pp. 231–252.

Allwright, D & Bailey, KM 1989, *Focus on the Language Classroom*, Cambridge University Press, Cambridge.

Arthur, J, Waring, M, Coe, R & Hedges, LV (eds) 2012, *Research Methods and Methodologies in Education*, SAGE, Thousand Oaks, CA.

Barkhuizen, G 2011, 'Narrative knowledge in TESOL', *TESOL Quarterly*, vol. 45, no. 3, pp. 391–414.

Cohen, L, Manion, L & Morrison, K 2007, *Research Methods in Education*, 6th edn, Routledge, New York, NY.

Cresswell, JW 2012, *Educational Research: Planning, Conducting and Evaluating Quantitative and Qualitative Research*, 4th edn, Pearson, Boston, MA.

Denzin, N & Lincoln, Y (eds), 2005, *The Handbook of Qualitative Research*, 3rd edn, SAGE, Thousand Oaks, CA.

Duff, PA 2007, 'Qualitative approaches to classroom research with English language learners', in J Cummins & C Davison (eds), *International Handbook of English Language Teaching*, Springer, New York, NY, pp. 973–986.

Flanders, NA 1970, *Analyzing Teacher Behaviour*, Addison-Wesley, Reading, MA.

Gebhard, JG & Oprandy, R 1999, *Language Teaching Awareness: A Guide to Exploring Beliefs and Practices*, Cambridge University Press, Cambridge.

Golombek, PR & Johnson, KE 2004, 'Narrative inquiry as a meditational space: Examining emotional and cognitive dissonance in second language teachers' development', *Teachers and Teaching: Theory and Practice*, vol. 10, no. 3, pp. 307–327.

Harbon, L 2000, 'Students gaining increased global awareness: Teacher research tracking implementation of LOTE curriculum policy', *Australian Association for Research in Education (AARE) Annual Conference Proceedings*, University of Sydney, Sydney December, Paper har00202, viewed 5 August 2014, http://www.aare.edu.au/publications-database.php

Harbon, L & Horton-Stephens, P 1997, 'It's what you do and the way you do it: The primary LOTE teacher in the classroom', in P Voss (ed.), *Conference Proceedings of the 11th AFMLTA National Languages Conference*, AFMLTA, Hobart, pp. 145–158.

Lightbown, PM 2000, 'Anniversary article. Classroom SLA research and second language teaching', *Applied Linguistics*, vol. 21, no. 4, pp. 431–462.

Lodico, MG, Spaulding, DT & Voegtle, KH 2006, *Methods in Educational Research: From Theory to Practice*, John Wiley & Sons, San Francisco, CA.

Mackey, A & Gass, SM 2005, *Second Language Research: Methodology and Design*, Lawrence Erlbaum Associates, Mahwah, NJ.

McKay, SL 2006, *Researching Second Language Classrooms*, Lawrence Erlbaum Associates, Mahwah, NJ.

Nunan, D 1989, *Understanding Language Classrooms*, Prentice Hall, New York, NY.

Nunan, D & Bailey, KM 2009, *Exploring Second Language Classroom Research: A Comprehensive Guide*, Heinle, Cengage Learning, Boston, MA.

Nunan, D & Choi, J 2011, 'Shifting sands: The evolving story of "voice" in qualitative research', in E Hinkel (ed.), *Handbook of Research in Second Language Teaching and Learning*, vol. II, Routledge, New York, NY, pp. 222–236.

Spada, N & Fröhlich, M 1995, *COLT Observation Scheme. Communicative Orientation of Language Teaching Observation Scheme: Coding Conventions and Applications*, National Centre for English Language Teaching and Research, Macquarie University, Sydney.

Wallace, MJ 1998, *Action Research for Language Teachers*, Cambridge University Press, Cambridge.

Zhao, HQ & Poulson, L 2006, 'A biographical narrative inquiry into teachers' knowledge: An intergenerational approach', *Asia Pacific Education Review*, vol. 7, no. 2, pp. 123–132.

Zhong, YX & Shen, H 2002, 'Where is the technology-induced pedagogy? Snapshots from two multimedia EFL classrooms', *British Journal of Educational Technology*, vol. 33, no. 1, pp. 39–52.

CHAPTER TWENTY SEVEN

Researching Language Testing and Assessment

John Read

Language testing, as a field of study in its own right, is conventionally considered to have been established around 1961, with the appearance of the first book on the subject (Lado 1961). Obviously, tests and examinations were being administered to second language learners long before this seminal publication, as Spolsky (1995) has documented in his comprehensive history of the area. What Lado did was to provide a systematic account of language testing as a sub-discipline within applied linguistics, rather than merely part of the normal work of language teachers and educators. Although the book was published in the United Kingdom, it drew on two distinctively American influences of the time: structuralist linguistics and psychometrics. Lado's book did not lack insights gained from the author's extensive experience as a language teacher, but it introduced a 'scientific' approach to the design and evaluation of tests that came to dominate language testing research for the next thirty years or more. The focus on objectively scored test items, reliability of measurement and ever more complex statistical procedures has meant that language testing has been commonly perceived as an esoteric field with little appeal for most language teachers whose academic background is in the arts and humanities. However, both the perception and the reality have been changing in recent years, in ways that are described below.

Testing and assessment

The dominance of the psychometric paradigm has been increasingly challenged, particularly by those who are primarily concerned with the progress and achievement of learners in the classroom. Thus, other approaches have developed with various labels such as educational assessment (Gipps 1994), assessment for learning (Gardner 2006) and classroom-based assessment (Turner 2012). Rather than ranking students and schools by means of standardized tests and examinations, this alternative paradigm seeks to monitor how well learners are working towards their learning objectives and to provide useful feedback on the process, using methods such as project work and take-home assignments; the compiling of portfolios, journals and diaries by learners; self-assessment and peer assessment; conferencing between teacher and learners; and the systematic monitoring of regular learning activities. The contrast in the two paradigms has been explored in language education by authors such as Teasdale and Leung (2000) and Rea-Dickins and Gardner (2000).

Within the alternative paradigm, there is a growing body of classroom-based research to investigate the beliefs and practices of teachers in the area of language assessment, using predominantly qualitative methods of inquiry: observation, recording, interviews and stimulated recall. A good starting point is to read the articles in a special issue of *Language Testing* (Rea-Dickins 2004).

Another recent trend has been, not to set up testing and assessment in opposition to each other, but to adopt 'assessment' as the general term for the process of designing and administering procedures to evaluate what language learners have achieved in terms of knowledge of, and ability in, the target language. Testing then becomes one very important form of assessment, particularly when large numbers of learners need to be assessed for high-stakes purposes such as university admission, employment or immigration. Brown and Hudson (1998) argue that we need to look broadly at 'alternatives in assessment', ranging from true-false and multiple-choice test items through to portfolios, selecting the most appropriate procedures according to the purpose of the assessment and the educational context. An example of this broader usage can be found in the title of the Cambridge Language Assessment Series, which is a comprehensive set of ten volumes published between 2000 and 2006. If the books had been published a decade or two earlier, it would almost certainly have been a language testing series. Similarly, a new journal first published in 2004 was named *Language Assessment Quarterly*, partly to differentiate it from the established journal *Language Testing*, but also to reflect the contemporary use of assessment as the cover term.

Nevertheless, neither of the distinctions outlined in the two preceding paragraphs is consistently maintained in the literature. There is a strong tendency for the two terms 'language testing' and 'language assessment' to be used interchangeably, and although the primary focus in this chapter is on formal tests and examinations, the general principles apply to other forms of assessment as well. Thus, both terms are used in the title of the chapter.

Test validity

The central preoccupation of research in language testing (and assessment, for that matter) is with the concept of validity. From taking an introductory course or reading a textbook, many people are familiar with the conventional formulation that a test is valid to the extent that it tests what it is supposed to test, and the idea that there are several so-called types of validity: face, content, concurrent, predictive, construct and maybe one or two others. This was always a somewhat simplistic account of what is involved in validation, but our understanding of test validity has been transformed over the past 20 years as language testers have become familiar with developments in validity theory in the general field of educational measurement, prompted by the work of two major scholars, Lee Cronbach (1989) and Samuel Messick (1989).

In the theoretical framework developed by Cronbach and Messick, construct validity has come to be the overarching concept. It is beyond the scope of this chapter to give a full account of the current theory of test validity (see McNamara & Roever 2006, Chapter 2; Xi 2008), but some key ideas can be summarized here:

- It is important to define carefully the construct underlying the test, that is, what specific language knowledge, skills or abilities are to be measured.

- Validity is not an inherent property of a test (as in the commonly seen statement 'This is a reliable and valid test'), but it is a function of the way in which the results can be meaningfully interpreted when the test is administered to a specified population of test-takers.

- In order to justify their intended interpretations of the results, test developers need to build an argument for the validity of their test, drawing on both theoretical reasoning and various kinds of empirical evidence obtained from trying out the test with actual test-takers.

The need for construct validation of tests can be seen as generating research at two levels. The first, which represents perhaps the purest form of investigation in the field, involves the broad construct that is the basis for test performance, particularly in general language proficiency tests. This construct has been given various labels and conceptual representations over the years: pragmatic expectancy grammar (Oller 1979), communicative competence (Canale & Swain 1980) and language ability (Bachman & Palmer 2010). Research at this level has been concerned with the question of whether language ability is divisible into components, and if so, what those components are. Is it meaningful to follow the common practice of assessing each of the four skills separately? To what extent should 'non-linguistic' aspects be taken into account in assessing speaking or writing ability? Recent developments have focused on the nature of performance in an oral interaction task such as an interview, role play or group discussion task (e.g. Bachman & Palmer 2010, esp. pp. 34–40; Chalhoub-Deville 2003). If the language that the test-takers produce is co-constructed through interacting with each other, what is the conceptual basis for rating each person's individual contribution?

The other level of construct validity relates to particular tests from a more practical perspective. The developers of a test need to gather various kinds of evidence to support their claims as to the meaningfulness of the results – and this can be seen as a major area of research activity in the field. Messick (1996) proposed that there are six main aspects of construct validation:

- Evidence that the test tasks are relevant to, and representative of, the domain of content to be assessed. For example, does a grammar test for high-school students contain a good sample of the grammatical structures and skills specified in the school curriculum?

- Evidence that, when they respond to the test tasks, the test-takers engage in cognitive processes that are predicted by a theory of task performance. For example, in a reading comprehension test, do learners actually apply higher-order reading skills in order to answer test items that target global understanding of the text?

- Evidence that the scoring criteria for a test are consistent with the way that the test construct is defined. For example, in an academic writing task, should the quality of the content be a scoring criterion, and what weight (if any) should be given to features such as spelling, punctuation and formatting?

- Evidence that the test results can be generalized, both in the sense that they are reliable and that they apply beyond the specific tasks in the test. For example, if an academic listening test includes a mini-lecture and a simulated tutorial discussion, can we infer from the results how well the test-takers can comprehend a seminar presentation or an individual consultation with a lecturer?

- Evidence that the test scores are consistent with external measures of the construct. For example, to what extent do the scores of health professionals on an oral proficiency test relate to ratings of their ability to communicate effectively with patients in a clinical setting?

- Evidence that the test results are being used appropriately and fairly, and not to the detriment of the test-takers. For example, if applicants for citizenship are required to pass a language test, has a suitable test been adopted for the purpose and does it assess their proficiency without bias against migrants from particular countries or language backgrounds?

This last area, which Messick called the consequential aspect, has become a major focus of discussion in testing. Given that tests are often used to make significant decisions about those who take them, it is important that such decision-making should be soundly based and not tainted by factors such as political expediency. Of particular concern in the modern world is the potential and actual misuse of tests by governments in dealing with refugees, asylum seekers and migrants applying for residence in the host country, as well as the use of assessment procedures to promote standards and accountability in national education systems (see McNamara & Roever 2006, Chapters 6 and 7). Thus, Messick somewhat controversially extended the scope of validation beyond the technical quality of the test instrument to a consideration of the impact of the test in operational use. This raises ethical issues for language testers involved in developing tests which may serve dubious political or educational purposes. In response, the International Language Testing Association has adopted a Code of Ethics and Guidelines for Good Testing Practice (both accessible at www.iltaonline.com, viewed 16 July 2014), and both major journals in the field have published special issues on ethical concerns (Davies 1997, 2004).

In terms of research on the consequential aspect, what has received most attention is the phenomenon of washback: the influence that major tests and exams exert on teaching and learning. Traditionally, washback has been seen in negative terms as encouraging students and their teachers to concentrate narrowly on intensive practice of test tasks at the cost of neglecting other important learning objectives. However, efforts have also been made to harness the washback effect in a positive way by introducing innovations into an exam, such as more communicative tasks, in order to modernize language teaching methods in schools. Inspired by a seminal article by Alderson and Wall (1993), numerous researchers have set out to investigate washback in a variety of national contexts, using classroom observation, teacher and student interviews, textbook analysis and other means. A definitive collection of articles on the topic can be found in Cheng et al. (2004).

Typical stages in language testing research

Research in language testing has become so diverse that it is difficult to identify any common set of steps that are taken in individual projects. However, what underlies research studies in the field is the process of developing a test, which is conventionally seen as comprising a series of stages following a broad linear sequence but also involving some cyclical processes.

The stages of test development are outlined in introductory textbooks (see e.g. Alderson et al. 1995; Hughes 2003). A more formal account, which has been influential in the field, is presented by Bachman and Palmer (2010). They divide the development process into five stages: (1) initial planning; (2) design; (3) operationalization; (4) trialling; and (5) assessment use.

Initial planning

This first step leads to a decision to proceed with developing the assessment (or not), based on considerations such as whether a suitable existing measure can be used and whether adequate resources are available for the project.

Design

At this stage, an overall plan called a Design Statement is written to guide the development of the assessment. It is necessary to clarify the purpose of the test and to define what it is supposed to be measuring in the form of at least one theoretical construct, which might be conversational proficiency in Spanish or academic writing ability in English. The developer should also describe the characteristics of the intended test-takers and the relevant domain of content for the test, either in terms of typical language use tasks or aspects of language knowledge (grammar, vocabulary, phonology, discourse features). For a large-scale testing project, the Design Statement should describe the resources required, in the form of personnel, funding, materials, equipment and so on.

Operationalization

The third stage yields a Blueprint which specifies the components of the assessment in much more detail than the Design Statement, to guide the writing of the actual assessment material, particularly when multiple forms of the test will be required. It spells out the tasks and items in terms of their key features: what kind of input material the test-takers are presented with, how they record their responses and how those responses are scored. The Blueprint should include information about how the test is to be administered, the timing of the various parts and the instructions to be given to the test-takers.

Trialling

The next step is to try out at least one complete form of the test with a group of students similar to those for whom the assessment is intended, to see how it works in practice. Even experienced test developers often cannot predict how particular tasks or items will perform when learners respond to them. The results are analysed, revisions are made to the materials and procedures and further trials are conducted as necessary.

Assessment use

Once the trialling stage has produced test material that is of acceptable quality, within the time and resources available, the assessment is ready for operational use with the intended population of students. However, ongoing monitoring is necessary, to address problems that may not have been identified through the trials and to check whether the assessment continues to function as expected.

The process of test development serves as a backdrop to research on language tests. The process does not really count as a research activity in itself; it is unlikely that a detailed account of how a particular test was developed according to the steps outlined above would be accepted as a research article in a journal or as a thesis or dissertation in language testing. Rather, research questions are generated as part of the development process when the test developers address problem areas or explore innovations in test design, the nature of the input material, the medium of delivery, rating procedures and so on. Here are some recent examples related to the assessment of writing:

- Knoch and Elder (2010) obtained somewhat mixed results in an academic writing test in Australia when they reduced the time allowed for the task from 55 to 30 minutes. Although the overall ratings were about the same, the longer time allowance was preferred by the test-takers and it produced better-quality essays in some respects.

- He and Shi (2012) found that post-secondary students taking an English proficiency test in Canada wrote significantly better essays on a general topic than one which required more specific background knowledge.

- Fritz and Ruegg (2013) investigated how raters scored vocabulary usage in essays by Japanese university students. The results showed that the raters were sensitive to lexical errors but not to the range or sophistication of the vocabulary that the students used.

A related point is that, particularly for postgraduate students, it is generally not feasible within a single study to develop a new test properly and tackle a research issue as well. Thus, most graduate researchers work with existing tests or test formats rather than creating their own, especially at the Masters level. Their university may have a testing program to place international students into language learning courses, or to assess the oral proficiency of international teaching assistants, and these programs offer opportunities for research. Another option is to be a member of a large-scale test development project directed by a professor at the student's university. A further possibility is that major testing organizations sometimes make test data available to approved outside researchers to conduct their own studies complementing those undertaken by in-house staff.

Whether researchers use an existing test or develop their own, it is an indispensable requirement that they should evaluate the technical quality of the instrument as a prelude to addressing their research questions. This means minimally reporting the reliability of the test when administered to the research participants. In this regard, language testers provide a model of good practice that should be emulated by those other frequent users of language tests, researchers in second language acquisition (SLA). As Norris and Ortega (2003) have pointed out, it is by no means a routine practice in published SLA studies to report on the reliability of the instruments used. This creates difficulties in determining to what extent measurement error has affected the results of individual SLA studies and also in building sound theory on the basis of a synthesis of research findings.

Research strategies and techniques

The most obvious tools to use in research on language tests are statistical procedures – the very thing that can deter mathematically challenged students of applied linguistics from considering language testing research in the first place. Before proceeding, then, I should make the point that not all research in the field involves the application of statistics, as we shall see below. The following section gives just a brief overview of test statistics; for more comprehensive yet accessible accounts, see Bachman (2004) or Green (2013).

Statistical methods

Introductory textbooks on testing usually present the basic statistics belonging to the classical model of psychometrics, allowing the user to summarize score distributions (mean and standard deviation), estimate the reliability of the test (KR-20, Cronbach's alpha), analyse the functioning of individual test items (item difficulty and discrimination) and calculate correlations for various purposes. When the number of test-takers is reasonably small (in the tens rather than hundreds or thousands), the statistics can be worked out manually on a scientific calculator. They are more usually computed these days by means of standard statistical software such as Microsoft Excel and SPSS (www.spss.com, viewed 16 July 2014), or by specialized programs like ITEMAN (www.assess.com, viewed 16 July 2014).

However, the classical statistics have significant limitations and since the 1980s they have been supplanted to a large extent in language testing by Item Response Theory (IRT) and especially the version of IRT known as the Rasch Model. A full discussion of the technical merits of the theory is beyond the scope of this chapter, but briefly, IRT has a number of advantages over the classical theory by, for instance, providing estimates of the reliability of individual test items rather than just the whole test, and making it easier to equate different forms of a test. In practical terms, IRT makes it possible to build a large bank of test items of known difficulty from which multiple forms of a test can be generated. This is the basis for computer-adaptive testing, with its promise of tests tailored to the ability level of individual test-takers – though for various reasons its potential remains only partly fulfilled (Chalhoub-Deville 1999).

The original Rasch Model, which applied just to test items scored right or wrong, has been extended to deal with items or questions worth more than one mark (the partial-credit model) and with rating scales. A further development is many-facet Rasch measurement, which provides a comprehensive evaluation of speaking or writing tasks, including on a single measurement scale estimates of the ability level of the test-takers, the difficulty of each task, the severity or leniency of the raters and the test-takers' relative performance on each of the rating criteria.

Another approach to the evaluation of tests, and in particular their reliability, is provided by Generalizability Theory (G-theory). Based on analysis of variance, a generalizability study (G-study) involves estimating the relative effects of the test-takers, the input texts, the items, the raters and other aspects of a test on the distribution of the scores. The primary purpose is to identify those facets of the measurement process that may be reducing the overall reliability of the test. The G-study can then be followed by a decision study (D-study), in which the test developer or researcher looks at how the reliability of the test might be improved by, say, adding twenty more items to the test or using three raters for each candidate's writing script rather than just two.

Perhaps the most sophisticated quantitative procedure in current use by language testing researchers is Structural Equation Modeling (SEM), which is used primarily in high-level research on the construct validation of tests. It involves calculating a complex set of correlations among numerous measures administered to the same group of learners in order to test a theoretical model of language ability. For instance, Shiotsu and Weir (2007) used SEM to demonstrate that syntactic knowledge was a better predictor than vocabulary knowledge of the reading comprehension ability of Japanese university students.

Although specialized software is available for IRT, G-Theory and SEM analyses, a great deal more is required to apply the procedures correctly than just entering test scores into the program and reporting the resulting statistics. Bachman quotes the authors of an introductory textbook on IRT as stating 'none of the currently available programs can be used with authority by researchers who are not well versed in the IRT literature' (Embretson & Reise 2000, quoted in Bachman 2004, p. 151). Thus, a researcher who plans to use one of these analyses should have an understanding of the mathematical basis of the statistical procedures as well as the underlying assumptions, the minimum amount of input data required and the accepted guidelines for interpreting the output – much of which, to complicate matters, may be the subject of ongoing debate among the experts. This means that a graduate student embarking on a study of this kind needs not only to read the relevant texts and take appropriate courses on quantitative methods and educational measurement but also to seek expert advice, which may be available only outside their own applied linguistics program.

Qualitative methods

However, although the statistical analyses have a central place in language testing research, there is an increasing trend towards the use of qualitative methods of inquiry to complement, if not replace, the traditional quantitative approaches. This reflects the general trend in applied linguistics and the social sciences generally towards a mixed methods approach to research methodology. Some types of non-statistical research have already been mentioned in the earlier discussion, such as the procedures for investigating educational assessment in the classroom and the methods involved in conducting washback studies.

It has become quite routine in testing research to obtain the perspective and insights of the test-takers themselves after they have completed the pilot version of a new test under development. By means of a questionnaire or interview, the test-takers can report on the level of difficulty of the test, any problems they had with the test instructions or with responding to novel test formats and also their perceptions of the fairness of the test as a measure of their ability. At a deeper level, researchers can probe the cognitive processes underlying test performance by eliciting verbal reports from individual test-takers either while they are responding to the test (think-aloud protocols) or immediately after they complete it. Such studies may seek to reveal the test-takers' reasons for choosing a particular response to multiple-choice or gap-filling items, or they may involve a more general investigation of test-taker strategies. For instance, the leading researcher in this area, Andrew Cohen, co-authored a study (Cohen & Upton 2007) of the reading and test-taking strategies adopted by learners responding to the reading formats of the internet-based TOEFL (iBT).

With the emphasis today on tests of communicative performance, the cognitive processes of raters are also of great interest to researchers. The quality of the assessment in speaking and writing tests depends on the raters having a shared understanding of the rating criteria as well as an ability to apply them consistently to particular performances. By means of interviews and verbal reports, researchers can evaluate the effectiveness of rater training, explore the extent to which raters have difficulty in following the prescribed guidelines and reveal cases where raters choose to ignore the official criteria in making their judgement. These qualitative procedures complement the more objective evidence provided by statistical analyses such as many-facet Rasch measurement and G-studies.

Another area of research opened by the assessment of productive skills is the investigation of spoken performance by means of discourse analysis. The most common template for a speaking test is the oral interview, in which an examiner (or interlocutor) presents a series of questions and perhaps other tasks to each test-taker in turn. Discourse analyses have shown, first, that a test interview is quite different from a normal conversation, and that the role of the interlocutor in the assessment is by no means a neutral one. For instance, Brown (2003) demonstrated that the style of interaction adopted by an examiner in the IELTS speaking test could have a significant impact on the rating the candidate received. This kind of research can lead to fairer assessment procedures as well as the development of alternatives to the standard interview, such as the paired format, in which two test-takers have opportunities to interact with each other rather than just with the examiner.

A sample study

As an example of research in language testing, let us look at a study I published some years ago (Read 2002). Although I was the sole author of the article, it reported a project conducted jointly with Kathryn Hill and Elisabeth Grove of the University of Melbourne. The work grew out of a desire to explore a new approach to the assessment of listening comprehension ability within the context of English for academic purposes. There were a number of facets of listening test design that could potentially have been investigated, such as what type of source to use for the input material, how to present the input to the test-takers and what type of test items to use. The focus in this case was on the form of the input.

At both universities involved (one in Australia and the other in New Zealand), there were existing listening tests based on scripted talks that were either pre-recorded on audiotape or presented live to the students. Such monologues can be seen at best as representing only part of the construct of academic listening ability, namely comprehension of formal lectures. We were interested in whether students could also understand more interactive forms of talk, such as the discussions that occur in seminars and tutorials.

There had been one previous study (Shohamy & Inbar 1991), conducted with high-school students in Israel, which was relevant to our emerging research question. These researchers prepared three versions of the input material with the same content, but one was a monologue designed to be like a news broadcast, whereas the other two involved varying degrees of interaction between the speaker and an interlocutor. Shohamy and Inbar found that the monologue was significantly more difficult for the students to understand than the other two versions. They argued that a typical monologue has key features of written language, like relatively dense content, limited redundancy and greater grammatical complexity, making the text more difficult for listeners to process than one which involves interaction between two or more speakers.

We decided to explore for ourselves the comparison between a scripted talk and a more interactive version of the same content. The first step was to prepare a talk on the topic of medical ethics, based on two cases that involved issues of informed consent and the acceptability of performing medical research on vulnerable patients. Once the script was written and edited, a set of thirty-six test items of the short-answer type was developed. Then, we set out to produce the interactive version. A first attempt, which was simply an unscripted discussion of the two cases by three people, did not produce a recording that could be meaningfully compared with the scripted talk. Instead, we adopted a 'semi-scripted' approach that was designed to shadow more closely the discourse structure of the monologue version. One of the speakers performed the role of a tutor, allocating turns and ensuring that all the content required to answer the test items was covered. The other two speakers acted as students, who took turns to review the facts of each case and comment on the ethical issues.

The study was conducted with six classes in an intensive English program at a New Zealand university. Most of the ninety-six students were from East or Southeast Asia and their main goal was to develop their proficiency in English for academic or professional purposes. In the eighth week of the course, the students took a pre-test in which they listened to a scripted talk about dreams. On the basis of the pre-test scores, they were divided into two groups that were matched in terms of listening ability. In Week 9 of the course, Group A took the monologue version of the experimental test, whereas Group B took the interactive version. For both groups it was quite a difficult test, with an overall mean score of just 16 out of a possible 36. When the two groups were compared, though, Group

A obtained a mean score of 18.0, which was significantly higher than the Group B mean of 14.16. In other words, the monologue version was easier to understand.

This result contrasted with the findings of Shohamy and Inbar (1991), whose participants found the interactive test versions more comprehensible. In considering why our results were different, we identified a number of reasons. One may simply have been a practice effect, in that Group A had taken a similar test based on a scripted talk as the pre-test the week before, whereas Group B had to cope with a new kind of input which they might not have experienced previously in a listening test. A second factor is that the test items had originally been written on the basis of the scripted talk and thus they fitted better with the monologue than with the interactive version of the test.

Another source of evidence was a questionnaire administered to all the participating students after they completed the test. With regard to the speed of the speech, the students in Group B reported significantly more often that the speakers in the discussion spoke too fast for them, and overall more of them rated the test as being very difficult. Thus, in the students' judgement, it was the interactive version of the test that was more challenging to comprehend.

The other main difference between the two studies was in the nature of the input texts. Shohamy and Inbar's (1991) monologue was deliberately designed to have the features of a formal written text in terms of its vocabulary, grammar and density of content, whereas ours was written more as a text to be read aloud, with simpler sentence structures, repetition of key vocabulary items and explicit discourse markers. In the case of the interactive versions of the tests, Shohamy and Inbar's dialogues were carefully scripted in order to incorporate the features of two distinct genres. By contrast, as described above, our discussion involved three speakers rather than two, and it was at the most semi-scripted, which meant that it was probably a more authentic sample of natural speech.

Thus, there are various ways in which the different outcomes of the two studies can be accounted for. At one level, they were both quite simple experiments, but they serve to highlight the complexity of the factors that can influence the difficulty level – and ultimately the validity – of a listening test. This in turn reinforces the point that, no matter how much thought and care go into the design and writing of a new test, it must be tried out with a suitable group of learners, analysed and revised before being used for operational purposes. The design of listening tests is an under-researched area, and there is certainly scope for studies of other variables besides the nature of the input texts. A lack of knowledge of statistics may seem like a deterrent, but it should not discourage anyone from conducting worthwhile research on this and a whole range of other topics in the field of language testing and assessment.

Resources for further reading

Books

Alderson, JC & Bachman, LF (eds), 2000–2006, *Cambridge Language Assessment Series*, Cambridge University Press, Cambridge.

This is an authoritative series of ten books written by specialist authors. Each volume includes a survey of relevant research and practice in a particular area of language assessment: listening, reading, speaking, writing, vocabulary, grammar, language for specific purposes, young language learners, the use of computer technology and statistical analysis.

Fulcher, G & Davidson, F (eds), 2012, *The Routledge Handbook of Language Testing*, Routledge, London.

This is a recent volume of thirty-four original papers by experts in language testing and assessment. The range of topics is indicated by these section headings: validity, classroom assessment and washback, the social uses of language testing, test specifications, writing items and tasks, prototyping and field tests, measurement theory and practice, administration and training, and ethics and language policy.

Kunnan, AJ (ed.), 2014, *The Companion to Language Assessment*, Wiley, Hoboken, NJ.

This is a comprehensive encyclopedia comprising 140 articles in four volumes, which is also available through the Wiley Online Library. Its all-inclusive coverage includes a volume devoted to Assessment Around the World, with thirty-six articles on the assessing of languages other than English.

McNamara, T & Roever, C 2006, *Language Testing: The Social Dimension*, Blackwell, Malden, MA.

This award-winning book gives an excellent overview of current concerns in language testing. The 'social dimension' in the title is interpreted broadly enough to encompass most of the major issues that researchers are addressing at the present time.

Journals

Assessing Writing: www.journals.elsevier.com/assessing-writing, viewed 16 July 2014.

Language Assessment Quarterly: www.tandf.co.uk/journals/titles/15434303.asp, viewed 16 July 2014.

Language Testing: http://ltj.sagepub.com, viewed 16 July 2014.

These three specialist journals publish research articles as well as reviews of books and tests.

Website

Resources in Language Testing: www.languagetesting.info, viewed 16 July 2014.

This is the single most useful website in the area of language testing. Maintained by Glenn Fulcher at the University of Leicester in the United Kingdom, it offers videos and podcasts by experts on a whole variety of topics: study materials on key subjects in the field; multiple web links to particular language tests, language testing organizations and relevant articles; as well as up-to-date news stories and a range of other resources.

References

Alderson, JC & Wall, D 1993, 'Does washback exist?', *Applied Linguistics*, vol. 14, no. 2, pp. 115–129.

Alderson, JC, Clapham, C & Wall, D 1995, *Language Test Construction and Evaluation*, Cambridge University Press, Cambridge.

Bachman, LF 2004, *Statistical Analyses for Language Assessment*, Cambridge University Press, Oxford.

Bachman, LF & Palmer, AS 2010, *Language Assessment in Practice*, Oxford University Press, Oxford.

Brown, A 2003, 'Interviewer variation and the co-construction of speaking proficiency', *Language Testing*, vol. 20, no. 1, pp. 1–25.

Brown, JD & Hudson, T 1998, 'The alternatives in language assessment', *TESOL Quarterly*, vol. 32, no. 4, pp. 653–675.

Canale, M & Swain, M 1980, 'Theoretical bases of communicative approaches to second language teaching and testing', *Applied Linguistics*, vol. 1, no. 1, pp. 1–47.

Chalhoub-Deville, M (ed.), 1999, *Issues in Computer-Adaptive Testing of Reading Proficiency*, Cambridge University Press, New York, NY.

—— 2003, 'Second language interaction: Current perspectives and future trends', *Language Testing*, vol. 20, no. 4, pp. 369–383.

Cheng, L, Watanabe, Y & Curtis, A (eds), 2004, *Washback in Language Testing: Research Contexts and Methods*, Lawrence Erlbaum, Mahwah, NJ.

Cohen, AD & Upton, TA 2007, '"I want to go back to the text": Response strategies on the reading subtest of the new TOEFL', *Language Testing*, vol. 24, no. 2, pp. 209–250.

Cronbach, LJ 1989, 'Construct validity after thirty years', in RL Linn (ed.), *Intelligence: Measurement, Theory and Public Policy*, University of Illinois Press, Urbana, IL, pp. 147–171.

Davies, A (ed.), 1997, 'Ethics in language testing (special issue)', *Language Testing*, vol. 14, no. 3.

—— 2004, 'The ethics of language assessment (special issue)', *Language Assessment Quarterly*, vol. 1, nos. 2 and 3.

Fritz, E & Ruegg, R 2013, 'Rater sensitivity to lexical accuracy, sophistication and range when assessing writing', *Assessing Writing*, vol. 18, no. 2, pp. 173–181.

Gardner, J (ed.), 2006, *Assessment and Learning*, Sage, London.

Gipps, C 1994, *Beyond Testing: Towards a Theory of Educational Assessment*, Falmer, London.

Green, R 2013, *Statistical Analyses for Language Testers*, Palgrave Macmillan, Basingstoke.

He, L & Shi, L 2012, 'Topic knowledge and ESL writing', *Language Testing*, vol. 29, no. 3, pp. 443–464.

Hughes, A 2003, *Testing for Language Teachers*, 2nd edn, Cambridge University Press, Cambridge.

Knoch, U & Elder, C 2010, 'Validity and fairness implications of varying time conditions on a diagnostic test of academic English writing proficiency', *System*, vol. 38, no. 1, pp. 63–74.

Lado, R 1961, *Language Testing*, Longman, London.

McNamara, T & Roever, C 2006, *Language Testing: The Social Dimension*, Blackwell, Malden, MA.

Messick, S 1989, 'Validity', in RL Linn (ed.), *Educational Measurement*, 3rd edn, American Council on Education and Macmillan, New York, NY, pp. 13–103.

———— 1996, 'Validity and washback in language testing', *Language Testing*, 13, no.3, pp. 241–256.

Norris, J & Ortega, L 2003, 'Defining and measuring SLA', in CJ Doughty & MH Long (eds), *The Handbook of Second Language Acquisition*, Blackwell, Malden, MA, pp. 717–761.

Oller, JW, Jr 1979, *Language Tests at School*, Longman, London.

Read, J 2002, 'The use of interactive input in EAP listening assessment', *Journal of English for Academic Purposes*, vol. 1, no. 2, pp. 105–119.

Rea-Dickins, P (ed.), 2004, 'Exploring diversity in teacher assessment (special issue)', *Language Testing*, vol. 21, no. 3.

Rea-Dickins, P & Gardner, S 2000, 'Snares or silver bullets: Disentangling the construct of formative assessment', *Language Testing*, 17, no. 2, pp. 215–243.

Shiotsu, T & Weir, CJ 2007, 'The relative significance of syntactic knowledge and vocabulary breadth in the prediction of reading comprehension test performance', *Language Testing*, vol. 24, no. 1, pp. 99–128.

Shohamy, E & Inbar, O 1991, 'Validation of listening comprehension tests: The effect of text and question type', *Language Testing*, vol. 8, no. 1, pp. 23–40.

Spolsky, B 1995, *Measured words: The development of objective language testing*, Oxford University Press, Oxford.

Teasdale, A & Leung, C 2000, 'Teacher assessment and psychometric theory: A case of paradigm crossing?', *Language Testing*, vol. 17, no. 2, pp. 163–184.

Turner, CE 2012, 'Classroom assessment', in G Fulcher & F Davidson (eds), *The Routledge Handbook of Language Testing*, Routledge, London, pp. 65–78.

Xi, X 2008, 'Methods of test validation', in E Shohamy & NH Hornberger (eds), *The Encyclopedia of Language and Education, Vol. 7, Language Testing and Assessment*, 2nd edn, Springer, New York, NY, pp. 177–196.

CHAPTER TWENTY EIGHT

Researching Teachers' Beliefs

Simon Borg

This chapter focuses on the study of teachers' beliefs, which has been an intense area of research in language teaching in the last fifteen years. Beliefs are often studied under the broader heading of *teacher cognition*, which also includes related constructs such as attitudes and knowledge, but here, I focus exclusively on beliefs. Following a brief discussion of the development of research on teachers' beliefs and a comment on definitional issues, I review the methodological features of research studies on language teachers' beliefs and provide a discussion of common research methods which can be used in such research. I end the chapter with the discussion of a recent sample study.

The study of teachers' beliefs

Figure 28.1 shows the number of social science articles with 'teacher(s')' beliefs' and 'language' in the title, abstract or keywords that were published (and which are cited in Scopus) between 2000 and mid-2014 (a total of 210 papers). The growth of research into language teachers' beliefs is clear from this figure, and the purpose of this chapter is to analyse the research methods which can be used to study the beliefs of second and foreign language (henceforth *L2*) teachers.

As I discuss in the opening chapter of Borg (2006), in the 1970s teaching was conceived of as a largely behavioural activity and little consideration was given to the mental side of teaching. This started to change in the 1980s, motivated in part by developments in cognitive psychology which posited strong links between human behaviour and underlying cognitive processes

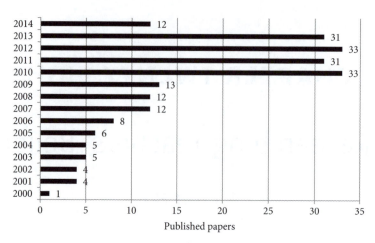

FIGURE 28.1 *Articles with 'teacher(s') beliefs' and 'language' in title, abstract or keywords: 2000–2014 (Source: Scopus)*

and which, therefore, implied that teaching, too, was shaped by teachers' thoughts, judgements and beliefs.

Beliefs, though, were not a major focus of early research on teacher cognition, which focused largely on understanding teacher planning (see the review in Clark & Peterson 1986), thinking (e.g. Calderhead 1987) and teacher judgement (e.g. Shavelson & Stern 1981). This early work was also heavily influenced by decision-making and information-processing theory (see Clark 1986), although from around the mid-1980s calls were emerging for research to go beyond the description of decision-making processes and to understand the beliefs underpinning such processes. The distinction implied here is what Ernest (1989) later described as that between teachers' thought *processes* (e.g. planning and decision-making) and the thought *structures* of teaching (e.g. knowledge and beliefs), and the latter has in the last twenty-five years become a much more significant focus of research than the former. Several reviews of research on teachers' beliefs have been written during this time (e.g. Calderhead 1996; Eisenhart et al. 1988; Fang 1996; Pajares 1992; Richardson 1996; Thompson 1992; Woolfolk Hoy, Davis & Pape 2006) and these reviews and many individual studies suggest (as summarized in Phipps & Borg 2009) that teachers' beliefs about teaching and learning:

- may be powerfully influenced (positively or negatively) by teachers' own experiences as learners and are well established by the time teachers go to university;

- act as a filter through which teachers interpret new information and experience;

- may outweigh the effects of teacher education in influencing what teachers do in the classroom;

- can exert a persistent long-term influence on teachers' instructional practices;

- are, at the same time, not always reflected in what teachers do in the classroom;

- interact bidirectionally with experience (i.e. beliefs influence practices and practices can also lead to changes in beliefs); and

- influence how teachers react to educational change.

The educational literature has also highlighted the definitional challenges that confront teacher cognition research more generally, and two particular questions that recur are (a) what is the definition of 'belief'? and (b) how is 'belief' distinct from 'knowledge'? Thirty years of intellectual consideration of these issues have not generated any consensus, so I will not attempt to resolve such matters here. Pajares (1992) provides perhaps the most detailed analysis of teachers' beliefs to date, suggesting that beliefs be defined as 'an individual's judgment of the truth or falsity of a proposition' (p. 316). Richardson (1996, p. 103) defines beliefs as 'psychologically held understandings, premises, or propositions about the world that are felt to be true', while, more recently, Murphy and Mason (2006, pp. 306–307) define beliefs as 'all that one accepts or wants to be true. Beliefs do not require verification and often cannot be verified'. In terms of the distinction between beliefs and knowledge, several discussions are available (e.g. Nespor 1987; Smith & Siegel 2004; Southerland, Sinatra & Matthews 2001), though the general view in the literature is summed up by Woolfolk Hoy, Davids & Pape (2006, p. 716), who state that 'in keeping with precedents set by other researchers … we discuss beliefs and knowledge as generally overlapping constructs'.

It is within this broader context of educational research on teachers' beliefs that the study of L2 teachers' beliefs has emerged since the mid-1990s, and I will now proceed to discuss the research methods used in this work.

Research on L2 teachers' beliefs

Recent studies

Table 28.1 summarizes the focus, context and sample of twenty recent studies of L2 teachers' beliefs. Apart from one study that looks at change in beliefs (Yuan & Lee 2014), this body of work focuses on identifying the beliefs teachers hold about a wide range of issues (in fact, grammar is the only issue that occurs more than once here). Eleven of the studies examined teachers' classroom practices (the comparison of teachers' stated beliefs and reported or actual practices is a recurrent theme in these papers). Context-wise, all except one of the studies (Alexander 2012, which used an online survey open to teachers in different countries) involved teachers working in one of nine different countries, with China being that most represented (seven studies) followed by Turkey (three). The majority of the studies (sixteen) examined the beliefs of practising teachers, with less attention to teacher candidates. In terms of sample sizes, nine of the studies had fewer than 10 participants, three between 11 and 50, four between 51 and 100, and four over 100 (two of which were particularly large with 753 and 1,091 respondents, respectively). Of the twenty studies, ten were qualitative, three quantitative and seven mixed methods.

Table 28.1 Focus, context and sample of twenty studies of L2 teachers' beliefs

	Focus	Context	Sample
Alexander (2012)	Teachers' beliefs about teaching EAP to low-level students	UK and international	126
Allen (2013)	French teachers' beliefs about developing foreign language proficiency	US	19
Borg and Al-Busaidi (2012)	Beliefs and practices regarding learner autonomy of EFL teachers	Oman	61
Büyükkarci (2014)	EFL teachers' beliefs and practices regarding formative assessment	Turkey	69
Chatouphonexay and Intaraprasert (2014)	Pre-service and in-service EFL teachers' beliefs about language learning.	Lao	1,091
Chimbutane (2013)	Teachers' beliefs and practices regarding code switching in L1 and L2 classroom contexts	Mozambique	3
Dincer and Yeşilyurt (2013)	Pre-service EFL teachers' beliefs about speaking	Turkey	7
Farrell and Bennis (2013)	Beliefs and practices of an experienced and a novice ESL teacher	Canada	2

(continued)

	Focus	Context	Sample
Graham, Santos and Francis-Brophy (2014)	Beliefs and practices of MFL teachers regarding the teaching of listening	UK	115
Hos and Kekec (2014)	Beliefs and practices of EFL teachers regarding grammar teaching	Turkey	60
Hu and Tian (2012)	Beliefs about learning strategies among teachers and students of Chinese as a foreign language	UK	75
Kissau and Algozzine (2013)	Beliefs about effective L2 teaching among university supervisors and teacher candidates	USA	41
Li (2013)	The beliefs and practices of an EFL teacher	China	1
Underwood (2012)	Beliefs of EFL teachers about the teaching of grammar	Japan	16
Yang and Gao (2013)	Beliefs and practices of EFL teachers concerning L2 writing	China	4
Yuan and Lee (2014)	Change in the beliefs of pre-service EFL teachers during the practicum	China	3
Zeng (2012)	Beliefs and practices of EFL teachers regarding postmethod	China	2
Zhang and Liu (2014)	EFL teachers' beliefs about teaching and learning English	China	753
Zheng (2013)	Beliefs and practices of EFL teachers	China	6
Zheng and Borg (2014)	Beliefs and practices of EFL teachers regarding task-based learning	China	3

In terms of research methods, most of these studies (sixteen) were multi-method in nature. This is a positive feature of this body of work given that it is generally acknowledged that multiple sources of data contribute to more trustworthy findings. In terms of the data-collection methods used, as in my earlier analysis of twenty-five teacher cognition studies (Borg 2012), interviews (see Wagner this volume) are here the most common strategy (occurring in fifteen studies). Observations (Harbon & Shen this volume) were utilized in twelve studies and questionnaires (Wagner this volume) in nine. These three research methods account for 80 per cent of the total number of individual methods in the studies listed above.

Research methods

Before proceeding to discuss different ways of researching L2 teachers' beliefs, it is appropriate to remind readers of the analysis of research methods in the study of L2 teacher cognition provided in Chapters 6–9 of Borg (2006). Other sources I draw on here and which provide reviews of research methods in the study of teachers' beliefs are Langan-Fox, Code and Langfield-Smith (2000), Calderhead (1996), Kagan (1990), Shavelson and Stern (1981), Kane, Sandretto and Heath (2002), Speer (2005), Clark and Peterson (1986), Jones and Carter (2007), Kalaja and Barcelos (2003) and Fang (1996).

Given the long list of individual research methods available for the study of teachers' beliefs, it is necessary to organize the discussion of these methods under broader headings. Various classifications are used in the reviews noted above, and here, I use the following:

- oral accounts,
- self-report instruments,
- observation,
- written accounts and
- visual methods.

Oral accounts

I used the label *oral accounts* here to include research methods which elicit teachers' beliefs through spoken accounts produced by respondents. The most obvious form of oral account is the interview, which, as noted above, is the most widely used research method in the study of L2 teachers' beliefs. In its most basic form, an interview involves oral interaction between two individuals who assume distinct roles – one, the researcher, asks questions, while the other, the participant, responds. Many variations on this simple definition are of course possible, and readers are referred to standard research methods texts for further discussions of these options.

Interviews seek to elicit beliefs by getting teachers to talk; one important methodological point, though, is that explicitly asking teachers to articulate their beliefs (i.e. by asking questions such as 'what are your beliefs about....') is not considered to be a productive strategy; as Munby (1982, p. 217) noted over thirty years ago, 'it is necessary to recognize that individually we may not be the best people to clearly enunciate our beliefs and perspectives since some of these may lurk beyond ready articulation'. It is thus necessary (and this applies more generally to the methods discussed below) to elicit beliefs indirectly. Another methodological problem that arises when teachers are asked directly about their beliefs in an interview is that of context; I have made the distinction (Borg 2006) between beliefs that reflect ideals and those that reflect reality; when teachers' beliefs are elicited in an abstract context, they are more likely to reflect ideals (i.e. professed beliefs). For this reason, it is valuable to create interview contexts (such as stimulated recall and photo-based interviews – see below) where the discussion of beliefs is related to concrete experiences or objects.

Stimulated recall (for examples in L2 teaching, see Kim 2011; Kuzborska 2011) is a form of interview where oral accounts are elicited with the help of a stimulus – typically a video of the respondent's teaching (this form of stimulated recall is called video-stimulated recall, or VSR). This strategy provides a concrete context for the elicitation of teacher beliefs and ensures that these are grounded in actual observed events rather than abstractions. While it is sometimes assumed that VSR can retrospectively capture the thinking that teachers were engaged in during the videotaped events, this is debateable; stimulated recall is best conceived of as an elicitational strategy for enabling teachers to talk, in concrete and situated ways, about the beliefs (and other factors) that underpin their teaching.

Another kind of interview where the discussion is mediated via a stimulus is *photo-based interviewing* (Hurworth 2003). As the name implies, this involves an interview situation where the discussion is guided by photographs (typically taken by respondents). I have not come across examples of this strategy used in the study of teachers' beliefs (e.g. based on teachers' photos of their classrooms), but it clearly has potential (see below for a discussion of visual methods).

Oral narratives are extended spoken accounts which can take the form of autobiographies and stories. They represent, in their own words and in substantial detail, teachers' lived experiences and may focus on the past as well as the present. In language teaching, for example, Hayes (2005) conducted oral life histories with teachers of English in Sri Lanka. His focus was not limited to the study of teachers' beliefs, but the accounts that were generated provide much insight into this dimension of teachers' professional lives. Carter and Doyle (1996) and Clandinin and Connelly (2000) provide good starting points for readers who want to explore narrative approaches to research on teaching in more detail (see also Barkhuizen this volume).

Think-aloud protocol is an oral elicitation strategy through which respondents verbalize what they are thinking while they complete a task (Gilhooly & Green 1996; Green & Gilhooly 1996). Some examples are available in the field of language teaching (Lumley 2002; Samuda 2005). During think-aloud protocols, respondents are asked to describe what they are doing, not to explain their behaviour; thus, this strategy, on its own, may not provide much evidence of teachers' beliefs (as opposed to, for example, teacher decision-making), and combining it with other strategies (e.g. subsequent interviews) may be more productive. One other limitation of think-aloud protocols in the study of teaching is that they often occur in contrived situations (i.e. naturally occurring contexts where teachers verbalize their thoughts are rare). And, of course, this research method cannot be used to study actual classroom teaching given that it is impractical (and perhaps impossible) for teachers to verbalize their thoughts while they teach.

Self-report instruments

Self-report instruments include any form of questionnaire, inventory, checklist and theoretical profiling tool which seeks to measure teacher beliefs (most typically, but not only, using Likert scale items). Such instruments are popular in the study of L2 teachers' beliefs, and it is easy to see why: they provide a relatively economical and very flexible way of collecting large amounts of data quickly and (especially where electronic instruments are used) from respondents in diverse geographical contexts. However, the prima facie simplicity of research designs which use self-report instruments can often blind researchers to methodological problems. The first challenge (and one that is unfortunately often not met in some recent studies I have reviewed) is simply technical incompetence – good-quality research of any kind cannot emanate from poor-quality instruments, and thus, the first requirement for researchers wanting to use questionnaires and similar tools to study teachers' beliefs is to ensure they understand – theoretically and in practice – how to design a robust instrument. A second critique about the use of self-report instruments in studying teachers' beliefs is that their limitations – which are widely discussed in the literature – are very often overlooked. For example, in their review of research methods in studying beliefs, Kane, Sandretto and Heath (2002) note that closed questionnaires can constrain what respondents say, lead respondents to give particular answers and prompt answers that reflect what respondents feel is the right or expected answer rather than what they believe. Kagan (1990, p. 426) thus concludes that 'any researcher who uses a short answer test of teacher belief (i.e. an instrument consisting of prefabricated statements) runs the risk of obtaining bogus data, because standardized statements may mask or misrepresent a particular teacher's highly personalized perceptions and definitions'. Additionally, as discussed in Borg (2006), theoretical measures of teachers' beliefs cannot be used to infer what teachers do in the classroom.

Given these substantial objections to the use of self-report instruments in studying teachers' beliefs, researchers need to take steps to minimize their exposure to criticisms which can seriously undermine their work. For example, instruments must be carefully designed, and researchers must engage critically with the limitations discussed above – ignoring them or adding a token comment in the 'limitations' section at the end of a paper is not adequate. Additionally, claims from self-report instruments should not extend beyond the limits of what is warranted – for example, if teachers *report* on what they do in the classroom this should not be presented as evidence of what they *actually* do. Another strategy to minimize the limitations of questionnaires in the study of teachers' beliefs is to combine them with other methods, such as interviews and observations.

Observation

In Borg (2006), I provided a detailed analysis of different parameters which can define the use of observation in the study of teacher cognition; for example, the researcher can be participant or non-participant, data can be captured using video, audio and fieldnotes, analytical categories can be predetermined or emergent and analysis can be qualitative or quantitative. As with interviews, then, the label 'observation' can mask significant diversity in the manner that teachers' beliefs are studied, and researchers will need to make decisions about the particular parameters to adhere to and, importantly, to justify these choices.

The major strength of observation in the study of teachers is that it allows for the collection of direct evidence about what happens in classrooms. This evidence can then provide the starting point for a grounded analysis of teachers' beliefs. At the same time, observation alters the context under study and causes reactivity – changes in the behaviour of those being observed. For this reason, repeated rather than one-off observations of teaching are recommended, on the assumption that reactivity decreases over time as teachers become accustomed to the presence of the observer.

It is essential that researchers acknowledge that while observation may allow for inferences about teachers' beliefs (such inferences generate *attributed beliefs*), observations alone are insufficiently robust as a source of evidence of what teachers believe; for example, a teacher may consistently correct students' oral errors in a particular way, but unless I ask the teacher why any conclusions I reach about their beliefs would be speculative. Deriving beliefs from behaviours is also problematic because different teachers may behave in similar ways for very different reasons. For these reasons, in studies of teachers' beliefs, observation is often combined (see examples in Table 28.1) with other data-collection strategies, particularly with interviews.

Written accounts

Teachers' beliefs can also be elicited via written accounts produced by teachers themselves and in response to specific questions or prompts. The term *account* implies that an extended volume of text is being produced, and the use of written accounts is thus most appropriate where teachers' beliefs are being studied qualitatively. Written accounts can take many forms such as open questionnaire responses, diaries, interpretive commentaries and autobiographical narratives (the written equivalent of the oral narratives discussed earlier). I will comment here on the first three of these.

An *open-ended questionnaire item* is one that allows respondents to answer the question in any way they want to and encourages them to do so in a relatively extended manner. One major disadvantage of open-ended questions is that they require more time and effort of the respondent, and for this reason, advice on good questionnaire design generally recommends that such questions be used sparingly. However, it is possible to explore teachers' beliefs through carefully designed prompts of this type. For example, Borg and Burns (2008) generated over just under 6,000 words of text from 136 teachers who wrote about their beliefs about the integration of grammar and skills in teaching English.

Diaries (also called *journals* and *logs*) are another strategy which can be used to elicited extended written accounts from teachers and which provide insight into their beliefs. A recent example is Allen (2013), who asked nineteen teachers of French to keep a diary for three weeks while they were on a course in France and analysed the teachers' accounts for insights into their beliefs about developing language proficiency. Allen discusses both the advantages and disadvantages of diaries; on the positive side, they are flexible and provide detailed information about specific experiences while these are still fresh in the writer's mind; less positively, the volume and quality of the writing that diarists produce can vary (in Allen's study, diary length ranged from two to thirty pages), diary writing requires commitment on the writer's part and the analysis of large volumes of written text can be problematic.

Diary writing in many cases will be a novel activity for teachers and its use to study teachers' beliefs must take this into account. This implies that teachers may benefit from some training in diary writing, from clear guidance on what they are expected to do (see Numrich 1996, for a good example of clear instructions) and from some form of template or guiding prompts to make it more likely that the writing produced will be relevant to the issues the researcher wants to examine.

Finally, *interpretive commentaries* are written texts through which teachers explain the beliefs that underpin some facet of their behaviour or which provide the basis for their evaluation of an object or event. For example, teachers might be given a sample of teaching material and asked to write about what they like or do not like about it, with explanations for their opinions. Or, as in the recent study by Borg et al. (2014) which I discuss further below, student teachers first drew pictures to represent their beliefs about effective EFL lessons and then produced written commentaries in which they explained what their pictures meant. The written accounts made explicit the beliefs about effective EFL teaching that were embedded in the pictures. Such commentaries could in theory be generated via an open-ended questionnaire item, though I would suggest that longer and deeper responses are more likely when an interpretive commentary is a separate task focused on the analysis of one particular phenomenon rather than being part of a longer instrument.

One proviso that applies to the study of beliefs through written accounts is that expecting teachers to spontaneously produce large volumes of written text about their beliefs is unreasonable. In selecting this methodological option, then, researchers should assess its suitability for the target participants and consider the kinds of support which are likely to enhance the volume and quality of the data that are elicited.

Visual methods

The final option for studying teachers' beliefs I will consider here is visual methods. Although there is a thriving literature on the use of visual methods in social science research more generally (e.g. Margolis & Pauwels 2011; Rose 2012), examples of their use in language teaching and teacher education contexts remain rare. As Spencer (2011, referring to Prosser 1998) explains, visual data take many forms and can occur naturally, be created by researchers or by respondents. My focus here is on the last of these and the examples I discuss below utilize drawings produced by respondents to examine their beliefs. Drawings can be valuable in the study of teachers' beliefs because, as Weber and Mitchell (1996, p. 304) state:

> Drawings offer a different kind of glimpse into human sensemaking than written or spoken texts do, because they can express that which is not easily put into words: the ineffable, the elusive, the not-yet-thought-through, the sub-conscious.

Kalaja, Dufva and Alanen (2013) review existing examples of visual narratives in language education contexts and report on their own ongoing work. In one study, they asked prospective language teachers in Finland to draw a picture of themselves giving a foreign language class in the near future. Respondents were also asked to write a brief explanation of the picture. One general finding, for example, was that most teachers depicted themselves as facilitators of learning ('smiling onlookers') rather than controlling the class from a central position. In a second example, Borg et al. (2014) used drawings with pre-service teachers of English in Spain to examine their beliefs about effective EFL teaching and also to monitor changes in these beliefs during their final year at university. The teacher candidates thus produced drawings at two points during the year and also produced written commentaries to explain them. Some of the respondents were also interviewed. Based on the analysis of four case study examples, the study concludes that the teacher candidates' beliefs were confirmed and extended rather than subject to any radical reform.

Visual methods clearly have much potential in the study of teachers' beliefs. Alone, though, drawings provide a limited basis on which inferences about teachers' beliefs can be made and that is why in both the studies above respondents also provided written and oral commentaries on their pictures. One other challenge that the use of visual methods raises relates to data analysis and researchers will need to familiarize themselves with, or indeed develop, new approaches to analysis through which visual data can be studied. Both the language education studies cited here provide valuable insight into such matters.

A sample study

Graham, Santos and Francis-Brophy (2014) is a recent study of L2 teachers' beliefs that illustrates many facets of good practice. The authors begin by acknowledging, as many such studies do, that the study of beliefs is valuable because they both influence and are influenced by what happens in the classroom. The substantive focus of this study – teachers' beliefs about second language listening – is justified, rightly so, with reference to the lack of research into this issue. The researchers also wanted to assess the extent that teachers' beliefs about second language listening were aligned with formal theory (as found in the literature) on this topic.

The study was conducted in England, where (at the time of the study), foreign language learning was only compulsory between the ages of eleven and fourteen. A mixed methods approach (see Ivankova & Greer this volume) was adopted, with an initial questionnaire followed by classroom observations, interviews and documentary analysis, although the paper focuses only on the questionnaire and addresses these research questions:

1 What are teachers' stated listening instructional practices?

2 What are teachers' stated beliefs about how listening should be taught and how listening activities should be carried out?

3 How do teachers' stated beliefs compare with their stated practice?

4 What factors if any are related to teachers' stated beliefs and stated practices?

Importantly, these questions are explicit in acknowledging their focus on stated (i.e. *professed*, rather than actual) beliefs and practices.

Participants were recruited through a mix of random stratified sampling using a national database and convenience sampling using schools associated with the researchers' university. One-hundred-and-fifteen teachers returned the questionnaire; 90 per cent of these taught in state schools with a mixed ability intake and most were non-native speakers of the foreign languages taught.

The design of the questionnaire is described in detail and well-justified with reference to the literature on studying teachers' beliefs. The instrument is reproduced almost in full in an appendix (this is important both to allow readers to assess the study and for other researchers to build on it). Respondents were asked both about their practices in teaching listening and about their beliefs. Importantly, the limitations of questionnaires for such research are acknowledged and discussed (e.g. the authors recognize that teachers' reported practices may not have always been their actual practices). The questionnaire was piloted with three teachers, though given the national focus of the study a larger pilot sample would have been desirable.

Questionnaires were sent out by hard copy to schools, though the manner in which they were returned to the researchers was not specified. The analysis of the data is described in detail and in particular clear information is supplied about the coding of the open-ended responses, including inter-rater comparisons. The amount of methodological detail provided adds transparency and rigour to the study and increases the reader's confidence in the results.

The results are organized around the research questions listed above and the key findings are that:

1 In line with the literature on second language listening, teachers agreed that effective listening is teachable, but their reported practices did not refer frequently to activities that develop effective listening skills.

2 Pre-listening activities were reported as being used quite frequently, though they seemed to focus on words rather than content.

3 There was little evidence that teachers' rationales for their approach to teaching second language listening were underpinned by formal theory.

4 Many teachers seemed uncertain about the most effective ways to help learners become better listeners.

5 Reported practices and beliefs were quite consistent across the sample, irrespective of length of teaching experience and how much focus of listening teachers had in their initial teacher education.

6 Assessment framework targets (i.e. the listening competences learners are expected to meet) and textbook activities were seen to be potential significant influences on how teachers taught L2 listening.

Overall, the approach to second language listening revealed by this study is one which emphasizes comprehension but 'which also involves institutional and contextual control, the following of almost ritualised procedures to ensure predictability, maximum correct answers and to shield learners from any challenge or uncertainty' (p. 54).

I would recommend this paper to readers looking for a good example of how questionnaire-based research into teachers' beliefs can be designed, conducted and reported. It is based on a sound understanding of key issues in the study of teachers' beliefs and, contrary to many current studies which use questionnaires, achieves a good level of theoretical, methodological and substantive rigour. One reason it does so is because it acknowledges and discusses the limitations of the methods used to study teachers' beliefs.

Conclusion

The major justification for studying L2 teachers' beliefs is that they provide insight into the psychological context for teaching and teacher learning which can inform the design of initiatives which encourage teachers to learn, change or behave in particular ways. Ultimately, research on L2 teachers' beliefs has a practical purpose. In several contemporary studies (see Table 28.1), though, the rationale for studying teachers' beliefs is very often unclear, and one is left with a sense that teachers' beliefs are being studied for their own sake. This phenomenon is a real threat to the continuing development of research on L2 teachers' beliefs; this is particularly true in questionnaire-based research, where it is very often convenience (e.g. the availability of ready-made instruments) that drives inquiry rather than any deeper consideration of the value of the work. Researchers investigating L2 teachers' beliefs, then, need to ensure that they provide a sound justification for their work and a persuasive answer to the question 'so what?' A disregard for such matters will turn research on L2 teachers' beliefs into a fashionable (and potential unethically exploitative) enterprise which has lost sense of the deeper professional and practical motivations which drove its growth.

Resources for further reading

Borg, M 2001, 'Teacher belief', *ELT Journal*, vol. 55, no. 2, pp. 186–188.

This is a short article which considers some key elements of beliefs and works towards a definition of the term.

Borg, S 2006, *Teacher Cognition and Language Education: Research and Practice*, Continuum, London.

This book provides an overview of the study of language teacher cognition and discusses in detail specific research methods which can be used in understanding what teachers know, think and believe.

Borg, S 2012, 'Current approaches to language teacher cognition research: A methodological analysis', in R Barnard & A Burns (eds), *Researching Language Teacher Cognition and Practice: International Case Studies*, Multilingual Matters, Bristol, pp. 11–29.

This chapter provides a methodological review of studies of language teacher cognition published in 2011. The book it is part of presents case studies from around the world which examine teacher cognition (including beliefs) from different angles.

Pajares, MF 1992, 'Teachers' beliefs and educational research: Cleaning up a messy construct', *Review of Educational Research*, vol. 62, no. 3, pp. 307–332.

A very detailed and widely quoted review of teachers' beliefs in the context of educational research generally.

Speer, NM 2005, 'Issues of methods and theory in the study of mathematics teachers' professed and attributed beliefs', *Educational Studies in Mathematics*, vol. 58, no. 3, pp. 361–391.

Much interesting research on teachers' beliefs has been conducted in the field of mathematics education. This paper provides an interesting review of literature in that field.

References

Alexander, O 2012, 'Exploring teacher beliefs in teaching EAP at low proficiency levels', *Journal of English for Academic Purposes*, vol. 11, no. 2, pp. 99–111.

Allen, LQ 2013, 'Teachers' beliefs about developing language proficiency within the context of study abroad', *System*, vol. 41, no. 1, pp. 134–148.

Borg, S 2006, *Teacher Cognition and Language Education: Research and Practice*, Continuum, London.

———— 2012, 'Current approaches to language teacher cognition research: A methodological analysis', in R Barnard & A Burns (eds), *Researching Language Teacher Cognition and Practice: International Case Studies*, Multilingual Matters, Bristol, pp. 11–29.

Borg, S & Al-Busaidi, S 2012, 'Teachers' beliefs and practices regarding learner autonomy', *ELT Journal*, vol. 66, no. 3, pp. 283–292.

Borg, S, Birello, M, Civera, I & Zanatta, T 2014, *The Impact of Teacher Education on Pre-Service Primary English Language Teachers*, British Council, London.

Borg, S & Burns, A 2008, 'Integrating grammar in adult TESOL classrooms', *Applied Linguistics*, vol. 29, no. 3, pp. 456–482.

Büyükkarci, K 2014, 'Assessment beliefs and practices of language teachers in primary education', *International Journal of Instruction*, vol. 7, no. 1, pp. 107–120.

Calderhead, J (ed.), 1987, *Exploring Teachers' Thinking*, Cassell, London.

———— 1996, 'Teachers: Beliefs and knowledge', in DC Berliner & RC Calfee (eds), *Handbook of Educational Psychology*, Macmillan, New York, NY, pp. 709–725.

Carter, C and Doyle, W 1996, 'Personal narrative and life history in learning to teach', in J Sikula (ed.), *Handbook of Research on Teacher Education*, 2nd edn, Macmillan, New York, NY, pp. 120–142.

Chatouphonexay, A & Intaraprasert, C 2014, 'Beliefs about English language learning held by EFL pre-service and in-service teachers in lao people's democratic republic', *English Language Teaching*, vol. 7, no. 3, pp. 1–12.

Chimbutane, F 2013, 'Codeswitching in L1 and L2 learning contexts: Insights from a study of teacher beliefs and practices in Mozambican bilingual education programmes', *Language and Education*, vol. 27, no. 4, pp. 314–328.

Clandinin, DJ & Connelly, FM 2000, *Narrative Inquiry: Experience and Story in Qualitative Research*, Jossey Bass Publishers, San Francisco, CA.

Clark, CM 1986, Ten years of conceptual development in research on teacher thinking', in M Ben-Peretz, R Bromme & R Halkes (eds), *Advances of Research on Teacher Thinking*, Swets and Zeitlinger, Lisse, pp. 7–20.

Clark, CM & Peterson, PL 1986, 'Teachers' thought processes', in MC Wittrock (ed.), *Handbook of Research on Teaching*, 3rd edn, Macmillan, New York, NY, pp. 255–296.

Dinçer, A & Yeşilyurt, S 2013, 'Pre-service English teachers' beliefs on speaking skill based on motivational orientations', *English Language Teaching*, vol. 6, no. 7, pp. 88–95.

Eisenhart, MA, Shrum, JL, Harding, JR & Cuthbert, AM 1988, 'Teacher beliefs: Definitions, findings and directions', *Educational Policy*, vol. 2, no. 1, pp. 51–70.

Ernest, P 1989, 'The knowledge, beliefs, and attitudes of the mathematics teacher: A model', *Journal of Education for Teaching*, vol. 15, no. 1, pp. 13–34.

Fang, Z 1996, 'A review of research on teacher beliefs and practices', *Educational Research*, vol. 38, no. 1, pp. 47–65.

Farrell, TSC & Bennis, K 2013, 'Reflecting on ESL teacher beliefs and classroom practices: A case study', *RELC Journal*, vol. 44, no. 2, pp. 163–176.

Gilhooly, K & Green, C 1996, 'Protocol analysis: Theoretical background', in JTE Richardson (ed.), *Handbook of Qualitative Research Methods for Psychology and the Social Sciences*, BPS Books, Leicester, pp. 43–54.

Graham, S, Santos, D & Francis-Brophy, E 2014, 'Teacher beliefs about listening in a foreign language', *Teaching and Teacher Education*, vol. 40, pp. 44–60.

Green, C & Gilhooly, K 1996, 'Protocol analysis: Practical implementation', in JTE Richardson (ed.), *Handbook of Qualitative Research Methods for Psychology and the Social Sciences*, BPS Books, Leicester, pp. 55–74.

Hayes, D 2005, 'Exploring the lives of non-native speaking English educators in Sri Lanka', *Teachers and Teaching*, vol. 11, pp. 169–194.

Hos, R & Kekec, M 2014, 'The mismatch between non-native English as a foreign language (EFL) Teachers' grammar beliefs and classroom practices', *Journal of Language Teaching and Research*, vol. 5, no. 1, pp. 80–87.

Hu, B & Tian, L 2012, 'Do teachers and students share similar beliefs about teaching and learning strategies?', *System*, vol. 40, no. 2, pp. 237–254.

Hurworth, R 2003, *Photo-Interviewing for Research*. Social Research Update, Issue 40, viewed 8 July 2014, http://sru.soc.surrey.ac.uk/SRU40.html

Jones, MG & Carter, G 2007, 'Science teacher attitudes and beliefs', in SK Abell & NG Lederman (eds), *Handbook of Research on Science Education*, Lawrence Erlbaum, Mahwah, NJ, pp. 1067–1104.

Kagan, DM 1990, 'Ways of evaluating teacher cognition: Inferences concerning the Goldilocks principle', *Review of Educational Research*, vol. 60, no. 3, pp. 419–469.

Kalaja, P & Barcelos, AMF (eds), 2003, *Beliefs About SLA: New Research Approaches*, Kluwer, Dordecht.

Kalaja, P, Dufva, H & Alanen, R 2013, 'Experimenting with visual narratives', in G Barkhuizen (ed.), *Narrative Research in Applied Linguistics*, Cambridge University Press, Cambridge, pp. 105–131.

Kane, R, Sandretto, S & Heath, C 2002, 'Telling half the story: A critical review of research on the teaching beliefs and practices of university academics', *Review of Educational Research*, vol. 72, no. 2, pp. 177–228.

Kim, EJ 2011, 'An activity theory analysis of a teachers' experience', in KE Johnson & PR Golombek (eds), *Research on Second Language Teacher Education*, Routledge, London, pp. 225–238.

Kissau, SP & Algozzine, B 2013, 'Foreign language student teaching: Do supervisor qualifications really matter?', *Foreign Language Annals*, vol. 46, no. 2, pp. 175–190.

Kuzborska, I 2011, 'Links between teachers' beliefs and practices and research on reading', *Reading in a Foreign Language*, vol. 23, no. 1, pp. 102–128.

Langan-Fox, J, Code, S & Langfield-Smith, K 2000, 'Team mental models: Techniques, methods, and analytic approaches', *Human Factors: The Journal of the Human Factors and Ergonomics Society*, vol. 42, no. 2, pp. 242–271.

Li, L 2013, 'The complexity of language teachers' beliefs and practice: One EFL teacher's theories', *Language Learning Journal*, vol. 41, no. 2, pp. 175–191.

Lumley, T 2002, 'Assessment criteria in a large-scale writing test: What do they really mean to the raters?', *Language Testing*, vol. 19, no. 3, pp. 246–276.

Margolis, E & Pauwels, L (eds), 2011, *The SAGE Handbook of Visual Research Methods*, Sage, London.

Munby, H 1982, 'The place of teachers' beliefs in research on teacher thinking and decision making, and an alternative methodology', *Instructional Science*, vol. 11, pp. 201–225.

Murphy, PK & Mason, L 2006, 'Changing knowledge and beliefs', in PA Alexander & H Winne (eds), *Handbook of Educational Psychology*, 2nd edn, Lawrence Erlbaum, Mahwah, NJ, pp. 305–324.

Nespor, J 1987, 'The role of beliefs in the practice of teaching', *Journal of Curriculum Studies*, vol. 19, no. 4, pp. 317–328.

Numrich, C 1996, 'On becoming a language teacher: Insights from diary studies', *TESOL Quarterly*, vol. 30, no. 1, pp. 131–153.

Pajares, MF 1992, 'Teachers' beliefs and educational research: Cleaning up a messy construct', *Review of Educational Research*, vol. 62, no. 3, pp. 307–332.

Phipps, S & Borg, S 2009, 'Exploring tensions between teachers' grammar teaching beliefs and practices', *System*, vol. 37, no. 3, pp. 380–390.

Richardson, V 1996, 'The role of attitudes and beliefs in learning to teach', in J Sikula, TJ Buttery & E Guyton (eds), *Handbook of Research on Teacher Education*, 2nd edn, Macmillan, New York, NY, pp. 102–119.

Rose, G 2012, *Visual Methodologies: An Introduction to Researching with Visual Materials*, 3rd edn, Sage, London.

Samuda, V 2005, 'Expertise in pedagogic task design', in K Johnson (ed.), *Expertise in Second Language Learning and Teaching*, Palgrave Macmillan, Basingstoke, pp. 230–254.

Shavelson, RJ & Stern, P 1981, 'Research on teachers' pedagogical thoughts, judgements and behaviours', *Review of Educational Research*, vol. 51, no. 4, pp. 455–498.

Smith, MU & Siegel, H 2004, 'Knowing, believing, and understanding: What goals for science education?', *Science and Education*, vol. 13, no. 6, pp. 553–582.

Southerland, SA, Sinatra, GM & Matthews, MR 2001, 'Belief, knowledge, and science education', *Educational Psychology Review*, vol. 13, no. 4, pp. 325–351.

Speer, NM 2005, 'Issues of methods and theory in the study of mathematics teachers' professed and attributed beliefs', *Educational Studies in Mathematics*, vol. 58, no. 3, pp. 361–391.

Spencer, S 2011, *Visual Research Methods in the Social Sciences*, Routledge, New York, NY.

Thompson, AG 1992, 'Teachers' beliefs and conceptions: A synthesis of the research', in DA Grouws (ed.), *Handbook of Research on Mathematics Teaching and Learning*, Macmillan, New York, NY, pp. 127–146.

Underwood, PR 2012, 'Teacher beliefs and intentions regarding the instruction of English grammar under national curriculum reforms: A Theory of Planned Behaviour perspective', *Teaching and Teacher Education*, vol. 28, no. 6, pp. 911–925.

Weber, S & Mitchell, C 1996, 'Drawing ourselves into teaching: Studying the images that shape and distort teacher education', *Teaching and Teacher Education*, vol. 12, no. 3, pp. 303–313.

Woolfolk Hoy, A, Davis, H & Pape, SI 2006, 'Teacher knowledge and beliefs', in PA Alexander & H Winne (eds), *Handbook of Educational Psychology*, 2nd edn, Lawrence Erlbaum, Mahwah, NJ, pp. 715–737.

Yang, L & Gao, S 2013, 'Beliefs and practices of Chinese university teachers in EFL writing instruction', *Language, Culture and Curriculum*, vol. 26, no. 2, pp. 128–145.

Yuan, R & Lee, I 2014, 'Pre-service teachers' changing beliefs in the teaching practicum: Three cases in an EFL context', *System*, vol. 44, no. 1, pp. 1–12.

Zeng, Z 2012, 'Convergence or divergence? Chinese novice EFL teachers' beliefs about postmethod and teaching practices', *English Language Teaching*, vol. 5, no. 10, pp. 64–71.

Zhang, F & Liu, Y 2014, 'A study of secondary school English teachers' beliefs in the context of curriculum reform in China', *Language Teaching Research*, vol. 18, no. 2, pp. 187–204.

Zheng, H 2013, 'The dynamic interactive relationship between Chinese secondary school EFL teachers' beliefs and practice', *Language Learning Journal*, vol. 41, no. 2, pp. 192–204.

Zheng, X & Borg, S 2014, 'Task-based learning and teaching in China: Secondary school teachers' beliefs and practices', *Language Teaching Research*, vol. 18, no. 2, pp. 205–221.

CHAPTER TWENTY NINE

Researching Language and Gender

Jane Sunderland

Language and gender is a wide-ranging field, the 'language' aspect encompassing 'use' (talk and writing, what is 'produced' and how it is understood) and 'code' (e.g. English, Gujarati, particular dialects). Modern, feminist-inspired language and gender studies first blossomed in the very early 1970s, prompted by what can be called the 'second wave' of the western women's movement.[1] Since then, 'use' and 'code' have increasingly converged for the field, with a shared movement towards and emphasis on *discourse* and on *diversity* (among women, among men). Accordingly, the thrust of much empirical research now is not on *speakers*, embodied as female or male, as in traditional variationist sociolinguistics and in the early days of gender and language study, but on *what is said or written*, about women, men, boys, girls and gender relations, and *how* – what we might term 'gendered discourse' and, more generally, *representation*. This is to conceptualize gender as including, but going far beyond, socially taught and learned 'differences' between women and men. It is also to see gender as not just a matter of socialization of children according to dominant gender stereotypes (though these may play a role). Gender is now largely seen as a question of social construction *of and by* social, embodied individuals, in linguistic and social (including institutional) practices, throughout those individuals' lifetimes, in ways which entail both individual agency and resistance (but see Motschenbacher & Stegu 2013, for more radical understandings, associated with post-structuralism and Queer Theory).

Approaches to researching language and gender

Gone are the days when a researcher, perhaps inspired by Noam Chomsky, could introspect and use themself as a source of data – as Robin Lakoff did in her pioneer work *Language and Woman's Place* (1975), providing a spirited defence of her methodology (pp. 4–5). *Language and Woman's Place* was the first monograph in the field. A child of its time, the book looked at sexist language ('Talking about women') but was mainly concerned with apparent differences between women's talk and men's talk. There has been debate about whether Lakoff's work should be characterized as an example of the 'deficit' (retrospectively named) approach to the interpretation of women's language use, or the '(male) dominance' approach (see e.g. Litosseliti 2006; Talbot 2010).[2] But she was clearly conceptualizing gender as a male–female *binary*. Current research has moved a considerable distance from this, and now (if it even asks about 'differences') assumes a prevalence of 'gender similarities' in language use, along with context-related nuancing and diversity among women and among men. Relatedly, it acknowledges the importance of intersectionality (i.e. weakly, gender in relation to class, ethnicity, age, and sexuality, *inter alia*, and, more strongly, sexism in relation to racism and homophobia, *inter alia*). In particular, the names of books and conferences in the field now accordingly often include both gender *and* sexuality, with *heteronormativity* a frequent target of critique. An obvious example is *The Handbook of Language, Gender and Sexuality* (Ehrlich et al. 2014), the first (Holmes & Meyerhoff 2003) edition of which was entitled *The Handbook of Language and Gender*.

Because the field is wide-ranging, so, accordingly, are the theoretical and methodological/empirical approaches used to research it. Indeed, it is hard to imagine an approach which is not suitable for some form of language and gender investigation. Below, I identify six different approaches, drawing on the collection *Gender and Language Research Methodologies* (Harrington et al. 2008), which readers are advised to consult for further detail and exemplification (the first part of this chapter is based on but goes beyond the introductory chapter, by Jane Sunderland and Lia Litosseliti). These six (non-comprehensive, non-mutually-exclusive) approaches are broadly theoretical, with associated data and methodologies. They are:

- sociolinguistics
- corpus linguistics
- conversation analysis
- discursive psychology
- critical discourse analysis
- feminist post-structuralist discourse analysis

Missing from this list (due to the need to select) are approaches drawing on stylistics (but see e.g. Mills 1995), pragmatics (see e.g. Cameron 1998) and Queer theory (see e.g. Motschenbacher & Stegu 2013; Sauntson 2008).

Sociolinguistics

Sociolinguistics has the longest history of the six, pre-dating the 1970s birth of (feminist-inspired) language and gender study. The original sociolinguistic paradigm was variationist (i.e. looking at differences in spoken language use in, say, people of different ages, social classes, geographical regions or biological sex) and correlational, hence quantitative. The typical methodology for early sociolinguistic studies of gender and language was large-scale *surveys* in which men's and women's language use – usually, their pronunciation and/or grammar (e.g. Labov 1966; Trudgill 1972) – was compared in terms of standard and vernacular usage. The notion of *gender* was largely unproblematized (rather, 'sex' was the key independent variable).

Some other pre-feminist 'gender differences' sociolinguistic work, though not carried out for feminist ends, produced findings of relevance to the later feminist project, in particular demonstrating the importance of context. Susan Gal (1978) revealed a striking tendency in Oberwart (on the Austrian-Hungarian border), that is, that men at the time of the study were more likely to retain their Hungarian than were women – for the highly situated reason that the women tended to want to marry out of the community, the men to remain within it, doing traditional farming work. Lesley Milroy (1980) found that a group of women in one Belfast community (the Clonard), who worked and socialized together, produced more of some vernacular forms than did their husbands (this in contrast to the findings of Labov (1966) and Trudgill (1972)) and concluded that social network (and its density and multiplexity) could be more relevant than gender. (Here, she was anticipating the notion of 'relevance' as applied to the field: that gender is sometimes, but sometimes is not, relevant to a given situation.) The notion of context is key to sociolinguistic work and has been considerably refined with the emergence of 'Communities of practice' (CofP) approaches (e.g. Eckert & McConnell-Ginet 1992), which emphasize the *local*, language as a form of social practice, and also the relevance of non-linguistic social practice. Eckert and McConnell-Ginet define a CofP as 'an aggregate of people who come together around mutual engagement in some common endeavour' (1992, p. 64): three examples might be a book club, a family breakfast and a school assembly. Gender will be enacted in different ways in each CofP, in terms of language use and other social practices, and may be more relevant in some CofPs than others.

Many modern gender and language studies (local, qualitative explorations of intersections of gender with other social identities, including race, class and sexuality), in which data is naturally occurring and contextualized, can be described as *sociolinguistic*. One example is Christine Mallinson and Becky Childs' (2007) investigation of language variation among rural Appalachian black women (two CofPs – the 'porch sitters' and the 'church ladies'). The two groups differed, *inter alia*, in their (non-)omission of the third person singular 's' (e.g. 'She like to eat'), omission being characteristic of the 'porch sitters' rather than the 'church ladies'. Mallinson and Childs see this variation as contributing to the identity construction of members of the two groups (for the benefit of themselves, and of others). Their study is concerned with diversity *among* women and does not involve binary or even nuanced comparisons between women and men. For a reminder that sociolinguistics goes beyond the private, see Janet Holmes' (2006) monograph on gender and workplace talk and Louise Mullany's (2014) *Sociolinguistics of Gender in Public Life*.

Corpus linguistics

Corpus linguistics quantitatively analyses corpora of up to several million words, of spoken or written language, enabling the researcher to establish frequencies and probabilities of words or phrases of interest, often together with demographic characteristics of their users. Corpus linguistics is ideally placed to investigate such 'traditional' questions as whether a particular word or phrase is used more by men or women (with, depending on the corpus, if the analyst wishes, inflections of age, ethnicity and/or social class). However, it can also be used to investigate how women and men are differentially *constructed* in the way they refer to themselves or are referenced by others. For example, Sally Johnson and Astrid Ensslin (2007) explore how gendered language use is represented in newspaper texts, basing their analysis on ninety-six instances of the terms <his language> and <her language>. As an example of a finding, in an analysis of *bachelor* and *spinster* in the British National Corpus, Paul Baker (2008) shows that while the former collocates with positive words such as *eligible* and the latter is constructed as unattractive and lonely, the corpus also reveals a conflicting *feminist* discourse surrounding spinsters. While many corpora already exist, a corpus can be built by the analyst and compared with another 'reference' corpus (see also Baker's (2010) *Sociolinguistics and Corpus Linguistics* and in particular his (2014) *Using Corpora to Analyse Gender*).

Corpus linguistics has the potential to make robust claims which other approaches cannot. Despite this, it faces a particular challenge in the current *qualitative* gender and language (indeed, social science) climate. However, frequencies and probabilities do not determine *interpretations*, and good corpus studies are by no means 'mechanical': the analyst often looks closely at at least a sample of their findings, deselecting as appropriate in interpretation; the 'co-text' (words on either side of the word/phrase in question) can be as wide as the analyst wishes to make it. Depth does not have to be sacrificed for breadth, and indeed, corpus linguistic studies can support and complement small-scale qualitative studies.

Conversation analysis

Conversation analysis (CA) is concerned particularly with the sequential organization of naturally occurring, interactive talk (everyday conversations or sometimes institutional talk) and 'accomplishments' in that talk. Using micro-analysis and very detailed transcription, CA identifies recurrent, structural characteristics – namely organizational patterns such as turn-taking, interruptions and repairs. For example, Celia Kitzinger (2008) shows how the details of the achievement of interruptions may point to positive outcomes for women (rather than 'male dominance') in particular interactional contexts.

The classic 'warrant' (see Swann 2002) for the relevance of gender in CA is *speakers' own orientation to gender*, for example, if a speaker starts an utterance with something like 'As a mother,…', or refers explicitly to women, men, boys or girls. Elizabeth Stokoe (2008) demonstrates the value for CA of looking *inter alia* at 'members' categories' in talk (such as *girls/women, fellas/men, secretary*; see also Speer & Stokoe 2011; Stokoe 2012).

In rejecting 'prior variables' or analyst agendas, such as gender, CA however can be seen as problematic for language and gender study, the 1990s' saw a long-running debate about claims for gender in a localized stretch of talk, together with the role of the analyst and insights she can bring (e.g. Schegloff 1997, 1998; Wetherell 1998).[3]

Discursive psychology

Discursive psychology, a branch of social psychology, arguably shares more with linguistics than with psychology. Whereas traditional work on 'sex differences' in psychology treated gender as a more-or-less fixed and monolithic entity, early work on discourse and gender in social psychology focused on ways in which gender identity positions 'emerged' from discourses and were 'accomplished' locally, in spoken texts (Edwards & Potter 1992). Key concepts are 'interpretive repertoires' and 'ideological dilemmas' (Billig et al. 1988; Edley 2001; see also below).[4] For a recent example of a study of 'interpretive repertoires', see Charlebois's (2010) work on the discursive construction of femininities by Japanese women.

Rather than being interested in cognitive processes, or the 'inner self', discursive psychologists look at the different sorts of things that are *said, how, to what purpose* and to what *effect* in interaction – including when the data is 'elicited', as in interviews and focus groups. Discursive psychology has taken two different directions (see McIlvenny 2002): one branch focusing on detailed fine-grained analysis and participants' concerns in talk, following the tradition of conversation analysis; the other branch being more closely related to post-structuralism and critical discourse analysis (CDA), drawing on the Foucauldian notion of *discourses*. Similar, but not identical to 'interpretative repertoires', these can be seen as ways of seeing or representing the world which 'systematically form the objects of which they speak' (Foucault 1972, p. 49), that is, are constitutive. A challenge for discursive psychology is (whether and how) to combine analytical principles from both branches. Nigel Edley and Margaret Wetherell (2008) argue precisely for such an integrative trajectory, claiming that an expanded and integrative discursive psychology that aims to work across both the micro and the macro could combine a focus on how speakers *do* gender in their talk and 'how they are simultaneously *done* (constructed) as gendered beings in that talk: how speakers construct (and use) gender categories and how they are constructed – as gendered beings – by those very categories' (2008, p. 166).

Critical discourse analysis (CDA)

Discourse analysis is concerned with naturally occurring language within a given context and usually beyond the sentence (though not always – consider interjections such as 'No!'), and with what 'work' certain discursive features do (e.g. close a conversation).

CDA goes beyond this to provisionally identify, analyse and often evaluate the workings of discourses (including gendered ones, of which many can be proposed (see Sunderland 2004)). CDA has very particular epistemological roots – including critical linguistics, with its Marxist underpinnings (see Fairclough 1992, 2003).

There are several different meanings of 'critical', and several forms of CDA (see Wodak & Meyer 2009), which can be seen as constituting a 'program' (Weiss & Wodak 2007). For example, Ruth Wodak (2008) has developed a 'discourse-historical' approach to CDA and, in a study of (female) migrant identities, deploys an analysis that is both macro- and micro-, addressing different levels of spatial, historical and linguistic context. Konstantia Kosetzi (2013) in turn applies Faircloughian CDA to Greek TV fictional texts and considers the special challenges of fiction for CDA. However, all CDA focuses on power (and agency, and contestation), works towards progressive social change, identifies presuppositions, challenges assumptions and opens up new possibilities through different readings of texts. It considers non-discursive as well as discursive practices. Its understanding of *discourse* extends to images, and hence to critical visual and critical multimodal analysis (see e.g. Kress 2009; van Leeuwen 2008). All CDA also assumes a dialectical relationship between discourse and the material, that is, that discourse shapes but is also shaped by some form of material reality (a position largely rejected by post-structuralist writers).

A question frequently raised is whether CDA's conventional focus on social class and on the 'dominant' and 'dominated' enables it to deal fully with gender (in which, for example, power and powerlessness may fluctuate – with context, conversational goal, within individuals and among gender groups; see Baxter (2003)). Some gender and language analysts self-identify as critical discourse analysts; others do not, though their work may well be feminist (hence 'critical') (see also Wodak 1997). One researcher who has explicitly used CDA effectively in her work on gender is Michelle Lazar (2005), who shows how the representation of the modern father in 'pro-natalist' ads in Singapore 'continue[s] to maintain, through subtle and seemingly innocuous ways, gender difference and inequality' (p. 140). Similarly, Busi Makoni (2013) uses 'feminist critical discourse analysis' to explore 'migration narratives' of 'dual career' Zimbabwean migrants.

Feminist post-structuralist discourse analysis

Developed by Judith Baxter, feminist post-structuralist discourse analysis (FPDA) (Baxter 2003, 2006, 2008, 2010, 2014) has roots in post-structuralism and feminism. Its concern is 'to release the words of marginalised or minority speakers' (2002, p. 9). FPDA also 'responds' to CDA and CA (it is informed by broad social issues *and* includes very detailed analysis of talk). It is intended in part to *supplement* CDA by focusing on instances of power (or powerlessness) which may fluctuate and/or be too fleeting or unconventionally manifested for conventional CDA to deal with (see Baxter 2003, 2008).

FPDA emphasizes individuals' *agency*, manifested in different linguistic forms, and their potential to recognize how and through which discourses they are being 'positioned', to *take up* particular subject positions and to *resist* others. FPDA thus rejects any notion of individuals being 'at the mercy of competing discourses' (Baxter 2003, p. 31). Agency does not entail, however, what Baxter characterizes as a 'liberal-humanist conception of the free individual in control of their destiny' (2003, p. 31), as the range of possible subject positions for women remains politically and socially limited.

It is not possible to identify a 'best' approach for gender and language study – or even for feminist language study. We already have 'feminist post-structural discourse analysis', 'feminist CDA', 'feminist conversation analysis' and indeed 'feminist stylistics' (Mills 1995) (see also Ergun 2013; and Holmes 2008 on 'feminist sociolinguistics') and there is no reason why we should not have feminist corpus linguistics/discursive psychology. Indeed, we already do, in all but name. However, discourse analysis (say) can be used in the interests of misogyny as well as feminism (see Gill 1995). A given researcher will choose her approach(es) in relation to her own epistemological stance, and of course her research question(s). Some approaches may be theoretically compatible, and hence 'combinable', and some can then be used to 'serve' others (corpus linguistics could serve CDA, for example). However, this may not be possible for all potential 'pairings' (CDA is unlikely to be used to 'serve' CA, say, because of the usual 'agenda-free' underpinning of CA). More than two compatible approaches can be combined, of course, as I show in the study below.

Data, research strategies and techniques

In the early days of language and gender study, data was characteristically transcripts of naturally occurring talk in private contexts between white middle-class heterosexual couples. Just as the 'spoken' field has widened and extended to public and institutional talk (e.g. Lazar 2008; Walsh 2001), written texts (including digital ones) of many genres have also come into their own (see e.g. Bengoechea (2011) on media representations of a Spanish woman Defence Minister). In either case, data for language and gender study does not have to be naturally occurring texts or talk, but rather *reported* beliefs or practices, elicited through questionnaires, interviews or focus groups (e.g. in discursive psychology projects). It can also be represented and/or mediatized talk (or indeed writing), for example in films, soap operas and novels, as well as multimodal representations of gender more widely.

As with approaches, it is not possible to exclude any research strategy or technique from the gender and language field. Data collection methods include questionnaires, diary studies, interviews, focus groups, observation (including fieldnotes, audio and video recording),[5] researcher participation (e.g. in a particular Community of Practice) and compilation of corpora, as well as methods often associated with research in education (there is huge scope for language and gender work across the curriculum (see Sauntson 2011; Sunderland 2000), such as stimulated recall and think-aloud protocols). When data is a set of written, visual or multimodal texts, we are talking about gender *representation* rather than naturally occurring spoken data, and the issue is data *selection* rather than *collection*. Needless to say, this is not a comprehensive list, neither are the strategies/techniques mutually exclusive.

A sample study

The following example of current language and gender research is an investigation of a written text: a set of electronically circulated jokes about women, and how such jokes can be 'dealt with' by (feminist) readers. As such, it contributes to the growing fields of gender representation (in a range of genres) and of gender and humour (e.g. Kotthof 2006). Here, a single text was *selected* after being identified as a fairly typical representative of a familiar genre: a written, digital set of jokes about women, men and gender relations, circulated electronically. Although data-driven, the study is a largely theoretical one – but *empirical* work on readings of these jokes would constitute an important subsequent project. The theoretical insights, I hope, have implications for texts beyond this particular illustrative dataset – for both language and gender study, in particular gender representation, and reading theory (for a fuller version, see Sunderland 2007). In terms of methodology, the study draws substantially on CDA in terms of close textual analysis and consideration of text 'consumption', and on discursive psychology (in particular the notion of 'ideological dilemma') and post-structuralism in its conceptualization. It can also be seen as falling within a modern sociolinguistic paradigm (in which written and indeed digital texts are increasingly of interest).

In their conceptualization of *ideological dilemma* for discursive psychology, Billig et al. (1998) cite examples of contradictory proverbs (e.g. 'look before you leap'/'he who hesitates is lost'). But we also *knowingly* use expressions such as 'On the one hand,...on the other...', and 'One part of me thinks...while the other part of me thinks...' And we draw on different discourses/interpretive repertoires at different times and in different situations: 'Academically selective schools are socially divisive' on the one hand, and 'Parents should do the best for their children (and my child would do best at an academically selective school)' on the other. We may be able to discursively reconcile these two positions ('Academically selective schools are socially divisive *but* I can live with that as I have to do the best for my child'), but we may still experience this 'reconciliation' as an uncomfortable ideological dilemma.

The jokes

The data/jokes in question were circulated by email – I received them from an ex-student who shared my interest in gender, who would have received them from someone else, and so on – and they may thus have been digitally altered, more than once, since their original launching. They are likely, I propose, to sound familiar to readers of this collection. The set of jokes (Figure 29.1) is entitled:

NEW COURSES AVAILABLE FOR WOMEN: *Training courses are now available for women on the following subjects.*

The list concluded: 'Please register immediately as courses are expected to be in great demand.'

- Silence, the Final Frontier: Where No Woman Has Gone Before.
- The Undiscovered Side of Banking: Making Deposits.
- Parties: Going Without New Outfits.
- Man Management: Minor Household Chores Can Wait until After The Game.
- Bathroom Etiquette I: Men Need Space in the Bathroom Cabinet Too.
- Bathroom Etiquette II: His Razor is His.
- Communication Skills I: Tears? The Last Resort, not the First.
- Communication Skills II: Thinking Before Speaking.
- Communication Skills III: Getting what you want without nagging.
- Driving a Car Safely: A Skill You CAN Acquire.
- Telephone Skills: How to Hang Up.
- Introduction to Parking.
- Advanced Parking: Backing Into a Space.
- Water Retention: Fact or Fat.
- Cooking I: Bringing Back Bacon, Eggs and Butter.
- Cooking II: Bran and Tofu are Not for Human Consumption.
- Cooking III: How not to Inflict Your Diets on Other People.
- Compliments: Accepting Them Gracefully.
- PMS: Your Problem ... Not His.
- Dancing: Why Men Don't Like To.
- Classic Clothing: Wearing Outfits You Already Have.
- Household Dust: A Harmless Natural Occurrence Only Women Notice.
- Integrating Your Laundry: Washing It All Together.
- Oil and Petrol: Your Car Needs Both.
- TV Remotes: For Men Only.
- Getting ready to go out: Start the day before.

FIGURE 29.1 *Training courses for women*

The above is clearly a 'spoof' list of Adult Education courses, workshop sessions or even academic conference sessions. As spoofs, they may be found amusing because of the recognizable structural features of the genre: the initial short, snappy phrase (a rather general noun, noun phrase or gerund), followed by a colon anticipating the specific focus of the 'course'.

But the jokes are also clear expressions of familiar gender stereotypes, with the first, seventh, eighth, ninth and eleventh being folklinguistic stereotypes/representations of women's talk. The jokes self-evidently, if jocularly, draw on a dominant 'gender differences' discourse (see Sunderland 2004) – 'a discourse', as indicated, being an important notion for both CDA and post-structuralism – 'gender differences' allowing neither for differences *among* women (or among men), nor similarities *between* women and men. So, assuming obvious contradictions between the premises of these jokes and our own largely feminist convictions, why did I (and my 'Gender and Language Research Group' members) simultaneously recognize the sexism *and* find the jokes, or at least the experience of reading them, mildly amusing? Did we experience an 'ideological dilemma'? What, precisely, were we laughing *at*?

What/who the text is about

CDA extends beyond texts and textual representation to their production and 'consumption' (see Fairclough 1992). As regards consumption, and informed also by Stylistics:

> A dissatisfaction with formalist accounts [of written texts] and with attempts to trace author intentions have led to concerns with the reader. Once the author is considered 'dead' [Barthes 1987], then it seems to be a logical move to try to institute the reader in that position of stability (Mills 1994, p. 8).

Some version of *reader response* may be particularly apposite when looking at digital, electronically circulated texts, whose original author is not traceable. A reader is normally capable of saying what they see a text they are reading as being 'about', partly through the guidance of the text itself. This includes its *interpellation* (Althusser 1998), that is, who is being addressed, and as what? Althusser's own example is of a policeman addressing a guilty person by 'hailing' him or her with 'Hey, you there!', and the person turning round, that is, accepting that she/he is being addressed. That person is, however, also being addressed by *ideology*, that is, she/he turns through acknowledgment of guilt *within a particular ideological framework*. Similarly, readers will recognize particular ideological workings of gender in these jokes.

On the surface, bolstered by the title, the pronouns *you* and *your* suggest that it is *women* who are being 'hailed' in these jokes: 'Getting what you want without nagging', and so on. Deeper and more inferential consideration of who the jokes are *actually* (if indirectly) interpellating however suggests that the 'ideal readers' or 'implied readers' (see Talbot 1995, 2010) are primarily *men*, who are being invited to laugh at women's behaviours which apparently merit correction, that is, talking without thinking, nagging and being:

- excessively talkative
- spendthrift
- vain

- preoccupied with appearance

- manipulative

- bad drivers

- irrational

- non-technical

- disorganized

Conceptually related to *interpellation* is *focalization*, the 'presentation of a scene through the subjective perception of a character' (Benwell 2002).[6] This is often achieved through direct speech or thought or a perception attributed to a particular speaker, or through first-person narration. Here, however, the focalization here is arguably that of those men who apparently find these alleged behaviours of women incomprehensible, in need of correction and/or simply amusing. More broadly, it is achieved because these 'behaviours' of women are all described in critical, prescriptive or proscriptive ways, which crucially also draw on existing, familiar, socially recognizable representations/stereotypes (e.g. talking too much, being serial clothes shoppers). Accordingly, it is *men's* interests that are being jocularly defended ('His razor is his'), and hence men whose perspective is shown. Note here the constructed opposition of interests (implicit or explicit) between the female (reader) and the implied male reader (see Sunderland 2004 on the 'Battle of the sexes' discourse). Even the 'gender-neutral' cases, like 'The Undiscovered Side of Banking: Making Deposits', can be read as being *about* (not addressed to) women, given the historical stereotype of women as spendthrift and serial shoppers, as well as the co-text (this joke follows 'Silence, the Final Frontier: Where No Woman Has Gone Before').

Exploring feminist readings of the jokes

If they do not simply dismiss the jokes, women sympathetic to feminism (as well as those who are not) may find them amusing in part if, like it or not, they recognize themselves in them. Pleasure, Freud notes, can come from recognition (1905/1976, p. 170). But, given post-structuralist insights that the meaning of a text is never fixed, and that any text affords more than one reading (e.g. about women, about men), we can also acknowledge not only that two readers can respond differently to a particular joke – with different conceptualizations (of what or who the joke is 'about') and evaluation (whether it is amusing, sexist, ironic or whatever) – but also that a *single* reader can also simultaneously entertain more than one reading of a text. This may not, of course, be a comfortable experience – an ideological dilemma. This takes us some way to looking at simultaneously critical and pleasurable responses to the same joke.

CDA takes as given that certain ways of seeing, representing, conceptualizing and evaluating the world are more hegemonic than others. And here, we return to *discourses* – value-laden and constitutive (within and potentially beyond texts themselves; manifested in and recognized through particular linguistic *cues* and *traces* (e.g. Talbot 2010, p. 121)). In these jokes, we can recognize an overall 'traditional', dominant gendered discourse: entailing that women are, *inter alia*, spendthrift and bad at reverse parking. Women readers are thus positioned by traditional discourses of gender as the very people who are the butt of the jokes. And, to make sense of such texts, women readers must *recognize* the indirect interpellation of women. If they do this, they must – however indirectly – have themselves been interpellated as such (Mills 1992).

However, importantly, feminist (and other) readers of the jokes are likely to be aware of other, intertextually related, oppositional, discourses – which as active readers they can 'invoke' or 'activate'. These, I suggest, include:

- a *critical anti-sexist discourse* (entailing awareness of sexism in its various historical, social and linguistic manifestations);

- a *feminist discourse of agency/non-victimhood/self-value* (entailing an awareness of women as strong, independent and worthy); and

- a *post-feminist discourse* (see below).

Feminist readers can thus be seen as 'multiply positioned', given the inter-discursive links of these sexist jokes with *competing* as well as supporting discourses. A feminist reader, while acknowledging the jokes' sexism, might at the same time find them – or at least their existence – amusing, given the awareness and self-confidence that can *simultaneously* come from also having access to the first two of these discourses (but see also Mills 2008).

Amusing, really? The above argument can be made more convincing, I suggest, if the feminist reader is seen as also able to access a 'Post-feminist discourse'. I propose five possible meanings of *post-feminism* – none of which is 'The need for feminism is over' or 'Feminism is dead'. ('We', here, refers to feminist readers of these jokes.)

- Although there is no longer a clear feminist platform for grievances, there has been in the recent past.

- We do and see things knowing about feminism and with the benefit of having experienced feminism.

- We can adopt a feminist perspective not just a 'sexism awareness' perspective.

- We see sexism (including 'indirect/subtle sexism' (Lazar 2005; Mills 2008) *and beyond* (e.g. its causes, but also its spin-offs and backlashes)).

- We can see sexist practices and ideas as dated, unthinking, foolish and ultimately of little value to *men*.

In other words, the relationship between such jokes and their readers can be seen broadly as: 'we know about feminism, others know, we know they know, and they know we know they know', where 'we' can be the reader *or* producer. This relationship holds true too for the producers and consumers of men's 'lifestyle' magazines such as *Loaded* (by-line: 'for men who should know better') – whose readership is now apparently in serious decline. Acknowledging this 'knowingness', Bethan Benwell writes: 'it seems that the reader is required to tread a subtle and practised course though a minefield of irony, ambiguity and double-voicing' (2002, p. 166).

The concept of *double-voicing* (Bakhtin 1984) can be used to refer to the possibility of two or more readings of a text being made available simultaneously, something Benwell (2002) also claims of *Loaded*: ('Yes, it's sexist, but we know that, and (so) we're [writers/publishers] being ironic'). Here, I am suggesting that our experience of double-voiced texts, together with the accessibility of a range of discourses, allows us to actively 'double-voice' a text *for ourselves*, as an active and productive form of 'reading against the grain' (see Cosslett 1996). As *active* readers, we can deliberately read these jokes in more than one way (including that not intended by the writer), simultaneously; together with the text, we can *co-construct* irony.

Feminist reading positions

What, then, are some alternative *reading positions* for the feminist who encounters these jokes?

Sara Mills (1992) looks at alternative positions in relation to the individual reading of a male-focalized poem, 'Valentine', and I have adapted these here. I suggest that there are four possible positions, which shade into each other, *vis á vis* the jokes: critical rejection, resistant reading, critical enjoyment and feminist reclamation.

A feminist reader may *critically reject* these jokes materially, by deleting them, or discursively, for example by adding a critical rejoinder (and/or perhaps asking the person who forwarded them not to do so again). If she engages in *resistant reading*, she may recognize and negatively evaluate the sexist discourse, positioning herself as an 'overhearer' of jokes addressed to men (though, as indicated, understanding means that she has been successfully interpellated (Mills 1992)).

Third, she may *critically enjoy* the text. For example, as suggested above, she may co-construct the text's ironic potential, 'double-discourse' the text and take intellectual pleasure in that process, rather than in the joke itself. This also allows her to see different possibilities for what or who the joke is about. In the fourth (related) reading, *feminist reclamation*, she can also co-construct the jokes as being *not so much* about women as about (foolish) *men*, the (presumed/ideal) consumers of the jokes. Cognitively more complex, but perhaps ultimately more satisfying, this is to 'refocalize' (ironize?) the jokes and take the woman's perspective (but far beyond the 'your laundry' reading), actively moving the 'object' of the joke (women) to subject position and make the original implied focalizers, men, the object. She can then see humour in the fact that some people *still* enjoy these tired old stereotypes which are *still* in circulation: 'Nice spoof – but how ridiculous these jokes *and* the people who find their presuppositions funny are!'[7]

The four reading positions may provide psychological survival strategies, allowing readings which constitute critique, enjoyment and/or an achieved refusal to be subject positioned as manipulative, a bad driver or irrational. The fourth position additionally helps us identify what exactly is amusing if we find ourselves smiling at these jokes: rather than their sexism, it is the dated and foolish assumptions behind them, and the amazing fact that these still retain some currency for some, that is, *as well as* worrying, entertaining. With the fourth position, the 'real joke' is thus at the expense of these particular social norms, and the butt is those who adhere to or uncritically enjoy them. It should be noted that the men in the jokes are also interpellated as not minding, or even as enjoying, being constructed as somewhat 'unreconstructed'.

All this raises the wider question of how feminists handle sexism (explicit, subtle or ironic) in a 'post-feminist' age. Saying to a man who is audibly enjoying such jokes, 'Your reaction does you no favours, you know', sounds unproductively pompous. More effective may be a humorous, playful riposte – in the spirit of 'fun feminism' (Kamada 2008). 'Double-voicing' facilitates sexism in *Loaded*, because of the potential for irony. Can it also be deployed to allow for the *contestation* of sexism? Can and does societal familiarity with double-voicing also work in favour of feminism?

A second question is whether – contradictions aside – such jokes point (in some sense) to a failure of feminism. Of *Loaded*, Benwell claims:

> [the] 'knowing' tone, the ambiguity, the double-voicing are all strategies employed to preserve [traditional, heterosexual] masculine values in the face of a disapproving world (2002, p. 170; see also Benwell 2004).

Johnson (1997) has similarly observed that, to survive, traditional institutions and practices simply need to *adapt* – and many do. The ironic potential of these polysemantic jokes can be seen as just such a form of adaptation. The trajectory of adaptation however will almost inevitably entail contradictions and dilemmas, and hence windows and avenues with progressive potential for both activists and analysts.

This example of a small-scale research project involving qualitative analysis of a naturally occurring written text has drawn on CDA, FPDA and the notion of *ideological dilemma*, from Discursive psychology. It will be clear that interpretation and evaluation, from a particular perspective, were key, as hence was a measure of subjectivity. Gender and language research is of course not alone here. What is important, I propose, is that interpretation precedes evaluation, and that both follow a description which is as denotative as possible: what is the text 'about', and how is it structured? Lastly, if the interpretation and evaluation of the analysis is to be informed by some form of feminism (as is the case in much gender and language research), then the researcher is likely to wish to make this explicit.

Notes

1 The 'first wave' is the campaign for women's suffrage in the early twentieth century; the 'third wave' is associated with postmodernist understandings and ways of being, sexuality (and Queer Theory) and 'post-feminism' (see Mills 2003; Mills & Mullany 2011).
2 A third 'gender differences' approach is widely referred to as '(cultural) difference' (see Litosseliti 2006; Talbot 2010).
3 CA has also been *reclaimed* by and for gender and language study (e.g. Kitzinger 2000, 2008; Speer & Stokoe 2011; Stokoe & Smithson 2001).
4 Another key concept of Discursive psychology is 'subject positioning' (Billig et al. 1988).
5 Transcription is associated with both naturally occurring and elicited spoken data, making the transcript the 'object' of analysis.
6 Focalization is a notion largely employed by Stylistics – a field regrettably absent from the above account of approaches to gender and language research. An early relevant text here is Sara Mills' (1995) *Feminist Stylistics*.
7 She can even reject the premises on which the jokes are based and consider, for example, the *value* of talk and of getting rid of dust. This also enables her to be *critical* of the specific masculine focalization. Actively making men the object of the jokes ('men simply do not appreciate the value of talk, etc.') allows her to see humour in this represented *lack* of appreciation.

Resources for further reading

Cameron, D, Frazer E,, Harvey, P, Rampton, B & Richardson, K (eds), 1992, *Researching Language: Issues of Power and Method*, Routledge, London.

Cameron et al. provide a penetrating examination of the ethics of research on language use. Gender is one of several foci here.

Gender and Genre Bibliography, 3rd edn, Centre for Language and Social Life, Lancaster University), viewed 22 July 2014, http://www.ling.lancs.ac.uk/groups/gal/projects/index.html

This includes references to studies of gender and language in relation to wide range of written (and spoken) genres, including dictionaries, posters and classroom talk.

Harrington, K, Litosseliti, L, Sauntson, H & Sunderland, J (eds), 2008, *Gender and Language Research Methodologies*, Palgrave Macmillan, Basingstoke.

This explores the six approaches detailed above, with exemplificatory empirical studies.

Ehrlich, S, Holmes, J & Meyerhoff, M (eds), 2014, *The Handbook of Language, Gender and Sexuality*, 2nd edn, Blackwell, Oxford.

This book is a very substantial 'state of the art' collection (with reviews of 'background' work) with contributions by key writers in the field. The book is divided into seven sections: Theory and History, Methods, Identities, Ideologies, Global and Cross-Cultural Perspectives, Domains and Institutions, and Engagement and Application. This second edition is thoroughly updated, with the topic of sexuality integrated throughout.

Miller, C & Treitel, C 1991, *Feminist Research Methods: An Annotated Bibliography*, Greenwood Press, Westport, CT.

This book is divided into disciplines. 'Language and speech' is a sub-section of 'Communication'.

Sunderland, J 2006, *Language and Gender: An Advanced Resource Book*, Routledge, London.

This includes extracts from classic and other important publications, as well as tasks which can be the basis of assignments or MA dissertations.

Sunderland, J 2000, 'Review article: Issues of gender and language in second and foreign language education', *Language Teaching*, vol. 33, no. 4, pp. 203–223.

This includes a substantial Bibliography, including references to work on achievement, 'ability', the 'four skills', motivation/investment, teacher perceptions, learning styles and strategies, classroom interaction, English as a sexist/non-sexist language, teaching materials, language testing, teachers and professional organizations, teacher education and identities (including masculinities).

References

Althusser, L 1998, 'Ideology and ideological state apparatuses', in J Rivkin & M Ryan (eds), *Literary Theory: An Anthology*, Blackwell Publishers, Malden, MA, pp. 294–304.

Baker, P 2008, '"Eligible" bachelors and "frustrated" spinsters: Corpus linguistics, gender and language', in K Harrington, L Litosseliti, H Sauntson & J Sunderland (eds), *Gender and Language Research Methodologies*, Palgrave Macmillan, London, pp. 73–84.

—— 2010, *Sociolinguistics and Corpus Linguistics*, Edinburgh University Press, Edinburgh.

———— 2014, *Using Corpora to Analyse Gender*, Bloomsbury Academic, London.

Bakhtin, M 1984, *Problems of Dostoevsky's Poetics* (ed. and trans. C Emerson), University of Minnesota Press, Minneapolis, MN.

Barthes, R 1987, 'The death of the author', in R Barthes (ed.), *The Rustle of Language*, Hill and Wang, New York, NY, pp. 49–55.

Baxter, J 2002, *Positioning Gender in Discourse: A Feminist Methodology*, Palgrave, Basingstoke.

————2003, *Positioning Gender in Discourse: A Feminist Methodology*, Palgrave Macmillan, London.

———— (ed.), 2006, *Speaking Out: The Female Voice in Public Contexts*, Palgrave Macmillan, Basingstoke.

———— 2008, 'Feminist post-structuralist discourse analysis: A new theoretical and methodological approach?', in K Harrington, L Litosseliti, H Sauntson & J Sunderland (eds), *Gender and Language Research Methodologies*, Palgrave, Basingstoke, pp. 243–255.

———— 2010, *The Language of Female Leadership*, Palgrave Macmillan, Basingstoke.

———— 2014, *Double-Voicing: Power, Gender and Linguistic Expertise*, Palgrave Macmillan, Basingstoke.

Bengoechea, M 2011, 'How effective is "femininity"? Media portrayals of the effectiveness of the first Spanish woman defence minister', *Gender and Language*, vol. 5, no. 2, pp. 405–442.

Benwell, B (2002), 'Is there anything "new" about these lads?: The textual and visual construction of masculinity in men's magazines', in L Litosseliti & J Sunderland (eds), *Gender Identity and Discourse Analysis*, John Benjamins, Amsterdam, pp. 149–176.

———— 2004, 'Ironic discourse: Evasive masculinity in men's lifestyle magazines', *Men and Masculinities*, vol. 7, no. 1, pp. 3–21.

Billig, M, Condor, S, Edwards, D, Gane, M, Middleton, D & Radley, A 1988, *Ideological Dilemmas: A Social Psychology of Everyday Thinking*, Sage, London.

Cameron, D 1998, '"Is there any ketchup, Vera?" Gender, power and pragmatics', *Discourse and Society*, vol. 9, no. 4, pp. 437–455.

Charlebois, J 2010, 'The discursive construction of femininities in the accounts of Japanese women', *Discourse Studies*, vol. 12, no. 6, pp. 699–714.

Cosslett, T 1996, 'Fairytales: Revising the tradition', in T Cosslett, A Easton & P Summerfield (eds), *Women, Power and Resistance*, Open University Press, Milton Keynes, pp. 81–90.

Eckert, P & McConnell-Ginet, S 1992, 'Communities of practice: Where language, gender and power all live', in K Hall, M Bucholtz & B Moonwomon (eds), *Locating Power: Proceedings of the Second Berkeley Women and Language Conference*, Women and Language Group, Berkeley, CA, pp. 89–99.

Edley, N 2001, 'Analysing masculinity: Interpretive repertoires, ideological dilemmas and subject positions', in Wetherell, M, Taylor, S & Yates, S (eds), *Discourse as Data: A Guide for Analysis*, Open University Press, Milton Keynes, pp. 189–228.

Edley, N & Wetherell, M 2008, 'Discursive psychology and the study of gender: A contested space', in K Harrington, L Litosseliti, H Sauntson & J Sunderland (eds), *Gender and Language Research Methodologies*, Palgrave Macmillan, London, pp. 161–173.

Edwards, N & Potter, J 1992, *Discursive Psychology*, Sage, London.

Ehrlich, S, Holmes, J & Meyerhoff, M (eds), 2014, *The Handbook of Language, Gender and Sexuality*, Blackwell, Oxford.

Ergun, E 2013, 'Feminist translation and feminist sociolinguistics in dialogue: A multi-layered analysis of linguistic gender constructions in and across English and Turkish', *Gender and Language*, vol. 7, no. 1, pp. 13–33.

Fairclough, N 1992, *Discourse and Social Change*, Polity Press, Cambridge.

────── 2003, *Analysing Discourse: Textual Analysis for Social Research*, Routledge, London.

Foucault, M 1972, *The Archaeology of Knowledge*, Tavistock Publications, London.

Freud, S 1905/1976, *Jokes and Their Relation to the Unconscious*, Pelican, London.

Gal, S 1978, 'Peasant men can't get wives: Language change and sex roles in a bilingual community', *Language in Society*, vol. 7, no. 1, pp. 1–17.

Gill, R 1995, 'Relativism, reflexivity and politics: Interrogating discourse analysis from a feminist perspective', in S Wilkinson & C Kitzinger (eds), *Feminism and Discourse: Psychological Perspectives*, Sage, London, pp. 165–186.

Harrington, K, Litosseliti, L, Sauntson, H & Sunderland, J (eds), 2008, *Gender and Language Research Methodologies*, Palgrave Macmillan, London.

Holmes, J 2006, *Gendered Talk at Work: Constructing Gender Identity Through Workplace Discourse*, Blackwell, Oxford.

────── 2008, *Introduction to Sociolinguistics*, 3rd edn, Longman, London.

Holmes, J & Meyerhoff, M (eds), 2003, *The Handbook of Language, Gender and Sexuality*, Blackwell, Oxford.

Johnson, S 1997, 'Theorising language and masculinity: A feminist perspective', in S Johnson & UH Meinhof (eds), *Language and Masculinity*, Blackwell, Oxford, pp. 8–26.

Johnson, S & Ensslin, A 2007, '"But her language skills shifted the family dynamics dramatically": Language, gender and the construction of publics in two British newspapers', *Gender and Language*, vol. 1, no. 2, pp. 229–253.

Kamada, L 2008, 'Discursive "embodied" identities of "half" girls in Japan: A multi-perspective approach', in K Harrington, L Litosseliti, H Sauntson & J Sunderland (eds), *Gender and Language Research Methodologies*, Palgrave Macmillan, London, pp. 174–192.

Kitzinger, C 2000, 'Doing feminist conversation analysis', *Feminism & Psychology*, vol. 10, no. 2, pp. 163–193.

────── 2008, 'Conversation analysis: Technical matters for gender research', in K Harrington, L Litosseliti, H Sauntson & J Sunderland (eds), *Gender and Language Research Methodologies*, Palgrave Macmillan, London, pp. 119–138.

Kosetzi, K 2013, 'The roles of the narrator, lexis, irony and visuals in the Greek TV series "Almost Never", Σχεδόν Ποέ (ΣΠ): Challenges to conservative themes and multiple readings', *Gender and Language*, vol. 7, no. 2, pp. 175–200.

Kotthof, H 2006, 'Gender and humour: The state of the art', *Journal of Pragmatics*, vol. 38, no. 1, pp. 4–25.

Kress, G 2009, *Multimodality: A Social Semiotic Approach to Contemporary Communication*, Routledge, New York, NY.

Labov, W 1966, *The Social Stratification of English in New York City*, Center for Applied Linguistics, Washington, DC.

Lakoff, R 1975, *Language and Woman's Place*, Colophon Books, New York, NY.

Lazar, M (ed.), 2005, *Feminist Critical Discourse Analysis: Gender, Power and Ideology in Discourse*, Palgrave Macmillan, Basingstoke.

——— 2008,'Language and communication in the public sphere: A perspective from feminist critical discourse analysis', in R Wodak & V Koller (eds), *Communication in the Public Sphere: Handbook of Applied Linguistics*, vol. 4, Mouton de Gruyter, Berlin.

Litosseliti, L 2006, *Gender and Language: Theory and Practice*, Hodder Arnold, London.

Makoni, B 2013, '"Women of the diaspora": A feminist critical discourse analysis of migration narratives of dual career Zimbabwean migrants', *Gender and Language*, vol. 7, no. 2, pp. 203–231.

Mallinson, C & Childs, B 2007, 'Communities of practice in sociolinguistic description: Analysing language and identity practices among black women in Appalachia', *Gender and Language*, vol. 1, no. 2, pp. 173–206.

McIlvenny, P 2002, 'Introduction: Researching talk, gender and sexuality', in P McIlvenny (ed.), *Talking Gender and Sexuality*, John Benjamins, Amsterdam, pp. 1–48.

Mills, S 1992, 'Knowing your place: A Marxist feminist stylistic analysis', in M Toolan (ed.), *Language, Text and Context: Essays in Stylistics*, Routledge, London, pp. 241–259.

——— 1994, *Gendering the Reader*, Harvester Wheatsheaf, Hemel Hempstead.

——— 1995, *Feminist Stylistics*, Routledge, London.

——— 2003, 'Caught between sexism, anti-sexism and "political correctness": Feminist women's negotiations with naming practices', *Discourse and Society*, vol. 14, no. 1, pp. 87–110.

——— 2008, *Language and Sexism*, Cambridge University Press, Cambridge.

Mills, S & Mullany, L 2011, *Language, Gender and Feminism: Theory, Methodology and Practice*, Routledge, Abingdon.

Milroy, L 1980, *Language and Social Networks*, Basil Blackwell, Oxford.

Motschenbacher, H & Stegu, M 2013, 'Queer linguistic approaches to discourse', *Discourse and Society*, vol. 24, no. 5, pp. 519–535.

Mullany, L 2014, *The Sociolinguistics of Gender in Public Life*, Palgrave, Basingstoke.

Sauntson, H 2008, 'The contributions of queer theory to gender and language research', in K Harrington, L Litosseliti, H Sauntson & J Sunderland (eds), *Gender and Language Research Methodologies*, Palgrave Macmillan, London, pp. 271–282.

——— 2011, *Approaches to Gender and Spoken Classroom Discourse*, Palgrave Macmillan, Basingstoke.

Schegloff, E 1997, 'Whose text? Whose context?', *Discourse and Society*, vol. 8, no. 2, pp. 165–187.

——— 1998,'Reply to Wetherell', *Discourse and Society*, vol. 9, no. 3, pp. 413–416.

Speer, SA & Stokoe, E (eds), 2011, *Conversation and Gender*, Cambridge University Press, Cambridge.

Stokoe, E 2008, 'Categories, actions and sequences: Formulating gender in talk-in-interaction', in K Harrington, L Litosseliti, H Sauntson & J Sunderland (eds),

Gender and Language Research Methodologies, Palgrave Macmillan, London, pp. 139–160.

—— 2012, 'Moving forward with membership categorization analysis: Methods for systematic analysis', *Discourse Studies*, vol. 14, no. 3, pp. 207–303.

Stokoe, E & Smithson, J 2001, 'Making gender relevant: Conversation analysis and gender categories in interaction', *Discourse and Society*, vol. 12, no. 2, pp. 217–244.

Sunderland, J 2004, *Gendered Discourses*, Palgrave Macmillan, London.

—— 2007, 'Contradictions in gendered discourses: Feminist readings of sexist jokes?', *Gender and Language*, vol. 1, no. 2, pp. 207–228.

Swann, J 2002, 'Yes, but is it gender?', in L Litosseliti & J Sunderland (eds), *Gender Identity and Discourse Analysis*, John Benjamins, Amsterdam, pp. 43–67.

Talbot, M 1995, *Fictions at Work*, Longman, London.

—— 2010, *Language and Gender*, 2nd edn, Polity, London.

Trudgill, P 1972, 'Sex, covert prestige and linguistic change in the urban British English of Norwich', *Language in Society*, vol. 1, no. 2, pp. 179–195.

Van Leeuwen, T 2008, *Discourse and Practice: New Tools for Critical Discourse Analysis*, Oxford University Press, Oxford.

Walsh, C 2001, *Gender and Discourse: Language and Power in Politics, the Church and Organisations*, Longman, Harlow.

Weiss, G & Wodak, R (eds), 2007, *Critical Discourse Analysis: Theory and Interdisciplinarity*, Palgrave Macmillan, Houndmills.

Wetherell, M 1998, 'Positioning and interpretative repertoires: Conversation analysis and post-structuralism in dialogue', *Discourse and Society*, vol. 9, no. 3, pp. 387–412.

Wodak, R 1997, 'Introduction', in R Wodak (ed.), *Gender and Discourse*, Sage, London, pp. 1–20.

—— 2008, 'Controversial issues in feminist critical discourse analysis', in K Harrington, L Litosseliti, H Sauntson & J Sunderland (eds), *Gender and Language Research Methodologies*, Palgrave Macmillan, Houndmills, pp. 193–209.

Wodak, R & Meyer, M 2009, 'Critical discourse analysis: History, agenda, theory and methodology', in R Wodak & M Meyer (eds), *Methods of Critical Discourse Analysis*, 2nd edn, Sage, London, pp. 1–33.

CHAPTER THIRTY

Researching Language and Identity

David Block

In recent years, identity has become a key construct in the social sciences in general, and applied linguistics in particular (Block 2013; Duff 2012; Norton 2010; Norton & Toohey 2011). Following current post-structuralism and social constructivist thinking on the topic from two decades ago (e.g. Giddens 1991; Weedon 1997), many applied linguists today understand identities to be socioculturally constructed ongoing narratives, which develop and evolve across different spatio-temporal scales, ranging from the micro, local and immediate to the macro, global and long term (Lemke 2008). These socioculturally constructed narratives are seen to emerge during individuals' engagements in activities with others, with whom to varying degrees they share beliefs, motives and values, in communities of practice, where a community of practice is defined as 'an aggregate of people who come together around mutual engagement in an endeavour' (Eckert & McConnell-Ginet 1992, p. 464). Such activity-based communication can take place either face-to-face or in an electronically mediated mode, with the latter becoming increasingly more prevalent. In addition, and consistent with the macro, global and long-term scale cited above, identity construction is seen as the negotiating of subject positions at the crossroads of the past, present and future.

Following Giddens's (1984) structuration theory, many researchers also take as axiomatic that individuals are shaped by ever-emergent and evolving social, cultural and historical structures, but at the same time – and indeed, in recursive fashion – they shape these same emergent and ever-evolving social, cultural and historical structures as their lives unfold. Among other things, negotiation means that such processes involve both self-ascription and self-positioning by individuals who in turn – and simultaneously – are ascribed identities and are positioned in particular ways by others with whom they come in contact. In this process, issues around perceived and invoked sameness and differences, and authenticity and inauthenticity, come into play.

All of this means that the process of identity construction is potentially and indeed often conflictive as opposed to harmonious, especially in situations involving movement across borders which are simultaneously geographical historical, cultural and psychological. In such circumstances, identity work is often characterized by the ambivalence that individuals feel about exactly who they are and where they belong (Block 2006; Meinhof & Galasiński 2005). In addition, following Bourdieu (1984), individuals are seen to be embedded in multiple social milieus, or fields, in which they constantly encounter unequal power relationships related to their access to and their legitimate control over and use of different capitals in these fields – economic, cultural and social. Finally, identities are related to different traditionally demographic categories such as ethnicity, race, nationality, migration, gender, sexuality, religion, social class and language (Block 2006, 2007).

This view of identity to varying degrees underlies a good deal of applied linguistics research that has been carried out over the past two decades, particularly work on multilingualism, language education and second language learning. On the one hand, there are publications in journals such as the *International Journal of Bilingual Education and Bilingualism* and the *Journal of Language, Identity and Education*. On the other hand, there is a long list of recent books on identity and language practices which include more general overviews (e.g. Benwell & Stokoe 2006; Block 2007; Edwards 2009; Joseph 2004; Kramsch 2010; Riley 2007), research monographs (e.g. Blackledge & Creese 2010; Block 2006; Byrd-Clark 2010; Jackson 2008; Kanno 2003; Miller 2003; Norton 2000, 2013; Pichler 2009; Preece 2009) and collections of chapters (Benson & Nunan 2005; Caldas-Coulthard & Iedema 2008; Csizér & Magid 2014; De Fina et al. 2006; Fishman & Garcia 2010; Higgins 2012; Llamas & Watt 2010; Nunan & Choi 2010; Omoniyi & White 2006; Pavlenko et al. 2001; Pavlenko & Blackledge 2004). In these and other publications, researchers have focused on migration, literacies, language policy, language learning and language use in a wide variety of contexts, emphasizing particular dimensions of identity – age, ethnicity, race, nationality, migration, gender, sexuality, religion, social class and so on.

Typical stages in carrying out the research

Applied linguists have tended to explore identity from two separate but often interlinked perspectives. On the one hand, many researchers have taken seriously the notion that all utterances constitute 'acts of identity in which people reveal both their personal identity and their search for social roles' (Le Page & Tabouret-Keller 1985, p. 14). As a first stage, these researchers typically collect samples of their informant's speech, either in the latter's day-to-day activities or in face-to-face interviews. The general view is that speakers' identities are indexed in how they draw on repertories of linguistic resources, which include language choice, accent, lexical choice, morphology and syntax. However, in recent years, the interest has moved beyond language, to a multimodal approach which examines semiotic resources, including body movements, gaze, clothing and space (Blommaert 2005). The upshot of this interest is that identity is seen as discursively constructed, where discourse, with a capital 'D', is understood in a broad sense as

> ways of combining and integrating language, actions, interactions, ways of thinking, believing, valuing, and using various symbols, tools, and objects to enact a particular sort of socially recognizable identity (Gee 2011, p. 201).

In addition, the process of indexing is not framed as two-dimensional, as was the case for early sociolinguistic work which focused on dyadic associations such as accent-social class and lexical choice-gender; rather, in keeping with the post-structuralist take on identity outlined above, indexing is reflexive and multidimensional. It is reflexive in that researchers generally do not posit a one-way deterministic flow from category to linguistic phenomenon (e.g. social class determines accent); rather, they see speech acts as constitutive of categories. Meanwhile, it is multidimensional and intersectional in that few researchers suggest that just one dimension of identity can be enacted at a time; rather, it is difficult to focus on just one dimension (e.g. gender) without considering others (e.g. social class and ethnicity) (Block & Corona 2014).

Over the past twenty-five years, many researchers have discussed and documented what has been termed the 'narrative turn' in the social sciences (Atkinson & Delamont 2006; Clandinin 2007; Clandinin & Connelly 2004; Czarniawska 2004; Dainute 2014; Elliot 2005; Goodson, Loveless & Stevens 2013; Goodwin 2012; Gubrium & Holstein 2009; Holstein & Gubrium 2000, 2012; Reissman 2008), whereby there is progressively more and more interest in how individuals present their life stories when communicating with others and how these stories might be analysed and interpreted. While life stories may be elicited by a variety of means, such as diaries or electronic logs, it is by far the face-to-face interview which has been the elicitation mode of choice in recent years. In such research, interviews are generally lengthy and relatively open-ended in nature, and they are often organized around particular stages in life, such as early childhood, early primary school, early adolescence and so on. The researcher may conduct just one life-story interview with an informant, or he/she may conduct a set of two or three interrelated ones, fairly close together in time

(Wengraf 2001). Alternatively, the researcher may adopt a longitudinal approach, which involves multiple interviews, carried out at intervals over a long period of time. Whatever the number of interviews per informants, in the end, the interest is generally the same: 'the story a person chooses to tell about the life he or she has lived, told as completely and honestly as possible, what is remembered of it, and what the teller wants others to know of it…' (Atkinson 1998, p. 3).

Research strategies and techniques: Doing narrative identity research

In her detailed discussion of narrative methods, Catherine Kohler Riessman (2008) suggests that there are four distinct ways of dealing with narratives, three of which I will present here: *thematic analysis, structural analysis* and *dialogic/performative analysis*. *Thematic* analysis is primarily a focus on the content of what is said, leaving to the side other aspects of narrative such as how it is produced. Although some see this approach as intuitive and overly simplistic, Riessman makes clear that it requires a great deal of rigour. First, once spoken data have been transcribed, the researcher has to identify key themes and strands in the narrative. Second, the researcher needs to have a solid background in other social sciences such as history, sociology and anthropology in order to be able to connect narrative content to bigger and broader issues and constructs.

A second approach, *structural analysis*, addresses first and foremost how narratives are produced. On the one hand, such an approach may focus on the micro-level linguistic phenomena, such as grammar, lexis and accent; on the other hand, it may examine how different clauses are assembled to produce a storyline or the strategies adopted by the storyteller as the story is told. Thus, while some researchers may focus on phenomena such as pronoun use and what it might mean, others may follow a variation on Labov and Waletzky's (1967) classic and oft-cited model, whereby narratives are seen to involve a series of steps, beginning with a brief synopsis of the story to be told and the provision of key background information, before moving to the crux of the story, its ending and its meaning to the narrator.

A third approach described by Riessman is what she calls *dialogic/performative*. In this case, the analyst draws on elements of the previous two approaches but, in doing so, creates a distinct third way beyond them. As Riessman notes, 'if thematic and structural approaches interrogate "what" is spoken and "how", the dialogic/performative approach asks "who" an utterance may be directed to, "when," and "why," that is, for what purposes?' (Riessman 2008, p. 105). Thus, the analyst works from the immediate context, in terms of the minutiae of interaction, discourse patterns, the background of interlocutors, the general sociohistorical backdrop and so on, eventually working up to border social categories, related to institutions and cultures and the identity inscriptions outlined earlier in this chapter (e.g. social class, gender and ethnicity).

A good example of a dialogic approach in action is Donald Freeman's research on teacher knowledge and cognition from two decades ago. Freeman (1996) self-consciously combines a thematic approach (what he calls a 'representational approach') with a structural approach (what he calls a 'presentational approach'). In doing so, he examines his interviews with teachers in terms of three types of relationship:

- *expression* (what is said and how it is said);

- *voice* (what is said to whom and therefore how it may be heard and understood); and

- *source* (what is said and where it comes from).

Being attentive to expression means a focus on the language that is used to say what is said. For example, Freeman examines the use of subject pronouns (I, you and they) and how speakers shift among them as they talk about different topics and personal and professional experiences. For Freeman, the uses of the different pronouns construct shifts in voice, which are related to, and indeed arise in, the changing affiliations of teachers over time. Thus, an informant might show shifts in affiliation in how she talks about her personal and singular experiences (using 'I'), her affiliation to fellow teachers (using 'we') or her lack of affiliation to fellow teachers with whom she does not agree (using 'they').

The idea that voices shift as an interaction unfolds is an essential characteristic of the dialogic/performative approach to narrative. Drawing on the work of Bakhtin (1981), Lemke makes the point that '[w]e speak with the voices of our communities, and to the extent that we have individual voices, we fashion these out of the social voices already available to us, appropriating the words of others to speak a word of our own' (Lemke 1995, pp. 24–25). Elsewhere, Stanton Wortham argues that '[s]peaking with a certain voice ... means using words that index social positions because these words are characteristically used by members of a certain group' (Wortham 2001, p. 38), a view echoed by Gubrium and Holstein (2009) and James Paul Gee (2011). What these authors are saying is that in the process of telling their stories, informants do not just produce unique individualized accounts; rather, their voices are saturated with the voices of others who have preceded them and who are their contemporaries.

In her research, focusing on young Greek women talking about their social lives in informal conversations, Alexandra Georgakopoulou (2006,

2007; De Fina & Georgakopoulou 2012) adopts an approach which sees her first of all examining how talk-in-interaction unfolds in terms of linguistic features such as code, register and style. These features are seen as foundational to an examination of different local 'small, here-and-now identities', specifically participants' 'telling identities', which are related to aspects of group interactions such as amount of participation, floor holding, how much one's talk is ratified (validated) by others and so on. The latter inform the researcher about how participants position themselves and are positioned during the course of their interactions. These positionings include 'expert/novice' and 'advice giver/advice receiver', which in turn can be connected to extra-interactional roles played by individuals in the communities of practice of which they are members, such as 'good student/bad' student. And with reference to the latter, there is a link to broader society-level identities related to gender, social class and so on. Thus, Georgakopoulou shows how her informants talk may be analysed, working from micro-level linguistic features, all the way up to macro-level social categories.

In the work of Freeman, Wortham, Georgakopoulou, De Fina and many others, I see something akin to a consensus emerging among researchers interested in narrative, both those who focus on narratives elicited in interviews and those who focus on narratives arising in informal conversations. In both cases, researchers negotiate an appropriation of Reismann's thematic and structural approaches as they move towards a dialogic/performative approach. Some researchers offer a great deal of detail as they navigate their way through their concern with micro-level language practices and how they connect with larger social constructs such as voice and broader identity inscriptions. Meanwhile, others work more elliptically, moving to the macro-level fairly quickly, although once there, they may go into great detail as regards what they think their data are saying. However, in both cases, there is a common willingness and desire to engage with the complexity of identity in narrative. There is, therefore, a position that what is needed is dialectic analysis which slides back and forth, between and among three general interacting levels:

- *micro:* at the basic level of utterances, examining how what is said is said;

- *meso:* at the intermediate level of positioning in the narrative, via the adoption of voices; and

- *macro:* at the broader, more macro-level, whereby what is said is related to identities and social groups in society.

And, in this sliding back and forth, there will inevitably be more emphasis on one level or another, a point to which I return in the next section.

Associated problems with narrative analysis

The approach to identity in narrative outlined in the previous section is not without problems, which in turn are directly related to the complex task that researchers set themselves. On the one hand, there are foundational and conceptual issues, which are beyond the scope of this chapter. More relevant to this book are problems related to data analysis in applied linguistics research on identity and language. Aneta Pavlenko (2007) identifies what she sees as five major problems common in much narrative research based heavily or exclusively on thematic analysis:

> The first is the lack of theoretical premise, which makes it unclear where conceptual categories come from and how they relate to each other. The second is the lack of established procedure for matching instances to categories. The third is the overreliance on repeated instances which may lead analysts to overlook important events or themes that do not occur repeatedly or do not fit into preestablished schemes. The fourth is an exclusive focus on what is in the text, whereas what is excluded may potentially be as or even more informative. The fifth and perhaps most problematic for applied linguists is the lack of attention to the ways in which storytellers use language to interpret experiences and position themselves as particular kinds of people. (Pavlenko 2007, pp. 166–167)

The overriding and unifying issue here would appear to be transparency and rigour in analysis. These problems are addressed to a large extent in the work cited in the previous section, where researchers adopt a dialogic approach which allows them to better articulate a multitude of analyses across scales, ranging from the micro-local to the macro-global. However, as Wortham (2008) notes, even in such dialectic research, problems remain, mainly concerning the lack of explanation of how big constructs, such as identities and social structures, come into existence and how they are maintained, strengthened and weakened over time. He proposes greater attention to the level of practice which means a close examination of the critical points in activities engaged in across space and time scales, where and when identities are, in a sense, made locally. This level of analysis then allows the researcher a clear path to making connections at higher levels (as regards structure) and longer scales (as regards time).

A sample study

As a way of concluding this chapter, I will now revisit a publication of mine (Block 2001) based on a study that I carried out over a decade ago, discussing it as a way *not* to proceed in this type of research as opposed to a way *to* proceed. I will reproduce a section of the publication to show the reader how I presented and analysed interview data and then, based on what has hitherto been discussed in this chapter, elaborate a brief critique of it. First, however, I provide some background.

The backdrop of the study which produced the publication was my reading about a shortfall in foreign language teachers in English secondary schools, which was being alleviated to a great extent by a flow of young adult French, German and Spanish nationals from their home countries to England. Interested in issues such as national identity and educational cultures in conflict, I conducted periodic interviews with nine such teachers between September 1999 and December 2002. The study began as the teachers started a Postgraduate Certificate of Education (PGCE) course in foreign language teaching and it then carried on subsequently as they settled into jobs in secondary schools in Greater London. Here, I present a section of a discussion of how study participants dealt with being positioned as different or foreign by the students with whom they came in contact as they did their PGCE teaching practice. The interviewees are two German nationals, whom I here call Arnold and Hilda. The interviews were carried out in English, and a language in which the two interviewees were extremely proficient.

The need for a reasoned response to national stereotyping was especially pronounced for German nationals, for if there is one nation which has inspired emotional responses in Britain since the Second World War, it is Germany. From the anodyne humour of Fawltey Towers and the classic line, 'Don't mention the war', to the spectacle of football fans celebrating wildly on any occasion that the English national side manages to beat Germany in an international competition, there is little ambivalence about the Germans: they were the enemy in the trenches during the two world wars of the twentieth century, and for many English fans today, they are perceived to be the ultimate rivals on the football pitch. The two German teachers commented about this phenomenon of Germans as the nemesis in the following way:

A = Arnold   H = Hilda   DB = David Block

A: You also feel sometimes that you are some kind of an ambassador or something for German culture, Germany, German politics, German history especially...

H: Oh, yeah. German history.

DB: Did that come up very much? You know, the whole sort of 'German Thing'...

H: The German thing, yes...

A: So you always had to be quiet but I was always quite relaxed about that... Sometimes they would draw some swastikas just to see 'what are you doing here?' (imitating dopey student voice) 'Ho-Ho-Ho'... Of course they just waited for me to explode or really be upset but I never was. So I really talked to them about it, although they were much too silly. But then in the end, they even listened, so I said 'OK, that's the way it is. We have to live with our past history. Imagine it is not always easy for Germans as well...' And I hope, even though it was year 10 and they are 16 and really silly and thick at times...I think they understood it a little...I mean it was just provoking me so they didn't expect that at all, that I would take it seriously and say something. I'm relaxed with that...I know that they all have some...Well, I have the feeling they have some prejudice and it's really just stereotypes and you just try to...open their mind up and say 'OK,...German people are exactly like you....What comes to your mind when you think about Germany? And what do you think is the media influence?' And they actually discuss things with you...

H: It's society, it's on TV, and it's every night.

DB: And it'll all come out now with the football again...

H: Exactly. I'm so glad I'm not at school at that time... And hopefully in two years' time when the World Championship is on...

A: And no matter if Germany or England wins, I will not be there the next day...

H: No, no way.

A: Especially if England wins. (6 June 2000)

Block (2001, pp. 297–298)

As regards the interview data discussed here, it is first of all noteworthy that they are transcribed orthographically (that is, in cleaned up form), as opposed to sociolinguistically (that is, with a view to capturing the detailed subtleties of spoken language). Suspension points (...) are used variably to convey either pauses or deleted words, which does little to recreate the interview as event. For example, the inclusion of pause times would perhaps have been useful to show any number of affective relationships with what was being said, such as hesitance or an inability to articulate thoughts. Also missing in the transcriptions are other features of conversations, such as overlapping speech or inflections on what is said (e.g. rising intonation), and we therefore do not get a clear sense of how Arnold and Hilda co-construct a version of events with their words. On the other hand, there is an attempt to mark with double quotation marks (") what Bakhtin (1981) called 'double voicing', that is, instances when Arnold is speaking as the protagonist in the story he is telling in his second turn. On the one hand, he double voices his students, putting on what I refer to here as a 'dopey voice', and on the other hand, he double voices the teacher (himself) with a more normal voice. Neither the telling of the story by Arnold nor the way it is told is commented on in my article, and thus, there is no consideration of Arnold's positioning himself as the more active interlocutor in this exchange (it is more his story than Hilda's), or how the double voicing draws lines between the sensible teacher and his students, described here as 'really silly and thick at times'. In sum, there is little that addresses what Pavlenko identifies as key problems in narrative research.

Instead, the content of the exchange is somewhat superficially linked to what is said in the paragraph that opens this excerpt from my article, in which I very briefly gloss English stereotypes of Germans revolving around the Second World War and football. There is, therefore, no overtly dialectic approach involving the moving back and forth across levels. There is no in-depth exploration, either sociologically or historically, of how Germany and Germans are discursively constructed in England today, and thus, no attempt at an explanation of how the stereotypes mentioned came into existence, and more importantly, how they are maintained and strengthened in day-to-day life in England and in the school setting described by Arnold. There is Hilda's comment – 'It's society, it's on TV, and it's every night' – but this is not explored further.

Space does not allow further dismantling and critiquing of my analysis and discussion from a decade and a half ago. However, I think I have done enough here to make my point. This, I should emphasize, has not been to position myself as a poor researcher in 2001; rather, I have used my work as a foil in my attempt to discuss very briefly what a researcher might do with life-story interview data, when working dialectically across levels and scales. Indeed, it should be noted that I have cited just a page-length section of a twenty-page article and that in other parts of it there is in-depth discussion of issues around national identity and educational culture, which in turn is filtered into my analysis of a fair number of interview excerpts.

Still, there is one inescapable problem with all research which attempts to link what people say about their lives to identity issues. Any such example of analysis – no matter how meticulously carried out, detailed and articulated across spatio-temporal scales – will always be partial in that there will always be more that could be said. The researcher can always dig more at the micro-level, relating findings to the meso-level, and he/she can always say a great deal more about social identities that serve as a backdrop to recounted experiences and indeed the interviews themselves as social events. In addition, there is the notion, introduced above, that identity is not only language-mediated, but more generally multimodally/semiotically mediated. If this notion is taken seriously, it means that any analysis which is exclusively language-based will be partial in that it misses many other aspects of communication, effectively ignoring the roles of other semiotic resources (gaze, posture, hand movements, dress and so on) as integral to identity construction. As Sigrid Norris (2004, 2011) argues, these other resources might even be more important than language at a given moment. From this point of view, researchers perhaps need to consider how phenomena such as gaze, posture and hand movements are part of interviews, and how they might contribute to attempts to link the interview to meso- and macro-level constructs.

Resources for further reading

Block, D 2007, *Second Language Identities*, Bloomsbury, London. NB Reissued in 2014 as part of the Bloomsbury Classics in Linguistics series.

This book is a selective but in-depth overview of how identity is an issue in different language learning environments. It begins with an overview of the post-structuralist approach to identity that has become dominant in applied linguistics, before moving to consider how identity is an issue in naturalistic, foreign and study abroad language learning contexts.

Caldas-Coulthard, C & Iedema, R (eds), 2008, *Identity Trouble: Critical Discourse and Contested Identities*, Palgrave, London.

This is a good state-of-the-art collection of chapters which also examines the interrelationships between language, discourse and identity. In thirteen chapters, contributors discuss conceptual issues related to the analysis of narrative from different perspectives, such as conversational analysis and social semiotics, focusing especially on contexts and events in which the emergence of identity is problematic in some way.

De Fina, A & Georgakopoulou, A 2012, *Analyzing Narrative: Discourse and Sociolinguistic Perspectives*, Cambridge University Press, Cambridge.

This is an excellent exploration of storytelling from a sociolinguistic perspective, situated more specifically in linguistic ethnography. It begins with a discussion of narrative studies in general before moving on to current scholarship in applied linguistics. Importantly, the book examines the different methodologies employed by researchers interested in stories elicited in research interviews, including conversation analysis and critical discourse analysis.

De Fina, A, Schiffrin, D & Bamberg, M (eds), 2006, *Discourse and Identity*, Cambridge University Press, Cambridge.

This is an excellent collection of work in sociolinguistics and linguistic anthropology, which explores the interrelationships between language, discourse and identity. In fifteen chapters, contributors examine conceptual issues and the specifics of research on public and private identities, masculinities and the interactions between person and place.

Riessman, CK 2008, *Narrative Methods for the Human Sciences*, Sage, London.

This book is a highly readable review of narrative methods in identity research. The author provides an excellent synthesis of her personal perspective and the work of other scholars, focusing on research processes and issues around data analysis.

Clandinin, J (ed.), 2007, *Handbook of Narrative Inquiry: Mapping a Methodology*, Sage, London.

This is still perhaps the most comprehensive and authoritative statement of what narrative research in the social sciences means today. It is extensive, although far more manageable than even more extensive collections such as Goodwin (2012).

References

Atkinson, R 1998, *The Life-Story Interview*, Sage, London.

Atkinson, P & Delamont, S (eds), 2006, *Narrative Methods*, Sage, London.

Bakhtin, M 1981, *The Dialogic Imagination: Four Essays*, University of Texas Press, Austin, TX.

Benson, P & Nunan, D (eds), 2005, *Learners Stories: Difference and Diversity in Language Learning*, Cambridge University Press, Cambridge.

Benwell, B & Stokoe, E 2006, *Discourse and Identity*, Edinburgh University Press, Edinburgh.

Blackledge, A & Creese, A 2010, *Multilingualism: A Critical Perspective*, Continuum, London.

Block, D 2001, 'Foreign nationals on PGCE in modern languages course: Issues in national identity construction', *European Journal of Teacher Education*, vol. 24, no. 3, pp. 291–312.

—— 2006, *Multilingual Identities in a Global City: London Stories*, Palgrave, London.

—— 2007, *Second Language Identities*, Bloomsbury, London.

—— 2013, 'Issues in language and identity research in applied linguistics', *ELIA (Estudios de lingüística inglesa aplicada)*, vol. 13, pp. 11–46.

Block, D & Corona, V, 2014, 'Exploring class-based intersectionality', *Language, Culture and Curriculum*, vol. 27, no. 1, pp. 27–42.

Blommaert, J 2005, *Discourse*, Cambridge University Press, Cambridge.

Bourdieu, P 1984, *Distinction: A Social Critique of the Judgement of Taste*, Routledge, London.

Byrd-Clark, J 2010, *Multilingualism, Citizenship, and Identity: Voices of Youth and Symbolic Investments in an Urban, Globalized World*, Continuum, London.

Caldas-Coulthard, C & Iedema, R (eds), 2008, *Identity Trouble: Critical Discourse and Contested Identities*, Palgrave, London.

Clandinin, J (ed.), 2007, *Handbook of Narrative Inquiry: Mapping a Methodology*, Sage, London.

Clandinin, J & Connelly, M 2004, *Narrative Inquiry: Experience and Story in Qualitative Research*, Jossey-Bass, San Fancisco, CA.

Csizér, K & Magid, M (eds), 2014, *The Impact of Self-Concept on Language Learning*, Multilingual Matters, Bristol.

Czarniawska, B 2004, *Narratives in Social Science Research*, Sage, London.

Dainute, C 2014, *Narrative Inquiry: A Dynamic Approach*, Sage, London.

De Fina, A & Georgakopoulou, A 2012, *Analyzing Narrative: Discourse and Sociolinguistic Perspectives*, Cambridge University Press, Cambridge.

De Fina, A, Schiffrin, D & Bamberg, M (eds), 2006, *Discourse and Identity*, Cambridge University Press, Cambridge.

Duff, P 2012, 'Issues of identity', in S Gass & A Mackey (eds), *The Routledge Handbook of Second Language Acquisition*, Routledge, London, pp. 410–426.

Eckert, P & McConnell-Ginet, S 1992, 'Think practically and act locally: Language and gender as community-based practice', *Annual Review of Anthropology*, vol. 21, pp. 461–490.

Edwards, J 2009, *Language and Identity*, Cambridge University Press, Cambridge.

Elliot, J 2005, *Using Narrative in Social Research*, Sage, London.

Fishman, J & Garcia, O (eds), 2010, *Handbook of Language and Ethnic Identity: Disciplinary and Regional Perspectives (Vol. I, Disciplinary & Regional Perspectives)*, Oxford University Press, New York, NY.

Freeman, D 1996, '"To take them at their word": Language data in the study of teachers' knowledge', *Harvard Educational Review*, vol. 66, no. 4, pp. 732–761.

Gee, JP 2011, *An Introduction to Discourse Analysis*, 3rd edn, Routledge, London.

Georgakopoulou, A 2006, 'Small and large identities in narrative (inter)action', in A De Fina, D Schiffrin & M Bamberg (eds), *Discourse and Identity*, Cambridge University Press, Cambridge, pp. 83–102.

—— 2007, *Small Stories, Interactions and Identities*, John Benjamins, Amsterdam.

Giddens, A 1984, *The Constitution of Society: Outline of the Theory of Structuration*, University of California Press, Berkeley, CA.

—— 1991, *Modernity and Self-Identity: Self and Society in the Late Modern Age*, Polity, Cambridge.

Goodson, IF, Loveless, AM & Stevens, D (eds), 2013, *Explorations in Narrative Research*, Sense, Rotterdam.

Goodwin, J (ed.), 2012, *Sage Biographical Research*, Sage, London.

Gubrium, J & Holstein, J 2009, *Analyzing Narrative Reality*, Sage, London.

Higgins, C (ed.), 2012, *Identity Formation in Globalizing Contexts: Language Learning in the New Millennium*, Mouton de Gruyter, Berlin.

Holstein, J & Gubrium, J 2000, *The Self We Live: Narrative Identity in a Postmodern World*, Oxford University Press, Oxford.

—— (eds), 2012, *Varieties of Narrative Analysis*, Sage, London.

Jackson, J 2008, *Language, Identity and Study Abroad: Sociocultural Perspectives*, Equinox, London.

Joseph, J 2004, *Language and Identity*, Palgrave, London.

Kanno, Y 2003, *Negotiating Bilingual and Bicultural Identities: Japanese Returnees Betwixt Two Worlds*, Lawrence Erlbaum Associates, Mahwah, NJ.

Kramsch, C 2010, *The Multilingual Subject*, Oxford University Press, Oxford.

Labov, W & Waletzky, J 1967, 'Narrative analysis: Oral versions of personal experience', in W Labov (ed.), *Language in the Iner City: Studies in the Black English Vernacular*, University of Pennsylvania Press, Philadelphia, PA, pp. 354–396.

Le Page, RB & Tabouret-Keller, A 1985, *Acts of Identity: Creole-Based Approaches to Language and Ethnicity*, Cambridge University Press, Cambridge.

Lemke, J 1995, *Textual Politics: Discourse and Social Dynamics*, Taylor and Francis, London.

———— 2008, 'Identity, development, and desire: Critical questions', in C Caldas-Coulthard & R Iedema (eds), *Identity Trouble: Critical Discourse and Contested Identities*, Palgrave, London, pp. 17–42.

Llamas, C & Watt, D (eds), 2010, *Language and Identities*, Edinburg University Press, Edinburgh.

Meinhof, U & Galasiński, D 2005, *The Language of Belonging*, Palgrave, London.

Miller, J 2003, *Audible Differences: ESL and Social Identity in Schools*, Multilingual Matters, Clevedon.

Norris, S 2004, *Analyzing Multimodal Interaction: A Methodological Framework*, Routledge, London.

———— 2011, *Identity in (Inter)action: Introducing Multimodal Interaction Analysis*, Mouton de Gruyer, Berlin.

Norton, B 2000, *Identity and Language Learning: Gender, Ethnicity and Educational Change*, Longman, Harlow.

———— 2010, 'Language and identity', in N Hornberger & S McKay (eds), *Sociolinguistics and Language Education*, Multilingual Matters, Bristol, pp. 349–369.

———— 2013, *Identity and Language Learning: Extending the Conversation*, 2nd edn, Multilingual Matters, Bristol.

Norton, B & Toohey, K 2011, 'Identity, language learning, and social change', *Language Teaching*, vol. 44, no. 4, pp. 412–446.

Nunan, D & Choi, J (eds), 2010, *Language and Culture: Reflective Narratives and the Emergence of Identity*, Cambridge University Press, Cambridge.

Omoniyi, T & White, G eds, 2006, *The Sociolinguistics of Identity*, Continuum, London.

Pavlenko, A 2007, 'Autobiographic narratives as data in applied linguistics', *Applied Linguistics*, vol. 28, no. 2, pp. 163–188.

Pavlenko, A & Blackledge, A (eds), 2004, *Negotiation of Identities in Multilingual Settings*, Multilingual Matters, Clevedon.

Pavlenko, A, Blackledge, A, Piller, I & Teutsch-Dwyer, M eds, 2001, *Multilingualism, Second Language Learning, and Gender*, Mouton De Gruyter, New York, NY.

Pichler, P 2009, *Talking Young Femininities*, Palgrave, London.

Preece, S 2009, *Posh Talk: Language and Identity in Higher Education*, Palgrave, London.

Riessman, CK 2008, *Narrative Methods for the Human Sciences*, Sage, London.

Riley, P 2007, *Language, Culture and Identity*, Continuum, London.

Weedon, C 1997, *Feminist Practice and Poststructuralist Theory*, 2nd edn, Blackwell, Oxford.

Wengraf, T 2001, *Qualitative Research Interviewing: Biographic Narrative and Semi-Structured Methods: Biographic Narrative and Semi-Structured Methods*, Sage, London.

Wortham, S 2001, *Narratives in Action: A Strategy for Research and Analysis*, Teachers College Press, New York, NY.

———— 2008, 'Shifting identities in the classroom', in C Caldas-Coulthard & R Iedema (eds), *Identity Trouble: Critical Discourse and Contested Identities*, Palgrave, London, pp. 205–228.

CHAPTER THIRTY ONE

Researching Language Teacher Education

Simon Borg

Various definitions exist (see e.g. Mann 2005), but in its broadest sense, *language teacher education* (henceforth *LTE*) encompasses all those activities which teachers, at any stage of their careers, engage in for the purposes of professional learning (which in turn can be defined as growth in one or more facets of teaching – behavioural, (meta)cognitive, attitudinal and emotional). In this chapter, though, I limit my focus to the discussion of what is often referred to as *in-service teacher education* – that is, professional learning for practising teachers, with specific reference to teachers of second and foreign languages. There are four reasons for my focus on practising teachers here: a comprehensive discussion of all forms of LTE would not be feasible in the space available; in-service teacher education has received less empirical attention in the literature than initial teacher preparation; there is increasing activity and interest worldwide in relation to the continuing professional development (CPD) of language teachers and systematic evaluations of its impact; and much of my own recent work has taken place in in-service contexts. Many of the issues I cover in discussing ways of researching LTE will be relevant to readers interested in pre-service work too; however, some of the theoretical issues I discuss and the examples of research I examine will relate specifically to work in in-service contexts from a range of language education settings internationally. Wright (2010) provides a detailed review dedicated to initial teacher preparation in language teaching.

I will first discuss two contrasting perspectives on in-service teacher education and summarize current thinking about how to promote teacher professional learning. I then consider key issues relevant to researching LTE, including the study of its impact, before concluding with a discussion of approaches and methods in LTE and a sample study.

Training-transmission models of LTE

Conventionally, as Johnson (2009b) notes, in-service teacher education has been done by others *to* teachers; typically, this might take the form of workshops or courses led by external trainers who provide teachers with knowledge and ideas. While I am not suggesting that such activity cannot contribute to teachers' growth, it is clear that, driven by a growing international dissatisfaction with the impact of in-service training on what happens in classrooms (Timperley 2011), serious questions have been raised in recent years about the efficacy of this approach to professional development. For example, when in-service teacher education is dependent on external activities led by others, professional learning by definition becomes an infrequent activity and one in which teachers rely on external agents for their own growth. Also problematic is the assumption that professional learning involves the acquisition through training of theoretical ideas and their subsequent application in the classroom – this is what Freeman (2009) describes as an input-application view of LTE. The classroom is thus viewed simply as the place where the application of new knowledge occurs. Further objections relate to the decontextualized and generic nature of training content and to the manner in which it has traditionally been defined:

> The problem... is that the need to know something new is identified by someone external to the group of teachers (e.g., a policy official or a researcher) without the participating teachers necessarily understanding the reason why it is important to know it or being committed to doing so (Muijs et al. 2014, p. 247).

Such concerns about the limited impact of training-transmission models of professional learning are not particularly new – 20 years ago Lamb (1995) lamented the lack of sustained practical impact of an in-service course on a group of language teachers in Indonesia; more recently, Kubanyiova (2012) has provided a detailed analysis of the failure of a year-long in-service initiative to achieve substantial impact on language teachers in Slovakia, while it has also been noted in China that 'teacher training at all levels for the new curriculum was found to be unable to help teachers solve practical problems or support their professional autonomy' (Wang & Zhang 2014, p. 223). Korea is another context where limited success has been reported in promoting more communicative language teacher practices through INSET (i.e. in-service teacher education) courses (Choi & Andon 2014; Hayes 2012).

Development-constructivist models of LTE

In contrast to the position outlined above, contemporary perspectives on in-service teacher education see the classroom as a powerful site for teacher learning and systematic inquiry by teachers into their own practices is a key professional learning process. Additionally, professional learning is not seen as the sequential, additive mastery and routine application of knowledge and skills but the development of 'adaptive expertise' (Hammerness et al. 2005) – that is, the capacity in teachers to modify, in creative ways, how they teach in response to evidence that existing practices are not effective. The constructivist nature of this perspective on teacher learning means that prior knowledge, beliefs and experience are recognized as important influences on how and what teachers learn. Another important feature of this perspective on INSET is that it is social – teacher learning is seen to be more effective when teachers learn together and share experiences and expertise. Darling-Hammond (2013, p. 150) thus notes that 'teaching improves most in collegial settings where common goals are set, curriculum is jointly developed, and expertise is shared', while Johnston (2009, p. 241) goes further (too far perhaps) by claiming that 'teachers can only learn professionally in sustained and meaningful ways when they are able to do so together'. An emphasis on collaboration and teachers' ownership of their professional learning does not rule out support from external agents; such support is actually recognized as a factor that can contribute to effective professional development (e.g. through university-school partnerships – see Wang & Zhang 2014).

Various strategies have been proposed through which this contemporary perspective on INSET can be implemented, such as peer observation (Richards & Farrell 2005), lesson study (Tasker 2011), critical friends groups (Poehner 2011), collaborative planning (Martin-Beltran & Peercy 2014), reading groups (Fenton-Smith & Stillwell 2011), exploratory practice (Allwright & Hanks 2009), teacher study groups (Hung & Yeh 2013) and action research (Burns 2010, this volume). Not all of these are, of course, particularly new – collaborative action research, for example, has been a feature of English language teaching in Australia for many years (Burns 1999) – but, globally, LTE is not characterized by the widespread adoption and study of such forms of professional learning. Even where they do exist, such as when peer observation schemes are mandated by Ministries of Education, evidence about their implementation is limited and that which does exist sometimes implies that the strategies are seen by teachers to be more of an administrative requirement than a learning opportunity (see, for example, A'Dhahab 2009). The simple existence within educational systems of the kinds of professional learning activities listed above cannot be taken, then, as a measure of effective professional learning; that is of course one reason why it is important for the use and impacts of such activities to be systematically researched.

Overall, though, there seems to be an emerging consensus in the literature (e.g. Avalos 2011; Beijaard, Korthagen & Verloop 2007; Broad & Evans 2006; Cordingley et al. 2003; Darling-Hammond & Lieberman 2012; Garet et al. 2001; Hammerness et al. 2005; Johnson 2009a; Leu & Ginsburg 2001; Muijs et al. 2014; Opfer & Pedder 2011; Richardson 1996; Schwille, Dembele & Schubert 2007; Timperley 2011; Timperley et al. 2008; Villegas-Reimers 2003; Waters & Vilches 2010) that professional learning can achieve positive and sustained impacts on teachers, learners and organizations when:

- it is seen by teachers to be relevant to their needs and those of their students

- teachers are centrally involved in decisions about the content and process of professional learning

- collaboration and the sharing of expertise among teachers is fostered

- it is a collective enterprise supported by schools and educational systems more broadly

- exploration and reflection are emphasized over methodological prescriptivism

- expert internal and/or external support is available

- classrooms are valued as a site for professional learning

- professional learning is recognized as an integral part of teachers' work

- classroom inquiry by teachers is seen as a central professional learning process

- teachers are engaged in the examination and review of their beliefs

- adaptive expertise is promoted

- student learning provides the motivation for professional learning

- teachers experience the cognitive dissonance that motivates change.

As I note below, though, it is important not to view these factors, uncritically, as a template for success in promoting professional learning.

Researching language teacher education

The study of in-service LTE is a growing area of activity and Table 31.1 lists recent illustrative studies, with brief notes on their focus and the research methods used. I will now discuss some key issues in this field of research.

Table 31.1 Recent studies of in-service language teacher education

Source	Focus	Research methods
Borg (2013a–c)	Impact of a mentoring program	Teacher narratives
Burns (2014)	Evaluation of an action research scheme	Written teacher evaluations, recordings of discussions during workshops, teachers' written reports
Choi and Andon (2014)	Impact of an INSET program on teachers' classroom practices	Document analysis, video recorded lessons, interviews, teacher assessment results
Choi and Morrison (2014)	Impact of a professional development program on teachers' classroom practices	Observations, on-line discussions
Collins and Liang (2013)	Teachers' evaluation of the relevance of on-line professional development tasks	Q study (ranking instrument), interviews
Fenton-Smith and Torpey (2013)	Evaluation of an induction program for EFL teachers	Surveys, written reports, interviews, focus groups
Hiver (2013)	The professional development choices of EFL teachers	Interviews
Huang and Papakosmas (2014)	Impact of teacher education program on teachers' beliefs and behaviours	Focus group interviews, lesson observations, student and teacher questionnaires, document analysis
Hung and Yeh (2013)	Impact of teacher study groups on teachers' beliefs and practices	Transcripts of teacher study group meetings, interviews
Kabilan and Veratharaju (2013)	EFL teachers' professional development needs	Questionnaire

(continued)

Table 31.1 Recent studies of in-service language teacher education

Source	Focus	Research methods
Lin (2014)	Teachers' views about on-line professional development	Questionnaires and interviews
Martin-Beltran and Percy (2014)	Teacher learning through collaborative teaching	Classroom observations, co-planning sessions, interviews
Molle (2013)	Facilitation processes during a professional development program	Audio recordings of professional development sessions, teacher coursework, interviews, pre-post course surveys
O'Dwyer and Atli (2014)	In-service teacher educators' perceptions of their roles and needs	Interviews, questionnaires
Walsh et al. (2013)	Using mobile phones in large-scale teacher development	Classroom observations, assessment of teacher and student English oral proficiency, attitude questionnaires, analyses of resources
Wang and Zhang (2014)	University-school collaborative action research	Pre-post project questionnaires, interviews, reflective journals, discussions, and research reports

Note: I have only included here studies of second and foreign language teachers' practices, beliefs knowledge, etc. as these relate to a teacher education initiative; many additional studies have provided descriptive analyses of such issues without a focus on LTE.

Professional learning as part of a system

Despite powerful arguments in the literature for the value of more job-embedded, collaborative and inquiry-based forms of professional learning, it is important that as a field we remain critical in the assumptions we make about how to support the development of practising teachers. One reason for this is that the outcomes of LTE are not simply determined by the activities teachers engage in (e.g. workshops, peer observation or action research). As discussed by Oper and Pedder (2011), who apply complex systems thinking to their analysis of professional learning, the learning activities teachers engage in interact with both the teachers' own prior knowledge, beliefs and experiences and with the school systems that teachers are part of. These interactions are also characterized by variability, meaning that the same professional learning activities will be differentially effective across contexts. For example, while collaborative teacher learning is generally seen to be desirable, there will be contexts where excessive emphasis on collaboration may prove counterproductive; similarly, action research will not be an appropriate professional learning option everywhere. And despite criticisms of 'workshops' as a strategy for professional development, they can be productive, particularly in combination with school-based work (Orr et al. 2013). What all this implies is that research on in-service LTE should not be simply about identifying the characteristics of teacher learning activities which seem to be effective; what is also important is an understanding of how particular learning activities interact with teacher and school system variables to shape the impact that LTE has. Oper and Pedder (2011) argue that attempts to understand teacher learning which focus solely on the activities teachers engage in 'must be understood as partial, incomplete, and biased' (p. 379).

So, for example, one important but understudied area of research in LTE relates to the relative effectiveness of different ways of structuring in-service initiatives. Many options are available, such as input-based training programs, two-phase programs which combine input and school-based practice, mentoring models, wholly online or blended models, teacher research programs (e.g. Borg 2014) and technology-driven programs (e.g. the English in Action project in Bangladesh, where mobile phones are used to deliver content to teachers – Walsh et al. 2013). It is not possible to empirically understand the contributions these (and other – see Orr et al. 2013) models make to the professional learning of language teachers without also understanding how the activities teachers engage in interact with their existing cognitions and experiences and with their school systems. As already noted, the complex ways in which these three influences may combine to shape professional learning will differ across contexts; the expectation that research will ever show that any one way of structuring INSET is universally more effective than others is therefore unrealistic. What we do need is detailed contextualized evidence of how different approaches to professional learning unfold, and as this becomes available our ability to make predictions about which approaches are most appropriate in which contexts will improve. Currently, though, our understandings of such matters in LTE remain limited. Thus, while I subscribe to many of the ideas about effective professional learning listed earlier (i.e. regarding collaboration and inquiry), I remain open-minded about their relative value in differing LTE contexts around the world.

Studying LTE and its impacts

Despite the need to consider LTE holistically, research projects typically delimit their focus, making particular facets of LTE salient. For example (see Table 31.1), LTE research can focus on:

- Teachers – for example, motivations for and evaluations of professional development, (the development of) their beliefs, attitudes, knowledge, skills, emotions, identities and classroom practices.

- Teacher educators – for example, their demographic characteristics, practices (such as facilitation and supervision[1]), cognitions and own professional development.

- Programs – for example, underlying philosophies, objectives, content, structure, resources, teaching/learning processes, modalities (e.g. face-to-face, on-line) assessment and evaluation.

- Strategies – specific approaches to professional learning such as peer observation, teacher support groups, teacher research and mentoring.

- Contexts – that is, how classrooms, schools, policies and cultures shape the nature and outcomes of teacher education.

- Impacts – the effects of teacher education on teachers, students and organizations.

In relation to the first of these points, while LTE has typically focused on the development of teachers' methodological skills, it is increasingly the case (especially in developing contexts) that improving teachers' language proficiency is the predominant focus of INSET; such work often happens at scale (i.e. with thousands of teachers), though to date the analysis of such work has been limited to largely internal project evaluations rather than the focus of empirical study. In relation to the last point on the list above, impact, from a research point of view as well as for practical accountability, understanding and demonstrating what difference LTE makes are important issues. However, impact can be defined and studied in a range of ways and researchers thus need to give due consideration to the way they operationalize this notion. At a broad level, professional learning can impact on teachers, students and organizations. And breaking this down further, Figure 31.1 illustrates a range of ways in which the impact on language teachers might be defined – this covers impacts on knowledge, teaching, affect and teachers' capacity for self-direction. Impact studies may or may not define their precise focus in advance; it is possible, for example, to adopt an initially broad orientation on impact to explore (e.g. with teachers) their perceptions of the different ways an in-service initiative is promoting change and to identify different kinds of impact from this analysis. In other studies, though, a concern for particular kinds of impact (e.g. on student learning) will be defined from the outset and studies will be designed with this specific focus in mind. Irrespective of whether impact is studied inductively or deductively, criticality is needed in considering what different kinds of evidence can actually tell us about professional learning. Oper and Pedder (2011) note the dangers of mistaking empirical evidence of change for evidence of professional learning; in LTE, for example, Scott and Rodgers (1995) compared teachers' conceptions of writing using a pre- and post-course survey and found that initially 58.5 per cent of the beliefs expressed were aligned with the principles and practices promoted on the course, compared to 89 per cent afterwards. There was clearly empirical evidence of change here; the lack of information about whether such change had any impact in the classroom, though, means caution is needed in the claims that are made about the effectiveness of the in-service program. Another important variable in the study of the impact of teacher education is timing – while evaluation data are commonly collected at the end of teacher education initiatives, it is less common for the longer-term impact of

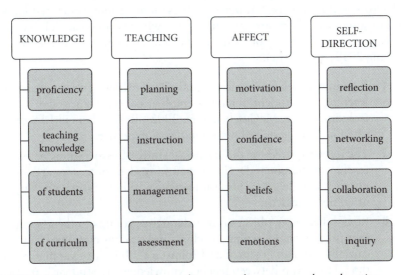

FIGURE 31.1 *Impacts on teachers of in-service language teacher education*

these initiatives to be studied (i.e. in terms of what happens when teachers return to the classroom). The formative study of impact is also an option for more extended programs.

Professional learning and student achievement

In recent analyses of INSET (e.g. Timperley et al. 2008), the key impact which has been used in defining effectiveness is student learning and Cochran-Smith and Fries (2008) note that this focus on student outcomes is currently the dominant paradigm for teacher education research in the United States. In LTE, Johnson (2009b, p. 26) has also noted that

> the next generation of research on L2 teacher education must tackle the thorny question of the relationship between teacher professional learning and student learning…. Probing the relationship between what teachers come to know through professional development and what, through their teaching, their students come to know and are able to do will be absolutely critical for the professional legitimacy of L2 teacher education in the future.

However, little progress has been achieved in this area and I am not aware of any research in LTE where links between professional learning and student outcomes have been explicitly studied. Poehner (2011), for example, provides a powerful account of how a teacher transformed her thinking and practices through a critical friends group but admits that 'we do not have evidence of student learning' (p. 202). Hutterli and Prusse (2011), to take just one more example, also report some success in transferring innovations into classrooms through INSET, but how these innovations benefitted students is not discussed. There are several reasons why research on LTE has yet to engage with student outcomes in any substantial manner (see also Hayes & Chang 2012; Tsui 2011):

1 Research which establishes causal relationships between professional learning and student outcomes employs complex statistical techniques (e.g. McCutchen et al. 2002). Researchers in LTE may often lack the required methodological expertise.

2 The data required for the statistical study of associations between teacher professional development and student outcomes are often not available (e.g. teachers on in-service LTE initiatives are very often not assessed).

3 Researchers may object on paradigmatic grounds to the assumption that professional learning, teaching and student outcomes can be causally studied. Freeman and Johnson (2005), for example, reframe the relationship between teacher knowledge and student learning as one of influence rather than causality.

4 Researchers may also find flawed the expectation that generalizable connections between professional learning and student outcomes can be established given the many other variables related to teachers, learners and school systems that interact in defining the impact that professional learning has on what students learn.

5 Another objection to process-product research on the effects of teacher education, as Borko, Whitcomb and Byrnes (2008) note, is that it does not generate findings that are of practical value and cannot explain why particular approaches to professional learning succeed or fail in particular contexts.

Despite these arguments, experimental and correlational studies demonstrating statistical links between professional learning and student achievement are very attractive to policy makers as well as to donors who may be investing substantial funds in INSET in order to raise student achievement and who can justifiably expect some measure of the difference it is making to what students learn. As a field, we need to engage more robustly with this issue and to develop frameworks which can support researchers in examining how professional learning influences student learning. Methodological pluralism should be encouraged, with space for both quantitative and qualitative approaches.

Approaches and methods in researching LTE

A survey of the available literature does not highlight any substantial discussion of methodological issues in the study of LTE. Many individual publications reporting research findings and discussing key relevant concepts do of course exist; deeper analyses of particular theoretical frameworks and their implications for the way teacher learning is conceptualized are also available; Johnson (2009a), for example, provides a detailed account of a sociocultural perspective on LTE; Borg (2006) outlines a framework centred on teacher cognition; Feryok (2010) draws on complexity theory while teacher conceptual change is the framework developed by Kubanyiova (2012). Despite their differences, such frameworks all reflect a move away from process-product and input-output models of professional learning and embrace more complex, dynamic notions of what it means to be and to grow as a teacher. However, frameworks which seek to classify different approaches and methods in the study of LTE are not readily available and I would now like to examine this issue.

The first point I will make is that there is nothing unique about the approaches and methods that are used in research on LTE. The broad processes for such inquiry – designing, conducting, reporting – are those which apply to educational research more generally. The options regarding paradigms, approaches and data collection strategies are similarly those which exist more generally in the social sciences literature and readers are referred to research methods texts for discussions of these. Also in common with research more generally, LTE research must strive for rigour to ensure that it generates trustworthy findings (what counts as 'rigour' and 'trustworthiness' will of course vary depending on one's perspective on social inquiry). It is also important that LTE research contributes in a productive way to the improvement of educational practice and, very importantly too, that it is ethical. Methodological diversity in LTE research should also be seen as a strength and quantitative, qualitative and mixed methods designs all have a role to play in the further development of the field (the examples in Table 31.1 suggest that qualitative work currently predominates).

Despite the above comments, there have been attempts in the mainstream teacher education literature to define different approaches to research and I will comment on just two examples here. The first, Zeichner (1999), discussed what he called 'the new scholarship' in teacher education research (in the United States) and proposed five kinds of research that were characterizing the field at the time. His categories were: survey research, case studies of teacher education programs, conceptual and historical research, studies of learning to teach and examinations of the nature and impact of teacher education activities, including self-study research. This list is problematic (as the author himself admits) as a framework for classifying different approaches to researching teacher education; for example, while survey research denotes either a research approach or a specific method of data collection, studies of learning to teach refer to a research focus (which may be examined through surveys). This analysis, though, does highlight potential differences of emphasis in the way that LTE might be approached. A second, more recent, framework for teacher education research consisting of four genres (see also Kennedy 2006, for an earlier discussion of genres in teacher education research) is provided by Borko, Whitcomb and Byrnes (2008), again largely with reference to the United States. The first genre discussed is the *effects of teacher education research*, which is the statistical approach to establishing links between teacher learning and student outcomes discussed earlier. Studies in this group use experimental and correlational designs and complex statistical procedures to study links between specific variables in teacher education and what students learn. A second genre is *interpretive research,* which utilizes qualitative methodologies (such as ethnography, case studies and narratives). Interpretive research in teacher education is concerned with understanding, from stakeholders' perspectives, the experiences, processes and outcomes of professional learning. Data are collected through a range of methods such as interviews, observations and journals and data analysis involves qualitative strategies such as thematic analysis (Braun & Clarke 2006) through which detailed contextualized descriptions of events and experiences are generated. *Practitioner research* is a third genre of research on teacher education. Here, we must be careful to distinguish practitioner research as a strategy for teacher professional development and practitioner research as a strategy through which teacher educators study their own practices – it is the latter which functions as a genre of teacher education research. This form of research is also called self study (see the special issue of the journal *Studying Teacher Education*, Vol. 8, No. 2, which is dedicated to this theme). In practitioner research, teacher educators are both the researchers and the focus of the research. They engage in the systematic study of themselves (rather than, as in conventional research, of others) and can collect data through a wide range of qualitative and quantitative methods. The final genre of teacher education research that Borko, Whitcomb and Byrnes (2008) mention is what they call *design research*. The characteristics of this approach are that it takes place in real settings (not experimental ones); consists of repeated cycles of design, application and redesign of an educational innovation, is theory-driven; and requires close collaboration between researchers and practitioners over an extended period of time (perhaps years). Multiple forms of data are collected in order to provide detailed insights into the processes and outcomes of the innovation being developed.

Applied to the LTE research in Table 31.1, the genres of teacher research described above are both useful and problematic. They are helpful in that they indicate that while interpretive research in LTE is common, practitioner research by in-service language teacher educators is less in evidence. They are problematic because they do not account in a comprehensive manner for the different ways in which LTE is being studied, most obviously (in the four genres proposed more recently) by not accounting for questionnaire-based studies of teachers' views about professional development. The distinction between interpretive research and practitioner research is also one I do not find particularly valuable in analytical terms given that the latter is very often interpretive in nature. What we require, then, is a scheme for describing different approaches to research in LTE which is comprehensive and provides relatively discrete categories that allow comparisons at different levels of analysis (e.g. research paradigms, approaches and methods). It may be that frameworks for classifying approaches to research more generally will serve this purpose well, supplemented with descriptors that link them explicitly to teacher education research. For example, Bryman (2012) classifies research through a matrix of research designs (experimental, cross-sectional, longitudinal, case study and comparative) and research strategies (quantitative and qualitative); Creswell (2013) presents a framework which combines philosophical worldviews, designs, research approaches and research methods; while, to take a final example, Saunders, Lewis and Thornhill (2012) propose the 'research onion' in which research parameters are described through a series of concentric circles which move inwards and become increasingly specific, covering (starting from the most general parameter) philosophy, approach, methodological choice (quantitative, qualitative or mixed methods), strategies, time horizon (cross-sectional or longitudinal) and techniques and procedures. Mapping LTE research onto such frameworks is beyond my scope here but would be a valuable activity to undertake.

A sample study

To conclude this chapter, I will now briefly discuss a sample study of in-service LTE. I have opted to focus on a project of my own, not to suggest this is necessarily better than others that are available but because I can comment with deeper insight on the processes that the study entailed. As already noted, though, the studies in Table 31.1 are all excellent candidates for further study by readers wanting to develop their understanding of research methods used in current research on LTE.

The study I discuss here (Borg 2011a, b) examined teacher learning during an INSET program called the Delta (Diploma in Teaching English to Speakers of Other Languages) and which is administered by Cambridge English Language Assessment. The study covered a range of questions but the two I will focus on here are:

1 What evidence is there of teacher learning – defined broadly as changes in knowledge, practices, awareness, attitudes, and beliefs – both in participants' own accounts of their experience on the Delta modules and in their assessed work and tutor feedback on it?

2 After completing the Delta, what impact on their professional practice do participants say the Delta modules have?

Data collection

The study was interpretive and longitudinal and data were collected from six teachers during the eight-week intensive program. The data took many forms, primarily detailed semi-structured interviews (six per teacher) and all the coursework the teachers produced during their program together with the tutor feedback they received on it. My role in this study was that of external researcher – I was not involved in the delivery of the course in any way. All the data for each teacher were compiled into chronologically ordered case files which allowed their experience of the program to be studied from just before the course started until two months after its completion.

Data analysis

Data analysis was qualitative and case studies were constructed for each teacher to narrate the stories of their learning during the program. The teachers read these accounts and provided comments on them. Methodologically, then, the study was underpinned by a belief in the value of studying teacher education qualitatively, narratively and longitudinally. The study also had a strong ethical dimension; for example, it was designed in negotiation with the course manager and the teachers to ensure data collection points did not clash with times when they were particularly busy.

Results

The results show that, collectively, through the course the teachers experienced enhancements in their practical skills, theoretical knowledge, planning and interactive decision-making skills, criticality, reflective ability, awareness of their beliefs, strengths and weaknesses, confidence and self-esteem, awareness of learners, attitudes to teaching and attitudes to professional development. Even where the observable impact of the Delta on teachers' classroom practices (during and after the course) was not felt to be significant, participants reported major changes in the thinking behind their work. Two months after the course, while contextual factors in the teachers' institutions did not always support their ability to apply learning from the Delta to their subsequent work, the teachers remained nonetheless positive of the considerable difference to their knowledge and thinking that the course had made. One area where impact varied was in changing teachers' beliefs about language teaching and learning. There was evidence that belief change did occur, but in some cases the teachers did not seem fully aware of or capable of articulating these changes.

Limitations

One limitation of the study relates to the lack of observational data about teachers' practices during and after the Delta. During the course, substantial data were collected about teachers' lessons through their lesson plans and from the lengthy written feedback they received from tutors on these lessons, but no direct observations of the teachers during practice teaching or input sessions during the course took place. Similarly, their classroom practices after the course were not observed. The study thus relied very heavily on teachers' own accounts of their professional learning.

Note

1   See Bailey (2006), Chapter 13, for a discussion of research on supervision in in-service contexts.

Resources for further reading

Borko, H, Jacobs, J & Koellner, K 2010, 'Contemporary approaches to teacher professional development', in P Peterson, E Baker & B McGaw (eds), *International Encyclopedia of Education*, 3rd edn, Elsevier, Oxford, pp. 548–556.

This chapter provides a concise analysis of contemporary understandings of what makes professional development for teachers effective.

Johnson, KE & Golombek, PR (eds), 2011, *Research on Second Language Teacher Education*, Routledge, London.

This collection of studies in both initial and in-service contexts illustrates the application of sociocultural perspectives to the study of LTE.

Muijs, D, Kyriakides, L, van der Werf, G, Creemers, B, Timperley, H & Earl, L 2014, 'State of the art – teacher effectiveness and professional learning', *School Effectiveness and School Improvement*, vol. 25, no. 2, pp. 231–256.

A recent review of literature on the factors that influence student learning, including teacher professional development.

Richards, JC & Farrell, TSC 2005, *Professional Development for Language Teachers*, Cambridge University Press, Cambridge.

This practical book on professional development strategies can provide researchers with ideas about the kinds of issues in LTE that can be researched.

Wedell, M 2009, *Planning Educational Change: Putting People and Their Contexts First*, Continuum, London.

While concerned with educational change more generally, this book provides analyses which are very relevant to the design and implementation of in-service LTE initiatives.

References

A'Dhahab, SM 2009, 'EFL teachers' perceptions and practices regarding reflective writing', in S Borg (ed.), *Researching English Language Teaching and Teacher Development in Oman*, Ministry of Education, Oman, pp. 1–15.
Allwright, D & Hanks, J 2009, *The Developing Language Learner: An Introduction to Exploratory Practice*, Palgrave Macmillan, Basingstoke.

Avalos, B 2011, 'Teacher professional development in Teaching and Teacher Education over ten years', *Teaching and Teacher Education*, vol. 27, no. 1, pp. 10–20.

Bailey, KM 2006, *Language Teacher Supervision*, Cambridge University Press, Cambridge.

Beijaard, D, Korthagen, F & Verloop, N 2007, 'Understanding how teachers learn as a prerequisite for promoting teacher learning', *Teachers and Teaching: Theory and Practice*, vol. 13, no. 2, pp. 105–108.

Borg, S 2006, *Teacher Cognition and Language Education: Research and Practice*, Continuum, London.

—— 2011a, 'The impact of in-service teacher education on language teachers' beliefs', *System*, vol. 39, no. 3, pp. 370–380.

—— 2011b, 'Teacher learning on the Delta', *Research Notes*, vol. 45, pp. 19–25.

—— (ed.), 2013a, *Narratives of Teacher Development 1: Reading and Speaking*, The British Council, Kuala Lumpur.

—— (ed.), 2013b, *Narratives of Teacher Development 2: Stories and Songs*, The British Council, Kuala Lumpur.

—— (ed.), 2013c, *Narratives of Teacher Development 3: Engaging Young Learners*, The British Council, Kuala Lumpur.

—— (ed.), 2014, *Teacher Research in Pakistan: Enhancing the Teaching and Learning of English*, British Council, Lahore.

Borko, H, Whitcomb, JA & Byrnes, K 2008, 'Genres of research in teacher education', in M Cochran-Smith, S Feiman-Nemser, JD McIntyre & KE Demers (eds), *Handbook of Research on Teacher Education: Enduring Questions in Changing Contexts*, 3rd edn, Routledge/Association of Teacher Educators, New York, NY, pp. 1017–1049.

Braun, V & Clarke, V 2006, 'Using thematic analysis in psychology', *Qualitative Research in Psychology*, vol. 3, no. 2, pp. 77–101.

Broad, K & Evans, M 2006, *A Review of Literature on Professional Development Content and Delivery Modes for Experienced Teachers*, Canadian Ministry of Education, Toronto.

Bryman, A 2012, *Social Research Methods*, 4th edn, Oxford University Press, Oxford.

Burns, A 1999, *Collaborative Action Research for English Language Teachers*, Cambridge University Press, Cambridge.

—— 2010, *Doing Action Research in English Language Teaching: A Guide for Practitioners*, Routledge, New York, NY.

—— 2014, 'Professional learning in Australian ELICOS: An action research orientation', *English Australia Journal*, vol. 29, no. 2, pp. 3–20.

Choi, DSY & Morrison, P 2014, 'Learning to get it right: Understanding change processes in professional development for teachers of English learners', *Professional Development in Education*, vol. 40, no. 3, pp. 416–435.

Choi, TH & Andon, N 2014, 'Can a teacher certification scheme change ELT classroom practice?', *ELT Journal*, vol. 68, no. 1, pp. 12–21.

Cochran-Smith, M & Fries, K 2008, 'Research on teacher education: Changing times, changing paradigms', in M Cochran-Smith, S Feiman-Nemser, JD McIntyre & KE Demers (eds), *Handbook of Research on Teacher Education: Enduring Questions in Changing Contexts*, 3rd edn, Routledge/Association of Teacher Educators, New York, NY, pp. 1050–1093.

Collins, LJ & Liang, X 2013, 'Task relevance in the design of online professional development for teachers of ELLs: A Q methodology study', *Professional Development in Education*, vol. 39, no. 3, pp. 441–443.

Cordingley, P, Bell, M, Rundell, B & Evans, D 2003, *The Impact of Collaborative CPD on Classroom Teaching and Learning*, EPPI Centre, Social Science Research Unit, Institute of Education, London.

Creswell, J 2013, *Research Design: Qualitative, Quantitative, and Mixed Methods Approaches*, 4th edn, Sage, Thousand Oaks, CA.

Darling-Hammond, L 2013, *Getting Teacher Evaluation Right: What Really Matters for Effectiveness and Improvement*, Teachers College, New York, NY.

Darling-Hammond, L & Lieberman, A 2012, *Teacher Education Around the World: Changing Policies and Practices*, Routledge, London.

Fenton-Smith, B & Stillwell, C 2011, 'Reading discussion groups for teachers: Connecting theory to practice', *ELT Journal*, vol. 65, no. 3, pp. 251–259.

Fenton-Smith, B & Torpey, MJ 2013, 'Orienting EFL teachers: Principles arising from an evaluation of an induction program in a Japanese university', *Language Teaching Research*, vol. 17, no. 2, pp. 228–250.

Feryok, A 2010, 'Language teacher cognitions: Complex dynamic systems?', *System*, vol. 38, no. 2, pp. 272–279.

Freeman, D 2009, 'The scope of second language teacher education', in A Burns & JC Richards (eds), *The Cambridge Guide to Language Teacher Education*, Cambridge University Press, Cambridge, pp. 11–19.

Freeman, D & Johnson, KE 2005, 'Towards linking teacher knowledge and student learning', in D Tedick (ed.), *Second Language Teacher Education: International Perspectives*, Lawrence Erlbaum Associates, Mahwah, NJ, pp. 73–95.

Garet, MS, Porter, AC, Desimone, L, Birman, BF & Yoon, KS 2001, 'What makes professional development effective? Results from a national sample of teachers', *American Educational Research Journal*, vol. 38, no. 4, pp. 915–945.

Hammerness, K, Darling-Hammond, L, Bransford, J, Berliner, D, Cochran-Smith, M, McDonald, M & Zeichner, K 2005, 'How teachers learn and develop', in L Darling-Hammond & J Bransford (eds), *Preparing Teachers for a Changing World*, Jossey-Bass, San Francisco, CA, pp. 358–389.

Hayes, D 2012, 'Mismatched perspectives: In-service teacher education policy and practice in South Korea', in C Tribble (ed.), *Managing Change in English Language Teaching: Lessons from Experience*, The British Council, London, pp. 99–104.

Hayes, D & Chang, K 2012, 'Theoretical perspectives on and international practice in continuing professional development for English teachers', *English Teaching*, vol. 67, pp. 107–129.

Hiver, P 2013, 'The interplay of possible language teacher selves in professional development choices', *Language Teaching Research*, vol. 17, no. 2, pp. 210–227.

Huang, L & Papakosmas, A 2014, 'The impact of TKT on Chinese teachers' teaching beliefs, knowledge and practice', *Research Notes*, vol. 57, pp. 13–23.

Hung, HT & Yeh, HC 2013, 'Forming a change environment to encourage professional development through a teacher study group', *Teaching and Teacher Education*, vol. 36, pp. 153–165.

Hutterli, S & Prusse, MC 2011, 'Supporting the transfer of innovation into foreign-language classrooms: Applied projects in in-service teacher education', in J Hüttner, B Mehlmauer-Larcher, S Reichl & B Schiftner (eds), *Theory and Practice in EFL Teacher Education*, Multilingual Matters, Bristol, pp. 145–163.

Johnson, KE 2009a, *Second Language Teacher Education: A Sociocultural Perspective*, Routledge, London.

—————— 2009b, 'Trends in second language teacher education', in A Burns & JC Richards (eds), *The Cambridge Guide to Second Language Teacher Education*, Cambridge University Press, Cambridge, pp. 20–29.

Johnston, B 2009, 'Collaborative teacher development', in A Burns & JC Richards (eds), *The Cambridge Guide to Language Teacher Education*, Cambridge University Press, Cambridge, pp. 241–249.

Kabilan, MK & Veratharaju, K 2013, 'Professional development needs of primary school English-language teachers in Malaysia', *Professional Development in Education*, vol. 39, no. 3, pp. 330–351.

Kennedy, M 2006, 'Research genres in teacher education', in F Murray (ed.), *Knowledge Base in Teacher Education*, McGraw-Hill, Washington, DC, pp. 120–152.

Kubanyiova, M 2012, *Teacher Development in Action: Understanding Language Teachers' Conceptual Change*, Palgrave Macmillan, Basingstoke.

Lamb, M 1995, 'The consequences of INSET', *ELT Journal*, vol. 49, no. 1, pp. 72–80.

Leu, E & Ginsburg, M 2001, *First Principles: Designing Effective Education Program for In-Service Teacher Professional Development*, USAID, Washington, DC.

Lin, Z 2014, 'In-service professional development in an online environment: What are South Australian English as an additional language or dialect teachers' views?', *Professional Development in Education*. DOI: 10.1080/19415257.2014.902860.

Mann, S 2005, 'The language teacher's development', *Language Teaching*, vol. 38, no. 3, pp. 103–118.

Martin-Beltran, M & Peercy, MM 2014, 'Collaboration to teach English language learners: Opportunities for shared teacher learning', *Teachers and Teaching: Theory and Practice*, vol. 20, no. 6, pp. 721–737.

McCutchen, D, Abbott, RD, Green, LB, Beretvas, SN, Cox, S, Potter, NS, Quiroga, T & Gray, AL 2002, 'Beginning literacy: Links among teacher knowledge, teacher practice, and student learning', *Journal of Learning Disabilities*, vol. 35, no. 1, pp. 69–86.

Molle, D 2013, 'Facilitating professional development for teachers of English language learners', *Teaching and Teacher Education*, vol. 29, no. 1, pp. 197–207.

Muijs, D, Kyriakides, L, van der Werf, G, Creemers, B, Timperley, H & Earl, L 2014, 'State of the art – teacher effectiveness and professional learning', *School Effectiveness and School Improvement*, vol. 25, no. 2, pp. 231–256.

O'Dwyer, JB & Atli, HH 2014, 'A study of in-service teacher educator roles, with implications for a curriculum for their professional development', *European Journal of Teacher Education*. vol. 38, no. 1, pp. 4–20.

Opfer, VD & Pedder, D 2011, 'Conceptualizing teacher professional learning', *Review of Educational Research*, vol. 81, no. 3, pp. 376–407.

Orr, D, Westbrook, J, Pryor, J, Durrani, N, Sebba, J & Adu-Yeboah, C 2013, *What are the Impacts and Cost Effectiveness of Strategies to Improve Performance* of *Untrained and Under-Trained Teachers in the Classroom in Developing Countries? A Systematic Review*, EPPI Centre, University of London, London.

Poehner, P 2011, 'Teacher learning through critical friends groups', in KE Johnson & PR Golombek (eds), *Research on Second Language Teacher Education*, Routledge, London, pp. 189–203.

Richards, JC & Farrell, TSC 2005, *Professional Development for Language Teachers*, Cambridge University Press, Cambridge.

Richardson, V 1996, 'The role of attitudes and beliefs in learning to teach', in J Sikula (ed.), *Handbook of Research on Teacher Education*, 2nd edn, Macmillan, New York, NY, pp. 102–119.

Saunders, M, Lewis, P & Thornhill, A 2012, *Research Methods for Business Students*, 6th edn, Pearson, London.

Schwille, J, Dembele, M & Schubert, J 2007, *Global Perspectives on Teacher Learning: Improving Policy and Practice*, UNESCO, Paris.

Scott, R & Rodgers, B 1995, 'Changing teachers' conceptions of teaching writing: A collaborative study', *Foreign Language Annals*, vol. 28, no. 2, pp. 234–246.

Tasker, T 2011, 'Teacher learning through lesson study', in KE Johnson & PR Golombek (eds), *Research on Second Language Teacher Education*, Routledge, London, pp. 204–221.

Timperley, H 2011, *Realizing the Power of Professional Learning*, Open University Press, Milton Keynes.

Timperley, H, Wilson, A, Barrar, H & Fung, I 2008, *Teacher Professional Learning and Development: Best Evidence Synthesis Iteration (BES)*, Ministry of Education, Wellington.

Tsui, ABM 2011, 'Teacher education and development', in E Hinkel (ed.), *Handbook of Research in Second Language Teaching and Learning*, Routledge, London, pp. 21–39.

Villegas-Reimers, E 2003, *Teacher Professional Development: An International Review of Literature*, International Institute for Educational Planning, Paris.

Walsh, CS, Power, T, Khatoon, M, Biswas, SK, Paul, AK, Sarkar, BC & Griffiths, M 2013, 'The "trainer in your pocket": Mobile phones within a teacher continuing professional development program in Bangladesh', *Professional Development in Education*, vol. 39, no. 2, pp. 186–200.

Wang, Q & Zhang, H 2014, 'Promoting teacher autonomy through university-school collaborative action research', *Language Teaching Research*, vol. 18, no. 2, pp. 222–241.

Waters, AV & Vilches, MLC 2010, '"*Tanggap, tiklop, tago*" (Receive, Fold, Keep): Perceptions of Best Practice in ELT INSET', The British Council, London.

Wright, T 2010, 'Second language teacher education: Review of recent research on practice', *Language Teaching*, vol. 43, no. 3, pp. 259–296.

Zeichner, K 1999, 'The new scholarship in teacher education', *Educational Researcher*, vol. 28, no. 9, pp. 4–15.

GLOSSARY OF KEY RESEARCH TERMS

Action research Research conducted by participants who are also members of the community where the research takes place (e.g. the school, classroom). It involves cyclical and iterative processes of planning, acting, observing and reflecting that allow for emergent findings and increased understanding about local practices.

Adaptive expertise The ability in teachers to be innovative and creative in using knowledge to solve novel problems. This is contrasted with routine expertise – a mastery of procedures which are used efficiently but not creatively.

Affective strategies Mental or behavioural techniques used to control the emotional aspects of language learning, such as stress.

Attributed beliefs Teacher beliefs that researchers infer on the basis of observations of what teachers do in their classrooms.

Auditory perceptual processing Phenomena associated with the bottom-up dimension of listening by providing listeners with an aural stimulus (word or short sentence presented with no contextual cues) and then asking the listener to choose from among several options in order to uncover listener word segmentation strategies.

Back-translation A process used to assure that a translated and original version of a questionnaire or a document is equivalent. The process involves translating the original version into the second language and then having a second person or group translate the second language version back into the original language. The original version and the (twice) translated version can then be compared to assure that they are equivalent.

Bootstrapping A nonparametric statistical procedure that produces a more stable and statistically accurate outcome.

Boundedness The delimitation of a case that enables us to distinguish what the case and its context do and do not consist of.

Breadth of vocabulary knowledge The number of words learners know.

Case study An approach which examines a single case, whether it be a single person, group, institution or community, either at one point in time or over a period of time. This allows for a project which produces in-depth descriptions of contexts, themes and issues.

Classroom observation A process whereby classroom events are observed, documented, analysed and interpreted.

Information is gathered and documented about processes and learning outcomes, participants' behaviours and actions, relationships as well as teaching/learning materials or other artefacts. Observation needs to be systematic to address validity and reliability concerns.

Codes Words and phrases that signify what is happening in the data – smaller pieces of meaning which when put together become themes.

Coding The process of searching for and recording codes within the data.

Cognitive dissonance Teachers' experience when they become aware of a tension or gap between their current beliefs and practices and others which they recognize as being of value. Cognitive dissonance is thought to play a role in facilitating changes in what teachers believe and do.

Cognitive strategies Techniques used to enhance memorization and recollection of language, such as lexical knowledge, grammatical knowledge, phonological knowledge, etc.

Collocation Words that frequently occur with other words in the language (e.g. chain smoker, domestic animal).

Component-skills approach An approach to reading research in which reading is viewed as being a set of sub-skills such as decoding, vocabulary knowledge, syntactic processing and metacognition.

Concurrent Quan + Qual MMR design A research design in mixed methods research (MMR) that consists of two independent quantitative and qualitative strands.

Confirmability A trustworthiness criterion in qualitative research which requires that researchers reveal the data they are basing their interpretation on or at least make such data available. Other researchers should be able to examine the data to confirm or reject the claim that is made. Confirmability is analogous to the concept of replicability in quantitative research.

Construct An abstract concept such as intelligence, motivation or English proficiency that cannot be observed directly and needs to be measured empirically.

Construct representation The processes whereby researchers construct texts that represent the participants and the researcher that are seen as constructed rather than 'true' presentations of an observed reality.

Construct validity of an instrument The extent to which an instrument measures or captures what it is intended to measure rather than measuring something else.

Constructivism A theory in which learning is seen to occur through the interaction of existing and new experience. What teachers already know and believe thus have a powerful impact on what they learn through teacher education.

Control group A group of participants in experimental research who are treated or taught in the traditional or typical way rather than undergoing the experimental treatment.

Conversation analysis (CA) A sub-discipline of discourse analysis. CA research is based on the fine-grained analysis of stretches of actual talk. The patterns and the principles that emerge from this analysis form the basis of the insights of the research. These findings can be related to wider generalizations – for instance how speakers interrupt one another politely in different circumstances or how laughter can show affiliation between speakers. CA differs fundamentally from corpus linguistics in that it is based on situated qualitative insights rather than frequency analyses.

Corpus/corpora A collection of texts, usually stored electronically, seen as representative of some subset of language and used for linguistic analysis. Corpora are designed to include certain types of language, for instance, teenagers' talk or broadcast radio or business meetings. Very large corpora are designed to allow researchers to find patterns in language and the greater the size of the corpus – as long as it is carefully designed – the stronger the conclusions are about these patterns.

Corrective feedback Feedback given to learners on their language errors.

Correlation coefficient A statistical measure ranging from –1 to +1 that indicates the strength of the relationship between variables. A correlation of 0 indicates no relationship at all, whereas a correlation of 0.9 indicates a strong positive relationship.

Correlational research A type of non-experimental research that investigates whether there is a true association between two variables. Correlational research differs from experimental research in that there is no manipulation of the independent variables under examination.

Credibility A trustworthiness criterion in qualitative research which requires researchers to accurately describe their definitions and the characterizations of the people or things under investigation. Credibility is more or less analogous to the concept of internal validity in quantitative research.

Credibility in action research In action research, internal credibility refers to the extent to which accounts of the research hold value and truth for the participants; external credibility relates to how convincing the outcomes appear to those outside the research.

Critical discourse analysis An approach which seeks to reveal the interests, values and power relations in any institutional and sociohistorical context through the ways that people use language.

Critical ethnography A strand of ethnography that seeks to understand the influence of class, race, gender and power relations on social relations and the production and reproduction of inequality with a view to facilitating social change.

Cross-cultural pragmatics Research that investigates differences between different native language groups in terms of pragmatic performance and perceptions of social variables.

Cross-sectional research Often associated with a quantitative research design, cross-sectional research involves collecting data on more than one case at a single point in time, typically with a relatively large number of participants.

Data coding A process of assigning codes to data. This process generally involves grouping instances in the data that share similarities together in categories. Data coding is related to data reduction as irrelevant data are not considered.

Data driven A model of language that begins from actual instances of written or spoken discourse and looks for patterns and generalizations that can be drawn from these instances.

Data Information gained through research that is used to respond to the research question or hypothesis.

Discourse Completion Task (DCT) A research instrument consisting of a situation description and a space for respondents to write what they would say in the situation. They are commonly used in pragmatics research but do not necessarily reflect real-world language use.

Deductive (top-down) reasoning The process of drawing a specific conclusion from a set of premises or theories (i.e. from general to particular).

Dependability A trustworthiness criterion in qualitative research which requires that researchers account for any shifting conditions directly related to the people and things they are studying and any modifications they have made in their study as it has progressed. Dependability is analogous to reliability in quantitative research.

Dependent variable The variable upon which the independent variable is acting. For example, improvement in writing proficiency (the dependent variable) as a result of a particular approach to teaching (the independent variable).

Depth of vocabulary knowledge The knowledge of individual words, including form, meaning, collocations and associations.

Descriptive statistics Basic statistics that describe measures of frequency (percentages), central tendency (mean, median, mode) and dispersion (such as standard deviation).

Direct vocabulary learning Language learning with a specific focus on vocabulary development (e.g. learning from word cards).

Discourse(s) Naturally-occurring, contextualized language use. For Critical Discourse Analysis (CDA) and Feminist post-structuralist discourse analysis (FPDA), discourse is social, ideological and constitutive – of behaviours and ideas – at least potentially. More specifically, a discourse, a Foucauldian notion drawn on by both CDA and post-structuralism, refers to a socially constructed way of seeing the world and then representing it in language (and perhaps images), for example, a 'Battle of the sexes' discourse may be identified when some stretch of language use seems to assume that women's and men's interests are automatically opposed.

Effect size A measure of the strength of the relationship between two variables. Effect size differs from a statistically significant effect in that it considers whether the size of the observed effects is robust enough or realistic. Different effect sizes are calculated for different inferential statistical tests, such as Cohen's d for two group mean differences, r squared for correlations, or eta squared for analysis of variance (ANOVAs).

Elicited data Data which is collected through a task that will trigger the use of a particular kind of reply or response. Elicited spoken data, by the nature of the process, restricts the type of data collected and reduces its authenticity. A recording of a dinner party conversation, then, would not be regarded as 'elicited'. Data gathered in this latter way will be more authentic but may not include some aspect of language that the researcher wishes to investigate.

Emic An insider's perspective on events – that is, as the events are experienced by the participants in the particular social setting.

Ethics Ensuring that research is conducted in an ethical manner, such as not abusing the participants in a study in any way, including abuses of time and effort.

Ethnographic approaches In wider research circles an 'ethnographer' is a researcher who embeds themselves in the social groups that they are investigating and carries out work from the perspective of that society. In this way, the insights gathered are less likely to be based on imposed or pre-existing models/ categories and new patterns of behaviour and social meaning can be uncovered. Ethnographic research investigates the naturally occurring behaviours of a group of people in their community; describes the beliefs, values and attitudes of a group; and provides a holistic description of contexts and cultural themes.

Etic An outsider's perspective on events.

Experimental group The group of learners in experimental research which receives a particular treatment or condition which is hypothesized to change the target behaviour (i.e. the dependent variable).

Experimental research A situation in which a researcher manipulates one or more variables (such as an approach to teaching speaking) while the others are kept constant in order to see the effect of manipulating the variable(s) on a dependent variable (such as speaking proficiency).

Explicit feedback An overt correction of erroneous utterances in learners' discourse with or without explanations.

Explicit grammar instruction Presenting and explaining a pre-determined set of grammar rules, usually but not necessarily followed by practice.

Explicit knowledge Conscious knowledge about a language (rules, conventions of use) that learners can often verbalize.

External validity The extent to which the results of quantitative research can be generalized to another situation (i.e. for different subjects/ participants, settings, times). That is, to what degree the inferred (causal) relationship or differences between groups can be generalized to other persons, settings and times.

Factor analysis A statistical analysis used to explore or confirm relationships between related variables. It can be exploratory (EFA) or confirmatory (CFA) and is often used to validate questionnaires or tests.

Field notes Notes from researchers' observations that are taken during the data collection process. The researcher may make brief notes during the observation and later expand these into field notes. These notes supplement information from other sources such as documents and interviews. There are two components of field notes: (1) description (e.g. setting, people, reaction, interpersonal relationship) and (2) reflection or observer comment (e.g. observer's personal feelings, impression about the events, comments, speculations about data analysis).

Focus group An interview strategy in which a small group of participants sharing similar characteristics are interviewed together by the researcher.

Focus on Form (FonF) Reactive grammar instruction which occurs spontaneously in response to learners' needs or errors as they arise when learners engage in meaning-focused activities.

Free recall protocols A form of comprehension verification where research participants listen to a text and immediately afterwards write, most often in their native language, as much information as possible to convey what they understood.

Gender Not just a polite word for 'sex'. While gender often refers to what are frequently seen as rather different learned, social attributes of women and of men (and girls and boys), it can also be used critically to refer to socially constructed ideas about such attributes.

Genre analysis A branch of discourse analysis which seeks to understand the communicative character of discourse by looking at how individuals use language to engage in particular communicative situations.

Goodness-of-fit indices The statistical fit indices of a hypothesized structural model. These include chi-quare, goodness-of-fit, root mean square residual fit indices. These indices are generated by the analytical software used, for example AMOS 21.

Grounded theory Grounded theory starts with data rather than theory. It employs a cyclical process of theory building and testing the developing theory against the data.

Hypothesis A predictive statement that can be tested empirically. It is mostly used in quantitative research.

Hypothesis testing This involves two types of hypotheses. A null hypothesis (H0) is the prediction that, for example, there is no linear relationship between variables. The alternative hypothesis (H1) is the opposite of the null hypothesis.

That is, that there will be a relationship between the variables.

Identity(ies) Ways of being in the world which are ongoing, individual and collective, socially and psychologically situated and socioculturally and sociohistorically constructed.

Implicit feedback The corrective intent of the feedback which is not self-evident (e.g. a recast).

Implicit knowledge Unconscious knowledge that can be quickly and easily accessed (e.g. in fluent speech).

Incidental vocabulary learning Acquiring new words while engaged with the language, such as while reading extensively.

Independent variable A variable that is hypothesized to be related to a change in something (e.g. language learning). For example, the type of writing feedback students receive could be an independent variable that affects subsequent writing performance, which is the dependent variable.

Inductive (bottom-up) reasoning The process of drawing a specific conclusion from a set of observations or data. To be absolutely certain of an inductive conclusion, researchers must observe all examples. Imperfect induction is a system in which researchers observe a sample of a group and infer from the sample what the characteristics of the entire population are likely to be.

Inferential statistics Statistics that are used to make inferences about population parameters, such as the relationship between two variables or between two groups on a variable of interest.

Informed consent The process whereby a research participant is informed of all potential risks and benefits associated with participating in the research before giving their consent.

Institutional review board/ethics committee The ethical review committee which oversees and approves research in universities.

Instrumental case study A study of a particular phenomenon, person, program or site that is motivated by interests and purposes beyond the case.

Interlanguage pragmatics Research that investigates learning of second language pragmatics; describes and explains development as well as the role of general target language proficiency in learning pragmatics.

Internal validity One of the fundamental types of validity in quantitative research (see external validity) which concerns the relationship between independent and dependent variables. It relates to the degree to which observed relationships between variables can be inferred to be causal-like (e.g. how strongly we can infer that variable A resulted in the observed effects (increased performance) in variable B.

Intervention A characteristic of research whereby innovative or changed practices may deliberately be introduced into the research.

Intrinsic case study A study of a particular phenomenon, person, program or site that is inherently interesting in itself.

Introspection A data collection technique that aims to have learners discuss their thoughts and behaviours while completing the event being studied, for example a think-aloud task.

Language ideologies Commonsense conceptions about language (e.g. as a communicative mode), specific languages (e.g. of a particular variety as more or less prestigious), language learning (e.g. that vocabulary is best learned through memorization) and language users (e.g. speakers of a given variety are more socially desirable than speakers of a different variety).

Language learner strategies Processes and actions that are consciously deployed by language learners to help them to learn or use a language more effectively. These include strategies applied by learners when learning a language, using a language or taking language tests.

Latent variable A variable that cannot be observed, for example, motivation. A model using observed variables is hypothesized and the model is accepted or rejected depending on the results.

Lexical coverage The proportion of tokens in a text represented by a word family or word list.

Likert-scale item A type of item commonly used in questionnaires. Usually it is in the form of a statement that the respondent has to respond to, often choosing from five response options (e.g. strongly agree, agree, don't know/ no opinion, disagree and strongly disagree).

Linguicism Prejudice or discrimination based on language. It can be traced to Skutnabb-Kangas and Phillipson's work in Linguistic Human Rights.

Literacy practices The ways people use written language in the home, the school and the community. These practices are socially constructed and are instrumental in shaping learner identity.

Longitudinal research A study in which data is collected from the same participants at more than one point in time. It is carried out over a relatively long period of time, often with a small number of participants.

Macroethics Ethical protocols stipulated by university ethical review committees and professional organizations.

Magnitude The relative size of a difference or the relative strength of a relationship (as opposed to probability which is the relative confidence that a finding is not a spurious fluke of chance).

Meta-analysis An approach to analysis that systematically combines the results of previous studies that examined related research questions. It is a type of research synthesis. A meta-analysis is usually carried out by identification of a common measure of effect size. Meta-analysis yields a more robust estimate of the true effect size than that derived from a single study (see Effect size).

Metacognitive instruction The pedagogical procedures that enable learners to better self-regulate their learning and by increasing awareness about (1) themselves as learners; (2) the nature and demands of learning; and (3) strategies for learning.

Metacognitive strategies Mental or behavioural techniques used to enhance the planning, monitoring and evaluation of one's learning.

Microethics Everyday ethical dilemmas that arise in specific research contexts.

Mixed methods research A study that has both quantitative and qualitative components. The purpose of mixed methods research is to achieve a fuller understanding of a complex issue and to verify one set of findings against the other.

Multimodal Traditionally, we might think of 'spoken mode' and 'written mode' as the two major ways that people communicate. However, it has always been the case that different modes can be in play at the same time – for instance, when someone dictates a message – and that other modes of communication have been used (for instance, miming or sign language). Increasingly, researchers into spoken language are becoming interested in 'multi-modal' settings and how these can be analysed. These range from the study of gesture in digitally captured video of speakers to online synchronous (real time) use of chat, video, pictures and talk.

Multimodal discourse Discourse which employs and integrates more than one mode of presentation, such as words and graphics, speech and gesture.

Narrative form The way stories are constructed, including the organization of ideas, the sequences of events, choice of words, textual coherence.

Narrative inquiry An approach to doing research that focuses on the stories people tell about their lives. Researchers are interested in understanding the meaning research participants make of their life experiences, often drawing on biographies, life stories, life narratives and oral histories.

Narrative knowledging The meaning making, learning and knowledge construction by participants, researchers and audience of the research reports that takes place during the entire narrative inquiry process.

Naturalistic data Data that is collected in a natural context without a researcher's attempt to control or manipulate the environment.

Neurolinguistics The study of language and the brain. It falls into two main areas in relation to researching speaking: study of the normal brain patterns during talk; study of the damaged brain as it affects talk. The second of these is the older discipline as various speech defects stem from particular areas of the brain becoming damaged. This allows researchers to connect brain function to speech processing and production. More recently, the capacity to scan the brain during different kinds of task has allowed more sophisticated understanding of lexical retrieval and speech processing.

Non-observational methods Methods of data collection used to capture people's reflections, thoughts, attitudes or feelings about the issue under investigation – that is, about things that cannot be directly observed.

Normal distribution A statistical term related to the spread of the data around the mean. Normal distribution is bell-shaped. In a perfect normal distribution, the mean, median and mode have equal values.

Null hypothesis The default hypothesis that there is no significant difference between two groups/populations.

Observation A basic method for obtaining data in qualitative research that involves the observation of a particular phenomenon, such as a particular set of lessons. The kind of observation carried out in qualitative research is more global and holistic than the systematic, structured observation used in quantitative research.

Observational methods Methods of data collection used to capture behaviours and interactions, for example audio/video recording, observational notes, descriptive journals or photographs.

Observed variable An item or a subscale of items measuring the same variable.

Outliers Extreme cases or values which are not typical of the group of participants in a study. Outliers can distort statistical results.

Participant observation Three terms are commonly associated with participant observation. *Complete observer* is when the observer does not take part in the activities but simply observes what is going on. *Participant as observer* is when the observer actively participates in the activities being examined. *Observer as participant* is when the observer interacts with the participants sufficiently to establish a rapport with them but does not become involved in the activities of the group.

Participants People (e.g. learners, teachers) who take part in research by providing information about themselves that is used as research data. The term 'participants' is preferred to the term 'subjects'.

Posttest A test instrument used to collect data following a research intervention period.

Pragmatism to research A philosophical position that underscores the idea that what has practical and functional value is important and valid in a research design.

Pretest A test instrument used to collect data before a research intervention period.

Probability The degree to which a statistical finding is likely to occur by chance (see statistical validity). The p-value (p = probability) is the likelihood that researchers will be wrong in the statistical inferences that they make from the data. $p < 0.05$ (i.e. there are 5 in 100 chances of being wrong) is commonly used in applied linguistics research. If the probability based on the result of the statistical analysis is less than the significance level, the null hypothesis can be rejected.

Process-oriented research Research that provides opportunities for participants to reveal or for researchers to uncover how or why research participants may have responded as they did.

Process-product research An approach to research which seeks to establish causal links between variables, such as between particular teaching behaviours and student learning.

Productive vocabulary knowledge Knowledge of words in spoken or written forms.

Product-oriented research Research that focuses on data only, as determined by some measurement instrument (e.g. test scores or questionnaire responses), without any interest in the processes that led to a given score.

Professed beliefs Teachers' stated beliefs, as expressed, for example, in questionnaires or interviews, also called espoused beliefs.

Psychometrics An approach to assessment derived from psychology which evaluates the quality of tests by using a range of statistical procedures.

Publication bias The tendency for statistically significant results to eventually appear published much more often than statistically non-significant results, which are more likely to remain unpublished.

Purposive sampling Researchers identify the characteristics of participants or samples prior to data collection and base the sampling on this. Purposive sampling is often associated with qualitative research.

Qualitative research An approach that seeks to make sense of social phenomena as they occur in natural settings. Rather than setting up a controlled environment, qualitative researchers are more interested in understanding contexts as they actually are. Qualitative researchers do not aim for quantification or standardization in the data collection and analysis of the data.

Quantitative data Numerical data derived from quantitative measures such as language tests and Likert-scale questionnaires.

Quantitative research A research approach that draws on numeric data. Variables are clearly defined, measurement is standardized and data are generally analysed using statistical methods.

Quasi-experimental research The underlying principles of quasi-experimental research are the same as experimental research. The difference is that there has been no random assignment of participants to groups.

Random assignment A process of randomization in assigning participants to the experimental treatments. With random assignment, each participant has an equal and independent chance of being assigned to any group. Thus, the assignment is independent of the researcher's personal judgement or the characteristics of the participants themselves.

Random selection A technique that aims to generate a sample that represents a larger population. Random selection is related to external validity in experimental and survey research.

Rater A trained person who judges the quality of a candidate's performance of a speaking or writing task according to specified criteria.

Reader response While there are many theories of reader response, the idea is that a given response to a text cannot be predicted by the text itself and that different readers will have different (perhaps equally valid) responses to the same text. Relatedly, the idea of the 'writer's intention' is deprivileged (Barthes' notion of the 'death of the author').

Reading fluency The ability to read rapidly with ease and accuracy. Fluency involves processing skills such as speed of word recognition and syntactic parsing.

Reading strategies Activities and behaviours that readers engage in to assist them in comprehending a text, such as predicting text content or guessing meaning from context.

Receptive vocabulary knowledge Recognition of word forms and meaning as evidenced when listening and reading.

Reflexivity Processes of critical self-reflection on a researcher's biases, theoretical predispositions, preferences that locate the researcher as a presence in the research and in the text.

Reliability The quality of instruments/ measures and results of a study. The reliability of an instrument or measure is concerned with the degree to which a research instrument or measure produces consistent information (e.g. whether the data would be the same if the instrument were administered repeatedly). The reliability of a result of a study is concerned with whether the result would be likely to reappear if the study were replicated under the same conditions.

Replicability A requirement that researchers provide enough information about a study to allow other researchers to replicate or repeat the study exactly as it was originally conducted. This includes information about the participants involved in the study, how they were selected, the instruments that were used and the data collection and analysis procedures.

Replication The process of conducting a new study closely based on a previous study. The aim is to find out whether the new study will yield the same finding as in the original study. However, exact replication is often impossible in applied linguistics research and hence *conceptual replication* may be achieved (i.e. the research concept is replicated, rather than the context and time).

Representation Representation tends to be of something or someone in a written, visual or multimodal text or set of texts. It can be seen as ideological as it invariably involves selecting from a pool of available choices and hence is not a 'mirror' on 'reality'. Representation can be seen as constitutive (as in Critical Discourse Analysis (CDA)).

Research synthesis An analysis of research evidence relating to a specific research question based on an analysis of previous studies on the topic. This can involve an examination of either quantitative or qualitative research. Research synthesis is a powerful tool in that it provides an overview of the overall body of research evidence.

Retrospection A data collection technique that aims to have learners introspect after completing the event being studied. Frequently used instruments can include interviews, questionnaires and diaries. Unlike introspection, retrospection occurs once a task has been completed. Participants are asked to report on what they were thinking while they carried out the task.

Reverse-coded items When creating a number of individual items to measure a particular construct, it sometimes is necessary to include items that are negatively stated. For example, one question in the scale might be 'Speaking English is necessary for my job', while a reverse-coded item measuring the same scale might state 'Learning English is not important for my occupation.' When inputting the data, it is imperative to input the value on the opposite end of the scale (e.g. if using a 5-point scale, a '2' response would be reverse-coded and inputted as '4').

Routine formula A fixed, situationally bound, highly frequent expression that can learned as a chunk, also known as conventional expression.

Sampling Because of the difficulty or impossibility of surveying an entire population, a sample of that population can be identified and used for research purposes. It is imperative that the process of sampling be well-planned, so that the sample used is representative of the intended population. Sampling can include probability sampling (e.g. random, stratified random, systematic, cluster) and nonprobability sampling.

Schematic structure The typical rhetorical patterning of a text in terms of an organized sequence of moves or discoursal acts. This can be seen as a system of conventions or resources of meaning for generating expected texts, sometimes also referred to as 'generic structure'.

Second language classroom research A term describing the number of ways that researchers study classroom language processes and phenomena in order to understand language classrooms better.

Self-regulation The underlying degree to which learners are proactively managing their language learning and language use.

Sensitivity analysis A planned investigation within a given study that allows the researcher to probe a suspected source of error in the analysis, that is, to ascertain the extent to which a result or observation may change when an alternative analysis is employed. Meta-analysts, for example, may decide to investigate the extent to which the average magnitude of an effect for a given group of primary studies would change when effect sizes from published and unpublished studies are aggregated together versus separately.

Sequential Qual → Quan MMR design A mixed methods research (MMR) design which consists of two chronological strands with a qualitative strand occurring first.

Sequential Quan → Qual MMR design A mixed methods research (MMR) design which consists of two chronological strands with a quantitative strand occurring first.

Significance level A pre-specified fixed probability of rejecting the null hypothesis when it is true. A significance level is determined by the researcher in consideration of the consequences of rejecting a true null hypothesis.

Small stories Snippets of talk-in-interaction, embedded in conversations and interviews. They are analysed discursively, more or less taking into account the local and broader context of construction and other ethnographic data, if available.

Sociocultural strategies Behavioural techniques used to enhance learning through planned interaction with the surrounding environment and people, such as working with more able learners, or seeking contexts conducive to learning.

Speech act An utterance that is performed with a certain intention of the speaker and effect on the hearer, for example promising, ordering, greeting, warning, inviting and congratulating.

SPSS Statistical Package for the Social Sciences – a statistical program to help with the analysis of quantitative data.

Statistical validity This validity is similar to internal validity in quantitative research. Researchers ask whether the observed relationship between the independent and dependent variables was a true relationship, incidental, or found by chance.

Stimulated recall A type of interview where the interviewee is encouraged to talk about a previous experience (e.g. a lesson) and a 'stimulus', such as a video recording of the lesson or some teaching material, is used to facilitate the conversation.

Strand in mixed methods research A component of a study that encompasses the basic process of conducting quantitative or qualitative research: posing a question, collecting and analysing data and interpreting results.

Strategies for language learning The strategies deployed by a learner when actively learning a language, such as cognitive, metacognitive, affective, or social strategies (when organized by function).

Strategies for language use The strategies deployed when a learner is using the language, such as coping strategies or communication strategies.

Structural equation modeling A series of statistical techniques that can be used to explore complex relationships between variables.

Style Socially identifiable ways of speaking (akin to but also different from notions of dialect).

Systemic functional linguistics A theory of language developed by Michael Halliday based on the idea that language is a system of choices used to express meanings in context.

Teacher cognition The study of the unobservable dimension of teaching, such as beliefs, attitudes, knowledge and emotions.

Teachers' beliefs Anything that a teacher considers to be true.

Test construct A defined skill or ability that is targeted by a test or assessment procedure.

Test reliability The extent to which a particular test or assessment procedure provides a consistent measure of the learners' knowledge or ability.

Test validation The process of obtaining evidence that a particular test or assessment procedure produces results which can meaningfully be interpreted as representing the level of the learners' language knowledge or ability.

Thematic analysis An analysis which looks for themes that emerge entirely from the data.

Thematic headings Headings which grow out of the thematic analysis which are used to structure the discussion of the data.

Thick description Devised by Geertz, the term thick description is often associated with ethnographic or case study research. Thick description refers to a detailed description of a phenomenon or event that includes the researcher's interpretation of what they have observed.

Think-aloud methodology A type of verbal report that attempts to tap the thought processes of learners while they are actually engaged in a learning activity. After some initial training in the process, participants 'think aloud' when prompted by the researcher.

Timing in mixed methods research A temporal relationship between the quantitative and qualitative strands within the study.

Tokens Individual occurrences of words (i.e. tokens = total number of words in a text).

Transfer The extent to which knowledge and skills possessed in one language transfer to another language.

Transferability A qualitative trustworthiness criterion which requires researchers to describe the research design, context and conditions so that other researchers can decide for themselves if the interpretations apply to another context with which they are familiar. Transferability is analogous to the concept of generalizability in quantitative research.

Transformative A philosophical perspective that defines knowledge as influenced by historical and contextual factors with special emphasis on issues of power and social justice.

Transmission models of teacher learning Strategies for teacher learning where the emphasis is on the communication of knowledge from trainers (who have the knowledge) to teachers (who lack it).

Triangulation A research strategy that involves analysing data from multiple sources (e.g. surveys and interviews), multiple groups of participants (e.g. students, teachers, and parents) and multiple research techniques (e.g. observation and interviews) to thoroughly examine the matter under investigation. Triangulation aims to collect multiple perspectives on an event so that the researcher can gain a more complete understanding of the topic under examination.

True mixed methods research study A study that implies mixing of quantitative and qualitative methods at different stages in a study process.

Trustworthiness The term for validity in qualitative research. Trustworthiness is often a preferred term in qualitative research because it takes account of the different nature of the research methods and epistemological assumptions made in qualitative research compared to those used in quantitative research.

Type I error An error type that occurs when the null hypothesis is rejected when it is true – that is, when a null hypothesis is wrongly rejected.

Type II error An error type that occurs when a false null hypothesis is not rejected.

Validation Procedures or steps taken by the researcher to make sure that the measure or instrument to be used for the research is valid and that proper inferences can be made about the construct of interest based on the data.

Validity The extent to which the research actually studies what it claims to study. The *validity of an instrument* concerns whether the instrument actually measures what it claims to measure. For instance, a questionnaire designed to explore language learners' motivation which actually examines learners' anxiety is not a valid instrument. The instrument may, however, be reliable because individuals may consistently provide the same responses on different occasions. The *validity of the research* refers to the accuracy of the inferences, interpretations or actions made on the basis of the data.

Variable An operationalized construct that can have different values or scores. Variable derives from the word 'vary', suggesting that individuals can vary in terms of their scores of the aspect under examination.

Vocabulary retention Storage of new word knowledge beyond short-term memory.

Warrant Providing justification or 'evidence' for one's analytic claims.

Talmy (this volume) argues that discourse analysis can be a fruitful way of warranting claims in critical ethnography.

Washback The way that a test influences the teaching and learning activities of students who are preparing to take the test.

Weighting in mixed methods research Relative importance of quantitative and qualitative methods for answering the study's questions.

Word family A word and its common derivatives and inflexed forms.

Word list A list of words grouped by frequency and/or specialization for research or teaching/learning purposes.

INDEX

Note: Locators followed by the letter '*f*' and '*t*' refer to figures and tables.